INTERNET SERVICE PROVIDER LIABILITY FOR COPYRIGHT AND TRADE MARK INFRINGEMENT

This book critically evaluates the EU regulatory framework for the liability of host Internet Service Providers (ISPs) for copyright and trade mark infringements and provides a cluster of novel recommendations for its improvement.

The book recommends the imposition of a duty of care to host ISPs to curb the dissemination of unauthorised works and counterfeit goods, the ascription of a transparency obligation to host ISPs towards their users, and the establishment of a supervisory authority for host ISPs.

Host ISPs have facilitated the dissemination of content amongst users and the purchase of goods online, enabling copyright holders and brand owners to attract a greater audience for their works and goods. However, their services have attracted a high number of copyright and trade mark violations, too. Neither Article 14 of the e-Commerce Directive nor Article 17 of the Copyright in the Digital Single Market Directive provides a solid response to the issue of host ISPs' liability.

This book is a valuable resource for researchers in IT and IP law and offers a new perspective for resolving online IP disputes.

Internet Service Provider Liability for Copyright and Trade Mark Infringement

Towards an EU Co-Regulatory Framework

Zoi Krokida

• HART •
OXFORD • LONDON • NEW YORK • NEW DELHI • SYDNEY

HART PUBLISHING
Bloomsbury Publishing Plc
Kemp House, Chawley Park, Cumnor Hill, Oxford, OX2 9PH, UK
1385 Broadway, New York, NY 10018, USA
29 Earlsfort Terrace, Dublin 2, Ireland

HART PUBLISHING, the Hart/Stag logo, BLOOMSBURY and the Diana logo are trademarks of Bloomsbury Publishing Plc

First published in Great Britain 2022

A catalogue record for this book is available from the British Library.

Library of Congress Cataloguing-in-Publication Data

Names: Krokida, Zoi, author.

Title: Internet service provider liability for copyright and trade mark infringement : towards an EU co-regulatory framework / Zoi Krokida.

Description: Oxford ; New York : Hart, 2022. | Includes bibliographical references and index.

Identifiers: LCCN 2022000357 (print) | LCCN 2022000358 (ebook) | ISBN 9781509948529 (hardback) | ISBN 9781509948567 (paperback) | ISBN 9781509948543 (pdf) | ISBN 9781509948536 (Epub)

Subjects: LCSH: Internet service providers—Law and legislation—European Union countries. | Copyright infringement—European Union countries. | Trademark infringement—European Union countries. | Tort liability of corporations—European Union countries.

Classification: LCC KJE7012 .K76 2022 (print) | LCC KJE7012 (ebook) | DDC 346.404/82—dc23/eng/20220331

LC record available at https://lccn.loc.gov/2022000357

LC ebook record available at https://lccn.loc.gov/2022000358

ISBN: HB: 978-1-50994-852-9
ePDF: 978-1-50994-854-3
ePub: 978-1-50994-853-6

Typeset by Compuscript Ltd, Shannon

ACKNOWLEDGEMENTS

It seems like it was only yesterday that I was a Bluebook trainee at the European Commission and attended the press release of the EU Digital Single Market Strategy in May 2015 at Berlaymont building in Brussels.

Fascinated about the idea of shaping the EU online world, a year later, I landed in the UK to pursue my PhD studies at the University of Reading and undertake research on the EU regulatory framework of ISPs.

The research of this book stems from my PhD thesis and turned into a manuscript during a global pandemic. Many people contributed with their mentoring, comments and support to the completion of this research. To those people I would like to express my gratitude.

First and foremost, I would like to thank my supervisor Professor Stavroula Karapapa whose constructive feedback on my research has given me the opportunity to develop the contents of my book and overcome any difficulties. I would also like to thank Professor Alina Tryfonidou and Professor Anne Thies; their guidance and expertise in European Law ultimately guided my research.

Also, I would like to thank Professor James Devenney and Professor Andres Guadamuz, who were in the panel of my Viva examination, for their valuable insights and constructive comments and for encouraging me to publish my work.

I am immensely indebted to Malcolm Langley who allowed me to use the facilities of the Queen Mary University Archive for IP law and advised me on the latest publications that were relevant to my research.

I am also particularly grateful to the anonymous reviewers and the editorial team at Hart Publishing. I would like to thank Dr Roberta Bassi who accepted my book proposal and final manuscript as well as Rosemarie Mearns and Linda Staniford for their continuous editorial support.

Further, I would like to express my gratitude to my colleagues and friends whose support has been of ultimate importance for my book. Dr Irene Antonopoulos for being the best academic mentor in my first year as a Lecturer at DMU and for believing in me, and Dr Oludara Akanmidu for offering me comments for the structure of my book. I would also like to thank Dr Athanassios Skourtis, Dr Adnan Farook and Dr Patsy Kirkwood for the fruitful conversations about the progress of our research.

Last but not least, I would like to thank my family: my sister Maria and my brother-in-law Miltos and my parents, my mother Asimina and my father Theodoros for their encouragement. It is to my parents that I would like to dedicate this book; without their emotional and financial support, I wouldn't have been able to start this research in the first place.

Zoi Krokida
Glasgow, 24 March 2022

CONTENTS

LIST OF ABBREVIATIONS

ARPANET	Advanced Research Projects Agency Network
ATVOD	Authority for Television on Demand
AG	Advocate General
ADR	Alternative Dispute Resolution
CJEU	Court of Justice of the European Union
Council	Council of the European Union
DMCA	Digital Millennium Copyright Act
DSMD	Copyright in the Digital Single Market
DNS	Domain Name System
ECD	E-Commerce Directive
EU Commission	European Commission
EU Parliament	European Parliament
ECHR	European Court of Human Rights
EU Charter	European Charter of Fundamental Rights
EUIPO	European Intellectual Property Office
EU Council	European Council
Enforcement Directive	Council Directive on the enforcement of intellectual property rights
GDPR	General Data Protection Regulation
INHOPE	International Association of Internet Hotlines
InfoSoc Directive	Information Society Directive
ICANN	Internet Corporation for Assigned Names and Numbers
IP	Internet Protocol
ISP	Internet Service Provider
ICO	Information Commissioner's Office

IFPI	International Federation of the Phonographic Industry
LCEN	Loi pour la confiance dans l'économie numérique
Host ISP	Host Internet Service Provider
OCSSP	Online Content Sharing Service Provider
OECD	Organisation for Economic Co-operation and Development
Ofcom	Office of Communications
PRS	Performing Right Society
Proposed DSA Regulation	Proposal for a Digital Services Act Regulation
TCP	Transmission Control Protocol
VERO	Verified Rights Owner Program
TMG	Telemediengesetz
VPN	Virtual Private Network
UNCTAD	United Nations Conference on Trade and Development
UN	United Nations
US Copyright Act	Copyright Act of 1976
UGC	Principles for user-generated content services published
UKWISPA	UK Wireless Internet Service Providers
URL	Uniform Resource Locator
UN Rapporteur	United Nations Rapporteur

TABLE OF CASES

European Court of Human Rights Case Law

Court of Justice of the European Union Case Law

UK Case Law

Irish Case Law

US Case Law

Belgian Case Law

Spanish Case Law

Italian Case Law

French Case Law

Swedish Case Law

German Case Law

Greek Case Law

Introduction

I. Historical Background: The Rise and Evolution of Intermediation in E-Commerce and Social Media

In the 1970s, the birth of the internet as a military experiment in a laboratory in the Massachusetts Institute of Technology signalled the beginning of the Information Society era. The internet, under the name Advanced Research Projects Agency Network (ARPANET), started as a computer network which aimed to facilitate military communication in the United States and, with the introduction of the Transmission Control Protocol/Internet Protocol (TCP/IP), evolved into the modern internet we experience today.[1]

In 1989, Sir Tim Berners Lee invented the world wide web (www) and, since 1995, the internet has grown to have a huge commercial orientation.[2] During its evolution, the internet has been revealed to have exponential dynamics and potential. One of its most significant innovations is intermediation which, according to a report from the Organisation for Economic Co-operation and Development (OECD), refers to 'the process by which a firm, acting as the agent of an individual or another firm, leverages its middleman position to foster communications with other agents in the marketplace that will lead to transactions and exchanges that create economic and/or social value'.[3] This means that digital entities can act as middlemen between internet users/consumers and the internet, and therefore have an impact on economic progress and on social norms. Representative examples are the internet service providers (ISPs), cache service providers, and host service providers[4] with the latter being at the epicentre of this book.

Host ISPs can be found in blogs, social media platforms, video-music exchange platforms, or online market place platforms. The first host ISP dates back to the 1970s. In particular, it is evidenced that in 1979 UseNet became the first blog to come to the surface and to enable users to post information online.[5] Following that, other business models appeared and enabled users to exchange information and communicate with each other. For instance, LunarStorm in 1996, and MySpace in 2006, were the first host ISPs to shape online communities of teenagers within their networks.[6]

[1] A Murray, *Information Technology Law: The Law and Society* (Oxford, Oxford University Press, 2019) 22–35.
[2] 'The birth of the web' (*Cern*, 7 October 2021) home.cern/science/computing/birth-web.
[3] OECD, 'The economic and social role of internet intermediaries' (2010) www.oecd.org/digital/ieconomy/44949023.pdf, 15.
[4] Hereinafter host ISPs.
[5] K McIntyre, 'The Evolution of Social Media from 1969 to 2013: A Change in Competition and a Trend Toward Complementary, Niche Sites' (2014) *The Journal of Social Media in Society* 8.
[6] S Edomsowan, 'The history of social media and its impact on business' (2011) 16 *The Journal of Applied Management and Entrepreneurship* 82.

In 2004, Facebook, the idea of a group of Harvard University students, emerged and enabled users to create profiles which showed their preferences, pictures, and hobbies. In 2005, YouTube enabled users to create and upload their videos within the platform,[7] while in 2006 Twitter offered a new type of blogging that was particularly appealing to celebrities.[8]

At the same time, intermediation facilitated the development of e-commerce. For instance, it is evidenced that in 1994 pizzahut.com and NetMarket.com were the first e-commerce platforms to emerge. Pizzahut.com was selling pizzas in California, while NetMarket.com was selling CDs. Later, Amazon started as an online bookstore and developed further to become a retail platform with a wide range of goods and services. In succession, in 1995 eBay, in 1999 Alibaba, and then in 2005 Etsy followed the same business model and displayed goods within their networks.

The services that host ISPs provided have increased their traffic and their popularity. For instance, as of October 2021, Facebook was considered the most popular online platform with 2,895 billion users.[9] At the same time, YouTube's dominance in respect of younger generations has been confirmed, with 91 per cent of its users being between 19–28 years old.[10] In similar fashion, online market places have given a tremendous boost to e-commerce services, with companies such as eBay and Amazon being the leaders in the market. The enormous success of online retail services has resulted in Amazon's CEO becoming the richest man worldwide in 2019.[11]

What is more, the annual revenues of host ISPs have skyrocketed. For instance, it has been reported that in 2009 Facebook had revenues of $777 million, while in 2020 revenues reached $85,965 billion.[12] In similar fashion, in 2020 YouTube reached $19,772 billion in revenue, and Instagram $24 billion.[13] In the e-commerce context, Amazon was the champion of host ISPs offering goods and services to consumers online. In particular, Amazon saw its revenues increase from millions to billions of dollars within 11 years. For instance, as per the OECD's report in 2009, Amazon was the leading online business generating $24,509 billion in revenues, while in 2020 the company achieved $386.06 billion.[14]

The popularity of host ISPs is depicted in a number of surveys and reports. For instance, a number of studies demonstrate the increase of sales within the European Digital Single Market. The EU Commission Communication entitled 'Towards a

[7] H Yu, L Xie and S Sanner, 'The Lifecyle of a Youtube Video: Phases, Content and Popularity' (2015) *Proceedings of the Ninth International AAAI Conference on Web and Social Media* 533.

[8] Edomsowan (n 6) 79–91.

[9] Number of users are available at www.statista.com/statistics/272014/global-social-networks-ranked-by-number-of-users.

[10] M Hills, 'Survey: YouTube Is America's Most Popular Social Media Platform' (*Forbes*, 23 March 2018) www.forbes.com/sites/meganhills1/2018/03/23/social-media-demographics/#59f74a57783a.

[11] R Frank, 'Jeff Bezos is now the richest man in modern history' (*cnbc*, 16 July 2018) www.cnbc.com/2018/07/16/jeff-bezos-is-now-the-richest-man-in-modern-history.html; OECD (n 3).

[12] Annual revenue of Facebook is available at www.statista.com/statistics/268604/annual-revenue-of-facebook/.

[13] YouTube revenues are available at www.businessofapps.com/data/youtube-statistics/; Instagram www.businessofapps.com/data/instagram-statistics/.

[14] OECD (n 3) 24; net revenue of amazon is available at www.statista.com/statistics/266289/net-revenue-of-amazon-by-region/.

modern, more European copyright framework', remarks that 49 per cent of European citizens have accessed music and films online.[15] A study conducted by the European Parliament reveals that in 2015, around 49 per cent of EU nationals purchased goods or services online, while in 2019 this percentage increased to 60 per cent.[16] At the same time, Denmark seems to have the greatest number of online consumers, Sweden and the Netherlands take second and third places, respectively.[17] With regard to the profiles of EU online consumers, it seems that individuals between 20–34 years old are more active in online shopping when compared with individuals in older age groups, such as 55–75 years old. At the same time, EU consumers can also be categorised according to their educational background and economic activity. In particular, one report outlines that 85 per cent of internet users who have attended higher education use online services, this compares with individuals with lower educational background of whom 35 per cent use online services.[18] Meanwhile, 78 per cent of internet users are employed (either as employees or self-employed), and only 55 per cent of users who are retired or unemployed make use of online platforms, such as purchasing online goods or posting content online.[19] A 2015 study initiated by the European Commission reveals that clothing, shoes, and accessories are the most popular items bought online, followed by electronic software and books.[20] Finally, the popularity of host ISPs has very recently been reinforced in light of the COVID-19 pandemic where a high number of individuals have been required to remain at home or self-isolate.[21] Specifically, a number of studies reveal the exponential increase in online purchases and the interaction of internet users through social media platforms. UNCTAD's report on COVID-19 and e-commerce shows that in May 2020 the retail turnover reached 40 per cent, this compares with just 10 per cent in July 2019, several months pre-pandemic.[22]

The popularity of host ISPs is warranted for various reasons. For instance, they facilitate information amongst internet users. A study conducted by the Digital News Oxford's Reuters Institute in 2019 indicates that 52 per cent of respondents between 25–34 years old reported Facebook to be their main source of information, while at the same time 32 per cent of the respondents between 18–24 years old claimed to rely on YouTube for their news.[23] What is more, these platforms enhance innovation and productivity.

[15] European Commission, 'Towards a modern, more European copyright framework' COM (2015) 626 final 2.

[16] M Negreiro, 'The rise of e-commerce and the cashless society' (2020) *European Parliamentary Research Service* 1.

[17] N Lomba and T Evas, 'Digital Services Act: European added value assessment' (2020) *European Parliamentary Research Service* 64.

[18] ibid.

[19] Negreiro (n 16).

[20] Directorate General for Justice and Consumers, 'Identifying the main cross-border obstacles to the Digital Single Market and where they matter most: DSM consumer survey (2015)' (*data.europa.eu*, 14 December 2018) data.europa.eu/data/datasets/dsm-consumer-survey-2015?locale=en.

[21] UNCTAD, 'How COVID-19 triggered the digital and e-commerce turning point' (*unctad.org*, 15 March 2021), unctad.org/news/how-covid-19-triggered-digital-and-e-commerce-turning-point.

[22] United Nations, 'Covid-19 and e-commerce: a global review' (2021) unctad.org/system/files/official-document/dtlstict2020d13_en_0.pdf.

[23] Reuters Institute for the Study of Journalism, 'Reuters Institute Digital News Report' (2019) 56; see also Edomsowan (n 4) 79–91.

For instance, as per the OECD's report on online platforms, host ISPs offer apps with tools for software development, or for open source technology where new developers can benefit and enhance their projects.[24] At the same time, it has been found that host ISPs can engage different actors and initiate a collaborative environment. This is because they could guide consumers or ISPs to other host ISPs, or engage other stakeholders such as the hospitality sector. Representative examples can be found in the business model of booking.com or yelp, both connect consumers with accommodation or food services.[25] Finally, host ISPs also enhance democratic values in society. This is because they can be compared with the Ancient Agora of Athens, ie, a place, in ancient Greece, where Athenians would gather to debate their views and criticise political developments and decisions. Similarly, host ISPs offer public spaces for internet users to exchange and debate their views. For this reason, Laidlaw describes host ISPs as vehicles of deliberative democracy where individuals can exchange information in online settings,[26] while the Rapporteur of the UN, referring to freedom of expression, argues that the internet 'contributes to the discovery of the truth and progress of society as a whole'.[27]

At the same time, e-commerce offers a number of benefits to online consumers in comparison to the physical environment. For instance, host ISPs offering goods or services online are accessible to their customers 24 hours a day, at the same time they offer a selection of goods, so customers have the opportunity to compare prices through price lists and to access detailed information about quality and about manufacturers through reviews.[28] Further, host ISPs have a positive economic function; certainly, through their platforms online advertising seems to be blooming. For instance, as per the Advertising Interactive Bureau, in 2009 online advertising within EU borders reached €12.9 billion, with Slovenia and Poland being the pioneers[29] while 10 years later, in 2019, online advertising amounted to €64.8 billion.[30] As per the Eurostat's report, it has been demonstrated that in 2018, 26 per cent of EU business was oriented towards online advertising, Denmark, Malta, and Sweden attracting the highest number of online advertising businesses.[31] Finally, a recent study conducted by the Advertising Interactive Bureau, in July 2020, reveals that the revenues from online advertising in 12 EU countries are above the EU average, UK and Sweden taking the first place with €338 and €260 spend per capita respectively.[32]

[24] OECD, 'An Introduction to Online Platforms and Their Role in the Digital Transformation' (2019) 28, 29.

[25] AB Rivares et al, 'Like it or not? The impact of online platforms on the productivity of incumbent service' (OECD, 2019) 12–13.

[26] E Laidlaw, 'Internet Gatekeepers, Human Rights and Corporate Social Responsibilities' (LSE PhD Thesis, 2012) 18.

[27] F La Rue, 'Report of the Special Rapporteur on the promotion and protection of the right to freedom of opinion and expression' (2011).

[28] M Negreiro, 'The rise of e-commerce and the cashless society' (2020) *European Parliamentary Research Service* 6.

[29] OECD (n 3) 19.

[30] IAB, 'AdEx Benchmark' (*iabeurope*, 2019) iabeurope.eu/knowledge-hub/iab-europe-adex-benchmark-2019-study/.

[31] Eurostat, 'Social media use by type, internet advertising' (2020).

[32] IAB, 'ADEX full report' (*iabeurope*, July 2020) iabeurope.eu/knowledge-hub/iab-europe-adex-benchmark-2020-study-highlights/.

II. Legal Problem

Internet Service Providers (ISPs) are described as the 'backbone of internet infrastructure'.[33] They do not only serve as a communication tool among internet users, but they also offer a multitude of services.[34] At the same time, they enable copyright holders and brand owners to address a broader audience for their works and brands.[35] However, the activities of ISPs, and in particular of host ISPs which are the main focus of this book, seem to attract many incidents of copyright and trade mark infringements. According to the summary responses to the public consultation on the modernisation of the enforcement of intellectual property rights launched by the EU Commission in September 2016, the emergence of new host ISPs has led to increased online piracy.[36] Likewise, the Global online piracy study[37] reveals that in 2017 a high percentage of internet users across the EU Member States have accessed music via illegal sources, with Spanish internet users being the pioneers in this regard – 35 per cent of the Spanish population are believed to have used such sources. At the same time, content owners see their work being circulated without their permission on video exchange platforms and social networks, as a result they suffer very high annual losses.[38] For instance, at European level, the average user consumed unlawful content 5.9 times each month in 2020,[39] while in the UK, the creative sector has faced annual losses of £9 billion due to copyright infringements occurring on the internet.[40]

[33] I Revolidis, 'Internet intermediaries and copyright enforcement in the EU: In search of a balanced approach' in M Corrales, M Fenwick and N Forgó (eds), *New Technology, Big Data and the Law* (Berlin, Springer, 2017) 224; a Costa Rican judgment considers internet access as a fundamental right, see in A Guadamuz, 'Text of the Costa Rican ruling declaring Internet as a fundamental right' (*Technollama*, 23 April 2012) www.technollama.co.uk/text-of-the-costa-rican-ruling-declaring-internet-as-a-fundamental-right; C Beaumont, 'Finland makes broadband a legal right' *The Telegraph* (15 October 2009) www.telegraph.co.uk/technology/broadband/6337698/Finland-makes-fast-broadband-a-legal-right.html.

[34] OECD (n 3) 9.

[35] A Bridy and D Keller, 'U.S. Copyright Office Section 512 Study: Comments in Response to Notice of Inquiry' (31 March 2016) 14–15.

[36] European Commission, 'Public Consultation on the evaluation and modernisation of the legal framework for the enforcement of intellectual property rights: Summary of responses' (2016) 8.

[37] J Poort and JP Quintais, 'Global online piracy study' (2018) *University of Amsterdam* 50, 51.

[38] OECD, 'The Economic Impact of Counterfeiting and Piracy' (2008) www.oecd.org/sti/ind/theeconomicimpactofcounterfeitingandpiracy.htm; UNODC, 'The Globalization of Crime: A Transnational Organized Crime Threat Assessment' (2010) www.unodc.org/documents/data-and-analysis/tocta/TOCTA_Report_2010_low_res.pdf; European Commission Staff Working Paper, 'Counterfeit and Piracy Watch List' SWD (2018) 492 final, trade.ec.europa.eu/doclib/docs/2018/december/tradoc_157564.pdf; 'YouTube law fight "threatens net"' (*bbc news*, 27 May 2008) news.bbc.co.uk/1/hi/technology/7420955.stm.

[39] European Intellectual Property Office, 'Online copyright infringement in the European Union: music, films and TV (2017–2020), trends and drivers' (November 2019) 22, euipo.europa.eu/tunnel-web/secure/webdav/guest/document_library/observatory/documents/quantification-of-ipr-infringement/online-copyright-infringement-in-eu/online_copyright_infringement_in_eu_en.pdf.

[40] Intellectual Property Office, 'IP Crime and Enforcement Report 2018–2019' (2019) 54, assets.publishing.service.gov.uk/government/uploads/system/uploads/attachment_data/file/842351/IP-Crime-Report-2019.pdf; Oxford Economics, 'The economic impact of the UK film industry' (June 2010), www.bfi.org.uk/sites/bfi.org.uk/files/downloads/economic-impact-of-the-uk-film-industry-2010-06.pdf; due to the expeditious increase of intellectual property infringements online, China has established specific online courts that deal with online disputes, see White Paper, 'Chinese courts and internet judiciary' (2019) 66, wlf.court.gov.cn/upload/file/2019/12/03/11/40/20191203114024_87277.pdf.

Against this background, feeling the deck tilting back and forth below them, content owners and brand owners have turned against host ISPs to seek compensation for the violation of their rights. Instead of turning against primary infringers, they are bringing proceedings against host ISPs.[41] Basing their legal claims on the provisions enshrined in the E-Commerce Directive (ECD),[42] they are asking for either monetary or injunctive relief against host ISPs.

However, the existing legal framework under the ECD that regulates host ISPs' activities appears to be outdated.[43] This is mainly because Article 14(1) of the ECD refrains from providing a definition of liability of host ISPs and leaves it to the discretion of European national jurisdictions. The result is a patchwork of miscellaneous tort law doctrines that either impose secondary liability rules to host ISPs or are difficult to apply within the online context. As a corollary, the rights of intellectual property holders might not be safeguarded, while the right of host ISPs to conduct business as per Article 16 of the EU Charter of Fundamental Rights might be restricted.[44]

This outdated framework has been aggravated by the introduction of the Copyright in the Digital Single Market Directive[45] (DSMD), which is in force in parallel with the ECD. While the DSMD has yet to be tested – indeed, it was only finalised on 17 April 2019 and is thus relatively new – there appear to be several problematic issues to be addressed.[46] After more than two years of intensive negotiations this much anticipated Directive provides a definition of the liability of host ISPs, but it also marks a seismic shift with regard to the kind of liability that is ascribed to host ISPs. Refraining from the secondary liability regime that exists under the ECD, the DSMD endorses a primary liability regime for host ISPs. This means that when an infringement takes place within the online network, the host ISP is liable for the infringement. Although this understanding might offer a higher degree of protection for the rights of intellectual property holders, it might have a detrimental effect on the rights of host ISPs and internet users/consumers.

The ascription of primary liability rules to a host ISP under Article 17 of the DSMD establishes a new era of liability regime for those host ISPs whose services aim at 'enabling users to upload and share a large amount of copyright-protected content with the purpose of obtaining profit from that activity'.[47] This is because the introduction of primary liability to ISPs seems to go against the main rationale of tortious secondary liability rules imposed by European policymakers in the ECD back in 2000. According to the secondary liability regime, host ISPs can be held liable if they have knowledge of the infringing content but fail to remove it upon being notified by the intellectual

[41] B Kleinschmidt, 'An International Comparison of ISP's Liabilities for Unlawful Third-Party Content' (2010) 18 *International Journal of Law and Information Technology* 332; C Waelde and L Edwards, 'Online Intermediaries and Liability for Copyright Infringement' (WIPO Workshop Keynote Paper, Geneva 2005) 3; JL Goldsmith and T Wu, *Who Controls the Internet? Illusions of a Borderless World* (Oxford, Oxford University Press, 2006) 107.

[42] Council Directive (EC) 2000/31 on certain legal aspects of information society services, in particular electronic commerce, in the Internal Market [2000] O.J. L 178.

[43] As I critically examine in ch 3 of this book.

[44] Analysis of the regulatory framework of host ISPs under the ECD in ch 3.

[45] The Copyright in the Digital Single Market Directive (hereinafter DSMD).

[46] As I critically examine in ch 4 of this book.

[47] Recital 62 of DSMD.

property holders. So, it is this defence of knowledge that has been widely used by host ISPs to exonerate them from liability, and which has allowed them to continue without disrupting the operation of their business model.

By contrast to secondary liability rules, primary liability rules do not require the element of knowledge. For instance, without the defence of knowledge, new players would be hesitant to enter the Digital Single Market, and existing host ISPs would be forced to develop or license highly advanced technology in order to prevent the emergence of online infringements in the first place. This might pose serious threats to innovation and competitiveness within the Digital Single Market and be in conflict with the main aims of the Digital Single Market Strategy that outlined the need to 'maximize the growth potential of the Digital Economy'.[48]

What is more, the imposition of primary liability rules to host ISPs might create a side effect for internet users' rights. Under the threat of being held primarily liable for the infringements of their users, host ISPs might 'over-remove' content without further investigating its illegality. This understanding has been exemplified in a number of studies which demonstrate that host ISPs are in favour of taking down content without a detailed examination of the notifications that they receive.[49] However, as these studies reveal, the content that has been removed by host ISPs upon notice is not always unlawful. For instance, it might be a parody or a work that belongs in the public domain. In this way, the removal of legitimate content by host ISPs might amount to censorship of users' speech and, thus violate Article 11 of the EU Charter of Fundamental Rights that guarantees the freedom of expression of individuals.

Finally, the Proposal for a Digital Services Act Regulation has been announced by the European Commission on 15 December 2020.[50] Its aim is to replace the ECD and offer an updated legal framework for host ISPs in order to safeguard the fundamental rights of the parties involved. To do so, it reinforces the defences of the ECD and fails to offer a solid response to the host ISPs' liability conundrum. What is more, while it enshrines some promising provisions, it seems unclear how the proposed DSA regulation would be compatible with the DSMD which is now in force within the EU borders.

On the basis of the above, it appears that the existing legal framework for ISPs' activities under Article 14(1) of the ECD and Article 17 of the DSMD either does not safeguard right holders, users, and ISPs or favour right holders' rights, and this undermines users and host ISPs' interests. For this reason, it is evident that a more robust legal framework is needed.

[48] European Commission, 'A Digital Single Market Strategy for Europe' (2015) COM 192 final 13–14.

[49] Lecture by S Nas, Bits of Freedom, 'The Multatuli Project ISP Notice & take down' (2004), available at www-old.bof.nl/docs/researchpaperSANE.pdf; C Ahlert, C Marsden and C Yung, 'How "Liberty" Disappeared from Cyberspace: The Mystery Shopper Tests Internet Content Self-Regulation' (2014), available at www.academia.edu/686683/How_Liberty_Disappeared_from_Cyberspace_The_Mystery_Shopper_Tests_Internet_Content_Self_Regulation; D Kiat Boon Seng, 'The State of the Discordant Union: An Empirical Analysis of DMCA Takedown Notices' (2014) 18 *Virginia Journal of Law and Technology* 369–37; D Keller, 'Empirical evidence of over removal by internet companies under intermediary liability laws: an updated list' (The Center for Internet and Society, 8 February 2021) http://cyberlaw.stanford.edu/blog/2021/02/empirical-evidence-over-removal-internet-companies-under-intermediary-liability-laws.

[50] Proposal for a Regulation of the European Parliament and the Council on a Single Market For Digital Services (Digital Services Act) and amending Directive 2000/31/EC COM/2020/825 final (hereinafter proposed DSA Regulation).

III. Research Question and Aims

In light of the issues discussed in the previous section, this book addresses the following question:

> How should the EU legal framework of host ISPs' liability be shaped in order to safeguard intellectual property right holders' rights as well as the interests of internet users/consumers and host ISPs?

This means the aim of this book is twofold. First, it aims to critically assess the current legal framework that regulates the activities of host ISPs at a normative level, and to then propose an array of recommendations to address how the regulatory framework of host ISPs should be shaped. It is important to mention that the proposed legal framework takes into consideration all the different interests of the parties at stake. On the one hand, the rights of intellectual property owners shall be protected. This understanding has been reinforced in a number of EU legislative tools. Indeed, Article 17(2) of the EU Charter of Fundamental Rights states that 'Intellectual property law shall be protected'. Likewise, Article 27(2) of the Universal Declaration of Human Rights states, 'Everyone has the right to the protection of the moral and material interests resulting from any scientific, literary or artistic production of which he is the author.' On the other hand, in *Scarlet v Sabam*, the Court of Justice of the European Union (CJEU) concluded that intellectual property rights are not inviolable, therefore their protection of intellectual property rights is not absolute.[51] As the CJEU outlined, intellectual property rights shall not be prioritised against other fundamental rights at stake.[52] Such fundamental rights include the rights of internet users and the rights of ISPs. Users' rights are safeguarded under Article 11(1) of the EU Charter of Fundamental Rights that states, 'Everyone has the right to freedom of expression. This right shall include freedom to hold opinions and to receive and impart information and ideas without interference by public authority and regardless of frontiers.' In similar fashion, Article 19(2) of the International Covenant on Civil and Political Rights states, 'Everyone shall have the right to freedom of expression; this right shall include freedom to seek, receive and impart information and ideas of all kinds, regardless of frontiers, either orally, in writing or in print, in the form of art, or through any other media of his choice.' Host ISPs' fundamental rights to conduct business are protected under Article 16 of the EU Charter of Fundamental Rights which notes that 'the freedom to conduct a business in accordance with Community law and national laws and practices is recognised'.

Therefore, an equilibrium between the interests of the parties involved shall be achieved. This equilibrium has been reinforced by a bedrock of case law at European level. As the CJEU noted in *Scarlet v Sabam*, it has been concluded that 'national authorities and courts must strike a fair balance between the protection of copyright and the protection of the fundamental rights of individuals who are affected by such measures'.[53]

[51] Case C-70/10 *Scarlet Extended SA v Société belge des auteurs, compositeurs et éditeurs SCRL (SABAM)* [2011] ECR I-11959, para 43.

[52] ibid para 44.

[53] ibid para 45.

In addition, in the *Promusicae* case, 'Member States must [...] take care to rely on an interpretation of the directives which allows a fair balance to be struck between the various fundamental rights protected by the Community legal order.'[54]

Further, in order to answer the research question, a number of sub-questions are addressed:

(i) How does the current legal framework under the ECD regulate the liability of host ISPs?[55]
(ii) How does the Copyright in the Digital Single Market Directive regulate liability of OCSSPs?[56]
(iii) How does the Proposal for a Digital Services Act regulate liability of providers of hosting services?
(iv) What is the impact of the current legal framework on the rights of internet users, right holders, and host ISPs?[57]
(v) Would a responsibility framework based on a co-regulatory approach for host ISPs have merits?[58]
(vi) What kind of responsibilities should be ascribed to host ISPs?[59]
(vii) What safeguards should be introduced in order to preserve host ISPs' right to operate their businesses, as well as internet users' right to free speech?[60]
(viii) Would the establishment of a host ISP supervisory authority have merits for host ISPs, right holders, and internet users?[61]

IV. The Need for this Book and Originality

A. Article 14(1) of the E-Commerce Directive 2000/31/EC (ECD) Adopts an Outdated Approach with Regard to Host Internet Service Providers' (Host ISPs) Liability

First, the need for this project is warranted in light of the outdated legal framework for host ISPs under the ECD. This outdated framework, as my findings indicate in chapter three, does not offer adequate protection for intellectual property holders' rights, while at the same time it subordinates internet users' interests and host ISPs' business operations.

[54] Case C-275/06 *Productores de Música de España (Promusicae) v Telefónica de España SAU* [2008] ECR I-271, para 70.
[55] This sub-question is addressed in ch 3.
[56] OCSSPs are a new sub-type of host ISPs and are enshrined in the DSMD. An analysis of this new type of host ISPs is presented in ch 4.
[57] This sub-question is in ch 5 of this book.
[58] A thorough analysis of the normative considerations is presented in ch 7. In a nutshell, a responsibility framework based on a co-regulatory approach lies on the ascription of a set of responsibilities to host ISPs through which they would be accountable to a host ISP supervisory authority.
[59] This sub-question is discussed in chs 7 and 8.
[60] This sub-question is addressed in chs 7 and 8.
[61] This sub-question is discussed in ch 9.

Article 14(1) of the ECD states that a host ISP can escape from liability if:

(a) the provider does not have actual knowledge of illegal activity or information and, as regards claims for damages, is not aware of facts or circumstances from which the illegal activity or information is apparent; or
(b) the provider, upon obtaining such knowledge or awareness, acts expeditiously to remove or to disable access to legal systems, of requiring the service provider to terminate or the information.

However, it does not define host ISPs' liability. As a result, national courts turn to their national tortious legal doctrines in order to ascribe liability to host ISPs. Given that secondary liability is not harmonised at EU level, heterogenous tortious secondary liability doctrines have been applied by national courts with conflicting outcomes. Further, disappointment over the regulatory framework for host ISPs' activities, as enshrined in Article 14(1) of the ECD, is mirrored in a handful of policy documents at European level. In these policy documents, different stakeholders, such as right holders, civil society organisations, and online platforms associations, have expressed their dissatisfaction. More specifically, pursuant to the public consultation on the role of host ISPs in 2015,[62] 49.6 per cent of 599 respondents admitted that the 'liability regime introduced in Section IV of the ECD (Articles 12–15) has proven not fit for purpose or has negatively affected market level playing field'.[63] At the same time, in a public consultation on the ECD in 2011,[64] stakeholders criticised the current legal framework under the ECD. This is mainly due to the lack of guidance on the concept of 'knowledge' and the term 'expeditious', which are included in Article 14(1) of the ECD which dictates that a host ISP that provides hosting services to its users can be exonerated from liability if it has no knowledge of the allegedly infringing material and, if upon receiving notification of the infringing material, the host ISP expeditiously removes the material.

B. Article 17 of the Copyright in the Digital Single Market Directive 2019/790 (DSMD): A Controversial Approach with Regard to Online Content Sharing Service Providers' (OCSSPs) Liability and a Problematic Intersection with Article 14(1) of the E-Commerce Directive (ECD)

The second need for this project is also justified in view of the controversial legislative attempts to amend and reconstruct the existing legal framework for host ISPs at

[62] European Commission, 'Results of the Public Consultation on the Regulatory Environment for Platforms, Online Intermediaries, Data and Cloud Computing and the Collaborative Economy' (26 January 2016) https://ec.europa.eu/digital-single-market/en/news/results-public-consultation-regulatory-environment-platforms-online-intermediaries-data-and/ [http://perma.cc/2CE8-MY3D].

[63] M Husovec and R Leenes, 'Study on the role of online intermediaries: Summary of the public consultation, a study prepared for the European Commission DG Communications Networks, Content & Technology' (25 May 2016) https://op.europa.eu/en/publication-detail/-/publication/12aa1485-23ce-11e6-86d0-01aa75ed71a1.

[64] European Commission Staff Working Paper, 'Online Services, Including E-Commerce, in the Single Market' SEC (2011) 1641 final 33–34, eur-lex.europa.eu/legal-content/EN/TXT/?uri=CELEX%3A52011SC1641; European Commission, 'Public Consultation on the future of electronic commerce in the Internal Market and the implementation of the Directive on electronic commerce: Summary of response' (2010) ec.europa.eu/information_society/newsroom/image/document/2017-4/consultation_summary_report_en_2010_42070.pdf.

European level with the introduction of the DSMD on 17 April 2019. The DSMD was endorsed in the aftermath of the impact assessment on the enforcement of copyright rules in the digital ecosystem, where rights holders expressed concerns about fair remuneration and control of the circulation of their works.[65] Although the DSMD has not yet been tested, a cluster of problematic issues have already been identified.[66] To name a few, Article 17 of the DSMD, which is relevant to this research, addresses the liability of a new type of host ISP, online content sharing service providers (OCSSPs). It introduces a primary liability regime which conflicts with the rationale of a secondary liability regime as set forth in Article 14(1) of the ECD. It endorses a licensing system for the OCSSPs and a notice and stay down mechanism. As corollary, Article 17 of the DSMD might give rise to tantamount concerns with regard to protection of different interests at stake, namely the rights of intellectual property holders, internet users, and host ISPs. For this reason, this research engages in a comprehensive analysis of the implications of the DSMD for the rights of OCSSPs, intellectual property holders, and internet users. This analysis forms chapter four of this book.

What is more, the DSMD does not only entail problematic features itself. Rather, it also presents a problematic intersection with the ECD since both legislative tools exist in parallel. As will be discussed in chapter four, Article 17 of the DSMD is a *lex specialis* to Article 14(1) of the ECD. While Article 14(1) of the ECD endorses a secondary liability regime, Article 17 of the DSMD introduces a primary liability framework for OCSSPs. This dual liability regime might trigger a fragmented framework of copyright law, split the existing case law at the European level, impede innovation within the Digital Single Market, as well as force the creation of a monopolistic market within the OCSSPs. A detailed analysis of this problematic intersection is presented in chapter four.

C. Proposal for Digital Services Act Regulation

The third need for this book is due to the emerging proposal for a Digital Services Act Regulation,[67] which the European Commission announced on 15 December 2020. The proposed DSA Regulation is about the liability of host ISPs for trade mark infringements and acts as a default for the liability of content sharing service providers for

[65] European Commission Staff Working document, 'Executive summary of the impact assessment on the modernisation of EU copyright rules' (2016) SWD/2016/0302 final.

[66] J Quintais et al, 'Safeguarding User Freedoms in Implementing Article 17 of the Copyright in the Digital Single Market Directive: Recommendations from European Academics' (November 2019); M Husovec and J Quintais, 'How to License Article 17? Exploring the Implementation Options for the New EU Rules on Content-Sharing Platforms' (1 October 2019) papers.ssrn.com/sol3/papers.cfm?abstract_id=3463011&download=yes; G Frosio and S Mendis, 'Monitoring and filtering: European reform or Global trend?' (2019) *Center for International Intellectual Property Studies Research Paper* 21; C Angelopoulos and J Quintais, 'Fixing copyright reform: a better solution to online infringement' (2019) 10 *Journal of Intellectual Property, Information Technology and E-Commerce Law* 153; M Vermeulen, 'Online content: to regulate or not to regulate – is that the question?' (2019) *Association for progressive communications* 10–11; Communia, 'Guidelines for the implementation of Article 17 of the DSMD' www.notion.so/Article-17-Use-of-copyrighted-content-by-online-platforms-8e9ab9aaa4ce42c2a6f35cb7415b8b83; K Grisse, 'After the storm – examining the final version of Article 17 of the new Directive (EU) 2019/790' (2019) 14 *Journal of Intellectual Property Law & Practice* 887.

[67] Proposed DSA Regulation.

copyright infringements. Although the proposed DSA Regulation is not legally binding at this stage of the EU legislative procedure, the proposed DSA Regulation is of interest to this book. Interestingly, the proposed DSA Regulation seems to be a promising approach and it has received a warm welcome from different stakeholders.[68] Yet, a number of flaws have already been identified. For instance, the proposed DSA Regulation maintains the liability exemptions of Article 14(1) of the e-Commerce Directive, and therefore it maintains the reverse logic of liability of host ISPs, while at the same time it imposes a very broad spectrum of obligations on very large platforms. Finally, one might wonder which provisions are also applicable to the copyright context and, more specifically, to Article 17 of the DSMD. A detailed analysis of the intersection of the proposed DSA Regulation and Article 17 of the DSMD is provided in chapter six.

D. Originality of the Book

The originality of this book draws on four main aspects. First, the work focuses on the host ISPs' liability for copyright and trade mark infringements. Although academic literature which addresses host ISPs' liability for copyright and trade mark protection exists separately, no research has been found which critically assesses host ISPs' liability for both copyright and trade mark infringements that occur within their networks. This is urgent for two main reasons. From an academic perspective, more attention should be drawn to these two intellectual property infringements since copyright and trade mark infringements constitute the most common intellectual property violations to occur online. Indeed, as elaborated in chapter three, a bedrock of case law reveals the frequency of copyright and trade mark violations online. The second reason is the dual liability regime which was endorsed with the DSMD. As explained at the outset of this chapter, Article 14(1) of the ECD includes a secondary liability regime for host ISPs. By contrast, Article 17 of the DSMD introduces a primary liability framework for copyright infringements that accrue within their networks. A detailed analysis of the implications of this dual liability regime for host ISPs and internet users seems crucial for innovation in the Digital Single Market, and for consumers' welfare in general.

Further, this research is the first to assess the current legislative framework under the DSMD, which was finalised on 17 April 2019. Even though the DSMD is a new Directive and its implications have not yet been tested in the courts' legal arena, the findings indicate a cluster of problematic aspects within Article 17 of the DSMD.

[68] EFF states that 'The DSA is an important opportunity to clarify the EU's commitment to fundamental rights online, and to secure basic rights that will be built upon in the years to come' in EFF, 'Preserve What Works, Fix What is Broken: EFF's Policy Principles for the Digital Services Act' (2020) www.eff.org/issues/eu-policy-principles; The Senior Director for Law and Policy of Article 19 noted that 'ARTICLE 19's preliminary analysis indicates that the DSA is looking to maintain the cornerstones of the E-Commerce Directive, including conditional immunity from liability and the prohibition on general monitoring. This is positive and corresponds to our recommendations in the consultations organised by the European Commission in ARTICLE 19, "EU: The draft Digital Services Act and the Digital Markets Act must protect freedom of expression"', www.article19.org/resources/digital-rights/.

So far, the existing literature has limited its discussion to the proposal for a DSMD and the compromise texts of the Council and the EU Parliament. For this reason, this book puts forwards a critical evaluation of the implications of the final draft of the DSMD, including a historical account of the whole legislative process which culminated in the DSMD. What is more, this book is the first work to address the intersection between Article 14(1) of the ECD and Article 17 of the DSMD. Under the scope of Article 14(1) of the ECD falls the host ISPs' liability for trade mark infringements, while Article 17 of the DSMD regulates OCSSPs' liability for copyright infringements. Given that this book addresses both copyright and trade mark infringements, a critical examination of the intersection between these two legislative tools is warranted. It is this intersection that is also problematic and, thus, might pose serious risks for the interests of intellectual property holders, internet users, and host ISPs.

In addition, this book is the first work to address the emerging legislative framework in the form of the proposed DSA Regulation announced on 15 December 2020 by the European Commission.[69] The proposed DSA Regulation addresses the liability of host ISPs and is followed by the outcomes of the impact assessment which revealed a broad consensus amongst different stakeholders for the need to update the current regulatory framework for host ISPs by imposing additional obligations.[70] More specifically, this book offers an analysis of the relevant provisions of the proposed DSA Regulation which aims to replace the ECD, while at the same time it critically examines the intersection of the proposed Regulation with Article 17 of the DSMD in relation to copyright infringements.

Finally, the main contribution of this book derives from the novel suggestions that it includes. It suggests a regulatory framework that takes into consideration, to a great extent, the different interests at stake. Although many scholars have addressed the thorny issues of host ISPs' liability, they mostly consider one-sided amendments in the legislation, with no attempt to balance the interests of intellectual property holders, internet users, and host ISPs. For this reason, this book aims to suggest plausible solutions for all the parties involved, and thus safeguard, to a great extent, fundamental rights as they are explicitly included in the EU Charter of Fundamental Rights. More specifically, these novel recommendations include the establishment of a responsibility framework based on a co-regulatory approach. This framework is about imposing a set of responsibilities to host ISPs, along with the establishment of a host ISP supervisory authority in cases of copyright and trade mark violations online. This authority will have specific duties do with enforcement, adjudication, and information awareness concerning the negative effects of online piracy. These recommendations, which are set out in Part III, are developed through an extensive analysis made on the basis of normative and theoretical underpinnings, a cluster of case law and policy initiatives at European level, and at national level across the EU Member States.

[69] Proposed DSA Regulation.

[70] European Commission staff working document, 'Executive summary of the impact assessment report' SWD (2020) 1–3.

V. Scope of the Book

The scope of this book covers copyright and trade mark infringements made online, a specific type of internet service provider, namely host ISPs, and the different types of liability that host ISPs might be ascribed for copyright and trade mark infringements that accrue within their networks.

A. Copyright and Trade Mark Infringements

Although there is a vast array of different kinds of violation in the digital ecosystem, the focus of this book is limited to copyright and trade mark violations online. This is because, within the online context, the kinds of intellectual property infringements that mostly occur rest in the field of copyright and trade mark law.[71] Previous literature has identified that digitisation and the internet have caused copyright holders, internet users, and host ISPs to enter into the arena of the so-called copyright wars. Copyright has become one of the most affected legal disciplines on the internet due to the ease and speed through which materials can be circulated online.

This understanding is exemplified by an increasing litigation as indicated by a bedrock of EU case law that was issued just over the last decade. Representative examples are the *Scarlet v Sabam*,[72] *Netlog v Sabam*,[73] *UPC Telekabel*,[74] *Svensson case*,[75] *GS Media*[76] and *Brein v Ziggo*[77] rulings, to name but a few. All the above cases are about the ascription of liability rules to host ISPs for unauthorised copyright content uploaded by their users, or for linking to material offered on third party websites without the right holders' permission.

Furthermore, the negative implications of digitisation on copyright has been mirrored in several policy documents where intellectual property holders have expressed their disappointment and concerns about the current legal framework, as depicted in the ECD.[78] More specifically, in the public consultation for the modernisation of the enforcement of intellectual property rights, almost 50 per cent of the respondents outlined that the current legal framework was no longer fit for purpose,[79] while the majority of the respondents viewed 'commercial scale IPR infringements as

[71] A joint project between the European Patent Office and the European Union Intellectual Property Office, 'IPR-intensive industries and economic performance in the European Union' (2019) 26.

[72] Case C-70/10 *Scarlet Extended SA* (n 51).

[73] Case C-360/10 *Belgische Vereniging van Auteurs, Com- ponisten en Uitgevers CVBA (SABAM) v Netlog NV* (2012) ECLI:EU:C:2012:85.

[74] Case C-314/12 *UPC Telekabel Wien* (2014) ECLI:EU:C:2014:192.

[75] Case C-466/12 *Nils Svensson and Others v Retriever Sverige AB* (2014) ECLI:EU:C:2014:76.

[76] Case C-160/15 *GS Media BV v Sanoma Media Netherlands BV and Others* (2016) ECLI:EU:C:2016:644.

[77] Case C-610/15 *Stichting Brein v Ziggo BV and XS4ALL Internet BV* (2017) ECLI:EU:C:2017:456.

[78] See also H Bosher, *The Human Element in Online Infringement* (London, Routledge, 2020) 6 where Bosher notes that 'at every advent of a new technology a fear rises in stakeholders that copyright is under threat; copyright law is claimed to be out of date and if immediate action is not taken, copyright will become obsolete'.

[79] EU Commission, 'Public Consultation on the evaluation and modernization of the legal framework for the enforcement of intellectual property rights: Summary of responses' (2016) 1.

a global business'.[80] Along similar lines, the outcomes of the public consultation on the future of electronic commerce in the Internal Market indicated 'the failure to respect copyright and the size of the illegal market'.[81]

Finally, the need to examine copyright infringements online is also warranted in light of the controversy that revolved around the DSMD, which was the result of intensive lobbying by publishers and content industries. It took two years and six months to finalise this controversial legislative instrument, even so, it has generated severe criticism from civil society associations, politicians, internet activists, and individuals, and its implications are yet to be seen since there is a timeframe of two years for its implementation by national Member States.[82] The main aim of the DSMD is to address the value gap between the creators of works and the economic benefits of disseminating content within the networks of OCSSPs. The term 'value gap' is understood as the non-fair remuneration of creators from the dissemination of their content in the digital ecosystem.[83] For instance, a report conducted by the International Federation of the Phonographic Industry outlines that whereas paid-online music platforms return $US20 to the creators per user, the return to authors per user from free online music platforms is limited to just $US1.[84] However, as many commentators argue, it seems that the DSMD might override this aim and may pose serious risks for the interests of OCSSPs and internet users.[85]

Apart from copyright law, trade mark law has been affected by the rapid increase of e-commerce services. There are emergent trends indicating that e-commerce has enabled infringements of registered trade marks, either through the unauthorised sale of counterfeit goods, or via the use of unlicensed Adwords. Indeed, a bedrock of court rulings indicate the high level of online piracy. Consider, for instance, the unauthorised sale of fake products. Examples at European level, such as landmark decisions in the cases *L'Oreal v eBay*[86] and *Google Adwords*,[87] have placed trade mark infringements at the forefront. At the same time, court rulings that impose liability are not rare at all. Indeed, national courts in France, Germany, Greece, and Spain have attempted to impose liability on host ISPs for trade mark violations within their networks.[88]

What is more, the negative implications of e-commerce services for brand owners have been illustrated in a joint study by the OECD and EUIPO.[89] More specifically, this

[80] European Commission, 'Public Consultation' (n 36) 6.

[81] European Commission, 'Summary of the results of the public consultation on the future of electronic commerce in the Internal Market and the implementation of the Directive on electronic commerce' (2016) 6.

[82] EU Member States needed to implement the DSMD into their national laws by 7 June 2021.

[83] See Explanatory Memorandum to the DSM Proposal 'It is therefore necessary to guarantee that authors and rightholders receive a fair share of the value that is generated by the use of their works and other subject-matter.'; see also N Elkin-Koren, Y Nahmias and M Perel, 'Is It Time to Abolish Safe Harbor? When Rhetoric Clouds Policy Goals' (2020) 31 *Stanford Law & Policy Review* 24.

[84] IFPI, 'Global Music Report 2018: annual state of the industry' (*Music Business Association*, 2018) https://perma.cc/SGZ3-PLHM.

[85] Frosio and Mendis (n 66).

[86] Case C-324/09 *L'Oreal SA V eBay Int'l AG* [2011] ECR I-6011.

[87] Case C-236/08 *Google France SARL and Google Inc. v Louis Vuitton Malletier SA* [2010] ECR I-2417.

[88] T Verbiest, G Spindler, G Riccio and A Van der Perre, 'Study on the Liability of Internet Intermediaries' (MARKT/2006/09/E) 4-115.

[89] European Commission, 'Trends in trade in counterfeit and pirated goods: the updated picture' (19 March 2019) ec.europa.eu/growth/content/trends-trade-counterfeit-and-pirated-goods-updated-picture_en.

study demonstrated that in 2016 counterfeit goods in international trade reached up to €460 billion in value, and the imports of fake products to Europe represent 6.8 per cent of all European imports.[90] Along similar lines, the EU Commission's public consultation on the modernisation of intellectual property rights' enforcement rules concluded, 'more than three quarters of respondents experiences an increasing intellectual property infringements over the last 10 years', while at the same time it has been noted that 'fighting IPR infringements in the online environment was becoming a regulatory and enforcement challenge'.[91]

However, the policy initiatives to curb online piracy are limited to a certain extent. For instance, in September 2016, the EU Commission announced the 'follow the money' approach which aimed to curb the circulation of fake goods online by blocking the revenue streams to websites that host such material.[92] However, at the time of writing this book, further guidance on the consistent implementation of this policy at European level has not been published. Likewise, a certain number of luxury brands have signed, with specific online marketplaces, a Memorandum of Understanding for counterfeit goods.[93] As per this Memorandum, online marketplaces are expected to verify the identity of the sellers who display their goods online, as well as undertake preventive measures when right holders notify them about trade mark infringements within their platforms. Yet, although this Memorandum might be a good start, its impact is limited since it only involves a certain number of brand owners and online marketplaces.

Finally, it is worthwhile to note that copyright and trade marks have different aims and, therefore, a different scope of protection. For this reason, it is imperative to specify the implications of the legal provisions and the novel recommendations in the context of copyright or trade marks when a solid response is missing. Should a common impact in the copyright and trade mark framework take place, the narrative will acknowledge this.

In light of the above developments, the legal problem addressed in this book focuses mainly on copyright and trade mark infringements taking place in the online environment. Given that this book examines the regulatory framework of host ISPs for copyright and trade mark infringements within their networks, the following section presents the specific type of host ISPs which this book assesses, in the context of copyright and trade mark violations, along with the reasons that justify this choice.

[90] OECD and EUIPO study, 'Trends in Trade in Counterfeit and Pirated Goods' (2019) read.oecd-ilibrary.org/trade/trends-in-trade-in-counterfeit-and-pirated-goods_g2g9f533-en#page13.

[91] European Commission, 'Public Consultation' (n 36) 8.

[92] European Commission, 'Commission one step closer to restricting revenues of websites that breach intellectual property rights' (25 October 2016) eur-lex.europa.eu/legal-content/EN/TXT/?uri=celex%3A52015DC0192.

[93] European Commission staff working document, 'Overview of the functioning of the Memorandum of Understanding on the sale of counterfeit goods via the internet' SWD(2017) 430 final 6; EU Commission, 'Memorandum of Understanding on the sale of counterfeit goods via the internet' ec.europa.eu/growth/industry/strategy/intellectual-property/enforcement-intellectual-property-rights/memorandum-understanding-sale-counterfeit-goods-internet_en.

B. Host Internet Service Providers (Host ISPs), Online Content Sharing Service Providers (OCSSPs) and Providers of Hosting Services

In the online world, ISPs are those entities that 'bring together or facilitate transactions between third parties on the Internet. They give access to, host, transmit and index content, products and services originated by third parties on the Internet or provide Internet-based services to third parties'.[94]

Authoritative legal definitions of ISPs are featured in the main legal instruments that regulate them, namely the ECD and DSMD. The ECD offers a definition of ISPs in Recital 17 where it notes that information society providers are those providers whose function 'covers any service normally provided for remuneration, at a distance, by means of electronic equipment for the processing and storage of data, and at the individual request of a recipient of a service'.[95] Different types of ISPs are set out in Articles 12, 13, and 14 of the ECD. As per Article 12(1), mere conduit ISPs are those whose service 'consists of the transmission in a communication network of information provided by a recipient of the service, or the provision of access to a communication network'. As per Article 13(1), the cache providers offer 'the automatic, intermediate and temporary storage of that information, performed for the sole purpose of making more efficient the information's onward transmission to other recipients of the service upon their request'. Finally, pursuant to Article 14(1) of the ECD, host ISPs are those ISPs whose services offer 'the storage of information provided by a recipient'.

Apart from the ECD, the DSMD adds what seems to be a subcategory to those ISPs that offer host services to internet users,[96] and thus endorses a new authoritative legal definition in Article 17 of the DSMD, namely the definition of an online content sharing service provider. Yet, an explanation of this new authoritative legal definition is found in Article 2(6) of the DSMD which notes that an online content sharing service provider is 'a provider of an information society service of which the main or one of the main purposes is to store and give the public access to a large amount of copyright-protected works or other protected subject matter uploaded by its users, which it organises and promotes for profit-making purposes'.[97] This means that online content sharing providers are those providers that offer services such as online audio or video streaming. Representative examples are Facebook, Dailymotion, YouTube, and Instagram. By contrast, online marketplaces, cloud to cloud businesses, and not for profit online encyclopaedias do not fall within the scope of Article 17 of the DSMD, as explicitly mentioned in Article 2(6) of the DSMD. Representative examples are eBay, Dropbox,

[94] OECD (n 3) 9.

[95] Council Directive 2000/31/EC of the European Parliament and of the Council of 8 June 2000 on certain legal aspects of information society services, in particular electronic commerce, in the Internal Market OJ L 178.

[96] Council Directive (EU) 2019/790 of the European Parliament and of the Council of 17 April 2019 on copyright and related rights in the Digital Single Market and amending Directives 96/9/EC and 2001/29/EC (2019) OJ L 130.

[97] ibid.

and Wikipedia. Therefore, these providers' activities are regulated by Article 14(1) of the ECD, which addresses the liability of host ISPs.[98]

Interestingly, the proposed DSA Regulation endorses the term of providers of hosting services. In particular, Recital 13 states that 'Online platforms, such as social networks or online marketplaces, should be defined as providers of hosting services that not only store information provided by the recipients of the service at their request, but that also disseminate that information to the public, again at their request.' This term seems to be the equivalent to host internet service providers as enshrined in Article 14(1) of the ECD.

In light of the above, I follow the terms that the main legal instruments include, namely the ECD and the DSMD as well as the term used in the proposed DSA Regulation. More specifically, the term host internet service provider (host ISP) as interpreted by the ECD is used throughout this book. Moreover, given that the book also deals with copyright infringements, I use the term online content sharing provider pursuant to the new legislative framework introduced by the DSMD in April 2019. The term addresses those information society service providers that provide access to a large amount of copyright-protected content and deal with copyright infringements online. Finally, I use the term providers of hosting services in chapter six where I critically discuss the proposed DSA Regulation.

Furthermore, it is important to mention the reasons for which the scope of this book is limited to two types of ISPs, namely host ISPs and their new subcategory, online-content sharing service providers (OCSSPs).[99]

I have chosen to examine the legislative framework of host ISPs under Article 14(1) of the ECD and OCSSPs under Article 17 of the DSMD due to the proximity of their roles in intellectual property infringements. First, with the services they provide to their internet users they facilitate users to commit wrongdoings within their networks. For instance, the business model of a video-music platform, which falls under the definition of OCSSPs, concerns the upload of music videos, among which some may be uploaded without right holders' authorisation and, thus, be in breach of copyright law. At the same time, online marketplaces, which fall under the definition of host ISPs, may not merely facilitate the use of electronic content, but also the sale of goods bearing intellectual property rights without the consent of the relevant right holders. Online marketplaces that enable their users to sell products may be at risk of liability when users advertise products that may be counterfeit or in breach of trade mark law. Secondly, they can control the material that is disseminated throughout their networks. This understanding is reinforced in YouTube's Content ID system[100] which is a database that comprises files of works that have been sent by their authors. Once an infringing video is uploaded by a user on YouTube's platform, it is automatically removed by the Content ID system.

What is more, further justification for the focus of this book to be on host ISPs and OCSSPs is the risk of over-enforcement of intellectual property rights and their negative implications for users' legitimate speech. Indeed, specialists in the field have frequently

[98] See also Frosio and Mendis (n 66).

[99] Hereinafter OCSSPs.

[100] T Margoni and M Perry, 'Online intermediary liability and privatised enforcement: the Content ID case' (2016) *The Tenth International Conference on Digital Society and eGovernments* 36.

warned that the imposition of liability rules on host ISPs might interfere with the freedom of expression of users.[101] This is because host ISPs and OCSSPs may be subject to economic risks by being held liable for intellectual property violations within their networks, thus they are prone to over-remove content online.

This focus on host ISPs and OCSSPs is also motivated by the lack of transparency within their operational business models. Although they have been entrusted with removing unlawful online content and counterfeit goods, it has been argued that there is a lack of transparency with regard to the processes they tend to follow. For instance, host ISPs and OCSSPs tend to use automated decision-making processes with regard to the removal of content online[102] without providing any safeguard for users whose material has been erroneously removed. Indeed, civil society organisations have heavily criticised the removal of content without justification or opportunity for users to appeal the decision.[103] In the absence of any legal remedy for users, the principles of due process may be threatened, and therefore users' right for equal weapons, as explicitly protected in Article 47 of the EU Charter of Fundamental Rights,[104] may be violated.

In addition, the investigation into OCSSPs, such as eBay and Amazon, is justified by the high rates of counterfeit goods within the networks of online marketplaces[105] which might pose a serious threat to e-commerce services. Online consumers lose their trust of online services when they are deceived and/or purchase fake goods online. In this sense, the cornerstone of e-commerce, which is the trust of online consumers, may be eroded.[106] This development may have a negative impact for the online world and consumers' trust of e-commerce platforms and online sales in general.[107]

Finally, it is important to mention that this book will not look at the regulatory framework of search engine machines, such as Google[108] or Bing.[109] This is because

[101] M Husovec, 'Why There Is No Due Process Online?' (*Balkin.com*, 7 June 2019) balkin.blogspot.com/2019/06/why-there-is-no-due-process-online.html; G De Gregorio, 'From Constitutional freedoms to the power of the platforms: protecting fundamental rights online in the algorithmic society' (2018) 11 *European Journal of Legal Studies* 82; D Rowland, U Kohl and A Charlesworth, *Information Technology Law*, 5th edn (London, Routledge, 2017) 85–87.

[102] Negative implications of automated decision-making process are presented in ch 8.

[103] European Digital Rights (EDRi), 'The Slide from "Self-Regulation" to "Corporate Censorship"' www.edri.org/files/EDRI_selfreg_final_20110124.pdf.

[104] Article 47 of the EU Charter of Fundamental Rights: Right to an effective remedy and to a fair trial: 'Everyone whose rights and freedoms guaranteed by the law of the Union are violated has the right to an effective remedy before a tribunal in compliance with the conditions laid down in this Article. Everyone is entitled to a fair and public hearing within a reasonable time by an independent and impartial tribunal previously established by law. Everyone shall have the possibility of being advised, defended and represented. Legal aid shall be made available to those who lack sufficient resources in so far as such aid is necessary to ensure effective access to justice.'

[105] OECD (n 38); UNODC (n 38); European Commission Staff Working Paper (n 38).

[106] World Economic Forum report on 'The Global Governance of Online Consumer Protection and E-commerce Building Trust' (2019) 4.

[107] European Commission, 'Online Platforms and the Digital Single Market Opportunities and Challenges for Europe' COM (2016) 0288 final 10 where it has been found that 'if consumers are properly informed of the nature of the products that they view or consumer online, this assist the efficient functioning of markets and consumer welfare'; EU Commission, 'Public Consultation on the future of electronic commerce in the Internal Market and the implementation of the Directive on electronic commerce: Summary of response' (n 64).

[108] www.google.com/.

[109] www.bing.com/?PC=JV01.

there is no common ground as to whether search engines qualify as host ISPs.[110] For instance, in the UK in *Designtechnica Corporation v Google*,[111] Justice Eady concluded that liability immunity provisions do not apply to search engines. Likewise, in France, in *SARL Publison System v SARL Google France*[112] the Court of Appeal of Paris concluded that search engines do not offer hosting services to their users. By contrast, at European level, in *Google France/Inc. v Louis Vuitton Malletier*,[113] the Advocate General noted that search engines fall into the scope of host ISPs as per Article 14(1) of the ECD. Therefore, the scope of this book is limited to the assessment of the regulatory framework of host ISPs and their subcategories, OCSSPs, with regard to their users' wrongdoings. Yet, if any court rulings or policy initiatives related to search engines are deemed relevant to the analysis and can be equally applied to the context of host ISPs and OCSSPs that host material, they are discussed.

C. Primary and Secondary Liability in Tort

As presented above, the scope of this book examines the liability of host ISPs and OCSSPs for trade mark and copyright violations that accrue within their networks. While intellectual property rights are considered property rights,[114] a tort law perspective is adopted here in order to examine the type of liability for these information society service providers. This is because the correlation between tort law and intellectual property violations is undeniable.[115] Indeed, this understanding has been exemplified in a number of rulings that treat individuals who commit an intellectual property

[110] For the debate on whether search engines qualify as host ISPs see European Commission, 'EU study on the New rules for a new age? Legal analysis of a Single Market for the Information Society, 6. Liability of online intermediaries' (2009) 24.

[111] *Designtechnica Corporation v Google* [2009] EWHC 1765 (QB), para 117 where it has been noted that with regard to liability immunity provisions as enshrined in Article 14 of the ECD 'the United Kingdom government has so far taken the view that it is unnecessary or inappropriate to extend protection expressly to search engines'.

[112] *SARL Publison System v SARL Google France* [2009] (Court of Appeal of Paris).

[113] Joined Cases C-236/08, C-237/08 and C-238/08 *Google France/Inc. v Louis Vuitton Malletier* (2009) ECLI:EU:C:2009:569, para 134 where the Advocate General Poiares Maduro notes that 'In any case, the provision of hyperlink services and search engines falls squarely within the notion of information society services and, most importantly – as I will argue next – their inclusion is consistent with the aims pursued by Directive 2000/31.'

[114] C Geiger, 'Fundamental Rights as Common Principles of European (and International) Intellectual Property Law' in M Leistner, *Common Principles of European Intellectual Property Law* (Heidelberg, Mohr Siebeck, 2012) 225 where he notes that 'in the case law of European Court of Human Rights, intellectual property has also entered the field of fundamental rights as the Court has issued more and more rulings interpreting IP relevant provisions of the European Convention on Human rights, and especially the right to property' and '… even though intellectual property is not explicitly named, there is no longer any doubt that the exploitation right is also protected by Art. 1 of Protocol 1 of the Convention, which protects property.'; P Goold, 'Unbundling the tort of copyright infringement' (2016) 102 *Virginia Law Review* 1842; *Anheuser- Busch Inc v Portugal* (11 January 2007) Application no. 73049/01 where it has been concluded that 'We therefore agree that Article 1 of Protocol No. 1 is applicable to intellectual property in general and to a duly registered trade mark.'

[115] R Arnold and P Davies, 'Accessory liability for intellectual property infringement: the case of authorisation' (2017) *The Law Quarterly Review* 1 where they have aptly remarked that '… intellectual property laws are treated as tort laws'.

infringement as tortious liable. For instance, in *Ted Browne Music Co. v Fowler*,[116] it was noted that the 'courts have long recognised that infringement of a copyright is a tort, and all persons concerned therein are jointly and severally liable as such joint tortfeasors'.[117] In similar fashion, in *Lawrence v Dana*[118] it was concluded that 'rights secured by copyright are property within the meaning of the law of copyright, and whoever invades that property beyond the privilege conceded to subsequent authors commits a tort, and is liable to an action'.[119] Moreover, it has been argued that intellectual property law has contributed to the development and shape of tortious liability doctrines and, in particular, tortious secondary liability.[120] Given that the tortious secondary liability doctrine is not harmonised at the European level, and is even under-analysed in many national jurisdictions,[121] intellectual property law cases have attempted to clarify, or offer a better understanding, of the different schemes of secondary liability.[122] For example, at UK level, Lord Templeman, in *CBS Songs Ltd v Amstrad Consumer Electronics Plc*,[123] framed the distinctive elements of the different schemes of tortious secondary liability doctrine, namely authorisation, common design, and procurement.[124] Following this, Kitchin Justice in *Newzbin I*[125] built on the *CBS Songs Ltd v Amstrad Consumer Electronics Plc* ruling and offered a narrower interpretation of the distinctive elements of tortious secondary liability.[126] A thorough analysis of the different schemes of tortious secondary liability doctrine is conducted in chapter three.

In connection with the above, this book looks at the two types of tortious liability which are attributed to OCSSPs and host ISPs for copyright and trade mark infringements carried out by their users. More specifically, their liability is examined through the lens of primary and secondary tortious liability rules.

With regard to the term of primary tortious liability, an individual is found primarily liable when she commits an intellectual property infringement. Within the online context, the concept of primary tortious liability has been endorsed with the DSMD, and in particular under Article 17 which notes that 'an online content-sharing service provider performs an act of communication to the public or an act of making available to the public for the purposes of this Directive when it gives the public access to copyright-protected works or other protected subject matter uploaded by its users'. This concept, as already explained at the outset of this book, introduces primary liability rules for online content sharing providers, and thus brings change to the liability regime for information society providers with regard to copyright violations within their networks.

[116] *Ted Browne Music Co. v Fowler* 290 F. 751, 754 (2d Cir. 1923).

[117] A Dorfman and A Jacob, 'Copyright as tort' (2011) 12 *Theoretical Inquiries in Law* 80–82.

[118] *Lawrence v Dana* 15 F. Cas. 26, 61 (Circuit Court, D. Mass 1869).

[119] Goold (n 114).

[120] P Davies, 'Accessory liability: protecting intellectual property rights' (2011) 4 *Intellectual Property Quarterly* 390.

[121] C. Angelopoulos, *European intermediary liability in copyright: A tort-based analysis* (Alphen aan den Rijn, Kluwer Law International, 2016) 19.

[122] Davies (n 120).

[123] *Amstrad CBS Songs v Amstrad* [1988] UKHL 15.

[124] Davies (n 120).

[125] *Twentieth Century Fox Film Corp v Newzbin Ltd* (2010) EWHC 608 (Ch).

[126] Davies (n 120).

Importantly, Article 17 of the DSMD has been considered as *lex specialis* to Article 14(1) of the ECD. This means that the services excluded from the scope of Article 17 of the DSMD fall into the scope of Article 14(1) of the ECD that employs secondary liability rules for host ISPs in cases of intellectual property infringements. Therefore, the activities of host ISPs that do not fall into the category of Article 17 of the DSMD are regulated under the existing law of the ECD where a secondary liability regime is in force.

However, by contrast to the term primary tortious liability, the term secondary tortious liability is not subject to an international consensus in the literature. Indeed, there are many and varied definitions that are used by scholars in order to define the concept of secondary tortious liability rules.[127]

The reason behind the existence of these multiple definitions for a secondary liability doctrine is mainly attributed to the different legal traditions that impose different requirements in order to trigger secondary liability rules for the actions carried out by the internet users of a host ISP, not by the host ISP itself. These examples, including joint-tortfeasance, accessory liability, contributory liability, and indirect liability, are employed by academic scholarship and different laws. Yet, the terms, as presented in chapter three, do not necessarily trigger the same outcomes. Therefore, this diversity of definitions in secondary tortious liability might create confusion among scholars. Indeed, Dinwoodie points out that this divergence may trigger 'some terminological difficulties for comparative analysis'.[128] This means that it would be complex for a scholar to find the equivalent of a secondary tortious liability doctrine for each jurisdiction, and thus to undertake a comparative analysis between different legal systems.

Hence, for the sake of clarity, this book uses the term 'secondary liability' in order to describe the liability of host ISPs for violations carried out by their internet users.[129] Yet, it is crucial to point out that the wrongdoing according to which a host ISP has been found secondarily liable, should not be confused with the wrongdoing of the primary infringer-user. This is because, as is pointed out in chapter three, host ISPs under the ECD may be held secondarily liable for enabling and facilitating the commission of copyright infringement by their users, not by committing a copyright or a trade mark violation themselves.

Finally, as already discussed in Section III of this chapter, the aim of this book is to critically assess the regulatory framework of host ISPs and OCSSPs under the existing laws. It does not look at the conditions that constitute a wrongdoing, namely it refrains from examining whether a copyright or a trade mark violation takes place. Further, the scope of this book is limited to two kinds of intellectual property infringements, namely copyright and trade mark violations. This means that the regulatory framework of host ISPs and OCSSPs for other violations, such as the violation of the right to privacy,

[127] GB Dinwoodie, 'A comparative analysis of the secondary liability of online service providers' in GB Dinwoodie (ed), *Secondary Liability of Internet Service Providers* (Berlin, Springer, 2017) 6–7.

[128] ibid 6.

[129] In light of the expeditious developments in host ISPs' liability at legislative and case law level, it seems now even more difficult to offer a definition for the liability of host ISPs with regard to the copyright and trade mark infringements within their networks.

defamation, or other types of intellectual property rights, are not examined. Yet, any case that may be equally applied to context of copyright and trade mark infringements is discussed.

VI. Structure of the Book

The book is divided into three parts, including an introduction and a conclusion. The first part consists of chapters one and two and offers an overview of internet regulatory theories and the rationale for ascribing liability rules to host ISPs. The second part encompasses chapters three, four, five and six and addresses a critical evaluation of the inefficiencies of the current legal framework that regulates host ISPs' activities for copyright and trade mark infringements that accrue within their networks. The third part includes chapters seven, eight and nine and presents an array of recommendations about how to structure a more robust legal framework for host ISPs with regard to copyright and trade mark violations online.

The introduction traces back to the birth and evolution of e-commerce and social media networks. It presents the legal problem, shapes the research question and the sub-questions, and defines the scope of the book. Following this, the rationale for the book, its originality, and an outline of the contents are provided.

Part I is entitled 'Theoretical and Policy Considerations' and introduces the theoretical underpinnings and policy background that revolves around internet regulation. It comprises chapters one and two. Chapter one commences by presenting internet regulatory theories that influence the cyberspace regulatory regime, namely self-regulation, co-regulation, and state regulation, their main pioneers and critics. Following that, chapter two places emphasis on moral and utilitarian theories that justify the ascription of liability rules to host ISPs. It also addresses the policy and practical considerations that warrant the liability rules with the aim to facilitate legal redress for rights holders for the violation of their rights.

Part II is entitled 'Evaluation of the Current Legislative Tools'. It examines the legislative tools that govern host ISPs' liability for copyright and trade mark infringements and includes chapters three, four, five and six. Chapter three critically evaluates the current legal framework that regulates host ISPs' activities under the ECD. It analyses the legal nature of host ISPs' liability, which is the secondary liability, the rationale for imposing secondary liability rules on host ISPs, and the theoretical background upon which host ISPs' liability relies. Then, it explores the requirements which trigger host ISPs' liability under Article 14(1) of the ECD, analyses their national implementation in selected jurisdictions, and identifies any flaws. Chapter four critically engages with the DSMD. At the outset, I offer a historical account of Article 13 of the DSMD (which has been renamed Article 17 in the final draft of the DSMD), where I discuss the EU Commission's Proposal and the compromised texts of the Council and Parliament.[130]

[130] European Parliament, 'European Parliament approves new copyright rules for the internet' (*Press release*, 26 March 2019) www.europarl.europa.eu/news/en/press-room/20190321IPR32110/european-parliament-approves-new-copyright-rules-for-the-internet.

Following this, I critically assess Article 17 of the DSMD where I identify a set of problematic features that reinforce the suggestion that this provision undermines the rights of OCSSPs and of internet users. Finally, the chapter assesses the national implementation of Article 17 of the DSMD into selected EU Member States. Chapter five offers an examination of the implications of liability rules on host ISPs and OCSSPs, intellectual property holders, and internet users. Chapter six presents the Proposal for a Digital Services Act Regulation[131] and, in particular, the legal provisions that are relevant to host ISPs. Following that, the chapter examines the intersection of the proposed Regulation with Article 17 of the Copyright in the Digital Single Market Directive.

Part III is entitled 'Introducing a Co-regulatory Framework'. It consists of the proposals for a co-regulatory framework for host ISPs and includes chapters seven, eight and nine. Chapter seven offers several normative insights towards the creation of a responsibility framework based on co-regulation for host ISPs with regard to copyright and trade mark infringements that take place within their networks. Further, it engages with one of the responsibilities that host ISPs have towards the dissemination of infringing content and counterfeit goods within their networks, namely the duty of care. In chapter eight, I explore another responsibility that host ISPs should have towards their users, namely a transparency obligation. In doing so, I observe the lack of a statutory transparency obligation and meticulously elaborate on the normative considerations for having such an obligation at European level. In light of this normative examination, I recommend how a transparency obligation should be implemented in practice by host ISPs in order to achieve, to a great extent, the equilibrium between the interests of the parties involved, namely the interests of host ISPs, internet users/online consumers and right holders. Following this, chapter nine builds upon the previous chapters and recommends the establishment of a host ISP supervisory authority. I demonstrate the normative considerations for creating such an authority, as well as suggest the principles and the functions under which the proposed authority would operate. In order to do so, I draw parallels with existing ISPs authorities in Greece and Italy, as well as authorities in other fields of law, such as those who deal with data protection and competition law.

The concluding chapter summarises the main findings and the novel recommendations for the establishment of a co-regulatory framework for host ISPs in the copyright and trade mark context.

[131] Hereinafter proposed DSA Regulation.

PART I

Theoretical and Policy Considerations

1

Internet Regulatory Theories: An Overview

I. Introduction

With the advent of internet, EU policymakers resorted to regulatory theories in order to govern host internet service providers' activities. Such regulatory theories differ from each other; they are based either solely on states' authority, are in the hands of the private sector, or they involve cooperation between state power and private party initiatives. The following Section discusses the main types of regulatory theories, namely state regulation, self-regulation, and co-regulation; it defines them and identifies their advantages and disadvantages.

II. State Regulation

State regulation, often called command and control regulation, addresses the role of the state as the main authority entitled to enforce rights within a specific jurisdiction. As Black notes, 'the state to have the capacity to command and control, to be the only commander and controller, and to be potentially effective in commanding and controlling'.[1] This means that through codified legal provisions the state governs the individual's activities, or intervenes in individuals' acts,[2] and can thus impose fines in cases of non-compliance.

The same interpretation has been adopted by other scholars who argue that in state regulation the rule of law is the predominant principle of ensuring the enforcement of rights. For instance, Easterbrook argues that legal rules need to be clearer so as to facilitate the bargains between the parties. Drawing on the example of copying, he states that low costs of copying might give rise to copyright violations, and therefore he suggests the modification of the US Copyright Act.[3] At the same time, Braithwaite explores the

[1] J Black, 'Decentring Regulation: Understanding the Role of Regulation and Self-Regulation in a "Post-Regulatory" World' (2001) 54 *Current Legal Problems* 106.

[2] C Koop and M Lodge, 'What is regulation? An interdisciplinary concept analysis' (2015) *Regulation and Governance* 7 where they argue that 'authors agree that regulation is about intervention in the behaviour or activities of individual and/or corporate actors'.

[3] FH Easterbrook, 'Cyberspace and the Law of the Horse' (1996) *University of Chicago Legal Forum* 210–11.

concept of regulatory state and discusses the evolution of the state as the main regulator from a liberal and Kensyan approach in the UK and US jurisdictions.[4] Finally, Finck also reflects on state regulation, calling it a top-down regulation, and notes that this 'is what typically comes to mind when thinking about regulating economic behaviour legislation'.[5]

Insofar as the theoretical framework of state-based regimes reach, it seems that state regulation characteristics are influenced by a plethora of different theories. In particular, they are influenced by liberal international relations theory, otherwise known as liberalism, which views the role of the state as guarantor of individuals' rights and interests. For instance, as Moravcsik, points out, 'the state is not an actor but a representative institution constantly subject to capture and recapture, construction and reconstruction by coalitions of social actors'.[6] This means that governmental authorities are assigned to the role of safeguarding citizens' fundamental rights.

Furthermore, another theory that could influence state regulation is the realist theory of international politics. This theory advocates that the state can control individuals' acts within a specific jurisdiction, as well as sanction any wrongdoing that takes place outside the jurisdiction but which targets the specific jurisdiction. This means that the state's boundaries reach beyond its jurisdiction. A representative example can be found in the CJEU's ruling on *Eva Glawischnig-Pieczek v Facebook*. This concerned a dispute between a former political member of the Green Party and Facebook over defamatory comments posted on the social platform about the politician. After careful consideration of the facts, Luxembourg judges acknowledged that the social media platform must remove the defamatory comments in whichever jurisdiction they appear. The court's reasoning drew on precedent allowing 'ordering a host provider to remove information covered by the injunction or to block access to that information worldwide within the framework of the relevant international law'.[7] This means Facebook, and similar social platforms, are obliged to remove any defamatory comments identical, or equivalent, to this one on a global basis since the comment violates the personality rights of the individual in a specific jurisdiction.

What is more, state regulation could also be influenced by the economic regulation theory developed by Stigler. This theory addresses how the state's power and public resources can boost or restrict industry activities. This is mainly due to tax legislation that can determine individuals' financial prosperity.[8] As Stigler points out,

> the state – the machinery and power of the state – is a potential resource or threat to every industry in the society. With its power to prohibit or compel, to take or give money, the state can and does selectively help or hurt a vast number of industries.[9]

[4] J Braithwaite, 'The Regulatory State?' in RE Goodin (ed), *The Oxford Handbook of Political Science* (Oxford, Oxford University Press, 2011) 219–20.

[5] M Finck, 'Digital Regulation: Designing a Supranational Legal Framework for the Platform Economy' (2017) *LSE Law, Society and Economy Working Papers* 15.

[6] A Moravcsik, 'Taking Preferences Seriously: A Liberal Theory of International Politics' (1997) 51 *International Organisation* 518; Harvard Law Association, 'Developments in the Law – The Law of Cyberspace' (1999) *Harvard Law Review* 1680.

[7] Case C-18/18 *Eva Glawischnig-Piesczek* [2019] ECLI:EU:C:2019:821.

[8] G Stigler, 'The theory of economic regulation' (1971) 2 *The Bell Journal of Economics and Management Science* 4.

[9] ibid 3.

This means that individuals can be burdened if taxation is high, while they may be favoured in the case of a light taxation scheme. For instance, in Spain the amended Intellectual Property Law required online platforms to pay a mandatory fee to the Association of Editors of Spanish Dailies for linking websites and snippets of articles from online journals.[10] This legislation seemed to be a severe burden for Google which decided in December 2014 to stop the operation of the Google News service.[11] Therefore, it seems that the state can constrain businesses' activities and development through taxation.

In the digital world, drawing upon the idiosyncrasies of state regulation, Goldsmith and Wu argue that state regulation can be applicable in the digital environment. In their writings, they describe the influence of the state on internet regulation, the legal disputes between Google and the French Government, and those between Yahoo and the Chinese Government.[12]

State regulation is the first type of regulation embraced by policymakers in order to govern e-commerce, and guide its baby steps, where the overall aim has been to make the EU Digital Single Market a competitive player against the US Market. Telling examples can be found in the e-Commerce Directive which constitutes the cornerstone of e-Commerce within the European Union.[13] It came into force in 2000 and consists of a cluster of legal rules that either enable host ISPs to exonerate liability under certain circumstances, or entail explicit prohibition of monitoring duties. Articles 12–14 of the ECD state that online intermediaries are exempt from liability if they do not have knowledge of the infringing activity within their networks, or if they remove the allegedly infringing content upon receiving notification of its existence.

Interestingly, state regulation theories have been subject to advantages and disadvantages. Insofar as the advantages are concerned, the primary asset of state regulation is accountability. The concept of accountability emerges from the Latin words *accomptare*, meaning to account, and *computare*, meaning to calculate. The concept itself is then divided into horizontal and vertical accountability. The former is defined as 'the obligation of a person to another person according to which the former must give account of, explain and justify her actions or decision in an appropriate way'.[14] A telling example is found in Ancient Greece where Athenians held public servants accountable for their actions, described by prominent historians as the 'hallmark of Athens'.[15] On the other hand, vertical accountability describes the state as accountable for the legislation

[10] J Malcolm, 'Google News Shuttered in Spain Thanks to "Ancillary Copyright" Law' (*EFF*, 10 December 2014) www.eff.org/deeplinks/2014/12/google-news-shuts-shop-spain-thanks-ancillary-copyright-law.

[11] D Rushe, 'Google News Spain to close in response to story links "tax"' *The Guardian* (11 December 2014) www.theguardian.com/technology/2014/dec/11/google-news-spain-to-close-in-response-to-tax-on-story-links.

[12] J Goldsmith and T Wu, *Who Controls the Internet?: Illusions of a Borderless* World (Oxford, Oxford University Press, 2006) 175.

[13] Council Directive (EC) 2000/31 on certain legal aspects of information society services, in particular electronic commerce, in the Internal Market [2000] O.J. L 178 (ECD).

[14] R Weber, 'The legitimacy and accountability of the Internet's governing institutions' in I Brown (ed), *Research Handbook on Governance of the Internet* (Cheltenham, Edward Elgar, 2013) 100.

[15] J Tolbert Roberts, *Accountability in Athenian Government* (Wisconsin, Wisconsin Studies in Classics, 1982) 4–5.

to a superior authority, namely the Constitutional Court. For instance, consider the case of Copyright in the Digital Single Market Directive.[16] Poland submitted an annulment of the Directive in front of the Court of Justice of the European Union (C-401/19) because its legal provisions violate freedom of expression as safeguarded in the Polish Constitution.[17]

What is more, legislation could offer a certain level of homogeneity. This means that the same rules can be applicable within different jurisdictions, and thus they promote legal certainty. A representative example can be found in the European legislation where European Directives and European Regulations offer the minimum standards in order to achieve harmonisation amongst the EU Member States in different policy areas, such as Copyright, Consumer Rights, and Agriculture. Indeed, the Directive on Consumer Rights, in 2011, offers a degree of harmonisation at the European level in distance and off-premises contracts.[18] In this way, as per Recital 7 of the Directive on Consumer Rights, the application of uniform rules would enhance legal certainty amongst consumers and limit the fragmentation barriers in the internal market. Likewise, the General Data Protection Regulation that came into force in 2018, aims to harmonise requirements for the processing of personal data in the healthcare sector.[19] For example, it offers specific conditions for the processing of special categories of personal data, such as the necessity of the processing and the consent of the data subjects. Therefore, legal certainty will prevail amongst individuals and the business sector.

However, state regulation theories also encompass disadvantages. As a plethora of scholars have argued, legislation might create legal uncertainty. This is because legal rules might be outdated for application in certain cases. This understanding has been accentuated by Husovec who expresses concern about whether the legal rules meet the idiosyncrancies and the speed of the digital progress; he notes that 'any statutory schemes are quickly outdated, and very slow to deploy'.[20] Likewise, a White Paper published by the World Economic Forum states that, '… relying only on government legislation and incentives to ensure the right outcomes is ill advised. These are likely to be out of date or redundant by the time they are implemented'.[21] For instance, consider the vast array of EU Directives and EU Regulations that succeeded each other

[16] Directive (EU) 2019/790 of the European Parliament and of the Council of 17 April 2019 on copyright and related rights in the Digital Single Market and amending Directives 96/9/EC and 2001/29/EC (Hereinafter DSMD).

[17] J Reda, J Selinger and M Servatius, 'Article 17 of the Directive on Copyright in the Digital Single Market: A Fundamental Rights Assessment' (2020) www.ssrn.com/abstract=3732223.

[18] Directive (EU) 2011/83/EU of the European Parliament and of the Council of 25 October 2011 on consumer rights, amending Council Directive 93/13/EEC and Directive 1999/44/EC of the European Parliament and of the Council and repealing Council Directive 85/577/EEC and Directive 97/7/EC of the European Parliament and of the Council Text with EEA relevance 2011 [32011L0083].

[19] Regulation (EU) 2016/679 of the European Parliament and of the Council of 27 April 2016 on the protection of natural persons with regard to the processing of personal data and on the free movement of such data, and repealing Directive 95/46/EC.

[20] M Husovec, *Injunctions Against Intermediaries in the European Union: Accountable but not liable* (Cambridge, Cambridge University Press, 2017).

[21] 'Values and the Fourth Industrial Revolution: Connecting the Dots Between Value, Values, Profit and Purpose' (*World Economic Forum*) 3, www.weforum.org/whitepapers/values-and-the-fourth-industrial-revolution-connecting-the-dots-between-value-values-profit-and-purpose/.

over the last years with the aim of capturing advanced technological developments in sector-specific issues. The Audiovisual Media Services Directive,[22] the DSMD, the General Data Protection Regulation, and the Directive on combating Terrorism[23] are but a few examples of legislative pieces which regulate the complex issues that arise with the rapid progress of technology. Meanwhile, the Proposal for a Digital Services Act Regulation[24] and a Proposal for a Digital Markets Act Regulation[25] have now been introduced in order to cover the latest developments in technology.

Furthermore, legal rules might prove ill-suited. This is because policymakers might not be in the right position to introduce the appropriate regime that would satisfy the online intermediaries' interests. For instance, it is questionable whether the policymakers have the relevant knowledge and experience to introduce measures that would take into consideration industry idiosyncrasies and interests. As a result, online intermediaries' business models are flourishing and, in general, innovation in the digital environment might be placed in jeopardy.[26]

Further, another discrepancy of the state regulation can be found in complexities in the decision-making procedures of legislation. As evidenced in the DSMD, the legislative process at the European level lasted more than two years before there was a final vote on it.[27] Intensive negotiations between the industry sector, digital rights associations, consumers' associations, and policymakers have prolonged the vote on the Directive.[28] Added to this, the disagreement between the EU Member States has led the Council to suggest a draft for the EU Directive three times,[29] while the EU Parliament had to vote twice to approve the Directive, given that the first time the EU Parliamentarians rejected the adoption of the DSMD.[30] This implies that the complex decision-making procedures might pose severe obstacles to an effective protection and enforcement of rights.

[22] Directive (EU) 2018/1808 of the European Parliament and of the Council of 14 November 2018 amending Directive 2010/13/EU on the coordination of certain provisions laid down by law, regulation or administrative action in Member States concerning the provision of audiovisual media services (Audiovisual Media Services Directive) in view of changing market realities.

[23] Directive (EU) 2017/541 of the European Parliament and of the Council of 15 March 2017 on combating terrorism and replacing Council Framework Decision 2002/475/JHA and amending Council Decision 2005/671/JHA.

[24] Proposal for a Regulation of the European Parliament and of the Council on a Single Market For Digital Services (Digital Services Act) and amending Directive 2000/31/EC COM/2020/825 final.

[25] Proposal for a Regulation of the European Parliament and of the Council on contestable and fair markets in the digital sector (Digital Markets Act) COM/2020/842 final. (An agreement about the Digital Markets Act between the Council and the Parliament was reached on 25 March 2022).

[26] Finck (n 5).

[27] F Ferri, 'The dark side(s) of the EU Directive on copyright and related rights in the Digital Single Market' (2020) 7 *China-EU Law Journal* 1; EU Commission, 'Questions and Answers – New EU copyright rules' (4 June 2021) ec.europa.eu/commission/presscorner/detail/en/QANDA_21_2821; EU Parliament, 'Legislative Train Schedule: Modernisation of EU Copyright Rules: Directive on Copyright in the Digital Single Market' www.europarl.europa.eu/legislative-train/theme-connected-digital-single-market/file-jd-directive-on-copyright-in-the-digital-single-market.

[28] Create, 'EU Copyright Reform: Evidence on the Copyright in the Digital Single Market Directive' www.create.ac.uk/policy-responses/eu-copyright-reform/.

[29] EU Council, 'EU adjusts copyright rules to the digital age' (15 April 2019) www.consilium.europa.eu/en/press/press-releases/2019/04/15/eu-adjusts-copyright-rules-to-the-digital-age/.

[30] M Khan, 'European copyright overhaul rejected by MEPs' *Financial Times* (5 July 2018) www.ft.com/content/4b2fdf68-8046-11e8-bc55-50daf11b720d; Results of votes on 26 March 2019 www.europarl.europa.eu/doceo/document/PV-8-2019-03-26-VOT_EN.pdf?redirect.

Moreover, state regulation might create a trend in forum shopping. This means that jurisdictions might introduce favourable legal rules in order to appeal to businesses. Such forum shopping, however, might undermine the rule of law and produce codified legal procedures that favour business interests and undermine individuals' interests. This is described by Burk as the Delaware effect.[31] For instance, the EU Antitrust Damages Directive states, 'This Directive should not require Member States to introduce collective redress mechanisms for the enforcement of Articles 101 and 102 TFEU'.[32] This means that the EU legislation refrains from offering a uniform approach and simply passes the controversial issue on to EU Member States to settle under their own legal rules. As a result, Denmark seems to be an appealing jurisdiction for collective actions in antitrust damages. This is because it offers collective opt-out mechanisms while it grants compensatory damages to all individuals in cases of successful collective opt-out actions.[33]

Finally, it is not the rule that state regulation leads to the creation of a harmonised legal framework. Rather, legal rules might trigger inconsistencies amongst jurisdictions. A telling example can be found in the disclosure of the identity of the alleged infringer in different jurisdictions. Whilst in the UK the disclosure of the personal data of the infringer shall satisfy the proportionality test in IP disputes, in Germany a disclosure of the identity of the alleged infringer is only warranted in cases of commercial scale infringements.[34] Therefore, as Burk notes, 'different result[s] would be expected where state regulations were inconsistent – if, for example, some jurisdictions required disclosure of certain facts about a product or service, but other jurisdictions forbade such disclosure'.[35]

Overall, state regulation amounts to the legislative tools that have been issued by state Institutions which aim to regulate individuals' and business' behaviour within the jurisdiction. This understanding, however, might be subject to advantages and disadvantages that either promote or harm legal certainty and innovation.

III. Self-regulation

Self-regulation is another type of regulation whereby individuals have the power to enforce their rights and govern their behaviour.[36] Hugenholtz defines it thus,

[31] DL Burk, 'How state regulation of the internet violates the commerce clause' (1998) 17 *Cato Journal* 151.

[32] Recital 13, 'Directive 2014/104/EU of the European Parliament and of the Council of 26 November 2014 on Certain Rules Governing Actions for Damages under National Law for Infringements of the Competition Law Provisions of the Member States and of the European Union Text with EEA Relevance' eur-lex.europa.eu/legal-content/en/ALL/?uri=CELEX%3A32014L0104.

[33] JL McGinnis and O Heinisch, 'Eyes across the Atlantic: coordination and management of global private antitrust litigation' (11 April 2017).

[34] C Angelopoulos *European Intermediary Liability in Copyright: A Tort-Based Analysis* (Alphen aan den Rijn, Kluwer Publications, 2016) 173.

[35] Burk (n 31) 158.

[36] H Maturana and F Varela, *Autopoiesis and Cognition* (Berlin, Springer, 1928) 32; The founders of self-regulation in social sciences, Varela and Maturana have developed the theory of autopoiesis and argue that 'the listener creates information by reducing his uncertainty through his interactions through its cognitive domain'.

'Self-regulation is a norm setting an enforcement by private actors, without the intervention of the state.'[37] This means that the power to regulate is now assigned to private entities and not to state authorities.

A representative example of self-regulation in the digital environment can be found in the code of conduct agreements signed between internet service providers which allow for the removal of infringing information from their networks. This is exemplified by the code which aims at countering illegal hate speech online, signed on 30 June 2016 by Facebook, Microsoft, Twitter, and YouTube.[38] The evaluation of the code's progress in July 2020 finds that 90 per cent of notifications of hate speech are reviewed within 24 hours, while 71 per cent of the reviewed content is taken down from the platform.[39] Another example are the UGC Principles which have been agreed between the film industry and internet service providers.[40] Such principles vary from blocking infringing content uploaded by users, to implementing advanced technological tools to identify links with illicit information, as well as offering counter-notice mechanisms to internet users whose content has been erroneously removed. A further example can be traced to the measures that internet service providers need to deploy in order to terminate, or prevent the reemergence of, infringements within their networks. As per Article 17 of the DSMD, online content sharing service providers need to demonstrate best efforts to prevent the reappearance of allegedly infringing content, or to obtain authorisation for the rights holders for making available the content within their platforms. This means that it is up to private entities to moderate the dissemination of content online and tackle any infringements within their networks. Finally, another initiative is the 'follow the money approach' by the European Commission in 2016. That approach involved different stakeholders such as online advertisers, big brands, host ISPs, mobile apps and payment agencies and aimed at blocking the revenue streams of websites with counterfeit goods through the aid of payment providers and advertisers.[41]

Self-regulation has been influenced by a cluster of theories that place economic actors at the epicentre of their analysis. For instance, Neoliberalism seems to support the self-regulatory framework. It is a theory that has been developed by Friedman, Hayek, and pioneers of economic thought school in Chicago, and as Ives has noted 'individual freedom is presented as the cornerstone value of the liberal regime; as such government action is illegitimate if it limits individual freedom in any way.'[42] This means that governmental

This means that the individuals receive and evaluate the information on its own, it is not contingent upon external factors and influence.

[37] P Hugenholtz, 'Codes of conduct and copyright enforcement in cyberspace' in IA Stamatoudi (ed), *Copyright Enforcement and the Internet* (Alphen aan den Rijn, Kluwer Law International, 2010) 307.

[38] EU Commission, 'The EU Code of conduct on countering illegal hate speech online' (30 June 2016) ec.europa.eu/info/policies/justice-and-fundamental-rights/combatting-discrimination/racism-and-xenophobia/eu-code-conduct-countering-illegal-hate-speech-online_en.

[39] D Reynders, '5th Evaluation of the Code of Conduct' (June 2020) 5, ec.europa.eu/info/sites/default/files/codeofconduct_2020_factsheet_12.pdf.

[40] ugcprinciples.com/.

[41] EU Commission-Directorate-General for Internal Market, Industry, Entrepreneurship and SME, 'The follow the money approach to IPR enforcement- stakeholders' voluntary agreement on online advertising and IPR' (2016) 1–2, ec.europa.eu/growth/industry/strategy/intellectual-property/enforcement-intellectual-property-rights/memorandum-understanding-online-advertising-and-ipr_en.

[42] A Ives, 'Neoliberalism and the concept of governance: Renewing with an older liberal tradition to legitimate the power of capital' (2015) *Mémoire(s), identité(s), marginalité(s) dans le monde occidental contemporain. Cahiers du MIMMOC*, journals.openedition.org/mimmoc/2263.

intervention is rejected, while at the same time individuals have the freedom to govern their own behaviours and actions. As per Neoliberalism, individual's freedom is divided into negative and positive. Negative freedom means that governmental authorities must not constrain individuals' rights, while positive freedom concerns the exercise of rights without limitations and constraints from the state.

Drawing upon the theory of neoliberalism, internet law theorists have developed internet self-regulation theories. For example, Barlow drafted the Declaration of Independence, arguing that the online world differs from the offline world and has separate jurisdictions and rules. He claims, 'Cyberspace does not lie within your borders. Do not think that you can build it, as though it were a public construction project. You cannot. It is an act of nature and it grows itself through our collective actions.'[43] This means that cyberspace is not influenced by external powers, while cyberspace citizens decide as a collective the procedures and the rules that govern them. Therefore, cyberspace is self-regulated and any rules imposed by the physical rulers of the offline world shall be rejected.

Following Barlow's Declaration, Post and Johnson argued in favour of a self-regulatory regime for the internet and developed their theory of Net Federalism.[44] This theory addresses cyberspace as an independent state with its own boundaries and legal rules that are applicable only within its jurisdiction. Taking the example of trade marks, the authors point out that due to cyberspace capacities, a trade mark will be accessible on a global basis. In this light, they express their concern that a website which advertises a company in the US could infringe a trade mark that is registered in Brazil since the website can be accessed in Brazil. Therefore, they argue that if cyberspace is considered a self-regulated state, a scheme for a global registration of trade marks needs to be introduced in order to avoid multiple claims of ownership of trade marks amidst different jurisdictions.

In line with this, Mifsud Bonnici and de vay Mestdagh develop further the idea of self-regulation in the digital environment.[45] They argue that a state regulatory solution cannot impede the dissemination of infringing information online. Rather, they tend to favour industry self-regulation where users shall be empowered with enforcement tools in order to limit the access to infringing content. Telling examples can be found in hotlines where internet users could call and report harmful content, and in the trusted flaggers' scheme where individuals can report infringing videos. Therefore, they conclude that the availability of user empowerment solutions would offer a higher degree of protection against harmful content. Moreover, Easterbrook tends to favour self-regulation and suggests, 'let us instead do what is essential to permit the participants in this evolving world to make their own decisions'.[46] This is because, he argues, legal rules of property law, and other rules of the offline world, cannot be applied in the online environment because they very soon become outdated, making any efforts futile.

[43] JP Barlow, 'A Declaration of the Independence of Cyberspace' (*EFF*, 8 February 1996) www.eff.org/cyberspace-independence.

[44] DR Johnson and D Post, 'Law and Borders: The Rise of Law in Cyberspace' (1996) 48 *Stanford Law Review* 1367.

[45] J Mifsud Bonnici and CNJ De Vay Mestdagh, 'Right Vision, Wrong Expectations: The European Union and Self-regulation of Harmful Internet Content' (2005) 14 *Information & Communications Technology Law* 138 where they provide the example of Hotlines for harmful content.

[46] Easterbrook (n 3) 216.

Finally, Murray leans in favour of a self-regulatory framework and developed the theory of network communitarianism, or symbiotic regulation.[47] Pursuant to his theory, regulated individuals are in constant interaction, or in a 'dynamic' relationship, with the state.[48] Such regulated individuals form micro-communities that are isolated from each other and can only interact with each other via the gatekeepers of the digital infrastructure. This means that gatekeepers, such as the internet service providers or host internet service providers, decide under which conditions these micro-communities can exchange information with each other, and thus regulate their activities.

Similar to state regulation, self-regulation theories are subject to advantages and disadvantages. As far as advantages are concerned, self-regulation provides flexibility in law. This means that the revision of rules is not subject to long legislative procedures by state authorities. Rather, rules can be updated or revised within shorter timeframes by the industry players.[49] Therefore, regulation can be easily adaptable to the rapid progress of technology, and thus can meet the peculiarities of digital developments.

Further, private entities might have a wide range of resources and highly trained staff in order to enforce rights online. A telling example can be found in Google's staff numbers, it has 139,995 employees[50] and its revenues in 2020 reached US$181.69 billion.[51] This means that Google has staff available to enforce rights online, as well as the necessary resources to develop highly advanced technology in order to do so. In this light, Google developed a Content ID system which is now used by YouTube in order to automatically remove allegedly infringing content once the video is uploaded to the platform.[52] Therefore, internet service providers seem to have the necessary expertise to identify allegedly infringing content.

In addition, self-regulation can achieve a higher degree of compliance. This is because industry players agree on certain principles and standards, thus consistency will be maintained. For example, major internet service providers have signed a Memorandum of Understanding about online advertising and intellectual property rights in order to terminate the stream of illicit revenues from websites that display counterfeit goods.[53] This Memorandum entails a set of guidelines which all parties involved need to deploy. In addition, major internet service providers can influence their parent companies, and thus integrate their policies into them. For instance, Google's policies can also be applicable to YouTube, Alphabet, Google X, and Fiber as they operate under the umbrella of Google.[54]

What is more, self-regulation can be more efficient from a cost-benefit perspective. This is because it gives incentives for complying with the rules, it relies upon the

[47] A Murray, *Information Technology Law: The Law and Society* (Oxford, Oxford University Press, 2019) 68.

[48] A Murray, *The Regulation of Cyberspace: Control in the Online Environment* (London, Routledge-Cavendish, 2006).

[49] Hugenholtz (n 37).

[50] Google number of employees 2021, google.com; see also E Lee, 'Recognizing Rights in Real Time: The Role of Google in the EU Right to Be Forgotten' (2016) *UC Davies Law Review* 1079.

[51] Annual revenue of Google, www.statista.com/statistics/266206/googles-annual-global-revenue.

[52] support.google.com/youtube/answer/2797370?hl=en-GB.

[53] 'Memorandum of Understanding on the Sale of Counterfeit Goods via the Internet' (2013); EU Commission, 'Report on the functioning of the Memorandum of Understanding on the sale of counterfeit goods on the Internet' (2020) ec.europa.eu/docsroom/documents/42701.

[54] Lee (n 50) 1023.

cooperation of private stakeholders and not on the expenses of the state. As Price and Verhulst point out, 'self-regulation can be seen as that range of activity by private actors undertaken to prevent more intrusive, and more costly action by government itself'.[55] This implies that self-relation can lead to the reduction of external costs that could arise within a state regulatory framework and mainly concerns the sanctions of private entities in cases of non-compliance with the legal rules.

Yet, self-regulation is not only a cost reduction for the state. Indeed, it could also be less expensive for the rights holders. This is because codes of conduct entail rapid redress mechanisms that mean rights holders do not need legal representation, nor do they need to be burdened with expensive legal proceedings in copyright cases.[56] For instance, it has been estimated that the costs for civil litigation procedures can be around US$500,000 for a copyright case that reaches trial in the United States.[57]

Crucially, self-regulation theories do not only entail advantages. Rather, a number of scholars have criticised the negative characteristics of self-regulation, arguing that it prioritises private sector's interests and undermines the rights of individuals. Such disadvantages might vary from a lack of accountability to a lack of transparency and a lack of due process.

With regard to the democratic deficit, private entities are not accountable to state authorities for their actions. This means that private entities can make decisions without considering the impact of those decisions on individuals' rights. This understanding can be worrisome in the case of internet service providers. This is because internet service providers' activities interact with internet users' rights of free speech and arts, namely Article 11 and Article 13 of the EU Charter of Fundamental Rights respectively. Consider, for instance, that internet service providers can block access to a website for users without prior notice, or terminate the accounts of users by alleging violation of its Terms of Service, with no opportunity for a user to challenge the termination.[58]

In line with this, self-regulation does not promote transparency in the decision-making process. This is because self-regulatory measures might be opaque. For example, the operation of filtering mechanisms with algorithms constitutes a 'black box' for internet users since they do not understand them.[59] A number of cases of biased or false removals from filtering-based tools have been reported. An experiment conducted by AlgorithmWatch revealed that Google's algorithms tagged a thermometer supported by a dark-skinned hand as a gun, while the same thermometer supported by a white-skinned hand was tagged as a thermometer.[60] Further, due process might be violated

[55] M Price and S Verhulst, 'The Concept of Self-Regulation and the Internet' (2000) in J Waltermann and M Machill (eds), *Protecting our children on the internet: Towards a new culture of responsibility* (Gütersloh, Bertelsmann Foundation Publishers) 75.

[56] Hugenholtz (n 37).

[57] M Palmese, 'Copyright litigation in the United States: overview' uk.practicallaw.thomsonreuters.com/w-012-9369?transitionType=Default&contextData=(sc.Default)&firstPage=true.

[58] Twitter Terms of services is available at twitter.com/en/tos which states that 'We reserve the right to remove Content that violates the User Agreement, including for example, copyright or trade mark violations …'.

[59] As Ursula von der Leyen, the President of the European Commission, states in her State of the Union speech, 'Algorithms must not be a black box and there must be clear rules if something goes wrong' (Ursula von der Leyen 2020).

[60] Algorithm, available at algorithmwatch.org/en/google-vision-racism/.

in self-regulatory regimes. This is because, as Angelopoulos points out, self-regulation tends to be a 'privatized enforcement'.[61] This means that private entities have business interests and tend to prioritise their interests and the interests of their business partners.

What is more, self-regulation might exceed the scope of legal rules. This means that private entities are developing their own enforcement rules and requirements that go beyond the legislation set forth by state authorities. This understanding has been exemplified by the taxi service Uber and its relationship with its drivers.[62] Uber is enforcing its own rules that seem to move far from the criminal law standards applicable in the United States. More specifically, according to Uber's policies, drivers are delisted from their account if they flirt with, or ask personal questions of, passengers, while any inappropriate post-trip contact could lead to the permanent termination of their account with Uber.[63]

Moreover, self-regulation might lead to fragmentation. This is because codes of conduct, or other agreements, might be open to limited participation. This means that while some private entities would participate and invest resources for the development of tools, other entities might simply ignore them. The phenomenon, or rather those that ignore it, are described by Price and Verhulst as 'free riders'.[64] For instance, with regard to internet service providers, participation within the UGG Principles is limited since major host internet service providers simply do not participate.[65] The same has been outlined in the Memorandum on the sales of counterfeit goods on the internet where limited actors have been involved.[66] This means that codes of conduct would have limited applicability,[67] and thus would create a patchwork of heterogenous practices by private entities. Therefore, any effort aimed at effective enforcement of rights online might be sabotaged.

To sum up, self-regulation relies upon a wide theoretical spectrum that finds its roots in neoliberalism and is developed through internet regulation theories. Such theoretical background places the private entities with business interests at the centre of the regulation, and activates a framework where the private entity plays the role of regulator and enforcer of rights. Similar to state-regulation, a self-regulatory regime might entail assets and flaws that could potentially dynamise, or promote, the enforcement of rights.

[61] C Angelopoulos, A Brody, W Hins, B Hugenholtz, P Leerssen, T Margoni, T McGonagle, O van Daalen and J van Hoboken, 'Study of fundamental rights limitations for online enforcement through self-regulation' (2015) *IVRi* 3.

[62] Finck (n 5) 11.

[63] Uber terms of service, www.uber.com/legal/en/document/?name=california-anti-sexual-harassment-policy&country=united-states&lang=en.

[64] Price and Verhulst (n 55).

[65] J Wang, *Regulating Hosting ISPs' responsibilities for copyright infringement: The freedom to operate in the US, EU and China* (Berlin, Springer, 2018) 228.

[66] EU Commission, 'Memorandum of understanding on the sale of counterfeit goods on the internet' ec.europa.eu/growth/industry/policy/intellectual-property/enforcement/memorandum-understanding-sale-counterfeit-goods-internet_en.

[67] Harvard Law Review Association, 'The Principles for User Generated Content Services: A Middle-Ground Approach to Cyber-Governance' (2008) 121 *Harvard Law Review* 1387, 1388; where it is stated that 'At the same time, the absence of certain parties at the negotiating table shows that there may be room for traditional regulators to step in and at least ensure fair representation at the time bar – gains are being struck.'

IV. Co-regulation

Co-regulation is the last type of regulatory regime that involves the cooperation of the state and individuals. At the European level, it was introduced in the Inter-Institutional Agreement for Better Law Making in 2003, and defined as 'the mechanism whereby a Community legislative act entrusts the attainment of the objectives defined by the legislative authority to parties which are recognised in the field (such as economic operators, the social partners, non-governmental organisations, or associations)'.[68] This means that the enforcement of rights is relied upon by private actors, while the state's involvement is limited to the role of supervisor.

The need for the development of a new type of regulation, namely co-regulation, is rooted in the rapid progress of developments and the inability of the legislation to keep track of them all. This understanding has been accentuated by Marsden; citing the White Paper on European Governance, noted that co-regulation 'is a pragmatic response to the common perception that regulatory frameworks must quickly adapt and continually be optimized to maintain relevance and effectiveness in rapidly evolving markets'.[69] This means that the main aim of co-regulation is to meet the markets' demands and, accordingly, be relevant and efficient with regard to the enforcement of rights.

Co-regulation seems to have common points with state and self-regulation. For instance, the Information report on the current state of co-regulation and self-regulation in the Single Market by the European Economic and Social Committee examines the self-regulation and co-regulation through the same lens and assumes that they have the same positive effect on the enforcement of rights.[70] More specifically, the report states that in the context of co-regulation and self-regulation, governments have introduced codes of conducts between private parties, declaration or agreements for adopting standards between private companies.[71] In another point, it notes that both types of regulation would make the legal rules easier, flexible, fast and make all key actors responsible for the implementation of rules.[72]

However, co-regulation does not only share common points with self- and state regulation. Indeed, it shall be borne in mind that co-regulation differs from state and self-regulation. This is because the state involvement and the individuals' involvement are not achieved to the same extent in co-regulation. With regard to self-regulation, Lulé notes that 'the main criterion for the distinction between co-regulation and self-regulation is the degree of autonomy of the co-regulatory organisation from state influence'.[73] This means that in self-regulation private entities have the discretion to exercise their power and not be subject to the state's approval. Likewise, co-regulation differs from

[68] Interinstitutional Agreement on better law making (2003) para 18.

[69] C Marsden, 'Co-Regulation in European Media and Internet Sectors' (2005) 33 *Intermedia* 28; European Commission, 'European governance – A white paper' (2001) COM/2001/0428 final.

[70] European Economic and Social Committee, 'Information report of the Section for the Single Market, Production and Consumption on the Current state of co-regulation and self-regulation in the Single Market' (18 January 2005) 1.3.

[71] ibid.

[72] ibid 1.5.

[73] C Palzer, 'Self-Monitoring v. Self-Regulation v. Co-Regulation' (2003) *IRIS Special: Co-Regulation of the Media in Europe* 31.

state-regulation because in the former the regulatory body can exercise its influence and authority regardless of the power of the governmental authorities. As Marsden notes, 'It is clearly a finely balanced concept, a middle way between state regulation and "pure" industry self-regulation.'[74] Therefore, it seems that co-regulation is in a dynamic relationship between private entities and state authorities.

Co-regulation has been discussed in the existing literature. Many scholars have based their interpretation of co-regulation as set forth at the European level and then developed it further. For instance, Kleinstuber defines co-regulation as a tool for enabling the collaboration between the state and the private sector, 'if the State and the private regulators co-operate in joint institutions'.[75] In line with this, Marsden views co-regulation as a tool for generating a dialogue between state and private entities but does not result into the common perceptions of state regulation with a bureaucratic authority or self-regulation with agreements between private parties.[76] Finally, Bredow points out that co-regulation deviates from the state regulatory framework and places individuals' interests and rights at the epicentre of the regulation. In this way, he noted that a co-regulatory framework seems to be a better form of regulation because it eliminates the drawbacks of command-and-control regulation and places the responsibility on individuals.[77]

Examples of co-regulation can be found in a number of EU legislative and international initiatives. More specifically, the Audiovisual Media Services Directive envisages the development of regulatory bodies in each EU Member State.[78] More specifically, as per Article 28(b)(5):

> Member States shall establish the necessary mechanisms to assess the appropriateness of the measures referred to in paragraph 3 taken by video-sharing platform providers. Member States shall entrust the assessment of those measures to the national regulatory authorities or bodies.

This means that regulatory bodies are assigned with supervisory duties and control whether online intermediaries adjust to the legal rules. Telling examples can be found in Belgium with the Conseil Supérieur de l'Audiovisuel de la Fédération Wallonie-Bruxelles, in Greece with the National Council for Radio and Television, and in Estonia with the Estonian Consumer Protection and Technical Regulatory Authority.[79] In addition, the DSMD envisages the creation of a co-regulatory regime.[80] More specifically, Article 17(9) envisages the creation of a mechanism whose main purpose is to

[74] C Marsden, 'Co- and Self-regulation in European Media and Internet Sectors: The Results of Oxford University's Study www.selfregulation.info' in OECD, *Self- Regulation, Co-Regulation and State Regulation* (2003) 80.

[75] HJ Kleinsteuber, 'State – Regulation – Media: OSCE Conference Amsterdam-Guaranteeing Media Freedom on the Internet' (2004) 3.

[76] Marsden (n 74).

[77] H Bredow, 'Final Report Study on Co-Regulation Measures in the Media Sector' (2006) 11.

[78] Directive (EU) 2018/1808 of the European Parliament and of the Council of 14 November 2018 amending Directive 2010/13/EU on the coordination of certain provisions laid down by law, regulation or administrative action in Member States concerning the provision of audiovisual media services (Audiovisual Media Services Directive) in view of changing market realities.

[79] Regulators in EU Member States: webcache.googleusercontent.com/search?q=cache:TWqijI11rgsJ:https://digital-strategy.ec.europa.eu/en/policies/audiovisual-regulators+&cd=3&hl=en&ct=clnk&gl=uk.

[80] Directive (EU) 2019/790 of the European Parliament and of the Council of 17 April 2019 on copyright and related rights in the Digital Single Market and amending Directives 96/9/EC and 2001/29/EC.

deal with users' complaints: 'Member States shall also ensure that out-of-court redress mechanisms are available for the settlement of disputes.' The creation of such a body has also been discussed in the course of the whole legislative process of drafting this Directive. The Council's compromised text noted in Article 13(7) that 'Member States shall endeavor to put in place independent bodies to assess complaints related to the application of the measures',[81] while in similar terms the EU Parliament's compromised text Article 13(2b) noted that, 'Member States shall ensure that users have access to an independent body for the resolution of disputes …'.[82] Finally, another example can be found in the UK White Paper for Online Harms which states that Ofcom can act as an independent body in order to supervise the compliance of online intermediaries with the rules on online harm. This means a regulatory body would be assigned with ensuring that online intermediaries are removing hate speech or offensive information circulated within their networks, as well as offering the appropriate redress mechanisms for complaints to their internet users.[83] Such a body could be new or could be an existing one with amendments made in regard to its duties.

Co-regulation is influenced by a number of theories that either envisage the dynamic cooperation of the state and the private sector, or accentuate the role of the private sector and limit the role of the state, as background. More specifically, a theory that influences co-regulation is liberal economic theory. This theory rejects any centralised governmental power and argues that private market actors shall be entitled to the enforcement of rights. As Sylvain, citing Buris and others, notes, 'Adherents of classic liberal economic theory, on the other hand, posit that centralised government administration (through, for example, the enforcement of network neutrality) is a hindrance to the efficient operation of the broadband market.'[84] This means that a decentralised model of regulation is preferred and is adjusted to market incentives.

This theory has its roots in the 1990s when Communism fell. More specifically, in Russia and the Czech Republic an economic movement towards privatisation has been put forward in order to boost the economy. This movement was about shifting ownership of public goods and services from the government to the private sector and is aptly described as capitalism. In this way, former Communist countries impeded any effort to regain communist status and the consequences of the state control of public goods.[85]

Yet, this theory leaves the back door open for governmental intervention into the regulatory framework established by private entities. This is because, as Baird notes, '… it is appropriate to set a high bar for failure before the government should intervene, that of significant and substantial market failure.'[86] This means that only if there is a significant and substantial market failure, can the state join the regulatory regime.

[81] For the full text of Article 13 of the Council text for the Copyright Directive in the Digital Single Market see Appendix II.

[82] ibid.

[83] HM Government, 'Online Harms White Paper: Full Government Response to the consultation' (2020) 53–54.

[84] O Sylvain, 'Internet Governance and Democratic Legitimacy' (2010) 62 *Federal Communications Law Journal* 207–08.

[85] H Appel, 'The Ideological Determinants of Liberal Economic Reform: The Case of Privatization' (2000) 52 *World Politics* 520, 528–29.

[86] S Baird, 'The Government at the standards Bazaar' (2007) *Stanford Law and Policy Review* 66, 84.

For example, in the case of standard-settings the state leaves the market to function on its own and, in particular, through the competition that it triggers between the companies with regard to the development of individual standards. However, if the development of individual standards might threaten the competition, or if there is a low level of cohesiveness within the stakeholders, such as the lack of codes of conduct of absence of potential methods to reach private agreements, then the state must intervene in the regulatory framework.[87]

Another theory which serves as a theoretical background for co-regulation is to be found in the public-private partnership theory. This theory is about the interaction and collaboration of the private and public sectors, deviating from its strict interpretation of public and private.[88] It does not place the private sector under the scrutiny of the public sector. Rather, it addresses the equal cooperation of both sectors. As Boni-Saenz notes, 'They are less likely to involve hierarchical relationships because their existence requires the consent of both the government and the private actors. In fact, their success depends crucially upon the buy-in of both parties.'[89]

The main rationale behind this theory is the development of a negotiated base for making decisions that relies upon a public agency whose aim is to accommodate the interests of the parties involved. As Freedman explains, this is about a process that engages different stakeholders with the aim to reshape the scope of application of the legal provisions.[90] He describes the Alternative Dispute Resolution as a representative example of this theory and notes that an agency could be responsible for negotiating, licensing, and solving the disputes of the parties involved.

Based on these theories, internet scholars have developed their own internet co-regulatory theories. More specifically, drawing parallels with *Lex Mercatoria*, Reindenberg – the prevailing law during medieval times – introduced the *Lex Informatica* theory.[91] This theory is based upon the idea of network decentralisation within which the state can influence the regulation of internet infrastructure through host ISPs.[92] This means that host ISPs would not be the sole entities to undertake the role of the enforcer of rights online. Rather, governmental authorities would be able to regulate online activities with the cooperation of host ISPs. Therefore, a regulatory framework for host ISPs could be built through public oversight, namely through the state as an external regulator.[93]

In similar fashion, Lessig's theory draws upon Reidenberg's *Lex Informatica* and further expands the concept of co-regulation within the internet infrastructure.[94]

[87] ibid 84; see also Regulation (EU) No 1025/2012 of the European Parliament and of the Council of 25 October 2012 on European standardisation, amending Council Directives 89/686/EEC and 93/15/EEC and Directives 94/9/EC, 94/25/EC, 95/16/EC, 97/23/EC, 98/34/EC, 2004/22/EC, 2007/23/EC, 2009/23/EC and 2009/105/EC of the European Parliament and of the Council and repealing Council Decision 87/95/EEC and Decision No 1673/2006/EC of the European Parliament and of the Council (Text with EEA relevance).

[88] Lee (n 50) 1083.

[89] A Boni-Saenz, 'Public-Private Partnerships and Insurance Regulation' (2008) *Harvard Law Review* 1367.

[90] D Freeman, 'Collaborative governance in the administrative state' (1997) *UCLA Law Review* 12.

[91] J Reidenberg, 'Governing Networks and Rule-Making in Cyberspace' (1996) 45 *Emory Law Journal* 911.

[92] J Reidenberg, 'Lex Informatica: The formulation of Information Policy Rules through Technology' (1997) 76 *Texas Law Review* 577.

[93] Murray (n 47) 60.

[94] L Lessig, *Code and other Laws of cyberspace* (New York, Basic Books, 1999) 43–44.

Pursuant to Lessig's theory, the internet can be regulated via four modalities, namely market, norms, code[95] and law.[96] This means that these four modalities could influence internet users' activities, and thus shape their online behaviour. In the brick and mortar environment, the four modalities could restrict citizens' actions. For instance, consider the case of tobacco regulations.[97] The state, under the threat to public health, aimed to reduce the consumption of tobacco and cigars. In order to achieve this policy, the state used some of the four modalities depicted in Lessig's theory. Therefore, states increased the price of tobacco products via the markets, prohibited the consumption of smoking in enclosed spaces, and prohibited the advertising of tobacco products via the media. In this way, the state achieved influence over the behaviour of individuals.

Further, Lee developed the theory of private administrative agency based on Weber's bureaucratic theory.[98] More specifically, Lee argued that Google's services and structure are similar to a bureaucratic agency. A bureaucratic agency, according to Weber, has the power of adjudication, investigation, and enforcement of duties, and contributes to the law-making processes. In this way, Google also shares those duties. Google is a private corporation with business interests and partners. However, it has adjudicative, enforcement, and lawmaking powers. With regard to adjudication, as Lee argues, Google receives requests from internet users and examines their validity. For instance, in January 2021 Google received 1,035,206 requests for delisting.[99] Further, it has enforcement duties because Google has the final word, in terms of the Right to be forgotten principle, in the removal of a link from the search engine. Finally, it has law-making power because it construed the CJEU's decision on *Costeja*[100] and integrated into its platform the Right to be forgotten option under all 27 EU Member States.

Another scholar, Castells, deviates from the public private partnership theories and provides another interpretation of co-regulation.[101] In particular, he views a co-regulatory framework as an information network. Information networks comprise nodes that are connected and interact with each other. In Information networks, the nodes exercise a decentralised authority and share the decision-making process. In this light, Castells states that 'these technologies allow for co-operation and management in complexity in an interactive system with feedback systems and communication patterns from anywhere to everywhere within their networks'.[102] This means that a network operates under the basis of a shared decision-making process amidst the nodes.

[95] ibid where Lessig argues that 'even if it is hard to regulate behaviour given the Net as it is, it is not hard for the government to take steps to alter, or supplement, the architecture of the Net' and 'if the government regulates the architecture of the Net, it could be regulated in the future'; A Guadamuz, *Networks, Complexity and Internet Regulation: Scale Free Law* (Cheltenham, Edward Elgar, 2011) 86–89 where Guadamuz notes that '… several countries started redesigning the entry points into their national networks in order to impose screening mechanism that would allow them to filter out undesired content if necessary'.

[96] L Lessig, *Code, version 2.0* (2006) 123.

[97] M Taddeo and L Floridi, 'The Debate on the Moral Responsibilities of Online Service Providers' (2016) 22 *Science and Engineering Ethics* 1575–1603.

[98] Lee (n 50) 1066–73.

[99] Transparency report Google, available at transparencyreport.google.com/eu-privacy/overview?hl=en_GB.

[100] Judgment of the Court (Grand Chamber) 13 May 2014, *Google Spain SL and Google Inc. v Agencia Española de Protección de Datos (AEPD) and Mario Costeja González* ECLI:EU:C:2014:317.

[101] M Castells, 'Materials for an Exploratory Theory of the Network Society' (2000) *The British Journal of Sociology* 5.

[102] ibid 15–16.

Finally, Marsden envisages a co-regulatory framework for the online world. In particular, he classifies twelve forms of self- and co-regulation.[103] Such co-regulatory forms may vary from approved compulsory co-regulation to scrutinised co-regulation and the government-imposed co-regulation with taxation. Insofar as the approved compulsory co-regulation is concerned, a telling example can be found in ICANN, an intergovernmental body where the state can impose fines and audit the process.[104] In scrutinised co-regulation a representative example is the Authority for Television on Demand (ATVOD),[105] which is an independent regulator for the supervision of the editorial content available on Television on Demand. With this form of co-regulation, the government supervises the function of the authority and approves its annual budget. Finally, another type of co-regulation is NOMINET, the UK registry for domain names.[106] In this form of regulation, the authority is subject to taxation while its operation could be under the supervision of the government.

In practice, this could mean that host ISPs would be assigned a set of responsibilities with regard to the dissemination of unlawful content. These responsibilities would be subject to a host ISP supervisory authority, which would be government based. Indicative examples can be found in the context of a number of European Member States that have introduced supervisory authorities which deal with blocking websites with infringing content, and the imposition of fines in cases of non-compliance with the legal rules. For instance, in Greece[107] and Italy,[108] intellectual property holders could resort to supervisory authorities in order to seek redress for infringements of their rights online. This recommended host ISP supervisory authority is addressed in chapter nine of this book.

As discussed in the state and self-regulatory regimes, theories that support co-regulation entail advantages and disadvantages. More specifically, co-regulation could reconcile different forms of governance, namely the centralised and decentralised initiatives and policies developed through the lens of state regulation and self-regulation.[109] This is because co-regulation will bring together elements of the state's involvement and industries expertise. For instance, the UK White Paper on online harms suggests the creation of a regulatory body that would oversee how the online platforms identify

[103] C Marsden, 'Internet Co-Regulation and Constitutionalism: Towards a More Nuanced View' (*SSRN*, 29 August 2011) ssrn.com/abstract=1973328 or dx.doi.org/10.2139/ssrn.1973328.

[104] ICANN, www.icann.org/.

[105] Ofcom, 'Ofcom brings regulation of "video-on-demand" in-house' (14 October 2015) www.ofcom.org.uk/about-ofcom/latest/media/media-releases/2015/1520333.

[106] Nominet, see www.nominet.uk/.

[107] General information on the Greek Committee on intellectual property violations, see www.opi.gr/en/committee/general-information.

[108] Regolamento in material di tutela del diritto d'autore sulle reti di comunicazione elettronica e procedure attuative as sensi del decreto legislative 9 April 2003, No. 70 is available at www.agcom.it/documents/10179/0/Documento/b0410f3a-0586-449a-aa99-09ac8824c945; in English it is available at wipolex.wipo.int/en/text/367415; Out of Laws News, 'Spain legislates for out-of-court copyright enforcement' (*Out of Law*, 29 November 2018) www.out-law.com/en/articles/2018/november/spain-out-of-court-copyright-enforcement/; ISP Review, 'UK Gov Aim to Make ISP Piracy Website Blocks Cheaper and Easier' (*ISP review*, 15 June 2018) www.ispreview.co.uk/index.php/2018/06/uk-gov-to-make-isp-piracy-website-blocks-cheaper-and-easier.html.

[109] Finck (n 5) 23.

and remove hate speech or defamatory comments.[110] This body will adopt a risk-based approach and would focus on companies with higher risks of dissemination of harmful content based on the industries' specifications and guidelines. This implies that a co-regulatory framework would be based on cooperation between state regulation and industry self-regulatory tools.

What is more, co-regulation signals a shift to a flexible form of regulation. This is because co-regulation avoids the complexities of state regulation and the questionable initiatives of industry's self-regulatory tools. Finck describes it as 'regulative facilitator'.[111] Consider, for instance, the role of Data Protection Authorities and the duties they undertake in order to ensure the compliance of companies with Data Protection Laws. On the one hand, they refrain from the peculiarities of legal provisions and they put forward their own guidelines. On the other hand, they are in close cooperation with industry players through the sharing of good practice and expertise, but without being subject to their influence. For instance, Ofcom has collaborated with the industry association of UK Wireless Internet Service Providers, UKWISPA in order to identify practices with regard to the coverage of their networks.[112] Therefore, co-regulation could be seen as a substitute for governmental authority with an essence of industry flexibility in terms of expertise and application of the rules.

Further, co-regulation would aim at promotion of a polyphonic and shared responsibility form of regulation.[113] As the European and Economic Social Committee points out in its Opinion on Simplification, 'Rather than mere co-existence of self-regulation and regulation, it involves the sharing of responsibilities between public and private partners.'[114] This is because governmental actors and private entities would collaborate and be accountable for their decisions with regard to the enforcement of rights. For instance, in the context of co-regulation, Koch discusses the role of administrative agencies in policymaking and how it differs from judiciary process. He also notes that administrative bodies would be subject to responsibility when they are undertaking policy-making procedures.[115] This implies that administrative bodies would be subject to responsibility for carving out policymaking. In this way, all views and interests would be taken into consideration while the entities that participate would be subject to oversight by citizens.

Moreover, co-regulation is seen as a form of regulation that achieves its regulatory aims through specific standards, not through the codification of legal rules.[116] This means that the efficiency of the regulation is contingent upon specific standards and not on compliance with legal rules. Consider, for instance, the issue of standards in

[110] HM Government, 'Online Harms White Paper' (2019) 54.

[111] Finck (n 5) 18.

[112] UKWISPA, 'Technical guidance for WISPS: Ofcom connected nations reporting' (2020) 1.

[113] Finck (n 5) 18 where it is stated that 'co-regulation in itself bears the promise of polycentric governance capable of bringing multiple actors to the table …'; RA Epstein, 'Can Technological Innovation Survive Government Regulation?' (2013) 36 *Harvard Journal of Law and Public* Policy 87.

[114] Opinion of the European Economic and Social Committee on 'Simplification' (2002) 130–41; Opinion of the European Economic and Social Committee on 'Self-regulation and co regulation' (2015) 22.

[115] CH Koch Jr, 'Policymaking by the Administrative Judiciary' (2005) Faculty Publications 1278 https://scholarship.law.wm.edu/facpubs/127.

[116] Finck (n 5) 21.

the ICANN. ICANN is the Internet Corporation for Assigned Names and Numbers and is responsible for the allocation of domain names. In order to allocate new generic top-level domains, ICANN has prepared a Guidebook for Morality and Public Order that sets forth four standards under which the right to freedom of expression can be restricted.[117] Those four standards are:

> (i) Incitement to or promotion of violent lawless action; (ii) incitement to or promotion of discrimination based upon race, color, gender, ethnicity, religion or national origin; (iii) Incitement to or promotion of child pornography or other sexual abuse of children; or (iv) a determination that an applied-for gTLD string would be contrary to equally generally accepted identified legal norms relating to morality and public order that are recognized under general principles of international law.

Should the Domain Names address one of those standards, ICANN has the right to refuse their registration under the reasoning of Morality and Public Order purposes.

Finally, co-regulation would lighten the workload for judicial authorities. National courts are the only way to seek redress in a state regulatory framework, thus they might be overburdened by the rising number of cases to adjudicate. For instance, a number of cases have preoccupied the EU national courts the last 20 years, namely the *Scarlet v Sabam*,[118] *Netlog v Sabam*,[119] *UPC Telekabel*,[120] *Svensson*,[121] *GS Media*[122] and *Brein v Ziggo* cases.[123] At the same time, co-regulation could prove more efficient than the judiciaries in the context of the enforcement of rights. More specifically, it has been argued that '[a]dministrative agencies adjudicate massive numbers of individual disputes, far exceeding the number resolved by courts'.[124] This implies that administrative bodies could undertake a higher number of cases, and thus prove to be more efficient than the courts.

Yet, it is worth mentioning that the limits of this responsibility regime based on co-regulation should be clearly carved out in order to avoid any shift from co-regulation to state regulation. Indeed, Reidenberg acutely warns that 'state governments cannot and should not attempt to expropriate all regulatory power from network communities'.[125] This is because the threat of state regulation could impede the boost of e-commerce since state regulation rules 'become outdated shortly thereafter'.[126] This means that the intervention of state regulation might act as a deterrent for innovation since legal rules cannot efficiently follow the rapid progress of technological developments. Furthermore, a lack of boundaries to the role of the state within internet regulation might pose

[117] ICANN, 'New gTLD Program Explanatory Memorandum Standards for Morality and Public Order Research' (2009) 2.

[118] Case C-70/10 *Scarlet Extended SA v Société belge des auteurs, compositeurs et éditeurs SCRL (SABAM)* [2011] ECR I-11959.

[119] Case C-360/10 *Belgische Vereniging van Auteurs, Com ponisten en Uitgevers CVBA (SABAM) v Netlog NV* (2012) ECLI:EU:C:2012:85.

[120] Case C-314/12 *UPC Telekabel Wien* (2014) ECLI:EU:C:2014:192.

[121] Case C-466/12 *Nils Svensson and Others v Retriever Sverige AB* (2014) ECLI:EU:C:2014:76.

[122] Case C-160/15 *GS Media BV v Sanoma Media Netherlands BV and Others* (2016) ECLI:EU:C:2016:644.

[123] Case C-610/15 *Stichting Brein v Ziggo BV and XS4ALL Internet BV* (2017) ECLI:EU:C:2017:456.

[124] Koch (n 115) 693.

[125] Reidenberg (n 91) 929.

[126] Easterbrook (n 3) 207.

a serious threat to the flow of content online since there might be a risk of abuse and censorship. This has already been exemplified in a number of countries outside Europe, such as China, where the authorities have deployed special routers, known as The Great Firewall, to prohibit internet users from accessing banned websites.[127] This means that if an internet user attempts to access a banned website, a network error message appears on the screen.[128] Finally, without any clear clarification of the role of the state in internet regulation, the decisions of the administrative body that would operate within the co-regulatory framework could be seen as political decisions. A telling example can be found in the Federal Communication Commission's Enforcement Bureau in the United States. The Commission is responsible for the policymaking of internet regulation and the enforcement of rights online. Its decisions have been criticised as 'political negotiations and resolved through deals made by the Chairman's office'.[129] This implies that the role of an administrative body might be contingent upon state authorities and its decisions might be biased.

What is more, while the theories discussed above have their own merits, the discussion prompts reflection on the legitimacy of those authorities that would allocate liability to host ISPs.[130] For instance, the proposed host ISP supervisory authority must entail an array of principles under which it would operate. These principles would act as a safeguard for all the parties at stake. This means that the proposed host ISP supervisory authority would guarantee the rights of the intellectual property holders whose rights have been violated, without undermining the rights of host ISPs to conduct business and internet users to access content and goods online. Otherwise, a lack of legitimacy would erode the validity of its decisions, and thus annul its own existence within the internet regulatory framework.

To sum up, co-regulatory theories provide another type of regulation which is based on cooperation between state authorities and industry key actors. While it has already been applied in the fields of finance, data protection, and competition law, it constitutes an emerging trend within online enforcement. Representative examples can be found in the DSMD,[131] the Audiovisual Directive[132] and the proposed DSA Regulation.[133] Similar to the state and self-regulatory theoretical frameworks, co-regulatory theories entail benefits for the rights of internet users, rights holders, and host ISPs, while at the same time they have been subject to criticism since the boundaries with the state and self-regulation might be blurred.

[127] A Guadamuz, 'Internet Regulation' in L Edwards (ed), *Law, policy and the internet* (Oxford, Hart Publishing, 2019) 20; Goldsmith and Wu (n 12) 96–97 where the author argues that China is using internet as a tool of political control.

[128] Goldsmith and Wu (n 12) 58.

[129] P Weiser, 'The Future of Internet Regulation' (2009) 43 *UC Davis* 585; see also Committee on energy and commerce majority staff report (2008) 18.

[130] V Mayer-Schonberger, 'Demystifying Lessig' (2008) *Wisconsin Law Review* 713.

[131] Council Directive (EC) 2019/790/EC of the European Parliament and of the Council of 17 April 2019 on copyright and related rights in the Digital Single Market and amending Directives 96/9/EC and 2001/29/EC (2019) OJ L 130.

[132] Council Directive (EU) 2018/1808 on the coordination of certain provisions laid down by law, regulation or administrative action in Member States concerning the provision of audiovisual media services (Audiovisual Media Services Directive) in view of changing market realities (2018) OJ L 303.

[133] Proposal for a Regulation of the European Parliament and the Council on a Single Market For Digital Services (Digital Services Act) and amending Directive 2000/31/EC COM/2020/825 final.

V. Conclusion

This chapter has provided an overview of the theoretical underpinnings of the three main types of regulation in the online world. These theories draw their characteristics from established regulatory theories in the off-line world and entail advantages and disadvantages.

More specifically, state regulation in the online world has its origins in the state regulatory theories of the brick and mortar environment. In particular, it could be influenced by liberal international relations theory, realist theory of international politics, and economic regulation theory. The main pioneers of state regulation in the online world are Goldsmith and Wu; under the influence of state regulatory theories, they argue that the internet is a reflection of legal and political regimes in different jurisdictions. Similar to the offline world, the state regulatory framework in the online world might have advantages and disadvantages. For instance, with regard to advantages, legal rules might offer homogeneity and accountability, while disadvantages might be found in the legal rules that might prove ill-suited and outdated.

Further, the narrative moved to another type of regulation in the online world, namely self-regulation. Self-regulation has been influenced by neoliberalism; its main pioneers in the digital ecosystem are Barlow, Post and Johnson, Lessig, and Murray. The common point for the theorists who support a self-regulatory framework is their belief that the internet is an independent state which can self-regulate without interference from state authorities. Self-regulation provides flexibility in law, a high level of compliance, and reduced costs for states and rights holders. However, as discussed, a self-regulatory framework runs the risk of violating the principles of due process and transparency. Finally, the chapter addressed the third type of regulation in the online context, namely co-regulation. Co-regulation in the online world is an emerging type of regulation and may draw its theoretical underpinnings from co-regulatory theories. For instance, liberal economic theory or public private partnership theory could influence co-regulatory theories. Drawing on these theories, Reidenberg's Lex Mercatoria, Lessig's theory, Marsden's theory, and Lee's theory of private administrative agency have further developed the concept of co-regulation in the digital world. The common point of these theories is to be found in the cooperation of private and state authorities in the regulatory framework. As discussed in relation to state and self-regulation theories, co-regulation could offer advantages, such as the reconciliation of different forms of governance, namely the centralised and decentralised initiatives and policies developed through the lens of state regulation and self-regulation, while depicting a polyphonic and shared responsibility-based framework. Yet, it shall be borne in mind that co-regulation should be clearly carved out in order to avoid any shift from co-regulation to state regulation. Otherwise, the objectives of co-regulation would be placed in peril.

Having discussed the different theories of internet infrastructure and their correlation with the regulatory theories of the physical environment, the following chapter moves to the analysis of the theoretical underpinnings and policy justifications for establishing the liability rules to host ISPs. This will enable the reader to gain an important insight of the theories that justify the ascription of liability to host ISPs for the infringements that have been committed by their users.

2

Liability of Host Internet Service Providers: Theoretical and Policy Background

I. Introduction

This chapter addresses the theoretical and policy perspectives for introducing liability rules to host internet service providers for the infringements that have been committed by their users. More specifically, the ascription of liability to host ISPs for copyright and trade mark violations within their networks have been influenced by a set of theories. Such theories either treat host ISPs as morally liable for the infringements or consider them as the most efficient entity to prevent or terminate the violations online. The following Section delves into the pioneers of the theories, their scope and their application into the host ISPs' context.

II. Theories for Liability for the Host ISPs in the Form of Secondary Liability

A. Moral Theory

In the physical environment, an individual can be held liable from a moral perspective if she has committed the illegitimate acts by herself.[1] This implies that an individual must not give account for third parties' actions; rather, she must be accountable only for her own actions.

Yet, within the online context, this view finds limited applicability since it has been argued that ISPs should be morally liable for the tortious acts of their users.[2] This understanding, as Spinello explains, depends on how the term of cooperation is construed.[3]

[1] P Davies, *Accessory Liability* (Oxford, Hart Publishing, 2015) 13.

[2] G Frosio, 'Why Keep a Dog and Bark Yourself? From Intermediary Liability to Responsibility' (2017) *25 Oxford International Journal of Law and Information Technology* 5; L Oswald, 'International issues in secondary liability for intellectual property rights infringement' (2008) 45 *American Business Law Journal* 247; M Bartholomew and J Tehranian, 'The secret life of legal doctrine: the divergent evolution of secondary liability in trademark and copyright law' (2006) 21 *Berkeley Technology Law Journal* 1419.

[3] R Spinello, 'Intellectual Property: Legal and Moral Challenges of Online File Sharing' in K Einar Himma and H Tavani (eds), *Handbook of Information and Computer Ethics* (Wiley Online library, 2008) 565.

The term 'cooperation' is understood as the act of facilitation or inducement. More specifically, for host ISPs it is understood as whether cooperation amounts to the facilitation or the inducement of a legitimate or an illegitimate activity.

From a general point of view, cooperation usually has positive connotations. Individuals cooperate with each other in communal activities in order to achieve a certain goal. However, there are stances where cooperation of individuals might lead to the commission of immoral acts. This may be the case for online intellectual property infringements. Representative examples of this line of thinking are the cases of file-sharing websites, online video exchange platforms or online marketplaces. For example, unauthorised content uploaded by internet users is circulated online via online platforms, or counterfeit goods are offered for sale by sellers and are displayed online. Therefore, host ISPs appear to cooperate with the wrongful acts of their users, who commit copyright or trade mark violations.

However, it could be argued that the abovementioned examples are not similar. This is because an online-exchange platform such as YouTube,[4] an online marketplace such as eBay, a file-sharing platform with unauthorised files such as the Pirate Bay, or a website that exclusively offers counterfeit goods,[5] are not based on the same business models. Rather, they are defined by different business goals and principles. This means that the main aim of an online video exchange platform or an online marketplace would be to enable their users to upload or download lawful content or to buy goods online respectively. By contrast, a file-sharing platform with illegitimate files or a website with fake products for sale engage in illicit activities by disseminating unlawful content online or deceiving potential customers with the offer of counterfeit goods. Therefore, to hold host ISPs liable for the tortious acts of their internet users requires a higher degree of granularity for the concept of cooperation.

In this light, a distinction should be made between formal and material cooperation.[6] Insofar as formal cooperation is concerned, a host ISP formally cooperates with the tortious acts of its internet users if its business model is deliberately designed to facilitate the dissemination of unlawful content or the circulation of pirated goods. As Spinello states, formal cooperation occurs when a 'person assists another person to commit a wrongful act, sharing its bad will and intention'.[7] Consider, for instance, the *eBay v Lancôme*[8] case where eBay enabled the circulation of counterfeit products of *Lancôme* cosmetics within its network. Hence, a host ISP may be considered morally liable if it formally cooperates with the wrongdoings of its users, who either share unauthorised material or offer for sale fake goods online.

Furthermore, another option for a host ISP to be considered morally liable for the intellectual property infringements that may occur within its platform is the material cooperation with the wrongdoings of its users. Material cooperation is understood as

[4] YouTube, 'Policies and safety' www.youtube.com/intl/en-GB/yt/about/policies/#community-guidelines.
[5] *Cartier International AG v British Sky Broadcasting Ltd* [2015] ETMR 1.
[6] (St.) Alphonsus Liguori, *Theologia Moralis* 4 volumes, ed by L Gaude (Rome, Ex Typographia, 1912) 357, available at archive.org/details/theologiamoralis01inligu; R Spinello, 'Secondary Liability in the Post Napster Era: Ethical Observations on MGM v. Grokster' (2005) 3 *Journal of Information, Communication and Ethics in Society* 126.
[7] Spinello (n 3).
[8] *eBay v Lancôme* [2008] (Brussels Commercial Court).

when an ISP designs its business model for legitimate purposes but accepts that, in the course of its operation, the emergence of illicit activities will be an unwanted side effect.[9] Indeed, this understanding emerges from Spinello's theory which suggests that the act of material cooperation triggers moral liability if most of the following conditions are fulfilled: the action of the individual must be unjust, proportionate to the gravity and the proximity of contributing to the wrongdoing and the individual must have rejected the possibility to deploy an alternative mechanism which could restrict any negative interference of the action.[10]

This theory implies that, within the online context, the imputation of moral liability to those host ISPs is excluded, insofar as those websites deploy appropriate technological measures and terminate, or at least curb to a great extent, the circulation of unauthorised content or pirated goods. Representative examples of this line of thinking can be found in video-music platforms and social networks.[11] The popularity of these host ISPs increased dramatically due to the services they offer to users.[12] Such services are focused on enabling users to upload and share authorised films, TV programmes or music files, without excluding the possibility of disseminating illegitimate content that has been uploaded by their users. Therefore, these websites are involved in the dissemination not only of legal content but also of unlawful content. Yet, in order not to be considered morally liable, those host ISPs deploy filtering-based technology that identify and remove online intellectual property infringements. For instance, eBay deploys the so-called VERO, Verified Rights Owner Program, which is a database where brand owners submit reports with regard to the selling of counterfeit products on the eBay platform.[13] In this way, while unauthorised content or counterfeit goods might be circulated, host ISPs undertake specific measures in order to curb or stop their circulation online. Hence, those host ISPs are not exposed to moral liability discourse.

By contrast, other host ISPs might be subject to moral liability if they refrain from deploying filtering-based technological systems. Consider, for instance, the example of a host ISP whose platform offers a number of counterfeit goods to its users. Indeed, a report conducted by the EU Commission on Counterfeit and Piracy Watch list demonstrates that a large amount of fake goods is circulated online.[14] Likewise, a bedrock of case law engages with the violation of trade marks in the digital ecosystem. A representative case is to found in *Amazon v Louboutin* where the Court of Justice of the European has now been requested to examine whether Amazon is liable for advertising, stocking and shipping counterfeit shoes of Louboutin.[15] Therefore, given the circulation of fake

[9] Spinello (n 6) 128.

[10] ibid 126.

[11] Case C-160/15 *GS Media BV v Sanoma Media Netherlands BV and Others* (2016) ECLI:EU:C:2016:644.

[12] '6 Reasons Why Social Networking is So Popular These Days' (Brandignity) www.brandignity.com/2012/11/6-reasons-why-social-networking-is-so-popular-these-days/.

[13] S Pilutik, 'eBay's Secondary Trademark Liability Problem and its VeRO Program' (2007) www.cs.cmu.edu/~dst/Secrets/E-Meter/eBay-VERO-pilutik.html; A Cheung and KH Pun, 'Comparative study on the liability for trade mark infringement of online auction providers' (2009) 31 *European Intellectual Property Review* 7.

[14] EU Commission Staff Working Paper, 'Counterfeit and Piracy Watch List' (2018) SWD 492 final, trade.ec.europa.eu/doclib/docs/2018/december/tradoc_157564.pdf.

[15] Case C-148/21, Request for a preliminary ruling from the Tribunal d'arrondissement lodged on 8 March 2021 – *Christian Louboutin v Amazon Europe Core Sàrl, Amazon EU Sàrl, Amazon Services Europe Sàrl.*

goods online, the absence of any precautionary measures to tackle online infringements could justify the moral liability of host ISP whose services address the online purchase of goods.

Therefore, in the light of the above, it could be extrapolated that a host ISP can be conceived as being morally liable for the wrongdoings of its users if it engages either in formal or material cooperation with the tortious acts of its users. On the one hand, the act of formal cooperation leads to moral liability if an ISP designs its business model in such a way that attracts only illegitimate content. On the other hand, material cooperation concerns a host ISP whose business model attracts a number of illegitimate content or counterfeit goods. However, for a host ISP, moral liability due to material cooperation may arise only under certain circumstances. This means that a host ISP is not morally liable if it installs technological measures in order to stop any illicit activity within its platform. Rather, moral liability might occur when the host ISP accepts the emergence of online infringements within its network and does not deploy any further measures to restrict them, thus accepting the harmful outcomes its business model on third parties' rights.

B. Utilitarian Theory

Another theory that could influence the imposition of a liability framework in the form of secondary liability is utilitarian theory. This theory is about allocating a right after assessing the impact of a specific action on third parties in comparison to the impact of another action to those third parties.[16] Transposing this theory into the host ISPs' liability regime means that the allocation of secondary liability rules on host ISPs is contingent upon the impact that host ISPs' activities might have on the different parties involved, namely content owners, brand owners and internet users/consumers.[17]

Host ISPs' liability in the form of secondary liability could find its roots in the gatekeeper liability theory.[18] One of the key proponents of gatekeeper theory is Kraakman. He developed the concept of gatekeeper liability, which can be described as liability 'that is imposed on private parties who are able to disrupt misconduct by withholding cooperation with wrongdoers'.[19] He noted that gatekeeping occurs when wrongdoings are not impeded by law authorities and the gatekeepers could identify the wrongdoing more efficiently without taking into consideration market standards and private incentives.[20] This implies that the role of gatekeepers is twofold, namely to prevent infringements and to identify those infringements at a reasonable cost.

[16] Pareto principle in Q Zhou, 'The Evolution of Efficiency Principle: From Utilitarianism to Wealth Maximization' (2005) SSRN 8; W Fisher, 'CopyrightX: Lecture: Supplements to Copyright: Secondary Liability' (2014) 81–82, copyx.org/files/2014/08/CopyrightX_-_Lecture_Transcripts_Book.pdf.

[17] Frosio (n 2); C Angelopoulos and S Smet, 'Notice and Fair Balance: How to reach a compromise between fundamental rights in European Intermediary Liability' (2016) 8 *Journal Media of Law* 266.

[18] E Laidlaw, 'A framework for identifying Internet information gatekeepers' (2010) 24 *International Review of Law, Computers & Technology* 264–67; A Tuch, 'The limits of Gatekeeper liability' (2017) 73 *Washington and Lee Law Review Online* 619; A Hamdani, 'Gatekeeper liability' (2003) 77 *Southern California Law Review* 98.

[19] RH Kraakman, 'Gatekeepers: The Anatomy of a Third-Party Enforcement Strategy' (1986) 2 *Journal of Law, Economics and Organization* 54.

[20] ibid 61.

i. Gatekeepers as a Source of Deterrence

First, in order to reinforce the role of gatekeepers as 'a source of deterrence' of the wrongdoings,[21] Kraakman selects examples from various professions. For instance, he argues that accountants and lawyers are natural gatekeepers of financial transactions because they can detect fraudulent money transfer with their audits or legal knowledge. Moreover, doctors and pharmacists are natural gatekeepers of medicines as they can terminate the abuse of medication through the prescription scheme.

This understanding could be applicable within the online world too. In this case, Barzilai- Nahon introduced the term of gatekeeper to the digital ecosystem and conceived ISPs as gatekeepers.[22] According to her theory, host ISPs appear to be the gatekeepers of hosted data and thus they can detect copyright infringements via their filter-based mechanisms. Following her writings, other scholars supported the notion that host ISPs seem to be the gatekeepers of the online world. For instance, Laidlaw argues that host ISPs are gatekeepers that control the content and information that pass through their gates[23] while Thompson goes one-step further and posits that due to their role as gatekeepers, host ISPs design the online word by choosing which information does and does not reach the end-users.[24] Therefore, the imposition of secondary liability rules to host ISPs might be justified due to their role as a source of deterrence of tortious acts online.

However, it is not only academic scholarship that is in favour of imposition of a secondary liability framework in light of the role of host ISPs as a source of deterrence of wrongdoings. Indeed, to treat host ISPs as a source of deterrence of wrongdoings has been outlined at legislative and judicial level too. With regard to legislative level, Recital 59 of the InfoSoc Directive notes that '… intermediaries are best placed to bring such infringing activities to an end'.[25] This means that European policymakers support the view that host ISPs are best situated to terminate violations that accrue online. At judicial level, the role of host ISPs as a source of deterrence has been exemplified in a bedrock of court rulings where the judiciaries have assessed whether online auction platforms or other social networks could have done more to terminate or at least mitigate the sale of counterfeit goods or the downloading of unauthorised content. For instance, at European level in *L' Oreal v eBay*, L'Oreal brought a legal action against eBay, alleging that eBay's efforts to prevent the selling of counterfeit goods on its network were insufficient.[26] Although the CJEU handed down that the ascription of liability rules on a matter left to the domestic courts of national Member States,[27] what is important to

[21] Bartholomew and Tehranian (n 2) 1366; they noted that 'shift injury costs to those who are in a position to prevent future injuries'.

[22] K Barzilai-Nahon, 'Toward a theory of network gatekeeping: a framework for exploring information control' (2008) 59 *Journal of the American Society for Information Science and Technology* 1493.

[23] Laidlaw (n 18) 26[illegible].

[24] M Thompson, 'Beyond Gatekeeping: The Normative Responsibility of Internet Intermediaries' (2016) 18 *Vanderbilt Journal of Entertainment & Technology Law* 783.

[25] Directive 2001/29/EC of the European Parliament and of the Council of 22 May 2001 on the harmonisation of certain aspects of copyright and related rights in the information society (hereinafter InfoSoc Directive).

[26] Case C-324/09 *L'Oreal SA V eBay Int'l AG* [2011] ECR I-6011.

[27] Case C-324/09 *L'Oreal SA V eBay Int'l AG*, 2011 ECR I-6011, para 23.

stress in this case, is that the CJEU views host ISPs as a source of deterrence of wrong-doings. In this regard, the Court referred to the opinion of Advocate General Jääskinen and described the role of website operators as follows:

> if the operator of the online marketplace does not decide, on its own initiative, to suspend the perpetrator of the infringement of intellectual property rights in order to prevent further infringements of that kind by the same seller in respect of the same trade marks, it may be ordered, by means of an injunction, to do so.[28]

This implies that host ISPs are seen by judicial authorities as a source of terminating the circulation of counterfeit goods online and for this reason host ISPs are secondarily liable for not installing the appropriate measures to deter the emergence of online infringements.

Such a stance has been maintained by EU national courts where host ISPs have been subject to secondary liability rules due to their role as a source of deterrence for online infringements. In particular, in Italy, Delta TV brought legal proceedings against Google and YouTube, alleging that a link to YouTube that included videos of episodes of Telenovelas without Delta TV's consensus appeared once the internet user had accessed Google's search results list.[29] In response to the allegations, Google and YouTube argued that they expeditiously removed the illegal content upon receipt of a valid notification from the rights holders. Interestingly, the Court of Torino handed down that, while YouTube was a host ISP and thus is eligible to invoke the immunity provisions to be exonerated from liability as per Article 14(1) of the ECD, it took down the illegal videos and deterred the upload of further videos of similar kind only within the Italian borders and not worldwide. For this reason, the Court of Torino reached the conclusion that YouTube was secondarily liable for the unauthorised videos uploaded by its users since it did not remove and prevent further uploads of illicit content by users outside Italian jurisdiction.

ii. Gatekeepers as Control Points that Identify the Wrongdoings at a Reasonable Cost

The utilitarian theory also views the role of host ISPs as a source of deterrence that warrants the ascription to them of a secondary liability framework. Indeed, as Kraakman acknowledges, gatekeepers can find wrongdoing at a reasonable cost.[30] This means that host ISPS can control and detect the online infringements at a reasonable cost; identifying illicit activity on their platforms faster and more efficiently than other parties, such as the rights holders.[31] This last-cost benefit understanding is supported

[28] ibid para 141; CJEU, Opinion of Advocate General Jääskinen, Case C-324/09 *L'Oréal v eBay International*, 9 December 2010, para 181.

[29] *Delta TV v Google and YouTube* (2017) (Turin Court of First Instance); see also E Rosati, 'Italian court finds Google and YouTube liable for failing to remove unlicensed content (but confirms eligibility for safe harbour protection)' *(IPKat*, 20 April 2017) ipkitten.blogspot.co.uk/2017/04/italian-court-finds-google-and-youtube.html.

[30] Kraakman (n 19) 61; B Martens, 'JRC Technical Support reports: An economic policy perspective on online platforms' (2016) *Institute for prospective technological studies digital economy working paper* 34.

[31] Frosio (n 2); see also Fisher (n 16) 281.

by Levinson who argues that in the physical environment, liability can be attributed to third parties that could identify wrongdoing more efficiently. Transposing the last-cost benefit approach into the online context, it means that host ISPs cannot only identify the primary wrongdoers that pass through their gates.[32] Rather, the imposition of liability rules might incentivise them to develop filtering-based technology that might reduce the transaction costs that would be generated by human review and achieve a higher degree of efficiency with regard to the removal of infringing content online.[33]

This view is also shared by Lichtman and Posner.[34] Following a number of failed attempts by the American Government to battle cyber-attacks, they posit that host ISPs could control the malicious software and viruses that pass through the online gates. For this reason, they argue that host ISPs might be in a better position than rights holders to mitigate the increasing amount of malicious software while at the same time they could more easily identify primary infringer-users that disseminate the malicious software in the first place.[35] In similar fashion, Katyal argues that 'ISPs could build software and hardware constraints into their systems' and therefore block internet users who attempt to access a website by using different credentials.[36] Along similar lines, in their influential paper, Mann and Belzley argue that the recent technological developments and the rapid advancement of knowledge of filtering means that filtering systems are now the cheapest tool to detect online wrongdoings more efficiently.[37] Therefore, it appears that host ISPs could deploy such filtering mechanisms and thus terminate online infringements in a more efficient manner.

What is more, apart from the academic scholarship that views host ISPs as the cheapest cost avoiders, this last-cost benefit understanding has preoccupied the courts as well. For instance, in the case of *Cartier v Sky*,[38] Cartier brought legal proceedings against five main UK internet service providers and requested they terminate access to websites where fake copies of luxury watches have been offered and sold to unsuspicious consumers. The English court did not find that ISPs that offered internet access to users were committing infringing acts, but it required them to block access to the particular websites with illicit activity. This is because the court considered that 'it is economically more efficient' to request host ISPs to deter the dissemination of counterfeit

[32] D Levinson, 'Collective sanctions' (2003) 56 *Stanford Law Review* 366 where he uses the example of last cost benefit approach in the context of child pornography.

[33] ibid 367.

[34] D Lichtman and E Posner, 'Holding Internet Service Providers Accountable' (2006) 14 *Supreme Court Economic Review* 221–2[illegible].

[35] ibid.

[36] NK Katyal, 'Criminal Law in Cyberspace' (2001) 149 *University of Pennsylvania Law Review* 1097 where he argues that 'ISPs could build software and hardware constraints into their systems. They may, for example, ensure that electronic traffic carries a specific source address consistent with the assigned address (a technique called egress filtering). ISPs might go further and only accept traffic from authorised sources (a technique called ingress filtering). Or ISPs could configure their systems to prevent subscribers from repeatedly trying to log in using different passwords.'

[37] RJ Mann and SR Belzley, 'The Promise of Internet Intermediary Liability' (2005) 47 *William and Mary Law Review* 268 who argue that 'advances in information technology make it increasingly cost effective for intermediaries to monitor more closely the activities of those who use their networks'.

[38] *Cartier International AG v British Sky Broadcasting Ltd* [2016] ETMR 43 307, 377.

goods online than to enable brand owners to seek legal redress against the primary infringers.[39] This understanding means that ISPs may be in a better position than rights holders to mitigate the increasing number of intellectual property violations at a reasonable cost.

However, the ascription of secondary liability rules to host ISPs is not backed up only by a theoretical framework. Indeed, policy and practical justifications reinforce the attribution of a liability regime in the form of secondary liability rules to host ISPs. An examination of these perspectives follows.

III. Policy and Practical Perspectives for Imposing Liability on Host ISPs

From a policy perspective, the concept of imposing a liability framework in the form of secondary liability to host ISPs rests on the premise of secondary regulation. Such concept was examined by Lessig in 1999 and stems from the idea that, by regulating host ISPs, policymakers can control internet users' behaviour. According to Lessig, governments can control an individual's conduct through four modalities, namely law, markets, architecture and social norms.[40] Lessig explains that, in the online world he treated the infrastructure of a host ISP, or as he called it the code, as law.[41] In this sense, he noted that if public authorities want to control internet users' activities, they must regulate online services. This is because, being subject to secondary liability rules, host ISPs may be incentivised to temper to a certain extent the dissemination of illegal material either by terminating the access to websites with illicit activities or undertaking proactive measures, such as filter-based technology, in order to identify unwelcome content. This means that the negative impact of illicit behaviour would be terminated or at least mitigated.

This view is supported by Balkin. According to him, the role of infrastructure can direct and control freedom of speech.[42] In order to clarify his view, Balkin draws parallels with the film industry and how films reach their audiences.[43] He notes that business organisations, contractual agreements, agents, actors and actresses, executive producers and directors, and other supporting entities cooperate before a film is distributed to the public.

This understanding could be equally applied to the digital ecosystem. So, in the online world, domain names, broadband networks, cloud companies and host ISPs, merely transmit or cache information – advertising ISPs and financial processors that form the infrastructure of the digital ecosystem cooperate in order to curb the

[39] *Cartier International AG v British Sky Broadcasting Ltd* [2015] ETMR 1, para 251; for an opposite view see M Husovec, 'Accountable, Not Liable: Injunctions Against Intermediaries' (2016) *TILEC Discussion Paper* 35–36; M Schellekens, 'Liability of Internet Intermediaries: A Slippery Slope?' (2011) *SCRIPTed* 154.

[40] L Lessig, *Code and other Laws of cyberspace* (NY, Basic Books, 1999) 3, 88.

[41] ibid.

[42] J Balkin, 'Old School/ new School speech regulation' (2014) 127 *Harvard Law Review* 2301.

[43] ibid.

dissemination of unlawful content. This implies that they decide which content is legitimate and non-legitimate, which information reaches the end-users, and how users can express their views. In this sense, the regulation of host ISPs via indirect regulation may decisively influence end users' actions.[44]

Furthermore, apart from the benefits of indirect regulation and its potential influence on internet users' behaviours, another policy reason that justifies the ascription of secondary liability framework to host ISPs is the fact that an entity can escape from liability if it does not have knowledge of the illicit activity. For this reason, secondary liability framework has been endorsed for host ISPs by the European policymakers. As will be discussed in Section IV of chapter three, the lack of knowledge is enshrined in Article 14(1) of the ECD, which notes that host ISPs are excluded from liability if they are not aware of the infringements that take place within their networks. This requirement of lack of knowledge was introduced in order to support e-commerce services, which were in an 'embryonic and fragile'[45] stage back in 2000 when the ECD was finalised, and it still continues to apply in order to boost competitiveness and innovation within the Digital Single Market[46] as well as to provide a free space for exchanging information between internet users.[47]

It is this requirement of lack of knowledge that has been used as a defence from host ISPs in order to be exonerated from liability for intellectual property infringements that accrue within their networks. In this sense, by arguing lack of knowledge of the infringements online, host ISPs can continue to operate their business without being afraid that the mere emergence of an online infringement within their network could amount to their liability. The defence of lack of knowledge has been seen as a shield of salvation from the pecuniary claims of content or brand owners and impedes any disruption to the operation of their business model.

However, apart from the policy considerations that influence the imposition of secondary liability rules to host ISPs, there are also other practical reasons. For instance, such reasons might be the difficulty to enforce intellectual property rights against primary infringers who are located in a foreign jurisdiction that provides a less favourable environment for enforcing intellectual property rights. Although courts can order the disclosure of the identity of the primary infringers,[48] the legal suit against them will not be reasonably practicable, as Riordan notes.[49] This is because the effectiveness of enforcing intellectual property rights is contingent upon the expenses of the enforcement

[44] A Murray, *Information Technology Law* (Oxford, Oxford University Press, 2019) 62, 63.

[45] D Friedmann, 'Sinking the safe harbour with the legal certainty of strict liability in sight' (2014) 9 *JIPLP* 148.

[46] G Frosio, 'Reforming Intermediary liability in the platform economy: a European Digital Single Market Strategy' (2017) 112 *Northwestern Law Review* 31.

[47] Joined Cases C-236/08, C-237/08 and C-238/08 *Google France/Inc. v Louis Vuitton Malletier* (2009) ECLI:EU:C:2009:569, para 142 where the Advocate General notes that 'To my mind, the aim of Directive 2000/31 is to create a free and open public domain on the internet. It seeks to do so by limiting the liability of those which transmit or store information, under its Articles 12 to 14, to instances where they were aware of an illegality.'

[48] Through Norwich Pharmacal orders; see also *Golden Eye (International) Ltd and others v Telefonica UK Ltd*, EWHC 723 (Ch) (2012).

[49] J Riordan, *The liability of the internet intermediaries* (Oxford, Oxford University Press, 2016) 54.

procedure, the remedy for which the claimant has applied, and the recognition and enforcement of a foreign decision.[50] Therefore, to turn against primary infringers might not be the ideal solution for rights holders that mainly wish to compensate their losses from the violation of their intellectual property rights.

Moreover, another practical reason that justifies host ISPs as the main target of rights holders with regard to compensate their losses are their high revenues or as Angelopoulos aptly points out 'their deep pockets'.[51] Undoubtedly, host ISPs' flourishing business model attracts the attention of rights holders.[52] This is because internet users, who are often the primary offenders, may not have the necessary assets to meet the compensatory expectations of intellectual property holders. In this regard, Facebook or YouTube, with annual incomes of approximately 77 billion euros in 2020, seem more likely to compensate rights holders in proportion to the harm triggered by their conduct.[53]

What is more, another practical consideration that favours holding host ISPs secondarily liable is the reputational harm that might arise if the rights holders bring legal proceedings against individual internet users who have downloaded or uploaded copyright infringing works.[54] For instance, in Europe, the French Government has been through severe public scrutiny and protests from civil society organisations with regard to the graduate response initiative aiming to fight music piracy.[55] According to this initiative, ISPs that offer internet access to users must send up to three notifications to alleged users-infringers. Lack of compliance with the notifications had resulted in harsh litigation proceedings against internet users. However, the picture of an average internet user who faces litigation procedures from multi-transnational music companies may cause feelings of sympathy and may lead to adverse reputation for the rights holders.

Further, another practical reason that warrants the imposition of secondary liability rules to host ISPs is the difficulty to identify the primary infringements. As Riordan remarked, rights holders face discrepancies to seek redress against primary wrongdoers due to the fact that they usually hide behind their IP addresses and it is not easy to identify them.[56] Indeed, this understanding has already been outlined in the case of *L'Oreal v eBay*.[57] In this case, the Advocate General Jääskinen recognised that there may be cases

[50] A Marsoof, *Internet intermediaries and Trade mark rights* (London, Routledge, 2019) 6–7; D Rowland, U Kohl and A Charlesworth, *Information Technology Law*, 5th edn (London, Routledge, 2017) 81–86; Riordan (n 49) 55–57.

[51] C Angelopoulos, '"Beyond the safe harbors": Harmonizing substantive intermediary liability for copyright infringement in Europe' (2013) 3 *Intellectual Property Quarterly* 253.

[52] N Jondet, 'The silver lining in Dailymotion's copyright cloud' (2008) *Juriscom. Net* 2; see also Case C-324/09 *L'Oreal SA V eBay Int'l AG* [2011] ECR I-6011; Case C-160/15 *GS Media BV v Sanoma Media Netherlands BV and Others* [2016] EU:C:2016:644.

[53] Facebook annual income in 2020, www.businessofapps.com/data/facebook-statistics/.

[54] Riordan (n 49) 57.

[55] P De Filippi and D Bourcier, 'Three-Strikes' Response to Copyright Infringement: The Case of Hadopi' in F Musiani, D Cogburn, L DeNardis and NS Levinson (eds), *The Turn to Infrastructure in Internet Governance* (London, Palgrave-Macmillan, 2016) 125; see also R Giblin, *Code Wars: 10 Years of P2P software litigation* (Cheltenham, Edward Elgar, 2011) 2 where she gives the example of an undergraduate student who has been sued for downloading songs from file sharing platforms and has been fined with 675, 000 dollars in statutory damages.

[56] Footnote 50 in GB Dinwoodie, 'Comparative analysis of the secondary liability of online service providers' in GB Dinwoodie (ed), *Secondary liability of internet service providers* (Berlin, Springer, 2017).

[57] Case C-324/09 *L'Oreal SA V eBay Int'l AG* (2011) ECR I-6011.

where 'a third party is using the services of a hosting ISSP to infringe an intellectual property right, but the true identity of that infringer remains unknown'.[58] By contrast, rights holders know host ISPs' establishments and therefore it is easier for them to turn against host ISPs and pursue compensatory claims for their losses.

IV. Conclusion

This chapter has provided an overview of the theoretical underpinnings and policy considerations for ascribing liability rules to host ISPs. Through the lens of the moral theory and the utilitarian theory, a host ISP can be seen either as morally liable due to its cooperation with the wrongdoings of its users, or from a utilitarian perspective, a host ISP could be held liable since it is seen as a source of deterrence for online infringements in a less expensive manner.

In particular, drawing upon the moral theory, a host ISP can be held morally liable if there is a formal or material cooperation with the illegal acts of the internet users. Yet, it is worthwhile to note that material cooperation can trigger ISP's liability if the host ISP does not accept practices or measures to curb the online infringements within their networks. Rather, it accepts the infringements to take place and therefore violate the rights of copyright holders or brand owners. Further, under the influence of the utilitarian theory, a host ISP can be held liable because it is placed in the best position to prevent the emergence of violations or it can detect and terminate the wrongful acts at a lower cost. Such theoretical justifications might justify the choice of European policy-makers to ascribe this specific liability regime to a host ISPs' activities.

However, the ascription of secondary liability rules to host ISPs is not backed up only by a theoretical framework. Indeed, policy and practical considerations reinforce the reasons that warrant the attribution of a liability regime in the form of secondary liability rules to host ISPs. Such rationale includes a plethora of reasons that are either based on the idea of secondary regulation as an instrument to influence internet users' behaviours as well as on practicality and efficiency. Especially the latter reasons address cases where host ISPs are targeted due to their high revenues, popularity and unknown domicile of primary infringers-users.

Having discussed the theoretical and policy considerations that warrant the imposition of a liability regime for hosting ISPs in the form of secondary liability, the discussion now moves to the concept of secondary liability for copyright and trade mark infringements. Given that host ISPs' liability, as enshrined in the ECD, is a form of secondary liability, the following chapter provides a discussion of the peculiarities of secondary liability doctrine with regard to intellectual property infringements and the liability of host ISPs as per Article 14(1) of the ECD.

[58] Case C-324/09 *L'Oreal SA V eBay Int'l AG* (2011) ECR I-6011, Opinion Jääskinen, para 179.

PART II

Evaluation of the Current Legislative Tools

3

The Host Internet Service Providers' (Host ISPs) Liability Framework under Article 14(1) of the E-Commerce Directive (ECD) for Copyright and Trade Mark Infringements: An Outdated Approach

I. Introduction

The introduction of the E-Commerce Directive[1] back in 2000 established the regulatory framework for host ISPs' activities in the European Union.[2] Following the rationale of the provisions that were included in its US counterpart, the Digital Millennium Copyright Act (DMCA),[3] the ECD offers immunity from liability to those ISPs which provide a mere conduit, caching and hosting services under specific circumstances. More specifically, under Article 14(1) of the ECD, the provision relevant to this research, host ISPs are exonerated from liability if they do not have knowledge of the infringing material or illicit activity that takes place within their networks, or when they expeditiously remove the infringing material upon receiving notification from the rights holder.[4]

These immunity liability provisions, for host ISPs, also known as safe harbour provisions, were justified on the basis of boosting innovation and development in the European Digital Single Market.[5] At that time, when the ECD was drafted at the European level, e-commerce was still in its infancy, but had promising perspectives for rapid

[1] Hereinafter ECD.

[2] Council Directive (EC) 2000/31 on certain legal aspects of information society services, in particular electronic commerce, in the Internal Market [2000] OJ L 178.

[3] 17 U.S.C. §§ 512 of Digital Millennium Copyright Act (hereinafter DMCA).

[4] Articles 12, 13 and 14 of the ECD.

[5] M Pélissié du Rausas et al, 'McKinsey Global Institute: Internet matters, the net's sweeping impact on growth, jobs, and prosperity' (May 2011) www.mckinsey.com/industries/technology-media-and-telecommunications/our-insights/internet-matters; C Wright, 'Actual versus legal control: Reading vicarious liability for copyright infringement into the Digital Millennium Copyright Act of 1998' (2000) 75 *Washington Law Review* 1005.

growth within the next few years.[6] In this way, host ISPs continued their business operation without fear of the imposition of liability rules.

However, with the rapid development of e-commerce services, a dramatic increase in the emergence of online infringements has been observed. This coincided with the increased occurrence of copyright and trade mark infringements on the internet. This thorny issue of online piracy has been aggravated by the advent of the Web 2.0 era.[7] Within this context host ISPs offer new services to their users, this can increase the risk of unauthorised material and the display of counterfeit goods appearing online.[8] This understanding has been supported by a number of studies that demonstrate the correlation between the digital ecosystem and online infringements. For instance, pursuant to the report of the European Intellectual Property Office (EUIPO) on intellectual property infringements in 2018, it has been found that the internet is a facilitator for the dissemination of unauthorised content and counterfeit goods online.[9] Likewise, in the recently published report by the EU Commission on Counterfeit and Piracy Watch list in 2018, it is possible to observe that the main type of host ISPs which offer, within their premises, the circulation of unauthorised material, are host ISPs.[10]

Witnessing this exponential growth in online copyright and trade mark infringements, rights holders decided to resort to courts with the aim of seeking compensation for their losses. However, while there have been cases where intellectual property holders have filed lawsuits against individual users,[11] there is increasing litigation where rights holders bring civil proceedings against host ISPs; asking the courts to hold them secondarily liable for enabling or facilitating copyright and trade mark violations that accrue within their networks. The rise of tort claims from rights holders can be

[6] EU Commission, 'Commissioner Bolkestein welcomes political agreement on electronic commerce Directive' (8 December 1999) europa.eu/rapid/press-release_IP-99-952_en.htm?locale=en; it has been noted that 'the global electronic commerce market is growing extremely fast and could be worth $ 1.4 trillion by the year 2003 (source: Forrester Research). In Europe, electronic commerce is already worth €17 billion and is expected to reach €340 billion by 2003'; A Wyckoff and A Colecchia, *The Economic and Social Impact of Electronic Commerce* (Paris, OECD, 1992) 12; T Verbiest, G Spindler, G Riccio and A Van der Perre, 'Study on the Liability of Internet Intermediaries: general trends in the EU' (2007) 4, papers.ssrn.com/sol3/papers.cfm?abstract_id=2575069.

[7] Web 2.0 era amounts to host ISPs that provide new online services to their users such as social networks, online marketplaces and online music platforms; T O' Reilly, 'What is Web 2.0' (*O'Reilly*, 30 September 2005) www.oreilly.com/pub/a/web2/archive/what-is-web-20.html; LW Friedman and HH Friedman, 'The New Media Technologies: Overview and Research Framework' (2008) 1; World Intellectual Property Organisation, 'Five Steps to Protect Your Trademarks in the Web 2.0 World' (*WIPO*, September 2010) www.wipo.int/wipo_magazine/en/2010/05/article_0006.html.

[8] A telling example can be found on Amazon. For what services Amazon has offered at its beginning and what services Amazon offers now to its online consumers, see A Hartmans, '15 fascinating facts you probably didn't know about Amazon' (*Business Insider*, 23 August 2018) www.businessinsider.com/jeff-bezos-amazon-history-facts-2017-4?r=US&IR=T#in-the-early-days-of-amazon-a-bell-would-ring-in-the-office-every-time-someone-made-a-purchase-and-everyone-would-gather-around-to-see-if-they-knew-the-customer-2.

[9] European Intellectual Property Office, 'Synthesis report on IPR infringement' (2018) 18 where it states 'Forty-six from the top 100 global companies were found to have at least one brand advertised on an infringing website', see euipo.europa.eu/tunnel-web/secure/webdav/guest/document_library/observatory/docs/Full%20Report/Full%20Synthesis%20Report%20EN.pdf.

[10] EU Commission Staff working document, 'Counterfeit and Piracy Watch List' (2018) SWD 492 final 8, available at trade.ec.europa.eu/doclib/docs/2018/december/tradoc_157564.pdf.

[11] *A&M Records v Napster* 9th Cir 2001; see also L Edwards and C Waelde, 'Online intermediaries and liability for copyright infringement' (2005) WIPO 27; L Edwards, 'The fall and rise of intermediary liability online'

justified due to the close connection between intellectual property law and tort law. This understanding has been reinforced in a bedrock of court rulings that perceive intellectual property infringements as torts and note that 'courts have long recognised that infringement of a copyright is a tort, and all persons concerned therein are jointly and severally liable as such joint tortfeasors'.[12] In this sense, host ISPs were subject to fines for damages as a result of infringements, or to injunctive relief which requires them to deploy a number of measures in order to prevent the illicit activities. Yet, as critically discussed in this chapter, to hold host ISPs secondarily liable for the illegitimate actions of their users seems challenging.

This is mainly due to the lack of harmonisation of secondary liability in tort at the European level, which has given rise to a sprawling patchwork of miscellaneous tortious secondary national doctrines across the European borders. Interestingly, in the absence of any harmonisation of secondary liability in tort, secondary liability rules have not been harmonised in a copyright context, nor in a trade mark context, but have only received peripheral attempts at harmonisation via the ECD. What is more, any attempts to offer a broader harmonisation perspective in the DSMD have not been fruitful.[13]

Against this background, this chapter explores the liability that host ISPs may incur for trade mark infringements that have been committed by their users under the ECD regime. What is worthy of mention here, is that until 17 April 2019, when the Copyright in the Digital Single Market Directive (DSMD) was finalised, the liability of host ISPs for copyright violations has been regulated under Article 14(1) of the ECD. For this reason, existing case law that examines the liability of host ISPs for copyright infringements under the ECD is also discussed in this chapter. In this respect, the narrative begins with the theoretical and policy considerations that justify the imposition of secondary liability rules to host ISPs. Following this, the discussion moves to the concept of secondary liability for trade mark infringements where the relationship between tort law and intellectual property law, as well as the peculiarities of tortious secondary liability doctrine, are discussed. Then, the concept of host ISPs' liability as a form of secondary liability is presented. This enables the reader to gain an understanding of the potential drawbacks that the concept of secondary liability in tort may have on host ISPs. Having defined the concept of host ISPs' liability, the chapter then critically assesses the conditions that trigger liability under the ECD and their national implementation in five selected legal systems, namely the UK, Germany, France, Spain, and Greece. These national legal systems have been chosen on the basis of them being the most representative legal traditions in Europe, with the UK representing the tradition of common law;[14] Germany, France, and Spain depicting the tradition of civil law; while Greece has been chosen on the basis of being one of the few EU countries to have an

in L Edwards and C Waelde, *Law and the Internet* (Oxford, Hart Publishing, 2009) 49; R Giblin, *Code Wars: 10 Years of P2P software litigation* (Cheltenham, Edward Elgar, 2011) 2–3 where she notes that 'From 2003–2007, members of the industry "filed, settled or threatened" lawsuits against more than 20.000 individuals.'

[12] Cited in A Dorfman and A Jacob, 'Copyright as tort' (2011) 12 *Theoretical Inquiries in Law* 80–82; *Ted Browne Music Co. v Fowler, 290 F. 751, 754* (2d Cir. 1923).

[13] A critical analysis of the DSMD will follow in ch 4 of this book.

[14] The UK withdrew its membership from the EU in January 2020 with the end of the transition period on the 31 December 2020. UK Laws will be addressed because as per Article 2 of the EUWA, EU-derived domestic legislation will continue to have effect and because the UK was an EU member state and thus has been influenced by the CJEU case law.

alternative framework for combatting intellectual property violations online. The presentation of these national legal systems offers a clearer insight into the key aspects of the legal nature of torticus secondary liability rules.

II. The Concept of Secondary Liability for Copyright and Trade Mark Infringements

In contrast to primary liability rules that penalise those actors who personally commit a tortious act, secondary liability is attributed to those actors who enable the commission of a wrongdoing by third parties.[15] Secondary infringement requires an act of primary infringement in order to take place. However, secondary liability may also be attributed to those involved in a wrongdoing, irrespective of the fact that it was not themselves carrying out the primary infringement.

Although in theory there are distinctive lines between primary and secondary liability, in practice it seems that the concept of secondary liability depends on primary liability. Indeed, secondary liability is attached to the existence of a primary wrongdoing. As Lord Hoffmann aptly pointed out, there is 'no secondary liability without primary liability'.[16] This has been referred to as its parasitic or derivative nature.[17] Rights holders cannot substantiate secondary liability claims without a primary infringement. This means that a defendant can only be held liable for the harm, which is triggered by the primary tortious acts of a third person. Otherwise, if a primary wrongdoing does not take place, secondary liability claims lack a legal basis, thus they cannot be invoked. Therefore, individuals who seek redress against secondary actors will not be compensated and legal uncertainty might arise.

What is more, a key difference between primary and secondary infringement is the mental element, in the sense that absence of knowledge of wrongdoing can be a defence against allegations for secondary infringement. This defence has been extensively used by defendants in order to be exonerated from liability from secondary infringements in tort or intellectual property law. A representative example of this line of thinking can be found in the *L'Oréal v eBay* ruling[18] where L'Oréal brought legal proceedings against eBay with an allegation of trade mark violation. In response, eBay claimed that it was

[15] M Sadeghi, 'The Knowledge Standard for ISP Copyright and Trademark Secondary Liability: A Comparative Study on the Analysis of US and EU Laws' (Unpublished PhD thesis, 2013) 13; C Angelopoulos, *European Intermediary Liability in Copyright: A Tort-Based Analysis* (Alphen aan den Rijn, Kluwer Law International, 2016) 13–14; GB Dinwoodie, 'A comparative analysis of the secondary liability of online service providers' in GB Dinwoodie (ed), *Secondary Liability of Internet Service Providers* (Berlin, Springer, 2016) 1.

[16] OBG, 31; Cited in J Riordan, *The liability of the internet intermediaries* (Oxford, Oxford University Press, 2016) 70; P Davies, 'Accessory liability for assisting torts' (2011) 70 *The Cambridge Law Journal* 362.

[17] P Davies, 'Accessory liability: protecting intellectual property rights' (2011) 4 *Intellectual Property Quarterly* 390; He notes that 'Accessory liability is parasitic upon the commission of a primary wrong, so unless and until the purchasing and selling of such keywords is recognised, at least potentially, to be wrongful, there can be no accessory liability.'; *OBG Ltd and another v Allan and others Douglas and others v Hello! Ltd and others (No 3) Mainstream Properties Ltd v Young* [2007] UKHL 21 para 31; Lord Hoffmann notes that 'there could be no secondary liability without primary liability, and therefore a person could not be liable for inducing a breach of contract unless there had in fact been a breach by the contracting party'.

[18] *L'Oreal S.A v eBay International AG* [2009] EWHC 1094 (Ch).

not aware of the illicit activity within its platform and was therefore eligible to apply the immunity provisions as set forth in Article 14(1) of the ECD.[19] In this way, by evoking the absence of knowledge, host ISPs can be exonerated from secondary liability rules under the principles of tort law.

However, it seems that the concept of secondary liability under the principles of tort law is subject to a blurred understanding. As Davies describes it, secondary liability in tort is considered an 'under-analyzed' area of law.[20] Mainly, this is because secondary liability in tort is seen as a new area of law.[21] That is, where the norms of secondary liability in criminal law have been extensively used in the courts in order to attribute criminal liability to alleged offenders,[22] and are considered 'well-established',[23] in tort secondary liability has not been well-developed.[24] This is probably because there have been very limited cases so far that have preoccupied the courts with the ascription of secondary liability norms from a tort law perspective in the physical environment.[25] For this reason, due to this limited applicability of secondary liability rules at judicial level, the need to clearly carve out the concept of secondary liability in tort law theory and doctrine has been neglected.

Furthermore, the blurred understanding in tort law relates to the miscellaneous definitions that have been attributed to secondary liability.[26] Although the concept of secondary liability remains the same, it has been interchangeably defined as accessory or vicarious liability, or indirect liability, or contributory liability. For instance, in the US legal system, instead of the broad term of secondary liability, the terms of vicarious or contributory liability are used exclusively. The former is about the defendant, 'with knowledge of the infringing activity, induces, causes or materially contributes to the infringing conduct of another',[27] while the latter emerges when the defendant 'unfairly reaps the benefits of another's infringing behaviour',[28] and 'has the right and the ability to supervise the infringing activity and also has a direct financial interest in such activities'.[29] At the European level, there is no harmonised framework of tort law and policy, the issue is left up to the laws of the various Member States who use various definitions, such as secondary liability, indirect liability, accessory liability, or joint-tortfeasance.[30] Whilst these are all subject to the same interpretation,

[19] A Rühmkorf, 'eBay on the European Playing Field: A Comparative Case Analysis of L'Oréal v eBay' (2009) 6(3) *SCRIPTed* 685.

[20] Davies (n 17) 390.

[21] Angelopoulos (n 15) 13–14.

[22] G Williams, *Joints Torts and Contributory Negligence* (London, Stevens & Sons Ltd, 1951) 11.

[23] Davies (n 16) 354.

[24] P Birks, 'Civil Wrongs: A New World' in P Birks and FMB Reynolds, *Butterworths Lectures 1990–1991* (London, Butterworths, 1991) 55, 100; P Birks considers secondary liability as an 'obscure and under-theorized' area of law.

[25] Angelopoulos (n 15) 13–14.

[26] Riordan (n 16) 13.

[27] *Gershwin Publishing Corp v Columbia Artists Mgmt*, Inc. 443 F. 2d 1159, 1162 (2D Cir. 1971).

[28] *Artists Music Inc. v Reed Publig.*, Inc. 31 U.S.P.Q 623 (S.D.N.Y 1994).

[29] *Fonovisa, Inc. v Cherry Auction*, Inc. 76 F. 3d 259 (9th Cir. 1996).

[30] J Wang, *Regulating Hosting ISPs' responsibilities for Copyright Infringement: The freedom to operate in the US, EU and China* (Berlin, Springer, 2018) 19–23; BM Farano, 'Internet Intermediaries' Liability for Copyright and Trademark Infringement: Reconciling the EU and US Approaches' (2012) *TTLF Working Paper No 14* 47.

ie, the allocation of liability to an actor for the acts of a third party, it seems that some of these definitions treat the actor as primarily liable, although such liability is secondary since it might arise only if the primary infringement takes place.[31] A telling example can be found in the UK joint-tortfeasance doctrine that treats joint-tortfeasors as equally liable next to the alleged primary infringers.[32] Further examination of different tortious secondary liability doctrines can be found in this chapter in section III(C).

Finally, the blurred understanding of secondary liability is aggravated by the lack of harmonisation of secondary liability at European level.[33] Unlike primary liability rules, which are harmonised, secondary liability rules in tort law do not fall under the umbrella of harmonisation. It is this lack of consensus over the main elements of secondary liability rules at European level that has led to the emergence of different doctrines within national jurisdictions. Such doctrines, as outlined with relevant case law in section III(C) of this chapter, include the joint-tortfeasance, authorisation, disturber liability (*Stoererhaftung*) and civil liability.[34] These might substantially differ from each other, and thus give rise to legal uncertainty to rights holders and defendants. For instance, in contrast to most EU national legal systems, the German legal system adopts the concept of disturber liability which excludes claims for damages and allows only injunctive relief. This contrasts with the system adopted in France where secondary infringers are subject to pecuniary claims, namely under Article 1382 of the French Civil Code which notes, 'any act whatever of man, which causes damage to another, obliges the one by whose fault it occurred, to compensate it'.[35]

In the midst of the uncertainty regarding a harmonised concept of secondary liability in tort or intellectual property law, the national examples discussed later in this chapter offer a clearer understanding of key aspects of the legal nature of secondary liability. Before entering this discussion, however, it is essential to establish how and why host ISPs' liability is a form of secondary liability according to the legislative framework set forth by the ECD. Such discussion is necessary to the extent that discrepancies and drawbacks in the definition of tortious secondary liability may also impact the scope and meaning of host ISPs' liability.

[31] Angelopoulos (n 15) 13; C Angelopoulos notes that 'these doctrines fail to identify cases of accessory liability as such, but instead formally categorise them as cases of primary liability, with the accessory treated either as a "joint tortfeasor", who stands alongside the person who committed the material act of infringement as an equal principal in a single tort, or as the perpetrator, not of a participation in the wrong of somebody else, but of an independent act of negligence consisting of that participation.'

[32] Angelopoulos (n 15) 13; *Football Dataco Ltd & Ors v Stan James Plc & Ors* [2013] EWCA Civ 27; *L' Oreal v eBay* [2009] EWHC 1094 (Ch).

[33] Angelopoulos (n 15) 13; M Leistner, 'Structural aspects of secondary provider liability in Europe' (2014) 9 *Journal of Intellectual Property Law and Practice* 75; Davies (n 17) 390; EU Commission, 'Proposal on certain legal aspects of electronic commerce in the internal market' COM (1998) 12; Max Planck Institute for Intellectual Property and Competition Law Munich, 'Study on the Overall Functioning of the European Trade Mark System' (2011) 213.

[34] Leistner (n 33) 78; C Angelopoulos, 'Beyond the safe harbours: harmonising substantive intermediary liability for copyright infringement in Europe' (2013) 3 *International Review of Industrial Property and Copyright Law* 262.

[35] Official translation of the French Civil Code, available at www.fd.ulisboa.pt/wp-content/uploads/2014/12/Codigo-Civil-Frances-French-Civil-Code-english-version.pdf.

III. Host ISPs' Liability as a Form of Secondary Liability: Article 14(1) of the ECD and Legal Traditions of EU Member States and the UK

This section addresses the concept of host ISPs' liability under Article 14(1) of the ECD at European level. It discusses the implementation of Article 14(1) of the ECD into the national legal systems of four representative EU Member States and the UK, as well as the liability of host ISPs under the legal traditions of those states.

A. Article 14(1) of the ECD: Concept of Host ISPs' Liability

ISPs' liability is about holding host ISPs liable for tortious acts committed by their users, notably acts of intellectual property infringement. It is set out in Article 14(1)(a)(b) of the ECD of 2000,[36] that a host ISP can escape liability if it does not have knowledge of the illicit activity or, if upon obtaining knowledge of the illicit activity it takes down the infringing content. Host ISPs' liability is established in a horizontal way[37] and it can be defined, as noted by Dinwoodie, both from a 'negative' and a 'positive' perspective.[38]

From the negative perspective, the definition of host ISPs' liability is set out in the provisions of the ECD. As Angelopoulos points out, host ISPs' liability is defined in the current legal framework in an 'evasive, negative fashion, dictating only when Member States can't impose liability for intermediary activities, not when they can'.[39] This means that the legal provisions determine only the conditions that shelter host ISPs from liability and dictate what host ISPs should not do in order to avoid liability. These legal provisions are known as immunity or safe harbour provisions. They are described by Husovec as 'a conditional liability-free zone, in which you can move freely as long as you respect its predefined boundaries'.[40]

Effectively, what the provisions of the ECD do is to carve out the specific circumstances that trigger instances where host ISPs are not liable. For instance, Articles 12 and 13 concern only the mere conduit and caching ISPs and prescribe the specific conditions of exemption from legal liability. Likewise, Article 14(1) of the ECD, which is relevant for

[36] Council Directive (EC) 2000/31 on certain legal aspects of information society services, in particular electronic commerce, in the Internal Market [2000] OJ L 178; K Parti and L Marin, 'Ensuring Freedoms and Protecting Rights in the Governance of the Internet: A comparative analysis on blocking measures and internet providers' removal of illegal internet content' (2013) 9 *Journal of Contemporary European Research* 149.

[37] This means that it addresses all types of unlawful content. In contrast to its counterpart in the US legal system; See M Peguera, 'The DMCA Safe Harbors and their European Counterparts: a comparative analysis of some common problems' (2008) 32 *Colum. J.L. & Arts* 482; EU Commission, 'First Report on the application of Directive 2000/31/EC of the European Parliament and of the Council of 8 June 2000 on certain legal aspects of information society services, in particular electronic commerce, in the Internal Market (Directive on electronic commerce)' COM (2003) 702 final 4.

[38] Dinwoodie (n 15) 19.

[39] Angelopoulos (n 34) 254.

[40] M Husovec, *Injunctions against Intermediaries in the European Union: Accountable but Not Liable?* (Cambridge, Cambridge University Press, 2017) 50.

this research, addresses the ISPs that host material. In particular, it dictates that a host ISP can avoid liability if it does not have actual knowledge of the illegal activity, or it expeditiously takes down the infringing material upon receiving a notification. In such cases, courts may rule out liability for the host ISP to the extent that the conditions that grant immunity apply.

The 'negative' understanding of host ISPs' liability under Article 14(1) of the ECD has been upheld at the European level in a number of rulings. According to those cases, the absence of knowledge and the prompt removal of infringing content upon notification are used as defences against ISPs' liability. Consider, for instance, the case of *L'Oreal v eBay*,[41] which was referred by the English High Court to the CJEU in order to clarify the concept of knowledge, as set forth in Article 14(1) of the ECD. In this case, the Court clarified that the requirement of knowledge addresses the cases where a host ISP is 'aware of facts or circumstances on the basis of which a diligent economic operator should have identified the illegality in question and acted in accordance with Article 14(1)(b) of Directive 2000/31'.[42] In this sense, given that host ISPs are not aware of the infringing content on the basis of a diligent economic operator, then they could evoke the defence of absence of knowledge. The concept of the diligent economic operator is comprehensively discussed in section III(A) of this chapter.

Along similar lines, national courts have also held that host ISPs could use the defence of absence of knowledge. A representative example can be found In *Audiencia Provincial Sentencia A.P.S. Madrid*,[43] where the Spanish broadcaster Telecinco sued YouTube, alleging that YouTube's users were uploading unauthorised content on the video music platform.[44] Amidst the arguments in its line of defence, YouTube claimed that it was not aware of the illicit activity and did not receive any notification with regard to the infringing nature of the content. In this way, YouTube evoked the lack of knowledge as set forth in Article 14(1) of the ECD in order to escape liability. Its allegations were further confirmed with the ruling from the Madrid Court of Appeals that held that YouTube cannot be held liable since the notifications that were sent by Telecinco do not entail removal requests for specific copyright infringements, thus they do not fall within the scope of actual knowledge.[45] Therefore, in this case YouTube was not liable because it lacked knowledge of the infringing content.

In similar fashion, the defence of prompt removal of infringing content upon being notified has been evoked in Belgium. More specifically, in the *Lancôme v eBay* case, Lancôme sued eBay for trade mark infringements.[46] eBay argued that it

[41] Case C-324/09, *L'Oreal SA V eBay Int'l AG* (2011) ECR I-6011.

[42] ibid para 120.

[43] *Audiencia Provincial Sentencia A.P.S. Madrid Jan* [2014] (Provincial Court Sentence).

[44] J Halliday, 'Google wins YouTube case in Spain Google wins case against Spanish broadcaster that claimed YouTube had damaged its business' *The Guardian* (23 September 2010) www.theguardian.com/technology/2010/sep/23/google-wins-youtube-case-spain.

[45] M Peguera, 'Internet Service Providers' Liability in Spain: Recent Case Law and Future Perspectives' (2010) 1 *Journal of Intellectual Property, Information Technology and E-Commerce Law* 159; M Peguera, 'Telecinco v. YouTube: the ruling in its context" (*ISP liability*, 26 September 2010) ispliability.wordpress.com/2010/09/26/telecinco-v-youtube-the-ruling-in-its-context/.

[46] *eBay v Lancôme* [2008] Unreported (Brussels Commercial Court).

removed the pirated goods as soon as it was notified and was thus eligible to evoke the defence of Article 14(1)b of the ECD, which notes that 'the provider, upon obtaining such knowledge or awareness, acts expeditiously to remove or to disable access to the information'. In response, Lancôme argued that eBay did not have a passive role towards the goods that were displayed on its platform. Rather, it had an active stance and exceeded its role as hosting provider.[47] For this reason, according to Lancôme's claims, eBay could not invoke the immunity provision of Article 14(1) of the ECD and had to be liable as per the general provisions of Belgian tort law. However, the Commercial Court in Brussels accepted eBay's defence, according to which eBay acted expeditiously upon being notified about the illicit activity on its network, namely by verifying the validity of the request and subsequently removing the counterfeit goods from its platform.[48] Such measures were considered realistic and efficient by the Belgian Court since eBay cooperated with the rights holders in order to terminate the circulation of counterfeit goods that infringed Lancôme's rights.[49] Hence, the Brussels court accepted eBay's defence to avoid liability pursuant to Article 14(1) of the ECD.

However, apart from the negative perspective, the host ISPs' liability can be defined in a positive manner too. This means that the courts define the conditions under which host ISPs can be held liable. For instance, the French Courts ascribe liability rules to host ISPs if there is a breach of duty. This understanding has been illustrated in *eBay v Louis Vuitton*[50] where the Court of Appeal held that that eBay was liable for circulating fake Louis Vuitton products within its networks. To the Court's reasoning, this is because eBay had a positive duty to prevent the dissemination of infringing material online. The lack of measures might result to the breach of duty and therefore trigger liability.

In light of the above, it is possible to observe that the ECD does not offer a definition of the concept of host ISPs' liability. Rather, it offers specific requirements that outline how host ISPs would avoid liability. Such requirements are used as defences by host IPs to allow them eligibility to immunity liability provisions under the ECD scheme. The absence of any definition of host ISPs' liability at European level shifts the narrative to EU Member States and the UK in order to identify how host ISPs' liability could be defined. For this reason, the following section looks at the implementation of the requirements of the ECD in five selected countries, namely the UK, Germany, France, Spain, and Greece.

[47] A Cheung and KH Pun, 'Comparative study on the liability for trade mark infringement of online auction providers' (2009) 31 *European Intellectual Property Review* 2; A Bain, 'Is it an infringement of trade mark law for the operator of an online marketplace (such as eBay) to allow counterfeit goods to be sold? As a matter of policy, should it be?' (2011) 33 *European Intellectual Property Review* 164.

[48] M Rimmer, 'Breakfast at Tiffany's': eBay Inc., Trade Mark Law and Counterfeiting' (2011) 21 *Journal of Law, Information, and Science* 150.

[49] ibid.

[50] Case 11-10505 *eBay Inc v LVMH* (French Court of Appeal, 3 May 2012).

B. Host ISPs' Liability under the National Implementation of Article 14(1) of the ECD into Four Selected EU Member States: Germany, France, Spain, Greece and the UK

This section examines the implementation of the ECD in four selected EU jurisdictions and the UK. Following the rationale of the ECD, these states refrain from defining to what host ISPs' liability refers and dictate under which requirements host ISPs can evade liability, namely with the claim of absence of knowledge and the expeditious removal of infringing content upon notification. What is more, these EU jurisdictions fail to offer a solid interpretation of the requirements, and thus trigger legal uncertainty among host ISPs.

First, with regard to the 'negative' understanding of host ISPs' liability, EU Member States follow the rationale of the ECD and refrain from defining to what host ISPs' liability amounts. This 'negative' understanding can be found in national laws that have been enacted for the purposes of implementing the ECD at national level. In the UK, the E-Commerce Regulations 2002/2013 were enacted in order to transpose the ECD onto the national legal system. The UK Laws followed verbatim the requirements set forth in Article 14(1) of the ECD, and Article 19(a) of the E-Commerce Regulations 2002/2013, which notes:

> The service provider (i) does not have actual knowledge of unlawful activity or information and, where a claim for damages is made, is not aware of facts or circumstances from which it would have been apparent to the service provider that the activity or information was unlawful; or (ii) upon obtaining such knowledge or awareness, acts expeditiously to remove or to disable access to the information …

Likewise, in the German legal system, the Telemediengesetz (TMG) was enacted for the purposes of implementing the provisions of the ECD. In § 10 of the TMG, which adopts the negative understanding of host ISPs' liability and dictates that a host ISP can be exonerated from liability if it has:

> 1. no knowledge of the illegal activity or the information and, as regards claims for damages, is not aware of any facts or circumstances from which the illegal activity or the information is apparent, or 2. upon obtaining such knowledge, have acted expeditiously to remove the information or to disable access to it.[51]

In a similar fashion in France, the Act on Confidence in Digital Economy (LCEN) has been enacted for implementing ECD provisions. So, Article 6(4) of LCEN dictates that a host ISP cannot be held liable if it has no knowledge of the illicit nature of the

[51] Telemediengesetz (TMG), English translation of the Telemediengesetz in Hunton Privacy blog, available at www.huntonprivacyblog.com/wp-content/uploads/sites/28/2016/02/Telemedia_Act__TMA_.pdf; in German § 10 TMG: 'Diensteanbieter sind für fremde Informationen, die sie für einen Nutzer speichern, nicht verantwortlich, sofern

1. sie keine Kenntnis von der rechtswidrigen Handlung oder der Information haben und ihnen im Falle von Schadensersatzansprüchen auch keine Tatsachen oder Umstände bekannt sind, aus denen die rechtswidrige Handlung oder die Information offensichtlich wird, oder
2. sie unverzüglich tätig geworden sind, um die Information zu entfernen oder den Zugang zu ihr zu sperren, sobald sie diese Kenntnis erlangt haben.'

infringement, or no awareness of the facts and circumstances that would make the illicit nature of the infringement apparent to the ISP, or if it reacts expeditiously in order to remove the infringing information or terminate access to it.[52]

Further, in Spain the Ley de servicios de la sociedad de la informacion y de commercio electronico has transposed the ECD provisions into the Spanish jurisdiction. Article 16(1)(a) of the Spanish Act notes that:

> Providers of an intermediary service consisting of hosting data provided by the recipient of this service shall not be liable for the information stored at the request of the recipient, provided that: (a) they have no effective knowledge that the activity or information stored is illicit or that it injures goods or rights of a third party liable for compensation, or (b) if they have such knowledge, they must act with diligence to withdraw the data or make access to them impossible and he service provider shall be understood to have the effective knowledge referred to in subparagraph (a) where a competent body has declared the illicit nature of the data, ordered its withdrawal, or ensured access to the data is impossible; (b) the existence of the injury was declared and the service provider knew the relevant decision, without prejudice to the procedures for the detection and removal of the content which the providers apply under voluntary agreements and of other means of effective knowledge that could be established.[53]

Finally, in Greece, the Presidential Decree 131/2003 has implemented the ECD provisions in the Greek legal system. In particular, Article 13 dictates that a host ISP cannot be held liable if it does not have knowledge of the infringing act, or in terms of pecuniary claims it lacks awareness of the illicit activity, or it removes the alleged infringing information upon being notified.[54]

[52] Loi n° 2004–575 du 21 juin 2004 pour la confiance dans l'économie numérique, French translation of Article 6(4) of LCEN '... si elles n'avaient pas effectivement connaissance de leur caractère illicite ou de faits et circonstances faisant apparaître ce caractère ou si, dès le moment où elles en ont eu cette connaissance, elles ont agi promptement pour retirer ces données ou en rendre l'accès impossible.', available at wipolex.wipo.int/en/text/276258.

[53] The translation in English is available at www.global-regulation.com/translation/spain/1450967/law-34-2002%252c-of-11-july%252c-services-of-the-society-of-information-and-electronic-commerce.html; Artículo 16. Responsabilidad de los prestadores de servicios de alojamiento o almacenamiento de datos. « 1. Los prestadores de un servicio de intermediación consistente en albergar datos proporcionados por el destinatario de este servicio no serán responsables por la información almacenada a petición del destinatario, siempre que: a) No tengan conocimiento efectivo de que la actividad o la información almacenada es ilícita o de que lesiona bienes o derechos de un tercero susceptibles de indemnización, o b) Si lo tienen, actúen con diligencia para retirar los datos o hacer imposible el acceso a ellos. Se entenderá que el prestador de servicios tiene el conocimiento efectivo a que se refiere el párrafo a) cuando un órgano competente haya declarado la ilicitud de los datos, ordenado su retirada o que se imposibilite el acceso a los mismos, o se hubiera declarado la existencia de la lesión, y el prestador conociera la correspondiente resolución, sin perjuicio de los procedimientos de detección y retirada de contenidos que los prestadores apliquen en virtud de acuerdos voluntarios y de otros medios de conocimiento efectivo que pudieran establecerse. »

[54] Article 14(1) in Greek; Άρθρο 13- Φιλοξενία, '1.Σε περίπτωση παροχής μιας υπηρεσίας της κοινωνίας της πληροφορίας συνισταμένης στην αποθήκευση πληροφοριών παρεχομένων από ένα αποδέκτη υπηρεσίας, δεν υφίσταται ευθύνη του φορέα παροχής της υπηρεσίας για τις πληροφορίες που αποθηκεύονται μετά από αίτηση αποδέκτη της υπηρεσίας, υπό τους όρους ότι:

(α) ο φορέας παροχής της υπηρεσίας δεν γνωρίζει πραγματικά ότι πρόκειται για παράνομη δραστηριότητα ή πληροφορία και ότι, σε ό,τι αφορά αξιώσεις αποζημιώσεως, δεν γνωρίζει τα γεγονότα ή τις περιστάσεις από τις οποίες προκύπτει η παράνομη δραστηριότητα ή πληροφορία, ή

(β) ο φορέας παροχής της υπηρεσίας, μόλις αντιληφθεί τα προαναφερθέντα, αποσύρει ταχέως τις πληρ οφορίες ή καθιστά την πρόσβαση σε αυτές αδύνατη.'

Therefore, it appears that a definition of host ISPs' liability cannot be found in the national laws of the above countries because they refrain from engaging in the difficult task of conceptualising host ISPs' liability and reproducing the requirements of the ECD, which dictate the stances where host ISPs cannot be held liable for the actions of their users.

However, they failed not only to offer a definition for host ISPs' liability, but also to provide a solid interpretation of the defences that host ISPs have available to them in order to be exonerated from liability for intellectual property infringements.

Indeed, at European level the public consultation on the ECD in 2011 illustrated that there were inconsistent views among different stakeholders with regard to the correct exegesis of the requirement of knowledge.[55] For instance, a number of stakeholders specified the notion of knowledge to be when they receive notification of the appearance of the illegal material. Others believe that a general awareness of the illicit content suffices to define actual knowledge, while a more stringent opinion supports that only a court order can be considered as actual knowledge. Finally, host ISPs subscribe to a broad notion of actual knowledge since this requires a general filtering obligation, which is prohibited as per Article 15 of the ECD.[56]

This broad notion of actual knowledge is possible because as Wang[57] and Sadeghi[58] point out, the ECD does not specify either the concept of knowledge of the illicit activity or the expeditious removal of infringing content, and thus passes the tricky problem of interpretation of those requirements to EU Member States. It is only with regard to the concept of awareness to which the CJEU has given guidance and which amounts to the principle of diligence. In this light, in *L'Oreal v eBay*,[59] the CJEU has construed the requirement of awareness through the lens of diligence[60] and concluded that a host ISP is not eligible to invoke the liability immunity provisions of Article 14(1) of the ECD if it is 'aware of facts or circumstances on the basis of which a diligent economic operator should have identified the illegality in question and acted in accordance with Article 14(1)(b) of Directive 2000/31'.[61] In this respect, the CJEU endorsed a subjective/objective standard which dictates that the host ISP should be aware on its own of facts or circumstances from which the illegal activity originates, and to examine this behaviour through the lens of a diligent economic operator.[62]

The notion of the diligent economic operator refers to the concept of a 'reasonable person' which stems from the idea of 'the ideal man'[63] as elaborated in Aristotle's work.[64]

[55] EU Commission Staff Working Paper, 'Online Services, Including E-Commerce, in the Single Market', SEC (2011) 1641 final 33–34.

[56] ibid.

[57] Wang (n 30) 19–23.

[58] Sadeghi (n 15) 103.

[59] Case C-324/09 *L'Oreal SA V eBay Int'l AG* (2011) ECR I-6011.

[60] Acting in a certain standard of care.

[61] Case C-324/09 *L'Oreal SA V eBay Int'l AG* (2011) ECR I-6011, para 120.

[62] Angelopoulos (n 15) 84–85; C Riefa, *Consumer Protection and Online Auction Platforms: Towards a Safer Legal Framework* (Farnham, Ashgate, 2015) 198–201.

[63] Σπουδαῖος ἀνήρ.

[64] J Kochanowski, 'The "reasonable man" standards in continental law' (2007) 1 *The Journal of Legislative studies* 1.

It appeared for the first time in the legislative text of Digesta of Justinian in the Byzantine Empire in 533 AD where it was used to examine the liability of debtors.[65] Since then, it has a broad application in all parts of law, but it is correlated mostly with tort law provisions.[66] It describes the actions of a person who acts according to societal expectations and does not prioritise her needs against third parties' interests.[67] The concept of a reasonable person has been integrated in many different jurisdictions, such as the UK, French, Spanish, and German legal systems. As Kulesza notes, 'This standard corresponds with the practical *bonus pater familias* estimate, present in national systems of civil law.'[68] For example, in the UK the reasonable man threshold is the 'the man of ordinary prudence and intelligence', in French Law 'bon père de famille or homme raisonnable et avisé', in Spanish Law 'Buen padre di familia', and in German Law 'a sorgfältiger Mensch von durchschnittlicher Umsicht und Tüchtigkeit'.[69]

Therefore, the idea behind the introduction of a subjective/objective threshold test for knowledge was mainly to give courts proper guidance on how to understand the requirement of knowledge with reference to a well-established principle of a reasonable person.[70] In this regard, a host ISP must on its own assess the illegality of an activity which becomes apparent to a diligent economic operator. This is why Angelopoulos comments that the objective/subjective test seems to 'provide the most logical answer consistent with the usual legal patterns governing such issues'.[71]

Yet, in the context of online infringements, the application of the diligent economic operator standard could be problematic.[72] This is mainly due to the lack of a uniform interpretation of the concept of diligence. This means that the notion of diligence could be construed following industry's practices and standards[73] which, however, might be defined by both industry representatives and host ISPs, and could therefore be biased towards their interests, thus undermining users' interests.[74]

Further, the notion of diligence is not harmonised at European level, national jurisdictions across Member States construe the term of diligence in different ways.[75] As Synodinou notes, 'the standards of duty of care imposed by national courts continue to

[65] ibid.

[66] J Gardner, 'The Many Faces of the Reasonable Person' (2015) *Law Quarterly Review* 2 is available at ora.ox.ac.uk/objects/uuid:9e724c9c-89c0-4ec0-bafd-4e3125081558.

[67] Angelopoulos (n 15) 297–99 where she notes that 'it stems from the Roman term of "bonus pater familias" that is translated as the good father of the family who acts with prudence and diligence after taking into consideration the outcomes of his actions for the others'.

[68] J Kulesza, 'Due diligence in International Internet Law' (2014) *Journal of Internet Law* 28.

[69] Angelopoulos (n 15) 297–99; C Van Dam, *European Tort Law* (Oxford, Oxford University Press, 2007) 231–32.

[70] Angelopoulos (n 15) 84–85; Wang (n 30) 19–23.

[71] Angelopoulos (n 15) 84–85.

[72] T Synodinou, 'Intermediaries' Liability for Online Copyright Infringement in the EU: Evolutions and Confusions' (2015) 31 *Computer Law & Security Review* 57.

[73] B Sander, 'Freedom of Expression in the Age of Online Platforms: The Promise and Pitfalls of a Human Rights-Based Approach to Content Moderation' (2020) 43 *Fordham International Law Journal* 939; U Carsten, 'Standards for Duty of Care? Debating Intermediary Liability from a Sectoral Perspective' (2017) 8 *Journal of Intellectual Property, Information Technology and E-Commerce Law* 114.

[74] S Jacques, K Garstka, M Hviid and J Street, 'Automated anti-piracy systems as copyright enforcement mechanism: a need to consider cultural diversity' (2018) 40 *European Intellectual Property Review* 218; E Rosati, 'Public Lecture on Copyright and the Court of Justice of the European Union: Role, Action, Legacy' (27 February 2019) University of Reading, Reading (UK).

[75] Kulesza (n 68) 28; Angelopoulos (n 34) 13.

differ significantly from jurisdiction to jurisdiction'.[76] For example, in France a diligent host ISP must act after being notified of the illicit activity, or when it has reasonable doubts that an unlawful content has been transmitted via its network.[77] Meanwhile in Germany, the notion of diligence is attributed to anyone whose actions can impinge upon others' rights and interests.[78] Hence, this implies that the CJEU gives leeway for EU national courts to construe the notion of diligent economic operator, with the potential risk for fragmented interpretations across European borders.

Interestingly, lack of guidance also exists in the case of expeditious removal of illicit activity. The ECD refrains from offering a solid interpretation, therefore EU Member States have adopted different approaches. An EU Commission working staff paper reveals that while some EU countries have adopted a specific timeframe within which host ISPs must remove allegedly infringing content, other EU countries remain silent and could be said to have passed this 'hot potato' to the host ISPs.[79] For instance, as per the Finnish Law, host ISPs must immediately remove intellectual property infringements for copyright infringements; in Spain host ISPs must act within 72 hours upon being notified; while in Hungary the timeframe is shorter, up to 12 hours. Finally, in Lithuania, intermediaries have to act within one day for intellectual property related infringements.[80]

What is more, it is not clear whether the removal of the illicit activity extends to the acts of preventing its reappearance. This is because the CJEU line of case law adopts either an expansive or a restricted interpretation and refrains from offering a solid approach. For instance, in *L'Oréal v Ebay*,[81] the CJEU offered an interpretation of the prevention of future infringements adopting the same identity approach. In this case, L'Oréal initiated legal proceedings against eBay alleging trade mark infringement, the CJEU concluded that a host ISP can be ordered to prevent the emergence of a specific trade mark infringement by the same infringer for the same trade mark. This means that it is the host ISPs who need to identify when the same infringement occurs by the same infringer.

However, in the *McFadden v Sony Music Entertainment* case,[82] the CJEU adopted an expansive interpretation with regard to the prevention of infringements. In this case, Sony Music Entertainment filed a lawsuit against McFadden alleging copyright infringement because the defendant offered his clients a wireless connection to the internet without a password requirement. After carefully examining the case, the CJEU concluded that copyright owners can request host ISPs to terminate future violations; taking into consideration the right to property, the right to conduct business, and the right to freedom of expression.[83] However, the CJEU refrained from providing guidance with regard to the type of violations and the alleged infringer.

[76] Synodinou (n 72) 65.
[77] Angelopoulos (n 34) 11; *Madame L. c/ les sociétés Multimania* (1999) (Tribunal de Grande Instance de Nanterre).
[78] Angelopoulos (n 34) 13.
[79] EU Commission Staff Working Paper (n 55).
[80] ibid.
[81] Case C-324/09 *L'Oreal SA V eBay Int'l AG* (2011) ECR I-6011, para 120.
[82] Case C-484/14 *Mc Fadden* (2016) ECLI:EU:C:2016:689.
[83] ibid para 100.

Interestingly, a later decision by the CJEU further expanded the scope for the prevention of such illicit activity. More specifically, in the *Glawischnig v Facebook* case,[84] the CJEU handled the dispute between Eva Glawischnig, a former member of the Green Party in Germany, and Facebook for offensive comments posted by internet users on Facebook's platform. While Facebook removed the defamatory comments, it failed to prevent the reappearance of offensive comments. In this light, the CJEU concluded that host ISPs are required to prevent the emergence of identical content of information that has already been declared unlawful, and equivalent information, without asking from host ISPs to examine the content. It added that such an obligation shall have a worldwide application. However, one might wonder how host ISPs would be in the position to identify content equivalent to the illicit information without deploying general monitoring obligations, thus in conflict with Article 15 of the ECD, which prohibits the imposition of general monitoring practices within the online networks.[85]

Finally, in the joined cases of *Peterson v YouTube*[86] and *Elsevier v Cyando*,[87] the CJEU adopted an interpretation of the prevention of illicit activity in reference to the fair balance approach and the disproportionate damage caused to the rights holder. More specifically, in the first of these cases, Frank Peterson filed a lawsuit against YouTube alleging that the latter failed to terminate the reappearance of unauthorised videos on its network; while in the second, Elsevier initiated legal proceedings against Cyando, a file-hosting platform, for neglecting to prevent the dissemination of copyright infringing works. Following a thorough analysis of the facts and relevant EU provisions, the CJEU handed down the ruling that host ISPs have an obligation to prevent the emergence of future infringements, considering a fair balance between different interests at stake. At the same time, the Court added that '… it is, however, for the national courts to satisfy themselves, when applying such a condition, that that condition does not result in the actual cessation of the infringement being delayed in such a way as to cause disproportionate damage to the rightholder'.[88] In this way, the CJEU reaffirmed the obligation for host ISPs to prevent the emergence of infringement upon being notified,[89] and stressed that such obligation shall be undertaken in order to avoid any disproportionate damage to the rights holder. Yet the Court did not provide guidance in terms of assessing the concept of disproportionate damage and appears to give leeway to the EU national courts for its interpretation.

[84] Case C-18/18 *Eva Glawischnig-Piesczek* [2019] ECLI:EU:C:2019:821.

[85] For a thorough analysis of the CJEU case see Z Krokida, 'Towards a wider scope for the duty of care of host internet service providers: The case of Eva Glawischnig-Piesczek v Facebook' (2021) 43 *European Intellectual Property Review* 313–21.

[86] Case C-682/18 *Peterson v YouTube* (2021) ECLI:EU:C:2021:503.

[87] Case C-683/18 *Elsevier v Cyando* (2021) ECLI:EU:C:2021:503.

[88] Joined Cases C-682/18 and C-683/18, para 145.

[89] C Angelopoulos, 'YouTube and Cyando, Injunctions against Intermediaries and General Monitoring Obligations: Any Movement?' (*Kluwer Copyright blog*, 9 August 2021) copyrightblog.kluweriplaw.com/2021/08/09/youtube-and-cyando-injunctions-against-intermediaries-and-general-monitoring-obligations-any-movement/; as Angelopoulos has rightfully pointed out 'The judgment in YouTube and Cyando does imply that after receiving a notification providers have an obligation to remedy the infringement and prevent it from recurring.'

Therefore, and in the absence of any clear guidance, it appears that these defences have been the subject of heterogenous interpretations in the above mentioned jurisdictions.[90] This means that each country has endorsed its own interpretation regarding the requirements of knowledge and expeditious removal of infringing content upon notification. Indicative examples of these interpretations are presented below.

i. UK: E-Commerce Regulations 2002/2013

With regard to the requirement of knowledge, it has been argued that a host ISP obtains knowledge of the infringing content only via a competent notice.[91] What amounts to a competent notice can be found in Article 22 of the E-Commerce Regulations 2002/2013[92] which states that a competent notice must include the name and address of the sender of the notice, the location of the information, and the unlawful nature of the activity.

This implies that a notice must include evidence of the illegality of the activity. Indeed, in the *Tamiz case*,[93] the claimant brought legal proceedings against a blog operator where defamatory comments about Tamiz were posted by users. Yet, in order to attribute liability to the blog, the English Court held that a complaint sent from the claimant regarding content posted on a blog does not constitute a notice. As Justice Eady noted, 'Liability may turn upon the extent to which the relevant ISP entity has knowledge of the words complained of, and of their illegality or potential illegality.'[94] Rather, the illegal nature of the content must be outlined in the notice.

However, the infringing nature of the content must not rely on general statements of unlawfulness. Rather, it must be demonstrated through specific acts. A representative line of such thinking can be found in *Bunt v Tilley and others*.[95] In this case, the claimant sued a number of individuals and the host ISP for libel comments made in a chat room. After careful consideration of the facts, Justice Eady did not find the host ISP liable since, as he noted, the notice about defamatory content which had been sent to the ISP by the claimant did not fulfil the conditions for a competent notice as per Article 22 of the E-Commerce Regulations 2002/2013. The notice did not include the location of the defamatory comment or the illicit nature of the activity.[96] For this reason, the ISP could not be held liable.

[90] EU Commission, 'Overview of the legal framework of notice and action procedures in Member States SMART 2016/0039' (2018) 2–3; L Essers, 'German, French Courts Disagree on Responsibility of ISPs for Illegal Content' (*PCWorld*, 16 July 2012) www.pcworld.com/article/259294/germany_french_courts_disagree_on_responsibility_of_isps_for_illegal_content.html.

[91] With regard to the threshold criteria for awareness, courts remain silent and thus no comprehensive interpretation of the concept of awareness exists until now, see Wang (n 30) 23.

[92] E-Commerce Regulations 2002/2013, available at www.legislation.gov.uk/uksi/2002/2013/contents/made.

[93] *Tamiz v Google* (2012) EWHC 449 (QB).

[94] ibid para 33.

[95] *Bunt v Tilley and others* (2006) EWHC 407 (QB) para 72.

[96] ibid para 70 which notes that 'In determining whether a service provider has actual knowledge for the purposes of regulations 18(b)(v) and 19(a)(i), a court shall take into account all matters which appear to it in the particular circumstances to be relevant and, among other things, shall have regard to – (a) whether a service provider has received a notice through a means of contact made available in accordance with regulation 6(1)(c), and (b) the extent to which any notice includes – (i) the full name and address of the sender of the notice; (ii) details of the location of the information in question; and (iii) details of the unlawful nature of the activity or information in question.'

What is more, in the UK there is debate on ways in which notice for infringing content may be generated, namely whether it should be an automatic or a human-based notification. The prevailing view leans in favour of a human-based approach. Indeed, in *McGrath v Dawkins and Amazon*,[97] a bookseller brought legal proceedings against Amazon for the posting of defamatory comments on the review of a book being sold on its site. In order to determine whether there was a competent notice to Amazon concerning the defamatory comments, HHG Moloney QC stated, 'A corporation can have actual knowledge only through a human representative, and given the vast size and diverse nature of Amazon's website there is no reason to suppose that anyone in Amazon was actually aware of these postings, let alone of their possible unlawfulness.'[98] This understanding excludes any possibility for Amazon to identify on its own any defamatory comments, thus it reinforces the view that a notice must be triggered by human providers.

Yet, apart from the defence of the absence of knowledge, Article 19(a)(ii) of the E-Commerce Regulations 2002/2013 states that a host ISP can be exonerated from liability if 'upon obtaining such knowledge or awareness, [it] acts expeditiously to remove or to disable access to the information'. What amounts to expeditious removal, however, has been subject to different interpretations. On the one hand, it has been argued that expeditious removal is about the sole act of removing the allegedly infringing content, while others claim that it extends to additional measures that impede the re-emergence of the allegedly infringing content within the network.

Insofar as the sole act of taking down the allegedly infringing content is concerned, the E-Commerce Regulations 2002/2013 refrain from specifying the timeframe within which an ISP must remove the content after being notified. In contrast, with regard to the additional steps taken by host ISPs to prevent the re-emergence of infringing content, guidance has been provided by the English High Court in *Twentieth Century Fox et al. v British Telecommunications*.[99] The English High Court ordered UK internet access ISPs to terminate the access of users to Newzbin2, a website that indexed and made available unauthorised works to its users. British Telecommunications argued that it was devoid of actual knowledge of the infringements that took place on its network and that a blocking injunction should not be allowed because it constituted a general monitoring obligation. After careful consideration of the facts, Justice Arnold noted that terminating access to a specific website does not amount to a general monitoring obligation since it does not require 'detailed inspection of the data of any of BT's subscribers'.[100] Rather, it is a blocking order based on the specific case and with the sole aim to address the targeted URLs.[101]

Accordingly, it seems that the UK transposed verbatim Article 14(1) of the ECD into its national legal system, and thus failed to define host ISPs' liability. At the same time, there is a lack of judicial guidance as to how the defences that host ISPs use in order to escape from liability shall be construed.

[97] *McGrath v Dawkins and Amazon* (2012) EWHC B3 (QB).
[98] *McGrath v Dawkins and Amazon* (2012) EWHC B3 (QB) para 42.
[99] *Twentieth Century Fox et al. v British Telecommunications PLC* (2010) EWHC 608 (Ch).
[100] *Twentieth Century Fox et al. v British Telecommunications PLC* (2011) EWHC 1981 (Ch) para 162.
[101] ibid para 70; Arnold Justice recommended the adoption of Cleanfeed, which is a filtering technology, and which has proved to be technically feasible and not easily circumvented by users.

ii. Germany: Telemediengesetz

In Germany, ECD provisions were transposed verbatim into the national legal system with the Telemediengesetz (TMG). This implies that German law follows the rationale of the ECD and does not define the liability of host ISPs. Rather, it provides defences to host ISPs in order to be exonerated from liability for infringements that take place online. However, it must be noted that TMG refrains from 'actual knowledge' which is used in Article 14(1) of the ECD and uses the term 'knowledge'.[102]

In this light, as per § 10 of the TMG, the host ISP must not have knowledge of the illegal act or of the information it contains in order to be exonerated from liability. Any negligent ignorance or conditional intent or general awareness does not fall within the scope of the concept of knowledge.[103] Rather, such a concept is about the knowledge of the specific infringement.[104] This means that an ISP can escape liability only if the host ISP can demonstrate that it lacks knowledge of the particular violation that took place within its platform.

Yet, in the German legal system the concept of knowledge of host ISPs has been the subject of different interpretations, which is enshrined in § 10 of the TMG and reads as follows: 'the hosting ISP avoids liability if it does not have knowledge of the illegal act or information'. On the one hand, many scholars argue that knowledge revolves around the illegality of the act and not the information itself.[105] This means that the court's focus is on the illegal conduct, such as unauthorised file-sharing or downloading, and not on the infringing copy of a film, book, or a song which is made available online.[106] On the other hand, scholars claim that the host ISP must not have knowledge of either the illegal conduct or the illegal information.[107] However, it was not until 2010 in the *Vorschaubilder* rulings, which concerned the downloading of unauthorised photographs,[108] that the German Supreme Court clarified that the host ISP must have knowledge of the illegal nature of the information and thus undertake the appropriate measures to terminate its dissemination.[109]

Further, with regard to the concepts of awareness and the diligent economic operator, there is no further guidance in German case law.[110]

What is more, as far as the second defence of expeditious removal of infringing content upon notification is concerned, it has been subject to different interpretations. Similar to the approach in the UK, the removal of infringing content upon the host ISP being notified can be construed either as a sole act of removal or the prevention of an infringement. First, the TMG does not include any provision that addresses the

[102] Verbiest et al (n 6).
[103] ibid 36–37.
[104] ibid 36–37.
[105] For the debate see Wang (n 30) 96.
[106] G Spindler, *Recht der elektronischen Medien: Kommentar*, 3rd edn (Munich, CH Beck, 2015) para 1531; G Spindler in G Spindler and A Wiebe (eds), *Internet Aktionen und Elektronische Marktsplaetze* (Verlag Dr. Otto Schmidt, 2005) ch 6.
[107] Wang (n 30) 97.
[108] Bundesgerichtshof, *Vorschaubilder III*, 21. September 2017 – I ZR 11/16.
[109] ibid.
[110] Verbiest et al (n 6) 36.

timeframe within which the infringing content must be removed by the ISP. By contrast, it is only recently with the introduction of the Network Enforcement Act that host ISPs have been required to remove allegedly infringing content upon being notified, according to the degree of severity of the infringement.[111] For instance, they must take down any blatantly illegal content within 24 hours, while a timeline of seven days is allowed in cases of unlawful content.[112]

As far as the prevention of infringements is concerned, the German legal system endorses the theory of the same nature of infringement, commonly known as *Kerntheorie*, which concerns the imposition of a duty of care on host ISPs with regard to infringements of the same nature.[113] According to this theory, host ISPs must prevent the reappearance of similar infringements through the use of monitoring technology. Similar infringements can be subject to different interpretations. For instance, they can either be described as those infringements that violate the same work but with a copy in another file, or those infringements that fall into the same category and are committed by the same infringing user.[114]

Interestingly, the application of *Kerntheorie* which was enshrined in the Internetversteigerung *I*[115] case was reaffirmed by the following court rulings of *Internetversteigerung II*[116] and *Internetversteigerung III*,[117] as well as the *Rapidshare II*[118] ruling in 2010. In the latter case, the Hamburg Court of First Instance examined the dispute between Rapidshare, a host ISP, and copyright holders. According to the line of reasoning, Rapidshare was providing financial benefits to its subscribers with a view to uploading files in high demand and increasing its website traffic. For this reason, the Hamburg Court noted that, upon notification, the deletion only of infringing links that directed users to files was not an adequate reaction. Rather, the operator of the website was under an obligation to detect and take down any future links of the same kind. In this way, the adequate reaction of a host ISP upon notification could be extended to specific monitoring duties with reference to infringing material or illicit activities that had already been notified.

However, it has been argued that the application of *Kerntheorie* might be in conflict with Article 15 of the ECD,[119] which notes that host ISPs are not obliged to deploy general monitoring obligations within their networks. In addition, an array of court rulings at European level have rejected the imposition of general monitoring obligations.

[111] G Spindler, 'Internet Intermediary Liability Reloaded: The new German act on Responsibility of Social Networks and its (In-) compatibility with European Law' (2017) 8 *Journal of Intellectual Property, Information Technology and E-Commerce Law* 166; H Tworek and P Leerssen, 'An Analysis of Germany's NetzDG Law' (2019) *Transatlantic High Level Working Group on Content Moderation Online and Freedom of Expression* 1 www.ivir.nl/publicaties/download/NetzDG_Tworek_Leerssen_April_2019.pdf.

[112] Spindler (n 111) 166.

[113] M Leistner, 'Störerhaftung und mittelbare Schutzrechtsverletzung' (2010) *GRUR-Beil* 1; Verbiest et al (n 6) 51.

[114] JB Nordemann, 'Liability for Copyright Infringements on the Internet: Host Providers (Content Providers) – The German Approach' (2011) 2 *Journal of Intellectual Property, Information Technology and Electronic Commerce Law* 37.

[115] Bundesgerichtshof, *Internetversteigerung I*, 11 March 2004, I ZR 304/01.

[116] Bundesgerichtshof, *Internetversteigerung II*, 19 April 2007, I ZR 35/04.

[117] Bundesgerichtshof, *Internetversteigerung III*, 30 April 2008, I ZR 73/05.

[118] Oberlandesgericht Düsseldorf, *Rapidshare I*, 27 April 2010, I-20 U 166/09.

[119] T Hoeren and S Yankova, 'The Liability of Internet Intermediaries – The German Perspective' (2012) 43 *International Review of Intellectual Property and Competition Law* 501.

Consider, for instance, the case of *Scarlet v Sabam*.[120] In this case, Sabam, which is the Belgian association that safeguards the rights of authors, requested a filtering injunction against Scarlet, an internet access provider, arguing that Scarlet's subscribers use its network in order to exchange copyright infringing works through the peer to peer software. However, the Court refused to issue an injunction under the reasoning that the imposition of a filtering obligation would 'oblige it to actively monitor all the data relating to each of its customers in order to prevent any future infringement of intellectual-property rights. It follows that that injunction would require the ISP to carry out general monitoring, something which is prohibited by Article 15(1) of Directive 2000/31'.[121]

A similar approach has been reinforced in *Sabam v Netlog* where the CJEU refused again to grant an order for a filtering injunction.[122] In this case, Sabam requested a filtering injunction against Netlog, a social network platform, arguing that Netlog's users uploaded copyright infringing content on the platform from its film repository. Yet, citing the conclusion from *Scarlet v Sabam* ruling, the CJEU refrained from issuing a filtering injunction on the basis that:

> [T]he injunction imposed on the hosting service provider requiring it to install the contested filtering system would oblige it to actively monitor almost all the data relating to all of its service users in order to prevent any future infringement of intellectual-property rights. It follows that that injunction would require the hosting service provider to carry out general monitoring, something which is prohibited by Article 15(1) of Directive 2000/31 (see, by analogy, Scarlet Extended, paragraph 40).[123]

By the same token, in the *McFadden* ruling on a dispute between the owner of a wifi connection that does not require a password to access the internet and Sony Music,[124] the CJEU delivered their finding that in 'monitoring all of the information transmitted, such a measure must be excluded from the outset as contrary to Article 15(1) of Directive 2000/31, which excludes the imposition of a general obligation on, inter alia, communication network access providers to monitor the information that they transmit'.[125]

Therefore, similar to the transposition of the ECD in the UK, the TMG fails to define the host ISPs' liability and does not provide adequate guidance to the existing defences that exonerate host ISPs from liability for violations that take place within their networks.

iii. *France: Act on Confidence in Digital Economy*

The provisions of the ECD have been transposed verbatim into the French legal system with the Act on Confidence in Digital Economy, known as LCEN Law.[126]

[120] Case C-70/10 *Scarlet Extended SA v Société belge des auteurs, compositeurs et éditeurs SCRL (SABAM)* [2011] ECR-I 11959.
[121] ibid para 36.
[122] Case C-360/10 *Belgische Vereniging van Auteurs, Com- ponisten en Uitgevers CVBA (SABAM) v Netlog NV* (2012) ECLI:EU:C:2012:85.
[123] ibid para 38.
[124] Case C-484/14 *Mc Fadden* (2016) ECLI:EU:C: 2016:689.
[125] ibid para 87.
[126] Loi n° 2004-575 du 21 juin 2004 pour la confiance dans l'économie numérique, available at www.legifrance.gouv.fr/affichTexte.do?cidTexte=JORFTEXT000000801164&dateTexte=&categorieLien=id.

So, similar to the UK and German Laws, LCEN provides host ISPs with defences which enable their exoneration from liability for infringements within their networks. As per Article 6-I-2 of LCEN, a host ISP is not liable if it does not have knowledge of the illegal nature of the stored data or the facts and circumstances that indicate the illegal nature of the data.[127] Knowledge can only be obtained if the host ISP receives a competent notice.[128] The requirements of a competent notice are set forth in Article 6 I(5) of LCEN which dictates that the notice must include the date of notification, the identity of the sender, the name and address of the recipient, the infringing material, and written evidence of communication between the sender and the recipient outlining the infringement and the request for removal.[129]

This understanding has been reinforced by several rulings where it has been concluded that a notice must entail precise information about the allegedly infringing content, as well as detailed information about senders and recipients of the notice. For instance, in the case of *Nord-Ouest v Dailymotion*,[130] the French Supreme Court handed down that the notice must not include a general statement about an unauthorised video on the online network. Rather, it must entail the precise location of the alleged infringing video, such as the URLs, so that the host ISP can effectively identify the unlawful content, and thus remove it.

However, apart from the notice which can trigger knowledge of the host ISP, another interpretation of the knowledge requirement can be found in the principle of the diligent economic operator. This principle was endorsed at European level in the case of *L'Oreal v eBay*.[131] As explained in section III(A) of this chapter, in this case the CJEU

[127] Article 6-I-2 of LCEN, 'Les personnes physiques ou morales qui assurent, même à titre gratuit, pour mise à disposition du public par des services de communication au public en ligne, le stockage de signaux, d'écrits, d'images, de sons ou de messages de toute nature fournis par des destinataires de ces services ne peuvent pas voir leur responsabilité civile engagée du fait des activités ou des informations stockées à la demande d'un destinataire de ces services si elles n'avaient pas effectivement connaissance de leur caractère illicite ou de faits et circonstances faisant apparaître ce caractère ou si, dès le moment où elles en ont eu cette connaissance, elles ont agi promptement pour retirer ces données ou en rendre l'accès impossible. L'alinéa précédent ne s'applique pas lorsque le destinataire du service agit sous l'autorité ou le contrôle de la personne visée audit alinéa.'; Wang (n 30) 97; S Nerisson, 'Intellectual Property Liability of Consumers, Facilitators and Intermediaries: The Position in France' in A Kamperman Sanders and C Heath (eds), *Intellectual Property Liability of Consumers, Facilitators and Intermediaries* (Alphen aan den Rijn, Kluwer Law International, 2012) 70.

[128] Wang (n 30) 98.

[129] Article 6-I-5 of LCEN 'La connaissance des faits litigieux est présumée acquise par les personnes désignées au 2 lorsqu'il leur est notifié les éléments suivant :

- la date de la notification;
- si le notifiant est une personne physique : ses nom, prénoms, profession, domicile, nationalité, date et lieu de naissance; si le requérant est une personne morale : sa forme, sa dénomination, son siège social et l'organe qui la représente légalement;
- les nom et domicile du destinataire ou, s'il s'agit d'une personne morale, sa dénomination et son siège social;
- la description des faits litigieux et leur localisation précise;
- les motifs pour lesquels le contenu doit être retiré, comprenant la mention des dispositions légales et des justifications de faits;
- la copie de la correspondance adressée à l'auteur ou à l'éditeur des informations ou activités litigieuses demandant leur interruption, leur retrait ou leur modification, ou la justification de ce que l'auteur ou l'éditeur n'a pu être contacté.'; Verbiest et al (n 6) 46.

[130] *Nord Ouest Production et al v Dailymotion, UGC Images* (2011) (Cour de Cassation).

[131] Case C-324/09 *L'Oreal SA V eBay Int'l AG* [2011] ECR I-6011.

offered guidance on the interpretation of the requirement of knowledge by equating an ISP with a diligent economic operator. This means that if a diligent economic operator could be aware of an illicit activity within its business model, an ISP could also be aware of the infringing content or counterfeit goods that are disseminated via its network.

In this vein, French courts were the first to apply this principle in the ruling of *LVHM v eBay*.[132] In this case, *LVHM* brought legal proceedings against the online market platform eBay on the basis of trade mark violations. The Paris Court of First Instance ruled that eBay was liable for the trade mark infringements which occurred on its platform since it had knowledge of the counterfeit goods. This is because eBay acted as a brokerage site and exercised commercial activity by sending notices to its users about upcoming offers. To the Court's reasoning, the commercial activity of eBay demonstrates knowledge and control of the goods that have been circulated within its platform.[133] Therefore, by virtue of its business model, the French judges thought that eBay should have stopped the distribution of counterfeit goods by either checking the originality of the products which were on sale, or by shutting down any seller's account who has been found liable for offering fake goods, or removing any displacement of illegal goods upon notification.[134]

With regard to the expeditious removal of infringing content upon notification, LCEN remains silent. Further guidance has been given by the French courts which offers different timeframes for the removal of infringing content.[135] For example, in *TF1 v YouTube*[136] the Court of First Instance in Paris concluded that YouTube was not eligible to the defence of Article 14(1) of the ECD since the removal of the infringing video five days after notification did not amount to expeditious removal. For this reason, YouTube was held liable for not removing, in a reasonable period of time, the unauthorised video. In similar fashion, in *TF1 v Dailymotion*[137] the Court of Appeal in Paris sanctioned Dailymotion for a delayed take down of infringing content upon being notified. Although the Court noted that Dailymotion qualifies as a host ISP under Article 14(1) of the ECD, it then concluded that the removal of the allegedly infringing video four days after notification did not exclude Dailymotion from being liable as per Article 14(1) of the ECD.

[132] *LVHM v eBay* (2008) (Commercial Court of Paris).
[133] *LVHM v eBay* (2008) (Commercial Court of Paris); see also J de Chavez, 'Building a Trademark Safe Harbor for Contributory Counterfeiting Liability After Tiffany v. eBay' (2012) 86 *St. John's Law Review* 267.
[134] See in Farano (n 30) 89–90 where the author notes that eBay was required to 'supply the sellers, upon request, the purchase invoice or a certificate of authenticity of the products offered for sale, in sanctioning any guilty vendor by finally terminating his account as soon as the breach is ascertained, in immediately withdrawing any illicit advertisements notified by the departments of Louis Vuitton Malletier in charge of combating infringement'.
[135] Wang (n 30) 168.
[136] *TF1 v YouTube* [2012] (Court of First Instance Paris); C Jassserand, 'France –Youtube guilty but not liable? some more precisions on the status of hosting providers' (*Kluwer copyright blog*, 18 June 2012) copyrightblog.kluweriplaw.com/2012/06/18/france-youtube-guilty-but-not-liable-some-more-precisions-on-the-status-of-hosting-providers/; cited in Wang (n 30) 168.
[137] *TF1 v Dailymotion* [2014] (Court of Appeal Paris); C Jasserand, 'France- Dailymotion heavily fined for the late removal of infringing content (*Kluwer copyright blog*, 18 September 2012) copyrightblog.kluweriplaw.com/2012/09/28/france-dailymotion-heavily-fined-for-the-late-removal-of-infringing-content/; cited in Wang (n 30) 168.

What is more, similar to UK and German courts, French courts have extended the removal of infringing content to the prevention of emergence of similar infringements within online platforms. Indicative examples can be found in an array of court rulings. For instance, in the case of *Andre Rau v Google and Aufeminin.com*[138] the Court of Appeal in Paris held that Google not only had an obligation to remove the infringing content upon notification, but it also had the duty to take all appropriate measures to impede the re-emergence of the same infringements online.[139]

Along similar lines, in *Zadig Productions v Google video*[140] the Paris Court of First Instance held Google liable for not undertaking the appropriate measures to terminate any further dissemination of the unauthorised video. Although the Court acknowledged Google's expeditious response to remove the unauthorised video of 'Tranquillity Bay' upon receiving a complaint, Google failed to deploy technological mechanisms that could prevent the re-uploading of the video.[141] It is this failure to prevent the emergence of similar infringements that obliged Google to pay damages to Zadig Productions, the owners of the 'Tranquillity Bay' video.

Overall, it appears that LCEN follows verbatim the provisions of the ECD and does not define ISPs' liability. By contrast, it offers defences for ISPs to use in order to escape liability. However, the interpretation of these defences seems to be examined on a case by case basis by courts, thus it offers legal uncertainty to rights holders and host ISPs.

iv. Spain: Ley de Servicios de la Sociedad de la Informacion y de Commercio Electronico

Similar to the previously discussed jurisdictions, in Spain the Spanish Law 34/2002[142] has followed the approach of the ECD and implemented Article 14(1) ECD into the national legal system. In particular, it offered the defences of host internet service providers' liability in order to evade liability in case of trade mark or copyright infringements.

However, with regard to knowledge, the Spanish Law refrained from the verbatim transposition of Article 14(1) ECD. In particular, Article 16 of the Spanish E-Commerce Law does not entail the concept of awareness. Rather, it states that host ISPs could avoid liability if they do not have effective knowledge of the illicit activity. This understanding has been criticised by scholars. For instance, as Peguera argues,

> A crucial issue regarding this exemption is the notion of actual knowledge, as the Spanish transposition departed from the language of E-Commerce Directive, crafting an extremely narrow concept of actual knowledge and moreover dispensing altogether with the requirement of lack of awareness of facts or circumstances from which the illegal activity or information is apparent.[143]

[138] *André Rau v Google and Aufeminin.com* [2011] (Court of Appeal Paris).

[139] Jurisprudence sur la communication en ligne is available at wiki.laquadrature.net/Jurisprudence_sur_la_communication_en_ligne, last accessed 18 October 2021.

[140] *SARL Zadig Productions, Jean-Robert Viallet et Mathieu Verboud c. Sté Google Inc. et AFA* [2007] (Court of First Instance Paris).

[141] YS Avocats, 'Google Video held liable for not doing all it could to stop the broadcasting of a film' (20 November 2007) copyrightfrance.blogspot.com/2007/11/google-video-held-liable-for-not-doing.html.

[142] Ley de servicios de la sociedad de la informacion y de commercio electronico.

[143] Peguera (n 45) 165.

This is mainly because this narrow approach might limit the defences for host ISPs, thus it may be in conflict with the existing EU case law.

What is more, the concept of effective knowledge is subject to different interpretations. On the one hand, it has been argued that a strict interpretation shall be adopted. Through such a strict lens, effective knowledge can be triggered in three ways, either following the issue of a decision by an administrative body or judicial authority,[144] or via voluntary notice and take down agreements initiated by host ISPs, or by the development of new regulatory mechanisms.[145] This understanding has been reinforced in an array of rulings. For instance, the Spanish Court of the Province of Alava dealt with a dispute between host ISPs and copyright holders. In that case, the Court held that the lack of a decision from judicial authority could not trigger effective knowledge, therefore the host ISP cannot be held liable for copyright infringements.[146]

On the other hand, others argue in favour of an open interpretation. This means that the ways that can trigger effective knowledge of host ISPs shall not be limited. For instance, in the *Telecinco* case,[147] the Spanish Court construed the concept of actual knowledge in a broad manner and concluded that only specific notices, and not general notices, for infringements can trigger actual knowledge of host ISPs.

Interestingly, it seems that the latter view now prevails. Indeed, the Supreme Court in *SGAE v Asociación of Internautas* examined the liability of Internautas for defamatory contents posted by users within its network and held the host ISP liable for the offensive comments.[148] To the Court's reasoning, Internautas should have been aware of the illegal nature of the content that appeared on its website under the domain name putasgae.org.[149] In this way, the Supreme Court adopted a broad interpretation of the concept of actual knowledge. This is because a narrow interpretation of actual knowledge would go against the rationale of Article 14(1) of the ECD. At the same time, any exclusion of the concept of awareness would also go against the ECD since the ECD equates actual knowledge of illegal facts with the concept of awareness of illegal facts and activities.[150]

As far as the expeditious removal is concerned, the Spanish E-Commerce Law remains silent and does not provide further guidance. This implies that it is up to the discretion of the court to assess whether the host internet service provider has removed the allegedly illicit activity.

In this light, the courts have construed the concept of removal. For instance, in the *Uploaded.to* case the Intellectual Property Commission examined the complaint submitted by the Association for phonographic producers about a website with copyright infringing works. In that case, the Commission ordered the removal of the infringing content within 48 hours.[151] Lack of compliance would trigger fines of up to

[144] Council of Europe, 'Comparative study on blocking, filtering and take-down of illegal internet content' (2015) 642.

[145] Peguera (n 45) 165.

[146] *Audiencia Provincial de Alava*, Section 2, Case 52/2012 of 3 February.

[147] *Audiencia Provincial Sentencia* A.P.S. Madrid Jan [2014] (Provincial Court Sentence).

[148] Supreme Court, Judgment 773/2009, Civil Chamber, 9 December 2009.

[149] For an opposite view see 'A focus on official notification may easily lead to a de facto exemption from liability of providers, even if they are clearly aware of illicit activities going on' in Verbiest et al (n 6) 15.

[150] Peguera (n 45) 153.

[151] Seccion Segunda de la Comission de Propriedad Intelectual, Codigo de expediente: E/ 2012/ 00012, Numero de registro.

€600.000 as per Articles 38.2 and 39.2 of the Spanish E-Commerce Law. In addition, the Spanish Court refrained from extending the removal of illicit activity in future infringements. Indeed, in *Telecinco v YouTube*,[152] the Spanish Court delivered that YouTube is not required to deploy measures in order to prevent or terminate any future copyright infringements. Otherwise, to the Court's reasoning, to ascribe additional obligations would result in the violation of Article 15 of the ECD which explicitly prohibits the imposition of general monitoring obligations on host ISPs.

To sum up, it seems that the Spanish E-Commerce Law follows the rationale of Article 14(1) of the ECD and refrains from defining host ISP liability. Similar to the previously discussed jurisdictions, it offers a set of defences to host ISPs in order to avoid liability. Interestingly, while the Spanish Law departs from the language of the ECD, it remains silent with regard to the interpretation of the defences. Therefore, the concepts of knowledge and removal have been subject to different interpretations by the courts, thus accentuating the existing legal uncertainty.

v. Greece: Presidential Decree 131/2003

Similar to France, Germany, and Spain, the ECD has been transposed in the Greek legislation with the Presidential Decree 131/2003. In particular, Article 14(1) of the ECD has been implemented verbatim in the Article and states that host ISPs are not liable if they do not have actual knowledge, or they are not aware of the infringing content.

While the legislation remains silent with regard to the interpretation of knowledge or awareness, the Greek Courts construed the concept of knowledge through the lens of criminal law. More specifically, in 2014, the Court of First Instance of Athens addressed the dispute between five collecting societies and host internet services.[153] In that case, five collecting societies initiated legal proceedings against internet service providers for hosting websites carrying unauthorised films and music. In order to assess whether knowledge is acquired, the Court concluded that there must be certainty in knowledge which shall be equivalent to direct intent as per Article 27 paragraph 2 of the Greek Penal Code. This element has not been found, therefore the application for blocking has been rejected.

Further, with regard to the removal of the allegedly infringing content, it seems that Article 14(2) has not been verbatim transposed into the Greek legislation. Instead, a structured notice and take down procedure has been implemented with the Law 4481/2017, following the transposition of the EU Directive on collective management only for copyright infringements.[154] As per the notice and take down procedure, an out of court Committee for copyright infringements would be responsible for copyright

[152] Commercial Court No. 7 Madrid, *Telecino v YouTube* Commercial Court No. 7 Madrid, Judgment No. 289/2010, 1 (2010).

[153] The decision 13478/2014 of the First Instance Court of Athens.

[154] Directive 2014/26/EU of the European Parliament and of the Council of 26 February 2014 on collective management of copyright and related rights and multi-territorial licensing of rights in musical works for online use in the internal market.

infringements by ordering host ISPs to either remove or block the allegedly infringing content.[155] In terms of trade mark law, the Greek Law remains silent.

In addition, the Greek Law seems to lean in favour of preventing the reappearance of infringing content or counterfeit goods online. In particular, the Greek Copyright Law sets forth, in Article 64A of the Presidential Decree, that online intermediaries could be required following the issue of an injunction to prevent the re-emergence of illicit activities online. Likewise, in the trade mark context, the Greek Trade Mark 4072/2012 offers, in Articles 153 and 154, the possibility to grant an injunction, and thus prevent the availability of counterfeit goods within the online networks.[156]

However, it has been observed that the Greek Courts have refrained, so far, from extending the removal to future uploads or counterfeit goods. For instance, in 2012 the First Instance Court of Athens ordered a specific website to be blocked without the obligation of deploying measures to prevent its reappearance.[157] In the case at hand, collecting societies had initiated legal proceedings requesting a blocking order against a particular webpage which carried unauthorised films and music. While the First Instance Court of Athens examined the detrimental effect on users' fundamental rights and the Information society, a blocking order has been issued against the particular webpage. Such blocking injunctions may also encompass future URLs and IP addresses with copyright infringing works.

Therefore, one might extrapolate that the Greek Presidential Decree implements verbatim Article 14(1) of the ECD and does not offer a solid definition of host ISP liability. In addition, instead of Article 14(1) of the ECD, the Greek legal system has implemented a structured notice and take down system that is operated under the auspices of the Hellenic Committee for Copyright infringements, while with regard to the removal of future infringing content or counterfeit goods a case by case approach is adopted by the Greek Courts.

In light of the above, it seems that the national implementation of the ECD does not offer answers to the host ISPs' liability conundrum. This is because, as presented above, the national implementation of the ECD in the EU Member States fails to provide a definition for host ISPs' liability, while at the same time it also fails to give concrete guidance with regard to the interpretation of the defences that host ISPs use in order to be exonerated from liability.

For this reason, national courts turn to their national tort law theories and doctrines in order to define host ISPs' liability in the form of secondary liability rules in tort law. Yet, while the EU Member States could offer a definition of host ISPs' liability, they seem to differ from each other. What is more, in many stances it seems challenging for EU national courts to fit tortious secondary liability rules into host ISPs' activities.

Against this background, the following section offers a critical examination of the legal traditions of selected jurisdictions. It identifies the key aspects of the legal nature of secondary liability rules, thus, it provides an understanding of the difficulties not only of harmonising secondary liability rules at European level, but also the underlying

[155] C Tsigou, 'Notice-and-Takedown Procedure under Greek Intellectual Property Law 4481/2017' (2018) 9 *Journal of Intellectual Property, Information Technology and Electronic Commerce Law* 203.
[156] Council of Europe (n 144) 291, national report of Greece.
[157] The Decision 4658/2012 of the Court of First Instance of Athens.

challenges for EU national jurisdictions to impose secondary liability rules on host ISPs' activities.

C. Host ISPs' Liability under the Legal Traditions of Four EU Member States: Germany, France, Spain, Greece and the UK

As discussed in the previous section, the national implementation of Article 14(1) of the ECD into four selected EU Member States and the UK fails to offer a solid answer to the ISPs' liability conundrum. For this reason, the following section examines how host ISPs' liability is defined outside the ECD and, in particular, how it is defined under the legal traditions of those legal systems.

i. UK

As already addressed, E-Commerce Regulations 2002/2013 fail to offer a comprehensive definition of host ISPs' liability. For this reason, English courts were forced to turn to national tort law doctrines for such establishment. In particular, the courts use the doctrine of joint tortfeasance which consists of three participation links; according to Carty's meticulous analysis these are authorisation, procurement, and combination.[158]

All three-participation links have been deployed by UK courts with limited success. Authorisation was the first attempt to ascribe liability on ISPs.[159] Yet, its success has been limited since a different interpretation from its traditional meaning has been offered by the courts in terms of online infringements.

The concept of authorisation stems from *Falcon v Famous Players Film Company Ltd* in 1929.[160] It amounts to 'sanction, approve and countenance'.[161] Authorisation requires a degree of authority. This understanding was exemplified in the *CBS Inc v Ames Records* ruling in 1981 where Whitford J noted:

> [A]ny ordinary person would, I think, assume that an authorisation can only come from somebody having or purporting to have authority and that an act is not authorised by somebody who merely enables or possibly assists or even encourages another to do that act, but does not purport to have any authority which he can grant to just the doing of the act.[162]

Such a view was reinforced in 1988 in *CBS v Amstrad* which was a legal dispute between CBS, a music production company, and Amstrad, a company that produced hi-fi technological tools.[163] In this case, Lord Templeman declared that authorisation requires

[158] H Carty, 'Joint tortfeasance and assistance liability' (1999) 19 *Legal studies* 10.
[159] Angelopoulos (n 34) 3.
[160] *Falcon v Famous Players* [1926] 2 KB 474.
[161] ibid para 48: as Atkin LJ put it more accurately, 'grant or purport to grant to a third person the right to do the act complained of, whether the intention is that the grantee shall do the act on his own account, or only on account of the grantor'.
[162] *CBS Inc v Ames Records and Tapes* [1981] 2 All ER 812; Cited in Davies (n 16) 359.
[163] T Hays, 'The evolution and decentralisation of secondary liability for infringements of copyright-protected works: Part 1' (2006) 28 *European Intellectual Property Review* 620; D Seng, 'Comparative analysis of the national approaches to the liability of internet intermediaries – Part I' (2010) *WIPO* 46.

authority, but he also distinguished authorisation from mere facilitation or assistance. In particular, the court noted that blank tapes can be used for lawful as well as unlawful recording. However, as has been noted 'no manufacturer and no machine confer on the purchase authority to copy unlawfully … By selling the recorder, Amstrad may facilitate copying in breach of copyright but does not authorise it'.[164] Otherwise, to hold Amstrad liable under the basis of facilitating copying seems unfair.

However, the tool of authorisation has been construed in a different way for online disputes. This is probably due to the impact of the ECD, which was endorsed in 2000, and the trend of case law at European level that equated a host ISP with a diligent economic operator. Following the impact of this EU legislation and case law, in the case of *Dramatico Entertainement*,[165] Justice Arnold carved out specific requirements that define authorisation in the online world. Such requirements include the nature of the relationship between the authoriser and the alleged infringer, the degree of control the authoriser has over the commission of infringements, the means the authoriser adopts in order to authorise the commission of infringements, and the steps the authoriser takes in order to prevent the infringement.[166]

Moreover, another interpretation of authorisation can be found in the inevitable consequence of the provision of torrent files by The Pirate Bay (TPB). This means that it was inevitable for infringements not to occur since TPB's business model was based on the provision of unauthorised material. To cite a few elements of its business model, TPB uses a pirated ship as its logo and states that it was founded by a Swedish anti-copyright organisation. Finally, the Judge found that while TPB could prevent the file-sharing of unlawful content, it did not take any preventive steps in order to terminate or at least curb the infringements. *A contrario*, the Court continued by saying that TPB has received many requests to block certain torrent files but has not complied with the notifications, while in other cases they mocked the notices they received from music industry representatives.[167]

This means that the interpretation of authorisation under the abovementioned criteria seems to be incompatible with the traditional notion of authorisation. This is because, as many commentators observed, it is dubious whether authority amounts to the refusal of the host ISP to remove the allegedly infringing material after receiving a notification, and therefore whether it justifies the attribution of liability rules to host ISPs.[168]

In light of this doubt, the courts resorted to other forms of joint tortfeasance in order to impose liability rules on ISPs. More specifically, the courts turned to the participation links of procurement or combination. Such links, however, find limited applicability since the courts experienced discrepancies in fitting them into the ISPs' context.

[164] *CBS Songs v Amstrad* [1988] UKHL 15.

[165] *Dramatico Entertainment Ltd & Ors v British Sky Broadcasting Ltd & Ors* [2012] EWHC 268 (Ch).

[166] *Dramatico Entertainment Ltd & Ors v British Sky Broadcasting Ltd & Ors* [2012] EWHC 268 (Ch) paras 75–80: 'TPB provides a sophisticated and user-friendly environment in which its users are able to search for and locate content.'

[167] M Manner, T Siniketo and U Polland, 'The Pirate Bay ruling: When the fun and game ends' (2009) 20 *Entertainment Law Review* 198.

[168] H Laddie, P Prescott, M Vitoria and A Speck, *The Modern Law of Copyright and Designs* (3rd edn, London, Butterworths, 2018) 19.3; Seng (n 163) 46.

Procurement, or inducement, is when an individual procures or induces another individual to commit an infringing activity. In this regard, as Davies explained 'procurement tends to give another person an idea he would not otherwise have had'.[169] Its definition stems from *Amstrad CBS Songs v Amstrad*[170] where Lord Templeman explained that procurement amounts to 'inducement, incitement or persuasion'. In particular, he added that 'inducement, incitement or persuasion to infringe must be by a defendant to an individual infringer and must identifiably procure a particular infringement …'.[171] This means that an individual must encourage a specific person to commit a specific infringement. However, such an interpretation is not easy to apply within the host ISPs' context. This is because it is problematic to prove that a host ISP encouraged a specific user to commit a tortious act.

Procurement should be distinguished from providing assistance. This is because procurement has a limited scope of liability, while to provide assistance covers a wider scope of liability.[172] Indeed, as Honoré notes, procurement aims to make an infringing act appealing to the alleged infringer who without procurement would not have considered committing the infringing act.[173] By contrast, providing assistance concerns any act which leads the primary infringer to commit the violation of the right.[174] Finally, while a procurer can be jointly liable,[175] mere assistance cannot affirm joint tortfeasance.[176] This is because the causal link between wrongdoing and providing assistance is weaker than the causal link between wrongdoing and inducing an infringing activity.[177]

By contrast, to provide mere assistance in terms of common design constitutes joint tortfeasance, in other words, assistance in combination amounts to participation in common design.[178] The participation link of common design stems from the *Koursk* ruling in 1924.[179] According to this ruling 'persons are said to be joint tortfeasors when their respective shares in the commission of the tort are done in furtherance of a common design'.[180] This means that two or more persons must commit a wrongful act under a common goal.[181] Yet, this does not mean that joint tortfeasors shall cause independent damage. Rather, as the *Koursk* ruling affirms, if only one commits the tortious act, then all independent actors are treated as jointly liable for the unlawful act.[182]

Within online infringements, this understanding has been mirrored in the *L'Oréal v eBay* ruling.[183] In this case, L'Oréal brought legal proceedings against eBay. L'Oréal argued that eBay had violated its trade mark in a common design under the reasoning

[169] Davies (n 16) 359.
[170] *Amstrad CBS Songs v Amstrad* [1988] UKHL 15.
[171] ibid.
[172] Davies (n 16) 360.
[173] LA Hart and T Honoré, *Causation in the Law*, 2nd edn (Oxford, Oxford University Press, 1985) 187–88.
[174] Davies (n 16) 359.
[175] Angelopoulos (n 15) 165.
[176] Leistner (n 33) 83; *Credit Lyonnais Bank Nederland NV v Export Credits Guarantee Department* [1996] C.L.C. 11.
[177] Davies (n 16) 359–60.
[178] Leistner (n 33) 83.
[179] *Koursk* [1924] P. 140.
[180] ibid 156.
[181] ibid.
[182] ibid, cited in *Koursk* [1924] P. 140, 156; 'concerted action to a common end'.
[183] *L'Oréal v eBay* (2009) (EWHC) 1094 (Ch).

that the defendants collaborated with eBay; using its services with the aim to infringe the trade mark of the claimants.[184] However, Justice Arnold dismissed these allegations. In his line of reasoning, he explained that eBay was a neutral online action platform that did not have control over the fake goods and did not have any duty to implement technological measures in order to stop the dissemination of counterfeit goods on its platform.[185] In this light, eBay cannot be held jointly liable for trade mark infringements.

Crucially, this ruling reveals the difficulty of holding a host ISP jointly liable for the actions of its users. On the one hand, Justice Arnold found the different standards of preventive measures eBay uses across EU Member States insufficient and added that neither the intention of a host ISP for profit nor the facilitation of a wrongful act with knowledge can trigger joint liability from a tort law perspective.[186] This is because eBay is considered a neutral online platform and liability rules cannot be easily ascribed to it. On the other hand, while eBay has not committed the infringing act itself, in the context of joint tortfeasance, a host ISP is considered a principal in the course of the commission of the tortious act. As Angelopoulos has pointed out,

> these doctrines fail to identify cases of accessory liability as such, but instead formally categorise them as cases of primary liability, with the accessory treated either as a 'joint tortfeasor', who stands alongside the person who committed the material act of infringement as an equal principal in a single tort, or as the perpetrator, not as a participator in the wrong of somebody else, but of an independent act of negligence consisting of that participation.[187]

This understanding could open a Pandora's box with a number of rulings in the future by considering ISPs as primary infringers, thus endangering their business welfare and innovation within the EU Digital Single Market, generally.[188]

In this light, through a theoretical lens, one might conclude that English tort law could offer a potential definition for host ISPs' liability. Yet, from an implementation perspective, domestic courts face difficulties in how to implement national tort law doctrines in the context of host ISPs' activities. This is because the traditional tort law doctrine of joint tortfeasance cannot fit into the host ISPs' business model and the services they provide. For instance, while most ISPs' business models are profit-based, they are considered neutral and without the duty to prevent the dissemination of unlawful material. Concomitantly, it is problematic to prove that a host ISP induces a specific user to commit a specific infringing act, such as in the offline world. Furthermore, in attempting to apply the joint tortfeasance doctrine, the courts interpret the participation links of procurement or authorisation or participation through common design in an excessive way, and thus negate their main essence. Finally, if the courts held host ISPs liable as joint tortfeasors, this means that they would be equally placed next to the primary infringers, and thus create the impression that they contributed to the wrongdoing through their participation.

[184] ibid para 360.
[185] ibid para 359.
[186] ibid para 382.
[187] Angelopoulos (n 15) 3.
[188] This is what has happened with the DSMD which ascribes primary liability rules to a specific type of ISPs, host ISPs.

However, it is not only the UK that does not offer a solid answer to host ISPs' liability conundrum. Indeed, the German legal system seems to face similar difficulties in establishing host ISPs' liability.

ii. Germany

Similar to the UK, the German legal system turned to its national tort law rules in order to grapple with the concept of host ISPs' liability. In this regard, German national courts have looked at disturber liability and joint-tortfeasance liability. Yet, these national tort law doctrines have limited success, either due to the inadequate degree of protection they offer to rights holders, or the difficulty to apply offline provisions to the online ecosystem.

The first type of liability which has been extensively used by German courts in order to define host ISPs' liability is the disturber liability. This type of liability is not enshrined in the German Civil Code and it is a case law fiction. It finds its roots in the ruling of *Constanze* II in 1954,[189] since then it has had an extensive application within case law. In order to establish disturber liability, a set of the following criteria must be met: a deliberate and adequately causal contribution to the infringement, and the breach of a reasonable duty of care.

In the context of online infringements, the principle of disturber liability was developed in the *Rapidshare* cases. In particular, in *Rapidshare II*[190] the Hamburg Court of First Instance held that apart from removing the disputed links upon being notified by rights holders, Rapidshare had to actively monitor any already notified infringing content, and thus prevent the emergence of future links that violate the rights of copyright holders. This is because, as the German judges highlighted, Rapidshare's business model was based on offering financial incentives to subscribers so that they could upload files containing popular films or TV series. Echoing *Rapidshare II*,[191] in *Rapidshare III*,[192] the German Supreme Court (BGH) noted that Rapidshare had a duty to monitor the already notified infringing content. The German Federal Court clearly noted that Rapidshare's business model was not deliberately designed to infringe the intellectual property holders' rights and it could also be used for legitimate purposes. However, the German court agreed that Rapidshare could not be exonerated from a duty to review with the excuse of the emergence of a high number of infringements in its business model, which is considered lawful.

Yet, this understanding does not mean that host ISPs must monitor all the material that passes through their networks. By contrast, as Leistner notes, 'only reasonable and technically possible measures in order to identify comparable infringements should be imposed'.[193] Reasonable measures, as established by BGH's case law, should take into

[189] BGH, *Constanze II*, 6 July 1954, I ZR 38/532.
[190] OLG Hamburg, *Rapidshare I*, 27 April 2010, I-20 U 166/09.
[191] BGH, *Rapidshare III*, 21 December 2010, I-20 U 59/10.
[192] BGH, *Rapidshare III*, 15 August 2013, I ZR 80/12.
[193] Leistner (n 33) 79.

consideration various factors. Such factors may vary from the role of the disturber in the commission of the wrongdoing, the risk of the wrongdoing, the possibilities to bring legal proceedings against the primary infringer[194] or, as declared in the *Jugendgfährdende Medien bei eBay* ruling,[195] the financial feasibility of the measures for the host ISP.[196] Otherwise, measures might put an additional burden on the host ISP, thus endangering its business model. In this light, the reasonable duties of a host ISP must not be limited to the removal of unlawful material, but must also be extended to the removal of infringements of the same nature in the future.[197] Crucially, the burden for the removal of future infringements should not be carried by the host ISP.

Likewise, lower German courts addressed the matter of adopting post measures. For instance, in 2012 in *GEMA v YouTube*,[198] the Hamburg District Court reached the conclusion that the music-video sharing platform had not expeditiously taken down the allegedly infringing content upon notification and did so only seven months later. While this finding does not come into conflict with Article 15 of the ECD, it enhanced its reasoning and addressed the obligation of YouTube to bear filtering duties for future infringements of similar nature and which have been already notified by the rights holders. For this reason, YouTube was required to use an automated tool of a Content ID system which provided the opportunity to rights holders to file their work on a database. If the video that was uploaded, matched a work that existed in the database, the Content ID system automatically removed the file. This means that YouTube was forced to use a specific filtering-based measure in order to identify the violations within its network and not be solely contingent upon rights holders' warnings.[199]

Crucially, the doctrine of disturber liability has been the subject of serious debate among German scholars.[200] This is because, as Hoeren and Yankova point out, it establishes a type of causal liability.[201] In this sense, the ISP might be held liable for any infringement that takes places on an online platform. Yet, in order to mitigate the negative consequences this kind of liability could cause, the courts endorsed that disturber liability may arise under the specific case of a breach of reasonable duties. This means that a host ISP could be treated as a disturber only if there is a breach of a reasonable duty. However, the concept of reasonable duties of host ISPs has been construed differently by the courts. As discussed earlier, for example, for host ISPs the rise of reasonable duties is contingent upon their technical and financial capability, or the impact of the violation of the rights, or the limitations by fundamental rights, such as the freedom of expression.[202] Thus, the concept of reasonable measures should be assessed on a case-by-case basis.

[194] ibid 88.

[195] BGH, *Jugendgefährdende Medien bei eBay*, 12 July 2007, I ZR 18/04; M Schellekens, 'Liability of Internet Intermediaries: a slippery slope?' (2011) 8 *SCRIPTed* 154.

[196] Leistner (n 33) 79.

[197] Parti and Marin (n 34) 149.

[198] Landesgericht Hamburg, *GEMA v YouTube*, 20 April 2012- 310 O 461/10.

[199] S Kulk, *Internet Intermediaries and Copyright Law: EU and US perspective* (Alphen aan den Rijn, Kluwer Law International, 2019) 224.

[200] G Spindler and M Leistner, 'Secondary Copyright Infringement – New Perspectives from Germany and Europe' (2006) 37 *International Review of Intellectual Property and Competition Law* 788; Hoeren and Yankova (n 119) 504.

[201] Hoeren and Yankova (n 119) 504.

[202] BGH, *Rapidshare III*, 15 August 2013, I ZR 80/12; BGH (n 195); Landesgericht Hamburg, *GEMA v YouTube*, 20 April 2012- 310 O 461/10.

Furthermore, given that disturber liability aims to address 'active' host ISPs that induced infringements within their networks, one might wonder why courts choose to limit their power to disturber liability which only applies to injunctive relief and not extend it to joint-tortfeasance doctrines, as do their UK counterpart courts. This concern has been noted by Angelopoulos who points out,

> [i]f however it is agreed that the neutrality or lack thereof of a service should make a difference and the courts wish to impose consequences on host ISPs for the "active" inducement of third party copyright infringement, it might would make more sense to bite the bullet and impose liability as a participant in the commission of a wrong.[203]

This implies that since the courts want to attribute liability to host ISPs, it seems reasonable to impose a type of liability which can compensate rights holders for their losses.

In light of the above disagreements, the courts resorted to an alternative route and treated host ISPs as direct infringers, namely as tortfeasors. However, as is demonstrated below, the application of tortfeasance doctrine is not compatible with the rationale of tortious secondary liability that is set forth in the ECD. This is because tortfeasance doctrine views host ISPs as primarily liable for violations that accrue within their networks.

Pursuant to the German Civil Code, primary liability is governed by § 823 (1) BGB which notes that '[a] person who, intentionally or negligently, unlawfully injures the life, body, health, freedom, property or another right of another person is liable to make compensation to the other party for the damage arising from this'.[204] This means that liability arises directly from unlawful activities or from a breach of a statutory tort. Within the copyright context, a statutory tort is enshrined in Section 97 of the German Copyright Act. Accordingly, this Act notes, 'Any person who intentionally or negligently performs such an act shall be obliged to pay the injured party damages for the prejudice suffered as a result of the infringement.'[205] Within the trade mark context, Section 14(6) of the German Trade mark Act notes, 'Any person who performs the act of infringement intentionally or negligently shall be obliged to compensate the proprietor of the trade mark for the damage incurred by the act of infringement.'[206]

Yet, to hold that host ISPs are direct infringers is a tricky matter. This is because host ISPs do not commit the unlawful acts themselves. Rather, their users commit unlawful activities. However, this understanding did not impede the German Federal Court from using the concept of 'adopting the information of others'.[207] In the case at hand, in *marions-kochbuch.de* the Court found that if the operator of a website checks the content of the material prior to its online availability to internet users, it has adopted the material as its own. More specifically, the requirements of 'one's own making'[208] are

[203] Angelopoulos (n 15) 256–57.

[204] Official translation of the German Civil Code is available at www.gesetze-im-internet.de/englisch_bgb/englisch_bgb.html#p3489.

[205] Official translation of the German Copyright Act is available at www.gesetze-im-internet.de/englisch_urhg/englisch_urhg.html.

[206] Official translation of the German Trade mark Act is available at www.gesetze-im-internet.de/englisch_markeng/englisch_markeng.html#p0092.

[207] Kulk (n 199) 194 where the author names it 'one's own making principle'; Angelopoulos (n 15) 261.

[208] Zu eigen macht.

to be met because the administrator of the website is editing the content and does not rely on third parties. At the same time, the logo with the chef's hat is placed next to the recipes while the information about the authors of the recipes are placed under the list of the ingredients. In light of the above factors, internet users have the impression that the operator of the website is controlling the content of the website.[209]

As a corollary, the operator of a website has been held liable under the general provisions as a content provider. This means that the host ISP is seen as primarily liable for violations which have been committed by its users.

The doctrine of 'one's own making' has been reinforced in the *Davidoff v Amazon*[210] ruling in 2016. In the case at hand, Davidoff, the perfume manufacturer filed legal proceedings against Amazon, arguing that Amazon placed infringing pictures of 'The Game' perfume within the platform. Although the selection of displaying of pictures and listings is made by an algorithm, the German Court in Berlin concluded that the algorithm equals to human acts that decide which goods and pictures are displayed to the platform and therefore are visible to online consumers. To the Court's reasoning, Amazon's algorithm intervenes into the autonomy of sellers who could have chosen to place next to their goods an authorised picture. For this reason, the Court has concluded that Amazon adapts the material as its own and has been held directly liable for copyright infringement.

However, this doctrine has been contested by prominent scholars. For instance, Hoeren and Yankova argue that the German Federal Court presumed that since the immunity provisions of the ECD are not applicable, then there is a need to impose liability on host ISPs.[211] This understanding, however, conflicts with the existing regulatory framework under the ECD whose main aim is to shield host ISPs from liability.[212] What is more, Dinwoodie argues that the lack of immunity provisions as set forth in Article 14(1) of the ECD does not amount to liability of ISPs. As he points out, 'the scope of the immunity provision in a particular country will not necessarily map to the scope of the secondary liability standard'.[213] This means that the inability of host ISPs to provide defences in order to be exonerated from liability for intellectual property infringements within their networks does not equate to their liability. Therefore, when a host ISP does not meet the requirements of liability immunity provisions of Article 14(1) of the ECD, this does not imply that the host ISP is liable for the wrongdoings of its users.

[209] BGH, Urteil v. 12.11.2009, Az. I ZR 166/07l; see the Press Release of the decision which states that 'Nach Ansicht des BGH betreibt die Beklagte nicht lediglich eine Auktionsplattform oder einen elektronischen Marktplatz für fremde Angebote. Sie habe vielmehr nach außen sichtbar die inhaltliche Verantwortung für die auf ihrer Internetseite veröffentlichten Rezepte und Abbildungen übernommen. Die Beklagte kontrolliere die auf ihrer Plattform erscheinenden Rezepte inhaltlich und weise ihre Nutzer auf diese Kontrolle hin. Nicht zuletzt kennzeichne die Beklagte die Rezepte mit ihrem Emblem, einer Kochmütze. Der Verfasser des Rezepts erscheine lediglich als Aliasname und ohne jede Hervorhebung unter der Zutatenliste. Zudem verlange die Beklagte das Einverständnis ihrer Nutzer, dass sie alle zur Verfügung gestellten Rezepte und Bilder beliebig vervielfältigen und an Dritte weitergeben darf.' Der Bundesgerichtshof, available at juris.bundesgerichtshof.de/cgi-bin/rechtsprechung/document.py?Gericht=bgh&Art=en&nr=52175&pos=0&anz=1.

[210] LG Berlin, *Davidoff v Amazon*, MMR 2016, 624.

[211] Hoeren and Yankova (n 119) 504.

[212] ibid 504; reinforced in Angelopoulos (n 15) 261.

[213] Footnote 150 in Dinwoodie (n 15) 25.

By contrast, whether a host ISP is liable is to be decided by national courts after a careful examination of national tort law provisions.

In light of the abovementioned discrepancies, German courts turn to the joint-tortfeasance doctrine as a base liability for ISPs. However, the application of joint-tortfeasance is a contested area. It is enshrined in Article 830(1) II BGB (German Civil Code) which notes, 'If more than one person has caused damage by a jointly committed tort, then each of them is responsible for the damage. The same applies if it cannot be established which of several persons involved caused the damage by his act.'[214]

In order to establish liability based on joint tortfeasance, the requirement of intent or knowledge have to be met. This concerns the intent of host ISPs to commit the infringing act, or the knowledge the host ISPs have about the unlawful nature of the act.[215] However, as Angelopoulos noted, 'this condition is not usually met by online intermediaries'.[216] This is because host ISPs are devoid of general monitoring obligations that concern the control of the transmission of material via their platforms. This, of course, does not imply that lack of knowledge could exonerate host ISPs from liability based on joint tortfeasance. By contrast, consistently ignoring notifications for allegedly infringing material could constitute liability. For instance, a ruling delivered by *OLG Hamburg*, handed down that a host ISP was an accessory to commission of the infringement because it ignored notifications for specific infringements and thus violated its duty of care.[217] This means that whereas ISPs are prohibited from engaging in monitoring activities, and are thus deprived of the requirement of knowledge, a violation of a duty of care can take place when the host ISP does not consider notifications for infringements within its platform. Therefore, in this case, pursuant to German scholarship, the host ISP could be held liable as joint-tortfeasor.

Moreover, apart from the joint-tortfeasance doctrine, German courts developed the concept of additional joint-tortfeasance. Additional joint tortfeasors include, as per Article 830(2) II BGB, those that participate in the commission of the wrongdoing, such as the instigators and the accessories of the unlawful act.[218] Based on this civil law provision, the Tenth Civil Senate of the German Supreme Court has further developed the notion of additional joint-tortfeasance which includes the willful causal contribution to the infringing act, the breach of a duty of care, and the possible prevention of the infringing act.[219] Additional tortfeasance has similarities with the disturber liability, but also covers punitive damages.[220] This is because, as Leistner notes, 'the standard for the duty of care can be structured along the lines of the case law on Stoererhaftung'.[221] Yet, additional tortfeasance has limited applicability and, in particular, it only applies to

[214] Official translation of the German Civil Code is available at www.gesetze-im-internet.de/englisch_bgb/englisch_bgb.html#p3489.

[215] Angelopoulos (n 15) 258.

[216] Angelopoulos (n 34) 14.

[217] OLG Hamburg, 13.05.2013–5 W 41/13.

[218] Official translation of the German Civil Code is available at www.gesetze-im-internet.de/englisch_bgb/englisch_bgb.html#p3489.

[219] Leistner (n 33) 80; M. Leistner, 'Common Principles of Secondary Liability?' in A Ohly (ed), *Common Principles of European Intellectual Property Law* (Heidelberg, Mohr Siebeck, 2012) 127.

[220] Angelopoulos (n 15) 269.

[221] Leistner (n 33) 80.

unfair competition law cases.[222] This understanding has been reiterated in the case of *the Jugendgefaehrdende Medien bei eBay*.[223] In this case, the German Federal Court of Justice found that eBay had a duty to prevent the commission of unfair competition acts within its platform. By not terminating the commission of unfair competition acts, the German court argued that for eBay the mere provision of a platform that enables unfair competition acts by internet users constitutes an act of unfair competition itself. This means that in order to be exonerated from liability for unfair competition acts, the host ISP must have undertaken all the appropriate measures and prevented unfair competition acts by its users.

However, it seems that this outcome is strictly limited to cases of unfair competition law.[224] This is because an extension of this understanding to copyright or trade mark law could be troublesome. Consider, for instance, the case of *Sommer unseres Lebens*.[225] In this case, the Court did not consider the operator of an insecure wireless connection liable. This is because, although the operator had a duty to secure her connection, the functioning of a wireless network without a password does not amount to an unauthorised act of communication to the public as per § 19 A of the German Copyright Act. In this light, although the operator of the connection violated its duty, the act of providing a connection without a password does not constitute copyright infringement itself.[226]

Bearing in mind the above, German courts have attempted to define host ISPs' liability on the basis of various tort law doctrines or general civil law doctrines. Such doctrines could vary from disturber liability to tortfeasance, to joint tortfeasance, and to additional tortfeasance. However, as illustrated throughout this section, these doctrines are difficult to apply in the context of online platforms. As has been seen, disturber liability is triggered upon the violation of a reasonable duty of care. However, how a reasonable duty of care should be understood depends on various factors and is mostly considered on a case by case basis. On the other hand, tortfesance or joint tortfeasance places ISPs next to the primary infringers and users, thus it creates the impression that they are also primary infringers for intellectual property violations within their networks. Finally, while the adoption of additional tortfeasance doctrine could make more sense, its applicability appears to be limited to unfair competition law matters and is not extended to copyright or trade mark contexts.

iii. France

Along similar lines, in France there is no special legal basis to establish host ISPs' liability. For this reason, French courts rely primarily upon the provisions of the French Civil Code, namely Articles 1382 and 1383.[227] That said, liability arises if the elements of fault,

[222] Hoeren and Yankova (n 119) 506.
[223] BGH (n 195).
[224] M Leistner, 'Common Principles of Secondary Liability?' in Ohly (n 219) 127.
[225] BGH, *Sommer unseres Lebens*, 12 May 2010- I ZR 121/0; M Leistner, 'Common Principles of Secondary Liability?' in Ohly (n 219) 127.
[226] Leistner (n 33) 80.
[227] X Amadei, 'Standards of liability for Internet for Internet Service Providers: A comparative study of France and the United States with a specific focus on copyright, defamation and illicit content' (2002) 35 *Cornell International Law Journal* 203.

damage, and a causal link between fault and damage are met.[228] Article 1382 notes, 'Any act whatever of man, which causes damage to another, obliges the one by whose fault it occurred, to compensate it',[229] and Article 1383 expands the duty to repair in cases of negligence or imprudence and reads as follows, 'Everyone is liable for the damage he causes not only by his intentional act, but also by his negligent conduct or by his imprudence.'[230]

In light of the above and following the German approach, French courts also imposed a general duty of care on host ISPs. A failure to comply with the obligation may give rise to fault. This general rule has been exemplified in a number of case laws which outline that host ISPs have a duty to take precautionary measures in order to be exonerated from liability. This understanding has been encapsulated in the *Lacoste* ruling[231] where the Nanterre Court of First Instance applied Articles 1382 and 1383 of the French Civil Code and specified three obligations that should be imposed on host ISPs, namely the obligations of information, proactive measures, and action against illicit activities.[232] This means that host ISPs must encourage their users to respect third parties' rights, undertake precautionary measures to prevent the reappearance of infringing material, as well as be alert to the circulation of infringing material within their networks and react appropriately upon being notified of an illicit activity.[233]

However, these obligations do not have a uniform interpretation,[234] thus they are divided into those before and those after the adoption of the ECD. On the one hand, before the implementation of the ECD, duty of care was interpreted in an excessive manner.[235] For instance, in the *Calimero*[236] ruling in 2000, the French Court held liable the host provider of a website with sadomasochistic material on the basis of Article 1382 of French Civil Code. In this case, the website operator named the domain name of the website after the popular cartoon Calimero and hosted pictures with sadomasochistic content. The host provider requested the operator of the website with unlawful material to move his website to another provider, but it still accepted its hosting of the website with illicit material.[237] In this regard, according to French Judges, it was the inaction of the host ISP to block access to the website, despite its ability to terminate access to it, that held the host ISP liable for violating its duty of care.

On the other hand, following the transposition of the provisions of the ECD into the French legal system through the LCEN Law in 2004, the principle of duty of care has been construed in a restrictive manner. This understanding has been exemplified

[228] Y Benhamou, 'Compensation of Damages for Infringements of Intellectual Property Rights in France, Under Directive 2004/48/EC and its Transposition Law – New Notions?' (2009) 40 *International Review of Intellectual Property and Competition Law* 126.

[229] Official translation of the French Civil Code by G Rouhette and A Rouhette-Berton, available at www.fd.ulisboa.pt/wp-content/uploads/2014/12/Codigo-Civil-Frances-French-Civil-Code-english-version.pdf.

[230] ibid.

[231] *Lacoste/multimania, Eterel and Cybermedia* (1999) (Tribunal de Grande Instance de Nanterre).

[232] Amadei (n 227) 204.

[233] Angelopoulos (n 34) 262.

[234] ibid.

[235] Angelopoulos (n 15) 221.

[236] *Cons P v Monsieur G.* [2005] (Tribunal de Grande Instance de Paris).

[237] Amadei (n 227) 205.

in the *SARL Zadig Productions* ruling in 2007[238] where the Court of First Instance in Paris held that upon notification of the infringing copies of film, Google was under obligation either to mitigate the diffusion of unauthorised works or block users from accessing the website with the infringing content.[239] This is because, as the French Court concluded, Google qualified as a host ISP which offers space to its users to commit infringing acts.[240] A failure to terminate the access, or at least impede infringing material from reaching end-users, could trigger ISPs' liability. This means that, upon being notified, ISPs have a duty to remove any unlawful material and prevent its re-emergence within their networks.[241]

This line of thinking has been reiterated by several French courts. For instance, in the landmark case of *Joyeux Noel* in 2007,[242] Nord Ouest Productions brought legal proceedings against Dailymotion alleging that its users uploaded the movie of Joyeux Noel without permission, and asked for €34,813 in damages for copyright infringements.[243] Responding to film production allegations, Dailymotion argued that it is a hosting provider, thus it is entitled to immunity liability provisions as enshrined in Article 14(1) of the ECD. However, after a careful examination of the facts, the Paris Court of First Instance found that Dailymotion's intention was to attract unauthorised material and thus increase its advertising revenue. In particular, it was found that 'the success of Dailymotion implied that the broadcasting of well-known works, the only ones enable to increase the site's audience, and thus ad revenues'.[244] For this reason, as the Court noted, Dailymotion had a duty to prevent illicit activities by adopting filtering mechanisms. Failure to comply with this duty would have resulted into holding Dailymotion liable for copyright infringements of its users.

Such a stance has been retained by the *Google Inc. c/ Les Films de la Croisade, Goatworks Films* case from the Court of Appeal in Paris.[245] In this case, it was decided that Google qualified as a host ISP under Article 14(1) of the ECD, and was thus under the obligation to take precautionary measures to prevent the dissemination of unlawful content within its network after being notified.[246] Otherwise, Google would have not been eligible to evoke the immunity liability provisions of the ECD, and therefore would be liable.

Yet, to define host ISPs' liability, imposing on them a duty of care to prevent the re-emergence of similar infringements might come into conflict with Article 15 of the ECD. This is in line with the German legal system, as discussed above. In *Google v Viaticom et Luteciel*,[247] the Court found Google liable because of its AdWords system.

[238] *SARL Zadig Productions, Jean-Robert Viallet et Mathieu Verboud c. Sté Google Inc. et AFA* [2007] (Tribunal de Grande Instance de Paris).
[239] Angelopoulos (n 15) 193–94.
[240] Farano (n 30) 74.
[241] Jasserand (n 137).
[242] *Christian C., Nord Ouest Production c. Dailymotion, UGC Images* [2007] (Tribunal de Grande Instance de Paris).
[243] N Jondet, 'The silver lining in Dailymotion's copyright cloud' (2008) Juriscom. Net 2.
[244] Translation from N Jondet, 'The silver lining in Dailymotion's copyright cloud' (2008) Juriscom. Net 5.
[245] *Google Inc. c. Les Films de la Croisade, Goatworks Films* [2011] (Cour d'appel de Paris).
[246] Farano (n 30) 75.
[247] *Google v Viaticum et Luteciel* [2011] (Court of Appeal in Versailles).

In particular, the Court considered that Google should have prevented the registration of trade mark keywords by deploying filtering technology, thus negating the need to be notified of the allegedly infringing act. Crucially, this outcome has been severely criticised since it goes against the existing EU Law and, more specifically, Article 15 of the ECD which prohibits the imposition of general monitoring obligations.[248] By the same token, in *Sedo GmbH v Hotel Meridien*,[249] the French Supreme Court examined the dispute between an online domain name's auction platform and the Hotel Meridien trade mark. In this case, the Court found Sedo secondarily liable because the selling of a specific domain name on its platform violated the trade marks of other parties. This is because, as the Court handed down, 'every operator acting in business owes to third party a duty not to harm third party's business'.[250] This outcome could imply that ex-ante control or regular screening should be performed in order to prevent the infringements of trade marks on its platform and thus give rise to concerns with regard to the compatibility of a duty of care for ISPs with Article 15 of the ECD.

For this reason, this line of thinking was reconsidered by the French Supreme Court in 2012 with three rulings, namely *Google & Aufeminin.com v Mr. X*,[251] *L'affaire Clearstream*,[252] and *Les dissimulateurs*.[253] In these cases, French judges reassessed the imposition of a duty for ISPs to prevent the reappearance of infringing material, which has been intensively used by the courts since 2007.[254] In particular, they disconnected the obligation to remove the infringing material with the subsequent monitoring obligation. In this regard, it has been argued that it is up to the copyright holders to monitor the network of host ISPs and detect any violation of their rights. This means that host ISPs must not be under any obligation to monitor the unwelcome content since this could contradict Article 15 of the ECD which advocates a general prohibition on filtering activities. This is because, as Angelopoulos has noted, if the host ISP wants to be exonerated from liability, it must maintain control of its network for future infringements of the same nature.[255] Otherwise, the host ISPs will be considered in violation of their duty of care, and thus be held liable.

In light of the above, under French tortious secondary liability rules, a host ISP can be held liable if it intentionally or negligently gives rise to copyright or trade mark infringements. This understanding has enabled the wide application of the concept of duty of care for host ISPs since the violation of duty of care would amount to negligence. How the general duty of care should be defined rests on the assessment of each domestic court. In this light, French courts have construed the general duty of care in different terms, either in a restrictive or excessive manner. Yet, while a restrictive interpretation of a duty of care for host ISPs is compatible with Recital 47 of the ECD, an excessive interpretation of a duty of care could incite severe criticism since it contradicts

[248] Leistner (n 33) 90.
[249] *Sedo GmbH v Hotel Meridien, Stephane H.* [2008] Cour de Cassation.
[250] Footnote 160 in Farano (n 30) 44.
[251] *Google & Aufeminin.com v Mr. X* [2012] Cour de Cassation.
[252] *La société Google France c. la société Bach films* (L'affaire Clearstream) [2012] Cour de Cassation.
[253] *La société Google France c. La société Bac films* (Les dissimulateurs) [2012] Cour de Cassation.
[254] Jasserand (n 137).
[255] Angelopoulos (n 15) 196.

existing EU Law provisions and, specifically, Article 15 of the ECD which prohibits the deployment of precautionary measures, such as ex-ante filtering of all the information that is transmitted online.

iv. Spain

Along similar lines, in Spain there is no special legal basis to establish host ISPs' liability. For this reason, Spanish courts could rely primarily upon the provisions of the Spanish Copyright Act, namely Article 138 which introduces secondary liability for infringements. In particular, Article 138 states that secondary liability arises for cases where anyone knowingly induces the infringement, or knowing or having reason to know about the infringement cooperates with it, or having a direct economic interest in the results of the infringement has the ability to control the infringer's conduct. This provision has been adopted since 2016 in order to offer a legal basis for identifying secondary liability and follows the rationale and the structure of the US secondary liability doctrine.[256] Interestingly, the Spanish Courts have refrained from adopting this provision so far and therefore they mainly examine host ISPs' liability in reference to the liability defences as per Article 14(1) of the E-Commerce Directive. At the same time, in trade mark law, there is not a similar provision that could offer the legal basis for establishing secondary liability for trade mark infringements.

Apart from this, another resort could be Article 1902 of the Spanish Civil Code which addresses the duty of care. In particular it states, 'the person who, as a result of an action or omission, causes damage to another by his fault or negligence shall be obliged to repair the damaged caused'.[257] This means that a host ISP could be liable if it violated its duty of care by not removing the allegedly infringing content or counterfeit good upon being notified. Yet, as Peguera notes, this provision is 'an unexplored argument in rights holders' civil rights lawsuits',[258] and therefore no court decision has addressed this possibility so far.

v. Greece

Similar to the previous jurisdictions, the Greek legal system does not offer a legal basis for the liability of host ISPs. For this reason, a legal basis can be found in the field of tort law. In particular, Article 914 of the Greek Civil Code addresses tort liability and states that 'Whoever is acting unlawfully and in fault causes a pecuniary damage to another party, is obliged to compensate same.' This means that liability for damages may arise if a causal link between the alleged infringer and the illicit activity can be established.

[256] M Peguera, 'Spanish Copyright Reform enters into force: special focus on online intermediaries' (*The Center for Internet and Society blog*, 27 January 2015) cyberlaw.stanford.edu/blog/2015/01/spanish-copyright-reform-enters-force-special-focus-online-intermediaries.

[257] Spanish civil code in English is available at derechocivil-ugr.es/attachments/article/45/spanish-civil-code.pdf.

[258] Peguera (n 45) 163.

Yet, this understanding has been subject to controversy. This is mainly because host ISPs are considered messengers of the information, so do not commit acts themselves. Under the Greek legal doctrine of messenger, a messenger cannot be held liable for the messages that it carries. For instance, the messenger of information is not responsible for examining the nature of the content transmitted and is not entitled to adjudicate whether it is illegal or legal. However, this view does not come without criticism. Beis argues that host ISPs are not only the messengers of information, but also are in a position which allows examination of the nature of content. For this reason, he urges the need to re-evaluate the current application of the concept of messengers in the context of host ISPs.[259] Yet so far, as per the prevailing view of scholarship and the courts' approach, host ISPs are seen as messengers of information, therefore it is impossible to establish a causal link and thus hold them liable.

However, in the light of ongoing lawsuits and the increasing numbers of intellectual property infringements on the networks, it has been argued that liability could emerge under the theory of adequate cause. This means that the alleged infringer could be held liable if her intervention could be considered as indispensable for the illicit activity. As Lianos aptly points out, 'The theory of adequate cause constitutes the archetype of a generalizing theory of causation in fact, as it focuses on the condition or conditions that would objectively produce the type of damage examined, not necessarily the specific damage or event.'[260] The roots of this theory stem from Von Kries who developed the theory of probability and applied it in the context of the law.[261] More specifically, he argued that adequate cause of harm can emerge under two conditions, namely there must be a sine qua non of the harm, and this action must have increased the objective probability of harm to a significant extent.[262]

Crucially, it is worthy of note that the Greek Courts have not yet applied the doctrine, instead they prefer to resort to the defences of Article 14(1) of the ECD and examine cases with reference to the defences offered, such as lack of knowledge or lack of expeditious removal of the illicit activity.

Bearing in mind the above, it could be concluded that the legal traditions of the UK, German, French, Spanish and Greek jurisdictions fail to offer a solid answer to the conundrum of host ISPs' liability. This is because, as presented in this section, each jurisdiction has its own secondary tort law doctrine. For instance, the French tort law system extends the direct breach of tort law provisions to additional actors and ascribes a duty of care to host ISPs which urges them to undertake precautionary measures to avoid future infringements. In line with this, the German legal system develops the notion of disturber liability and places a reasonable duty of care on host ISPs. Insofar as the UK tortious legal tradition is concerned, whereas the doctrine of joint-torfeasance is applicable to host ISPs' activities, to endorse a duty of care for ISPs seems to be out of

[259] Cited in K Χριστοδούλου, 'Ουσιαστικού και δικονομικού δικαίου ιδιαιτερότητες του καθεστώτος των ηλεκτρονικών δικτύων' (μετά τις οδηγίες.2002/ 19–22, 58 και τον Κανονισμό της ΕΕΤ για τα Domain Names).

[260] I Lianos, 'Causal Uncertainty and Damages Claims for the Infringement of Competition Law in Europe' (2015) *Yearbook of European Law* 182.

[261] Hart and Honoré (n 173) 469.

[262] ibid.

the question. At the same time, the Spanish Copyright Act includes a secondary liability doctrine inspired by the vicarious liability as set forth in the US jurisdiction, while the Greek legal system endorses the theory of the adequate cause of harm in order to establish secondary liability. This creates a patchwork of miscellaneous tort law doctrines that differ from each other and offer legal uncertainty to the parties at stake. Given the lack of a uniform approach towards host ISPs' liability, rights holders might not be able to compensate their losses in cases of intellectual property infringements on the online networks, while host ISPs might overzealously remove material which could be lawful, thus preventing lawful material to reach end-users.

What is more, there have been many instances where national courts have faced discrepancies in order to fit secondary tortious liability doctrines to host ISPs' activities. This is either because some tortious secondary liability doctrines require a duty of care for host ISPs, or because secondary liability doctrine does not fit within the role of host ISPs. For example, under French jurisdiction a duty of care shall be imposed on hos ISPs. This means that once host ISPs are notified of the allegedly illicit activity, they have a duty to act and prevent the dissemination of unlawful material within their networks. Failure to comply with the duty of care amounts to their liability. However, what falls under the scope of duty of care is subject to a case by case assessment, leading to contradictory outcomes. Another example can be found in the Greek jurisdiction, where secondary liability is considered through the lens of the adequate cause of harm. In the context of host ISPs, however, it is tricky to establish secondary liability for intellectual property law infringements because host ISPs are seen as messengers of information, therefore it is impossible to establish a causal link and thus hold them liable. Finally, another reason that reiterates the difficulties that national courts face in order to find host ISPs liable is the fact that some secondary tortious liability rules in some jurisdictions consider host ISPs as primary infringers. For instance, the joint-tortfeasance doctrine which has a wide application in Germany and the UK, places the host ISPs next to the principal infringer of the tortious act. This is because the joint-tortfeasor is also considered a direct infringer. This understanding, however, prompts further reflection on the appropriateness of fitting joint-tortfeasance doctrines into host ISPs' activities. To treat a host ISP as a direct infringer does not only negate the main intention of European policymakers to offer a secondary liability regime for host ISPs, but also aggravates, without reason, the role of ISPs with regard to intellectual property infringements committed on its platform.

IV. Conclusion

This chapter has critically engaged with the secondary liability of host ISPs under the ECD. After demonstrating the theoretical, practical, and policy approaches that warrant the ascription of liability rules to ISPs, the narrative delved into the regulatory framework of ISPs under Article 14(1) of the ECD.[263] Since 2000, the ECD has been the main

[263] See ch 3 section III(A), (B) and (C).

instrument that regulates ISPs' liability for infringements that may accrue within their networks and are committed by their users. It had been warmly welcomed by ISPs since its main intention was to enhance e-commerce, which was at its infancy at that time, and boost innovation at European level.

However, a critical analysis of the ECD, and in particular of Article 14(1), demonstrated that the regulatory framework of host ISPs is outdated. This is because Article 14(1) of the ECD defines host ISPs' liability with reverse logic. This means that host ISPs are offered a number of defences in order to be exonerated from liability, or to put it more accurately, Article 14(1) offers the specific conditions under which host ISPs are not liable for intellectual property infringements that take place within their networks. For instance, host ISPs can escape from liability if they are not aware of the illicit activity, or if they remove the unlawful content upon being notified. Hence, this means that the ECD does not provide a definition of host ISPs' liability.

What is more, the findings indicate that the transposition of the ECD in five selected jurisdictions follows the rationale of the ECD, therefore it does not offer a solid answer to host ISPs' liability. For instance, Germany, UK and France follow *verbatim* Article 14(1) of the ECD and endorse defences for ISPs that they could invoke in order to defend themselves against allegations of liability, while Greek and Spanish jurisdictions follow the rationale of Article 14(1) of the ECD with some minor alterations. Therefore, the implementation of Article 14(1) of the ECD into national legal systems fails to provide a solid answer to the conundrum of host ISPs' liability.

In this light, many courts have turned to their national secondary tortious liability rules in order to attribute liability to ISPs. Given the lack of harmonisation of secondary liability rules at European level, each jurisdiction applies its national tort law system in order to seek the appropriate tortious liability doctrines, and thus define ISPs' liability. While from a theoretical perspective secondary tortious liability could offer a definition of host ISPs' liability, it appears that national courts face difficulties fitting them into online disputes. This is either because tortious secondary liability doctrines require a duty of care for host ISPs, which can only be assessed on a case-by-case basis, or because other secondary tortious liability rules in some jurisdictions treat host ISPs as primary infringers of the unlawful act, or because the secondary liability doctrine is incompatible with the role of host ISPs as messengers of information as set forth in the Greek jurisdiction.

Further, the idea of each jurisdiction adopting its own national tort rules could create a puzzle of different secondary tortious liability doctrines that stem from the legal traditions of each national jurisdiction, respectively. However, this understanding could result in legal uncertainty for the parties involved, and thus undermine their interests.

In light of the above, legal reform is extremely urgent in order to clarify the liability that host ISPs might incur in the case of intellectual property infringements within their networks. Yet, before presenting a number of recommendations, it is necessary to critically assess the second legislative piece that regulates host ISPs' liability for copyright infringements within their networks. This new legislative tool is the Copyright in the Digital Single Market Directive (DSMD). As discussed in the introduction to this book, this legislative tool was introduced in April 2019 and has created severe controversy among different stakeholders at European level. Although the DSMD has not yet been tested in the courts' legal arena, and given that its transposition into the national legal systems of the 27 European Member States has not yet been completed despite the fact that the deadline was on 7 June 2021, an array of structural problems have already been identified. For this reason, the next chapter critically examines the DSMD, and in particular Article 17 which addresses the liability of online content sharing service providers, which seems to be a new type of host ISP, who host material on their networks uploaded by users.

4

The Regulatory Framework of Online Content Sharing Service Providers (OCSSPs) under Article 17 of the Copyright in the Digital Single Market Directive (DSMD) for Copyright Infringements: A Controversial Approach

I. Introduction

As discussed in chapter three, the regulatory framework for host ISPs as set forth in the ECD[1] seems outdated. This is because in Article 14(1) it offers a set of defences for host ISPs[2] in order for them to be exonerated from liability for infringements committed by their users.[3] What is more, the transposition of the ECD into national legal systems follows the rationale of the ECD, thus it fails to provide an answer to the ISPs' liability conundrum. Finally, given that the ECD does not define host ISPs' liability, national courts turn to their national secondary tortious legal doctrines. However, given that tortious secondary liability rules are not harmonised at European level, the result is a landscape of different secondary liability rules in tort that not only differ in each jurisdiction, but which are also difficult to apply within the context of online disputes.

However, as well as the ECD, there is another legislative tool that regulates ISPs' liability for copyright infringements. The Copyright in the Digital Single Market Directive (DSMD) was finalised on 17 April 2019.[4] Given that this research addresses trade mark as well as copyright infringements online, a critical evaluation of the Directive introduced DSMD framework of host ISPs at the European level.

[1] Council Directive (EC) 2000/31/EC of the European Parliament and of the Council of 8 June 2000 on certain legal aspects of information society services, in particular electronic commerce, in the Internal Market (hereinafter ECD).

[2] As discussed in ch 3, Article 14(1) notes that host ISPs can exonerate from liability if they lack knowledge or they are not aware of the infringement or take down the infringement upon obtaining knowledge of it.

[3] Chapter 3 section III(A), (B) and (C).

[4] Council Directive (EC) 2019/790/EC of the European Parliament and of the Council of 17 April 2019 on copyright and related rights in the Digital Single Market and amending Directives 96/9/EC and 2001/29/EC (2019) OJ L 130 (hereinafter DSMD).

Following the outcomes of the impact assessment on the modernisation of European copyright rules launched by the European Commission,[5] it has been concluded that there is an unfair distribution of the revenues with regard to the content that is circulated online between host ISPs and rights holders. In order to resolve this mismatch,[6] the EU Commission initiated the Proposal for a new Copyright in the Digital Single Market Directive (DSMD).[7] In this light, Jean Claude Juncker stated that the DSMD entails 'clear rules that guarantee fair remuneration for creators, strong rights for users and responsibility for platforms. When it comes to completing Europe's Digital Single Market, the copyright reform is the missing piece of the puzzle'.[8]

Among the provisions of this Directive, the most relevant to the current discussion is Article 17 (formerly Article 13) which deals with the liability of Online Content Sharing Service Providers (OCSSPs), a new type of host ISPs, for copyright infringements. It is this provision in the DSMD that has raised severe controversy among different stakeholders. Here, it bears noting that Article 17 has not yet been tested in the courts' legal arena, while its transposition to EU national Member States remains ongoing.[9] However, a number of problematic aspects of Article 17 have been identified.[10] This is because Article 17 of the DSMD is complex and not easy to follow, even by legal experts. What is more, it has been argued that Article 17 of the DSMD is biased in favour of rights holders[11] since it appears to promote the rights of copyright holders and subordinates the interests of OCSSPs and internet users.[12]

[5] European Commission Staff working document, 'Executive summary of the impact assessment on the modernisation of EU copyright rules' (2016) SWD 302 final 1.

[6] T Madiega, 'EU Legislation in Progress: Copyright in the digital single market' (2019) *European Parliamentary Research Service* 1–3; S von Lewinski, 'Comments on the "value gap" provisions in the European Commission's Proposal for a Directive on Copyright in the Digital Single Market (Article 13 and Recital 38)' (*Kluwer Copyright Blog*, 10 April 2017) copyrightblog.kluweriplaw.com/2017/04/10/comments-value-gap-provisions-european-commissions-proposal-directive-copyright-digital-single-market-article-13-recital-38/; A Bridy, 'EU Copyright Reform: Grappling with the Google Effect' (2019) 22 *Vanderbilt Journal of Entertainment & Technology Law* 334.

[7] DSMD.

[8] European Commission, 'Copyright reform clears final hurdle: Commission welcomes approval of modernised rules fit for digital age' (15 April 2019) europa.eu/rapid/press-release_IP-19-2151_en.htm.

[9] Although the deadline for the transposition into EU member was 7 June, the majority of the EU Member States have not implemented the DSMD yet. For a detailed analysis of all the provisions of the DSMD see E Rosati, 'Copyright in the Digital Single Market Article-by-Article Commentary to the Provisions of Directive 2019/790' (Oxford University Press 2021).

[10] 'Safeguarding User Freedoms in Implementing Article 17 of the Copyright in the Digital Single Market Directive: Recommendations from European Academics' (November 2019); S Stalla-Bourdillon et al, 'Open Letter to the European Commission – On the Importance of Preserving the Consistency and Integrity of the EU Acquis Relating to Content Monitoring within the Information Society' (2016); C Angelopoulos and JP Quintais, 'Fixing copyright reform: a better solution to online infringement' (2019) 10 *Journal of Intellectual Property, Information Technology and E-Commerce Law* 153; S Dusollier, 'The 2019 Directive on Copyright in the Digital Single Market: Some Progress, a few bad choices and an overall failed ambition' (2020) 57 *Common Market Law Review* 979.

[11] E Rosati, 'Public Lecture on Copyright and the Court of Justice of the European Union: Role, Action, Legacy' (27 February 2019) University of Reading, Reading (UK); A Guadamuz, 'New EU Directive threatens the Internet as we know it' (*TechnoLlama*, 23 February 2019) www.technollama.co.uk/new-eu-directive-threatens-the-internet-as-we-know-it.

[12] M Husovec, 'How Europe wants to redefine global online copyright enforcement' in T Synodinou (ed), *Pluralism or Universalism in International Copyright Law* (Alphen aan den Rijn, Kluwer Law International, 2019) 529; G Frosio, 'To filter or not to filter? That is the question in EU Copyright Reform' (2018) 36 *Cardozo*

Indicative of its controversy are the sizeable protests that have been organised across EU Member States[13] as well as numerous speeches and signed statements by prominent public figures and large inventors.[14] For instance, the UN Representative on freedom of expression and opinion, David Kaye, noted that while it is imperative that Europe modernises its copyright rules, 'this should not be done at the expense of the freedom of expression that Europeans enjoy today'.[15] Meanwhile, at the same time the founder of the world wide web, Sir Tim Berners-Lee, stated that 'the DSM transforms the internet from open platform for sharing and innovation, into a tool for the automated surveillance and control of its users'.[16] What is more, a set of stakeholders' dialogues have already taken place at the University of Amsterdam[17] and in the EU Commission[18] in order to provide more guidance to Member States on how to implement the DSMD into their national legislation. Finally, the controversy that revolves around the DSMD led Poland to file a challenge before the CJEU and request the annulment of Article 17. As for the reasoning for the application, the Polish Minister of Culture and Heritage outlined that 'in our opinion this mechanism introduces solutions with preventive censorship features. Such censorship is forbidden by both the Polish Constitution and EU law – the Charter of Fundamental Rights guarantees freedom of expression.'[19] On the application, the Advocate General Saugmandsgaard Øe held that Article 17 is compatible with Article 11 of the European Charter of Fundamental Rights and in particular that the contested provisions 'are sufficiently clear and precise …' while they respect the essence of the right because it imposes a specific monitoring obligation.[20] However, it remains to be seen whether the CJEU will follow his recommendation or reach a different conclusion.

Arts and Entertainment Law Journal 122; G Frosio and S Mendis, 'Monitoring and Filtering: European Reform or Global Trend' (2019) *Center for International Intellectual Property Studies Research Paper* 21.

[13] M Maker, 'Inside the giant German protest trying to bring down Article 13' (*Wired*, 26 March 2019) www.wired.co.uk/article/article-13-protests.

[14] P Samuelson, 'The EU's Controversial Digital Single Market Directive – Part I: Why the Proposed Internet Content Filtering Mandate Was So Controversial' (*Kluwer Copyright Blog*, 10 July 2018) copyrightblog.kluweriplaw.com/2018/07/10/eus-controversial-digital-single-market-directive-part-proposed-internet-content-filtering-mandate-controversial/; D Kaye, 'Mandate of the Special Rapporteur on the promotion and protection of the right to freedom of opinion and expression' (13 June 2018) www.ohchr.org/Documents/Issues/Opinion/Legislation/OL-OTH-41-2018.pdf.

[15] Office of the High Commissioner, United Nations Human Rights, 'EU must align copyright reform with international human rights standards', available at https://www.ohchr.org/EN/NewsEvents/Pages/DisplayNews.aspx?NewsID=24298&LangID=E, last accessed 9 September 2021.

[16] Samuelson (n 14).

[17] European Copyright Roundtable, 'Over-blocking: How to safeguard creators' and users' rights? & Closing Remarks' (17 June 2019) www.youtube.com/watch?v=9zRjXr6xxSQ.

[18] EU Commission, 'Organisation of a stakeholder dialogue on the application of Article 17 of Directive on Copyright in the Digital Single Market' (28 August 2019) digital-strategy.ec.europa.eu/en/news/organisation-stakeholder-dialogue-application-article-17-directive-copyright-digital-single-market.

[19] N Mileszyk, 'The Copyright Directive challenged in the CJEU by Polish government' (*Communia*, 1 June 2019) www.communia-association.org/2019/06/01/copyright-directive-challenged-cjeu-polish-government/; Action brought on 24 May 2019 – Republic of Poland v European Parliament and Council of the European Union (Case C-401/19), available at curia.europa.eu/juris/document/document.jsf?text=&docid=216823&pageIndex=0&doclang=EN&mode=lst&dir=&occ=first&part=1&cid=8371710.

[20] Opinion of Advocate General SAUGMANDSGAARD ØE delivered on 15 July 2021 (1), Case C-401/19 *Republic of Poland v European Parliament, Council of the European Union*, paras 95 and 110.

Against this background, this chapter aims to critically assess the DSMD. The narrative starts with a historical account of Article 17 that provides a comprehensive discussion of the legislative process that led to the final vote of the DSMD. This historical account includes the EU Commission's original Proposal, the Council's Proposal, and the EU Parliament's final compromised text after the dialogue between the EU Institutions. The narrative on the legislative process that preceded the final text of the DSMD will not be analysed since most of the problematic features that were included in the EU Commission's Proposal, the Council's, and the EU Parliament's texts also exist in the final text of the DSMD. Thus, in order to avoid repetition, but also to draw attention to the final text of the DSMD, the historical account is condensed. Following this, the discussion moves to the final draft of Article 17 of the DSMD and critically addresses its problematic features. These issues entail the introduction of primary liability rules, the dual liability regime with the ECD, as well as a number of obligations that contradict the *EU acquis*. Finally, this chapter offers a critical examination of the national implementation of Article 17 of the DSMD in EU Member States and its problematic intersection between Article 17 of the DSMD and Article 14(1) of the ECD.

II. Brief Overview of the Historical Account of Article 17 of the DSMD

The following section discusses the different legislative stages of the implementation of Article 17 of the DSMD from the EU Commission Proposal to the texts of the Council and the EU Parliament.

A. EU Commission's Proposal for the Copyright in the Digital Single Market Directive (DSMD)

In September 2016 the EU Commission published its Proposal for a Copyright in the Digital Single Market Directive at the State of the Union.[21] This Proposal, as the Commissioner for Digital Affairs stated, was expected to provide a 'copyright environment that is stimulating, fair and rewards investment'.[22] This Proposal was part of the Digital Single Market Strategy that was announced in March 2015[23] and whose aim was to modernise intellectual property rights' enforcement rules in the online world.[24]

[21] Hereinafter European Commission Proposal, for the full text of Article 13 of the EU Commission Proposal for a Copyright Directive in the Digital Single Market see Appendix I.

[22] European Commission, 'State of the Union 2016: Commission proposes modern EU copyright rules for European culture to flourish and circulate' (Strasbourg 14 September 2016) europa.eu/rapid/press-release_IP-16-3010_en.htm.

[23] European Commission, 'A Digital Single Market Strategy for Europe' {SWD (2015) 100 final} Brussels, 6.5.2015 COM (2015) 192 final.

[24] European Commission, 'Press release on Digital Single Market Creating a Digital Single Market European Commission actions since 2015' (June 2018) ec.europa.eu/information_society/newsroom/image/document/2018-25/creatingadigitalsinglemarket-europeancommissionactionssince2015pdf_996FEA88-AD3C-940E-050B64C947B33CF5_53055.pdf.

It traces back to the EU Commission's Public Consultation on the Review of European Copyright rules that outlined the need for modernising copyright rules at the European level.[25]

However, this much anticipated legislative proposal, whose main purpose was to fight against the value gap and ensure fair remuneration for creators whose works are disseminated in the digital ecosystem, seems to be biased. This means that rights holders' rights were prioritised while host ISPs' and internet users' interests were subordinated.[26]

The provision that addressed the liability of host ISPs is to be found in Article 13 of the EU Commission's Proposal, which is now Article 17 of the final draft of the DSMD. The former introduced a set of obligations for ISPs. Following the definition of internet service providers (ISPs) as enshrined in the ECD, Article 13 of the Proposal noted that host ISPs shall enter into a licence agreement with rights holders and deploy appropriate measures to ensure the correct functioning of those agreements. Yet, as Article 13 of the Proposal noted, this is an obligation only for those ISPs who are not eligible for the liability immunity provisions set out under Article 14(1) of the ECD. *A contrario*, for those ISPs who fall outside the scope of Article 14(1) of the ECD, Article 13 of the Proposal assumes that they have an active role. What amounts to an active role has been described in Recital 38 of the Proposal, it notes that the provider must go 'beyond the mere physical facilities' or 'optimising the presentation of the uploaded works or subject matter or promoting them, irrespective of the nature of the means used therefor'.[27] While the latter understanding of what constitutes an active provider has already been confirmed at judicial level with the *L'Oreal v eBay* case in the CJEU,[28] this does not mean that ISPs with an active role are excluded from liability immunity provisions. Rather, pursuant to the *L'Oreal v eBay* ruling, host ISPs who offer hosting services and have an active role may still be eligible to the liability exemption under Article 14(1) of the ECD.[29] Therefore, confusion has emerged with regard to the stances where host ISPs are subject to liability immunity provisions and on which stances they are not.

Further, another point of the EU Commission Proposal that has been subject to criticism is the notion of storing and providing access to large amounts of copyrighted material. Both definitions were new and might be subject to different interpretations. Some scholars have argued that the notion of providing access to large amounts of copyrighted works amounts to communication to the public.[30] If so, this means that the Proposal slightly opens the door for attributing primary liability rules to host ISPs.

[25] European Commission, 'Public Consultation on the Review of EU Copyright Rules' (2013) 1.

[26] O Fischman Afori, 'Universal measures in the service of global challenges: proportionality, blocking orders, and online intermediaries as hybrid bodies' in T Synodinou, *Pluralism or Universalism in international copyright law* (Alphen aan den Rijn, Kluwer Law International, 2019) 657.

[27] Recital 38 of the Proposal for a Directive of the European Parliament and of the Council on copyright in the Digital Single Market COM/2016/0593 final.

[28] Case C-324/09 *L'Oreal SA V eBay Int'l AG* (2011) ECR I-6011, para 116.

[29] S Stalla-Bourdillon, 'Internet intermediaries as responsible actors? Why it is time to rethink the e-Commerce Directive as well' in M Taddeo and L Floridi (eds) *The Responsibilities of Online Service Providers* (Berlin, Springer, 2017) 281; E Rosati, 'Why a Reform of Hosting Providers' Safe Harbour is Unnecessary Under EU Copyright Law' (2016) 38 *European Intellectual Property Review* 668.

[30] Frosio (n 12) 342.

Yet, given that the wording is vague, it was not possible to be sure about the intentions of the European policymakers at the time they drafted this provision.

Moreover, pursuant to Article 13, the obligations that host ISPs must follow give rise to mounting concerns. This is because they are either non-feasible as such, or they might pose serious threats to internet users' fundamental rights. In particular, Article 13 notes that host ISPs must enter into licensing agreements or deploy filtering mechanisms. On the one hand, with regard to licensing agreements, it seems an 'impossible feat'[31] for host ISPs to license all the works. On the other hand, this means that in order to comply with the obligation and prevent the availability of unauthorised works on their networks, host ISPs are forced to deploy filtering technologies. Such filtering mechanisms have attracted negative criticism and, without any safeguard, might encroach upon users' fundamental rights.[32] This is mainly due to the 'dangers' this kind of technological measure could trigger.[33]

It is these risks of violations of the rights of internet users that urged Germany to address a question to the legal service of the Council to clarify the issue of content identification filtering technology, as set forth in Article 13 of the Proposal for the DSMD. The question reads as follows:

> How do Article 13 and Recital 38 of the draft relate to the liability privileges for service providers that have been established in the Directive on electronic commerce (2000/31/EC)? How could Article 13 of the draft be put in more clear terms?[34]

This question seems plausible since filtering or blocking technology could create a serious threat for host ISPs, namely encroaching upon their freedom to conduct business. The right to conduct business is guaranteed pursuant to Article 16 of the EU Charter of Fundamental rights and dictates the right of each person to 'pursue a business without being subject to either discrimination or disproportionate restrictions'.[35] Within the context of ISPs, the right of freedom to conduct business was invoked for the first time in the *Scarlet Extended* case[36] where the CJEU examined the issue of an injunction for the implementation of filtering technology in order to terminate or mitigate the online infringements. According to the Court, while intellectual property rights are fundamental rights as per Article 17(2) of the Charter of Fundamental Rights of the European Union, this does not mean that the right is inviolable. Rather the protection

[31] J Reda, 'The text of Article 13 and the EU Copyright Directive has just been finalised' (*Julia Reda's website*, 13 February 2019) juliareda.eu/2019/02/eu-copyright-final-text/.

[32] F La Rue, 'Mandate of the Special Rapporteur on the promotion and protection of the right to freedom of opinion and expression' (13 June 2018) www.ohchr.org/Documents/Issues/Opinion/Legislation/OL-OTH-41-2018.pdf.

[33] M Senftleben et al, 'The Recommendation on Measures to Safeguard Fundamental Rights and the Open Internet in the Framework of the EU Copyright Reform' (2017) 40 *European Intellectual Property Review*.

[34] Council of the European Union (18 September 2017) Interinstitutional File: 2016/0280 (COD) data.consilium.europa.eu/doc/document/ST-12291-2017-INIT/en/pdf.

[35] European Union Agency for Fundamental rights, 'Report on Freedom to conduct a business: exploring the dimensions of a fundamental right' (2015) 21, available at file:///C:/Users/bc810741/Downloads/fra-2015-freedom-conduct-business_en.pdf.

[36] Case C-70/10 *Scarlet Extended SA v Société belge des auteurs, compositeurs et éditeurs SCRL (SABAM)* [2011] ECR-I 11959.

of intellectual property rights should be in conjunction with the other fundamental rights. For this reason, 'in the context of measures adopted to protect copyright holders, national authorities and courts must strike a fair balance between the protection of copyright and the protection of the fundamental rights of individuals who are affected by such measures'.[37] In this light, the Court found that a filtering system would constitute a serious infringement of the host ISPs' freedom to conduct business since the system would be expensive and the host ISP would also bear the costs for its implementation. The equilibrium between different interests at stake has not been reached because the measure is disproportionate and comes in conflict with Article 3 of the Enforcement Directive which notes, 'Those measures, procedures and remedies shall also be effective, proportionate and dissuasive and shall be applied in such a manner as to avoid the creation of barriers to legitimate trade and to provide for safeguards against their abuse.'[38]

What is more, the implementation of filtering or blocking-based technology may impinge upon the freedom of expression of the users. As Zittrain points out, blocking or filtering injunctions against online platforms should be treated with skepticism as they must abide by 'changes to information technologies which are themselves quite frequently speech-related'.[39] This is because the filtering technology cannot distinguish the lawful and unlawful content and might block the dissemination of legal material or the continuation of lawful activities. There are many examples where the legal activities of users have been restricted by filtering software, regardless of the fact that YouTube declares that this kind of measure performs satisfactorily.[40] This can be seen in a case where YouTube removed a video of a University lecture delivered by a Harvard Law Professor. This happened because the Professor, during his lecture, included samples of lyrics of popular songs. However, the video was lawful because it was for educational purposes.[41] Hence, the filtering obligation could restrict the freedom of speech, to a certain extent.

The importance of respecting the freedom of expression of the subscribers in light of blocking or filtering injunctions has been highlighted at European level. For instance, the preamble of the InfoSoc Directive stresses that any measure to be adopted must be in 'compliance with the fundamental principles of law and especially of property, including intellectual property, and freedom of expression and the public interest'.[42] In this vein, paragraph 1.3.1. of the Recommendation of the Council of Europe states that 'Any request, demand or other action by public authorities addressed to internet intermediaries to restrict access (including blocking or removal of content), or any other measure that could lead to a restriction of the right to freedom of expression, shall be prescribed

[37] ibid.

[38] Council Directive (EC) 2004/48/EC on the enforcement of intellectual property rights (2004) O.J. L 157.

[39] J Zittrain, 'A History of Online Gatekeeping' (2006) 19 *Harvard Journal of Law and Technology* 253; see also KM Schmidt and M Schnitzer, 'Public Subsidies for Open Source? Some Economic Policy Issues of the Software Market' (2003) 16 *Harvard Journal of Law and Technology* 473, 476.

[40] J Reda, 'When filters fail: These cases show we can't trust algorithms to clean up the internet' (*Julia Reda's website*, 28 September 2017) juliareda.eu/2017/09/when-filters-fail/.

[41] ibid.

[42] Preamble of the Directive 2001/29/EC of the European Parliament and of the Council of 22 May 2001 on the harmonisation of certain aspects of copyright and related rights in the information society.

by law, pursue one of the legitimate aims foreseen in Article 10 of the Convention, be necessary in a democratic society and be proportionate to the aim pursued.'[43]

The importance of respecting the freedom of expression of the users has also preoccupied the court's legal arena. In the landmark case of *Yildirim v Turkey*,[44] the European Court of Human Rights highlighted the danger of violating the rights of expression of users and endorsed more precise circumstances on how the blocking technology should be implemented in order to strike a fair balance between the different interests at stake. In the case at hand, a Turkish national operated a website hosted by the 'Google Sites' portal. In 2009, the Criminal Court in Turkey ordered a blocking injunction against a website that insulted the memory of Kemal Ataturk. That website was also hosted by the 'Google Sites' portal. The Turkish Telecommunication and Data Protection Authority advised the Criminal Court to block access to the entire 'Google Sites' portal, thus blocking access to the website of Yildirim as well. For this reason, Yildirim submitted an application to the European Court of Human Rights in Strasbourg arguing that the blocking of Google Sites had resulted into collateral censorship, ie, termination of access to his own website. In this way, the blocking of his website constituted violation of the right to freedom of expression as enshrined in Article 10 of the European Convention of Human Rights.[45] According to the Court, a restriction is compatible with Article 10 only if the restriction 'is prescribed by law' and meets the demands of a democratic society.[46] This understanding implies that when a court orders a blocking injunction, it must take into consideration 'the scope of the website ban'[47] and 'the guarantee of the judicial review',[48] in order to avoid any violation of European fundamental rights, such as the freedom of expression of users. After careful consideration of the facts, the Court held that blocking Yildirim's website was not warranted since there was no connection between the allegedly infringing site and Yildirim's website, but also the block itself was decided on after the recommendations of an administrative body, the Telecommunications Directorate, so was not based on judicial scrutiny. Therefore, it is clear that website

[43] Council of Europe, 'Recommendation of the Committee of Ministers to member States on the roles and responsibilities of internet intermediaries' CM/Rec(2018)2; See also Article 11 of the EU Charter of Fundamental Rights – Freedom of expression

1. Everyone has the right to freedom of expression. This right shall include freedom to hold opinions and to receive and impart information and ideas without interference by public authority and regardless of frontiers. This article shall not prevent States from requiring the licensing of broadcasting, television or cinema enterprises.
2. 'The exercise of these freedoms, since it carries with it duties and responsibilities, may be subject to such formalities, conditions, restrictions or penalties as are prescribed by law and are necessary in a democratic society, in the interests of national security, territorial integrity or public safety, for the prevention of disorder or crime, for the protection of health or morals, for the protection of the reputation or rights of others, for preventing the disclosure of information received in confidence, or for maintaining the authority and impartiality of the judiciary.'

[44] *Ahmet Yildirim v Turkey* (18 December 2012) Application no. 3111/10; for a commentary of the case see globalfreedomofexpression.columbia.edu/cases/ahmed-yildirim-v-turkey/.

[45] European Union, Charter of Fundamental Rights of the European Union, 26 October 2012, 2012/C 326/02.

[46] ibid.

[47] M Husovec, 'Injunctions against Innocent Third Parties: The case of Website Blocking' (2013) 4 *Journal of Intellectual Property, Information Technology and E-Commerce Law* para 40.

[48] ibid para 40.

blocks should stem from a clear legal basis and on the grounds of a thorough assessment by the court.[49] Otherwise, restricting the freedom of expression without any clear legal basis is unnecessary and disproportionate.

Furthermore, the installation of filtering technology might pose serious risks for the protection of users' personal data. This is because, as the Court noted in *Scarlet v Sabam*, 'a filtering system would involve a systematic analysis of all content and the collection and identification of users' IP addresses from which unlawful content on the network is sent'.[50] This means that in the process of filtering, filtering software identifies the IP addresses of users which are considered, according to the prevailing view, to be personal data of the users.[51] This understanding was mirrored in the opinion of the Article 29 Working Party,[52] an independent body of data privacy experts that advises the European Commission on data protection issues.[53] In particular, the Working Party noted that IP addresses are personal data since 'Internet access providers and managers of local area networks can, using reasonable means, identify Internet users to whom they have attributed IP addresses as they normally systematically log a file of the date, time, duration, and dynamic IP address given to the Internet user. The same can be said about Internet Service Providers that keep a logbook on the HTTP server. In these cases, there is no doubt about the fact that one can talk about personal data in the sense of Article 2 a) of the Directive …)'.[54]

The view that IP addresses are considered personal data becomes more relevant in cases where the purpose of IP addresses aims to unveil the identity of primary infringers. There are a number of cases outlining an obligation on ISPs to give all the necessary details to the rights holders in order to attack direct infringers. This has also reached the CJEU, which in its *Promusicae* ruling[55] held that Member States are entitled to request ISPs to unveil the identity of individual infringers who are also users of their networks. In this regard, should Member States decide to allow this possibility, rights holders will be provided with information in order to pursue actions against primary infringements. This has not been without challenge however. In Ireland, for instance, in *EMI V Eircom*,[56] the Irish High Court found that the settlement which had been agreed between record companies and Eircom, an internet service provider, did not infringe privacy and other data protection laws since IP addresses are not personal data and cannot identify the subscribers.[57]

[49] EDRi, 'ECtHR: Blocking Google Sites in Turkey breaches human rights' (19 December 2012) edri.org/our-work/edrigramnumber10-24ecthr-google-blocking-decision-foe/; Dr. Agnes Callamard, ARTICLE 19 Executive Director noted that 'a victory for online freedoms at a time when governments around the world increasingly seek to regulate the Internet'.

[50] CJEU C-70/10 *Scarlet Extended SA v Société belge des auteurs, compositeurs et éditeurs SCRL* (2011) ECR I- 11959.

[51] ibid para 51.

[52] Article 29 Working Party, 'Opinion 4/2007 on the concept of personal data' (WP 136, 20 June 2007) 16.

[53] It is now replaced by the European Data Protection Board.

[54] Recommendations, 'WP 37: Privacy on the Internet – An integrated EU Approach to On-line Data Protection' adopted on 21.11.2000.

[55] CJEU, C-275/06 *Productores de Musica de Espana (Promusicae) v Telefonica de Espana SAU* (2008) ECR I-00271; M Frabboni, 'File-sharing and the role of intermediaries in the marketplace' in I Stamatoudi (ed), *Copyright enforcement and the Internet* (Alphen aan den Rijn, Kluwer Law International, 2010) 132 where she outlines the debate between property versus privacy.

[56] High Court, *EMI v Eircom* [2009] IEHC 411.

[57] T Train, '"Three Strikes" settlement between EMI and Eircom approved by Irish court' (*Weblog of the Journal of Intellectual Property Law and Practice*) jiplp.blogspot.co.uk/2010/08/three-strikes-settlement-between-emi.html.

Finally, filtering technology itself has an 'opaque nature'.[58] This means that, unlike usual practices for censorship that specify the content which should be restricted,[59] automatic filtering does not entail specific guidance on which material should be targeted. This is because, as the Advocate General stressed in his opinion for *Scarlet v Sabam*, in order for filtering to be effective, 'it must be systematic, universal and progressive'.[60] This implies that filtering cannot be targeted or narrowed. Rather, filtering is about the monitoring of all the data that is transmitted through the internet service provider.[61] Yet, this understanding is not compatible with EU Law provisions and mostly it conflicts with Article 15 of the ECD which prohibits general monitoring obligations. Moreover, the opaque nature of filtering enables manufacturers of filtering technology to control which information can reach the end-users and which cannot.[62] For instance, it has been reported that in Saudi Arabia the filtering software Smart Filter has blocked access to websites with non-pornographic gay material. After severe criticism from human rights organisations, the Saudi Arabian government abolished the unreasonable blocking and permitted access to these websites.[63] Thus, the opaque nature of filtering leaves space for potential abuses which could be used by states or private entities in order to satisfy their own interests.

What is more, these obligations must be undertaken indiscriminately by all host ISPs. This means that commercial as well as non-commercial host ISPs must either enter into licence agreements or deploy filtering technologies. As mentioned earlier, the obligation to enter into licensing agreements is non-feasible. For this reason, host ISPs might resort to filtering mechanisms. However, to force non-commercial ISPs to apply filtering technology might have a corrosive effect on their business welfare. For instance, the non-profit website Wikipedia, which lacks any financial resources to either develop its own technology in-house, or to license filtering technology from others, would be forced to terminate its business.[64]

Finally, Article 13 of the EU Commission Proposal encourages the cooperation between rights holders and host ISPs. For instance, it urges providers to inform rights holders for the functioning of the agreements. In case they do not enter into agreement, they will cooperate with host ISPs to develop best practices to tackle infringement online. However, such cooperation might prompt reflection on the methods that would be agreed between rights holders and host ISPs[65] and whether such methods would

[58] TJ McIntyre and C Scott, 'Internet Filtering: Rhetoric, Legitimacy, Accountability and Responsibility' in R Brownsword and K Yeung (eds), *Regulating Technologies: Legal Futures, Regulatory Frames and Technological Fixes* (Oxford, Hart Publishing, 2008).

[59] ibid.

[60] Case C-70/10, Opinion of AG Cruz Villalon on *Scarlet Extended SA v Société Belge des auteurs compositeurs et éditeurs (SABAM)* (2011) ECLI:EU:C:2011:255, para 48.

[61] C Angelopoulos, 'Filtering the Internet for copyrighted content in Europe' (2009) *Legal Observations of the European Audiovisual Observatory* 3.

[62] McIntyre and Scott (n 58) 3.

[63] N Villeneuve, 'The Filtering Matrix: Integrated Mechanisms of Information Control and the demarcation of borders in cyberspace' (*First Monday*, 2006) 11, firstmonday.org/ojs/index.php/fm/article/view/1307.

[64] G Sartori, 'Providers liability: From the ECD to the Future: In depth analysis for the IMCO Committee' (2017) IMCO Committee 14, www.europarl.europa.eu/RegData/etudes/IDAN/2017/614179/IPOL_IDA(2017)614179_EN.pdf.

[65] U Carsten, 'Standards for Duty of Care? Debating Intermediary Liability from a Sectoral Perspective' (2017) 8 *Journal of Intellectual Property, Information Technology and E-Commerce Law* 116; E Bonadio, 'File Sharing, Copyright and Freedom of Speech' (2011) 33 *European Intellectual Property Review* 628 where

be 'one-sided', and thus would not take into consideration the fundamental rights of internet users.

B. Council's Text for the Copyright in the Digital Single Market Directive (DSMD)

The Council's text of 25 May, 2018 follows the pathway of the European Commission's Proposal, but with a few problematic amendments on board.[66]

Firstly, Article 13 of the Council's compromised text deviates from the definition of host ISPs.[67] Instead, it uses the term online content sharing service providers (OCSSPs).[68] Such a term, however, is a novelty for the online world and marks a shift from the definition of host ISPs which is enshrined in the ECD. As per the ECD, host ISPs are online marketplaces, social networks and blogs, and are, broadly speaking, all those providers who offer hosting services to users' content. However, under the definition of content sharing providers, only those providers who store and provide access to content are included. Such providers are those profit-based providers such as Facebook, YouTube, and Google. In contrast, Wikipedia and other non-profit websites are excluded from the scope of OCSSPs.[69]

Further, the Council's text endorses primary liability rules for OCSSPs. This is because it notes, 'Member States shall provide that an online content sharing service provider performs an act of communication to the public or an act of making available to the public when it gives the public access to copyright protected works or other protected subject matter uploaded by its users.' This means that OCSSPs will be liable for any infringing material their users' upload without having the defence of knowledge. This is because knowledge is a requirement for the establishment of secondary liability, not primary liability. Yet, as a corollary to the introduction of primary liability rules, a paradox might emerge. Two different regimes occur, which might create confusion for the parties involved. For instance, consider when a right holder initiates legal proceedings against an OCSSP for copyright infringement within its platform.

E Bonadio argues that 'the "transformation" of ISPs into copyright enforcement agents is probably a consequence of a quid pro quo strategy. There are signals that ISPs act as entertainment industry enforcement agents in exchange for them acquiring the right to transmit copyright holders' programmes over their internet networks' in; at US level, A Bridy, 'Graduated Response and the Turn to Private Ordering in Online Copyright Enforcement' (2010) 89 *Oregon Law Review* 101 where Bridy found that 'In 2005, the same year the Eighth Circuit decided Charter, Verizon entered into an agreement with Disney to forward notices of infringement, in return for which it received the right to transmit certain Disney programming over its network' in; See also N Anderson, 'Verizon to forward RIAA warning letters (but that's all) Verizon looks set to forward RIAA copyright infringement notices to its …' (*Arstechnica*, 13 November 2009) arstechnica.com/tech-policy/2009/11/verizon-to-forward-riaa-warning-letters-but-thats-all/.

[66] For the full text of Article 13 of the Council text for the Copyright in the Digital Single Market Directive see Appendix II.

[67] For the full Council text on DSMD see Appendix II.

[68] Hereinafter OCSSPs.

[69] V Moscon, 'The Council Negotiating Position on Article 13: Warning, Creators are also Part of the Game!!!' (*Kluwer copyright blog*, 4 July 2018) copyrightblog.kluweriplaw.com/2018/07/04/council-negotiating-position-article-13-warning-creators-also-part-game/.

On the one hand, OCSSPs might argue that under the e-commerce framework they were exonerated from liability since they did not have knowledge of the illicit activity, while rights holders under the DSMD might argue that OCSSPs are still liable since knowledge is not a requirement for primary liability.[70]

However, in order to avoid primary liability, OCSSPs must take authorisation from rights holders. By taking this authorisation through the conclusion of agreements, users would benefit since their activities would no longer amount to copyright infringement. However, as already discussed in the European Commission Proposal, taking authorisation for all copyrighted works seems impossible. This is because rights clearance licences provided by collecting societies cover only works from their members, not those works from non-members. In this sense, there would always be an option for holding OCSSPs liable since the licence cannot cover all types of content users upload on their platforms.[71]

If no such authorisation is given, the Council's text notes that OCSSPs can escape liability if they fulfil the following requirement. They must demonstrate either that they made their best effort to prevent the availability of infringing works within their platforms, or that they have acted expeditiously and removed it upon being notified. However, when it comes to the interpretation of the term 'best effort', one might wonder what that constitutes and, in particular, what kind of measures OCSSPs must deploy.

Further, Article 13 of the Council's text specifies that the measures which must be deployed shall be effective and proportionate, and that for this to occur a number of factors must be taken into consideration. In particular, 'the size and the nature of the services' provided by the online content sharing provider, 'the amount and type of uploaded works', and 'the availability and costs'. While this understanding seems reasonable, it can only be assessed case by case. For this reason, legal uncertainty may arise.

What is more, the provision notes that such measures shall be defined by rights holders and OCSSPs so that they function effectively. However, as already discussed in the EU Commission Proposal, the cooperation between OCSSPs might result in one-sided methods, thus subordinating the rights of internet users. This understanding is aggravated by the fact that the measures will be economically affordable and effective for the OCSSPs. This provision might lead to the use of cheap and limited efficiency filtering technology that might be prone to a high margin of error, and thus lead to over-blocking of lawful content.

In order to appeal the blocking of legitimate content, users can resort to the complaints and redress mechanisms offered by the OCSSPs. Following the line of the EU Commission's Proposal, the Council's text encourages the establishment of complaints and redress mechanisms as well.[72] Yet, here it could be argued that self-regulatory measures do not always guarantee the fundamental rights of users. For instance, it has been

[70] Frosio (n 12) 352.

[71] M Senftleben, 'Bermuda Triangle – Licensing, Filtering and Privileging User-Generated Content Under the New Directive on Copyright in the Digital Single Market' (2019) *Vrije Universitat* 3.

[72] See Appendix II.

found that YouTube's complaints dispute procedure can last up to one month, thus leaving users in legal uncertainty about their rights.[73]

Finally, the Council's text suggests the establishment of independent bodies. Such independent bodies will be in charge of evaluating complaints with regard to the measures OCSSPs have deployed in order to prevent the availability of infringing material within their platforms. However, while the creation of an independent authority would be welcome, this shift from judicial control to administrative control might prompt reflections on the legitimacy and accountability of this authority since the principles under which the it functions are not clearly carved out.

C. EU Parliament's Text for the Copyright in the Digital Single Market Directive

In similar fashion, the EU Parliament's compromised Text adopts the same approach with the Council, with few amendments.[74] Following its rejection as a result of the first vote in July 2018, the EU Parliament voted again in September 2018 in its plenary session in Strasbourg. This time 438 MEPS voted in favour of the DSMD, with 226 against.[75]

Thus, the EU Parliament's text redeploys the language of the Council's text and notes that OCSSPs perform an action of communication and, therefore, they should conclude licensing agreements. Again bringing forward primary liability rules, the EU Parliament confirms the seismic shift from secondary liability norms to primary liability rules for host ISPs' activities as this has also been observed in the Council's text.

The EU Parliament's text continues by noting that if OCSSPs do not wish to conclude licensing agreements with rights holders, then they shall cooperate with rights holders to prevent the availability of copyright infringing works within their networks.[76] In order to do so, they shall decide methods which must be compatible with fundamental rights, do not restrict lawful content from being available, and avoid the use of automated blocking mechanisms. Yet, one might wonder what practices will be decided on between rights holders and OCSSPs in order to tackle the circulation of infringing material within their networks. As explained earlier, in the Council's text, practices defined between industry representatives and OCSSPs might be biased towards the interests of rights holders and providers, thus undermining users' interests.

[73] A Bridy and D Keller, 'U.S. Copyright Office Section 512 Study: Comments in Response to Notice of Inquiry' (30 March 2016) 18, available at cyberlaw.stanford.edu/publications/us-copyright-office-section-512-study-comments-response-notice-inquiry.

[74] For the full text of Article 17 of the EU Parliament for a Copyright Directive in the Digital Single Market see Appendix III.

[75] N Bernal, 'EU Parliament approves sweeping digital copyright reforms' *The Telegraph* (12 September 2018) www.telegraph.co.uk/technology/2018/09/12/eu-parliament-approves-sweeping-copyright-reforms-reshape-internet/.

[76] See Appendix III, IV.

Moreover, following the Council's text, the EU Parliament's text encourages a self-regulatory approach by addressing the establishment of effective redress mechanisms where users can submit their complaints in case their content has been unreasonably removed. Such complaints will be dealt with without delay and be subject to human review. Here, however, it is possible to add that the review of all complaints by users will require a high number of employees with expertise knowledge in copyright law, which in turn will give rise to the transaction costs of online service providers. Yet, this review of complaints will be in accordance with the General Data Protection Regulation (GDPR)[77] which prohibits any inaccurate and non-proportionate processing of personal data.[78]

Finally, Member States shall establish an independent body for disputes, as well as provide an alternative resolution mechanism for users whose rights have been violated by the measures adopted by OCSSPs. However, as already observed, it is crucial to specify the principles under which this independent body will operate with a view to enhancing the legitimacy of its decisions. Otherwise, such an independent body will lack legitimacy.

Hence, it seems that the EU Parliament's text of the DSMD includes the problematic features that have already been identified in the previous texts of the EU Commission and the Council.

Yet, in order to finalise the definitive text of the DSMD, the following step in the legislative process is the dialogue between the three main European Institutions, ie, the EU Commission, the EU Parliament, and the Council. Thus, after the EU Parliament's vote on its compromised text in September 2018, dialogue began. However, due to the severe controversy that revolved around this Directive, instead of them lasting four months, as initially planned, they lasted until March. It was in February 2019 when these three Institutions compromised and finalised the ultimate draft of the DSMD which was passed by the EU Parliament in its plenary session in Strasbourg in March 2019; 348 EU Parliamentarians voted in favour, 274 against.

Overall, it could be extrapolated that the EU Commission's Proposal and the texts of the Council and the EU Parliament have raised problematic aspects. These relate to the introduction of primary liability rules for OCSSPs, the creation of a specific category of host ISPs, the imposition of monitoring obligations, licensing requirements, and the creation of self-redress mechanisms operated by OCSSPs in case of complaints by their users. Unsurprisingly, as demonstrated below, many of these problematic aspects are to be found in the final draft of Article 17 of the DSMD. They are critically assessed in the following section to underline the need for the legal reform that is presented in Part III of this book. This examination provides a discussion of the flaws in Article 17 of the DSMD which address the OCSSPs' liability for copyright infringements.

[77] Council Regulation (EU) 2016/679 of the European Parliament and of the Council of 27 April 2016 on the protection of natural persons with regard to the processing of personal data and on the free movement of such data, and repealing Directive 95/46/EC (2016) OJ L 119 (hereinafter GDPR).

[78] G Buttarelli, 'Comments of the European Data Protection Supervisor on Article 13 of the proposal for a directive of the European Parliament and of the Council on copyright in the Digital Single Market' (3 July 2018) edps.europa.eu/sites/edp/files/publication/18-07-03_cover_letter_comments_copyright_en.pdf.

III. Article 17 of the DSMD: Problematic Features

Recital 64 of the DSMD notes, 'It is appropriate to clarify in this Directive that online content-sharing service providers perform an act of communication to the public or of making available to the public when they give the public access to copyright protected works or other protected subject matter uploaded by their users.' This means that one of the underlying objectives of Article 17 of the DSMD[79] is to provide clarification on the existing *EU acquis* that deals with ISPs' liability. However, instead of clarifying it, Article 17 makes fundamental amendments to the law. Indeed, Bridy points out that the DSMD 'changes the rules of the game'.[80]

This is because Article 17 deviates from the existing liability regime of ISPs and introduces not only new liability rules, but also an array of amendments that create legal uncertainties and are highly controversial. As demonstrated below, the final text of Article 17 (previously named Article 13 in the EU Commission's Proposal, Council's and EU Parliament's texts) follows the same rationale of the compromised texts. In particular, in some stances it adopts the same wording while other controversial aspects identified in the compromised texts have been reduced due to the high controversy that revolved around them.

In light of this, the following section aims to identify and critically assess the problematic aspects of Article 17 of the DSMD. Features include the new definition of OCSSPs, the introduction of primary liability rules, the option of OCSSPs to conclude a licence agreement with rights holders, the option of OCSSPs to demonstrate that they made their best effort to terminate any illicit activity within their networks, the provision which addresses the prohibition of general monitoring obligations, and the creation of redress mechanisms for online disputes with regard to copyright infringements.

A. The New Definition of Online Content Sharing Service Providers (OCSSPs)

The first problematic feature of Article 17 of the DSMD is that it introduces a new definition for those ISPs that host copyright content online into the regulatory framework of ISPS. Following the definition that has been used in the Council's and EU Parliament's texts, and abandoning the definition which has been adopted in the EC's Proposal, this new type of host ISP is called an Online Content Sharing Service Provider (OCSSP), which seems to be a sub-set of host ISPs as set forth in Article 14(1) of the ECD. Falling under the scope of OCSSPs are popular music-exchange platforms such as YouTube, Vimeo, Dailymotion, and Instagram, as well as any platform where users can upload content online. This understanding has been clearly illustrated in Recital 62 of the DSMD which narrows the scope of the OCSSPs to those whose services are 'to store and enable users to upload and share a large amount of copyright-protected content

[79] For the full text of Article 17 of the DSMD see Appendix V.

[80] A Bridy, 'The Price of Closing the "Value Gap": How the Music Industry Hacked EU Copyright Reform' (2020) 22 *Vanderbilt Journal of Entertainment & Technology Law* 358.

with the purpose of obtaining profit therefrom, either directly or indirectly, by organizing it and promoting it in order to attract a larger audience, including by categorizing it and using targeted promotion within it'.[81]

This, of course, does not mean that all online platforms that host content fall within the scope of Recital 62. Rather, certain platforms are excluded from the scope of OCSSPs; indeed, non-profit platforms, online marketplaces, and cloud services do not fall within its scope. Thus, as per Article 2(6) of the DSMD,

> Providers of services, such as not-for-profit online encyclopedias, not-for-profit educational and scientific repositories, open source software-developing and sharing platforms, electronic communication service providers as defined in Directive (EU) 2018/1972, online marketplaces, business-to-business cloud services and cloud services that allow users to upload content for their own use, are not 'online content-sharing service providers' within the meaning of this Directive.[82]

Otherwise, Article 17 would include all the host ISPs that fall under the scope of Article 14(1) of the ECD and, in this sense, two provisions at the European level would regulate the same types of host ISPs with a different legal system.[83] What is more, the non-exclusion of certain host ISPs from the scope of Article 17 would supersede the aim of the DSMD, which is to close the value gap between creators and host ISPs.[84] This would imply that host ISPs that are not connected with the music or film industry sector would fall under the regime of Article 17, and this would pose serious threats to their business model. For instance, if Wikipedia, a non-profit platform, fell under the scope of Article 17, it would be forced to shut down its business since it would be impossible for a non-profit platform to access the resources needed to prevent the posting of unlawful content, while at the same time it would be impossible to pay damages to the relevant rights holders in the event of violation being established.

Interestingly, whilst the exclusion from the scope of OCSSPs non-profit platforms, such as Wikipedia, and open source software platforms seems sensible,[85] it raises the question as to why cyber lockers, online marketplaces, and cloud services do not fall under the scope of OCSSPs since they also give access to copyrighted content. For example, online marketplaces, such as Amazon and eBay, offer tangible as well as non-tangible goods to their online consumers. Non-tangible goods are understood as online seminars or eBooks which are offered by online marketplaces and can be viewed as YouTube videos.[86] In addition, with regard to cloud services, although the main

[81] Recital 62 of Council Directive (EU) 2019/790 of the European Parliament and of the Council of 17 April 2019 on copyright and related rights in the Digital Single Market and amending Directives 96/9/EC and 2001/29/EC.

[82] Council Directive (EU) 2019/790 of the European Parliament and of the Council of 17 April 2019 on copyright and related rights in the Digital Single Market and amending Directives 96/9/EC and 2001/29/EC.

[83] Bridy (n 80) 339.

[84] Frosio and Mendis (n 12) 21.

[85] See ch 4.

[86] M Husovec, 'Compromising (on) the Digital Single Market? A Quick Look at the Estonian Presidency Proposal(s) on Art 13' (*Kluwer copyright blog*, 8 September 2017) copyrightblog.kluweriplaw.com/2017/09/08/compromising-digital-single-market-quick-look-estonian-presidency-proposals-art-13/.

function of cloud service providers is to store material online, they can also give access to copyright-protected content by providing links via Dropbox files.[87]

Finally, the need to introduce a new definition for OCSSPs could be questioned since there has been no criticism or concern raised regarding the definition of host ISPs as set forth in Article 14(1) of the ECD. For instance, to my knowledge, the outcomes of the European Commission's Public Consultation on the Review of European Copyright rules raised problematic issues that revolve around online regulation, but it seems that the relevant stakeholders did not argue that a need for a new definition for host ISPs was required.[88] Likewise, the outcomes of the Public Consultation on e-commerce did not demonstrate any need for amending or introducing a new definition for host ISPs.[89] In contrast, they focused on the need for legal reform with regard to liability rules that regulate ISPs' online activities by noting that the 'liability regime introduced in Section IV of the ECD (Articles 12–15) has proven not fit for purpose or has negatively affected market level playing field'.[90] Finally, the summary of the outcomes of the Public Consultation on the modernisation of IPR enforcement did not include the importance of the need for a new definition for ISPs.[91] In contrast, many stakeholders argued that the introduction of a new definition might create inconsistency with the definition set forth in Article 14(1) of the ECD, and thus lead to legal uncertainty.

Therefore, the introduction of a new type of host ISPs, namely OCSSPs, might prompt reflections among rights holders and host ISPs as to which host ISPs fall within its scope. The question may be raised as to what would happen if a host ISP does not qualify as an OCSSP but its services fall within the scope of Article 17 of the DSMD, in addition to the practical necessity for the introduction of this new type of host ISP.

B. The Introduction of Primary Liability Rules

Another problematic feature of Article 17 of the DSMD is the introduction of primary liability rules for this new type of host ISPs, the so called OCSSPs. Following the EU Commission's Proposal and EU Parliament's texts, this understanding was reiterated in the final text of the DSMD. So, Article 17 confirms the departure from secondary to primary liability rules by noting, 'Member States shall provide that an online content-sharing service provider performs an act of communication to the public or an act of making available to the public for the purposes of this Directive when it gives the public

[87] ibid.

[88] European Commission, 'Report on the responses to the Public Consultation on the Review of the EU Copyright Rules', Directorate General Internal Market and Services, Directorate D – Intellectual property, D1 – Copyright (July 2014).

[89] ibid.

[90] European Commission, 'Summary of the results of the Public Consultation on the future of electronic commerce in the Internal Market and the implementation of the Directive on electronic commerce (2000/31/EC)' (2010).

[91] European Commission, 'Public Consultation on the evaluation and modernisation of the legal framework for the enforcement of intellectual property rights: Summary of responses' (2016).

access to copyright-protected works or other protected subject matter uploaded by its users.'[92] As per Article 3 of the InfoSoc Directive,[93] communication to the public constitutes primary infringement. Therefore, OCSSPs commit a primary infringement by carrying out acts of communication to the public.

This new provision signals a landmark shift from the traditional legal regime for host ISPs which is dictated under Article 14(1) of the ECD. As per Article 14(1)(a), host ISPs can escape liability if they have not become, or are not made to become, aware of the illicit activity. This means that knowledge is a requisite element in order to attribute liability rules to host ISPs. In contrast, primary liability rules, which are now endorsed in Article 17 of the DSMD do not require the element of knowledge. So, under Article 17 OCSSPs are held liable for any copyright infringement that might take place on their networks without being aware they exist.

The new liability regime under Article 17, however, conflicts with secondary tortious liability theories which are the legal basis upon which the ISPs' regulatory framework has been developed. Given that OCSSPs are a sub-set of host ISPs, this conflict applies to host ISPs as well. Secondary tortious liability theories, as presented in chapter two, are the main theoretical underpinning for ascribing liability rules to host ISPs for the actions of their users. Such theories support the point that there may be moral or utilitarian reasons[94] for host ISPs to be held liable for enabling the circulation of infringing content within their networks. However, secondary liability rules might arise only if host ISPs are aware of the infringing content that is disseminated within their networks. What is more, these theories constitute the main tool that offers a safe harbour to host ISPs and boosts e-commerce in its infancy.[95] Without secondary liability rules, it would be doubtful that European host ISPs could compete with their American rivals since the relevant legislative tool, the DMCA, dictates that OCSSPs can be held liable only under the specific condition of having knowledge of the infringing content online.

Nevertheless, while primary liability rules seem to contradict secondary tortious liability, upon which the rationale of host ISPs' regulatory framework has been developed, there is a line of case law that reiterates the trend towards primary liability rules for host ISPs. Indeed, at both European and national level, a number of courts imposed primary liability on ISPs for hyperlinking unauthorised content.[96] Interestingly, although the line of case law addresses hyperlinking cases, the trend towards primary liability rules could be applied more broadly. To put it more clearly, the trend towards primary liability can be equally applied to cases where material is circulated within online platforms without the permission of the creators.

[92] Directive (EU) 2019/790 of the European Parliament and of the Council of 17 April 2019 on copyright and related rights in the Digital Single Market and amending Directives 96/9/EC and 2001/29/EC.

[93] Council Directive (EC) 2001/29 on the harmonisation of certain aspects of copyright and related rights in the information society (2001) O.J. L 167 (Hereinafter InfoSoc Directive).

[94] See ch 2 section II(A) 1, 2.

[95] Frosio and Mendis (n 12) 5.

[96] JP Quintais, 'Untangling the hyperlinking web: In search of the online right of communication to the public' (2018) 21 *The Journal of World Intellectual Property* 408.

At European level, this judicial trend began with the *Svensson*[97] case in 2014, it continued with the *GS Media*[98] case in 2016, and in the *Brein v Ziggo*[99] case in 2017.[100] In all three cases, under the umbrella of communication to the public as per Article 3 of the InfoSoc Directive,[101] the CJEU endorsed primary liability rules for host ISPs which redirect users via hyperlinks to unauthorised content.

In particular, the *Svensson* case,[102] which was a referral from the Stockholm District Court, addressed a dispute between Retriever Sverige, which was a website that redirected its users via links to articles published on the websites of journals, and a number of journalists. The thorny question that the CJEU was asked to examine was whether hyperlinking constitutes an act of communication to the public within the meaning of Article 3(1) of the InfoSoc Directive. After a careful examination of the facts, the CJEU concluded that hyperlinking constitutes communication to the public if two requirements are fulfilled, namely, if there is an act of communication and if there is a new public. The concept of a new public, as the CJEU noted, addresses the public that the right holder has not included in the initial transmission of her work. Therefore, if those two cumulative requirements are to be fulfilled, a host ISP can be held primarily liable for copyright infringement.

Such a stance was maintained in the *GS Media* ruling[103] where the CJEU went two steps further by adding two more requirements in order to find a host ISP primarily liable for providing hyperlinks with unauthorised content. This case was about a dispute between Sanoma, the publisher of *Playboy Magazine* and GS Media, a lifestyle website which contained hyperlinks that redirected internet users to third parties' websites where nude pictures of a Dutch celebrity had been placed prior to their official release in the *Playboy Magazine*. In this case too, the problematic question was whether hyperlinking constitutes an act of communication to the public. Following the *Svensson* ruling,[104] the CJEU responded in a positive way but added two further requirements. According to the Court's reasoning, hyperlinking constitutes an act of communication to the public if it is an act of communication to a new public and the host ISP knows the illegal nature of the link if it operates on a commercial basis.[105]

This outcome implies that the profit-making motive plays a fundamental role in whether the link provider is primarily liable for hyperlinking unauthorised content.

[97] Case C-466/12 *Nils Svensson and Others v Retriever Sverige AB* (2014) ECLI:EU:C:2014:76.

[98] Case C-160/15 *GS Media BV v Sanoma Media Netherlands BV and Others* (2016) ECLI:EU:C:2016:644.

[99] Case C-610/15 *Stichting Brein v Ziggo BV and XS4ALL Internet BV* (2017) ECLI:EU:C:2017:456.

[100] Meticulous analysis of the three cases in ch 4 section III(B); see also E Papadaki, 'Hyperlinking, making available and copyright infringement: lessons from European national courts' (2017) 8 *European Journal of Law and Technology* 2–14.

[101] Council Directive (EC) 2001/29 on the harmonisation of certain aspects of copyright and related rights in the information society (2001) O.J. L 167.

[102] Case C-466/12 *Nils Svensson and Others v Retriever Sverige AB* (2014) ECLI:EU:C:2014:76; A Ohly, 'The broad concept of "communication to the public" in recent CJEU judgments and the liability of intermediaries: primary, secondary or unitary liability?' (2018) 13 *Journal of Intellectual Property Law and Practice* 670.

[103] C-160/15 *GS Media BV v Sanoma Media Netherlands BV and Others* (2015) ECLI:EU:C:2016:644.

[104] *Nils Svensson and Others v Retriever Sverige AB*, C-466/12, ECLI:EU:C:2014:76.

[105] T Rendas, 'How Playboy Photos Compromised EU Copyright Law: The GS Media Judgment' (2017) 20 *Journal of Internet Law* 11; E Rosati, 'GS Media and Its Implications for the Construction of the Right of Communication to the Public within EU Copyright Architecture' (2017) 54 *Common Market Law Review* 1242.

Therefore, if the link provider does not run on a commercial basis, knowledge of the illicit activity is not presumed.[106] This means that linking is not a primary infringement, thus the link provider is not liable for a primary copyright infringement.

A contrario, if the posting of hyperlinks is carried out for profit, it can be expected that the link provider knows the possible lack of consent of the right holder, thus this amounts to an act of communication to the public. This is because the CJEU noted that if the posting of links pursues financial gains, then the link provider 'should carry out the checks necessary to ensure that the work concerned is not illegally published. Therefore, it must be presumed that that posting has been done with the full knowledge of the protected nature of the work and of the possible lack of the copyright holder's consent to publication on the internet'.[107] Hence, in this case, hyperlinking amounts to an unauthorised act of communication to the public, unless the lifestyle website can prove that it does not pursue financial gains.

In similar fashion, the CJEU in the *Brein v Ziggo* case confirmed the requirements set out in the *GS Media* case.[108] This case, a referral from the Dutch Supreme Court, was about a dispute between Sichting Brein, an anti-piracy association, that brought legal proceedings against Ziggo, an internet access service provider, requesting Ziggo to block access to Pirate Bay. Here again, the difficult question that the CJEU had to examine was whether hyperlinking constitutes an act of communication to the public within the meaning of Article 3(1) of the InfoSoc Directive. Following the line of reasoning in the *Svensson* and *GS Media* cases, the CJEU held that hyperlinking constitutes an act of communication to the public, thus the operators of Pirate Bay might be held primarily liable since 'by making that platform available and managing it, provide their users with access to the works concerned … They can therefore be regarded as playing an essential role in making the works in question available'.[109]

Unsurprisingly, all three rulings have been the subject of heated debate. Many commentators have argued that the rulings are controversial. This is because they not only give a new interpretation to hyperlinking since they equate the act of linking to the act of communication to the public,[110] but also because they introduce primary liability

[106] Case C-160/15 *GS Media V Sanoma Media Netherlands BV and Others* (2016) ECLI:EU:C:2016:644, paras 47–48; Rosati (n 105) 1229.

[107] Case C-160/15 *GS Media V Sanoma Media Netherlands BV and Others* (2016) ECLI:EU:C:2016:644, para 51.

[108] C Angelopoulos, 'CJEU Decision on Ziggo: The Pirate Bay Communicates Works to the Public' (*Kluwer copyright blog*, 30 June 2017) copyrightblog.kluweriplaw.com/2017/06/30/cjeu-decision-ziggo-pirate-bay-communicates-works-public/; C Angelopoulos, 'AG Szpunar in Stichting Brein v Ziggo: An Indirect Harmonisation of Indirect Liability' (*Kluwer copyright blog*, 23 March 2017) copyrightblog.kluweriplaw.com/2017/03/23/ag-szpunar-stichting-brein-v-ziggo-indirect-harmonisation-indirect-liability/.

[109] Case C-610/15 *Stichting Brein v Ziggo BV and XS4ALL Internet BV* (2017) ECLI:EU:C:2017:456, para 37.

[110] Case C-160/15 *GS Media* V Sanoma Media Netherlands BV and Others (2016) ECLI:EU:C:2016:644, para 45: 'In that regard, it should be noted that the internet is in fact of particular importance to freedom of expression and of information, safeguarded by Article 11 of the Charter, and that hyperlinks contribute to its sound operation as well as to the exchange of opinions and information in that network characterised by the availability of immense amounts of information.'; Rosati (n 105) 1229; see also M Leistner, 'Intermediary liability in a global world' in T Synodinou (ed), *Pluralism and Universalism in international copyright law* (Alphen aan den Rijn, Kluwer Law International, 2019) 488 where he argues that this controversy has restricted the spread of the presumption of knowledge at national level and gives the example of Germany where 'accordingly, the German Federal Court of Justice has refused to apply the presumption to frame links containing Google's image search function, since the social utility of such search services as well as their automated, passive mass character precluded a presumption of specific knowledge'.

rules for hyperlinking that can also be applicable to any copyright infringement online. The latter concerns, which are relevant to the core of this book, have been confirmed with the DSMD that endorses a primary liability regime for OCSSPs for copyright infringements committed by their users.

Here, it is worthy of mention that the trend of primary liability rules to OCSSPs for copyright violations within their networks has influenced the trade mark context as well. In particular, Advocate General Campos Sanchez-Bordona has opined, in *Coty v Germany*,[111] that Amazon can be held primarily liable for trade mark violations within its networks. This is because Amazon is involved in the distribution of fake goods since it offers its premises for their storage. For this reason, the online market place, as the Advocate General points out, is reasonably expected to identify the pirated goods and prevent their circulation.[112] Yet, while the CJEU did not follow the opinion of the Advocate General,[113] his opinion nonetheless gives a hint of the potential impact of the new DSMD on trade mark infringements which are ruled under the ECD, as already discussed in chapter three.[114]

What is more, this new type of liability rules for OCSSPs have raised long term discussions among prominent scholars. These discussions surround the legal uncertainties that revolve around the introduction of primary liability rules for OCSSPs and their parallel force to the secondary liability regime as set forth in Article 14(1) of the ECD. In this vein, many scholars argue that Article 17 of the DSMD is considered a *lex specialis* for Article 14(1) of the ECD.[115] This means that if Article 17 of the DSMD does not apply, for instance because the host ISP is an online market retailer, Article 14 of the ECD continues to apply. Therefore, Article 14(1) of the ECD is the general rule and covers a wide spectrum of ISPs that host and store content online. Should the host ISPs provide services similar to those that are provided by YouTube, Dailymotion, or Vevo, and are not those that are explicitly excluded pursuant to Article 2(6) of the DSMD,[116] then Article 17 of the DSMD applies.

Further, other scholars argue that Article 17 of the DSMD constitutes a *sui generis* communication to the public right.[117] This means that Article 17 introduces a new communication to the public right that does not share common elements with the right to communication to the public as enshrined in Article 3 of the InfoSoc Directive. Indeed, Husovec points out that 'the newly constituted exclusive right is a communication to the public right only in name'.[118]

This is because pursuant to Article 3 of the InfoSoc Directive, 'Member States shall provide authors with the exclusive right to authorise or prohibit any communication

[111] C- 567/18 *Coty Germany v Amazon*, Opinion of the Advocate General (2019) ECLI:EU:C:2019:1031.

[112] ibid para 84.

[113] C-567/18 *Coty Germany GmbH v Amazon Services Europe Sàrl and Others* (2020) ECLI:EU:C:2020:267.

[114] Article 14(1) of the ECD addresses the liability of host ISPs in the form of secondary liability rules.

[115] JP Quintais, 'The New Copyright Directive: A tour d'horizon- Part II (of press publishers, upload filters and the real value gap)' (*Kluwer Copyright Blog*, 17 June 2019) copyrightblog.kluweriplaw.com/2019/06/17/the-new-copyright-directive-a-tour-dhorizon-part-ii-of-press-publishers-upload-filters-and-the-real-value-gap/.

[116] Council Directive (EU) 2019/790 of the European Parliament and of the Council of 17 April 2019 on copyright and related rights in the Digital Single Market and amending Directives 96/9/EC and 2001/29/EC.

[117] Husovec (n 12) 536.

[118] ibid.

to the public of their works, by wire or wireless means, including the making available to the public of their works in such a way that members of the public may access them from a place and at a time individually chosen by them.'[119] This means that the alleged infringer may be held primarily liable if she broadcasts the work and makes the work available to the public who can access it at a specific place and time chosen by them.

By contrast, communication to the public under Article 17 of the DSMD does not require the act of making the work available to the public. Rather, the communication to the public under Article 17 of the DSMD is fulfilled 'by the legal presumption of the provision'.[120] This means that an infringement of communication to the public takes place if this act is committed by an OCSSP. Therefore, this implies that OCSSPs are subject to primary liability rules which are triggered from a new communication to the public right that applies in parallel with the right of communication to the public under Article 3 of the InfoSoc Directive.[121]

However, in order to offer a solid interpretation of the legal relationship between Article 17 of the DSMD and Article 3 of the InfoSoc Directive, the European Commission in its Guidance on 4 June 2021 clarified that 'Article 17 is a lex specialis to Article 3 of Directive 2001/29/EC and Article 14 of Directive 2000/31/EC. It does not introduce a new right in the Union's copyright law'.[122] This means that Article 17 does not represent a new right to communication to the public. Rather, it operates under the umbrella of Article 3 of the InfoSoc Directive and therefore introduces primary liability to OCSSPs that communicate a work to the public without prior permission of the creator.

In order to escape from primary liability rules, Article 17 of the DSMD provides two possibilities for OCSSPs. As per Article 17(2)(3), OCSSPs must either seek the authorisation of rights holders by concluding licensing agreements with them with regard to the use of their works, or make their best effort to terminate the dissemination of unlawful content within their networks. Both requirements, which are discussed below, seem to be contested areas as to how they should be construed in order for OCSSPs to avoid liability for the copyright infringements that their users have committed within their networks.

C. The Possibility for OCSSPs to Conclude a Licence

Following the wording of the EU Commission's Proposal, as well as the texts of the Council and the EU Parliament, the final text of Article 17 of the DSMD envisages

[119] Council Directive (EC) 2001/29 on the harmonisation of certain aspects of copyright and related rights in the information society (2001) O.J. L 167.

[120] Husovec (n 12) 536

[121] ibid.

[122] European Commission, 'Communication on the Guidance on Article 17 of Directive 2019/790 on Copyright in the Digital Single Market' (2021) COM/2021/288 final 2; see also for criticism on the Guidance provided by the European Commission. C Geiger and JB Jütte, 'The EU Commission's Guidance on Article 17 of the Copyright in the Digital Single Market Directive – A Guide to Virtue in Content Moderation by Digital Platforms?' (2021) *European Intellectual Property Review* 1; The criticism is mainly focused on the lack of safeguards for internet users' fundamental rights. For instance, the earmarking of works by rights holders seems to lead to opposite results and thus undermine users' free speech. In particular, the authors note that the Guidance '… does not depart from a system based on monitoring and automated filtering and thus is likely to fail protecting fundamental rights in an appropriate manner'.

the introduction of a licensing system. This constitutes another problematic feature of Article 17 which places licensing as a default rule for host ISPs in order to exonerate them from liability for copyright infringements that accrue within their platforms. More specifically, Article 17(2) notes,

> Member states shall provide that when an authorisation has been obtained, including via a licensing agreement, by an online content sharing service provider, this authorisation shall also cover acts carried out by users of the services falling within Article 3 of the Directive 2001/29/EC when they are not acting on a commercial basis or their activity does not generate significant revenues.

This implies that a licensing system constitutes the main way for OCSSPs to avoid liability, thus they must adopt it in their business model. A failure to license content that is disseminated via their networks might result in liability of OCSSPs.[123]

However, this emphasis on a licensing system might be complex[124] as it seems difficult to license all material that is disseminated online.[125] Indeed, as Senftleben points out, it burdens OCSSPs with a clearance rights task which cannot be fulfilled.[126] The full licensing of the circulated content can only be achieved via umbrella licences. However, such licences issued by collective societies cover only works by their members,[127] they do not extend to the works of rights holders who are not their members. In this sense, the dissemination of works by authors without their prior permission might automatically amount to the primary liability of host ISPs, despite the fact that they concluded licensing agreements with collective societies.[128]

What is more, at European level, there is no uniform approach with regard to the extended collective licences or, as they are more commonly referred to, umbrella licences.[129] This means that even if OCSSPs decide to resort to collective licences, they would face a vast array of different licences from each jurisdiction. This is because the licensing system has not yet been harmonised at European level. For instance, while Article 12 of the DSMD offers a hint of harmonisation for extended collective licensing schemes, it is unclear how this provision will be transposed in each of the 27 European Member States and whether a desirable level of harmonisation would be achieved.[130] What is more, the possibility of a pan-European licence is limited since a pan-European licence issued by collective societies is restricted to works within a specific jurisdiction and does not cover works within other jurisdictions.[131]

Finally, the conclusion to the use of licensing agreements seems to be rejected by the intellectual property holders themselves, even though the aim of European policy

[123] Bridy (n 6) 22.

[124] Husovec (n 12) 531; See also for another view in M Husovec and JP Quintais, 'How to License Article 17? Exploring the Implementation Options for the New EU Rules on Content-Sharing Platforms' (1 October 2019) papers.ssrn.com/sol3/papers.cfm?abstract_id=3463011.

[125] Reda (n 31).

[126] Senftleben (n 71) 3.

[127] JP Quintais, 'The New Copyright in the Digital Single Market Directive: A Critical Look' (2019) 1 *European Intellectual Property Review* 18.

[128] Husovec (n 12) 535.

[129] Senftleben (n 71) 4.

[130] ibid 4; see section IV of this chapter.

[131] ibid 4.

makers to introduce the option of licensing copyrighted content was to safeguard those very rights. The licensing of copyright content would bridge the value gap between rights holders' revenues and the dissemination of content online. However, although the rationale for licensing was to protect their rights, rights holders seem to disagree with this option. Indeed, at the stakeholders meeting organised by the European Commission on 15 October 2019,[132] rights holders expressed their opposition to the inclusion of licensing agreements with the OCSSPs. This is because, as they argue, the experience of collective licensing with ISPs thus far is not appealing. For instance, a number of issues arise with regard to the functioning tools that host ISPs deploy in order to identify the allegedly infringing content. Such tools are mainly sound-recordings, and thus do not prevent the dissemination of infringing content online. Further, many rights holders argue that collective licensing agreements are not transparent in relation to the monetisation of authors; they also lack accuracy in reporting the use of works and the revenues of ISPs when they enable the circulation of copyrighted content online.[133]

It is this disagreement that comes to accentuate the problematic feature of concluding licensing agreements as set forth in Article 17(2) of the DSMD.

Therefore, it seems that concluding licensing agreements would turn out to be a very difficult task for OCSSPs. This of course might imply that in order to avoid liability, OCSSPs are forced to resort to the second possibility as envisaged in Article 17(4) of the DSMD. This possibility, which is analysed in the following section, addresses the duty of OCSSPs to make their best effort either to conclude authorisation from copyright holders to use their works, or to prevent the dissemination of unauthorised content within their platforms.

D. The Possibility for OCSSPs to Demonstrate their Best Effort

The second possibility for OCSSPs to be exonerated from liability is to demonstrate that they made their best efforts to seek authorisation from copyright holders, or made the best efforts to impede the circulation of copyright infringing content online or act expeditiously upon being notified and remove the allegedly infringing work. More specifically, Article 17(4) of the DSMD reads as follows:

> (a) made best efforts to obtain an authorisation, and (b) made, in accordance with high industry standards of professional diligence, best efforts to ensure the unavailability of specific works and other subject matter for which the rights holders have provided the service providers with the relevant and necessary information; and in any event (c) acted expeditiously, upon receiving a sufficiently substantiated notice from the rights holders, to disable access to, or to remove from their websites, the notified works or other subject matter, and made best efforts to prevent their future uploads in accordance with point (b).

Similar to the previous paragraphs of Article 17 of the DSMD, this paragraph also seems problematic for many reasons.

[132] European Commission, 'Press release on first meeting of the Stakeholder Dialogue on Art 17 of the Directive on Copyright in the Digital Single Market' (15 October 2019).

[133] Copyright Stakeholders dialogue (15 October 2019) digital-strategy.ec.europa.eu/en/policies/stakeholder-dialogue-copyright.

Firstly, as per Article 17(4)a, OCSSPs must prove that they made their best efforts to gain the permission of rights holders for the dissemination of their works. In this way, the impetus to seek authorisation is placed on OCSSPs. Yet, it could be asked what level of diligence must be demonstrated by OCSSPs.[134] However, a clear understanding of the level of diligence is missing. As Erikson notes, there is only one unsuccessful attempt to define the concept of diligence in the Orphan Works Directive, but, in the end, it seemed that this had not been fruitful.[135]

Secondly, as per Article 17(4)b of the DSMD, such best efforts must be in accordance with industry practices. At the outset, it seems that this paragraph has been agreed in order to minimise the negative criticism that the European Commission's Proposal has received with the introduction of the concept of 'content effective recognition technologies'.[136] This concept has drawn severe criticism from academics who, with a number of public signed statements, were against the imposition of filtering-based technologies and accentuated its negative implications for internet users' fundamental rights.[137] So, instead of using this term, the final text of the DSMD used the concept of 'industry standards of professional diligence', while in the end it refers to the vague concept of 'suitable and effective means'.[138] Undoubtedly, the wording seems problematic.

Insofar as industry practices are concerned, a number of examples provide evidence that OCSSPs can conclude agreements with rights holders that undermine the rights of internet users, and thus lead to censorship. Moreover, with regard to suitable and effective means, this wording can entail a number of tools that could prove efficient in identification of the unlawful content and block it. Such tools have already been developed by a number of OCSSPs.[139]

Thirdly, Article 17(4)c of the DSMD states that the OCSSPs must make best efforts and not only terminate the dissemination of unlawful content but also prevent the emergence of these infringements in the future. Following the pathway of the texts of the EU Commission, the Council, and the EU Parliament,[140] the final draft of the DSMD introduces a notice and stay down scheme that obliges OCSSPs to stop infringements from reappearing. Yet, this notice and stay down scheme, as already explained in section II(A), has prompted mounting concerns for its compatibility with the *EU acquis* and, in particular, with existing EU legal provisions and case law. For example, a notice and stay down scheme would require the imposition of filtering-based technological tools that would identify the allegedly infringing content, and thus prevent it

[134] K Erikson, 'The EU copyright directive creates new legal uncertainties' (*LSE Blog*, 6 April 2019) blogs.lse.ac.uk/businessreview/2019/04/06/the-eu-copyright-directive-creates-new-legal-uncertainties/.

[135] ibid.

[136] Article 13 of the Proposal for a Directive of the European Parliament and of the Council on copyright in the Digital Single Market COM/2016/0593 final – 2016/0280 (COD).

[137] CREATe, 'The Copyright Directive: Articles 11 and 13 must go – Statement from European Academics in advance of the Plenary Vote on 26 March 2019' (*CREATe blog*, 24 March 2019) www.create.ac.uk/blog/2019/03/24/the-copyright-directive-articles-11-and-13-must-go-statement-from-european-academics-in-advance-of-the-plenary-vote-on-26-march-2019/.

[138] See also Bridy (n 80) 353.

[139] See ch 4 section III(D).

[140] See Appendices II, III and IV.

from reappearing. While European policy makers attempted to eliminate the criticism by endorsing (in paragraph 7) that notice and stay down schemes shall take into consideration copyright exceptions such as parody or caricature,[141] it is doubtful whether the notice and stay down does not conflict with the prohibition of general monitoring as envisaged in Article 15 of the ECD, as well as with Articles 8, 11, and 16 of the EU Charter of Fundamental Rights that safeguards users' personal data, right to conduct business, and right to information.

With regard to Article 15 of the ECD, it has been argued that the imposition of content identification technologies seems to be in conflict with Article 15 of the ECD, which is about the prohibition of imposing general monitoring obligations on host ISPs.[142] In particular Article 15(1) reads as follows, 'Member States shall not impose a general obligation on providers, when providing the services covered by Articles 12, 13, and 14, to monitor the information which they transmit or store, nor a general obligation actively to seek facts or circumstances indicating illegal activity.' This has been considered the bottleneck of the host ISPs' regulatory framework since it prevents host ISPs from policing the digital world.[143]

Undoubtedly, a notice and stay down might lead to the use of content identification technology, which is all about general monitoring. By general monitoring it is meant, as Riordan notes, 'a systematic arrangement requiring random or universal inspection'.[144] The use of such technology will make host ISPs examine their platforms and remove any unlawful material. Therefore, content identification measures are in clear contrast with the prohibition of general monitoring.

The prohibition of general monitoring has been clearly outlined by the CJEU in a number of landmark cases. One of those is to be found in *Scarlet v Sabam*.[145] Sabam, the Belgian association for authors, requested a filtering injunction against Scarlet, an internet service provider, alleging copyright infringement. Sabam argued that Scarlet's subscribers used its network in order to file-share unauthorised material via peer-to-peer systems. However, the Court refused to issue an injunction under the reasoning that the imposition of a filtering obligation would 'oblige it to actively monitor all the data relating to each of its customers in order to prevent any future infringement of intellectual-property rights. It follows that that injunction would require the ISP to carry out general monitoring, something which is prohibited by Article 15 (1) of Directive 2000/31'.[146] This means that the adoption of a filtering mechanism would contravene the *EU acquis* that explicitly prohibits the obligations for general monitoring of a network.

The incompatibility of filtering technological tools with Article 15 of the ECD has also been accentuated by a growing body of academic scholarship. For instance, a handful of scholars published an open letter entitled, 'The Recommendation on Measures to

[141] See Appendix V.
[142] ECD.
[143] Frosio (n 12) 332.
[144] J Riordan, *The Liability of Internet Intermediaries* (Oxford, Oxford University Press, 2016) 421.
[145] Case C-70/10 *Scarlet Extended SA v Société belge des auteurs, compositeurs et éditeurs SCRL (SABAM)* [2011] ECR-I 11959.
[146] ibid para 36.

safeguard fundamental rights and open internet in the framework of the EU Copyright Reform.'[147] In this letter, they outlined the conflict with Article 15 of the ECD and urged the European Commission to reassess the imposition of monitoring obligations. Drawing their analysis from the CJEU case law, they outlined that Article 15 of the ECD applied to online platforms which host material, and stated that the imposition of content identification technologies would come into direct conflict with Article 15 of the ECD. Such a stance has been maintained by Bourdillon, Rosati, and others who have stressed that the imposition of content identification technologies will erode legal certainty of the *EU acquis*.[148] For this, as they clearly point out, the need to ensure the maintenance of filtering mechanisms is urgent for many reasons. Such reasons address the need to maintain legal certainty, boosting innovation within the Digital Single Market and protecting internet users' fundamental rights.[149] Along similar lines, Senftleben stressed that filtering mechanisms will change the goals of copyright law.[150] This is because, as he notes, instead of being 'an engine of content creation and dissemination',[151] copyright tends to restrict the circulation of works in the online world.[152]

However, it is not only a body of academics who have raised serious concerns about the incompatibility of filtering technologies with Article 15 of the ECD. Indeed, a number of Member States have submitted a series of questions to the legal service of the Council. More specifically, Belgium, the Czech Republic, Finland, Hungary, and The Netherlands have asked for clarification on the applicability of Article 15 of the ECD:

> Is Article 15 of the Directive on electronic commerce to be understood that the prohibition for Member States to impose general monitoring obligations does not apply in the situation where Member States' legislation would oblige certain platforms to apply technology that identifies and filters all the data of each of its users before the upload on the publicly available services?[153]

In light of the above, it seems that a body of academic scholars, a handful of Member States, and the CJEU's rulings reject the application of monitoring mechanisms on the host ISPs, arguing that Article 17 of the DSMD contradicts Article 15 of the ECD. Interestingly, it has been argued that this conflict with Article 15 of the ECD might generate 'systemic inconsistency'[154] with other provisions of the *EU acquis*, such as Article 14(1) of the ECD which guarantees immunity from liability to host ISPs under circumscribed conditions.

Another problematic aspect of Article 17(4)a of the DSMD revolves around how to assess that the OCSSP has made its best effort to seek authorisation from the rights holders with regard to the legitimate use of their works online. From a judicial perspective, the answer to this question could be found in Article 17(5) of the DSMD, which

[147] Senftleben et al (n 33) 149–63.
[148] Stalla-Bourdillon et al (n 10) 1–5.
[149] M Senftleben, 'Content censorship and Council carelessness – Why the Parliament must safeguard the open, participative web 2.01' (2018) 4 *AMI – tijdschrift voor auteurs-, media- en informatierecht* 139.
[150] ibid.
[151] ibid 142.
[152] ibid 142.
[153] Senftleben et al (n 33) 149–63.
[154] Frosio (n 12) 352.

dictates that the principle of proportionality could examine the requirement of best efforts. Article 17(5) of the DSMD notes,

> In determining whether the service provider has complied with its obligations under paragraph 4, and in light of the principle of proportionality, the following elements, among others, shall be taken into account: (a) the type, the audience and the size of the service and the type of works or other subject matter uploaded by the users of the service; and (b) the availability of suitable and effective means and their cost for service providers.

This means that the concept of best efforts shall be examined through the lens of proportionality. Certainly, the principle of proportionality has been one of the cornerstones of European Law.[155] As Stone, Sweet, and Matthews point out, the principle of proportionality is equally placed next to the principles of supremacy and direct effect at the European level.[156]

The principle of proportionality was officially included for the first time in Article 52 of the EU Charter of Fundamental rights, which dictates that,

> any limitation on the exercise of the rights and freedoms recognised by this Charter must be provided for by law and respect the essence of those rights and freedoms. Subject to the principle of proportionality, limitations may be made only if they are necessary and genuinely meet objectives of general interest recognised by the Union or the need to protect the rights and freedoms of others.

This implies that proportionality is the most appropriate mechanism to warrant the limitation of fundamental rights, thus it could serve as a legitimate basis to examine the best efforts of OCSSPs with regard to the termination of unauthorised content online.

Yet, discrepancies may be found in using the principle of proportionality to assess such efforts to prevent the circulation of the content. Indeed, Stamatoudi describes the principle of proportionality as 'an ambiguous oracle of Pythia: it says everything and nothing at the same time',[157] while Riordan reports that the principle of proportionality is 'a notoriously difficult test to apply'.[158] This is mainly due to its nature.

Firstly, the concept of proportionality lacks clarity. This understanding has been illustrated in the different views expressed by academic scholarship which attempts to define 'proportionality'. For instance, within the framework of the enforcement of intellectual property rights in the digital ecosystem,[159] Husovec suggests a cluster of guidelines in order to specify the elements of proportionality.[160] He notes that in order for the measures to be proportionate, the following elements should be met: (1) effectiveness; (2) method of implementation; (3) collateral damage to innovation; (4) operator's right to fair trial; (5) abusive use; (6) legality of blocking (out-of-court private agreements);

[155] J Schwarze, *European Administrative law* (Sweet and Maxwell, 2006) 677.

[156] A Stone Sweet and J Matthews, 'Proportionality Balancing and Global Constitutionalism' (2009) *47 Columbia Journal of Transnational Law* 86.

[157] I Stamatoudi, 'Data Protection, Secrecy of Communications and Copyright: Conflict and Convergences – The Example of Promusicae v. Telefonica' in Stamatoudi (n 55) 231; Frabboni (n 55) 133 where she criticises the principle of proportionality 'Interpretation of the meaning of proportionality is problematic and could hardly be seen to have established a common ground for the rules existing in each of the Member states.'

[158] Riordan (n 144) 98.

[159] Schwarze (n 155) 664–65.

[160] Husovec (n 47) para 116.

(7) degree of illegality; (8) subsidiarity; and (9) shifting of costs. Lodder and Meulen consider the directness, the effectiveness, and the costs of the measure, the host ISP's level of cooperation in the past, the time element, and the adequate safeguards to be taken.[161] Finally, a more widely accepted definition of the elements of proportionality has been put forward by Savola who submitted five interrelated criteria to evaluate proportionality,[162] namely the legal basis of blocking, the effectiveness of the measure, not burdening the host ISPs, subsidiarity, and avoiding collateral damage.

Secondly, it has been argued that the principle of proportionality has been construed in different ways, depending on the jurisdiction. Indeed, Finnish courts balance the different interests at stake without first considering the suitability of, or necessity for, the measures to be ordered.[163] German courts preclude from the suitability test only the most irrelevant measures, while limitations that minimally restrict the exercise of the right are considered sufficient on the condition that the legislative objective is accomplished.[164] This vague nature of proportionality may lead to ambiguity, thus eroding its applicability when national judges include it in their reasoning, leading to conflicting outcomes from jurisdiction to jurisdiction as to whether OCSSPs have undertaken best efforts to seek authorisation from rights holders with regard to the use of their works.

Therefore, it seems that the principle of proportionality might not be suitable to assess whether the OCSPs have fulfilled the requirement of best efforts, and thus avoid liability.

What is more, the concept 'suitable and effective' is vague and gives the right to OCSSPs to deploy any measure they believe could identify online infringements. This might entail a number of tools which could prove efficient to identify and block the unlawful content. Such tools have already been developed by a number of ISPs. The most prominent examples are the Content ID system used by YouTube,[165] and the Copyright Match used by Vimeo,[166] both are filtering-based technologies and enable rights holders to file their works in a database.

Nevertheless, it could be argued that not all OCSSPs own the appropriate resources to prevent the dissemination of infringing content. Indeed, in order to counter-balance the criticism expressed in the EU Commission's Proposal, and the Council's and EU Parliament's compromised texts, the requirement of best efforts does not apply to all OCSSPs indiscriminately. Article 17(6) of the DSMD excludes a number of OCSSPs with regard to the requirement of best efforts. This limitation entails those OCSSPs whose services 'have been available to the public in the Union for less than three years and [have] an annual turnover of 10 million euros'. Those OCSSPs which fulfil

[161] A Lodder and N van der Meulen, 'Evaluation of the Role of Access Providers: Discussion of Dutch Pirate Bay Case Law and Introducing Principles on Directness, Effectiveness, Costs, Relevance, and Time' (2013) 4 *Journal of Intellectual Property, Information Technology and E-Commerce Law* 138.

[162] P Savola, 'Proportionality of Website blocking: Internet Connectivity Providers as Copyright Enforcers' (2014) 5 *Journal of Intellectual Property, Information Technology and E-Commerce Law* 125–40.

[163] P Savola, 'Proportionality in Fundamental Rights Conflicts in National Measures Implementing EU Law' (2014) dx.doi.org/10.2139/ssrn.2432260.

[164] ibid.

[165] support.google.com/youtube/answer/3244015?hl=en.

[166] vimeo.com/help/guidelines.

the criteria do not have to demonstrate best efforts with regard to the prevention of unlawful content from reappearing. Rather, they must comply only with Article 17(4)(a) and (b), which state that OCSSPs must demonstrate best efforts to seek authorisation from rights holders and act expeditiously upon receiving notification of allegedly infringing content.

Yet, while this particular paragraph has its own merits since the rationale behind it is to dispense with the burden of OCSSPs to undertake the appropriate measures to seek authorisation or prevent the dissemination of infringing content, it remains problematic. This is because there is a lack of evidence that could justify those limitations.[167] To my knowledge, to date there are no empirical studies that conclude that OCSSPs with less than three years of operation could take advantage of this exclusion or, even better, whether OCSSPs with annual turnover could benefit from it. What is more, the paragraph might trigger more complicated questions, rather than offer solid answers. For instance, it is not clear how these OCSSPs would benefit from this limitation of liability,[168] or whether the threshold of five million users per month is too low.[169] It is worth pointing out that, within two years, YouTube managed to increase its traffic and reach 72 million users monthly.[170] It may even be that the threshold of the annual turnover of €10 million is too high. Hence, it seems that the thresholds for OCSSPs are subject to different interpretations and do not clarify which of them would be entitled to a limited liability regime.

Finally, another problematic aspect of the term 'best efforts' is that it could be subject to interpretation by national jurisdictions. So, in the course of the transposition of the DSMD to the national legal systems of the 27 EU Member States, the translation of the term 'best effort' might substantially differ from national jurisdiction to national jurisdiction. Indeed, there is evidence that in Spain the term 'best effort' translates to 'greater efforts', in Italy it amounts to 'greatest effort', while in Germany it is construed as 'all efforts'.[171] It is this divergence in the interpretation of the term that could lead to conflicting outcomes with regard to court rulings, and thus accentuate legal uncertainty among OCSSPs and rights holders. For instance, whereas in Spain if an OCSSP demonstrates that it undertook greater efforts to prevent the circulation of infringing content, it would be exonerated from liability. By contrast, if in Italy an OCSSP proves that made greater efforts and not the greatest to tackle the online dissemination of illicit content, it runs the risk of being held responsible for committing copyright infringements. Undoubtedly, the translation of various terms that are enshrined in Directives and Regulations in one of the 24 EU national languages is not a novelty. Yet, this problematic aspect confirms the stance of this book that harmonisation of the liability of OCSSPs seems to be far from reality.

[167] Quintais (n 115).
[168] JP Quintais describes this paragraph 'window dressing' in Quintais (n 127) 19.
[169] ibid.
[170] BBC News, 'Google buys YouTube for $1.65bn' (*bbc news*, 10 October 2006) news.bbc.co.uk/1/hi/business/6034577.stm.
[171] 'DSM Directive Series #5: Does the DSM Directive mean the same thing in all language versions? The case of "best efforts" in Article 17(4)(a)' (*IPKat blog*, 22 May 2019) ipkitten.blogspot.com/2019/05/dsm-directive-series-5-does-dsm.html.

E. No General Monitoring: A Void Provision

To mitigate any criticism that could emerge from the requirement of best efforts to prevent the reappearance of infringing content, Article 17(8) of the DSMD outlines the prohibition of general monitoring obligations. In particular, it states, 'the application of this Article shall not lead to any general monitoring obligation'.

In this way, European policymakers want to be compliant with the *EU acquis* and EU case law. More specifically, Article 17(8) is compliant with Article 15 of the ECD which prohibits general monitoring. Article 15 of the ECD is considered one of the cornerstones of e-commerce since it removes from host ISPs any obligation to develop technological tools in order to identify any illicit activity within their networks. Therefore, host ISPs continue their business operation without disruption and without investing in content-identification technologies.

With regard to EU case law, Article 17(8) is in accordance with a number of EU rulings that reinforce the importance of not having general monitoring duties for the OCSSPs.[172]

However, this paragraph is void. Its existence seems to be for aesthetic reasons alone. This is because it seems impossible to satisfy the requirement of best effort to seek termination of the circulation of infringing content, or to prevent the reappearance of infringing content within the OCSPs' networks, without deploying monitoring obligations.

This understanding has been reiterated in the words of European and national policymakers. After the final vote of the DSMD in Strasbourg, the French Minister stated, 'I also announce that the Higher Council of Literary and Artistic Property, the HADOPI and the CNC will jointly launch in the coming days a "Mission to promote and supervise content recognition technologies"'.[173] Likewise, the former Commissioner for Digital Affairs admitted that Article 17 of the DSMD implies the imposition of filtering obligations to OCSSPs by noting, 'As things stand, upload filters cannot be completely avoided.'[174] These statements illustrate the rationale of the DSMD and reinforce the suggestion that the use of filtering technologies would be an essential part of the new European e-commerce legislation.[175]

Therefore, it seems that Article 17(8) of the DSMD becomes void since its application in practice is problematic.

[172] Case C-70/10 *Scarlet Extended SA v Société belge des auteurs, compositeurs et éditeurs SCRL (SABAM)* [2011] ECR-I 11959; Case C-360/10, *Belgische Vereniging van Auteurs, Com- ponisten en Uitgevers CVBA (SABAM) v Netlog NV* (2012) ECLI:EU:C:2012:85; Case C-484/14 *Mc Fadden* (2016) ECLI:EU:C:2016:689.

[173] M Maschnik, 'After Insisting That EU Copyright Directive Didn't Require Filters, France Immediately Starts Promoting Filters' (*techdirt*, 28 March 2019) www.techdirt.com/articles/20190327/17141241885/after-insisting-that-eu-copyright-directive-didnt-require-filters-france-immediately-starts-promoting-filters.shtml.

[174] M Maschnik, 'EU Commissioner Gunther Oettinger Admits: Sites Need Filters To Comply With Article 13' (*techdirt*, 3 April 2019) www.techdirt.com/articles/20190329/15501341902/eu-commissioner-gunther-oettinger-admits-sites-need-filters-to-comply-with-article-13.shtml.

[175] Interestingly, companies that develop content identification technologies already advertise their technical tools in relation to Article 17 of the DSMD, see for instance audible magic's website where it states that 'Article 17 impacts most social networks in existence today. The clock is ticking, and companies need to put in place technical measures to comply', www.audiblemagic.com/article-17/.

F. Redress Mechanisms and Out of Court Mechanisms: Not Legitimate without Safeguards?

Another problematic feature of the DSMD is found in Article 17(9). Following the EU Commission's and EU Parliament's compromised texts, the final text of the DSMD states, in Paragraph 9, that 'OCSSPs must put in place an effective and expeditious complaint and redress mechanism that is available to users of their services'.

Undoubtedly, the role of paragraph 9 is to decrease the negative criticism that could emerge from the requirement of best effort to prevent the circulation of infringing content. However, this mechanism might give rise to concerns around the its legitimacy and whether it fulfils its aim, ie, to offer access to justice for internet users whose material has been removed erroneously. This is because there have been many examples that outline the inefficiency of such a mechanism operated by host ISPs. For instance, YouTube rejected a counter-notification from a user on the basis of existing contractual relations with rights holders.[176] Another example that outlines the inefficiency of this kind of mechanism is the long process that might be needed in order to examine the counter-notifications. For example, it has been found that the process can take more than a month – during this period, and until the decision is handed down, internet users' accounts are blocked so that they do not upload any new content.[177] It is this long process that encroaches upon the access to justice since, as Husovec points out, 'justice delayed is justice denied'.[178] This implies that while this redress mechanism has been designed to offer access to justice for internet users, the long process to examine the content might have the opposite effect and take this right away from end-users.

What is more, Article 17(9) fails to specify which entity would examine the counter-notices made by internet users. For instance, one might wonder if the rights holders would examine the counter-notices of end-users and under what conditions? Or would it be the OCSSPs that would assess the validity of the counter-notices and decide whether the content will be reinstated. In any case, this article lacks clarity and gives rise to legal uncertainty.

Finally, another problematic issue of the DSMD revolves around the creation of an impartial body to deal with complaints from users whose material has erroneously been removed by OCSSPs. As Article 17(9) paragraph 2 states, 'Member states shall ensure that out-of-court redress mechanisms are available for the settlement of disputes. Such mechanisms shall enable disputes to be settled impartially and shall not deprive the users of the legal protection afforded by national law, without prejudice to the rights of users to have recourse to efficient judicial remedies.' This means that an alternative dispute resolution mechanism will be offered to internet users in order to protect their

[176] M Perel and N Elkin-Koren, 'Accountability in Algorithmic Copyright Enforcement' (2016) 19 *Stanford Technology Law Review* 496.

[177] S Wodinsky, 'YouTube's copyright strikes have become a tool for extortion – Scammers are threatening to shut down channels – unless the owner pays up' (*The Verge*, 11 February 2019) www.theverge.com/2019/2/11/18220032/youtube-copystrike-blackmail-three-strikes-copyright-violation.

[178] M Husovec, 'Why There Is No Due Process Online?: New Controversies in Intermediary Liability Law' (*Balkan.com*, 7 June 2019) balkin.blogspot.com/2019/06/why-there-is-no-due-process-online.html.

fundamental rights, namely the freedom of expression. Although this initiative has its own merits, it could be void due to the lack of identifying criteria under which it would operate. This is because, as will be discussed in chapter nine, sections IV and V, it is crucial to specify the principles that shape this impartial body with regard to the validity of the decisions issued. A lack of accountability, legitimacy, or proportionality might erode the mission of this impartial body, and thus fail to safeguard the fundamental rights of internet users.

In light of the above, it is possible to observe that the Copyright in the Digital Single Market Directive entails a vast array of problematic features that could not only undermine OCSSPs' right to conduct business, but also interfere with internet users' fundamental rights and rights holders' rights. This controversial approach of the DSMD shifts the narrative to the implementation of this provision into EU Member States in order to identify how the liability of OCSSPs has been illustrated in EU national jurisdictions. In this light, the following section critically engages with the transposition of Article 17 of the DSMD in the Netherlands, France, Germany, Hungary, Denmark, and Malta. These EU Member States have already finalised the implementation of Article 17 of the DSMD into their national legal systems.

IV. National Implementation in EU Member States

Article 17 of the Copyright in the Digital Single Market Directive has now been implemented in a number of EU Member States, although the transposition deadline was 7 June 2021. This is not surprising since most of the EU Member States have been waiting for the EU Commission's Guidance, this was published three days before the implementation deadline[179] and the CJEU had not delivered its decision on the annulment action submitted by Poland.[180]

Crucially, although some Member States have transposed Article 17 of the DSMD, the national implementation seems to be fragmented, so far. This is because

[179] A bedrock of scholars have highly criticised the Guidance provided by the European Commission with regard to the implementation of Article 17 of the DSMD. One of the thorny issues addresses the concept of earmarking and states that 'When providing the relevant and necessary information to the service providers, rightsholders may choose to identify specific content which is protected by copyright and related rights, the unauthorised online availability of which could cause significant economic harm to them. The prior earmarking by rightsholders of such content may be a factor to be taken into account when assessing whether online content-sharing service providers have made their best efforts to ensure the unavailability of this specific content and whether they have done so in compliance with the safeguards for legitimate uses under Article 17(7) …'. This guidance reveals that if OCSSPs disregard the information provided by copyright holders, they will not be able to evidence that they made the best efforts to prevent or terminate the circulation of allegedly infringing material, thus being liable. Otherwise, it seems that the use of automated means or human review would be the most plausible solution; see also Geiger and Jütte (n 122) 625.

[180] Action brought on 24 May 2019 – *Republic of Poland v European Parliament and Council of the European Union* (Case C-401/19); Case C-401/19 *Republic of Poland v European Parliament, Council of the European Union* (2021) ECLI:EU:C:2021:613 where the Advocate General Saugmandsgaard ØE states in para 220 that 'It follows from all of the foregoing considerations that the limitation on the exercise of the right to freedom of expression and information resulting from the contested provisions, as interpreted in this Opinion, satisfies all of the conditions laid down in Article 52(1) of the Charter. In my view, that limitation is therefore compatible with the Charter. Consequently, the action brought by the Republic of Poland must, in my view, be dismissed.'

the majority of the EU Member States that have already implemented the Directive have either adopted Article 17 of the DSMD verbatim without any safeguards for internet users' rights, while only the minority so far has introduced additional provisions with the aim of safeguarding copyright exceptions.

In particular, on 15 May 2020, the Netherlands became the first country to transpose DSMD into its national legal system. The Dutch Parliament refrained from introducing separate legislation and instead added Article 17 and the relevant provisions of the DSMD to the current Dutch Copyright Act.[181]

The Dutch bill follows Article 17 of the DSMD verbatim. In particular, it adopts a definition of OCSSPs as per Article 29(c)(8), while at the same time it offers the conditions for evading liability. More specifically, Article 29(d)(2)(2) notes that the OCSSP must 'upon receipt of a sufficiently substantiated notification from the author or his successor in title, promptly remove the reported works from his website or make access to them impossible and make every effort to prevent the reported works from being offered again in the future'. This means that OCSSPs are required to prevent the reappearance of infringing content. Such prevention may take place either through the use of filtering-based tools or by human review; there is no obligation to justify their choice. Finally, it is worthy of note that the Dutch Parliament retained the right to impose additional rules at a later stage in order to facilitate the application of the provision. However, there is no indication so far that it intends to do this.

Similarly, France has implemented verbatim the Copyright in the Digital Single Market Directive into the national legal system in Article L. 137-1 and Article L. 137-2 of the existing Code of Intellectual Property Law. Article L. 137-1 addresses the scope of OCSSPs, while Article L. 137-2 discusses the liability of OCSSPs for copyright infringements within their networks and the requirements for evading liability.[182] Following Article 17 of the DSMD, OCSSPs are required to demonstrate their best efforts to obtain authorisation for using the disputed work, or to prevent the emergence of allegedly copyright infringing works. Crucially, in the case of OCSSPs deploying filtering-based tools, the national transposition does not deliver any relevant provisions that would protect legitimate uses of copyright, therefore it does not safeguard users' rights. This is not surprising given the support of the French government for the DSMD, which is evident in the EU Commission's stakeholders consultation with regard to the implementation of Article 17 of the DSMD.[183]

Further, another country that has transposed the Copyright in the Digital Single Market Directive, and in particular Article 17, is Germany. On 20 May 2021, the German

[181] R Chavannes, 'The Dutch DSM copyright transposition bill: safety first (up to a point) – Part 2' (*Kluwer Copyright blog*, 11 June 2020) copyrightblog.kluweriplaw.com/2020/06/11/the-dutch-dsm-copyright-transposition-bill-safety-first-up-to-a-point-part-2/.

[182] Ordonnance n° 2021-580 du 12 mai 2021.

[183] Note des autorités françaises, available at www.communia-association.org/wp-content/uploads/2020/10/201001french_consultation_response.pdf where the French government responded to the Commission's stakeholders Consultation with regard to the implementation of Article 17 of the Copyright in the Digital Single Market Directive by noting that Article 17 of the DSMD takes into consideration the fundamental rights framework and provides safeguards for internet users.

Parliament transposed Article 17 of the DSMD through the Act on Copyright Liability of Online Content Sharing Service Providers.[184] Following the rationale of the provision of the Copyright in the Digital Single Market Directive, the German Act implements the conditions for liability of OCSSPs and states that they are primarily liable for copyright infringement if they give access to the work to the public. In particular, § 4 of the Act notes:

> A service provider is obliged to make every effort to acquire the contractual rights of use for communication to the public and the reproduction required for this purpose of copyright-protected works.

Interestingly, the German Act inserts an additional provision which aims to protect copyright exceptions online. Under the term 'presumably authorised uses', § 9 states that user-generated content must remain online if it includes less than half of the work of a third party, or other works of other parties, and is combined with another work, as well as if it makes minor use of works of third parties as per § 10, or is flagged by trusted users as per § 11. The allegedly infringing content can be removed from the network after the outcome of the complaint's procedure is provided. Otherwise, there is an underlying risk of over-enforcement and, therefore, over-blocking of lawful material.[185]

This implies that OCSSPs might use filtering-based tools in order to identify copyright infringing works. However, in the case of presumably authorised uses by law, if the work matches a work that already exists in the database, the filtering-based technology cannot automatically take it down. This is because, as per § 9 paragraph 3, the OCSSP has the responsibility to inform the copyright holder about the right to lodge a complaint about the allegedly infringing content. In the meantime, the content is still available on the platform and can only be removed following manual review by humans. In this way, the German Act safeguards the legitimate uses of copyright and, therefore, the fundamental rights of users.[186]

However, it is crucial to emphasise that the Act does not provide rules with regard to the moderation of content that does not fall within the abovementioned categories. For instance, consider an uploaded work that quotes the whole work of a creator, or belongs in the public domain, or even in cases where copyright holders submit false notifications for infringements;[187] such cases do not fall within the categories of § 9, thus it is highly likely that OCSSPs which use filtering tools would remove them.[188]

[184] Urheberrechts-Diensteanbieter-Gesetz-UrhDaG.

[185] See further in Z Krokida, 'Use of Filters by Online Intermediaries and the Rights of Users: Developments in the European Union, Mexico, India and China' in IFLA, *Copyright Reader for Librarians* (Berlin, De Gruyter 2022).

[186] ibid.

[187] T Nobre, 'The German Model to Protect User Rights when implementing Article 17' (*Communia*, 27 January 2021) www.communia-association.org/category/eu-policy/dsm-implementation/page/2/; J Reda, 'Germany attempts to square the circle in its implementation of Article 17 CDSMD – Part 1' (*Kluwer Copyright blog*, 2 June 2021) copyrightblog.kluweriplaw.com/2021/06/02/germany-attempts-to-square-the-circle-in-its-implementation-of-article-17-cdsmd-part-1/; T Gerken, 'YouTube's copyright claim system abused by extorters' (2019) www.bbc.co.uk/news/technology-47227937 where two popular YouTubers have reported that they have been asked for paying up to £309 in exchange of removing the copyright strikes against their YouTube channels.

[188] See further in Krokida (n 185).

Hungary has also transposed Article 17 of the Copyright in the Digital Single Market Directive. With 136 votes, the Hungarian Parliament accepted the Act to implement the Copyright in the Digital Single Market Directive. Similar to the Netherlands and France, the Hungarian Act adopted Article 17 without any additional measures which would safeguard users' fundamental rights. Rather, § 57. E (4) only restates that the measures shall not result in the prevention of legitimate uses.[189] This means that OCSSPs must not prevent the dissemination of lawful content when they take measures against the availability and prevention of re-appearance of copyright infringing works. What is more, the Hungarian Act offers a separate provision for the creation of a complaint redress mechanism. In particular, § 57.G (1) notes that OCSSPs need to offer to users the opportunity to counter claim the removal of content, and therefore an effective resolution mechanism.

Denmark implemented Article 17 of the Copyright in the Digital Single Market Directive verbatim, with 90 votes in favour, on 3 June 2021. In particular, in 52c. Stk. 2 the Danish Act transposes the definition of OCSSPs and in Stk.4 it provides the liability exemptions.[190] In order to avoid any misuse of the prevention of legitimate uses, the Danish Act refrains from providing ex-ante safeguards. Therefore, a risk of censorship would impinge upon users' fundamental rights.[191]

Finally, Malta implemented Article 17 of the DSMD on 7 July 2021. Similar to the previous jurisdictions, Malta did not provide additional provisions in order to mitigate risks for users' free speech. Rather, the Maltese Act reinstated features of Article 17, and thus prioritised copyright holders' rights, while at the same time subordinated users' fundamental rights.

Interestingly, it is not only the national implementation of EU Member States so far that seems to fail to provide a solid response to the conundrum of OCSSPs' liability. Indeed, the much-awaited Guidance of the European Commission on the implementation of Article 17 of the Copyright in the Digital Single Market Directive appears to fail to provide a solid interpretation of the contested provision. In particular, in order to mitigate any risk to the fundamental rights of the users, the European Commission's Guidance introduced the concept of earmarking and stated,

> When providing the relevant and necessary information to the service providers, rightholders may choose to identify specific content which is protected by copyright and related rights, the unauthorised online availability of which could cause significant economic harm to them. The prior earmarking by rightholders of such content may be a factor to be taken into account when assessing whether online content-sharing service providers have made their best efforts to ensure the unavailability of this specific content and whether they have done so in compliance with the safeguards for legitimate uses under Article 17(7) …

This means that if online content sharing service providers disregard that information, they will not be able to demonstrate that they made their best effort to prevent the

[189] A (2) bekezdésben meghatározott intézkedések tartalommegosztó szolgáltató általi alkalmazása nem eredményezheti a jogszerű felhasználások megakadályozását.

[190] Folketinget, 'L 205 Forslag til lov om ændring af lov om ophavsret' www.ft.dk/samling/20201/lovforslag/l205/index.htm.

[191] CREATe, available at www.create.ac.uk/cdsm-implementation-resource-page/.

dissemination of copyright infringing content within their networks. Therefore, they will be subject to liability. In order to avoid liability, as Reda and Keller rightfully point out, OCSSPs would either have to apply for human review or to block, via automated means, every upload that contains a work or parts of a work that has been earmarked by copyright holders.[192]

Overall, the national transposition of Article 17 of the DSMD fails to address the discrepancies with regard to the legal framework of OCSSPs and does not take into account the current copyright exceptions.

Yet, it is not the national transposition of Article 17 of the DSMD into the EU Member States that might trigger legal uncertainties. Indeed, it is important to keep in mind that Article 17 of the DSMD is in parallel force with the provisions of the ECD. Both legislative tools regulate the liability of ISPs and OCSSPs for trade mark and copyright infringements within their networks, respectively. Crucially, as demonstrated below, it is this intersection between the DSMD and the ECD that might be problematic and might accentuate the existing legal uncertainties.

V. Problematic Intersection between Article 17 of the DSMD and Article 14(1) of the ECD

Article 17 of the DSMD addresses the liability of OCSSPs for copyright infringements within their networks. Given that OCSSPs seem to be a sub-category of the host ISPs, this provision acts as a *lex specialis* to Article 14(1) of the ECD whose scope has been limited to regulation of the liability of host ISPs for trade mark infringements.

However, as noted in this chapter in section III(B), Article 17 of the DSMD introduces primary liability rules for OCSPs and marks a shift from a secondary to a primary liability regime. Yet, as explored in chapter three, the ECD, which is still in force, offers a secondary liability regime for those ISPs who are aware of the infringing content or who do not act expeditiously to remove it upon being notified.

This understanding implies that there is a dual liability regime, ie, one set forth in Article 17 of the DSMD and Article 14(1) of the ECD. Such a dual liability regime, however, might trigger legal uncertainties and fragmentation at European level since copyright protected works are not only disseminated on YouTube, Facebook, Twitter, or Instagram.[193] In fact, they are also disseminated on Amazon, by eBooks, audio files or 3d printing files and online courses and among Cloud service providers via Dropbox files which offer links to material.

In this respect, this dual liability regime might split the existing case law. Consider, for instance, the case where the ISP falls outside the scope of the definition of Article 17 of the DSMD, but the services it provides fall within it. A representative example of this

[192] J Reda and P Keller, 'European Commission back-tracks on user rights in Article 17 Guidance' (*Kluwer Copyright Blog*, 4 June 2021) copyrightblog.kluweriplaw.com/2021/06/04/european-commission-back-tracks-on-user-rights-in-article-17-guidance/.

[193] European Commission, 'EU study on the New rules for a new age? Legal analysis of a Single Market for the Information Society 6. Liability of online intermediaries' (2009).

line of thinking is eBay. As discussed in section III(A) of this chapter, eBay offers both tangible and non-tangible goods to its online consumers. Tangible goods amount to anything that is tangible. Non-tangible goods amount to eBooks, audio files or online seminars which can be viewed as YouTube videos.[194] In this way, eBooks or online seminars that are listened or viewed as videos via music video exchange platforms, such as Dailymotion, fall within the meaning of copyrighted content, and thus come under the scope of Article 17 of the DSMD. Accordingly, if a brand owner brings legal proceedings against an online marketplace alleging trade mark infringement, the principle of the diligent economic operator comes into play. More specifically, following the *L'Oreal v Ebay* case,[195] to attribute liability to the online marketplace, the court shall examine whether the online marketplace is 'aware of facts or circumstances on the basis of which a diligent economic operator should have identified the illegality in question and acted in accordance with Article 14(1) (b) of Directive 2000/31'.[196] In contrast, it is questionable which principle would be applicable if a rights holder brings legal suit against an online marketplace for copyright infringements that accrue within its platform.[197] Whether the principle of a diligent economic operator would be applicable in the case where the online marketplace offers copyrighted content would be open to discussion. In any case, the stance of this book, given the novelty of the DSMD, is that further guidance from the CJEU in following years would be very much expected.

What is more, this dual liability regime could lead to a fragmented enforcement of copyright law since there would be a dual regime in locating the burden of proof. Consider, for instance, that within the copyright framework, as a default a right holder must prove that their rights have been violated. This rationale has been followed by the ECD whereby, under Article 14(1), intellectual property holders would need to prove the copyright violations. More specifically, under Article 14(1) of the ECD, rights holders must prove that they identified the infringing content and sent a valid notification of the allegedly infringing content to ISPs. By contrast, under Article 17 of the DSMD that sets forth a notice and stay down regime, OCSSPs must demonstrate that they undertook all the precautionary measures to terminate the unauthorised content and prevent its reappearance in the future. Thus, for OCSSPs such as YouTube, Facebook, and Instagram, the right holder does not need to prove a copyright infringement in order to seek redress for the violations of her rights. Therefore, a copyright law of two velocities would incur, and thus amend the existing harmonised practices in copyright law.

Finally, this dual liability regime might act as a deterrent for innovation in the Digital Single Market. This is because a dual liability regime might pose a strict limitation for those host ISPs that may wish to offer either copyrighted content or goods within their networks, or for those host ISPs that wish to offer both services. This means that if host ISPs would like to engage in a business model that offers the ability to internet to view videos and at the same time to provide online shopping to consumers, they are subject to different obligations as per Article 14(1) of the ECD and Article 17 of the DSMD, thus

[194] Husovec (n 86).
[195] Case C-324/09 *L'Oreal SA V eBay Int'l AG* (2011) ECR I-6011.
[196] ibid para 120.
[197] Angelopoulos and Quintais (n 10) 153.

placing an additional burden on its business model. For instance, a host ISP may wish to combine different services in its business model. When it gives access to copyrighted material, its activities fall under the scope of Article 17 of the DSMD. This means that in order to be exonerated from liability, a host ISP must conclude licensing agreements with rights holders. If a host ISP decides not to license the material that users upload within its networks, it must provide evidence that it made its best effort either to acquire the permission of creators for the material that is circulated on the platform, or to prevent the availability of infringing material within the platform. The latter, as many scholars have pointed out, amounts to the use of filtering technology that prevents the emergence of online infringements. In parallel with this, a host ISP who might also wish to engage in online retail must comply with Article 14(1)(b) of the ECD. This implies that in order to be exonerated from liability, a host ISP must expeditiously remove, upon being notified, the allegedly infringing material. Therefore, excessive costs might arise for host ISPs who wish to commercially operate in both services.

This dual liability regime might lead to the creation of a monopoly in the field of OCSSPs that disseminate content. For instance, the role of OCSSPs such as YouTube and Instagram would be empowered in the market since they already own highly sophisticated technology to identify infringements. Given that the burden of proof is lower in the case of notice and take down, many host ISPs would prefer to invest in online retail markets whose schemes to avoid liability do not place an impetus on host ISPs. As a corollary, the DSMD might erode the main aim of the ECD, namely to facilitate e-commerce players.

Therefore, it seems that the intersection between the ECD and DSMD is also problematic. This is because, firstly, the imposition of a dual liability regime, might contradict the rationale of the ECD which has been introduced with the aim to offer ISPs a friendlier environment for innovation within the European Digital Single Market. Secondly, it might give rise to a fragmented enforcement of copyright rules or, as I have discussed, to a copyright framework of two velocities. Thirdly, the intersection between the ECD and DSMD might lead to a monopolistic market and pose serious impediments to innovation.

VI. Conclusion

This chapter has critically discussed Article 17 of the DSMD and addressed the liability of OCSSPs for copyright infringements within their networks. Although the DSMD is a new Directive and has not yet been tested in the courts across EU borders, this chapter has identified a number of problematic aspects that might give rise to legal uncertainties.

Firstly, it was noted that a problematic feature of Article 17 of the DSMD is what appears to be a new sub-type of host ISPs, the OCSSPs. Under the definition of OCSSPs fall those platforms that store, and enable users to upload, copyright protected content while, as per Recital 62, providers of business-to-business cloud services and cloud services, cyber lockers, and online marketplaces are excluded. It is questionable as to why online marketplaces, cloud services, and cyber lockers do not fall within the definition of OCSSPs since they also give access to publicly-protected content. This understanding might lead to limitations of innovative business ideas, such as new online platforms that could offer a multiple of services to their users which combine the provision of copyright content and the sale of goods.

Secondly, another problematic feature of Article 17 of the DSMD is the introduction of primary liability rules. In particular, Article 17(1) states that an OCSSP performs an act of communication to the public, or an act of making content available to the public. This means that, when a copyright infringement takes place, OCSSPs are primarily liable. However, primary liability rules go against the rationale of a secondary liability regime as set forth in Article 14(1) of the ECD. This is because, as discussed in this chapter and as per Article 14(1) of the ECD, host ISPs can escape liability if they are aware of the illicit activity, or upon them being made aware of it, by expeditiously removing the infringing content. The imposition of primary liability rules goes against the rationale of secondary liability theories which have been the cornerstone of e-commerce for more than 20 years; these have safeguarded the operation of business for many host ISPs since the defence of knowledge enabled them to be exonerated from liability in cases where intellectual property holders initiated proceedings against them. In contrast, primary liability rules, which are now endorsed in Article 17 of the DSMD, do not require the element of knowledge, and thus OCSSPs would be held liable once the copyright violation takes place within their networks.

In order to evade primary liability for copyright infringements, OCSSPs must fulfil two requirements. As per Article 17(4) of the DSMD, they must either make their best effort to seek concluding licensing agreements or terminate the dissemination, as well as prevent the reappearance of copyright infringements. However, both requirements are not without criticism. As discussed in this chapter, given that OCSSPs operate within a primary liability regime, this implies that the burden of evidence is now placed on them, meaning OCSSPs have to prove that they took all the necessary precautions in order to avoid the dissemination of unlawful material. In contrast, under the secondary liability regime, set forth in Article 14(1) of the ECD, rights holders have to prove that they notified host ISPs for infringing material within their network. Further, it promotes one-sided agreements between rights holders and OCSSPs since it states that the best efforts OCSSPs must undertake must be compliant with 'high industry standards of professional diligence'. Such practices might prompt reflections as to whether they take into consideration users' rights, and thus guarantee the dissemination of content online. For this reason, Ramahlo concludes that the current framework 'is partly industry-orientated'.[198]

Thirdly, this paragraph endorses a notice and stay down mechanism without defining its limits. On the one hand, it could be assumed that the notice and stay down system requires the implementation of filtering technology. Certainly, the prevention of the reappearance of infringements cannot rest on human review, technological tools are needed. Otherwise, OCSSPs would have to hire a huge number of reviewers in order to examine the infringements case by case. On the other hand, it is extremely urgent to

[198] A Ramahlo, 'Copyright law-making in the EU: what lies under the "internal market" mask?' (2014) 9 *Journal of Intellectual Property Law & Practice* 224.

clarify whether this notice and stay down mechanism shall address the emergence of copyright infringements of the same nature, or copyright infringements by the same user, or copyright infringements of the same nature by different users, or copyright infringements of the same nature by the same user.[199] Otherwise, notice and stay down would be the subject of different interpretations, and thus inconsistencies.

What is more, another problematic aspect revolves around Article 17(8) of the DSMD which explicitly prohibits general monitoring obligations. As discussed in this chapter, this paragraph also seems problematic since it might be subject to different interpretations. On the one hand, it could be argued that the paragraph is void because Article 17(4) of the DSMD requires OCSSPs to prevent the dissemination of infringing content. The only understandable way to follow this requirement is to deploy filtering mechanisms. On the other hand, it could be argued that the explicit prohibition of general monitoring obligations implies that specific filtering obligations are allowed under the DSMD. If this is the case, however, does this mean that filtering is allowed only in specific cases, as already set forth in Recitals 47 and 48 of the ECD and, if so, how those specific cases shall be examined.

Finally, the problematic framework of Article 17 of the DSMD is aggravated by the establishment of a redress mechanism which would be operated by OCSSPs as well as the creation of an out of court mechanism that would deal with the disputes between OCSSPs and internet users. This is because, as explained in this chapter, if those self and out of court mechanisms come without safeguards, the principles of due process and the right to access to justice for internet users would be in peril.

Overall, it appears that the attempts to offer greater harmonisation in terms of host ISPs' liability have not been fruitful. While Article 17 of the DSMD offers a definition for OCSSPs by noting that OCSSPs commit an act of communication with the public by giving the public access to copyright protected works, the rationale behind this definition and the constituents of this new regulatory framework for OCSSPs, which seems to be a sub-type of host ISPs, appear to be problematic. In particular, this definition does not only come into conflict with the secondary liability doctrine that has served as the foundation for e-commerce within the EU, but it might also have a detrimental effect on the interests of OCSSPs and internet users' fundamental rights.

Crucially, to fix this controversial approach seems far from reality. This is because the problematic issues of Article 17 of the DSMD seems to be integrated into the EU national jurisdictions. Whereas some of the EU Member States have implemented the DSMD and in particular Article 17 of the DSMD, it appears that the majority had transposed the provision verbatim without any safeguards for internet users' rights. At the same time, the European Commission's Guidance on the transposition of Article 17 clarifies a number of thorny issues such as the correlation between Article 17 of the DSMD and Article 3 of the Infosoc Directive but it seems be insufficient in terms of safeguarding internet users' rights.

However, as the findings of this book indicate, what is even more troublesome with Article 17 of the DSMD is the fact that it does not only entail problematic features.

[199] This is the so called Kerntheorie and has been discussed in ch 3 section III(B)ii; see also in *Case* C-494/15 *Tommy Hilfiger Licensing* (2016) ECLI:EU:C: 2016:528, para 34.

Rather, it also performs a problematic intersection with the existing *EU acquis* and, in particular, with Article 14(1) of the ECD. As discussed, this intersection reveals the existence of a dual liability regime under the ECD and DSMD respectively. This dual liability regime might lead to a monopolistic market with big OCSSPs prevailing since the new host ISPs might find the secondary liability regime more appealing and, subsequently, develop services such as cloud services, cyber lockers, and online market retailers. The creation of such a monopolistic market might lead to the erosion of Web 2.0, the main aim of which is the dissemination of diverse information to which the direct involvement of internet users is required. Finally, a dual liability regime might create confusion for OCSSPs and ISPs as, in order to avoid liability rules, they may over-remove material that might be lawful. In this way, internet users' right to freedom of expression and information would be violated.

In addition, there is a dual scheme for host ISPs and OCSSPs in order to avoid primary and secondary liability. Within the scope of Article 17 of the DSMD, OCSSPs must undertake their best efforts not only to terminate the infringement, but also to prevent any future reappearance. In contrast, pursuant to Article 14(1) of the ECD, ISPs must remove the infringing content upon being notified. Any obligation to prevent the reemergence of content is not stated in the ECD. However, this dual scheme for avoiding liability might create confusion for host ISPs, OCSSPs, and rights holders. This is because the burden of proof is different in each scheme. For instance, under Article 14(1) of the ECD, rights holders must prove that they identified the infringing content and sent a valid notification for the allegedly infringing content to host ISPs. In contrast, under Article 17 of the DSMD OCSSPs must demonstrate that they deployed preventive mechanisms in order to stop the violation online, and to impede its reappearance.

Hence, it seems that the DSMD fails to offer a solid answer to the OCSSPs' liability conundrum. Although it remains to be seen in coming years how this Directive would be transposed into the national legal systems of the 27 EU Member States, it is undeniable that Article 17 of the DSMD attempted to provide a uniform aspect to the OCSSPs' liability. Yet, its problematic features seem to erode this aspect. This makes this Directive, along with the ECD, which offers an outdated approach to host ISPs' liability, two legislative tools that do not meet the needs of the parties at stake. In contrast, the outdated approach of the ECD and its problematic aspects might pose serious risks to ISPs' business operations and interfere with internet users' fundamental rights.

In light of the above, and in order to examine the legal consequences of the approaches adopted by the ECD and DSMD, respectively, the following chapter examines the rights holders, OCSSPs and host ISPs and internet users/consumers in the context of the existing legislative framework. This enables the reader to illustrate the impact of these two legislative tools on the parties involved, as well as offering a strong normative justification for a legal reform with a cluster of recommendations, which follow in Part III of this book. It is worthy of mention here that, given OCSSPs appear to be a new sub-type of host ISPs, for the sake of convenience and to avoid repetitions, I will use the umbrella term of host ISPs in order to critically examine the implications of the current regulatory framework under the ECD and DSMD to the rights of intellectual property holders, internet users, and host ISPs and OCSSPs. Yet, I will use the term OCCSPs when the specific implications emerge from the DSMD.

5

Host ISPs, OCSSPs and Parties Involved under Article 14(1) of the E-Commerce Directive and Article 17 of the Copyright in the Digital Single Market Directive

I. Introduction

As discussed in the previous chapters, the current legislative framework fails to offer a solid response to host ISPs' liability. Article 14(1) of the ECD seems to be outdated while Article 17 of the DSMD has been subject to a high degree of controversy. This implies that both legislative tools do not take into consideration the parties involved, namely the rights holders, the host ISPs and internet users/consumers. In this vein, the following section critically examines the impact of the specific articles of the EU Directives on the business model of host ISPs, internet users' fundamental rights to free speech and culture as well as the right of rights holders to protect their works and brands.

II. Article 14(1) of the ECD and Article 17 of DSMD and Host ISPs/OCSSPs

The main rationale of liability rules on host ISPs and OCSSPs is to safeguard the rights of trade mark owners and copyright holders respectively. However, as the findings indicate in chapters three and four, the outdated and problematic framework under Article 14(1) of the ECD and Article 17 of the DSMD respectively for host ISPs and OCSSPs' liability might cause a level of legal uncertainty to host ISPs and OCSSPs.

The need to ascribe clear legal rules has been expressed by private stakeholders, academic scholars and policymakers. With regard to private stakeholders, a report conducted by Oxera on behalf of Google demonstrates that clear rules may reduce the transaction costs of host ISPs. This is because host ISPs would be aware of the level of enforcement and the processes they need to follow in order to avoid liability.[1] Clear legal rules could have a positive impact in cases where the notification sent to ISPs

[1] Oxera report on behalf of Google, 'The economic impact of safe harbors on Internet intermediary start-ups' (2015) 10, available at www.oxera.com/wp-content/uploads/2018/07/The-economic-impact-of-safe-harbours-on-Internet-intermediary-start-ups.pdf.pdf.

lacks clarity, but host ISPs would still prefer to remove the allegedly infringing material without further investigation with the aim to avoid liability.[2] An example of this is the case of the Liberty project.[3] In this case, the researchers submitted a complaint for a legitimate content to a UK and a US ISP that offered internet access. The content at stake was part of the book of John Stuart Mill which belonged in the public domain since it was published in 1869. While researchers submitted the same complaint to both ISPs offering access to internet, the responses differed. In particular, the US ISP that offered internet access responded to this notice with a list of questions regarding the claims of copyright ownership while the UK ISP expeditiously removed the legitimate material without any further investigation of the claim.

Therefore, with the adoption of clear legal rules, host ISPs would be urged to follow a specific process in order to investigate the notices that they receive and thus take down the allegedly infringing material. Otherwise, this ambiguity may result in over-removal of lawful content or additional costs for host ISPs. This is because ISPs might undertake expensive precautionary measures in order to avoid liability, thus increasing their transaction costs. Such measures would amount to the use of highly sophisticated technology that could detect infringing material online or the hire of experienced employees that could monitor the traffic within the networks.

In line with this, the Council of Europe's recommendation on cyberspace stresses the need for a clear legal framework. In order to promote the public value of the internet, the Council of Europe points out a number of recommendations for Member States with the aim to establish legislation between cyberspace entities and public authorities that have '... a clear legal basis and respects privacy regulations'.[4] This is warranted because internet and all relevant digital technologies have high public service value and must promote the respect of human rights and other fundamental rights within the online environment. At the same time, the policymakers in EU Cyber Forum declares that 'legal certainty is key for a better international cooperation against cybercrime'[5] while the Open Forum Europe's report on intermediary liability stresses the need for clear legal rules in order for ISPs to be aware of liability conditions and how they can avoid them.[6]

[2] D Rowland, U Kohl and A Charlesworth, *Information Technology Law*, 5th edn (London, Routledge 2017) 86; Lecture by Sjoera Nas, Bits of Freedom, 'The Multatuli Project ISP Notice & take down' (2004) www-old.bof.nl/docs/researchpaperSANE.pdf; C Ahlert, C Marsden and C Yung, 'How "Liberty" Disappeared from Cyberspace: The Mystery Shopper Tests Internet Content Self-Regulation' (2014) www.academia.edu/686583/How_Liberty_Disappeared_from_Cyberspace_The_Mystery_Shopper_Tests_Internet_Content_Self_Regulation; D Kiat Boon Seng, 'The State of the Discordant Union: An Empirical Analysis of DMCA Takedown Notices' (2014) 18 *Virginia Journal of Law and Technology* 369; D Keller, 'DMCA classic, DMCA turbo: major new empirical research on notice and takedown operations' (*The Center for Internet and Society*, 20 April 2016) cyberlaw.stanford.edu/blog/2016/04/dmca-classic-dmca-turbo-major-new-empirical-research-notice-and-takedown-operations.

[3] Ahlert, Marsden and Yung (n 2).

[4] Committee of Ministers, 'Recommendation to member states on measures to promote the public service value of the Internet' CM/Rec (2007) 16, available at wcd.coe.int/ViewDoc.jsp?id=1207291.

[5] EU Cyber Forum, available at www.coe.int/en/web/cybercrime/glacyplusactivities/-/asset_publisher/uKE6ShlCfApw/content/eu-cyber-forum-legal-certainty-is-key-for-a-better-international-cooperation-against-cybercrime?inheritRedirect=false&redirect=https%3A%2F%2Fwww.coe.int%2Fen%2Fweb%2Fcybercrime%2Fglacyplusactivities%3Fp_p_id%3D101_INSTANCE_uKE6ShlCfApw%26p_p_lifecycle%3D0%26p_p_state%3Dnormal%26p_p_mode%3Dview%26p_p_col_id%3Dcolumn-4%26p_p_col_count%3D1.

[6] Open Forum Europe, 'Intermediary liability through the back door: Consequences of extending digital copyright for the open internet' (2016) 19, www.openforumeurope.org/wp-content/uploads/2016/05/White-Paper-Intermediary-Liability.pdf.

Along similar lines, the Public Consultation on the evaluation and modernisation of the legal framework for the enforcement of intellectual property rights outlines the need for legal certainty.[7] The majority of respondents supported the introduction of specific requirements that would prevent the dissemination of unlawful content along with a uniform level of enforcement of intellectual property rights at European level. Such requirements could promote legal certainty among rights holders. Likewise, the EU Human Rights Guidelines on Freedom of Expression Online and Offline by the Council of European Union notes that any restrictions on free speech in the online and offline world shall be clear and accessible to everyone. In particular, the Guidelines state that 'They must be provided for by law, which is clear and accessible to everyone (principle of legal certainty, predictability and transparency).'[8]

Likewise, prominent scholars lean in favour of clear legal rules. For example, Garstka argues that legal certainty is directly related with the 'quality of a desirable system of regulation'.[9] This implies that a legislative framework that aims to balance the interests involved must set out clear legal rules. Another scholar, Husovec, stresses the need for establishing clear legal rules with the aim to take into consideration the interests of the parties involved. In particular, he notes that 'The solution to this dilemma is to draw up clear and stable rules, which are flexible enough to accommodate diverse interests and technical solutions. In this way, legal certainty and flexibility can be promoted together at the same time.'[10]

In addition, Angelopoulos outlined the need for legal certainty at European level.[11] She argues that the current legal framework triggers legal uncertainty. This is because the non-uniform approach of liability rules at European level might create legal uncertainty to host SSPs, rights holders and internet users. Likewise, Stalla- Bourdillon stresses the need for legal certainty with regard to host ISPs' regulatory framework.[12] She argues that the diverse interpretations of legal provisions in the ECD, along with their inconsistent application, would turn host ISPs into key players of content regulation while at the same time users' freedom of expression would be subordinated.

Without clear legal rules, a great degree of confusion would have a detrimental effect on host ISPs. For instance, legal uncertainty might lead to excessive removal of content from host ISPs as host ISPs would be unaware of the level of enforcement and would tend to take down material in order to avoid liability. In this way, host ISPs might

[7] European Commission, 'Public Consultation on the evaluation and modernisation of the legal framework for the enforcement of intellectual property rights: summary of responses' (2016) 37.

[8] Council of the European Union, Council of the European Union, 'EU Human Rights Guidelines on Freedom of Expression Online and Offline' (2014) 5, www.consilium.europa.eu/uedocs/cms_data/docs/pressdata/EN/foraff/142549.pdf.

[9] K Garstka, 'Looking above and beyond the blunt expectation: specified request as the recommended approach to intermediary liability in cyberspace' (2016) 7 *European Journal of Law and Technology* 10.

[10] M Husovec, 'Accountable, not liable: injunctions against intermediaries' (2016) *TILEC Discussion Paper* 33.

[11] C Angelopoulos, 'Beyond the safe harbors: harmonizing substantive intermediary liability for copyright infringement in Europe' (2013) 3 *Intellectual Property Quarterly* 254.

[12] S Stalla-Bourdillon, 'Sometimes one is not enough! Securing freedom of expression, encouraging private regulation, or subsidizing Internet intermediaries or all three at the same time: the dilemma of Internet intermediaries' liability' (2012) 7 *Journal of International Commercial Law and Technology* 154.

turn into censorship machines that would violate users' fundamental rights in order to preserve their business operation.[13]

Moreover, legal uncertainty created by the outdated and problematic approach under the ECD and the DSMD might pose serious interference to the legitimate uses of host ISPs and thus threaten their business model. While OCSSPs, a sub-type of host ISPs, such as Pirate Bay focus on the dissemination of copyright infringing material, many host ISPs offer legitimate services to users. This is the case of dual use technologies which can 'be used to violate third parties' rights as well as promote social beneficial uses'.[14] This understanding might undermine their business models since host ISPs may be unsure in which cases they would be subject to liability. So, in order to avoid any risk of liability, host ISPs may undertake proactive measures with the aim to mitigate the dissemination of infringing content within their platforms and thus be exonerated from liability. This scenario has been illustrated by Landes and Lichtman. They refer to the case of a flea market.[15] In order to battle counterfeit goods, flea market organisers might use technology in order to screen the goods that are displayed.[16] Yet, whereas the use of technology might protect sellers from liability, it might increase the costs of operating a flea market and thus impede sellers of goods to participate in the flea market.[17]

However, this outdated framework of Article 14(1) of the ECD and the problematic approach set forth in Article 17 of the DSMD do not have a negative impact only on host ISPs. Indeed, new tech companies may be hesitant to enter the Digital Single Market. In light of legal uncertainty, new host ISPs under Article 14(1) of the ECD and OCSSPs under Article 17 of the DSMD may be forced to adopt expensive proactive measures in order to avoid liability.

Within the context of a digital ecosystem, consider for instance the case of YouTube. Being uncertain of the level of enforcement, YouTube may be encouraged to use filtering technology in order to curb the illicit content that accrues within its platform. At the same time, the adoption of filtering technology would increase the transaction costs

[13] Rowland, Kohl and Charlesworth (n 2) 86.

[14] G Frosio, 'Why keep a dog and bark yourself? From intermediary liability to responsibility' (2017) *Centre for International Intellectual Property Studies* 8.

[15] WM Landes and D Lichtman, 'Indirect Liability for Copyright Infringement: An Economic Perspective' (2003) 16 *Harvard Journal of Law and Technology* 409.

[16] WM Landes and D Lichtman, 'Indirect Liability for Copyright Infringement: Napster and Beyond' (2003) 16 *The Journal of Economic Perspectives* 20; Landes and Lichtman (n 15) 404–05.

[17] Landes and Lichtman (n 15) 409; M Daly, 'Life after Grokster: analysis of US and European approaches to file-sharing' (2007) 29 *European Intellectual Property Review* 2; T Hays, 'The evolution and decentralisation of secondary liability for infringements of copyright-protected works: Part 1' (2006) 3 *European Intellectual Property Review* 620 where Hays notes that from a judicial perspective, this understanding has been exemplified in the *Sony* case which was the first ruling that has preoccupied the courts and shed light on whether dual-uses technologies should be held liable for copyright infringements or not. In the case at hand, Universal City Studios have brought legal proceedings against Sony Betamax because Sony manufactured home video recorders which were used by its users also for unlawful copying of films. Having found that Sony's products can commercially contribute to the home video industry while at the same time home video recorders' main aim was non-infringing uses, the Court refrained from imposing liability on Sony Betamax. Otherwise, if Sony was held liable for the infringing actions of its users, piracy might be decreased but the whole market of home video recording will be disrupted; *Sony Corp of Am. v Universal City Studios*, Inc 464 U.S. 417, 220 U.S.P.Q. (BNA) 665 (1984).

and thus act as a deterrent for new OCSSPs with similar services to enter the market. This dual effect has been criticised by Lichtman who argues that:

> … the best reason to impose liability on YouTube is that it is in an enormously good position to filter for and in other ways discourage online infringement. The best reason to decline is that there will be some cost associated with filtering, and that cost might discourage future technologists from experimenting with similar products …[18]

This means that legal uncertainty on the level of enforcement might impede innovation in the Digital Single Market. This because the development of sophisticated technology would require high resources from new host ISPs and OCSSPs, which they would not possess. Lacking resources, new host ISPs and new OCSSPs may be hesitant to enter the market. Therefore, one of the substantial elements of the Digital Single Market (DSM), innovation,[19] would be under threat at supranational and national level.

Finally, with regard to the DSMD, new OCSSPs might be willing to enter into licensing agreements with content owners in order to avoid liability. Given that enforcement rules are not clear to rights holders and host ISPs and OCSSPs, both parties might adopt a more cautious approach in the course of the negotiations of licensing agreements. This is what Coase describes as a 'prisoner's dilemma'.[20] This describes the difference in the behaviour of the prisoners in prison when they live in their own cells and when they live all together. According to this dilemma, if prisoners were not restricted in their own cells, they would have more chances to contact each other and negotiate in a more liberal way. As they live in separate cells they follow a more personal way of making contact with other prisoners.[21] This understanding could be applied in the context of host ISPs and rights holders. Given that OCSSPs and intellectual property holders are not aware of the level of enforcement, they might act with more precautions than necessary. It is this precautionary approach that might lead to the cancellation of the negotiations for licensing agreements between intellectual property holders and new tech companies.[22]

Nevertheless, this outdated and problematic framework under Article 14(1) of the ECD and Article 17 of the DSMD that revolves around the regulatory regime of ISPs might prove harmful not only for host ISPs and OCSSPs. Indeed, it could also have a

[18] D Lichtman, 'Copyright as Information Policy: Google Book Search from a Law and Economics Perspective' in J Lerner and S Stern (eds), *Innovation Policy and The Economy* (National Bureau of Economic Research, 2008) 19.

[19] JS Marcus, G Petropoulos and T Yeung, 'Contribution to Growth: The European Digital Single Market Delivering economic benefits for citizens and businesses' (*IMCO Committee*, 2019) 11, www.europarl.europa.eu/RegData/etudes/STUD/2019/631044/IPOL_STU(2019)631044_EN.pdf; EU Commission, 'A Digital Single Market Strategy for Europe' COM (2015) 192 final 3.

[20] FE Guerra-Pujol and O Martínez-García, 'Does the Prisoner's Dilemma Refute the Coase Theorem?' (2013) 47 *John Marshall Law Review* 1290.

[21] ibid.

[22] J Blevins, 'Uncertainty as Enforcement Mechanism: The New Expansion of Secondary Copyright Liability to Internet Platforms' (2013) 34 *Cardozo Law Review* 1829; see also MA Carrier, 'Copyright and Innovation: The Untold Story' (2012) 2012 *Wisconsin Law Review* 914 where Carrier notes that 'VCs are Venture capitalists (VCs) provide money and play an active role in the company's operations, typically occupying a position on the board of directors'. Carrier stresses that legal uncertainty forced VCs to adopt a more cautious approach towards the new entrants in the markets and thus led to a 'loss of new disruptive technologies that deliver content to people'; Husovec (n 10) 33.

detrimental effect on internet users' fundamental rights. For this reason, a critical evaluation of the implication of liability rules on users' rights follows.

III. Article 14(1) of the ECD and Article 17 of DSMD and Internet Users/Online Consumers

The outdated and problematic approaches under Article 14(1) of the ECD and Article 17 of the DSMD might restrict users' freedom of expression as per Article 11 of the EU Charter of Fundamental rights, namely the right to freedom of expression that encompasses the right to receive and impart information. To hold host ISPs under the uncertainty of whether or not to impose on the liability rules, as Zittrain argues, could lead to paradoxical scenarios.[23] For instance, while host ISPs are forced to function as gatekeepers by policymakers, they have a lack of expertise and judiciary duties.[24] In this regard, under the threat of sanctions, they may act as 'overzealous police officers'.[25] Subsequently, this could lead to an overzealous notice and take down or even an intensive blocking of websites without prior consideration of their illicit activities. This would reduce the amount of content available on public and deprive internet users from obtaining information.

A representative example of this line of thinking can be found in a handful of empirical studies where notice and take down mechanisms were eroded. For instance, in a study conducted in the Netherlands,[26] it was found that the ISP that offered internet and was located in the UK removed the allegedly infringing material upon notification without verifying the validity of the claim. In this case, the claim was fake since the allegedly infringing material was in the public domain. In this regard, one might assume that other ISPs might adopt the same stance in order to avoid liability. This understanding seems persuasive since, if an ISP unreasonably or unjustifiably removes a content, it is not liable. In contrast, the non-expeditious removal of allegedly infringing content upon notification might trigger the liability of host ISPs.

With regard to users' right to impart information, legal uncertainty could have a negative impact too. For instance, it could cause disincentives for the host ISPs' side. This concerns the concept of collateral censorship which occurs 'when a (private) intermediary suppresses the speech of others in order to avoid liability that otherwise might be imposed on it as a result of that speech'.[27] In order to be exonerated from liability, host ISPs could unreasonably restrain the sphere of action of internet users, prohibiting legal activities and lawful content which has been placed or exchanged by the users.[28] In this

[23] J Zittrain, 'A History of Online Gatekeeping' (2006) 19 *Harvard Journal of Law and Technology* 253.
[24] Rowland, Kohl and Charlesworth (n 2) 86.
[25] ibid 87.
[26] Lecture by Nas (n 2).
[27] FT Wu, 'Collateral Censorship and the Limits of Intermediary Immunity' (2011) 87 *Notre Dame Law Review* 295–96; The concept of collateral censorship has been first developed in Balkin's writings; see J Balkin, 'Old School/ new School speech regulation' (2014) 127 *Harvard Law Review* 2309.
[28] G Sartor, 'Providers Liability: From the e-commerce Directive to the future' (2017) *IMCO Committee* 12; A Kuczerawy, *Intermediary Liability and Freedom of Expression in the EU: from Concepts to Safeguards* (Wellington, Intersentia, 2018) 96–97 where she argues that 'legal uncertainty is problematic because vague

way, whereas online infringements could be curbed, lawful activities of internet users would be restricted. Therefore, the benefit of terminating illicit activities online could not outweigh the negative effect of restricting lawful activities online.

A telling example can be found in the *Lenz v Universal* case.[29] In this case, a video with a baby dancing under the rhythms of the Prince's song 'Let's go crazy' has been removed by YouTube for copyright purposes. Likewise, a video from NASA that was about the landing of Curiosity robot in Mars has been removed for copyright violation.[30] Therefore, under the reasoning of copyright infringement, users are deprived from expressing themselves by uploading videos with parodies or videos with educational purposes.

In addition, the current legislative tools might undermine consumers' interests. This is because host ISPs might erroneously remove legitimate listings or non-counterfeit goods from their networks. Given that goods and services are messengers of information and cultural aspects of the society, the removal of legitimate material might pose a risk to consumers' right to receive and impart information. For instance, Senftleben notes that 'The creation of a brand image demonstrates that trademarks are capable of serving as carriers of complex, additional information referring to a specific lifestyle, behaviour or attitude. Viewed from this perspective, trademarks can be qualified as the focal point of communication with consumers.'[31] As a corollary, online consumers would be deprived of information about the availability of goods and services that are offered within their networks.

Finally, the legal uncertainty with regard to the level of enforcement of rights would underestimate the internet users' rights in the online public domain. This is because, as Advocate General Poiares Maduro in Joined Cases C-236/08, C-237/08 and C-238/08 of *Google France/Inc. v Louis Vuitton Malletier*[32] pointed out, 'the aim of Directive 2000/31 is to create a free and open public domain on the internet'. This means that internet users should be able to exchange and receive information online. Yet, if the dissemination of content is restricted online due to the legal uncertainty that revolves around the level of enforcement of rights, one of the main objectives of the ECD would be placed in peril.

However, apart from the right to free speech, the uncertainty with regard to the enforcement of rights and the application of the existing legislative tools might undermine the right of internet users to arts. As per Article 13 of the EU Charter of Fundamental Rights, 'the arts and scientific research shall be free of constraint …'. This understanding has been accentuated in a study conducted by Jacques, Garstka, Hviid and Street. The study demonstrated that whilst 1845 parody videos have been

rules can push intermediaries to adopt overly cautious behaviour. When not sure about their legal situation, they may prefer to err on the side of caution, which means that they eliminate disputed content, even if it is actually legitimate'.

[29] *Lenz v Universal Music Corp.* (9th Cir. Mar. 17, 2016).

[30] J Reda, 'When filters fail: These cases show we can't trust algorithms to clean up the internet' (*Reda's website*, 28 September 2017) juliareda.eu/2017/09/when-filters-fail/; see also T Lee, 'As Curiosity touches down on Mars, video is taken down from YouTube' (*arstechnica*, 8 June 2012) arstechnica.com/tech-policy/2012/08/as-curiosity-touches-down-on-mars-video-is-taken-down-from-youtube/.

[31] M Senftleben, 'An uneasy case for notice and takedown: context-specific trademark rights' (2012) *VU Centre for Law and Governance* 8.

[32] Joined Cases C-236/08, C-237/08 and C-238/08 of *Google France/Inc. v Louis Vuitton Malletier* (2009) ECLI:EU:C:2009:569, para 142.

uploaded on YouTube in 2012, 32.1 per cent of them were removed under the reasoning of copyright infringement in December 2016.[33] In addition, the Advocate General Saugmandsgaard Øe on *Peterson v YouTube*[34] has stressed the negative effects of the existing legal framework with regard to the use of automated technology. In particular, he noted that filtering technology 'would introduce a risk of undermining online creativity, which would be contrary to Article 13 of the Charter. The danger in that regard is that maximum protection of certain forms of intellectual creativity is to the detriment of other forms of creativity which are also positive for society'.[35] Therefore, the current legal framework might deprive internet users from their right to culture.

Yet, the negative implications of the liability rules under Article 14(1) of the ECD and Article 17 of the DSMD might not be limited to internet users and host ISPs' and OCSSPs' business models. Indeed, they can also extend to rights holders themselves.

IV. Article 14(1) of the ECD and Article 17 of DSMD and Copyright Holders/Brand Owners

With regard to the rights of intellectual property holders, the outdated framework under the ECD and the problematic approach as set forth in DSMD create legal uncertainty. As already discussed in chapter three, Article 14(1) of the ECD does not provide a definition for host ISPs. Rather, it entails a set of defences for host ISPs in order for them to be exonerated from liability. For this reason, in order to define liability for host ISPs, national courts resort to secondary liability rules. Given the lack of harmonisation on secondary liability rules, each legal jurisdiction offers its own legal rules. The result is a patchwork of miscellaneous tortious secondary liability doctrines among the EU Member States with different criteria to claim legal protection. In addition, as discussed in chapter four, Article 17 of the DSMD provides a definition for OCSSPs, which is a sub-type of ISPs, but entails an array of problematic features that accentuate the existing legal uncertainty for copyright holders. As discussed in chapter four section III(B), it is questionable under which liability regime copyright holders could seek redress if their copyrighted content has been violated within the platform of an online marketplace. A representative example of this line of thinking is to be found on eBay. In this case, eBay offers tangible as well as non-tangible goods to its online consumers. For instance, tangible goods amount to anything that is tangible such as bags, watches, furniture while non-tangible goods could amount to eBooks or online seminars which can be viewed as YouTube videos. With regard to non-tangible goods, this means that eBooks or online seminars that are viewed as video via music video exchange platforms such as Dailymotion fall within the meaning of copyrighted content and thus under the scope

[33] S Jacques, K Garstka, M Hviid and J Street, 'The Impact on Cultural Diversity of Automated Anti-Piracy Systems as Copyright Enforcement Mechanisms: An Empirical Study of YouTube's Content ID Digital Fingerprinting Technology' (2018) 15 *SCRIPTed* 298.

[34] Case C-682/18 Opinion of Advocate General SAUGMANDSGAARD ØE on *Peterson v YouTube* (2021) ECLI:EU:C:2021:503.

[35] ibid para 243.

of Article 17 of the DSMD.[36] However, if a copyright holder brings legal proceedings against an online marketplace, which is considered a host ISP under Article 14(1) of the ECD, alleging copyright violation, one might wonder under which liability regime would her lawsuit fall and how she will protect her copyright.

Therefore, neither legislative frameworks can guarantee the protection of the rights of creators or brand owners. Whether or not a host ISP is liable for copyright or trade mark infringements that accrue within their networks is subject to a case-by-case assessment and might differ from jurisdiction to jurisdiction depending on the courts' examination.

Further, apart from the legal uncertainty that might arise among rights holders, the imposition of liability rules may not be a panacea for the intellectual property holders. This is because, even if the courts find host ISPs liable, this does not automatically guarantee that rights holders will be compensated. Consider, for instance, the case of The Pirate Bay.[37] In 2009, the Stockholm District Court found Pirate Bay liable and thus ordered it to pay damages up to 30 million kronor. However, when the rights holders requested the damages, it was found that Pirate Bay did not have the necessary assets to satisfy the pecuniary orders of the court.[38] Therefore, the rights holders could not collect the award of damages and thus be compensated for the massive infringement of their rights. Hence, in such cases it appears that liability rules cannot provide adequate protection to the rights holders.

Finally, the problematic approach under the DSMD might give rise to negative publicity for intellectual property holders. Although the aim of the DSMD was to bridge the value gap between rights holders' revenues and the dissemination of their content online, it might have an opposite effect for rights holders. This is because it presents rights holders as the main threat for users to access copyrighted content online and for OCSSPs to disruptively continue the operation of their business model. For example, it urges OCSSPs to license the content that is disseminated online. Given that it seems impossible to license all the content available online, internet users would be deprived of content that could not license. What is more, the introduction of primary liability rules, as presented in chapter 4 section III(B), would act as a threat for the operation of OCSSPs since they would be subject to damages once a copyright infringement takes place within their networks.

V. Conclusion

Overall, one might conclude that the current legislative tools that regulate host ISP's and OCSSPs' liability undermine their business models, and internet users' and rights

[36] M Husovec, 'Compromising (on) the Digital Single Market? A Quick Look at the Estonian Presidency Proposal(s) on Art 13' (*Kluwer copyright blog*, 8 September 2017) copyrightblog.kluweriplaw.com/2017/09/08/compromising-digital-single-market-quick-look-estonian-presidency-proposals-art-13/.

[37] A Murray, *Information Technology Law: The law and society* (Oxford, Oxford University Press, 2009) 250.

[38] N Anderson 'Swedish court rules TPB admins too broke to pay damages' (*Arstechnica*, 24 August 2009), available at <https://arstechnica.com/tech-policy/2009/08/swedish-court-rules-tpb-admins-too-broke-to-pay-damages, last accessed 18 October 2021; M Manner, T Siniketo and U Polland, 'The Pirate Bay ruling' (2009) 20 *Entertainment Law Review* 198.

holders' rights. While the CJEU outlined in the *Scarlet Extended*[39] ruling that 'in the context of measures adopted to protect copyright holders, national authorities and courts must strike a fair balance between the protection of copyright and the protection of the fundamental rights of individuals who are affected by such measures',[40] the findings presented in this book indicate that the ECD and DSMD fail to provide a regulatory framework that could take into consideration all the rights at stake. For this reason, a legal reform is imperative in order to suggest legislative amendments so as to balance the interests of the parties involved. These suggestions will be thoroughly discussed in Part III of this book

However, before delving into the recommendations for a robust legal framework, there is a need to discuss the Proposal for a Digital Services Act Regulation,[41] which has been announced by the European Commission on 15 December 2020. This Proposal aims to replace the ECD and the relevant provisions on host ISPs. In this way, the reader will have a complete picture of the EU legislative framework and initiatives on host ISPs' activities.

[39] Case C-70/10 *Scarlet Extended SA v Société belge des auteurs, compositeurs et éditeurs SCRL (SABAM)* [2011] ECR-I 11959.

[40] ibid para 45.

[41] Hereinafter proposed DSA Regulation.

6

Liability of Providers of Hosting Services under the Proposal for a Digital Services Act for Trade Mark and Copyright Infringements: A Promising Approach

I. Introduction

On 17 September 2020, Ursula von der Leyen, the President of the European Commission, in her State of the European Union address, announced the main priorities for the EU Commission for the next five years.[1] Similar to the former EU Presidency's priorities, one of the main priorities is to ensure Europe is fit for the Digital Age, thus ensuring a fair and competitive digital economy.[2] In order to achieve this, the EU Commission initiated an EU Public Consultation with regard to the current regulatory framework of host ISPs. The consultation invited comments and views from different stakeholders and conducted an impact assessment. The outcomes of the EU Public Consultation showed that a high numbers of stakeholders urge harmonisation of the obligations of ISPs in terms of content moderation, standardised notice and action mechanisms, and transparent policies.[3] At the same time, the impact assessment revealed that there is a broad consensus amongst different stakeholders for the need to update the current regulatory framework for host ISPs by imposing additional obligations.[4] Likewise, leading voices in scholarship urge for an update to the current legal framework. For instance, Geiger and Frosio argue that, 'Given the rapid technological development in the past two decades there is a

[1] Ursula von der Leyen, 'State of the Union Address 2020 by Ursula von der Leyen', available at www.youtube.com/watch?v=q8eThxTJxRk&t=188s; The President of the European Commission noted in the event of 'Masters of Digital 2021' that 'the Digital Services Act defines the responsibilities of all digital actors operating in Europe …'; EU President, 'A Union that strives for more – My agenda for Europe' (2021) 13.

[2] European Commission, 'Shaping Europe's Digital Future' (February 2020) 2.

[3] European Commission, 'Open Public Consultation on the Digital Services Act Package: Summary Report on the open public Consultation on the Digital Services Act Package' (2020) 5.

[4] European Commission staff working document, 'Executive summary of the impact assessment report' SWD (2020) 1–3 which states that 'The annexed evaluation of the Directive shows that its core principles remain valid, but some of its specific rules require an update in light of the specific challenges emerging around online intermediaries and online platforms in particular.'

widespread agreement that an update of the legal framework for digital services is needed.'[5]

In light of this, on 15 December 2020, the EU Commission announced the Proposal for a Regulation on Digital Services Act.[6] Its aim is 'to ensure the best conditions for the provision of innovative digital services in the internal market, to contribute to online safety and the protection of fundamental rights, and to set a robust and durable governance structure for the effective supervision of providers of intermediary services'.[7]

The proposed DSA Regulation accompanies the sector-specific legislation with regard to online intermediaries and illegal content online. This means that the proposed Regulation would apply as *lex specialis* for the cases that are not covered by the current legislative pieces, such as the DSMD or the Directive on video-sharing platform providers.[8]

This proposed DSA Regulation is of interest for this book because it addresses the liability of host ISPs for trade mark infringements and acts as a default for the liability of content sharing service providers for copyright infringements. The proposed DSA Regulation seems to be a promising approach. It has received a warm welcome from civil society organisations, human rights activists, and business platforms.[9] This is mainly because it stresses the need for transparency in the online world, including online advertising, as well as ensuring public oversight for the operation of host ISPs. At the same time, it seems that EU Member States have also considered the proposed DSA Regulation in a positive manner.[10] For instance, Poland welcomes the provisions of the DSA Regulation but would like more competences for the appointment of Digital Services Coordinators[11] while Italy requires more clarification with regard to the measures against the reappearance of illegal material within the online networks.[12] However, a number of flaws have already been identified. For instance, the proposed DSA Regulation maintains the liability exemptions of Article 14(1) of ECD, thus it preserves the

[5] C Geiger and G Frosio, 'Taking fundamental rights seriously in the Digital Services Act's platform liability regime' (2021) *European Law Journal* 35.

[6] Proposal for a Regulation of the European Parliament and the Council on a Single Market For Digital Services (Digital Services Act) and amending Directive 2000/31/EC COM/2020/825 final (hereinafter proposed DSA Regulation).

[7] European Commission, 'Proposal for a Regulation of the European Parliament and of the Council on a Single Market For Digital Services (Digital Services Act) and amending Directive 2000/31/EC' COM/2020/825 final.

[8] C Angelopoulos, 'Digital Services Act and Digital Markets Act: Commission presents legislative proposals' (2020) *EU Law live* 30–31.

[9] EFF states that 'The DSA is an important opportunity to clarify the EU's commitment to fundamental rights online, and to secure basic rights that will be built upon in the years to come' in EFF, 'Preserve What Works, Fix What is Broken: EFF's Policy Principles for the Digital Services Act' (2020) www.eff.org/issues/eu-policy-principles; The Senior Directive for Law and Policy of Article 19 noted that 'ARTICLE 19's preliminary analysis indicates that the DSA is looking to maintain the cornerstones of the E-Commerce Directive, including conditional immunity from liability and the prohibition on general monitoring.' This is positive and corresponds to our recommendations in the consultations organised by the European Commission in ARTICLE 19, 'EU: The draft Digital Services Act and the Digital Markets Act must protect freedom of expression' www.article19.org/resources/digital-rights/.

[10] DSA Observatory, available at dsa-observatory.eu/.

[11] Position of Polish Government in the Council, available at www.gov.pl/web/digitalization.

[12] Position of Italian Government in the Council, available at secure.ipex.eu/IPEXL-WEB/document/COM-2020-0825/itcam.

reverse logic of liability of host ISPs and imposes a very broad spectrum of obligations to very large platforms while it is unclear which provisions are applicable to copyright issues and, in particular, to Article 17 of the DSMD. Crucially, given that it is an emerging legislative piece, such flaws could be rectified in the process of the legislative process through the Compromised Texts of the Council, the trilogues and the final text voted on by the EU Parliament.

Against this background, this chapter critically examines the proposed DSA Regulation. For the purposes of this book, the narrative focuses on the legal provisions that are relevant to host ISPs.[13] In particular, the provisions that reinforce the legal rules of the E-Commerce Directive, the concept of a diligent economic operator, and the interpretation of actual knowledge are each evaluated. The discussion then moves to the proposed Good Samaritan clause, the attribution of additional obligations to very large platforms with regard to trace the traders and the use of automated technology to curb online infringements, the proposed statutory provision for transparency in online advertising and the establishment of a proposed Digital Services Coordinator as a supervisory authority. Finally, the chapter examines the intersection of the proposed Regulation with Article 17 of the DSMD.

II. Proposed DSA Regulation: A Good Start but More Clarity is Required

A. Reinforcing the Provisions of the E-Commerce Directive about Liability Exemptions

The provisions of the proposed DSA Regulation reinforce the provisions of the e-Commerce Directive. More specifically, Article 3 of the proposed Regulation, which addresses the liability of mere conduit ISPs, incorporates Article 12 of the e-Commerce Directive and Article 4 of the proposed Regulation, which concerns the liability of caching ISPs; it also repeats Article 13 of the e-Commerce Directive.

Further, Article 5 of the proposed DSA Regulation is about the liability of providers of hosting services and reinforces Article 14(1) of the ECD. In particular, it states that providers of hosting services would be exempt from liability if they are not aware, or do not have actual knowledge, of the illicit activity, or if they expeditiously remove the infringing content upon being notified. The need to maintain the liability exemptions of the e-Commerce Directive has been outlined in a number of EU policy documents. For instance, the Impact Assessment of the Digital Services Act reveals that the great majority of stakeholders agree to preserve its fundamental principles.[14]

[13] For the purposes of this chapter, the authoritative definition of providers of hosting services, which has been included in the proposed DSA Regulation, will be adopted.

[14] European Commission, 'Staff working document on executive summary of the impact assessment report' (2020) SWD 349 final 2.

Unlike Article 14(1) of the ECD, Article 5 of the proposed Regulation takes a step forward and specifies in Recital 22 that actual knowledge shall be correlated with a specific infringement. This understanding is also reinforced at the European level. In particular, in the *Peterson/ YouTube*[15] case the Advocate General (AG) discussed the dispute between a copyright owner and YouTube for the latter's failure to remove a video from a song, alleging copyright infringement and clarifying that this should be assessed in relation to specific illicit content. In the AG's opinion, 'the applicant must show that the provider had "knowledge" or "awareness" of that information in particular or whether it need only demonstrate that the provider had general and abstract "knowledge" or "awareness" of the fact that it stores illegal information and that its services are used for illegal activities'.[16] In addition, Article 8 of the proposed DSA Regulation specifies that knowledge shall be related to a specific infringement and could be acquired through a court order which shall specify the reasons and the URL location.

Further, Recital 22 of the proposed Regulation uses the concept of the diligent economic operator in order to assess the knowledge of the providers of hosting services. This means that if it is possible for a diligent economic operator to be aware of an illicit activity within its business model, a provider of hosting services should also be aware of the infringing content or counterfeit goods that are disseminated via its network. This understanding has already been reinforced in a cluster of case law at the European level. For instance, in the *L'Oreal v Ebay* ruling, the CJEU stated that in order to attribute liability to providers of hosting services national courts need to examine whether the online marketplace is 'aware of facts or circumstances on the basis of which a diligent economic operator should have identified the illegality in question and acted in accordance with Article 14(1) (b) of Directive 2000/31'.[17]

What is worthwhile to note is that Article 5 of the proposed DSA Regulation endorses a higher degree of protection for the consumers of online platforms. More specifically, paragraph 3 states that the actual knowledge of a specific violation shall not be applied to the consumer protection context in order to protect the average and reasonably well-informed consumer. This means that a provider of hosting services would not be exempt from liability in cases of online purchases and the online transactions between consumers and traders. Therefore, the objectives of the proposed Regulation, such as to contribute to online safety, would be fulfilled.

In addition, the proposed Regulation maintains the prohibition for the implementation of general monitoring obligations. More specifically, Article 7 of the Proposed DSA Regulation repeats Article 15 of the ECD and notes that providers of hosting services shall not be subject to general monitoring obligations or an obligation to actively seek for illegal information within their networks. The prohibition for general monitoring obligations has been the cornerstone of the e-commerce framework since it enabled online intermediaries to escape from the burden of monitoring the content that is transmitted online. This is mainly because online intermediaries did not need to license

[15] AG Saugmandsgaard Øe in his Opinion in Joined Cases C-682/18 and 683/18 *YouTube*, 16 July 2020.
[16] ibid para 171.
[17] Case C-324/09 *L'Oreal SA V eBay Int'l AG* (2011) ECR I-6011, para 120.

expensive filtering technology or develop their technology in order to monitor their networks.[18] Therefore, their right of host ISPs to operate business has been safeguarded.

B. Different Terms for Host ISPs

Another complex issue of the proposed DSA Regulation is to be found in the multiple definitions offered for the host ISPs. For instance, Article 2 notes that a host ISP 'consists of the storage of information provided by, and at the request of, a recipient of the service; while an "online platform" means a provider of a hosting service which, at the request of a recipient of the service, stores and disseminates to the public information'. Finally, Article 25 of the proposed DSA Regulation introduces the definition of very large platforms that have a monthly-based traffic of 45 million internet users.

Crucially, the use of diverse definitions might be confusing. This is mainly because the proposed DSA Regulation does not carve out the differences between the diverse definitions for ISPs. For instance, one might wonder what is the functional difference between a provider of hosting services and an online platform. In the Explanatory Memorandum of the proposed DSA Regulation, it is stated that online platforms encompass social media and online market places. This means that both hosting services and online platforms can fall within the definition of providers of hosting services. Given that providers of hosting services and online platforms are ascribed different obligations under the proposed DSA Regulation, it is plausible to ask how obligations can be attributed. For instance, would it be based on objective requirements or on a case-by-case basis?[19]

Furthermore, the terms entailed in the proposed DSA Regulation are already used in other legislative tools, but their definitions differ. Indeed, the Committee of the Regions noted in the Opinion on DSA that 'there seem to be many closely-related definitions in different instruments, which may become too cumbersome from the perspective of compliance, imposing additional costs on companies and consumers'. Telling examples can be found in the term 'online platform', and its use in the DSMD and the proposed DSA Regulation. While the proposed DSA Regulation introduces the terms 'online platforms' and 'very large platforms', the Proposal for a Digital Markets Act Regulation entails the definitions of core platform services and digital platforms.[20] In addition, although the proposed DSA Regulation encompasses the term 'provider of hosting services', the DSMD uses the term 'online content sharing service providers', and the Audiovisual Media Services Directive[21] uses the term 'video-sharing platforms'. The notion of very large online platforms is broadly defined while it does not correspond with the concept of dominant position as set

[18] Geiger and Frosio (n 5) 31.

[19] A Castillo, 'The Digital Services Act Package: Reflections on the EU Commission's policy options' (2021) *ETUI Policy Brief* 4.

[20] Proposal for a Regulation of the European Parliament and of the Council on contestable and fair markets in the digital sector (Digital Markets Act) COM/2020/842 final.

[21] Council Directive (EU) 2018/1808 on the coordination of certain provisions laid down by law, regulation or administrative action in Member States concerning the provision of audiovisual media services (Audiovisual Media Services Directive) in view of changing market realities (2018) OJ L 303.

forth in Article 102 Treaty on the Functioning of the European Union (TFEU).[22] As a result, the interplay between similar terms and different interpretations might have a detrimental effect on their business model and create an additional burden for rights holders aiming to enforce their rights.

What is more, a number of EU policy documents criticise the use of diverse terms in legislative tools that address the online regulatory framework, thus it favours consistent and clear terminology. For instance, the Opinion of the European Data Protection Supervisor outlines the need for the proposed DSA Regulation to use the same wording for the prohibition of general monitoring obligations as set forth in Article 15 of the ECD.[23] In this way, the proposed DSA Regulation would align with the precedent line of case law delivered by the Court of Justice of the European Union.[24] In addition, the Opinion of the Regulatory Scrutiny Board urges the need to offer clear terms in the new legislative tools and in particular with regard to the terms of 'public spaces', or of the concept of 'fundamental rights by design, and the definition of a platform'.[25] Otherwise, the enforcement of intellectual property rights online would be jeopardised.[26]

C. Introducing a Quasi-Good Samaritan Clause

Another new provision is to be found in Article 6 of the proposed DSA Regulation that introduces a quasi-Good Samaritan clause. In particular, it states that providers of hosting services can apply the defences of knowledge and expeditious removal in order to exonerate from liability even though they integrate into their business models proactive measures and practices in the battle against piracy. This means that providers of intermediary services would be subject to liability exemption despite undertaking measures against infringements on a voluntary basis. Therefore, the use of mechanisms against infringements would not lead to the liability of providers of intermediary services because those providers would not be able to identify the illicit activity.

Within this context, many scholars have argued that Article 6 of the proposed DSA Regulation resembles the Good Samaritan clause in the US legal system. The roots of the Good Samaritan clause are to be found in Section 230 C 1 and Section 2 of the Communications Decency Act (CDA) which states that 'No provider or user of an interactive computer service shall be treated as the publisher or speaker of any information provided by another information content provider.'[27]

[22] JB Nordemann, 'Annex III: Digital Services Act: Improving the functioning of the single market' (2020) 299.

[23] European Data Protection Supervisor, 'Opinion 1/2021 on the Proposal for Digital Services Act' (2021) 8.

[24] ibid.

[25] Regulatory Scrutiny Board Opinion, 'Proposal for a Regulation of the European Parliament and of the Council on a Single Market For Digital Services (Digital Services Act) and amending Directive 2000/31/EC' 6.11.2020SEC(2020) 432 2.

[26] See also F Wilman, 'The EU's system of knowledge-based liability for hosting service providers in respect of illegal user content – between the e-Commerce Directive and the Digital Services Act' (2021) 12 *Journal of Intellectual Property, Information Technology and E-Commerce Law* 340.

[27] 47 U.S.C. § 230, a Provision of the Communication Decency Act.

The rationale for imposing such a privilege[28] stems from the case of *Stratton-Oakmont v Prodigy*.[29] In the case at hand, Stratton and Oakmont filed legal proceedings against Prodigy, a computer network for libel comments that were posted on Prodigy's network. The Supreme court held that Prodigy exercised editorial control over the material the users had posted since it uses filtering technology to detect offensive comments, and therefore is able to remove it. In this sense, it exercises a type of censorship over the information that is transmitted online.[30] Interestingly, although Prodigy took voluntarily action and removed the unlawful information, the court found Prodigy liable for the defamatory comments under the reasoning that it did not remove all the offensive comments which had been visible to internet users on its bulletin board.[31]

However, the current proposed provision does not correspond to the US provision in its entirety. As Kuczerawy notes, 'it has very little in common with its Section 230 counterpart'.[32] This is because Article 6 of the Proposed DSA Regulation does not state that providers of hosting services would be exempt from liability if they do not remove the allegedly infringing work regardless of knowledge, as set forth in section 230 of the CDA. Rather, Article 6 focuses solely on noting that providers of hosting services would be eligible for liability exemptions even if they undertake measures on their initiatives and terminate, or curb, the re-emergence of copyright infringing works.[33]

Further, it is unclear whether providers of hosting services would be liable if they acquire knowledge of the illicit content through voluntary measures. Recital 25 of the proposed DSA Regulation explains that the use of proactive measures do not exonerate providers of hosting services from the defences of Article 5 of the proposed DSA Regulation, but it remains silent with regard to knowledge of the illicit content. Consider, for instance, providers of hosting services that deploy filtering technology in order to identify copyright infringing works, but fail to identify defamatory or terroristic comments.[34] In this vein, it is plausible to ponder if the use of filtering tools would lead to the assumption of knowledge of the provider of intermediary services, and thus make them liable for the offensive comments within the network.

Crucially, this uncertainty might lead to over-removal of content. This is because providers of hosting services might be incentivised to take down illicit content without conducting prior investigation to ensure exemption from liability.[35] This understanding has been already accentuated in a number of studies at the European and International level where host ISPs were prone to remove information irrespective of their lawful

[28] A Kuczerawy, 'The EU Commission on voluntary monitoring: Good Samaritan 2.0 or Good Samaritan 0.5?' (*CITIP blog*, 24 April 2018) www.law.kuleuven.be/citip/blog/the-eu-commission-on-voluntary-monitoring-good-samaritan-2-0-or-good-samaritan-0-5/.

[29] US Supreme Court, *Stratton Oakmont Inc and Daniel Porush v Prodigy Services Company* (24 May 1995) h2o.law.harvard.edu/cases/4540.

[30] ibid.

[31] Kuczerawy (n 28).

[32] A Kuczerawy, 'The Good Samaritan that wasn't: voluntary monitoring under the (draft) Digital Services Act' (*Verfassungsblog*, 12 January 2021) verfassungsblog.de/good-samaritan-dsa/.

[33] ibid.

[34] ibid.

[35] ibid.

nature. For instance, a study case conducted in 500 Blogger accounts and 500 Twitter accounts in the context of the DMCA notices in the US legal system revealed that 441 of blog posts that that have been taken down due to copyright infringement were still offline while only 58 of them have been reinstated.[36] With regard to Twitter accounts, 483 Twitter accounts have been taken down while only 17 have been made available again. However, as the study outlines, the users whose accounts have been removed did not file for a counter-notice in order to ask for taking back the content online. This implies that lawful information might still be offline.[37]

Finally, should the final draft of Article 6 not incorporate any clarification with regard to knowledge of the provider of intermediary services, the objectives of the Regulation, namely the protection of fundamental rights, would be placed in peril.[38]

D. New Obligations for Providers of Hosting Services with Regard to Trade Mark Infringements

The proposed DSA Regulation introduces new obligations for providers of hosting services that are not entailed in the ECD. In particular, it addresses the need for transparency reporting, the respect of fundamental rights and the creation of the points of contact and appointment of legal representative for providers of hosting services, the transparency in online advertising and the traceability of traders.

With regard to transparency obligations, Article 13 of the proposed DSA Regulation requires providers of hosting services to publish transparency reports on a yearly basis. This statutory provision seems to be very much welcome. This understanding is also reinforced in the Opinion of the European Data Protection Supervisor who welcomes the transparency obligation. More specifically, the Opinion states, 'In the same vein, the EDPS also welcomes Article 13 of the proposed DSA Regulation, which institutes transparency reporting obligations requiring publication, at least once a year, of reports on any content moderation engaged in during the relevant period.' Furthermore, the High Commissioner for Human Rights Affairs noted that the role of the proposed DSA Regulation shall 'require more transparency on how platforms used by millions of people function'.[39] In addition, this provision is aligned with the provisions of the General Data Protection Regulation (GDPR) that notes, in Article 13, that the data controller must provide information to the data subject whose personal data has been collected with regard to the identity and the contact details of the controller, the purposes for collecting the data, the legitimate basis and the legitimate interests of the data controller.

However, it has been argued that transparency obligations for providers of hosting services might be subject to controversy. For instance, the structure and information

[36] J Penney, 'Privacy and Legal Automation: The DMCA as a Case Study' (2019) 22 *Stanford Technology Law Review* 456.

[37] ibid 458.

[38] Kuczerawy (n 32).

[39] High Commissioner for Human Rights, 'Letter to the President of the European Commission on the Proposal on a Digital Services Act Regulation' (September 2020).

contained in transparency reports may differ from one hosting ISP to another. A study conducted by Keller and Leerssen demonstrates that transparency reports differ from each other.[40] In particular, YouTube's transparency reports show the infringements that take place within the platform under each category, namely copyright, violation of community guidelines, and hate speech. Facebook's transparency reports show the number of counter notices that internet users submit in order to reinstate their videos,[41] while Twitter's transparency reports mainly present the accounts that have been blocked due to the violation of their policy guidelines under four categories, namely information requests, removal requests, copyright notices and trade mark notices.[42] For this reason, it is imperative to clarify how the transparency reports are structured and what information is entailed. A harmonised structure would facilitate internet users and researchers to be aware of the transparent operation of the providers of hosting services. Otherwise, a patchwork of different transparency policies would undermine the objectives of the proposed DSA Regulation.

Further, Article 24 of the proposed DSA Regulation requires online advertising transparency. It states:

> Online platforms that display advertising on their online interfaces shall ensure that the recipients of the service can identify, for each specific advertisement displayed to each individual recipient, in a clear and unambiguous manner and in real time: (a) that the information displayed is an advertisement; (b) the natural or legal person on whose behalf the advertisement is displayed; (c) meaningful information about the main parameters used to determine the recipient to whom the advertisement is displayed.

This provision is warranted due to the risks that online advertising might reveal. In particular, a study conducted by IMCO Committee demonstrates that targeted online advertising could manipulate online consumers and influence their user experience.[43] This is mainly because, as the study points outs, the advertising power is monopolised by two companies, namely Facebook and Google. In addition, online advertising requires the process of personal data of consumers through the cookies[44] or the history of accessing the websites. Yet, a study conducted by the European Commission reveals that 47 per cent of the respondents express their concerns about the volume of personal data that is processed and the purposes for which the data can be used from third parties.[45] They also feel uncomfortable with this practice and thus urge for a higher degree of transparency.

[40] D Keller and P Leerssen, 'Facts and Where to Find Them: Empirical Research on Internet Platforms and Content Moderation' in N Persily and J Tucker (eds), *Social Media and Democracy: The State of the Field and Prospects for Reform* (Cambridge, Cambridge University Press, 2020) 14–17.

[41] Facebook, Transparency reports, available at transparency.fb.com/data/.

[42] Twitter, Transparency reports, available at transparency.twitter.com/.

[43] N Fourberg et al, 'Online advertising: the impact of targeted advertising on advertisers, market access and consumer choice' (2020) IMCO Committee 39–40.

[44] N Lomba and T Evas, 'Annex II: Digital Services Act: Adapting commercial and civil law rules for commercial entities operating online: legal assessment' (2021) *European Parliamentary Research Service* 73.

[45] European Commission, 'Consumer market study on online market segmentation through personalised pricing/offers in the European Union' (2018) 131; European Commission, 'Consumer Conditions Scoreboard' (2019) 14.

Interestingly, while this provision seems to offer a higher degree of protection for online consumers, it might raise criticism with regard to the concept of main parameters of transparency. Indeed, the Opinion of the European Data Protection Supervisor urges that the parameters of transparency obligations shall be clearly carved out. In particular, it states that what is required is 'further clarification as to what parameters would need to be disclosed at a minimum to constitute "meaningful information" within the meaning of Article 24 and 30'. This is because one might wonder what is meant by meaningful information. Would it be information about the location of previously accessed products, or how many times the product information has been accessed by online consumers?

What is more, Article 22 of the proposed DSA Regulation requires traceability of the traders, thus it offers a higher degree of protection for online consumers. More specifically, Article 22 of the proposed DSA Regulation sets forth the information that is required from traders in order to register on the relevant online platforms and sell their products. In particular, requirements would include: the contact details of the trader; a copy of the identification of the trader; the trader's bank account details; the trade register on which the trader is registered; and confirmation from the trader that the products displayed would conform with the EU law provisions.

Interestingly, this provision endorses the principle of know your customer. This means that providers of hosting services need to know specific information about their customers before accepting their engagement. This provision is already applicable, on a voluntary basis, by providers of hosting services that require the provision of information about trade sellers in their policies. For instance, Alibaba's policy states, 'you will be asked to provide certain contact information that is necessary for the registering for a Platform account on behalf of a Buyer or Seller, including name, address, phone number, email address, job title and department; you will be asked to provide certain identity information, tax registration and/or related information about your business, such as your company name, business type and industry, corporate registration details and information about your business licence; if you are a Seller we will also ask you to provide details about the goods and products that you intend to sell via the Platform and details about your sales/transactions on Alibaba.com'.[46] Likewise, Amazon notes that 'In accordance with EU regulations, Amazon Payments Europe requires sellers to provide information about themselves and their business so that they can begin or continue to sell on Amazon and receive the proceeds of their transactions on Amazon EU Marketplaces.'[47]

In addition, this provision conforms with Article 3(5) of the Regulation on promoting fairness and transparency for business users of online intermediation services that require providers of hosting services to visibly demonstrate the details of the business trader offering the goods online.[48] Also, it aligns with the existing legislative

[46] Alibaba, Privacy Policy, available at rule.alibaba.com/rule/detail/2034.htm.

[47] Amazon seller central, Information Required to Sell on Amazon, available at sellercentral.amazon.co.uk/gp/help/external/201200780?language=en_GB&ref=efph_201200780_cont_901.

[48] Regulation (EU) 2019/1150 of the European Parliament and of the Council of 20 June 2019 on promoting fairness and transparency for business users of online intermediation services (Text with EEA relevance) PE/56/2019/REV/1, OJ L 186.

framework that requires the provision of information about traders. More specifically, Article 4 of the Regulation on market surveillance and compliance of products[49] states in paragraph 4,

> Without prejudice to the respective obligations of economic operators under the applicable Union harmonisation legislation, the name, registered trade name or registered trade mark, and contact details, including the postal address, of the economic operator referred to in paragraph 1 shall be indicated on the product or on its packaging, the parcel or an accompanying document.

This means that full details of the manufacturer of the product shall be indicated. Finally, the European Commission's report on the functioning of the Memorandum of Understanding on the sale of counterfeit goods on the internet reveals that brand owners urge online platforms to adopt stricter measures with regard to the verification of the identity of the sellers and identify ways to connect the sellers with previous accounts that have been suspended, or terminated, due to the counterfeit allegations.[50]

However, a number of scholars have accentuated the risks for introducing know your customer obligations for providers of hosting services.[51] In particular, Nordemann[52] explains that a know your customer obligation is already applicable in the financial sector with the 5th Anti-Money Laundering Directive.[53] Yet, he argues that the know your customer duty in the context of the proposed DSA Regulation shall be moderated and thus refrain from adopting strict standards similar to the finance. Therefore, a clear articulation of the know your customer principle, taking into consideration the context of its application, is needed.

E. Additional Obligations for Very Large Platforms with Regard to Trade Mark Infringements

Section 4 of the proposed DSA Regulation endorses a new type of provider of intermediary services and describes them as very large platforms. These very large platforms have traffic equal to, or higher than, 45 million users clients and have additional obligations with regard to the operation of their business.

More specifically, Article 26 notes that very large platforms need to undertake risk assessment once per year with regard to the operation of their business model. In particular, they need to fulfil risk assessments with regard to: the dissemination

[49] Regulation (EU) 2019/1020 of the European Parliament and of the Council of 20 June 2019 on market surveillance and compliance of products and amending Directive 2004/42/EC and Regulations (EC) No 765/2008 and (EU) No 305/2011.

[50] European Commission, 'Report on the functioning of the Memorandum of Understanding on the sale of counterfeit goods on the internet' (2020) 19.

[51] A Bertolini, 'Liability of online platforms' (2020) *European Parliamentary Research Service 78*; N Lomba and T Evas, 'Digital Services Act: European added value assessment' (2020) *European Parliamentary Research Service* II.

[52] Nordemann (n 22) 283.

[53] Directive (EU) 2018/843 of the European Parliament and of the Council of 30 May 2018 amending Directive (EU) 2015/849 on the prevention of the use of the financial system for the purposes of money laundering or terrorist financing, and amending Directives 2009/138/EC and 2013/36/EU (2018) OJ L 156.

of illegal content within their networks; the protection of fundamental rights within their services; and the protection of health, minors, or any issues related to public security and elections. Further, Article 27 requires very large platforms to mitigate the potential risks, and thus deploy content moderation systems, cooperate with trusted flaggers, and initiate codes of conducts with other platforms. In addition, Article 28 states that very large platforms undertake audit, Article 32 requires them to appoint compliance officers to ensure the compliance of the business with the legal provisions while Article 33 introduces a statutory duty for transparency obligations for this group.

The additional obligations to very large platforms have been very much welcomed. A great number of academic scholars and civil society organisations ask for a framework based on accountability and due diligence. This is mainly because some very large platforms have business interests, while others act as governmental authorities. For instance, consider a recent contribution on Amazon's blog about creating a trustworthy consumer experience. It states that, 'in the first three months of 2021, we reported more than 1.000 such groups, with social media services taking a media time of five days to take them down',[54] it then notes that, 'while we appreciate that some social media companies have become much faster at responding, to address this problem at scale, it is imperative for social media companies to invest adequately in proactive controls to detect and enforce fake reviews ahead of our reporting the issue to them'.[55] This demonstrates that although Amazon is a private corporation, it is also acting in the manner of a state which reports on, and stresses, the imperative need for enforcement against fake reviews.

Interestingly, while the attribution of additional obligations to very large platforms might prove to be a good start, it might also seem, as Leistner notes, 'overextended'.[56] This is because a number of additional obligations might undermine the operation of the business of the very large platforms. For instance, it is questionable whether very large platforms would be burdened with the set of the new obligations, and whether they would prefer to resort to other business models. Therefore, one of the objectives of the proposed Regulations, namely to contribute to the proper functioning of the internal market for intermediary services, would be undermined.

What is more, it seems unclear that the additional obligations would guarantee the protection of internet users/consumers. This is because individual remedies, such as injunctive relief or compensatory claims, are not available in the proposed DSA Regulation.[57] This understanding is also reinforced in the Opinion of the Committee of the Regions. More specifically, it has been noted that the Proposal needs to provide the appropriate redress schemes to consumers in cases where their rights have been undermined and the providers of intermediary services do not comply with the rules.[58]

[54] Amazon, 'Creating a trustworthy reviews experience' (16 June 2021) www.aboutamazon.com/news/how-amazon-works/creating-a-trustworthy-reviews-experience?ots=1&tag=curbedcom06-20&linkCode=w50.

[55] ibid.

[56] M Leistner, 'The Commission's vision for Europe's Digital Future: Proposals for the Data Governance Act, the Digital Markets Act and the Digital Services Act–Acritical primer' (2021) 10.

[57] ibid.

[58] Opinion of the European Economic and Social Committee, Proposal for a Regulation of the European Parliament and of the Council on a Single Market For Digital Services (Digital Services Act) and amending Directive 2000/31/EC [COM(2020) 825 final – 2020/0361 (COD)] 3.4.

This implies that greater clarity is required with regard to the remedies available to consumer or internet users.

An additional complicated issue lies in the obligations for very large platforms to use content automation tools in order to detect infringements within their networks. In particular, Article 12 states:

> Providers of intermediary services shall include information on any restrictions that they impose in relation to the use of their service in respect of information provided by the recipients of the service, in their terms and conditions. That information shall include information on any policies, procedures, measures and tools used for the purpose of content moderation, including algorithmic decision-making and human review.

This understanding is reinforced in the Explanatory Memorandum of the proposed Regulation which states that 'the provisions of this Regulation relating to liability should not preclude the development and effective operation, by the different interested parties, of technical systems of protection and identification and of automated recognition made possible by digital technology within the limits laid down by Regulation 2016/679'.

However, as already discussed in chapter four, the use of filtering technology is controversial. A bedrock of studies indicate that automated technological tools perform a high margin of error, and thus remove legitimate content from their networks.[59] In addition, this understanding is evidenced from a set of practical examples that reveal the issue of the high number of counter-notifications for content that has been removed from their networks. A representative example can be found in YouTube's counter-claim procedure. During the COVID-19 pandemic, it has been reported that while 11 million videos were removed during March and September 2020, 320,000 videos were appealed and 160,000 were reinstated back to the platform.[60] As well, YouTube's transparency report between January and March 2020, states that while 6,111,008 videos have been removed from the platform due to violation of Community guidelines, 41,059 have been reinstated following a successful counter-notification.[61] At the same time, filtering tools fail to identify counterfeit goods online. In particular, the European Commission's report on the functioning of the Memorandum of Understanding on the sale of counterfeit goods on the internet in 2020 indicates that filtering tools cannot identify original and counterfeit products, especially in the categories of sporting and luxury brands.[62] Those products that cannot be identified fall within the unable to determine category. In this light, only with rights holders' assistance can a product be classified.

[59] A Holland et al, 'NOC online intermediaries case studies series: intermediary liability in the United States' (18 February 2015) *Berkman Center for Internet and Society* 60; J Urban, J Karaganis and B Schofield, 'Notice and Takedown in everyday practice' (2017) *Berkley Law* 9; S Jacques et al, 'An Empirical Study of the Use of Automated Anti-Piracy Systems and their Consequences for Cultural Diversity' (2018) 15 *Scripted* 277; N Elkin-Koren and S Bar- Ziv, 'Behind the Scenes of Online Copyright Enforcement: Empirical Evidence on Notice & Takedown' (2017) 50 *Connecticut Law Review* 3.

[60] J Vincent, 'YouTube brings back more human moderators after AI systems over-censor' (*The Verge*, 21 September 2020) www.theverge.com/2020/9/21/21448916/youtube-automated-moderation-ai-machine-learning-increased-errors-takedowns.

[61] G Sartor and A Loreggia, 'The impact of algorithms for online content filtering or moderation: Upload filters (2020) *Report for the JURI Committee* 50.

[62] European Commission (n 50) 12.

F. The Establishment of the Digital Services Coordinator

Another innovative provision of the proposed Regulation is the establishment of a Digital Services Coordinator. This provision is similar to the GDPR, and more specifically to Articles 51–59 which require the creation of Independent Supervisory Authorities and classify its competences, power, and tasks. For instance, in France the relevant authority is the Commission Nationale de l'Informatique et des Libertés (CNIL), in Belgium it is the Autorité de la protection des données; – Gegevensbeschermingsautoriteit (APD-GBA); in Greece, the Hellenic Data Protection Authority; and in Italy, the Garante per la protezione dei dati personali.

In this vein, drawing upon the relevant provisions of the GDPR, Article 38 of the proposed DSA Regulation envisages the creation of competent authorities, otherwise called the Digital Services Coordinators, in each EU Member State. Such authority would be responsible for the application and enforcement of the rules in the Regulation while, at the same time, channels for cooperation shall be carved out amongst the authorities in national jurisdictions. The creation of the Digital Services Coordinators shall operate, as per Article 30, under the principles of transparency and impartiality, be timely, and coordinate with each other.

Crucially, the exchange of data and the audits performed by the proposed Digital Services Coordinators needs to comply with the principles set forth in the GDPR. In particular, the processing of personal data must be in accordance with Article 5 of the GDPR which states that processing of personal data shall be conducted under a transparent, fair and lawful manner.[63] This understanding has been reiterated by the Civil Liberties Committee that argues that a new legislative tool shall take into account the provisions of the GDPR and the EU Directive on privacy and electronic communications.[64]

The creation of a supervisory authority seems to be endorsed by a number of scholars who argue in favour a supervisory entity. For instance, Geiger and Frosio noted that the creation of an independent body would ensure the compliance of providers of hosting services with the rules and lower the risks of removing lawful material posted by internet users.[65]

What is more, the creation of an independent authority is not only encouraged by a cluster of academic scholars. Indeed, at policy level, the EU Parliament's Committees agree. This understanding has been illustrated in the JURI's Committee Opinion that suggested the assignment of compliance controls to an independent entity at the European level.[66] In particular, it stresses the lack of oversight as to how the providers of hosting services are handling illicit activity within their networks and suggests:

> the application of the regulation should be closely monitored by a European entity tasked with ensuring compliance by content hosting platforms with the provisions of the regulation, in

[63] Council Regulation (EU) 2016/679 of the European Parliament and of the Council of 27 April 2016 on the protection of natural persons with regard to the processing of personal data and on the free movement of such data, and repealing Directive 95/46/EC (2016) OJ L 119 (hereinafter GDPR).

[64] Opinion of the Civil Liberties Committee, 'P9_TA(2020)0274- Digital Services Act and fundamental rights issues posed European Parliament resolution of 20 October 2020 on the Digital Services Act and fundamental rights issues posed' (2020/2022(INI)) 19.

[65] Geiger and Frosio (n 5) 35.

[66] European Parliament resolution of 20 October 2020 with recommendations to the Commission on a Digital Services Act: adapting commercial and civil law rules for commercial entities operating online.

particular by monitoring compliance with the standards laid down for content management on the basis of transparency reports and monitoring algorithms employed by content hosting platforms for the purpose of content management.

In addition, the EU Parliament's Committee on Internal Market and consumer protection echoes and notes that the structure of the independent body that would supervise the hosting services shall be based on a hybrid scheme and shall take into consideration current regulatory bodies. Telling examples can be found in the Consumer Protection Cooperation (CPC) Network, the European Regulators Group for Audiovisual Media Services (ERGA), the European Data Protection Board (EDBP) and the European Competition Network (ECN).[67]

Such an independent authority could be an existing, or a new, European Agency. Finally, the Opinion of the Committee on Civil Liberties, Justice, and Home Affairs echoes the imposition of measures to providers of hosting services and notes that the battle against illicit activities online shall be placed on the arms of private corporations through self-regulatory or co-regulatory schemes. Rather, public authorities shall initiate practices and rules in order to terminate the circulation of unlawful information in the digital ecosystem.[68]

In this way, it seems that the proposed DSA Regulation envisages a co-regulatory framework for online platforms. As the EU Parliament briefing aptly points out, 'the DSA constitutes a step away from the self-regulation approach towards more cooperative, co-regulation and regulatory mechanisms'.[69]

Overall, the proposed DSA Regulation introduces a set of provisions which aim to combat trade mark infringements. Such provisions concern the providers of hosting services and very large platforms and address transparency obligations, establishment of a supervisory authority, and maintenance of the liability exemptions. Whether or not those provisions would also be applicable to copyright issues is critically discussed in the following section.

III. Blurred Intersection with Article 17 of the DSMD

The proposed Regulation aims to act as *a lex specialis* to the existing legal framework. While its application in cases of trade mark infringements is straightforward, its application to copyright issues and, more specifically, its intersection with Article 17 of the DSMD, appears to be subject to debate.

Firstly, the intersection between DSA and the DSMD is ambiguous. This is because Article 1(5) of the proposed Regulation notes that its application is without prejudice to copyright issues. This is reinforced in Recital 11 of the proposed DSA Regulation which notes the new provisions in the Proposal shall be applied without prejudice to the current

[67] Opinion of the Committee on Internal Market and Consumer Protection, 'Report with recommendations to the Commission on the Digital Services Act: Improving the functioning of the Single Market' (2020/2018(INL)) para 38.

[68] Opinion of the Committee on Civil Liberties, Justice and Home Affairs, 'Opinion of the on the proposal for a Regulation Single Market for Digital Service' (2021) 4.

[69] European Parliament, 'Briefing Legislation on Digital Services Act' (2021) 1.

legal system that governs copyright law. This means that the provisions in the InfoSoc Directive and in the DSMD remain active and applicable. Therefore, the proposed Regulation does not affect the issues that are already regulated in the relevant copyright provisions. Rather, it still affects those areas that are not taken into consideration.[70] At the same time, Article 1(5) of the proposed Regulation seems to contradict Recital 12 of the DSA which identifies the non-authorised use of copyright protected material as illegal content.[71] Therefore, one might wonder when the provisions of the DSA apply to copyright issues and to what extent.

Secondly, it seems unclear whether specific provisions of the proposed DSA Regulation are applicable to copyright issues and, in particular, to the OCSSPs' activities. In particular, one might wonder whether the additional obligations on very large platforms would apply to OCSSPs. Given that the DSMD does not entail provisions related to transparency obligations, risks assessments, or measures to mitigate risks, it is plausible to argue that those provisions might also applicable in the field of OCSSPs. In particular, very large platforms, such as YouTube, Facebook, and Instagram, might be required to issue transparency reports about online advertising on a mandatory basis, also to appoint compliance officers and to be accountable for their actions to the Digital Services Coordinator. The application of those provisions to OCSSPs would be highly recommended since it would enhance the principles of due process, fair trial, and transparency within the operation of their business.

However, apart from the obligations to very large platforms, the proposed DSA Regulation requires a set of obligations to all providers of intermediary services. Indeed, Article 10 is about establishing points of contact, Article 11 about the appointment of legal representatives for those providers that do not have a legal establishment within the EU borders, Article 12 is about the terms and conditions for the operation of the providers of hosting services and Article 13 entails a provision for the issue of transparency reports on a yearly basis. Yet, whilst it is not clear whether those obligations might be applicable within the DSMD context, their applicability would be of an ultimate importance for the internet users' fundamental rights. For instance, Article 12 requires providers of intermediary services to offer clear and specific information about the moderation of content, either by algorithmic review or human review. In this way, one of the objectives of the proposed DSA Regulation, namely to promote a safe and transparent online environment, would be achieved.

What is more, it is questionable whether the provisions related to voluntary own initiative investigation and legal compliance are directly applicable to Article 17 and, in particular, to OCSSPs. For instance, Article 6 of the proposed DSA Regulation notes:

> Providers of intermediary services shall not be deemed ineligible for the exemptions from liability referred to in Articles 3, 4 and 5 solely because they carry out voluntary own-initiative investigations or other activities aimed at detecting, identifying and removing, or disabling of access to, illegal content, or take the necessary measures to comply with the requirements of Union law, including those set out in this Regulation.

[70] JP Quintais and SF Schwemer, 'The Interplay between the Digital Services Act and Sector Regulation: How special is copyright?' (2022) *European Journal of Risk Regulation* 1–31.

[71] Angelopoulos (n 8) 30–31.

Given that those provisions directly refer to the liability exemptions as set forth in Articles 3, 4, and 5 of the proposed Regulation, it might be concluded that they are not applicable in the case of copyright infringements and OCSSPs. In this light, more clarification would be much welcomed.

What is more, it seems unclear whether the remedy of injunctive relief and provision of information to online consumers about the removal of listings or material could be applicable to the DSMD context. In particular, Article 8 of the proposed DSA Regulation is about the injunctive orders against providers of intermediary services in order to act against illegal content, and Article 9 of the proposed DSA Regulation addresses the provision of information to internet users. If those Articles are applicable for copyright issues, a dual enforcement regime might occur. This is because Article 17 of the DSMD does not include the opportunity for injunctions for the purposes of removing copyright infringing works or provision of information to the users whose work has been removed. Rather, the provision requires OCSSPs to demonstrate the best efforts to terminate or prevent the reemergence of copyright infringing works.

Further, the same uncertainty is to be found in the provisions related to information about the reasons for removal of the allegedly infringing material, the creation of an internal mechanism for providers of hosting services and the establishment of an out of court dispute settlement scheme. More specifically, Article 15 is about the statements of reasons for the removal of the information, Article 17 addresses the internal complaint system and Article 18 concerns the out of court dispute settlement. It is questionable whether the provisions fall within the scope of the activities of OCSSPs. On the one hand, the Explanatory Memorandum of the proposed DSA Regulation points out that sector-specific instruments do not cover all regulatory gaps, especially with regards to 'fully-fledged rules on the procedural obligations related to illegal content and they only include basic rules on transparency and accountability of service providers and limited oversight mechanisms'. On the other hand, Quintais and Schwemer argue that detailed mechanisms would be in favour of legal certainty and the protection of users' fundamental rights and platforms' right to operate business.[72] In that case also, more guidance on the application of the provisions would provide clarity.

Moreover, it seems blurred whether the measures against online piracy might be applicable in the DSMD context. This is mainly because Article 19 which is about the use of trusted flaggers, and Article 20 on the termination of accounts of allegedly infringers, refer directly to the notice and action mechanisms that are only applicable to providers of hosting services. This might mean that the use of trusted flaggers and the termination of infringing accounts might not apply in the case of OCSSPs. However, as Quintais and Schwemer point out, the use of trusted flaggers would be a benefit to OCSSPs since it would enable them to curb the increasing number of copyright infringements within their networks.[73] This understanding is also reinforced at policy level. In particular, the EU Commission's Communication on tackling illegal content online urges the use of trusted flaggers in order to alert online platforms to illegal content

[72] Quintais and Schwemer (n 70) 17–18.
[73] ibid.

within their networks.[74] In addition, a number of OCSSPs have already applied this measure on a voluntary basis with effective results. For instance, it has been reported that YouTube's trusted flaggers contributed to the identification of 400,000 copyright infringing videos.[75] Likewise, the EU Commission's assessment of the implementation of the Code of Practice on Disinformation reveals that 89 per cent of content that has been considered illegal by trusted flaggers is examined by host ISPs within 24 hours.[76] At the same time, enforcement Units in Europol and INHOPE act as trusted flaggers for terroristic and child abuse content, respectively.[77] Yet, as already said, more clarification is required.

IV. Conclusion

This chapter has critically engaged with the proposed DSA Regulation. The Proposal seems to be a promising approach since it clarifies existing vague issues, such as the interpretation of actual knowledge, while at the same time it proposes a number of provisions that safeguard the rights of online consumers, internet users, and providers of intermediary services. Of course, the 'DSA is not an IPR toolbox'; as the Commission stated.[78] However, to clarify the boundaries and the conditions for application will be to the advantage of the parties at stake. Indeed, this understanding has been reinforced by Savin who noted that 'the success of the act will depend not so much on its ability to bring a solution to all questions (as this can be corrected by subsequent legislation) as on its power to strike the right balance between competing fundamental rights'.[79] Otherwise, the proposed DSA Regulation will place in jeopardy the fundamental rights of users and the rights of the providers of intermediary services.

Further, the proposed DSA Regulation entails innovative provisions, such as the quasi-Good Samaritan provision, the notice and action mechanisms, the trusted flaggers, and the additional obligations for very large platforms. Such additional obligations include the issue of transparency reports, transparency in online advertising, the appointment of compliance officers, and the establishment of Digital Services Coordinators in each Member State. Interestingly, while those provisions might be a promising approach with regard to the combat of illicit activity online, more clarity is required. For instance, the provisions related to the use of different terminology among ISPs, the provision of information with regard to the removal of illicit activity online, the quasi-Good Samaritan clause, as well as the Digital Services Coordinator, all need to

[74] European Commission, 'Communication on tackling illegal content online: Towards an enhanced responsibility of online platforms' (2017) COM/2017/0555 final.

[75] E Munn, 'YouTube Reveals It Removed 8 Million Videos From The Site In The First Three Months Of 2018' (*alphr*, 24 April 2018 www.alphr.com/google/1009171/youtube-removes-8-million-videos/.

[76] European Commission, 'Study for the assessment of the implementation of the code of practice on disinformation: final report' (2020) 67.

[77] European Commission (n 74).

[78] See Quintais and Schwemer (n 70) 20.

[79] A Savin, 'The EU Digital Services Act: Towards a more responsible Internet' (2021) *Copenhagen Business School Law Research Paper Series No. 21-04*.

be further enhanced to take into consideration the principles of legal certainty, proportionality, and consistency. What is more, while it is evident that such provisions of the proposed DSA Regulation are applicable for trade mark infringements within the networks, it is questionable whether they could be applied to copyright issues. In particular, it is not clear whether the provisions would be applied to OCSSPs for copyright and non-copyright related issues.

Finally, it is worthwhile to note that this is only the proposed DSA Regulation and that there is a long process in the EU legislative procedure until the final draft is complete. This means that it is highly likely that the proposed DSA Regulation be subject to a set of amendments, minor or major, and we might need to wait some time to see the final version. At the moment of writing this book, the Proposal is debated in the Council where EU Member States pursue to adopt a common position.[80] In any case, drawing upon our experience of the EU legislative process for the DSMD, the roadmap from the Proposal to the final vote of the Regulation might be long and uncertain. In addition, it is noteworthy to mention that during the final stages of editing this book, the Council has reached a compromised text with regard to the proposed DSA Regulation. The text introduces stricter rules on very large online platforms and assigns additional obligation to very large online search engines too. Amidst the important provisions, Recital 35 clarifies that the compliance with due diligence obligations is separate from liability of online platforms for third-party content. Further, while Recital 15 reinforces the ban of general monitoring obligations, it allows the issue of orders requiring providers of hosting services to remove information which it stores, the content of which is identical or equivalent to the content of information which was previously declared to be unlawful, or to block access to that information. With regard to the transparency obligation, Article 23 of the Council's text requires the creation of a structured database that is managed by the EU Commission and that be accessible to researchers. Finally, another key provision is Article 32 which is about the compliance function. The Council's text offers detailed requirements for the compliance function of the platforms by appointing a team with specific professional qualifications and the responsibilities of the head of the compliance team.[81]

With the discussion of the proposed DSA Regulation, the landscape for the liability of host ISPs for copyright and trade mark infringements has been completed. Based on the critical examination of the current legislative tools in Part II, the narrative now moves to Part III of this book which offers a set of recommendations for a robust legal framework on host ISPs' liability.

[80] Legislative train schedule, a Europe fit for digital age, available at www.europarl.europa.eu/legislative-train/theme-a-europe-fit-for-the-digital-age/file-digital-services-act.

[81] Council's text on the proposed DSA Regulation https://data.consilium.europa.eu/doc/document/ST-13203-2021-INIT/en/pdf.

PART III

Introducing a Co-regulatory Framework

7

Redefining the Concept of Duty of Care

I. Introduction

As discussed in Part II of this book, the current legislative landscape that regulates host ISPs' and OCSSPs', which is a sub-type of host ISPs, liability for trade mark and copyright infringements respectively fails to strike a fair balance between the interests of host ISPs, intellectual property holders and internet users. Firstly, the legal framework under Article 14(1) of the ECD is outdated. As already presented, Article 14 of the ECD endorses a secondary liability regime for host ISPs. This means that host ISPs could only be held liable for the infringements committed by their users only if they are aware of the illicit activity within their networks. However, Article 14 of the ECD fails to define host ISPs' liability. Instead of defining host ISPs' liability, it offers a set of defences to host ISPs. Unfortunately, the national transposition of the ECD to EU Member States fails to offer a solid answer to host ISPs' liability conundrum as well. What is more, national courts resort to their tortious secondary liability doctrines to define the secondary liability of host ISPs. Yet, while secondary liability rules could define host ISPs' liability, this solution does not seem ideal. The findings suggest this is mainly due to two reasons. Firstly, it seems that national courts have difficulties in applying tortious secondary liability rules within the online context. Secondly, these tortious secondary liabilities differ from each other. As corollary, a puzzle of miscellaneous secondary liability doctrines has emerged and aggravated the existing legal uncertainty among the parties involved.

Likewise, the DSMD seems to favour the interests of intellectual property holders while at the same time it undermines the rights of OCSSPs and internet users. More specifically, Article 17 of the DSMD has attempted to define OCSSPs' liability[1] with regard to copyright infringements but with limited success. While it offers a definition of OCSSPs' liability, it endorses a primary liability regime for them. This means that OCSSPs are held liable if a copyright infringement takes place within their network. The defence of knowledge cannot be used since it does not constitute a requisite for primary liability. This understanding comes against the rationale upon which internet infrastructure has been developed and which is based on the ideal of secondary

[1] Council Directive (EU) 2019/790 of the European Parliament and of the Council of 17 April 2019 on copyright and related rights in the DSM and amending Directives 96/9/EC and 2001/29/EC (hereinafter DSMD).

liability rules. What is more, Article 17 of the DSMD is misaligned with Article 14 of the ECD as it introduces a dual liability regime that might accentuate the existing legal uncertainty.

Further, the Proposal for a Digital Services Act Regulation seems to be a promising approach.[2] This is because the EU policymakers introduced provisions that would enhance transparency of the host ISPs at operational level and promote online consumers' trust through the provision of sellers' identification and redress methods. Yet, several provisions such as the ascription of different responsibilities to different types of host ISPs, the introduction of new definitions for host ISPs and the establishment of Digital Services Coordinators require further granularity. Finally, while the Proposal addresses trade mark infringements, it is applicable without prejudice to copyright context as well. However, it is still unclear which provisions of the proposed Regulation would apply in the copyright context and to what extent it would be in conformity with the DSMD, which regulates copyright disputes in the digital world.

These findings offer normative reasons to justify the need for a legal reform with regard to host ISPs' regulatory regime. In this vein, Part III of this book explores an array of legal amendments on host ISPs' liability with a view to balance the interests of host ISPs, intellectual property holders and internet users. In order to propose the amendments, this chapter draws upon the establishment of a responsibility framework for host ISPs based on a co-regulatory approach. This means that host ISPs would undertake a number of responsibilities and the state would step in the EU regulatory framework with the establishment of a proposed host ISP supervisory authority. In other words, host ISPs would be assigned to a set of responsibilities through which they would be accountable to a proposed host ISP supervisory authority. In this light, this chapter considers the normative considerations upon which a set of responsibilities of host ISPs could lie. Finally, this chapter explores one of the constituents of this responsibility framework, namely the duty of care of host ISPs towards the infringements that might occur within their networks.

II. Normative Justifications for Ascribing a Duty of Care to Host ISPs' Business Model

With the advent of Web 2.0, there has been a plethora of arguments that might warrant the ascription of a responsibility framework for host ISPs. The underlying basis of these arguments is the new role of host ISPs. Such a role no longer represents host ISPs as mere conduit platforms. Rather, this role depicts host ISPs as controllers of the information that passes through their networks, implementers of public policies and enforcers of rights in the digital ecosystem. However, this new role also comes with challenges for internet users/online consumers, intellectual property holders and host ISPs.

[2] Proposal for a Regulation of the European Parliament and of the Council on a Single Market For Digital Services (Digital Services Act) and amending Directive 2000/31/EC COM/2020/825 final.

A. Host ISPs as Information Gatekeepers

Firstly, host ISPs are now considered *information gatekeepers*.[3] This is because the great majority of internet users are informed by host ISPs. Indeed, a number of policy documents and reports reinforce that new role of host ISPs. For instance, the Digital Single Market Strategy outlines that one of the main social functions of host ISPs nowadays is to inform internet users.[4] A study conducted by the Digital News Oxford's Reuters Institute in 2019 indicates that Facebook is the most important source of information while at the same time 32 per cent of the respondents between 18–24 years old rely on YouTube for their news.[5] Host ISPs are now compared with the public squares where citizens express and exchange views on political, social and cultural aspects of life.[6]

However, what is critical about host ISPs as information gatekeepers is that they can decide which information reaches the end-users. As Mansell pointed out, host ISPs 'have the power to influence what ideas citizens are able to find easily'.[7] An example of this is the removal of a political video on YouTube.[8] This video concerned the speech of a Member of the EU Parliament who advocated the termination of selling trade goods that are used for tortures and death penalties. The video has been removed under the justification of violating the community guidelines of the online music-exchange platform. However, the removal of this video has deprived EU citizens from obtaining knowledge of a highly important discussion topic.[9] In this sense, the music exchange platform could control the information received by its users through the take down of a video. Likewise, Perel and Elkin-Koren argue that host ISPs can decide which information reaches the end-users. For instance, they note that the mere removal of videos by YouTube or the blocking of a link of a website by Google denies users from obtaining useful information which otherwise would have been accessible by the public.[10]

[3] E Laidlaw, 'Private Power, Public Interest: An Examination of Search engine accountability' (2009) *17 International Journal and Information Technology* 114.

[4] EU Commission, 'A Digital Single Market Strategy for Europe' COM (2015) 192 final where it states that host ISPs have 'an ever more central role in social and economic life: they enable consumers to find online information …'.

[5] Reuters Institute for the Study of Journalism, 'Reuters Institute Digital News Report' (2019) 56; Reuters Institute for the Study of Journalism, 'Reuters Institute Digital News Report 2016' (Reuters Institute, 2016) 176, reutersinstitute.politics.ox.ac.uk/sites/default/files/research/files/Digital%2520News%2520Report%25202016.pdf; 'We increasingly get our news on social media (44 percent of the overall U.S. population accesses news on Facebook), shop on e-commerce platforms (Amazon accounts for 43% of US online retail sales) stream videos on YouTube (80% of European internet users had used the digital video platform within the past month).'

[6] A Starzak, 'When the Internet (Officially) Became the Public Square' (*Cloudfare*, 21 June 2017) blog.cloudflare.com/internet-became-public-square/; the US Supreme Court has held that access to social media is a constitutional right, see US Supreme Court of United States, *Packingham v North Carolina* 582 U.S. (2017); in addition, a Costa Rican ruling confirmed that access to internet is a fundamental right, see A Guadamuz, 'Text of the Costa Rican ruling declaring internet as a fundamental right' (*TechnoLlama*, 23 April 2012) www.technollama.co.uk/text-of-the-costa-rican-ruling-declaring-internet-as-a-fundamental-right.

[7] R Mansell, 'Platforms of power' (2015) 43 *Intermedia* 20–24.

[8] J Reda, 'When filters fail: These cases show we can't trust algorithms to clean up the internet' (*Julia Reda's website*, 28 September 2017) juliareda.eu/2017/09/when-filters-fail/.

[9] Marietjschaake's website, medium.com/@marietje.schaake/when-youtube-took-down-my-video-412d945012aa.

[10] M Perel and N Elkin-Koren, 'Accountability in Algorithmic Copyright Enforcement' (2016) 19 *Stanford Technology Law Review* 483.

Subsequently, a level of censorship is performed by host ISPs that restrict internet users' fundamental right to obtain information which is a constituent of freedom of expression as set forth in Article 11 of the EU Charter of Fundamental Rights.

B. Host ISPs as Policymakers

Furthermore, given that host ISPs control the flow of information,[11] they could also shape public policy. From a normative perspective, the impact that host ISPs might have on the public sphere and the influence as to how policies can be implemented in practice might warrant the ascription of a set of responsibilities to host ISPs. Although they are not political or public institutions, they contribute to the development of public policies such as copyright and trade mark policies.[12] This is illustrated by the example of YouTube, which carves out copyright policies through the provisions in their Terms of Service and in particular through Content ID system and the Copyright School tutorial. Content ID system is a software that entails a database where copyright holders have submitted files of their works and that scans any video that is uploaded by internet users within this music exchange platform.[13] Within the context of Content ID system, YouTube amends the main copyright law principle which states that the owner of a work is the author of the work. This is because copyright holders do not own their works anymore. Rather, they are subject to the options that YouTube offers them in case this advanced software identifies a copyright infringement.[14] More specifically, once a piece of work which is uploaded matches a copyrighted work that is already in the database of the Content ID system, the copyright owner is notified and provided with specific options with regard to the unauthorised video such as the blocking of the whole video,

[11] D Rowland, U Kohl and A Charlesworth, *Information Technology Law*, 5th edn (London, Routledge, 2017) 85–86.

[12] An example with regard to privacy issues can be found in the right to be forgotten case. More specifically, given that Google is the most popular search engine worldwide, it contributed to the imposition of the right to be forgotten pursuant to the ruling of *Google Spain SL, Google Inc. v* Agencia *Española de Protección de Datos (AEPD), Mario Costeja González* by enabling the users in the 27 EU Member States to request the deletion of their personal data. Case 131/12 *Google Spain SL, Google Inc. v Agencia Española de Protección de Datos and Mario Costeja González* [2014] ECR I-000; see also O Lynskey, 'Control over personal data in a digital age: Google Spain v AEPD and Mario Costeja Gonzalez' (2015) 78 *Modern Law Review* 522–34; In this case, a Spanish citizen Mario Costeja González sent a formal notice to the Spanish Data Protection Agency requesting a Spanish newspaper and Google Spain to remove information about his social security debts which were no longer overdue. While the Spanish Data Protection Agency rejected Costeja's arguments against the newspaper, it tilted in favour of his claims against Google. In this regard, Google appealed to the Spanish Court of Appeal which subsequently made a referral of three questions to the CJEU; See also O Fischman Afori, 'Universal measures in the service of global challenges: proportionality, blocking orders, and online intermediaries as hybrid bodies' in T Synodinou, *Pluralism or Universalism in international copyright law* (Alphen aan den Rijn, Kluwer Law International, 2019) 663 where the author describes host ISPs as 'hybrid private/public bodies'; E Lee, 'Recognizing Rights in Real Time: The Role of Google in the EU Right to Be Forgotten' (2016) 49 *UC Davis Law Review* 1066 where Lee argues that Google is 'a private administrative agency administering the right to be forgotten'.

[13] Youtube, 'How to manage your copyrights in Youtube', see support.google.com/youtube/answer/2797370?hl=en-GB.

[14] L Edwards, 'With Great Power Comes Great Responsibility? The Rise of Platform Liability' in L Edwards (ed), *Law, Policy and the Internet* (Oxford, Hart Publishing, 2019) 276.

the monetisation of the video by running ads before its viewing, or sharing revenues with the user that uploaded the video.[15]

Further, another example of the role of host ISPs in curtailing copyright policies can be found in the Copyright School tutorials offered by YouTube and in which users are educated as to how they shall comply with copyright law.[16] Users who upload material that has been blocked are encouraged to attend YouTube's Copyright School. In this tutorial, the video stresses the negative consequences for the users if they upload infringing material on the platform. Such consequences may vary from taking the infringer-users to court or suspending users' accounts for an unlimited period of time. In this way, users are educated to comply with copyright policies and be cautious before uploading any material regardless of the fact that it may have been legitimately obtained by third parties.[17] However, what is critical about shaping copyright policies is that host ISPs are not state authorities and thus they are not granted any legitimacy to curtail policies on copyright or trade mark issues. This role belongs to the national authorities and not to private entities with business interests. What is more, it might be the case that the copyright policies that host ISPs adopt are one-sided and thus a risk to remove lawful content, such as fair use content, might occur.[18] As corollary, an over-enforcement of copyright law may emerge and therefore impinge upon the rights of users, such as the right of freedom of expression, and violate the rights of the authors of fair use works.

C. Host ISPs as Enforcers of Intellectual Property Rights Online

Moreover, the growing power of host ISPs due to their function as information gatekeepers and implementers of public policies is increased when their role as enforcers of intellectual property rights in the digital ecosystem is added. It is this role of enforcers of intellectual property rights online that could also justify the ascription of a set of responsibilities to them. Under the guise of indirect regulation of the online behaviour

[15] See support.google.com/youtube/answer/2797370?hl=en; in addition, it is worth mentioning that since mid-September 2019 YouTube has changed its policy in its manual claiming tool for copyright holders with regard to the monetisation of the videos. In particular, the new terms and conditions state that copyright holders cannot monetise videos that entail 'very short or unintentional uses unclaimed'. Without defining these concepts, this might result, as commentators observe, to a high degree of blocking videos. In other words, copyright holders would be in favour of blocking the video entirely since they do not have the option of monetising it if the video entails only short uses of their copyright protected works in H Boscher, 'YouTube takes copyright law into their own hands with new policy on music infringement' (*IPKat*, 2 September 2019) ipkitten.blogspot.com/2019/09/youtube-takes-copyright-law-into-their.html.

[16] www.youtube.com/copyright_school.

[17] L Belli, P Augusto Francisco and N Zingales, 'Law of the Land or Law of the Platform? Beware of the Privatisation of Regulation and Police' in L Belli and N Zingales (eds), *Platform Regulations: How Platforms are Regulated and How They Regulate Us* (2017) 57.

[18] Perel and Elkin-Koren (n 10) 491: An example is the removal of the campaign video of a candidate for the US Presidential Elections in 2008 on the basis that it included snippets from popular TV programmes, although the use of snippets being considered fair use is found in A Marsoof, 'Notice and take down: a copyright perspective' (2015) 5 *Queen Mary Journal of Intellectual Property Law* 19; W Seltzer, 'Free speech unmoored in copyright's safe harbour: chilling effects of the DMCA on the first Amendment' (2010) 24 *Harvard Journal of Law & Technology* 172.

of the users,[19] host ISPs now filter, block or remove allegedly infringing material that harms the rights of the content industries or trade mark holders.[20] However, what is critical about their role as enforcers of rights is that it is not limited to the enforcement of rights but is also extended to adjudication needs. As Huszti-Orban notes, 'the end decision is ultimately delegated to private entities who are thereby effectively given law enforcement and quasi-adjudicative responsibilities'.[21] This means that host ISPs are those entities that take the last decision to leave or remove any allegedly unwelcome content that is uploaded on their networks. In this respect, they out turn to be 'police, judge, jury and executioner'.[22]

Yet, it is worth questioning whether this dual role of host ISPs acts against the rule of law and in particular whether it is legitimate to engage concomitantly a private entity such as a host ISP with enforcement and judicial demands. For this reason, Elkin-Koren criticises this dual role of host ISPs and argues that enforcement and judicial duties have a public interest and shall be assigned to government institutions and authorities.[23] Otherwise, this dual role of host ISPs could prompt reflections on the legitimacy of the decision of host ISPs to remove material depending on their judgement while at the same time they lack any authority to adjudicate.

This concern about the dual role of host ISPs could be aggravated by the fact that they are private entities that might need to adjust their business interests with their enforcement and adjudication duties.[24] In particular, it could be argued that host ISPs might abuse the power they enjoy and favour their own interests or the interests of their business partners, which could threaten competition and innovation within the Digital Single Market. Insofar as the interests of the host ISPs are concerned, consider, for example, Google which has been accused and fined by the European Commission by virtue of abuse of its dominant position.[25] In this case, Google placed its own shopping services on higher ranking in the search listings while at the same time downgrading rival services. However, while market dominance is acceptable under European competition rules, it is forbidden to take advantage of the dominant position in the market and restrict competition.[26] On this basis, the European Commissioner for Competition

[19] L Lessig, *Code and Other Laws of Cyberspace* (New York, Basic Books, 1999) 85; M Schruers, 'Copyright, Intermediaries and Architecture' in F Mesiani, Cogburn, L Denandis and N Levinson (eds), *The Turn to Infrastructure in Internet Governance* (London, Palgrave Macmillan, 2016) 108.

[20] N Tusikov, *Chokepoints: Global Private Regulation on the Internet* (Berkeley, University of California Press, 2017) 49–50.

[21] K Huszti-Orban, 'Countering Terrorism and Violent Extremism Online: What Role for Social Media Platforms?' in Belli and Zingales (eds) (n 17) 202.

[22] European Digital Rights (EDRi), 'The Slide from "Self-Regulation" to Corporate Censorship', www.edri.org/files/EDRI_selfreg_final_20110124.pdf.

[23] Perel and Elkin-Koren (n 10) 485.

[24] ibid.

[25] R Price, 'Google has been hit with a record-breaking €2.4 billion fine by the EU over its antitrust case' (*UK Business Insider*, June 2017) uk.businessinsider.com/eu-fines-google-record-breaking-antitrust-shopping-case-2017-6; European Commission, 'Antitrust: Commission fines Google €2.42 billion for abusing dominance as search engine by giving illegal advantage to own comparison shopping service' (27 June 2017) europa.eu/rapid/press-release_IP-17-1784_en.htm.

[26] European Commission, 'Antitrust: Commission fines Google €2.42 billion for abusing dominance as search engine by giving illegal advantage to own comparison shopping service' (27 June 2017) europa.eu/rapid/press-release_IP-17-1784_en.htm; K von Blanckenburg, 'Google search abuses dominant position to illegally favour Google Shopping: an economic review of the EU decision' (2018) 20 *Digital Policy, Regulation and Governance* 211.

Affairs, Margaret Verstager, acutely pointed out that 'what Google has done is illegal under European antitrust rules. It denied other companies the chance to compete on the merits and to innovate. And most importantly, it denied European consumers a genuine choice of services and the full benefits of innovation'.[27] This means that by giving preference to its own services, Google did not only undermine the services provided by its competitors, rather, it also deprived internet users of a number of choices in terms of comparative shopping services.

Drawing further insights, due to their growing power[28] host ISPs might not only favour their own interests and violate competition rules. Rather, they may also favour their business partners' interests. Indeed, the European Commission stated in 2018 in relation to the market power of host ISPs that 'the providers of those services often have superior bargaining power, which enables them to effectively behave unilaterally in a way that can be unfair and that can be harmful to the legitimate interests of their businesses users and, indirectly, also of consumers in the Union'.[29] This implies that host ISPs may give priority to their business partners' interests and disregard their users' rights and the interests of other business players in the market. This was illustrated in the case of an American singer who uploaded a parody video on YouTube.[30] Due to the fact that the video included a number of lyrics from popular songs, YouTube removed the video on the basis of copyright infringement. In order to respond to the removal, the singer submitted a counter-notice highlighting that he uploaded the video for fair use. Despite his legitimate claims for the fair use purposes, YouTube refused to reload the video under the justification that it had a contractual agreement with the specific copyright holders and thus the counter-notification that had been submitted could not be further processed and examined. Therefore, the video that had been removed could not be reinstated to the platform.[31] This response reveals that YouTube gives priority to rights holders with whom the video-music platform has concluded agreements.[32] Indeed, having a closer look at YouTube's policies, it appears that counter-notification processes are not available if the work belongs to music copyright owners who have entered into agreements with YouTube with regard to the use of their music.[33]

A similar example where host ISPs gave priority to the interests of their business partners can be found in the android's Google Play application store.[34] While Google

[27] ibid.

[28] O Lynskey, 'Regulating "Platform Power"' (2017) *LSE Law, Society and Economy Working Papers* 3; see also the Communication of the EU Commission, 'A DSM Strategy for Europe' COM (2015) 192 final 12 which states that some host ISPs are now key actors in many sectors and it is worrisome how they are using their market power; J Cohen, 'The Regulatory State in the Information Age' (2016) 17 *Theoretical Inquiries in Law* 6 where Cohen names it 'platform power'.

[29] Proposal for a Regulation of the European Parliament and of the Council on promoting fairness and transparency for business users of online intermediation services, COM/2018/238 final.

[30] Perel and Elkin-Koren (n 10) 507.

[31] 'YouTube's Deal with Universal Blocks DMCA Counter Notices' (*Torrentfreak*, 5 April 2013) torrentfreak.com/youtube-deal-with-universal-blocks-dmca-counter-notices-130405/.

[32] Perel and Elkin-Koren (n 10) 507.

[33] YouTube, 'Videos removed or blocked due to YouTube's contractual obligations', support.google.com/youtube/answer/3045545?hl=en.

[34] O Lynskey, 'Regulation by Platforms: The Impact on Fundamental Rights' in Belli and Zingales (eds) (n 17) 90.

is considered a search engine and does not fall within the scope of the host ISPs, this example could be equally applied to host ISPs as well. In this case, the Google play app store did not include in its store the Disconnect's application which was about a software that prevents third parties tracing Android users' data when they use applications on their mobile devices. The exclusion of this app in its store was achieved under the guise that this specific application was in conflict with existing applications by diminishing the functionality of the existing applications or forcing them to amend their business model.[35] In this way, Google can exert control over which information reaches end-users and thus might deprive users of important content to them.

D. Host ISPs as Architects of E-Commerce Infrastructure

Further, within the context of e-commerce, host ISPs play a pivotal role. Their function is no longer limited to acting as middlemen between information and internet users.[36] Rather they are architects of the e-commerce infrastructure. This means that they design their business model in such a way that allows them to be aware of the material that is hosted and in particular the value of the goods as well as their demand among consumers.[37] In this way, they can grasp the needs of the consumers and distribute material that is appealing to the internet users, thus turning themselves into 'critical market access points'.[38] This means that they are the main entities that consider which content shall be circulated within the digital ecosystem.

However, if counterfeit goods are displayed on host ISPs and are sold to innocent consumers, the trust of consumers will be lost. Given that e-commerce's primary aim is to gain trust from consumers when they interact with online auction platforms via the transactions,[39] a lack of trust could not only restrict the growth of the e-commerce business models and prevent new players to enter the market, it could also drive back internet users from using their services.

[35] FY Chee, 'Privacy app maker files EU antitrust complaint against Google' (*Reuters*, 2 June 2015) www.reuters.com/article/us-eu-google-antitrust/privacy-app-maker-files-eu-antitrust-complaint-against-google-idUSKBN0OI1Z220150602; in the words of Google's spokesperson, 'Our Google Play policies have long prohibited apps that interfere with other apps – such as altering their functionality or removing their way of making money. We apply this policy uniformly and Android developers strongly support it.'

[36] As OECD describes 'internet intermediaries bring together or facilitate transactions between third parties on the internet. They give access to, host, transmit and index content, products and services originated by third parties on the internet or provide internet-based services to third parties' in OECD, 'Report on the economic and social role of internet intermediaries' (2010) 9. M Tessier, J Herzog and L Madzou, 'Regulation at the Age of Online Platform-Based Economy: Accountability, User Empowerment and Responsiveness' in Belli and Zingales (eds) (n 17) 178.

[37] ibid 179.

[38] ibid 178.

[39] See C Riefa, *Consumer Protection and Online Auction Platforms: Towards a Safer Legal Framework* (London, Routledge, 2015) 67–123 where Riefa elaborates on the control of pre-contractual information in online auctions and the right of consumers to withdraw from online auctions; I Lianos and K Botwright, 'Five ways to increase trust in e-commerce' (*World Economic Forum*, 22 March 2019) www.weforum.org/agenda/2019/03/five-ways-to-restore-trust-in-e-commerce/; World Economic Forum, 'White Paper on The Global Governance of Online Consumer Protection and E-commerce Building Trust' (22 March 2019) www3.weforum.org/docs/WEF_consumer_protection.pdf.

E. Host ISPs as Inducers of Illicit Activity Online

Finally, another reason that warrants the ascription of a set of responsibilities to host ISPs is the fact that their power could induce illegal activity on the part of internet users. A representative example of this line of thinking can be found in autocomplete suggestions that search engines offer to their users.[40] Whereas search engines do not fall into the scope of host ISPs, this example can be equally applied to host ISPs. This is because host ISPs might offer a search list to their users in order to navigate themselves better within their websites.[41] Autocomplete suggestions concern the suggestions that are provided in the search bar lists once the internet user starts typing a term. In that case, the French Supreme Court has found that the use of the terms Rapidshare and Megaupload that showed up next to suggested websites of the search results 'systematically orients internet users'[42] towards the commission of illicit activities.[43] In this way,

[40] S Karapapa and M Borghi, 'Search engine liability for autocomplete suggestions: personality, privacy and the power of the algorithm' (2015) 23 *International Journal of Law and Information Technology* 261–89.

[41] Another important reason addresses that host ISPs' power has political dimensions. There are cases where host ISPs do not exert their power within the limits of a business corporation. Rather, they manage to influence the public with regard to political issues such as the national elections or important Referendums. With regard to national elections, an outstanding example is the Cambridge Analytica scandal. Cambridge Analytica is a UK data profiling organisation that uses a number of psychological tools in order to predict the outcome of important political events based on voters' personal profiles. In light of the US elections in 2016, Facebook gave access to Cambridge Analytica's experts so that they collect via an app its users' data within the US jurisdiction and create psychological profiles for each of them. After collecting users' data and without their permission, Cambridge Analytica offered this database to Trump's campaigners with the aim to influence voters' choices at the day of the US elections. In this way, despite Zuckerberg's refusal, Facebook has enabled the manipulation of US voters through the non-authorised use of its users' personal data. Hence, it seems that major political outcomes could be influenced by host ISPs' services. A documentary on Netflix with the title *The Great Hack* explores allegations of Facebook selling its users' data without their consensus to Brexit campaigners ahead of the Brexit Referendum; 'The Cambridge Analytical files: key stories' *The Guardian* (17 March 2018) www.theguardian.com/news/series/cambridge-analytica-files; L Edwards, 'Privacy and Data Protection' in Edwards (n 14) 56–57; I Lapowsky, 'How Cambridge Analytica Sparked the Great Privacy Awakening Repercussions from the scandal swirling around the data analytics firm continue to be felt across the tech industry' (*Wired*, 17 March 2019) www.wired.com/story/cambridge-analytica-facebook-privacy-awakening/. See for instance, the free Basics service aimed to launch an initiative in India in order to offer free services to low-income citizens. The service enabled the user to access the internet via their mobile phones after entering Facebook's website. With this service, Facebook's CEO claimed that they fight social inclusion and the digital divide. However, this initiative has been subjected to severe criticism. Its opponents argue that the Free Basics programme is a walled garden whose function is directly manipulated by Facebook. Subsequent to these allegations, the Indian government decided to ban this initiative. Yet, Facebook invoked the status of an international actor that contributes to the development of lower-income countries and put pressure on the Indian government by sending emails and stressing the importance of the right to connectivity. Thus, it appears that host ISPs can exercise influence to a certain degree on political governments and participate in the discussion of seminal agendas such as the international economic and social developments of the poorer countries; for more see D Broeders and L Taylor, 'Does Great Power Come with Great Responsibility? The Need to Talk About Corporate Political Responsibility' in M Taddeo and L Floridi (eds), *The Responsibilities of Online Service Providers* (Berlin, Springer, 2017) 319; J Kiss, 'Mark Zuckerberg defends Facebook's motives in free internet project in India' *The Guardian* (28 December 2015) www.theguardian.com/technology/2015/dec/28/mark-zuckerberg-facebook-india-internet-free-basics; J Hempel, 'Zuckerberg to the UN: The Internet Belongs to Everyone' (*Wired*, 28 September 2015) www.wired.com/2015/09/zuckerberg-to-un-internet-belongs-to-everyone/.

[42] Karapapa and Borghi (n 40) 282.

[43] *Syndicat National de l'Édition Phonographique (SNEP)/Google*, Cour de Cassation, 12 July 2012 (France).

search engines could induce internet users to commit infringing acts such as the download of unauthorised films or songs. Likewise, in the *LUSH* case,[44] the English Court of Appeal has found that Amazon's search list that offered a number of competitive products once the online consumer started typing LUSH violates the origin function of the trade mark and therefore consumers can be misled.[45] Hence, the suggestion of competitive goods by the autocomplete function could lead to the violation of trade marks online.

In the light of the above, one may conclude that the ascription of a responsibility framework is justified due to the emerging role of host ISPs. Such a role, in contrast with the role of host ISPs as perceived in the ECD in 2000, represents host ISPs as powerful market players that control information flow,[46] shape public and political discourse as well as enforce and adjudicate rights online. Yet, whilst host ISPs are entitled to enforcement and adjudication duties, this does not mean that they should subordinate their business interests. However, those business interests may lead them to undermine the rights of their less powerful individual users and rights holders and therefore adopt a 'lowest common denominator'[47] for the protection of their rights. For this reason, the establishment of a responsibility framework for host ISPs might offer a greater degree of protection for the rights of internet users and right holders respectively.

However, the introduction of a handful of responsibilities for host ISPs does not only relate to the new role they exercise in the Web 2.0 era. Indeed, it is also backed up by a cornucopia of legislative and policy documents.

III. A Duty of Care for Host ISPs at Legislative and Policy Level

Within the context of online infringements, this book argues that host ISPs need to take care of the safe operation of their business model. In particular, they need to eliminate or terminate any misuse which arises on their networks and thus filter, scan or block any allegedly infringing content within their platforms.[48] In other words, they should have a duty of care. This duty of care describes the proactive role that a host ISP should adopt against the illicit material that is disseminated within its network and safeguard the rights of rights holders.

[44] *Cosmetic Warriors Ltd v Amazon.co.uk Ltd* [2014] EWHC 181 (Ch).

[45] ibid.

[46] As Revolidis has rightfully summarised 'the activities of internet intermediaries constitute the basic backbone of current internet technology' in I Revolidis, 'Internet intermediaries and copyright enforcement in the EU: In search of a balanced approach' in M Corrales, M Fenwick and N Forgó (eds), *New Technology, Big Data and the Law* (Berlin, Springer, 2017) 224.

[47] In other words, a lower standard; see O Lysnkey, 'Regulation by Platforms: The Impact on Fundamental Rights' in Belli and Zingales (eds) (n 17) 92.

[48] G Frosio describes the imposition of a duty of care as 'ongoing move towards privatization of law enforcement' in G Frosio and M Husovec, 'Accountability and Responsibility of Online Intermediaries' in G Frosio (ed), *The Oxford Handbook of Online Intermediary Liability* (Oxford, Oxford University Press, 2020) 3.

The imposition of a duty of care on host ISPs is not a novelty. Rather, its legal basis has been envisaged in Recitals 47 and 48 of the ECD.[49] According to Recital 48, Member States may require from 'service providers, who host information provided by recipients of their service, to apply duties of care, which can reasonably be expected from them and which are specified by national law, in order to detect and prevent certain types of illegal activities'.[50] This means that host ISPs might be forced to deploy preventive measures against the circulation of infringing material within their networks.

At policy level as well, the duty of care has been endorsed in a handful of several European policy documents that include recommendations on how host ISPs would tackle the increasing number of online intellectual property infringements within their networks.[51] In these documents, host ISPs are expected to adopt proactive measures in order to curb the dissemination of infringing material online. A duty of care has been for the first time endorsed in the DSM Strategy that addressed the steps to be taken in order to offer better enforcement of intellectual property rights in the online world. It has been noted that 'the Commission will analyse the need for new measures to tackle illegal content on the internet, with due regard to their impact on the fundamental right to freedom of expression and information, such as rigorous procedures for removing illegal content while avoiding the take down of legal content, and whether to require intermediaries to exercise greater responsibility and due diligence in the way they manage their networks and systems – a duty of care'.[52] Likewise, after rights holders' requests for better enforcement of intellectual property rights online, the European Commission's staff working document outlines the need for due diligence. More specifically, it notes that 'another is whether to ask intermediaries to exercise greater responsibility and due diligence in the way they manage their networks and systems'.[53] This demonstrates the need for a higher degree of responsibility of host ISPs towards the dissemination of content within their networks.

[49] Council Directive (EC) 2000/31/EC of the European Parliament and of the Council of 8 June 2000 on certain legal aspects of information society services, in particular electronic commerce, in the Internal Market (hereinafter ECD).

[50] Recital 48 of the ECD.

[51] European Commission, 'A DSM Strategy for Europe' {SWD (2015) 100 final 12; European Commission, 'Recommendation on measures to effectively tackle illegal content online' (2018) 1177; see also HM Government, 'Online Harms (White Paper)' (April 2019) 57; see also Theresa May's speech on Davos where she announced the creation of a Digital Charter 'The Digital Charter we are developing in the UK sets out the principles of our approach to agree the rights and responsibilities of the online world and to put them into practice' in World Economic Forum, Theresa's May speech in Davos 2019 is available at www.weforum.org/agenda/2018/01/theresa-may-davos-address/; a duty of care has already been applied in the context of terroristic content, hate speech and pornographic content; see European Parliament, 'Legislative resolution of 17 April 2019 on the proposal for a regulation of the European Parliament and of the Council on preventing the dissemination of terrorist content online' (COM(2018)0640 – C8-0405/2018 – 2018/0331(COD)); Council Directive (EU) 2018/1808 on the coordination of certain provisions laid down by law, regulation or administrative action in Member States concerning the provision of audiovisual media services (Audiovisual Media Services Directive) in view of changing market realities (2018) OJ L 303; EU Commission, 'The EU Code of conduct on countering illegal hate speech online', ec.europa.eu/info/policies/justice-and-fundamental-rights/combatting-discrimination/racism-and-xenophobia/countering-illegal-hate-speech-online_en.

[52] European Commission, 'A DSM Strategy for Europe' (SWD (2015) 100 final 12.

[53] European Commission, 'A DSM Strategy for Europe – Analysis and Evidence' (COM (2015) 192 final) 56–57.

Such a stance has been reinforced in the public consultation the EU Commission has conducted on the evaluation of the certain aspects of the Enforcement Directive.[54] More specifically, the right holders outlined that 'a duty of care for intermediaries at EU level would be a step in the right direction and should extend to all intermediaries'.[55] Further, the consultation notes that a number of respondents find that there is no balance between the interests at stake. In this light, they argue that host ISPs must have a duty of care so as to prevent the circulation of infringing material within their networks.[56] Likewise, the EU Commission's citizens' summary on the EU action plan for enforcing intellectual property rights has stressed that the 'idea is to encourage due diligence by all parties involved in these transactions – from suppliers and advertising agencies to payment service providers, even the rights-holders themselves'.[57] Finally, the EU Commission Communication on a balanced intellectual property rights' enforcement system warned about the negative impact of not imposing the concept of due diligence on host ISPs. A lack of due diligence on host ISPs would be detrimental for the e-commerce infrastructure since it would allow the circulation of counterfeit goods to a great extent, thus questioning the security of online purchases. Therefore, businesses and online consumers would be placed in a weak position.[58]

However, while the imposition of a duty of care is not only legally admissible but also encouraged at the policy level as well, many scholars have reflected on the ascription of a duty of care to host ISPs.[59] Firstly, scholars have debated the choice of a duty of care over existing mechanisms such as notice and take down mechanism or notice and notice mechanism. Secondly, they question the imposition of a duty of care on 'neutral' host ISPs. Thirdly, they express concerns on the conflict between Recital 48 of the ECD, which envisages a duty of care for host ISPs and Article 15 of the ECD, which prohibits the imposition of general monitoring obligations on host ISPs and has been a cornerstone for the development of the e-commerce infrastructure. An evaluation of these concerns follows.

IV. Criticism and Counter-Arguments for Imposing a Duty of Care for Host ISPs

This section critically engages with the relevant criticism that has been flagged and in particular addresses the choice of a duty of care against notice and take down and notice

[54] Council Directive (EC) 2004/48/EC on the enforcement of intellectual property rights (2004) O.J. L 157.

[55] European Commission, 'Public consultation on evaluation and modernisation of the legal framework for the enforcement of intellectual property rights' (2016) 52.

[56] ibid 43.

[57] European Commission, 'Citizens' summary EU action plan – enforcing intellectual property rights', ec.europa.eu/docsroom/documents/10058.

[58] European Commission, 'A balanced IP enforcement system responding to today's societal challenges' (SWD (2017) 430 final) 9.

[59] C Angelopoulos and S Smet, 'Notice and Fair Balance: How to reach a compromise between fundamental rights in European Intermediary Liability' (2016) 8 *Journal Media of Law* 287–88; G Frosio, 'Why Keep a Dog and Bark Yourself? From Intermediary Liability to Responsibility' (2017) 25 *Oxford International Journal of Law and Information Technology* 5; D Mac Sithigh, 'The road to responsibilities: new attitudes towards internet intermediaries' (2019) *Information and Communications Technology Law* 18.

and notice mechanisms, its imposition to neutral host ISPs and its conflict with the general prohibition of monitoring obligations as set forth in Article 15 of the ECD.

A. Duty of Care v Notice and Take-down Mechanism and Notice and Notice Mechanism

As discussed earlier, a duty of care on host ISPs is envisaged at legislative and policy level. Yet, the majority of European Member States have integrated the notice and take down system into their national legislations.[60] For this reason, it is worth considering whether a notice and take down mechanism with the appropriate safeguards for users' rights could be recommended instead of imposing a duty of care. The majority of European Member States have integrated the notice and take down system into their legislations.[61] Pursuant to this system, a host ISP can examine the validity of the claim and react either by rejecting the claim for removal of the content or taking down the content.[62] For this reason, despite a number of empirical studies that demonstrate several flaws of the notice and take down system,[63] the introduction of this mechanism in 2000 has been warmly welcomed by scholars. As Van Eecke has pointed out, through the notice and take down system all the interests of the parties involved are taken into consideration.[64] This is because through the notice and take down system, the rights holder sends a notice to the ISP alleging copyright or trade mark violation. Upon examining the validity of the notice, the host ISP reaches the decision whether to remove the allegedly infringing material or not. It is this examination on the part of the host ISP that might protect internet users' fundamental rights to information and expression.

However, the imposition of a duty of care could have advantages over the notice and take down system. This is mainly because the aim of a duty of care is to prevent the emergence of the same infringement online. Conversely, with the notice and take down system, the same infringement might occur again 'hydra-like' within the online platform.[65] This is because while Hercules cut Learnean Hydra's one head,

[60] A Kuczerawy, *Intermediary Liability and Freedom of Expression in the EU: from Concepts to Safeguards* (Wellington, Intersentia, 2018) 210.

[61] Report of the Swiss Institute of Comparative Law commissioned by the Council of Europe, 'Comparative study on filtering, blocking and take-down on illegal content on the internet' (2015); For an overview of EU Member States that adopt the notice and take down process see Kuczerawy (n 60) 331–77.

[62] P Van Eecke, 'Online service providers and liability: A plea for a balanced approach' (2011) 48 *Common Market Law Review* 1455 where Van Eecke noted that 'the notice-and-take-down procedure is one of the essential mechanisms through which the E-Commerce Directive achieves a balance between the interests of right holders, online intermediaries and users'.

[63] C Ahlert, C Marsden and C Yung, 'How "Liberty" Disappeared from Cyberspace: The Mystery Shopper Tests Internet Content Self-Regulation' (2014) www.academia.edu/686683/How_Liberty_Disappeared_from_Cyberspace_The_Mystery_Shopper_Tests_Internet_Content_Self_Regulation; Lecture by Sjoera Nas, Bits of Freedom, 'The Multatuli Project ISP Notice & take down' (2004) www-old.bof.nl/docs/researchpaperSANE.pdf; it has been found that the number of notices might increase compliance costs as well as encroach upon the principle of due process in K Erickson and M Kretschmer, 'Empirical approaches to intermediary liability' (2019) 6 *CREATe Working Paper* 6.

[64] Van Eecke (n 62) 1455.

[65] See in A Giannopoulou, 'Copyright enforcement measures: the role of the ISPs and the respect of the principle of proportionality' (2012) 3 *European Journal for Law and Technology* 1; JC Ginsburg, 'Separating the

two heads emerged.[66] In this sense, a notice and take down system might not impede the increasing number of infringements in the digital world since it is considered a 'Sisyphean task'.[67]

Further, it could be argued that a notice and notice system would be more preferable over the imposition of a duty of care. Policymakers should endorse a notice and notice mechanism with the appropriate safeguards for users' rights. This mechanism treats a host ISP as an intermediary since, after being notified of the infringement, intermediary's duties are limited to sending a notification to the allegedly infringing user. As Angelopoulos notes, this mechanism 'restricts intermediaries to their natural role as middlemen and returns the job of enforcing rights and obligations to the courts'.[68] This implies that host ISPs would no longer be treated as enforcers and adjudicators of intellectual property rights since judicial authorities would now decide on the illegal nature of the content and offer redress to the intellectual property holders.

However, this assumption can be misleading. This is because the crucial point here is not to give host ISPs immunity for circulating infringing material. Rather, since their services, as Friedmann notes, 'shapes infringements',[69] host ISPs should undertake in principle a higher degree of participation in the battle against online infringements. This is illustrated in the case of the Pirate Bay website. Due to its infrastructure, internet users are able to file exchange unauthorised files. Moreover, in order to increase traffic on its website and increase advertisement revenues, the website invited internet users to share their illegal files with each other. In this sense, the business model of Pirate Bay shaped the infringements through inducing its clients to exchange files via its peer-to-peer network.

B. From Neutral to Active Host ISPs

Another concern to be addressed is the imposition of a duty of care to host ISPs whose function does not address an active involvement in the dissemination of content online. In this respect, it could be questioned how plausible it is to ascribe a duty of care to those host ISPs whose nature is neutral and whose services are limited to hosting and storing content uploaded by their users.

Sony Sheep from the Grokster Goats: Reckoning the Future Business Plans of Copyright-Dependent Technology Entrepreneurs' (2008) 50 *Arizona Law Review* 591.

[66] Hydra Greek Mythology (Encyclopedia Britannica), available at www.britannica.com/topic/Hydra-Greek-mythology.

[67] L Helman and G Parchomovsky, 'The best available technology standard' (2011) 111 *Columbia Law Review* 1204.

[68] Angelopoulos and Smet (n 59) 266.

[69] D Friedmann, 'Sinking the Safe Harbour with the legal certainty of strict liability in sight' (2014) 9 *Journal of Intellectual Property Law and Practice* 148–55 where Friedmann gives the example of the algorithm 'if one assumes that the algorithms of an OSP to optimise the transactions between a third party and internet users, were merely technical, automatic and passive, but have the result that they induce infringements, the OSP has the option to fix this problem in the algorithm under their control after it becomes aware of the problem'.

Host ISPs are understood as neutral entities in view of the passive nature of the services they provide to the end-users.[70] This understanding has been outlined in the *Google v Louis Vuitton case*[71] where Louis Vuitton initiated legal proceedings against Google alleging trade mark violation via Google's AdWords.[72] Google AdWords is a paid service which offers to advertisers the option to advertise their products when users enter specific search terms. In this case, Google AdWords offered advertisements of fake Louis Vuitton bags when users typed the keywords Louis Vuitton into the search engine. After a careful consideration of the facts, the court did not attribute liability to Google for trade mark infringement because it perceived its role as neutral. By neutral is understood, as the CJEU noted, the conduct that is 'merely technical, automatic and passive, pointing to a lack of knowledge or control of the data which it stores'.[73] This means that the concept of neutrality amounts to the passive function of host ISPs provided that they are deprived of knowledge and control of the content that is hosted via their platforms. Therefore, host ISPs were treated as neutral entities since they did not engage with the circulation of content and goods within their platforms.

Nonetheless, while host ISPs would have incentives to maintain the rhetoric of neutrality so as to evade any accountability,[74] the concept of neutrality does not align with the technological developments of 2022. This is because this provision was drafted in 1999 when the host providers were related to forums and blogs.[75] Yet, with the advent of Web 2.0, host providers are no longer neutral and thus do not limit their services to hosting content. Rather, they are seen as active entities that index material, decide which content reaches the end-users and circulate the content within their networks. As van der Sloot pointed out 'in the modern internet landscape however, providers have become much more active, for example by providing the platform on which information is shared by users, by indexing this information, by making it searchable and by publishing and distributing the information over the internet'.[76] This means that following the technological evolution, the business model of host ISPs has been transformed.

[70] See discussion on the passive nature of host ISPs in P Jougleux, 'The role of internet intermediaries in copyright law online enforcement' in T Synodinou, P Jougleux, C Markou and T Prastitiou (eds), *EU Internet Law: Regulation and Enforcement* (Berlin, Springer, 2017) 273.

[71] Case C-236/08 *Google France and Google* (2010) ECLI:EU:C:2010:159.

[72] C Volkmann, 'Trademark Use and Liability of Referencing Service in Keyword Advertising – Google AdWords and Trademark Law' (2011) 3 *European Journal of Risk* Regulation 450.

[73] Case C-236/08 *Google France and Google* (2010) ECLI:EU:C:2010:159, para 114.

[74] U Kohl, 'Google: The rise and Rise of online intermediaries in the Governance of the Internet and Beyond (Part 2)' (2013) 21 *International Journal of Law and Information Technology* 187.

[75] A Lodder, 'Directive 2000/31/EC on certain legal aspects of information society services, in particular electronic commerce, in the internal market' in A Lodder and A Murray (eds), *EU Regulation of E-Commerce: A commentary* (2017) 51; The French High Council for Literary and Artistic Property notes that 'Although all parties noted that the above activities do not match the assumptions made by the European authorities in 2000 when the legislation was drafted', in The French High Council for Literary and Artistic Property, 'Mission to Link Directives 2000/31 and 2001/29 – Report and Proposals (2016) 7 *Journal of Intellectual Property, Technology and E-Commerce*, see www.jipitec.eu/issues/jipitec-7-2-2016/4436.

[76] B van der Sloot, 'Welcome to the Jungle: The Liability of Internet Intermediaries for Privacy Violations in Europe' (2015) 6 *Journal of Intellectual Property, Information Technology and E-Commerce Law* 212.

More specifically, host ISPs nowadays govern a wide range of activities and are active towards the usage of the content[77] since they index it and choose which information reaches the end-users.[78] As Hurwitz notes 'active intermediaries now are capable of using and manipulating user data in ways that were never before possible …'.[79] For example, social network platforms or video sharing networks or digital auction platforms are not merely hosting the content posted by users or enabling sellers to display their goods within their networks. Rather, they are suggesting links to content which users may find more appealing on the basis of their preferences or make it easier for users to search for their favourite material.[80] Hence, it appears that host ISPs adopt a more dynamic role that is far from passivity and neutrality.

This active role of host ISPs has been mirrored in a bedrock of court rulings where host ISPs have been treated as active entities at the European level. For instance, in the cases of *Delfi v Estonia*,[81] *Google Spain*,[82] *Sichting Brein v Ziggo*[83] and *GS Media*,[84] the CJEU endorsed an active role for host ISPs since they are now more active in the dissemination of content throughout their platforms. Whereas the first two rulings addressed defamatory and privacy issues, it seems worth mentioning them since they were the first rulings that introduced the active role of host ISPs. For example, in the *Delfi* ruling delivered by the European Court of Human Rights,[85] an individual user requested that Delfi, a news portal with very high traffic in Estonia, remove offensive comments which also entailed threats against him. After a careful consideration of the facts, the Court did not find Delfi liable, but in light of the 'comments' section on the website, the Strasbourg Judges considered Delfi as an active entity. In particular, they noted that '… in the case of active intermediaries who host their own content and actively monitor all data (that is to say, are in a position to read it and remove it after the data are made accessible), as in the case of Delfi'[86] and have concluded that with the comments' part it offers to the users, Delfi's role went 'beyond that of a passive, purely technical service provider'.[87]

[77] Whilst the ECD provisions consider host ISPs as passive entities and limit the scope of their functions into storing temporary data, transmitting information or offering space for users to upload content, P Van Ecke thinks that although mere conduit and caching providers have a neutral role, the hosting providers exercise greater involvement with their users. To explain his view, Van Eecke cites the following example 'For example, when offering a website on which users can upload and store their personal photos or videos, the website operator must make available some tools to allow users to upload, categorize and display the information towards the usage of the content transmitted via their networks, the hosting providers exercise greater involvement in distributing the information' in van Eecke (n 62) 1483. However, Revolidis criticises this view and notes that 'the neutral role of internet service providers is not to be measure only on their function per se, but it must also be projected on their participation in the production of information. It is the knowledge and the control of information that would take them out of the realm of intermediaries not the mere distribution of information that would take them out of the realm of intermediaries not the mere distribution of it, even if they are relatively highly involved in it' in Revolidis (n 46) 231; see also Kuczerawy (n 60) 97–98.

[78] van der Sloot (n 76) 211.

[79] J Hurwitz, 'Trust and Online Interaction' (2013) 161 *University of Pennsylvania Law Review* 1593.

[80] C Yoo, *The Dynamic Internet: How Technology, Users, and Businesses are Transforming the Network* (AEI Press, 2012) ch 9.

[81] ECtHR, Grand Chamber, *Delfi AS v Estonia*, 16 June 2015, Application no. 64569, (2015) E.M.L.R.

[82] Case C-131/12 *Google Spain SL and Google Inc. v Agencia Española de Protección de Datos (AEPD) and Mario Costeja González* (2014) ECLI:EU:C:2014:317.

[83] Case C-610/15 *Stichting Brein v Ziggo BV and XS4ALL Internet BV* (2017) ECLI:EU:C:2017:456.

[84] Case C-160/15 *GS Media BV v Sanoma Media Netherlands BV and Others* (2016) ECLI:EU:C:2016:644.

[85] ECtHR, Grand Chamber, *Delfi AS v Estonia*, 16 June 2015, Application no. 64569, (2015) E.M.L.R 78.

[86] ibid.

[87] ibid note 146.

Furthermore, in the *Google Spain* ruling[88] the CJEU examined the dispute between a Spanish citizen and Google Spain which declined his request to take down search results that linked to a Spanish online newspaper. These search results were about a past social security debt that had been paid back and thus was no longer relevant. At the outset, the Luxembourg judges outlined that Google's search services play a seminal role in the spread of information online.[89] Such dissemination could occur with the processing of personal data conducted by Google. For this reason, the Court explained that '... it is undisputed that that activity of search engines plays a decisive role in the overall dissemination of those data in that it renders the latter accessible to any internet user making a search on the basis of the data subject's name, including to internet users who otherwise would not have found the web page on which those data are published'.[90] This means that the courts perceive that search engines do not maintain a passive role towards the searching results. Rather, it is presumed that search engines adopt an active role since they process data with a view to provide a list of searching results.[91] Although this conclusion has been applied to search engines, a similar stance could be equally applied to host ISPs. This understanding has been reinforced in the following case at the European level.

Similar to the cases that deal with privacy and defamatory issues, the CJEU then endorsed an active role for host ISPs with regard to copyright infringements in the *Stichting Brein v Ziggo BV and XS4All Internet BV* ruling.[92] In this case, the CJEU examined the question of whether Pirate Bay's activities which enable users to download files via a peer-to-peer software constitute communication to the public as per Article 3 of the InfoSoc Directive. This case was referred from the Dutch Court of Appeal where Stichting Brein, a Dutch foundation that protects the rights of creators, requested a blocking injunction against Ziggo and XS4All Internet, two internet service providers, to terminate the access to their users to the Pirate Bay website. After careful consideration of the facts, the CJEU held that Pirate Bay's actions to redirect users to websites with unauthorised content amounted to communication to the public on the basis that The Pirate Bay is 'a sharing platform which, by means of indexation of metadata relating to protected works and the provision of a search engine, allows users of the platform to locate those works ...'.[93] This means that to index files and enable users to find them via search engine service implies the active involvement of The Pirate Bay towards the circulation of unauthorised content. Therefore, while this ruling has been severely criticised since it attributes primary liability rules to The Pirate Bay,[94] it shows clearly that the Court treats host ISPs with file-sharing function as active host ISPs.

[88] Case C-131/12 *Google Spain SL and Google Inc. v Agencia Española de Protección de Datos (AEPD) and Mario Costeja González* (2014) ECLI:EU:C:2014:317.

[89] Ibid, para 33.

[90] Case C-131/12 *Google Spain SL and Google Inc. v Agencia Española de Protección de Datos (AEPD) and Mario Costeja González* (2014) ECLI:EU:C:2014:317, para 36.

[91] S Stalla-Bourdillon, 'Internet intermediaries as responsible actors? Why it is time to rethink the e-Commerce Directive as well ...' in Taddeo and Floridi (n 41) 287.

[92] Case C-610/15 *Stichting Brein v Ziggo BV and XS4ALL Internet BV* (2017) ECLI:EU:C:2017:456.

[93] ibid para 50.

[94] This ruling prompted reflections on the academic scholarship. JB Nordemann, 'Liability of Online Service Providers for Copyrighted Content – Regulatory Action needed?' (2017) *IMCO Committee* notes that 'the role of The Pirate Bay as a platform to connect users of the BitTorrent protocol for infringing activity was evaluated

Finally, in the *GS Media* ruling, the active status of host ISPs was confirmed. This case was a referral from the Dutch Supreme Court to the CJEU and it examined the liability of linking a provider to unauthorised content, in this case the nude photos of a Dutch celebrity prior to their publication in a magazine. Upon assessing the facts, the CJEU held that since GS Media, as operator of the website GeenStijl, has a profit-gain aim, it must conduct the necessary control to ensure the legality of the material to which the users are redirected via the link that is provided.[95] In this way, GS Media is assumed that it has knowledge over the illegal content and thus could be held liable for copyright infringements via hyperlinking.[96] To counter the presumption of knowledge, the host ISPs shall provide evidence that it carried out all the necessary controls in order to confirm the lawful nature of the content.[97] Therefore, it appears that GS Media shall undertake an active role towards the dissemination of content online in order to escape liability.

Bearing in mind the above, there is an emergent trend in judicial rulings that confirms an active role for host ISPs. These rulings dictate that host ISPs are not neutral but are actively engaged in the distribution of goods and transmission of information that reaches the end-users. Therefore, the idea of host ISPs as neutral entities seems to have been replaced by host ISPs as entities who index content and make it subsequently available to the audience online. This understanding might offer a solid justification for the recommendation of this book for establishing a responsibility framework for host ISPs based on co-regulation.

C. Duty of Care v General Monitoring: Lack of Clash

As discussed earlier, a duty of care has been envisaged in Recital 48 of the ECD. This provision dictates that host ISPs might deploy preventive measures in order to prevent the emergence of online infringements. Yet, a number of commentators argue that the imposition of a duty of care might not be in accordance with the prohibition of general monitoring obligations as set forth in Article 15 of the ECD.[98]

by the CJEU as primary liability for communication to the public'; Angelopoulos states that 'the result would be a judge-made harmonisation of indirect (ie accessory) copyright liability and one, moreover, that engulfs it within primary liability' in C Angelopoulos, 'AG Szpunar in *Stichting Brein v Ziggo*: An Indirect Harmonisation of Indirect Liability' (*Kluwer copyright blog*, 23 March 2017) copyrightblog.kluweriplaw.com/2017/03/23/ag-szpunar-stichting-brein-v-ziggo-indirect-harmonisation-indirect-liability/; Rosati as well, 'Further to the CJEU decision in The Pirate Bay situations like the one examined by the CJEU should be assessed by national courts under the lens of primary – rather than secondary – liability' in E Rosati, 'The CJEU Pirate Bay judgment and its impact on the liability of online platforms' (2017) 39 *European Intellectual Property Law Review* 12.

[95] Case C-160/15 *GS Media BV v Sanoma Media Netherlands BV and Others* (2016) ECLI:EU:C:2016:644, para 51.

[96] See also E Papadaki, 'Hyperlinking, making available and copyright infringement: lessons from European national courts' (2017) 8 *European Journal of Law and Technology* 12.

[97] For further analysis see also E Rosati, 'GS Media and Its Implications for the Construction of the Right of Communication to the Public within EU Copyright Architecture' (2017) 54 *Common Market Law Review* 1242.

[98] Council Directive (EC) 2000/31/EC of the European Parliament and of the Council of 8 June 2000 on certain legal aspects of information society services, in particular electronic commerce, in the Internal Market (hereinafter ECD).

Pursuant to Article 15 of the ECD the imposition of general monitoring obligations to host ISPs is precluded. This means that host ISPs are not obliged by law to deploy mechanisms in order to identify the allegedly infringing content online. Nonetheless, a growing body of academic scholarship argues that the prohibition of general monitoring shall not be construed as an absolute exclusion of filtering mechanisms by host ISPs.

To restrict host ISPs' reaction to mere removal of the infringing content upon being notified might be against the *EU acquis*, firstly, it could be against Recital 47 of the ECD that allows the imposition of monitoring obligations to host ISPs in specific cases. Indeed, Recital 47 states that 'Member States are prevented from imposing a monitoring obligation on service providers only with respect to obligations of a general nature; this does not concern monitoring obligations in a specific case and ….' It is this conflict between a Recital and an Article that has generated mounting concerns as to which of the two prevails. However, this concern is but an illusion. This is because Recitals are considered 'interpretative tools'[99] of the provisions of the Directive. This interpretation takes into consideration the purpose of the Directive. Given that the overall purpose of the Directive is to curb the dissemination of infringing content within the online world, it could be implied that proactive measures are allowed.

Indeed, this understanding has been reinforced at policy level. The Director General of the DG Internal Market stated that Article 15 is about '… certain duties of care which can be reasonably be expected from service providers and which are specified in national law. Such duties of care could for instance consist in making available of complaint-systems or in the operation of notice and take down procedures ….'[100] This implies that host ISPs are expected to adopt a proactive stance towards the circulation of infringing content. Otherwise, the exclusion of all proactive measures would force host ISPs merely to remove content.[101]

Secondly, it could be against the established line of CJEU case law that ascribes not only take down duties but also preventive duties on host ISPs. A representative example can be found in the *L'Oreal v Ebay* case.[102] In this case, the CJEU handed down that eBay shall prevent the displacement of counterfeit goods of L'Oreal on its platform, outlining that 'the measures, procedures and remedies to be provided for should include prohibitory measures aimed at preventing further infringements of intellectual property rights.'[103] This means that eBay's role would not amount only to the termination of the illicit activity but also to the prevention of future infringements.

[99] R Baratta, 'Complexity of EU Law in the domestic implementing process' (2014) 2 *The Theory and Practice of Legislation* 296 where he states that 'It seems worth noting in particular that the Commission rightly refers to recitals as interpretative tools. In that respect, the preamble of a legal act is a useful means for interpreting it.'

[100] Letter of Director of DG Internal Market J Mogg to MEP Cederschild (13 June 2000), www.asktheeu.org/en/request/2250/response/7914/attach/2/letter%20Mogg%20to%20MEP.pdf.

[101] JB Nordemann, 'Are preventive duties on hosting service providers in line with EU law? Some comments from a legal perspective on Art. 13 Draft DSM Directive and upload filters' (*Kluwer Copyright blog*, 28 June 2018) copyrightblog.kluweriplaw.com/2018/06/28/preventive-duties-hosting-service-providers-line-eu-law-comments-legal-perspective-art-13-draft-dsm-directive-upload-filters/.

[102] Case C-324/09 *L'Oreal SA V eBay Int'l AG* [2011] ECR I-6011.

[103] ibid.

In a similar fashion, in *Scarlet v Sabam*,[104] although the court outlined the prohibition of general monitoring obligations, it explicitly noted that host ISPs are allowed 'to take measures aimed not only at bringing to an end infringement already committed against intellectual-property rights using their information-society services, but also at preventing further infringements'.[105] This implies that under certain conditions Scarlet shall exercise a proactive role and thus undertake any precautionary measures in order to prevent its customers from downloading unauthorised films.

Similarly, in the *UPC Telekabel* ruling,[106] which was a referral from the Austrian Appeal Court, two film production companies requested the issue of a blocking injunction against UPC Telekabel, an ISP that gave access to websites with unauthorised films. After careful consideration of the facts, the CJEU reinforced the compatibility of outcome injunctions with the European fundamental rights. This is because, as the Court noted, it does not violate the fundamental right of host ISP to conduct business as per Article 16 of the EU Charter of Fundamental Rights while at the same time it enables the recipient of the injunction to undertake all reasonable measures to avoid liability.[107] For the current narrative, the second explanation seems the most interesting. This is because the Court introduced the concept of reasonable measures that host ISPs must have taken in order to exonerate liability.[108] Such measures imply a proactive nature. This means that they should prevent the emergence of online infringement or at least to curb at a greater extent the online infringements. As the Court noted, the measures to adopt shall be effective in the sense that they must protect the fundamental right to property as enshrined in Article 11 of the European Charter of Fundamental Rights but also in the sense that they must prevent the access of internet users to unauthorised content that could place into peril the right of content owners and brand owners to safeguard their property.[109] In this light, with this ruling the CJEU explicitly carved out the path for the imposition of obligations on host ISPs by endorsing the concept of reasonable measures.

Finally, the most recent ruling in the line of the CJEU's case law that affirms the preventive duties of host ISPs is the *Eva Glawischnig-Piesczek* case.[110] This case was a referral from the Austrian Supreme Court and was about the dispute of *Eva Glawischnig-Piesczek*, an internet user against Facebook with regard to the post of defamatory comments online. After careful consideration of the facts, the Court handed down that a host ISP is obliged to prevent the reemergence of content that has already been declared unlawful. This means that in this case, the reposting of defamatory comments

[104] Case C-70/10 *Scarlet Extended SA v Société belge des auteurs, compositeurs et éditeurs SCRL (SABAM)* [2011] ECR-I 11959.

[105] Case C-360/10 *Belgische Vereniging van Auteurs, Com- ponisten en Uitgevers CVBA (SABAM) v Netlog NV* (2012) ECLI:EU:C:2012:85, para 18; see also Edwards (n 14) 280 where Edwards notes that 'Nonetheless, Scarlet still upheld the principle that a filtering injunction might be possible if properly tailored and constrained.'

[106] Case C-314/12 *UPC Telekabel Wien GmbH v Constantin Film Verleih GmbH (2014)* ECLI:EU:C:2014:192, paras 51–52.

[107] ibid paras 51–52.

[108] ibid para 53.

[109] ibid para 62.

[110] Case C-18/18 *Eva Glawischnig-Piesczek v Facebook Ireland Limited* (2019) ECLI:EU:C:2019:821.

should have been removed by Facebook, without notifying the internet user. In this line of reasoning, the CJEU found that 'EU law does not preclude a host provider such as Facebook from being ordered to remove identical and, in certain circumstances, equivalent comments previously declared to be illegal'.[111] This means that the existing European law does not exclude the order of a host ISP to take down information that is stored within its network and whose illegality has already been declared given that the host ISP does not need to take an independent examination to identify the illegal nature of the content.[112]

Therefore, it appears that a duty of care is allowed within the scope of the existing *EU acquis* since the rationale of Article 15 of the ECD is not to prohibit the imposition of all preventive measures in the battle against copyright and trade mark infringements.

Finally, a reason that could offer a counter-argument to those scholars who insist that the wording of Article 15 of the ECD prohibits the imposition of monitoring obligations to host ISPs is the fact that Article 15 of the ECD is outdated. Article 15 of the ECD was drafted in the 1990s.[113] This means that European policymakers had in mind the limited technological capacities of filtering at that time. More specifically, it was around 1999–2000 when scientists started developing filtering technology in laboratories around the world. Representative examples are the MIT Butterfly Project and the Information Retrieval and Information Systems in the Netherlands that reveal the development of applications and software on filtering information.[114] Given the premature stage of all these projects at the time, one might understand that such a nascent filtering technology could not distinguish between illegitimate and lawful material without a high margin of error.[115] It is probably for this reason that the European policymakers endorsed Article 15 of the ECD and thus exempted host ISPs from deploying ill-fitted filtering technologies in order to monitor their networks.

[111] Press release No. 128/19 on the Judgment of Case C-18/18 *Eva Glawischnig-Piesczek v Facebook Ireland Limited*, 3 October 2019.

[112] Case C-18/18 *Eva Glawischnig-Piesczek v Facebook Ireland Limited* (2019) ECLI:EU:C:2019:821, para 55; see also A Kuczerawy, 'General Monitoring obligations: a new cornerstone of Internet Regulation in the EU?' in KU Leuven Centre for IT and IP Law (ed), *Rethinking IT and IP Law* (Wellington, Intersentia, 2019) 146 where she criticises the Advocate's General decision on differentiating between software tools and sophisticated monitoring solutions. As she explains, the former do come in conflict with Article 15 of the ECD while the latter might encroach upon it.

[113] Lodder (n 75) 53; The French High Council for Literary and Artistic Property notes that 'Although all parties noted that the above activities do not match the assumptions made by the European authorities in 2000 when the legislation was drafted', in The French High Council for Literary and Artistic Property, 'Mission to Link Directives 2000/31 and 2001/29 – Report and Proposals' (2016) 7 *Journal of Intellectual Property, Information Technology and E-Commerce Law* is available at www.jipitec.eu/issues/jipitec-7-2-2016/4436.

[114] SM Bohte, WB Langdon and H La Poutre, 'Report on Current Technology for Information Filtering and User Profiling in Agent-Based Systems, Part I: A Perspective' (2000) 9, www0.cs.ucl.ac.uk/staff/W.Langdon/TA/reports/profiling.pdf.

[115] Center for Democracy and Technology, 'Mixed Messages? The Limits of Automated Social Media Content Analysis' (November 2017) 18 where it is noted that 'Among studies using NLP to judge the meaning of text (including hate speech detection and sentiment analysis), the highest accuracy rates reported hover around 80%; in many studies, the highest accuracy rates reported were around 70 to 75%.73 These accuracy rates may represent impressive advancement in NLP research, but they should also serve as a strong caution to anyone considering the use of such tools in a decision-making process.'

Yet, the current digital ecosystem it not similar to the 'embryonic state of electronic commerce'[116] of 2000. This is because, as Frosio notes, 'the theoretical and market background against which the intermediary liability debate developed has changed considerably since the first appearance of online intermediaries almost two decades ago'.[117] This means that host ISPs' business models, along with the environment in which they operate, have been transformed into a more complex digital ecosystem with myriad online services and risks as well.

So, in contrast to 2000 when the ECD was introduced, in 2022 it cannot be denied that existing filtering technologies are way more advanced and sophisticated.[118] A telling example is the Content ID system of YouTube.[119] This is a rights management system based on digital fingerprinting technology, and its costs for its development were about US$60 million.[120] Without overlooking the errors, such as the lack of detecting works that belong to the public domain,[121] it is undoubtfully a representative example of high quality filtering technology of our time and consists of a 'set of copyright policies and content management tools'.[122] It has been estimated that its Database includes 50 million works which amount to a period of 600 years' audiovisual material.[123] Another example can be found in PhotoDNA software developed by Microsoft. It is a digital fingerprint-based software otherwise known as hashes that detect images that relate to terroristic content.[124] Under the initiative of the EU Commission, a number of host ISPs have already deployed this software in order to cope with terrorism in the digital ecosystem.[125] Finally, the technology of LTU Tech offers image recognition services that can detect pirated goods or child abuse content.[126]

Accordingly, one might conclude that the clash between a duty of care and general monitoring obligations does not exist in practice. This is mainly because the interpretation of Article 15 of the ECD that prohibits any general monitoring obligations is not

[116] A Wyckoff and Al Colecchia, 'Report on the Economic and Social Impact of Electronic Commerce' (1992) 12 where he notes that 'the embryonic state of electronic commerce, policies should be crafted with care and with due recognition of its fragile and evolving nature'.

[117] Frosio (n 59) 3.

[118] M Schellekens, 'Liability of Internet Intermediaries' a slippery slope?' (2011) 8 *SCRIPTed* 154 where he cites the examples of eBay's Fraud Engine and VeRo-software; Edwards (n 14) 258; in a study conducted by N Koren and M Perel it has been found that 25% of video-sharing websites and 10% of image-sharing websites adopt ex-filtering systems in order to identify unauthorised content online in N Koren and M Perel, 'Black Box Tinkering: Beyond Disclosure in Algorithmic Enforcement' (2017) 69 *Florida Law Review* 181.

[119] B Boroughf, 'The Next Great YouTube: Improving Content ID to foster creativity, cooperation and fair compensation' (2015) 25 *Albany Law Journal Science and Technology* 8; Helman and Parchomovsky (n 67) 1209; L Shinn, 'YouTube's content ID as a case study of private copyright enforcement systems' (2015) *AIPLA Quarterly Journal* 359.

[120] S Jacques, K Garstka, M Hviid and J Street, 'Automated anti-piracy systems as copyright enforcement mechanism: a need to consider cultural diversity' (2018) 40 *European Intellectual Property Review* 218.

[121] ibid.

[122] C Sims and E Figueira, 'YouTube, Google find safe harbour in New York Court' (2010) *Communications Lawyer* 3.

[123] Footnote 84 in Jacques, Garstka, Hviid and Street (n 120) 218.

[124] Frosio and Husovec (n 48) 613–30.

[125] EU together we protect is available at europa.eu/euprotects/our-safety/awareness-prevention-how-eu-combating-radicalisation across-europe_en.

[126] A Gann and D Abecassis, 'The Impact of a Content Filtering Mandate on Online Service Providers' (2018) 6.

to be understood as precluding all preventive measures. Such interpretation would be in conflict with *EU acquis*. Furthermore, Article 15 of the ECD seems to be outdated. This is because it was drafted in the 1990s when filtering technology was at its infancy. Nowadays, it is undeniable that filtering technology is more sophisticated and can, with a low margin of error, distinguish unlawful information from legitimate information.

Having discussed the reasons that warrant the imposition of a duty of care on host ISPs drawing evidence from the *EU acquis*, namely from legislation and the line of CJEU case law, this brings us to the next question, namely how such a duty of care should be shaped. This discussion is of seminal importance since however necessary a measure might be, it is the clear articulation of the limits within which this measure can be exercised that would enable the measure to achieve its goals. Otherwise, the imposition of that measure might be biased towards the interests of one of the parties involved and thus fail to reach its full potential. The following section aims to answer which host ISPs shall implement a duty of care towards the circulation of infringing content and fake goods and what the scope of that duty of care shall be.

V. How Should a Proposed Duty of Care for Host ISPs be Shaped?

In this light, this section discusses whether a duty of care shall be treated as a matter of outcome or as a matter of principle as well as how the scope of a duty of care shall be defined based on legal principles, existing trends in case law and academic scholarship.

A. A Duty of Care as a Matter of Outcome or as a Matter of Principle

In the current policy and scholarly landscape, a duty of care is subject to different interpretations. It is either construed as a matter of principle or as a matter of outcome. As a matter of principle, it means that all host ISPs must be assigned with proactive duties towards the circulation of unlawful material within their networks. In contrast, a matter of outcome means that host ISPs are attributed a number of proactive duties according to their business model. For instance, this encompasses their ability to control the usage of the content or the likelihood to attract a number of unlawful contents within their networks.

On one hand, the ascription of a duty of care as a matter of principle might raise concerns as to its implications on the business welfare of certain websites. For instance, for a non-profit host ISP such as Wikipedia,[127] it would be an excessive burden to adopt a filtering mechanism in order to monitor its platform for copyright infringements. It might be difficult for Wikipedia to develop its in-house technology as YouTube did

[127] G Sartori, 'Providers' Liability: From the e-commerce directive to the future: In depth analysis for the IMCO Committee' (2017) *IMCO Committee* 29.

or excessively costly to license an existing one. Secondly, should the host ISPs not be in compliance with the set of responsibilities, then they will be subject, as elaborated in chapter four, to primary liability rules.

Further, an additional concern on imposing a duty of care on host ISPs as a matter of principle is that a number of host ISPs attract a decimal rate of infringements. In this sense, it would not be fair for these host ISPs to be ascribed a duty of care since their business model does not enable any circulation of infringing material within their platforms. An illustration of this is Github, an open-source platform where software developers use its service so as to share their own codes with other developers.[128]

In the light of the above, it is argued that a duty of care should be imposed as a matter of outcome. This means that a duty of care should not be imposed on each host ISP, rather, it should be imposed on those host ISPs whose business models might also attract unlawful content or on those which have control over the dissemination of material within their networks. This approach, however, is not new. There have been stances in law where different entities were assigned different duties depending on their impact on others' rights.[129] For instance, Recital 68 of the DSMD excludes from the scope of OCSSPs the non-profit host ISPs such as Wikipedia. This means that while OCSSPs such as Facebook would be assigned to a number of obligations with regard to the dissemination of infringing content online, non-profit host ISPs would be free from complying with those obligations. Accordingly, this will enable those non-profit host ISPs to continue their operation without disruption and thus not deprive internet users of information that is available online.

So, in this respect, with regard to copyright violations, those host ISPs that appear to be the borderline of online infringements or have a certain degree of control towards the usage of content that is disseminated within their networks should have a duty to prevent the emergence of online infringements.

From a normative perspective, this book argues that the imposition of a duty of care to host ISPs depending on their business model seems fairer. First of all, without their services, the allegedly infringing material would not have been stored nor transmitted via their networks and thus not reach end-users.[130] Secondly, in selecting which information is made publicly available, host ISPs exercise editorial discretion.[131] This means that, like the editors in newspapers, host ISPs are in the pursuit of content that would be more appealing to their subscribers and thus increase the traffic to their sites.[132] For instance, this was the case of Google which managed to beat its competitors such as AltaVista. What Google did was to deploy an algorithm that offered more effective

[128] J Reda, 'Censorship machines are coming: It's time for the free software community to discover its political clout' (*Julia Reda's website*, 6 April 2018) juliareda.eu/2018/04/free-software-censorship-machines/.

[129] C Angelopoulos, 'EU Copyright Reform: Outside the Safe Harbours, Intermediary Liability capsizes into incoherence' (*Kluwer Copyright blog*, 6 October 2016) copyrightblog.kluweriplaw.com/2016/10/06/eu-copyright-reform-outside-safe-harbours-intermediary-liability-capsizes-incoherence/.

[130] A Marsoof, *Internet Intermediaries and Trade Mark Rights* (London, Routledge, 2019) 106.

[131] Yoo (n 80) ch 9 where Yoo notes that they 'manage the daily barrage of wanted and unwanted content'; E Goldman, 'Search Engine Bias and the Demise of Search Engine Utopianism' (2006) 8 *Yale Journal of Law and Technology* 189.

[132] Yoo (n 80) ch 9.

search listing results to its users than its rivals. In this way, Google became the leader in the search engines market.[133]

What is more, the ascription of a duty of care according to the business model of the host ISP has been supported by a handful of scholars. These scholars argue that since those host ISPs who have more control over the dissemination of the infringing content, or whose business model attracts illicit activity, should have a duty of care. For instance, it has been implied in Riordan's taxonomy of host ISPs[134] that it is fairer to attribute a greater responsibility to those host ISPs that are 'closest to the end-users'. Along similar lines, Marsoof argues that 'an intermediary that is proximate to an infringing activity, in that it possesses control over the means of infringement, has a greater responsibility to terminate, if not mitigate, the infringement'.[135] Such a stance has been maintained by Sartor who in his report for the IMCO Committee outlines that 'business models and available means should also be considered in determining duties of care'.[136]

What is more, successful examples of duty care can be traced to various sectors. A telling example can be found in trade marks. At policy level, for instance, following the introduction of the 'follow the money' approach, a handful of online auction platforms signed a Memorandum of Understanding on the sale of counterfeit goods via the internet.[137] In this Memorandum, large corporations such as luxury, fashion brands and sporting goods signed agreements with popular host ISPs such as Amazon and Alibaba in order to initiate actions which could terminate the display and circulation of counterfeit goods on their online marketplaces.

Apart from such policy initiatives that encourage cooperation among host ISPs to combat the circulation of counterfeit goods, there are also voluntary private initiatives in order to prevent the dissemination of fake goods within the networks. This can be seen in the case of Amazon which is one of the most popular online auction platforms. After the platform faced an unprecedented number of lawsuits from brand owners due to the counterfeit goods that are circulated within its platform,[138] Amazon decided to change its policy against fake goods online. This policy is the Brand Registry that enables trade mark owners to register their brand in a Registry.[139] Once the brand is registered, Amazon may identify instances where the brands are being unlawfully used. For instance, it includes listings with products that use the trade marks in their title that are not correlated with the brands, images that include the logo but belong to products that are not relevant to the brands, and suppliers that display brands'

[133] ibid.

[134] J Riordan, *The Liability of Internet Intermediaries* (Oxford, Oxford University Press, 2016) 40.

[135] Marsoof (n 130) 106; see also MJ Sørensen, 'Draft Model Rules on Online Intermediary Platforms' in B Devolder (ed), *The Platform Economy: Unravelling the Legal Status of Online Intermediaries* (Wellington, Intersentia, 2019) 181 where Sørensen argues that 'there is a big difference between the very active platforms and the more passive platforms. The latter might have less control over the main contract and the users of the platform'.

[136] Sartori (n 127) 29.

[137] Memorandum of Understanding on the online sale of counterfeit goods (21 June 2016).

[138] A Samuels, 'Amazon May Have a Counterfeit Problem: The company is facing multiple lawsuits from brands who say it does not do enough to prevent fakes from being listed on its website' (*The Atlantic*, 20 April 2018) www.theatlantic.com/technology/archive/2018/04/amazon-may-have-a-counterfeit-problem/558482/.

[139] brandservices.amazon.co.uk/benefits.

products from countries where the brands do not have promises for manufacturing or distributors.[140] However, while it may be argued that this policy is primarily aimed at the benefit of the right holders, it has a tantamount positive advantage to the online consumers. This is because the circulation of counterfeit goods under the guise of lawful brands will be eliminated to a great extent.

Importantly, to allow a massive scale of online infringements might attract a bad reputation for the online platform itself and drive off existing as well as potential clients. Further, another crucial point to consider is the loss of trust from other brands within the market. A representative example of such a line of thinking is the Birkenstock decision to withdraw its products from Amazon.[141] In light of the wide availability of fake copies of Birkenstock shoes, the CEO of Birkenstock accused Amazon of being an 'accomplice' to the infringements and characterised its functioning as 'pathetic'.[142]

With regard to copyright infringements, a representative example can be found in the private voluntary initiative undertaken by YouTube with the use of content identification technology, the Content ID system.[143] This is because such technology can prevent the emergence of copyright infringement in the first place. Without neglecting its flaws,[144] it is considered a highly sophisticated technology that was developed by YouTube and, so far, has been extensively used in order to mitigate the circulation of unauthorised works within its video-exchange platform.[145] A study conducted on the impact of cultural diversity of automated anti-piracy systems as copyright enforcement mechanisms demonstrates the unique technological infrastructure of the Content ID system along with the efforts to keep it up to date, competitive and efficient.[146] In particular, the authors of the study applauded the work of YouTube employees to develop the Content ID system and fix its flaws.[147]

[140] www.cpcstrategy.com/blog/2018/07/amazon-brand-registry/ states that 'Product listings that aren't for your brand and incorrectly use your trademarked terms in their titles.; images that contain your logo, but are for products that don't carry your brand name; sellers shipping products from countries in which you do not manufacture or distribute your brand; product listings being created with your brand name when you have already listed your full product catalogue on Amazon.'

[141] Letter from David Kahan, CEO Birkenstock Americas to Birkenstock Retail Partners (*Washington post*, 20 July 2017), available at www.washingtonpost.com/news/business/wp-content/uploads/sites/8/2017/07/Amazon-retailer-letter-7.20.17.pdf?tid=a_inl&noredirect=on.

[142] S Smith, 'Birkenstock accuses Amazon of failure to tackle fake replicas' *The Telegraph* (22 December 2017) www.telegraph.co.uk/business/2017/12/22/birkenstock-accuses-amazon-failure-tackle-fake-replicas/.

[143] T Margoni and M Perry, 'Online intermediary liability and privatised enforcement: the Content ID case' (2016) *The Tenth International Conference on Digital Society and eGovernments* 36.

[144] P Tassi, 'The Injustice Of The YouTube Content ID Crackdown Reveals Google's Dark Side' (*Forbes*, 19 December 2013) www.forbes.com/sites/insertcoin/2013/12/19/the-injustice-of-the-youtube-content-id-crackdown-reveals-googles-dark-side/#5336a67866c8; A Bridy and D Keller, 'U.S. Copyright Office Section 512 Study: Comments in Response to Notice of Inquiry' (31 March 2016) 20; T Ingham, 'YouTube's content ID fails to spot 20%-40% of music recordings' (*Music Business Worldwide*, 13 July 2016) www.musicbusinessworldwide.com/youtubes-content-id-fails-spot-20-40/.

[145] Edwards (n 14) 275 where Edwards notes that '… with the rise of machine learning, automated blocking has begun to look more feasible …'.

[146] S Jacques, K Garstka, M Hviid and J Street, 'The Impact on Cultural Diversity of Automated Anti-Piracy Systems as Copyright Enforcement Mechanisms: An Empirical Study of YouTube's Content ID Digital Fingerprinting Technology' (2017) 40 *European Intellectual Property Review* 218–29.

[147] ibid where the authors note that 'it is undeniable that YouTube continues to devote tremendous efforts and resources to improve its Content ID system, altering the algorithm's operation in relation to specific circumstances. Its customisation of various policies is impressive and offers tailored control of content for its

In the light of the above, a duty of care based on the business model of host ISPs seems to be fairer in contrast with the imposition of duty of care as a matter of principle. This is because the ascription of a duty of care to all host ISPs indiscriminately might undermine host ISPs' business welfare while right holders' rights are not safeguarded. Conversely, it seems fairer to require from host ISPs whose services might attract online infringements and from host ISPs that exert control over the dissemination of material within their platforms to adopt proactive measures. In this way, not only would right holders' rights be safeguarded, but also host ISPs would be more engaged in the battle of online piracy, which has been aggravated due to the services they offer to the internet users.

B. The Scope of a Duty of Care

Another aspect of a duty of care to be addressed is the scope. It is important to carve out the scope of a measure since the appropriate articulation of the scope of a measure would enable the measure itself to fulfil its aim without encroaching upon the rights of third parties. To my understanding, the scope of a duty of care for host ISPs addresses the obligation of host ISPs to prevent any illicit activity within their networks. Such prevention is to be achieved either through human review of unlawful content or via the use of advanced technological tools that could identify the infringing content.

i. Trends in Case Law

At the outset, the concept of prevention of unauthorised content stems from Recital 48 of the ECD that states that host ISPs shall '… prevent certain types of illegal activities'.[148] However, one might wonder how the concept of prevention of illicit activities shall be construed. In this respect, there are two main trends in case law at the European level with regard to the prevention of reemergence of further online infringements. The first trend in case law addresses the need for host ISPs to prevent any further infringements without carving out its boundaries.[149] A representative example can be found in the landmark judgment of *L'Oreal v eBay*.[150] In this case, L'Oreal brought legal proceedings against eBay alleging trade mark infringement. After a careful consideration of the facts, the CJEU concluded that eBay shall terminate the trade mark infringements within its platform but must also prevent the further infringements of that kind. This implies that eBay must adopt a proactive role towards the online infringements aiming at terminating and preventing the reappearance of online infringements. What is more, reiterating point 182 of the Opinion of the Advocate General, CJEU stated that

partners across borders. Dedicated engineers work daily to help right-holders control their works online by enabling them to enforce their intellectual property rights on the platform directly, without the need to go to court'.

[148] Recital 48 of the ECD.

[149] See A Guadamuz, 'Developments in Intermediary Liability' in A Savin and J Trzaskowski (eds), *Research Handbook on EU Internet Law* (Cheltenham, Edward Elgar, 2014) 312.

[150] Case C-324/09 *L'Oreal SA V eBay Int'l AG* [2011] ECR I-6011, para 141.

'if the operator of the online marketplace does not decide, on its own initiative, to suspend the perpetrator of the infringement of intellectual property rights in order to prevent further infringements of that kind by the same seller in respect of the same trade marks, it may be ordered, by means of an injunction, to do so'. This implies that preventive measures shall address infringements of the same nature of the same brands by the same internet users. However, one might wonder if this obligation would be applicable in the copyright context. For instance, shall the proactive measures address copyright works from the same creator or different creators. Under the definition of 'infringement of that kind', one might wonder whether all exceptions of copyrighted works such as parodies and works that belong to public domain would apply.

In similar fashion, *Tommy Hilfiger Licensing v Delta Center*[151] reinforced the principle concluded in the case of *L'Oreal v eBay*.[152] While this judgment examines the case of an intermediary in the brick and mortar environment, it can be equally applied within the activities of host ISPs who act as intermediaries. In this light, this judgment advances the existing case law with regard to the prevention of infringements at the European level and offers a narrower interpretation of the scope of a duty of care for intermediaries. The case at hand is about a dispute between Hilfiger and the Delta Center company that sublets spaces to traders in the Prague Market Hall. While Delta Center has warned sellers not to sell counterfeit goods, Tommy Hilfiger brand has identified that some sales areas have sold fake copies of the popular brand's products. In this light, Tommy Hilfiger has filed a lawsuit against Delta Center, alleging violation of its trade mark and requesting Delta Center to adopt preventive measures such as for instance the non-conclusion of rental agreements with sellers that have sold fake goods of the brand.[153] After a careful consideration of the facts, CJEU concluded that preventive measures shall address 'new infringements of the same nature by the same market-trader from taking place'.[154] This means that a duty of care amounts to the prevention of the infringement of the same nature by the specific seller. So, transposing this outcome within the context of host ISPs, it means that host ISPs shall prevent the emergence of infringements that have been committed by a specific user whose activities have already been declared illicit.[155] However, the judgment refrained from specifying whether the principle could also be applicable in the copyright context.

This conclusion, however, is not a novelty. Indeed, it could find its roots in the *Kerntheorie*[156] case which is a peculiarity of German case law and which concerns the imposition of duty of care on online intermediaries with regard to infringements of the same nature.[157] This theory has been reiterated in a bedrock of German

[151] Case C-494/15 *Tommy Hilfiger Licensing* [2016] ECLI:EU:C:2016:528.
[152] Case C-324/09 *L'Oreal SA V eBay Int'l AG* [2011] ECR I-6011.
[153] H Berendschot, 'Summary and analysis of Case C-494/15' in H Berendschot and K Janssens (eds), *Landmark IP decisions of the European Court of Justice 2014–2018* (ELS Belgium, 2019) 139–44.
[154] Case C-494/15 *Tommy Hilfiger Licensing* [2016] ECLI:EU:C:2016:528, para 34.
[155] See also C Angelopoulos, 'C-494/15 – Tommy Hilfiger: No Difference between Online and Real World Marketplaces for IP Enforcement' (*Kluwer Copyright blog*, 10 August 2016) copyrightblog.kluweriplaw.com/2016/08/10/c-49415-tommy-hilfiger-no-difference-online-real-world-marketplaces-ip-enforcement/.
[156] See ch 4.
[157] M Leistner, 'Störerhaftung und mittelbare Schutzrechtsverletzung' (2010) *GRUR-Beil* 1.

rulings that examined the disputes of host ISPs and copyright holders for copyright infringements that accrue within their networks and have been committed by internet users. To name a few, *Internetversteigerung I*,[158] *Internetversteigerung II*[159] and *Internetversteigerung III*[160] as well as the *Rapidshare I*[161] outlined that the host ISPs shall not only delete the infringing links that directed internet users to unauthorised files, rather, host ISPs are under the obligation to detect and take down any future links of the same kind or, as the Kerntheorie states, of the same nature.[162]

The second trend in case law has been found in the recently issued judgment of *Glawischnig-Piesczek v Facebook* of 2019.[163] That case was about a dispute between Eva Glawisching, a former member of the Green Political Party and Facebook on defamatory comments that have been posted by internet users online. The question was whether Article 15(1) of the ECD precludes host ISPs from monitoring their networks for unlawful content. Following a consideration of the facts, the CJEU concluded that host ISPs can be required to remove identical content of information that has already been declared illicit, and equivalent information, without any individual assessment of its illegal nature.[164] By equivalent information is meant 'information conveying a message the content of which remains essentially unchanged and therefore diverges very little from the content which gave rise to the finding of illegality'.[165] However, one might wonder what is meant by essentially unchanged content or content which differs very little from that which has been declared unlawful or how host ISPs would be able to identify equivalent content to illegal information.[166] This implies that the CJEU refrained from carving out the precise boundaries of a duty of care and passed the hot potato to the host ISPs. They would decide the circumstances under which the infringing content shall be removed and thus adopt a stricter or a lighter approach with regard to the take down of content. As a corollary, this understanding might lead to the fragmentation of intellectual property rights' enforcement or might result to collateral censorship of lawful content that has been uploaded by internet users.

In my opinion, a narrow scope of a duty of care might have merits. For instance, it would offer clarity to the parties involved. As already discussed in chapter five, legal certainty would make the parties involved aware of the level of enforcement that is required and enable them to adjust their business model to new legal rules. In addition,

[158] Bundesgerichtshof, *Internetversteigerung I*, 11 March 2004, I ZR 304/01.

[159] Bundesgerichtshof, *Internetversteigerung II*, 19 April 2007, I ZR 35/04.

[160] Bundesgerichtshof, *Internetversteigerung III*, 30 April 2008, I ZR 73/05.

[161] OLG Düsseldorf, *Rapidshare I*, 27 April 2010, I-20 U 166/09.

[162] JB Nordemann, 'Liability for Copyright Infringements on the Internet: Host Providers (Content Providers) – The German Approach' (2011) 37 *Journal of Intellectual Property, Information Technology and E-Commerce Law* 41–42.

[163] Case C-18/18 *Glawischnig-Piesczek* [2019] ECLI:EU:C:2019:821; see for the analysis of the case Z Krokida, 'Towards a wider scope for the duty of care of host internet service providers: The case of Eva Glawischnig-Piesczek v Facebook' (2021) 43 *European Intellectual Property Review* 313–21.

[164] Case C-18/18 *Glawischnig-Piesczek* [2019] ECLI:EU:C:2019:821, para 55.

[165] Case C-18/18 *Eva Glawischnig-Piesczek* [2019] ECLI:EU:C:2019:821, para 39.

[166] See for commentary in D Keller, 'Filtering Facebook: introducing dolphins in the net, a new Stanford CIS White Paper – or- why internet uses and EU policymakers should worry about the Advocate General's opinion in Glawischnig- Piesczek' (*The Center for Internet and Society*, 5 September 2019) cyberlaw.stanford.edu/blog/2019/09/filtering-facebook-introducing-dolphins-net-new-stanford-cis-white-paper-or-why.

a clear articulation of the scope of a measure would decrease the chances of abuse of rights of third parties. For example, a precise context, within which the host ISP could exercise its duty of care, would not leave any margin for abuse of the rights of third parties.[167] What is more, any shift from specific obligations to general monitoring obligations would be avoided since the boundaries of specific obligations would be clearly carved out and distinct from general monitoring. Otherwise, a wide scope of a duty of care for host ISPs might conflict with the prohibition of general monitoring obligations, which constitute one of the cornerstones of the development of e-commerce.

ii. How to Prevent the Dissemination of Unlawful Content and Counterfeit Goods Online

Another aspect that relates to the scope of a duty of care is the tool that could prevent the dissemination of illegitimate content online. Pursuant to the existing academic scholarship, host ISPs could prevent the emergence of further infringements either through the use of advanced filtering technology or through human review.

On the one hand, the adoption of filtering technology would have merits for rights holders and host ISPs. With regard to intellectual property holders, filtering mechanisms would curb to a great extent the dissemination of illegitimate content online. This is mainly due to the large volume of data that is transmitted per minute within the networks of host ISPs. For instance, consider that in 2020, 4.7 million videos have been viewed on YouTube per minute, 1,400 downloads were taking place per minute on TikTok while 194,444 users were posting their tweets per minute on Twitter.[168] In this light, the use of technological tools might prevent the reemergence of unlawful information and therefore might be a panacea for the right holders. Insofar host ISPs are concerned, they would be encouraged to develop in-house technology and thus compete their American rivals. Therefore, the adoption of filtering might boost innovation within the Digital Single Market.

Yet, it could be argued that the adoption of filtering mechanisms cannot guarantee the removal of unlawful content.[169] A number of situations have been reported where filtering technology could not differentiate between legitimate and unlawful material. Consider, for instance, the announcement of YouTube at the beginning of the COVID-19 pandemic which stated that Artificial Intelligence technology would replace human employees in the battle against illicit content online. However, it has recently been announced that YouTube will turn back to human moderators as far as content related to hate speech and misinformation is concerned. This is because the Artificial Intelligence moderators have taken down a high degree of lawful content, reaching double figures in the margin of errors. In particular, it has been evidenced that while 11 million videos were removed during March and September 2020, 320,000 videos

[167] See also Krokida (n 163) 313–21.

[168] G Sartor and A Loreggia, 'The impact of algorithms for online content filtering or moderation: Upload filters' (2020) *Report for the JURI Committee* 35.

[169] See also F Wilman, *The responsibility of online itnermediaries for illegal user content in the EU and US* (Cheltenham, Edward Elgar, 2020) 259 where he notes that 'There is also somewhat of a chicken and egg dimension to the debate about the use of automated means.'

were appealed and 160,000 were reinstated to the platform.[170] Therefore, it appears that the adoption of filtering mechanisms might give rise to censorship and thus encroach upon the right to freedom of expression of internet users.[171]

However, it should be borne in mind that those challenges to distinguish lawful and illegitimate content should not act as a deterrent for host ISPs from not using advanced filtering technology. Although host ISPs cannot undertake a meticulous fair use assessment,[172] other criteria can be taken into consideration in assessing whether a material is fair use or not. Such criteria might be, for instance, whether the work has been published already or the size of the portion of the work that has been used.

Moreover, apart from concerns about the efficiency of filtering technology to distinguish lawful and illegitimate content, it could be argued that the imposition of filtering technology might be excessively burdensome for host ISPs. For example, it is estimated that YouTube's technology cost about 60 million dollars to develop. Thus, the imposition of a duty of care might pose serious threats on host ISPs' business welfare. This is because filtering can be expensive to develop while the conclusion of licensing agreements for the use of copyrighted works might increase the transaction costs of host ISPs.

To circumvent the issue of high transaction costs, the creation of an archive with filtering technologies could be recommended,[173] managed by the proposed supervisory authority for host ISPs. How this authority could be shaped, as well as its functions, is further elaborated in chapter nine. This authority would have a list of filtering technologies which could be licensed to host ISPs in order to deploy them and prevent the online infringements within their networks.[174] In this way, host ISPs would comply with their duty of care and any liability would be excluded.

Finally, another opponent of filtering might argue that, with filtering a process of data without lawful basis takes place. This argument was included in the *Scarlet v Netlog* case[175] where the CJEU handed down that filtering would pose serious threats on users' personal data. Without explaining how filtering would violate users' data, the Court noted that 'requiring installation of the contested filtering system would involve the identification, systematic analysis and processing of information connected with the profiles created on the social network by its users'.[176] Given that information is personal data, any systematic analysis without users' consent might encroach upon users' right

[170] J Vincent, 'YouTube brings back more human moderators after AI systems over-censor' (*The verge*, 21 September 2020) www.theverge.com/2020/9/21/21448916/youtube-automated-moderation-ai-machine-learning-increased-errors-takedowns.

[171] Center for Democracy and Technology, 'Mixed Messages? The Limits of Automated Social Media Content Analysis' (November 2017) 18 where it is stated that 'an accuracy rate of 80% means that one out of every five people is treated "wrong" in such decision-making; depending on the process, this would have obvious consequences for civil liberties and human rights.'; See also ECtHR, Grand Chamber, *Delfi AS v Estonia*, 16 June 2015, Application no. 64569, (2015) E.M.L.R where it is noted that 'This is an invitation to self-censorship at its worst.'

[172] Ernesto, 'YouTube's copyright protection is a total mess. Can it be fixed?' (*Torrentfreak*, 22 December 2018) torrentfreak.com/youtubes-copyright-protection-system-is-a-total-mess-can-it-be-fixed-181222/.

[173] See in K Garstka, 'Looking above and beyond the blunt expectation: specified request as the recommended approach to intermediary liability in cyberspace' (2016) 7 *European Journal of Law and Technology* para 3; see also Wilman (n 169) 269.

[174] ibid.

[175] Case C-70/10 *Scarlet Extended SA v Société belge des auteurs, compositeurs et éditeurs SCRL (SABAM)* [2011] ECR-I 11959.

[176] ibid para 45.

to privacy as enshrined in Article 8 of the European Charter of Fundamental Rights. However, this argument was overturned in 2022. This is because as per the GDPR,[177] which is in force since March 2018, any personal data processing must fulfil a set of principles. Such principles are lawfulness, transparency, accountability and data minimisation. Yet, one might argue that the use of filtering would be in conflict with Article 22 of the GDPR that states that 'the data subject shall have the right not to be subject to a decision based solely on automated processing, including profiling, which produces legal effects concerning him or her or similarly significantly affects him or her'.[178] However, this obstacle can be overcome if the internet user gives her consent to the process of her data. This option, as Frosio notes, could be included in the terms of use of host ISPs.[179] In this regard, given that host ISPs abide by these rules, any unlawful process of personal data would be eliminated.

On the other hand, a duty of care of host ISPs could amount to the human review of the content that is disseminated within the networks. Human review could distinguish between the legitimate and illegitimate nature of content.[180] In this respect, in Germany according to the Network Enforcement Law that combats hate speech online, Facebook hired 1,200 employees who, in parallel with algorithmic review, review videos that might include hate speech and remove them.[181]

However, this can be tricky for host ISPs, especially the ones with high traffic, since a high number of employees are required to be hired. In addition, such employees must be skilled in order to distinguish between legitimate and illegitimate content online. Otherwise, a margin of error might occur and lawful content would be removed.

Nonetheless, human review might not be equal to algorithmic review. For instance, there have been instances where human review has performed less efficiently than algorithmic review. A telling example can be found in the case of Garry Kasparov where a computer software managed to beat the World Chess Champion.[182] In this case, computer programmers developed a software, which is known as Deep Blue and could predict 200,000,000 moves in chess. However, as already explained, in some instances a human review is warranted,[183] such as copyright infringements. To judge whether a copyright infringement has occurred, an understanding of its context is deemed necessary.[184]

[177] The EU General Data Protection Regulation (GDPR) is the most important change in data privacy regulation in 20 years and is available at eugdpr.org/.

[178] See for further analysis in S Kulk, *Internet Intermediaries and Copyright Law: EU and US perspective* (Alphen aan den Rijn, Kluwer Law International, 2019) 142.

[179] G Frosio, 'Algorithmic enforcement online' in P Torremans (ed), *Intellectual Property and Human Rights*, 4th edn (Alphen aan den Rijn, Kluwer Law International, 2020) 17.

[180] See also in F Pasquale *New Laws of Robotics: Defending human expertise in the age of AI* (Cambridge, Harvard University Press, 2020) 3 where he argues that 'Robotic systems and AI should complement professionals, not replace them.'

[181] ARTICLE 19, 'Germany: Responding to 'hate speech: Country report' (2018), www.article19.org/wp-content/uploads/2018/07/Germany-Responding-to-%E2%80%98hate-speech%E2%80%99-v3-WEB.pdf.

[182] MR Anderson, 'Twenty years on from Deep Blue vs Kasparov: how a chess match started the big data revolution' (*The Conversation*, 11 May 2017) theconversation.com/twenty-years-on-from-deep-blue-vs-kasparov-how-a-chess-match-started-the-big-data-revolution-76882.

[183] D Citron Keats and B Wittes, 'The Internet Will Not Break: Denying Bad Samaritans Section 230 Immunity' (2017) 86 *University of Maryland Legal Studies* 17.

[184] This means where the work can be considered as fair dealing or not.

In the light of the above, this book argues that a duty of care shall address either the use of technological tools or human review without excluding the possibility to combine them. This means that both options might be used separately but also in a complementary way. However, it shall be up to the host ISPs as to which option they would adopt according to their business model. This is because filtering-based technology might prove cost-efficient for those host ISPs that have resources while for other smaller host ISPs this would be an obstacle for their continuous operation since they would be deprived of the appropriate resources to develop such tools or at least license ones. On the other hand, the review by humans of content that is disseminated could eliminate potential errors that technological tools might perform while at the same time it might prove non-efficient since a high number of employees shall be employed and trained. Last but not least, both options could be used by host ISPs. For instance, the use of technological tools would faster identify the infringing content whereas in cases where the host ISPs could not reach a decision on the illegal nature of the content a human review of the allegedly infringing content shall be provided. It is worth stressing that the adoption of filtering mechanisms must fall into the narrow scope of a duty of care. This is because any extension beyond the scope of a duty of care might pose risks to fundamental rights of internet users and thus lead to censorship. For instance, a wide scope of duty of care might take down lawful content since specific conditions under which content could be removed are not carved out. Therefore, following this recommendation and due to the pivotal role that host ISPs play in the digital ecosystem, as already discussed in section II of this chapter, host ISPs would be able to fulfil their duty of care and combat online piracy.

To sum up, it was concluded that a duty of care shall be imposed on host ISPs as a matter of outcome. This means that it shall be attributed to those host ISPs that attract online infringements and not indiscriminately to ISPs that provide host services to its users. As Sartori has pointed out, a duty of care shall be assigned after taking into consideration the business model of the host ISP.[185] Further, it was concluded that a narrow scope of a duty of care would have merits over a wide scope of a duty of care. This is because a narrow scope of a duty of care would not only achieve its aim, which is to decrease the online piracy, but also would have more possibilities to strike a fair balance between the interests of the parties involved, namely host ISPs, right holders and internet users. Finally, how duty of care would be fulfilled shall be contingent on the host ISPs. This means that they could either deploy filtering-based technological tools or resort to human review of the content and goods that are circulated online.

iii. Copyright Context

For copyright infringements, host ISPs would need to deploy a hybrid model of technical and human practices. This hybrid model could be divided into two stages. The first stage consists of the use of technology in flagging copyright infringing works and the second stage sets forward the deployment of human reviewers for the content that is disseminated.

[185] Sartori (n 127).

With regard to the first instance, a set of technological filtering measures are available in many fields and could be used in order to fight online piracy. Without overlooking their flaws and inaccuracies, technological tools that could be used are metadata, hashes, fingerprint technology natural language processing or blacklisting. Metadata constitutes the information that accompanies the work while hashes represent a unique signature for each work and examine infringements based on audio, video or images.[186] Fingerprint technology checks the content online against a database with files submitted by rights holders. Representative examples can be found in audible magic, cleanfeed and echoprint.[187] Finally, natural language processing or blacklisting makes a contextual and semantic analysis in order to identify the copyright infringements and check the works against a database. Should the text match with an unlawful text in the registry, the software technology removes the infringing content.[188]

In addition, another layer of measures would address human moderators. A number of host ISPs have already deployed human review in order to identify copyright infringing works and curb the erroneous removal of legitimate content. For instance, human moderators would be trained to identify the copyright infringements that have been flagged by the technological tools. For instance, they would examine whether the work is about non-commercial research, quotation for parody or criticism, news reporting, works that belong to the public domain or incidental including of a work in artistic works.[189] In this way, the scope of copyright protection will be safeguarded while copyright exceptions will be taken into consideration.

iv. Trade Mark Context

In trade mark infringements, a similar approach could be adopted. Host ISPs that display goods within their networks would need to deploy measures that would detect fake goods within their networks. As already discussed, a number of host ISPs offer a service to brand owners that could register their brands and notify for any counterfeit goods online. For instance, Amazon offers the VERO programme which allows brand owners to report counterfeit goods through the online platform.[190] Other host ISPs, such as Etsy, offer the opportunity to rights holders to complete a form for intellectual property infringements.[191]

Further, the use of filtering-based technology would also enable host ISPs to identify counterfeit products. Such filtering, as rights holders have noted in the Memorandum,

[186] See also Z Krokida, 'Use of Filters by Online Intermediaries and the Rights of Users: Developments in the European Union, Mexico, India and China' in International Federation of Library Associations and Institutions (ed), *A copyright reader for librarians* (Berlin, De Gruyter 2022).

[187] ibid.

[188] Sartor and Loreggia (n 168) 41.

[189] S Karapapa and L McDonagh, *Intellectual Property Law* (Oxford, Oxford University Press, 2019) 110.

[190] brandservices.amazon.co.uk/progressreport where it has been stated that 'over 10 billion suspected bad listings blocked by Brand Protection's robust verification processes before they were published to Amazon's stores'.

[191] Etsy report on intellectual property infringements, available at help.etsy.com/hc/en-us/articles/360000344448-How-to-File-a-Report-of-Intellectual-Property-Infringement.

would need to focus on keywords that are used by sellers to offer counterfeit goods as well as address specific time zones since it has been stated that counterfeit goods are mainly displayed during the nights and the weekends.[192]

Finally, a human review would also be an additional layer of protection for trade marks. For instance, Amazon employs human reviewers in order to capture counterfeit goods. This measure would safeguard to a great extent the scope of protection of trade marks while at the same time it would eliminate the categories of undetermined products. In particular, the human reviewers would take into consideration the different function of trade marks, namely the origin, product differentiation, guarantee, advertising and investment function.[193] In addition, human reviewers would be in the position to examine whether a trade mark infringement takes place. This is because they could detect whether the sign has been affixed to goods or to their packaging or whether the goods are offered for purchase under the infringing sign or whether the infringing sign is used for comparative advertising purposes in a way that goes against the provisions of the Comparative Advertisement Directive.[194] In this way, rights holders would safeguard their brands to a great extent while at the same time online consumers would receive information about the available goods and services.

Yet, whereas a duty of care shall be imposed on host ISPs in accordance with their business model and shall entail a narrow scope with regard to the reemergence of infringing content, it could be argued that it might assume knowledge of the illicit activity from the part of the host ISP or interfere with fundamental rights of internet users such as the right to information. For this reason, a duty of care cannot be introduced without limitations. Those limitations aim at safeguarding the rights of host ISPs, to which a duty of care has been assigned, as well as the rights of third parties, such as internet users, without cancelling the positive effect of a duty of care of host ISPs in the battle against online piracy.

VI. Limitations Upon a Proposed Duty of Care

This section endorses certain limitations for a duty of care on host ISPs in order to safeguard the interests of host ISPs and internet users/consumers. With regard to host ISPs, drawing parallels with the US legal system, a Good Samaritan clause is suggested with the aim to safeguard the fundamental right of host ISPs to conduct business. A transparency obligation for host ISPs is also suggested in order to guarantee the fundamental right of users to freedom of expression.

[192] European Commission, 'Commission staff working document: Report on the functioning of the Memorandum of Understanding on the sale of counterfeit goods on the internet' (2020) 11.

[193] See the different functions in Karapapa and McDonagh (n 189) 292.

[194] Directive 2006/114/EC of the European Parliament and of the Council of 12 December 2006 concerning misleading and comparative advertising (2006) OJ L 376.

A. Host ISPs' Perspective: Endorsing a 'Good Samaritan Clause'

As concluded from the discussion in section IV, a duty of care is allowed under the *EU acquis* and it is its precise articulation that would enhance the completion of its goals, namely the combat of online infringements. However, it could be argued that the introduction of a duty of care might endanger the business model of host ISPs. Indeed, despite the great benefits for right holders, a duty of care might run the risk of threatening the operation of the business welfare of host ISPs. This is because one might argue that the use of filtering mechanisms or human review of content that is disseminated online might amount to knowledge of host ISPs of any allegedly infringing content. In this way, a knowledge of host ISPs about illicit activities could be presumed in case copyright holders or brand owners identify infringing content or counterfeit goods online. As Stalla-Bourdillon pointed out, if the host ISPs remove in good faith infringing content by deploying proactive means, then host ISPs shall not be held liable if infringing content has been found in their networks.[195] This means that since host ISPs take the initiative and deploy the appropriate mechanisms, they should be given liability immunity due to their direct involvement in the battle against online piracy.

This understanding is envisaged at policy level too. More specifically, the proposed DSA Regulation includes a provision related to a quasi-Good Samaritan clause and states in Article 6 that providers of hosting services can apply the defences of knowledge and expeditious removal in order to exonerate from liability even though they deploy measures in order to curb or terminate online piracy within their networks.[196]

In similar fashion, this understanding has been mirrored in a handful of court rulings where the commentators observed that a duty of care might result in knowledge or awareness of the illegal activities taking place in their networks. For instance, in the case of *Gisele Spiegel v YouTube*,[197] YouTube voluntarily adopted a filtering mechanism in order to detect unauthorised works. Yet, it was this act of deploying filtering identification technology that led the German Supreme Court to conclude that YouTube had actual knowledge of the infringing acts due to the availability of filtering mechanisms.[198]

Similar reflections have been raised in light of the *L'Oreal v eBay* case.[199] This is because, as the court explicitly pointed out, there are instances where host ISPs could be aware of illicit activity after deploying mechanisms in order to identify any wrongdoing within its platform on a voluntary basis.[200] This understanding means that in order to impose liability rules on host ISPs, the court could take into consideration any proactive action on behalf of the host ISPs. Such action could amount to knowledge or

[195] S Stalla-Bourdillon, 'On Delfi v Estonia … Is it time to adopt a good-Samaritan style exemption?' (*Inforrm's Blog*, 24 June 2015) inforrm.org/2015/06/24/on-delfi-v-estonia-is-it-time-to-adopt-a-good-samaritan-style-exemption-sophie-stalla-bourdillon/.

[196] Proposal for a Regulation of the European Parliament and the Council on a Single Market For Digital Services (Digital Services Act) and amending Directive 2000/31/EC COM/2020/825 final (hereinafter Proposed DSA Regulation).

[197] Landesgericht Hamburg, 5 March 2010, ref. no. 324 O 565/08.

[198] ibid.

[199] Case C-324/09, *L'Oreal SA V eBay Int'l AG* [2011] ECR I-6011.

[200] ibid para 122.

awareness of the unlawful activity.[201] Therefore, as Van Eecke pointed out 'a hosting provider would be disincentivized from voluntarily keeping an eye on some parts of its platform'.[202] This implies that host ISPs would not be motivated to deploy the appropriate mechanisms in order to prevent the reappearance of online infringements since any application of filtering-based technology would deprive them of their main defence, which is the lack of knowledge of the illicit activity.

However, to deprive host ISPs from adopting the defence of knowledge, as the Advocate General pointed out, seems 'surreal'.[203] This is because it is beyond the current understanding of host ISPs' policy framework and the reasons that justified the imposition of the secondary liability regime. Such liability provisions aimed to further develop innovation and the entrance of new digital players in the market. As Edwards acutely points out, 'future innovation which brought with it prosperity required a feeling of safety against future liability'.[204] Otherwise, liability rules would deter new host ISPs from actively engaging within the Digital Single Market or leading the current ones to bankruptcy, as happened in the Napster case.[205]

Finally, such concerns may be evoked in cases of non-commercial host ISPs. A representative example of such thinking is Wikipedia.[206] In this case, Wikipedia hired employees to monitor the content that was uploaded online so as to verify the validity of the information that is edited along with the accuracy of such information. Should the employees notice any unlawful information, they remove it from the online platform. However, such removal implies a control over the content.[207] This understanding could be taken into consideration by the courts and could subsequently lead to the imposition of damages on Wikipedia. This outcome could either shut down Wikipedia's website or non-incentivise Wikipedia to monitor its website for unlawful information.[208]

In the light of the above criticism, many commentators have argued in favour of a Good Samaritan privilege.[209] For instance, in the context of proposing amendments on the EU Commission's Proposal for the DSMD, Angelopoulos noted that if host ISPs are required to take down material under their own initiatives, a 'Good Samaritan' protection for them shall be granted.[210] In similar fashion, a number of European policy documents lean in favour of a 'Good Samaritan' clause. To name a few, according to

[201] See also R Harvey, 'Host providers may be subject to obligations resulting in content removal on a worldwide basis, says AG Szpunar' (2019) 14 *Journal of Intellectual Property Law & Practice* 836.

[202] Van Eecke (n 62) 1483–84.

[203] Case C-324/09 *L'Oréal v eBay International*, Opinion of Advocate General Jääskinen (2011) ECR I-6011, para 146 where he noted 'I would find it surreal that if eBay intervenes and guides the contents of listings in its system with various technical means, it would by that fact be deprived of the protection of Article 14 regarding storage of information uploaded by the users'.

[204] Edwards (n 14) 260.

[205] J Koranteg, 'Napster considers bankruptcy' (2002) 20 *Music and Media* 1. It has been noted that due to expensive ongoing copyright litigation pursued by major Music Industry labels against Napster, Napster had to file for bankruptcy.

[206] Van Eecke (n 62) 1483–84.

[207] ibid.

[208] ibid.

[209] Stalla-Bourdillon (n 195); M Leistner, 'Copyright law on the internet in need of reform: hyperlinks, online platforms and aggregators' (2017) 12 *Journal of Intellectual Property Law & Practice* 136–49; Kuczerway (n 112) 142 where she outlines the negative implications resulting from the lack of a Good Samaritan clause.

[210] C Angelopoulos, 'On Online Platforms and the Commission's New Proposal for a Directive on Copyright in the DSM' (2017) 11.

EU Commission Public Consultation on e-commerce, stakeholders and in particular host ISPs argue in favour of the introduction of a Good Samaritan clause.[211] This understanding, as the EU Commission's staff working document explains, is based on Recital 40 of the ECD that notes that 'the provisions of this Directive relating to liability should not preclude the development and effective operation, by the different interested parties, of technical systems of protection and identification and of technical surveillance instruments made possible by digital technology within the limits laid down by Directives 95/46/EC and 97/66/EC'.[212] Therefore, this means that the development of technology that filters the online infringements should not be correlated with the imposition of liability rules to host ISPs.

The concept of the Good Samaritan privilege has its roots in the US jurisdiction and more precisely is enshrined in Section 230 C 2 of the CDA.[213] It states that a host ISP shall not be liable for taking actions in good faith aiming to terminate the circulation of infringing content online or the reappearance of infringing content online.[214] The rationale for imposing such a privilege[215] stems from the case of *Stratton-Oakmont v Prodigy*.[216] This case addressed the dispute between Prodigy, a computer network and Stratton and Oakmont for libel comments that were posted on their network. The Supreme Court held that Prodigy exercised editorial control over the material the users had posted since it uses monitoring systems to detect unlawful information and thus remove it. In this sense, it exercises a type of censorship over the information that is transmitted online.[217] Interestingly, whereas Prodigy took action on its own initiative and deleted the offensive material, the court found Prodigy liable for the defamatory comments under the reasoning that it did not remove all the defamatory comments, which had been posted on its bulletin board.[218]

In this regard, at European level, the introduction of a Good Samaritan clause may prove to counterbalance the negative criticism for deploying filtering technologies in order to curb online infringements. From the perspective of host ISPs' business model, host ISPs would deploy filtering mechanisms so as to terminate infringements online but without considering such proactive actions as equal to knowledge or awareness of the infringing material. Without any Good Samaritan clause, such proactive actions

[211] European Commission, 'Public Consultation on the future of the electronic commerce in the Internal Market and the implementation of the Directive on electronic commerce' (2000) 11.

[212] Recital 40 of the ECD.

[213] Communications Decency Act, 47 U.S.C. §230.

[214] Electronic Frontier Foundation, 'Section 230 of the Communications Decency Act: 47 U.S.C. § 230, a Provision of the Communication Decency Act', available at www.eff.org/issues/cda230; Section 230 C 2 of the CDA Act states that '(2) Civil liability. No provider or user of an interactive computer service shall be held liable on account of – (A) any action voluntarily taken in good faith to restrict access to or availability of material that the provider or user considers to be obscene, lewd, lascivious, filthy, excessively violent, harassing, or otherwise objectionable, whether or not such material is constitutionally protected; or (B) any action taken to enable or make available to information content providers or others the technical means to restrict access to material described in paragraph (1).'

[215] A Kuczerawy, 'The EU Commission on voluntary monitoring: Good Samaritan 2.0 or Good Samaritan 0.5?' (24 April 2018) www.law.kuleuven.be/citip/blog/the-eu-commission-on-voluntary-monitoring-good-samaritan-2-0-or-good-samaritan-0-5/.

[216] US Supreme Court, *Stratton Oakmont Inc and Daniel Porush v Prodigy Services Company* (24 May 1995) h2o.law.harvard.edu/cases/4540.

[217] ibid.

[218] Kuczerawy (n 215).

could make host ISPs aware of the illicit activity and thus lead to their liability. This is because host ISPs could no longer resort to the defence of knowledge which is a requisite of secondary liability regime. In contrast, a Good Samaritan clause may safeguard host ISPs from being held liable under the reasoning that they knew the existence of the infringing material.

B. What about Internet Users'/Consumers' Perspective?

Apart from the introduction of a Good Samaritan clause in order to safeguard host ISPs' business model, it is also important to establish some safeguards for users in order to achieve a better balance between the different interests at stake. This is because proactive measures, as elaborated in section IV might pose risks to internet users' fundamental right to freedom of expression.[219] Such safeguards should be explicitly included in the new regulatory framework and not be left to the discretion of host ISPs.

Such safeguards are about a statutory obligation for transparency which should be imposed on host ISPs. This transparency obligation would enable users and consumers to be aware of the management policies on content removal and the actions of host ISPs against the circulation of fake goods within their platforms. An analysis of this transparency obligation is undertaken in the following chapter.

VII. Conclusion

This chapter hitherto has critically discussed the establishment of a responsibility framework for host ISPs based on co-regulation. It did so by analysing the normative considerations of this framework. It was argued that a responsibility framework is warranted due to the new role of host ISPs. Although at the beginning of e-commerce host ISPs have been considered passive entities, they are now given an active role. That new role depicts host ISPs as enforcers of intellectual property rights, adjudicators of intellectual property rights and implementers of public policies.

Having discussed the normative considerations of the proposed regulatory framework for host ISPs, this chapter also looked at one of the constituents of this responsibility framework which is the imposition of a duty of care to host ISPs. A duty of care is not a novelty since it has already been exemplified at policy and judicial level. However, as my findings indicate, to which host ISPs shall be assigned and its scope have not been set up. For this reason, it was noted that it seems fairer to assign a duty of care to those host ISPs that are closer to the infringements or at least they should control their dissemination. In addition, it was noted that the scope of the duty of care shall be narrow. Although there are two lines of case law with regard to the scope of duty of care, in my

[219] See also J Van Hoboken, 'Hosting intermediary services and illegal content online: an analysis of the scope of article 14 ECD in light of the developments in the online service landscape' (2018) 27 op.europa.eu/en/publication-detail/-/publication/7779caca-2537-11e9-8d04-01aa75ed71a1/language-en.

opinion the narrow scope of a duty of care shall be preferred. This is because a narrow scope would contribute to legal certainty so that host ISPs would be aware of the level of enforcement that is needed and enable them to comply their business model with the new legislative requirements. Otherwise, a wide scope of a duty of care would leave many decisions to the discretion of host ISPs and thus might lead to excessive removal of content that could be lawful as well. Finally, a set of suggestions for adjusting a duty of care to host ISPs in the copyright and trade mark context has been offered.

However, the ascription of a duty of care shall have limitations in order to avoid any interference of a duty of care with the business model of host ISPs and the abuse of third parties' rights. So, with regard to the limitations upon a duty of care in order to safeguard the business model of host ISPs, I looked at the Good Samaritan principle in the US legal system. This principle would be beneficial since from the perspective of host ISPs' business model such proactive actions would not be considered as equal to knowledge or awareness of the infringing material. In contrast, if there is not a Good Samaritan clause, such proactive actions that are entailed in the duty of care could amount to knowledge and thus would lead to the liability of host ISPs. With regard to the limitations of a duty of care in order to protect the rights of internet users, I argue that a transparency obligation, a thorough analysis of which follows in chapter eight, would be necessary. By disclosing more information about the operation of host ISPs relating to the removal of content and goods online, the right of internet users to freedom of expression would be safeguarded as well as the confidence of consumers towards online platforms and online sales in general being increased.

8

Introducing a Statutory Provision for Transparency

I. Introduction

As previously discussed in chapter seven, the proposed imposition of duty of care might offer a higher degree of protection to rights holders while at the same time with the appropriate safeguards would enable host ISPs to sustain their business welfare. This duty of care that host ISPs would have towards the dissemination of infringing material within their networks might include filtering-based technological tools. However, as this chapter discusses, the use of filtering technology which is based on automated algorithmic decision-making procedures has been subject to severe criticism.

On the one hand, scholars characterise algorithms as 'fundamental enablers in modern society'[1] or 'sovereign over important aspects of individual lives'.[2] By gathering news in one single website through aggregation applications or mitigating the dissemination of illegal material via filtering or spam applications, algorithms become important constituents of modern society. On the other hand, others argue that algorithms are 'black boxes'.[3] This is because their internal structure is obscure to users.[4] It is this obscure nature of algorithms that gives rise to mounting concerns over their operation. For instance, it could be asked under what conditions host ISPs remove material from their platforms, how they process the notifications for illegal material, or to what extent their actions might amount to censorship.[5]

[1] European Commission's Directorate-General for Communications Networks. Content and Technology, 'Algo: aware; Raising awareness on algorithms' (December 2018).

[2] DK Citron and F Pasquale, 'The Scored Society: Due Process for Automated Predictions' (2014) 89 *Washington Law Review* 19.

[3] F Pasquale, *Black Box Society: The secret algorithms that control money and information* (Harvard University Press, 2015) 9; S Stalla-Bourdillon, 'Online Monitoring, Filtering, Blocking … What is the Difference? Where to Draw the Line?' (2013) *Southampton Research Paper* 19.

[4] PJ Dittrich, 'Online Platforms and how to regulate them: an EU overview' (2018) *Policy Paper No. 227* 5; J Zerilli, A Knott, J Maclaurin and C Gavaghan, 'Transparency in Algorithmic and Human Decision-Making: Is there a double standard?' (2018) 9 *Philosophy and Technology* 2 where they noted that 'the worry seems to be that because deep learning systems arrive at their decisions unaided, i.e. in a manner that is not specified in advance, it is not possible to interpret the system's internal processes except only approximately and imperfectly'.

[5] M Perel (Filmar) and N Elkin-Koren, 'Accountability in Algorithmic Copyright Enforcement' (2016) 19 *Stanford Technology Law Review* 473 (2016) 530; EDRI, 'Leaked document: Does the EU Commission really plan to tackle illegal content online?' (21 September 2017) edri.org/leaked-document-does-the-eu-commission-actually-aim-to-tackle-illegal-content-online/.

Against this background, the EU Communication on online platforms of 2016 found that the majority of the respondents to the public consultation on host ISPs 'called for greater transparency on platform content policy'.[6] This means that internet users demand more information on the procedures that host ISPs adopt in order to remove material from their networks. In a similar fashion, the importance of a transparency obligation has been reinforced in the behavioural study on transparency on online platforms of 2018.[7] In particular, it was concluded that transparency is of great benefit to both online consumers and host ISPs.

Against this background, this chapter argues that the introduction of a transparency obligation at European level is necessary. In the context of a responsibility framework, as discussed in chapter seven, host ISPS shall have a transparency obligation. In this regard, this chapter firstly examines the current European and national framework with regard to a transparency obligation. Following this, it examines the normative considerations of transparency so as to identify which goals a transparency obligation aims to pursue. Having explored the need for a transparency obligation, the narrative moves to the interpretation of the proposed transparency obligation. Undoubtedly, while the introduction of transparency mainly safeguards users' rights, the interests of host ISPs are also taken into consideration. This is because, however useful a transparency obligation might be, the outcome may be detrimental to host ISPs if the limits of a transparency obligation are not clearly articulated. This is of special concern for this research, since its main aim is to maintain an equilibrium between the different interests at stake. For this reason, the last part of this chapter examines how transparency should be construed so as to accommodate users' interests without subordinating host ISPs' rights.

II. Current Initiatives for a Transparency Obligation and Trends

This section addresses the initiatives and trends for a transparency obligation for host ISPs undertaken at European level as well as at national level within the EU Member States.

A. EU Initiatives for a Transparency Obligation

To address the opacity of host ISPs' operation with regard to the management of online content, initiatives aiming at establishing a transparency obligation have emerged at European level as well as in a handful of national jurisdictions. However, as illustrated below, it seems that all these initiatives are insufficient.

A transparency obligation for host ISPs is not included in the ECD or in the DSMD. Instead at European level, suggestions to set out a transparency obligation for host

[6] European Commission, 'Online platforms and the DSM opportunities and challenges for Europe' (2016) 7.
[7] European Commission, 'Behavioural Study on the transparency of online platforms- Executive summary' (2018) 6.

ISPs are included in non-binding documents. These documents concern the battle against unlawful content that is disseminated online, including instances of unauthorised content within online platforms. For instance, in 2017 the European Commission published a Communication outlining the importance of a transparency obligation in the Digital Single Market.[8] This transparency obligation concerns the publication of transparency reports on a voluntary basis. In particular, it notes that transparency reports shall encompass a disclosure of information on content policy and the notices for removals host ISPs receive as well as the timeframe within which they respond. In this way, the Communication invites host ISPs to adopt more transparent policies for their internet users while at the same time it attempts to mitigate any abuse of users' rights resulted from filtering mechanisms. As already discussed in chapter four, such abuse might include the violation of information rights and freedom of expression of internet users.

By the same token, the European Commission's Recommendation of 1 March 2018, discussing measures to effectively tackle illegal content online, notes in paragraph 20 that:[9]

> In order to ensure transparency and fairness and to avoid the unintended removal of content which is not illegal content, content providers should, as a matter of principle, be informed of the decision to remove or disable access to the content stored at their request and be given the possibility to contest the decision through a counter-notice.

This recommendation is about the notification to users for the removal of their videos and the availability of counter-notification procedures in order to appeal the unreasonable removal. In doing so, users who may not have observed that their uploaded video has been removed will be able to submit a counter-notification. Hence, users' rights, such as the right to effective trial as enshrined in Article 47 of the EU Charter of Fundamental Rights, would be safeguarded.

In line with this, paragraph 23 of the European Commission's Recommendation notes that:

> In order to better assess the effectiveness of notice-and-action mechanisms and other activities of host ISPs in respect of content considered to be illegal content and to ensure accountability, there should be transparency vis-à-vis the general public. Host ISPs should therefore regularly publish reports about those mechanisms and other activities, which should be sufficiently complete and detailed to allow for an adequate insight.[10]

This recommendation addresses the need for transparency reports to be published by host ISPs. Such reports should include information on host ISPs' content policies as well as information on where they store content that has been removed from their platforms. In this way, host ISPs' practices would be under public scrutiny, thus eliminating risks of misconduct from their part.

[8] European Commission, 'Tackling illegal content online: Towards an enhanced responsibility of online platforms' COM (2017) 555 final 16.

[9] European Commission, 'Recommendation of 1.3.2018 on measures to effectively tackle illegal content online' COM (2018) 1177 final 5.

[10] Ibid.

Along similar lines, following the European Commission's Recommendation guidelines, the Council of Europe published a Recommendation on the role and the responsibilities of host ISPs.[11] In particular, it invites host ISPs to adopt clear and transparent information regarding their operation. It notes that '[i]nternet intermediaries should clearly and transparently provide meaningful public information about the operation of automated data processing techniques in the course of their activities'.[12] At the same time, the Recommendation encourages host ISPs to publish transparency reports every year and include all the requests for content removals. Such requests for removing content online may be sent from governmental authorities or individual users.[13]

What is more, the Proposal for harmonised rules for artificial intelligence stresses the need for transparency in algorithmic context.[14] More specifically, Article 52 paragraph 1 states that 'Providers shall ensure that AI systems intended to interact with natural persons are designed and developed in such a way that natural persons are informed that they are interacting with an AI system, unless this is obvious from the circumstances and the context of use.' This means that host ISPs whose services or actions have an impact on internet users/online consumers shall adopt a transparent approach with regard to the use of algorithmic technology within their networks. Finally, the proposed DSA Regulation envisages a higher degree of transparency for the operation of providers of hosting services.[15] In particular, the proposed Regulation urges the need for transparency in the context of online advertising so that online consumers are aware of the characteristics of the products, the traceability of the sellers as well as internal mechanism disputes and out of court remedies in order to protect their rights.

In light of the above, it is possible to observe that a transparency obligation with regard to the removal of copyright infringing contents exists at European level. However, its soft law approach is not legally binding for host ISPs. Therefore, a margin of manoeuvre is entirely left to the discretion of host ISPs.

However, apart from the recommendations for a transparency obligation at European level, a handful of European national jurisdictions have endorsed legislative pieces towards a transparency obligation. Yet, on closer inspection of European national approaches, it appears that the landscape of initiatives for a transparency obligation differs from country to country. These divergent policies might trigger legal uncertainty among the parties involved, namely host ISPs, internet users and rights holders.

[11] Committee of Ministers, 'Recommendation of the Committee of Ministers to member States on the roles and responsibilities of internet intermediaries' CM/Rec (2018) 1, see rm.coe.int/CoERMPublicCommonSearchServices/DisplayDCTMContent?documentId=0900001680790e14.

[12] ibid.

[13] ibid.

[14] Proposal for a Regulation of the European Parliament and of the Council laying down harmonised rules on artificial intelligence (2021) COM/2021/206 final.

[15] Proposal for a Regulation of the European Parliament and the Council on a Single Market For Digital Services (Digital Services Act) and amending Directive 2000/31/EC COM/2020/825 final (hereinafter Proposed DSA Regulation).

B. National Initiatives for a Transparency Obligation

Firstly, it can be observed that across European Member States, any initiatives for transparency do not address copyright or trade mark violations in the digital world. In contrast, they either explicitly touch upon transparency of host ISPs with regard to the removal of illegal content, such as hate speech or fake news, or solely focus on imposing a transparency obligation on algorithmic decision-making procedures. This understanding was exemplified in Germany where the Network Enforcement Law came into force in 2018 and addressed issues relating to the removal of offensive comments from host ISPs within 24 hours.[16] In addition, this imposed a transparency obligation on host ISPs; forcing them to publish transparency reports twice a year and reveal the procedures to remove the infringing content and how the users have appealed the decisions.[17] In similar fashion, the UK government published in April 2019 a White Paper on online harms which includes a number recommendations such as the issue of transparency reports by ISPs annually. These annual transparency reports include the practices that ISPs deploy in order to delete offensive or hate speech content online.[18] Further, other countries have introduced a transparency obligation for algorithmic decision-making processes. A telling example can be found in Estonia where the government recently passed a law about the algorithmic-liability of artificial intelligence schemes.[19] This new law aims to clarify potential liability from algorithmic decision-making and addresses a wide range of stakeholders, such as private sectors, individuals and public authorities, which could make use of algorithms in the course of their operation.

Secondly, other initiatives across European borders impose a transparency obligation in the digital world without limiting the scope of applying a transparency obligation to host ISPs. This means that a transparency obligation is placed in order to enhance Digital Growth from a broader perspective. For example, the Denmark government published a strategy that provides several guidelines to Danish corporations that deal with digital services.[20] In this strategy, the role of transparency as one of the most important requirements for online growth and innovation is outlined. In a similar fashion, in the Netherlands, the Dutch Digitalisation Strategy stresses the need for transparency in the digital services.[21] In particular, it notes that a disclosure of information on supplier's identity for goods online is recommended and stresses the need for transparency in algorithmic decision-making process in the digital world.[22]

[16] ARTICLE 19 Working Party, 'Germany: The Act to Improve Enforcement of the Law in Social Networks' (August 2017) www.article19.org/wp-content/uploads/2017/09/170901-Legal-Analysis-German-NetzDG-Act.pdf.

[17] P Oltermann, 'Tough new German law puts tech firms and free speech in spotlight' *The Guardian* (5 January 2018) www.theguardian.com/world/2018/jan/05/tough-new-german-law-puts-tech-firms-and-free-speech-in-spotlight.

[18] HM Government, 'Online Harms (White Paper)' (April 2019) 7, 57.

[19] Estonian Government, 'Prime minister: to implement artificial intelligence, countries need a unified approach and ability to adapt' (16 October 2018) www.valitsus.ee/en/news/prime-minister-implement-artificial-intelligence-countries-need-unified-approach-and-ability.

[20] The Danish Government, 'Strategy for Denmark's Digital Growth' (2018) eng.em.dk/media/10555/digital-growth-strategy-report_uk_web-1.pdf.

[21] Government of the Netherlands, 'Dutch Digitization Strategy' (2018) www.government.nl/documents/reports/2018/06/01/dutch-digitalisation-strategy.

[22] ibid.

Thirdly, among these national jurisdictions, it seems that a number of Member States limit their initiatives for a transparency obligation at policy level while others take a step further and include it in their legislation. For instance, the Italian government has issued a policy document regarding the challenges of algorithmic decision-making process for citizens. In particular, this document stresses any risks that stem from algorithms and concludes with suggesting potential safeguards.[23] In addition, in the UK, there is an initiative to establish a Centre for Data Ethics and Innovation whose main aim is to assist regulators in order to identify ethical issues that arise from the use of algorithms, cooperate with other research institutes and promote awareness of the use of algorithms among citizens and consumers.[24] In contrast, France has not restricted itself only to policy attempts. Rather, the French government introduced a legislative piece in 2017 endorsing a transparency obligation for host ISPs. More specifically, the newly issued French Consumer Code urges as per Article L. 111-7 II ISPs to provide transparent information to consumers with regard to the removal, indexing and ranking of the content within their networks.[25] Hence, while some countries are more decisive towards the application of a transparency obligation and incorporate them into their national legislation, others prefer to limit any transparency initiatives at policy level.

Therefore, it is possible to conclude that initiatives on a transparency obligation are limited and fragmented. As these findings indicate, this is due to various reasons. At a European level a transparency obligation has been introduced but it is enshrined in non-binding documents and thus has limited applicability so far. Further, European national jurisdictions either address transparency in the context of online platforms or recommend a transparency obligation for algorithmic decision-making procedures without limiting their scope on host ISPs. Finally, some European Member States have limited themselves to recommend a transparency obligation at policy level while others have already integrated a transparency obligation into their national legislation. As a corollary of this divergent landscape, parties involved might face legal uncertainty. More specifically, internet users and consumers may be in doubt about their legal rights if the content that they upload is erroneously removed. Rights holders may be unsure of the adequate protection of their works and goods online. Lastly, this lack of a uniform approach at European level might either impede new host ISPs from entering the Digital Single Market or create confusion for the existing host ISPs that operate in different European national jurisdictions.

On this basis, I argue that a statutory transparency obligation for host ISPs should be introduced at a European level. For this reason, the following section elaborates on the normative considerations of this transparency obligation.

[23] AI White Paper, 'Artificial Intelligence at the service of the citizen', see ai-white-paper.readthedocs.io/en/latest/.

[24] Department for Digital, Culture, Media and Sport, 'Centre for data ethics and innovation consultation' (June 2018), see assets.publishing.service.gov.uk/government/uploads/system/uploads/attachment_data/file/715760/CDEI_consultation__1_.pdf.

[25] Propriete Industrielle et economie numerique, 'Part 1: A law for a digital French Republic – online platforms' (21 February 2017) www.dreyfus.fr/en/new-technologies/part-1-a-law-for-a-digital-french-republic-online-platforms/.

III. Normative Considerations of a Proposed Transparency Obligation

From a normative perspective, the introduction of a transparency obligation for host ISPs appears to be warranted due to an array of reasons. As discussed below, these reasons mainly address the promotion of democratic values and the respect of online users' and consumers' rights.

Firstly, it has been argued that transparency would promote the rule of law.[26] This is because under the current practice, the thresholds and the conditions that generate the automatic removal of material from host ISPs are unknown to end-users. A telling example can be found in the erroneous removal of a video from the Black Lives Matter protests.[27] This video was removed from YouTube and Facebook under the justification of copyright infringement because snippets of songs were played at the background of the protests. Under the generic statement of copyright violation, the creators of videos were not aware of the reasons that led to the removal of their video and thus were left in doubt about their legal rights. However, setting out a transparency obligation would give internet users ample opportunity for reviewing the conditions that trigger the removal. Given reviewability is an important constituent of the rule of law, such obligation might reinforce democratic governance.[28]

Moreover, the disclosure of information would increase users' awareness towards the practices that host ISPs follow.[29] This understanding is considered to be a cornerstone for European Law since via transparency, users would have the opportunity to verify the compatibility of the procedures with the existing legal requirements.[30] In other words, as Buizje notes, it would enable users to 'ensure that it is actually doing what it should be doing'[31] or, as Article 29 Data Protection Working Party noted, 'it is about engendering trust in the processes which affect the citizen by enabling them to understand, and if necessary, challenge those processes'.[32] Therefore, cases that might amount to censorship of free speech and thus contradict the current legal system would be prevented.[33] A similar approach has already been adopted in the case of rights holders on a voluntary basis. In this light, a number of host ISPs have already voluntarily approached groups of rights holders and given them the opportunity to gain an understanding of their practices. For instance, it has been reported that Google signed an agreement with the French audio-visual sector that enables rights holders access to the filtering-based

[26] M Hildebrandt, 'The new imbroglio – living with machine algorithms' (2016) *Vrije Universiteit Brussel* 2; Perel (Filmar) and Elkin-Koren (n 5) 483.

[27] M Masnick, 'Copyright Blocks Interview Of Protesters Because Marvin Gaye's "Let's Get It On" Was Playing In The Background' (*Techdirt*, 3 June 2020) www.techdirt.com/articles/20200602/21391944634/copyright-blocks-interview-protesters-because-marvin-gayes-lets-get-it-was-playing-background.shtml.

[28] Zerilli, Knott, Maclaurin and Gavaghan (n 4) 3.

[29] T Zarsky, 'The trouble with algorithmic decisions: an analytical road map to examine efficiency and fairness in automated and opaque decision making' (2016) 41 *Science, Technology and Human Values* 129.

[30] Perel (Filmar) and Elkin-Koren (n 5) 483.

[31] A Buijze, *The Principle of Transparency in EU Law* (Unpublished PhD thesis, 2013) 56–57.

[32] Article 29 Data Protection Working Party, 'Guidelines on transparency under Regulation 2016/679' (2016) 5.

[33] F Pasquale, 'Secret Algorithms Threaten the Rule of Law' (*MIT Technology Review*, 1 June 2017) www.technologyreview.com/s/608011/secret-algorithms-threaten-the-rule-of-law/.

technology that host ISPs adopt in order to curb the online infringements.[34] Therefore, it is possible to argue that since similar steps to make rights holders aware of the procedures of host ISPs are available to rights holders, users shall also take advantage of them.

Therefore, having the opportunity to review the conditions and be aware of the practices host ISPs adopt, users would thus know the reasons upon which the decisions for removal have been made. In this way, it may be posited that transparency would enhance due process.[35] Due process, as Pasquale notes, is 'critical to a legitimate legal system',[36] since it permits users to challenge a decision after obtaining information of the facts of the removal.[37] Otherwise, it seems impossible to challenge a decision without knowing the reasons that led to this decision. This lack of information would be in conflict with the right to a fair trial right or the right to effective remedy, as enshrined in the European Charter of Fundamental Rights and the European Convention of Human Rights accordingly.[38] Both rights, as the Council of Europe outlines, are 'fundamental to the respect and protection of individual rights'.[39]

However, it could be argued that the principles of due process are only relevant to the environment of public authorities and cannot be applicable to the activities of private entities such as the host ISPs. In this sense, internet users cannot question the decisions of private platforms and appeal against them. Yet, this view lies on unstable ground. It seems that, although host ISPs are not governmental institutions, their activities appear to be tightly correlated with fundamental rights such as intellectual property rights, the right to freedom of expression, or the right to privacy. For instance, host ISPs nowadays enforce intellectual property rights by removing illegal material from their platforms or detecting counterfeit goods within their networks.[40] Hence, they shape our 'informational environment' by deciding which information reaches the end-users and which information does not.[41] Finally, social networks such as Facebook process a large amount of users' personal data every day. In light of the power of host ISPs,[42]

[34] F Romero-Moreno 'Notice and stay down and social media: amending Article 13 of the Proposed Directive on Copyright' (2018) 33 *International Review of Law, Computers and Technology* 187.

[35] Perel (Filmar) and Elkin-Koren (n 5) 478.

[36] Pasquale (n 33).

[37] Zerilli, Knott, Maclaurin and Gavaghan (n 4) 3.

[38] G Noto La Diega, 'Against the Dehumanization of Decision-Making: Algorithmic Decisions at the Crossroads of Intellectual Property, Data Protection and Freedom of Information' (2018) 9 *Journal of Intellectual Property, Information Technology and E-Commerce Law* 23.

[39] Committee of Ministers, 'Guide to good practice in respect of domestic' (adopted on 18 September 2013) www.echr.coe.int/Documents/Pub_coe_domestics_remedies_ENG.pdf.

[40] T Synodinou, 'Intermediaries' liability for online copyright infringement in the EU: evolutions and confusions' (2015) 31 *Computer Law and Security Review* 58–59.

[41] M Taddeo and L Floridi, 'The Debate on the Moral Responsibilities of Online Service Providers' (2016) 22 *Science and Engineering Ethics* 1575–1603.

[42] A number of scholars have pointed out the power of online intermediaries: S Stalla-Bourdillon, 'Internet intermediaries as responsible actors? Why is it time to rethink the E-Commerce Directive as well' in M Taddeo and L Floridi (eds), *The Responsibilities of Online Service Providers* (Berlin, Springer, 2017) 275; D Broeders and L Taylor, 'Does Great Power come with Great Responsibility? The need to talk about corporate political responsibility' in M Taddeo and L Floridi (eds), *The Responsibilities of Online Service Providers* (Berlin, Springer, 2017) 315; D Rowland, U Kohl and A Charlesworth, *Information Technology Law*, 5th edn (London, Routledge, 2017) 81–99; J Wang, *Regulating Hosting ISPs' Responsibilities for Copyright Infringement: The Freedom to Operate in the US, EU and China* (Berlin, Springer, 2018); M Thompson, 'Beyond Gatekeeping: The Normative Responsibility of Internet Intermediaries' (2016) 18 *Vanderbilt Journal of Entertainment & Technology Law* 783–84.

it seems that the need to safeguard fundamental rights of users is crucial. Otherwise, without due process, a new era of unaccountable host ISPs may emerge. This is what Citron and Pasquale have described as 'a new feudal order of unaccountable reputational intermediaries'.[43]

Further, it has been argued that transparency would enhance the legitimacy of host ISPs' activities.[44] This view is important due to the questionable enforcement and quasi-adjudication duties that host ISPs have been assigned to undertake. In particular, there is a pressing concern that revolves around whether host ISPs compromise their enforcement tasks with their own private business interests and their partners' interests.[45] However, being aware of the grounds upon which host ISPs reach a decision, users would show more willingness to accept the specific decision.

In line with this, and given that there is legitimacy, trust comes to the forefront as well. If users were aware of the importance of the role of host ISPs, they would trust, to a greater extent, the services host ISPs offer. This is because users would make sure that host ISPs that are entitled to remove online material from their platforms exercise their activities in a fair way.[46] In this sense, transparency could act as a guide to users on what to expect from the online services and have a deeper understanding of the practices they use. As Brill notes 'transparency should also include helping consumers navigate the complex ecosystem of data, devices, and big data analytics operating behind the scenes, so that consumers understand the practices that can affect them, and exercise choices about the practices'.[47] Therefore, users may have more confidence and faith in online services. They may also be less sceptical about undertaking transactions with host ISPs, and less reluctant to do so.

A representative example of such a line of thinking can be found in a European Commission's Study on the transparency of host ISPs, which claims that providing information for a specific product in a host ISP can enhance the trust of online consumers.[48] In particular, this study demonstrates that the lack of information about the identity of the seller could prevent the users from choosing this specific product. In contrast, it has been observed that when there is information on the third party, the percentage of users that select these goods could reach up to 50 per cent. Furthermore, the study highlights the importance of reviews. While there is low likelihood of purchasing the precise goods when reviews are not available, the likelihood of buying it in cases where there are reviews could increase sales by up to 200 per cent. This means that the provision of information for the third party or the existence of reviews for the products attracts online consumers and preserves online business welfare. As the study

[43] Citron and Pasquale (n 2) 19.

[44] Perel (Filmar) and Elkin-Koren (n 5) 494.

[45] M Tessier, J Herzog and L Madzou, 'Regulation at the Age of Online Platform-Based Economy: Accountability, User Empowerment and Responsiveness' in L Belli and N Zingales (eds), *Platform Regulations – How to Regulate Them and How They Regulate Us* (2017) 181.

[46] R Binss, M Van Kleek, M Veale, U Lyngs, J Zhao and N Shabolt, 'It's reducing a human being to a percentage: perceptions of justice in algorithmic decisions' (2018) *Proceedings of the 2018 CHI Conference on Human Factors in Computing Systems.*

[47] J Brill, 'Keynote Address Before Coalition for Networked Information: Transparency, Trust, and Consumer Protection in a Complex World' (15 December 2015) 5, www.ftc.gov/system/files/documents/public_statements/895843/151216cnikeynote.pdf.

[48] European Commission, 'Behavioural Study on the transparency of online platforms- Executive summary' (2018) 6.

effectively summarises, transparency in the online word aims to accommodate not only consumers' interests but also host ISPs' business interests since a great number of consumers will show a higher amount of trust towards their online activities.[49]

However, transparency would not only enhance the legitimacy of the host ISPs' decisions and thus promote users' trust. Indeed, it would also have benefits for host ISPs' business models. In particular, transparency would contribute to the quality of the services they offer as it would encourage host ISPs to adopt good methods and thus perform better. Drawing parallels with the concept of transparency in public institutions, Addink and Ten Berge point out that a transparency obligation is tightly correlated with 'socially accepted standards and values and with the principles of democracy and the rule of law'.[50] This means that higher standards of achievement will be set out, thus reinforcing important democratic values. Likewise, within the framework of online copyright and trade mark infringements, transparency would induce host ISPs to adopt better practices. For instance, given that there have been cases where algorithms have been criticised for biased outcomes and practices,[51] host ISPs would first examine the efficiency and the accuracy of those algorithms before putting them into practice. In this way, as Elkin-Koren points out, under the fear of disgrace or public criticism about their methods, 'decision-makers who function in a transparent environment are discouraged from engaging in problematic conduct'.[52] This implies that host ISPs would be afraid to deviate from the rules since information regarding their actions would be made available to users. Therefore, higher rates of good performance would be achieved, and marginal errors would be tempered to a great extent.

Further, it is possible to argue that a transparency obligation would mitigate any information asymmetries that exist between host ISPs and internet users. Information asymmetry takes place 'when one party to a transaction has pertinent information that the other party lacks'.[53] While this understanding seems difficult to apply in the copyright context, it finds fertile ground in the trade mark framework. For instance, in the offline world, the trader and the consumer have knowledge of the features of a product.[54] They can both verify the origin and the quality of a product, characteristics that are fundamental to consumers in order to make a decision and purchase a specific product among others.[55] This is in contrast with the online environment where only the trader and the host ISP have knowledge over the characteristics of

[49] European Commission, 'Study on Behavioral study on the transparency of online platforms: Final report' (2018) 48 where it has been found that 'online transparency is clearly in the interests of consumers. Equally, it might be argued that it is in the interests of platforms and traders who could expect to see a growth in online activity as a result of increased consumer confidence and trust'.

[50] GH Addink and JBJM ten Berge, 'Study on Innovation of Legal Means for Eliminating Corruption in the Public Service in the Netherlands' (2007) *Netherlands Comparative Law Association* 12.

[51] Data and Society, 'Algorithmic Accountability: A Primer' (18 April 2018) 6; S Venkant, 'When an algorithm isn't' (*Medium*, 2 October 2015) medium.com/@geomblog/when-an-algorithm-isn-t-2b9fe01b9bb5.

[52] Perel (Filmar) and Elkin-Koren (n 5) 495.

[53] Ch Shen, J Chiou and B Kuo, 'Remedies for information asymmetry in online transaction: An investigation into the impact of web page signals on auction outcome' (2011) 21 *Internet Research* 156.

[54] N Economides, 'The Economics of Trademarks' (1988) 78 *Trademark Reporter* 526.

[55] ibid.

the goods.[56] This is because, as Sørensen points out 'the need to secure transparency through information is based on the assumption that the contracting parties have different levels of knowledge relevant to their choice to enter into a contract'.[57] Hence, this implies that it is up to host ISPs to control the dissemination of goods. Otherwise, online consumers are vulnerable to confusion and deception when purchasing products online.[58]

Finally, transparency would enhance the right to information. This is because in the online world, a number of host ISPs might indiscriminately remove material without justifying the reasons for its removal. This understanding can be exemplified by a handful of ISPs such as Google[59] where it has been found that this search engine removes links from their search listing results that do not favour their business partners or as a response to individual requests.[60] In particular, in its terms and conditions, Google notifies users that they will 'remove pages from their results if they believe the page violates their Webmaster Guidelines, if they believe that they are required to do so by law, or at the request of the webmaster who is responsible for the page'.[61] In a similar fashion, Twitter includes in its terms of service the statement 'We reserve the right to remove Content that violates the User Agreement, including for example, copyright or trade mark violations …'.[62] It is this element of the policy that has been criticised as resulting in the indiscrete removal of web results and content online. This is because this broadly defined statement could imply that host ISPs have a margin of manoeuvre and could thus remove links or material after receiving individual requests without clarifying their reasoning. In this way, host ISPs could either grace its business partners or be subject more easily to external political influence that could give those rewards.

Bearing in mind the above, it is possible to argue that the role of transparency is very important in the online world as it is a great asset for internet users, online consumers and subsequently the business model of host ISPs. In particular, with regard to internet users and online consumers, this is because transparency would enhance the rule of law and due process. For instance, it would give users information with regard to the removal of their content. In doing so, users would be able to observe whether the host ISP has complied with the rules and either accept or challenge the decision. In contrast, the lack of information about the conditions that trigger the removal of material would undermine the rule of law and the principle of due process since users would be deprived of the right to effective remedy and to a fair trial as set out in the EU

[56] A Marsoof, *Internet Intermediaries and Trade Mark Rights* (London, Routledge, 2019) 12; Shen, Chiou and Kuo (n 53) 156.

[57] MJ Sorensen, 'Draft Model Rules on Online Intermediary Platforms' in B Devolder (ed), *The Platform Economy: Unravelling the Legal Status of Online Intermediaries* (Wellington, Intersentia, 2019) 182.

[58] See also E Rubin, 'The internet, consumer protection and practical knowledge' in J Winn, *Consumer Protection in the Age of the 'Information Economy'* (London, Routledge, 2006) 37.

[59] E Laidlaw, 'Private Power, Public interest: an examination of search engine accountability' (2008) 17 *International Journal of Law and Information Technology* 133.

[60] ibid.

[61] Webmaster Guidelines, support.google.com/webmasters/answer/35769?hl=en.

[62] Twitter Terms of services is available at twitter.com/en/tos.

Charter of Fundamental Rights and European Convention of Human Rights. Further, the ascription of a transparency obligation would justify the legitimacy of the decisions undertaken by the host ISP's activities and thus generate trust to online consumers. This is because with transparency users would be aware of the thresholds that generate the removal of their material. Otherwise, users would be suspicious of the principal reasons their material was taken down and whether this decision had a legitimate basis.

In addition, transparency would have a positive impact on transactions between host ISPs and online consumers. This is because it would eliminate the information asymmetries in online purchases since consumers in the online world would have more information about the quality and the origin of goods. Therefore, consumers would not be deceived and their trust and confidence in the online services would increase.

Yet, apart from safeguarding internet users/online consumers' rights, a transparency obligation would induce host ISPs to adopt better practices in the operation of their business and therefore the principle of good governance would be enhanced. This is because under the fear of being publicly criticised about their business policies, host ISPs would be incentivised to undertake a prior examination of their practices in order to eliminate any errors or malfunctions.

In light of the above, it could be posited that a transparency would have benefits not only for users but also for host ISPs' interests. Yet, as mentioned at the beginning of this chapter, however necessary a transparency obligation might be, it is crucial to articulate the limits within which such a transparency obligation would be exercised. Otherwise, the potential advantages a transparency obligation might have could lead to adverse results for host ISPs. It is to these limits the following section of this chapter now turns.

IV. How Should a Proposed Transparency Obligation be Shaped?

In order to frame the limits within which a transparency obligation would take place, it is important to take into consideration in which context a transparency obligation would be applicable and how it would be construed. This is because, as explained at the beginning of this chapter, it has been argued that 'different contexts require different levels of transparency'.[63] This means, for instance, that a full disclosure of an algorithm would have a detrimental effect on the business model of host ISPs since third parties would be able to take advantage of it and find pathways to circumvent or, as referred to by Yakowitz and others, to 'game the algorithm'.[64] Indeed, a transparency obligation shall take into consideration the interests of internet users/online consumers as well as the host ISPs. In particular, with regard to online consumers, Devenney argues that 'care must be taken to recognise the limits on the extent to which the provision of

[63] R Caplan, J Donovan, L Hanson and J Matthews, 'Algorithmic Accountability: A primer: Tech Algorithm Briefing: How algorithms perpetuate racial bias and inequality' (2018) 7.

[64] J Yakowitz Bambauer and T Zarsky, 'The Algorithm Game' (2018) 94 *Notre Dame Law Review* 11.

information can cure the many varied and complex disadvantages under which different consumers may be operating'.[65] This implies that in the case of online consumers, the provision of information relating to the functioning of the online marketplace must take into consideration the position of online consumers, such as the information asymmetries that exist,[66] while at the same time the disclosure of information shall not harm the business model of the online marketplace.

Against this background, the narrative continues by examining the different contexts in which a transparency obligation should be applicable and how it should be articulated so as to maintain a balance between the different interests at stake. In particular, on the basis of the normative considerations that have been discussed in the previous section, I assess how a transparency obligation should be construed in relation to the algorithms that host ISPs use, to their terms and conditions and to the issue of transparency reports.

A. Transparency in Algorithmic Decision-making Process

As mentioned at the beginning of this chapter, to curb the increasing number of online infringements, host ISPs mainly use algorithms. These algorithms decide the removal of the material based on an automated decision-making process. While this process excludes any human intervention, which can be 'cost-saving' for host ISPs,[67] average users may perceive it as a 'black box'.[68] This is because algorithms are inscrutable, as Introna notes, and users cannot oversee them and thus gain an understanding of their function.[69]

It is this inscrutable and opaque nature of algorithms that has raised calls for transparency.[70] Such calls dictate that host ISPs should disclose their algorithms to users so that users would be aware of, and could challenge, the reasons that triggered the removal of their content online.[71]

[65] J Devenney, 'The legacy of the Cameron-Clegg coalition programme of reform of the law on the supply of goods, digital content and services to consumers' (2018) 6 *Journal of Business Law* 488.

[66] See ch 8 section III.

[67] D Citron, 'Technological Due Process' (2008) 85 *Washington University Law Review* 1252.

[68] Citron and Pasquale (n 2) 5 where the authors note that 'the lack of transparency of credit scoring systems leaves consumers confounded by how and why their scores change.'; G Frosio, 'Algorithmic enforcement online' in P Torremans (ed), *Intellectual Property and Human Rights*, 4th edn (Alphen aan den Rijn, Kluwer Law International, 2021) 30 where Frosio notes that 'algorithmic enforcement finds its primary Achilles' heel in algorithms' transparency.'

[69] L Introna, 'Algorithms, Governance and Governmentality: on governing academic writing' (2016) 41 *Science, Technology and Human Values*; D Heaven, 'Not like us: Artificial Minds we can't understand' (2013) *New Scientist* 32–35; Heaven argues that there are cases where algorithms are not understood by their manufacturers as well; in addition in Caplan, Donovan, Hanson and Matthews (n 63) where they argue that 'the more complex and sophisticated an algorithm is, the harder it is to explain, even by a knowledgeable algorithmic engineer'.

[70] Zarsky (n 29) 121; M Marchill, C Neuberger and F Schindler, 'Transparency on the Net: Functions and Deficiencies of Internet Search Engines' (2003) 5 *The Journal of Policy, Regulation and Strategy for Telecommunications* 52; E van Couvering, 'Is relevance relevant? Market, Science and War: Discourses of search engine quality' (2007) 12 *Journal of Computer-Mediated Communication* 866.

[71] Citron (n 67) 1308.

The main proponent of full transparency of the algorithm is Lessig.[72] In his landmark book *Code and Other laws of Cyberspace*, he argues that in order to understand how internet infrastructure works, an 'open' code is needed.[73] This is because, as he explains, internet infrastructure is regulated by lawmakers who, through internet infrastructure, aim to control the behaviour and the activities of internet users. By disclosing the code, users would be aware of the practices that their governments follow in order to regulate their behaviour.

Other proponents of full disclosure of algorithms are Introna and Nissenbaum. They outline the need for full disclosure of algorithms that the search engines use in order to index material or facilitate the search of information.[74] This is because, as they argue, algorithms may, either intentionally or unintentionally, downgrade or upgrade specific websites. By excluding certain information while at the same time prioritising other material, algorithms undermine the importance of the internet as a public good and erode the main principles upon which has been built.[75] Such principles mainly concern the boost of free flow of information and free access to an open internet.[76]

However, the full disclosure of the algorithm to end-users seems problematic. This is mainly due to three specific reasons. The first reason touches upon the consideration of an algorithm as a business trade secret,[77] a notion which lies at the core of the business model of a company.[78] As Pasquale notes 'trade secrecy is a business tool'.[79] Many host ISPs have developed their own algorithms and integrated them into their business operation.[80] These algorithms hugely increased the popularity and the revenues of several host ISPs[81] by either addressing the way information is presented to end users or focusing on detecting illegal content that is circulated within a platform without author's permission. For instance, Facebook has developed its own algorithm in order to manage its News Feed section, which concerns the posts Facebook's users can view, taking into consideration different parameters such as gender, education, and location of the users.[82]

Given the importance of algorithms as business tools, many host ISPs abstain from disclosing the algorithm because they are afraid that their competitors will take advantage of them.[83] As Diakopoulos points out, such a full disclosure 'may undermine their

[72] L Lessig, *Code and Other Laws of Cyberspace* (New York, Basic Books, 1999) 139.

[73] ibid.

[74] L Introna and H Nissenbaum, 'Shaping the web: Why the Politics of search engines matters' (2000) 16 *The Information Society* 181.

[75] ibid 178.

[76] OECD, 'OECD Principles for Internet Policy Making' (2014) 5–6 is available at www.oecd.org/internet/ieconomy/oecd-principles-for-internet-policy-making.pdf.

[77] R Wexler, 'Life, Liberty, and Trade Secrets: Intellectual Property in the Criminal Justice System' (2018) 70 *Stanford Law Review* 1383. Citron and Pasquale (n 2) 17.

[78] F Pasquale, 'Restoring transparency to automated authority' (2011) *Seton Hall Research Paper* 237.

[79] ibid.

[80] Citron (n 67) 1290; Citron notes that 'Because vendors typically build these systems, the source code is proprietary and closed.'

[81] C Cheung, P Chiu and M Lee, 'Online social networks: Why do students use facebook?' (2011) 27 *Computers in Human Behaviour* 1337.

[82] J Martin, 'The New Facebook Algorithm: Secrets Behind How It Works and What You Can Do To Succeed' (*Carney*, 15 February 2018) carney.co/daily-carnage-feature/new-facebook-algorithm-secrets-behind-works-can-succeed/.

[83] Citron and Pasquale (n 2) 5.

competitive advantage'.[84] This is because the competitors of a company might copy its algorithm and thus provide the same services to internet users.[85] This understanding has been exemplified in a handful of court rulings. In those cases, the courts rejected the claims of rights holders and refrained from ordering the full disclosure of an algorithm under the reasoning that an algorithm is protected under Trade Secrecy Laws. For instance, in the dispute between Viacom, a film and TV industry corporation, and YouTube,[86] Viacom brought legal proceedings against YouTube, requesting the Court to order YouTube to disclose its algorithm that identifies copyright infringing material within its platform. After a careful examination of the facts, the District Court declared that a company's algorithm is protected under Trade Secret Law and outlined its commercial importance for a company along with the tremendous labour and economic effort that is needed in order to develop such an algorithm.[87] Subsequently, as a corollary to this approach, the Court declined the request of Viacom and did not order the disclosure of the algorithm. Otherwise, as the Court has noted, the disclosure of an algorithm might mean the end to the owner's competitive edge.[88] This means that either the owner could lose the dominant position they may have in the market or that their competition would be detrimentally affected. For instance, YouTube's competitors, such as Dailymotion, could have benefitted from the revelation of the algorithm and attempted to create a similar one, potentially becoming more competitive and thus attract more customers to their services.

Further, so important are trade secrets for a business that any disclosure without the corporation's consensus could give the right to the business to ask for damages.[89] This is because a trade secret is the intellectual property of a business and must be protected against infringers.[90] Such an understanding was reinforced in the long-running legal battle of the Linux case.[91] In this case, SCO, a software company, brought legal proceedings against IBM, alleging that IBM used SCO's algorithm without its authorisation. More specifically, after SCO and IBM concluded an agreement to use certain technological knowledge, IBM decided to change its business strategic plan and invest more on Linux promotion. Despite the dismissal of SCO's allegation for misuse of trade secrets, this case demonstrates the importance of an algorithm as a trade secret since a company can bring legal proceedings against another company alleging the misuse of its trade secret. Therefore, drawing conclusions from this case, one might extrapolate that trade secrets are fundamental parts of a business model and any disclosure could have a detrimental effect on the company with regard to its competitiveness.

[84] N Diakopoulos, 'Algorithmic accountability reporting: on the investigation of black boxes' (2013) *Town Center for Digital Journalism* 12.

[85] Pasquale (n 3) 142.

[86] *Viacom Intern. Inc. v YouTube Inc.* 676 F.3d 19 United States Court of Appeals, Second Circuit 2012, see cyber.harvard.edu/people/tfisher/cx/2012_Viacom.pdf; M Perel (Filmar) and N Elkin-Koren, 'Black box tinkering: beyond disclosure in algorithmic enforcement' (2017) 69 *Florida Law Review* 193.

[87] *Viacom Intern. Inc. v YouTube Inc.*, United States District Court, S.D. New York, Jul 1, 2008 253 F.R.D. 256 (S.D.N.Y. 2008), see casetext.com/case/viacom-intern-inc-v-youtube-inc.

[88] ibid.

[89] Pasquale (n 78) 238.

[90] ibid.

[91] A LaFontaine, 'Adventures in software licensing: SCO v. IBM and the future of the open source model' (2006) 4 *Journal on Telecommunications and High Technology Law* 449.

The second reason that justifies the rejection of any request towards the revelation of an algorithm can be found in the risks of circumvention by potential infringers-users. This risk has been outlined by Facebook's representative who argued that Facebook refrains from any revelation of its algorithm so that the users do not know about its 'workarounds'.[92] This is mainly because, with the disclosure of the full algorithm of the company, many users would know the operation an online intermediary operates and thus might identify potential loopholes. Such loopholes can be circumvented with the use of certain services such as Smart DNS or VPN services. These services have been extensively used by a number of internet users already in order to download illegal content from file-sharing websites. For instance, it has been reported that many companies, such as Smart DNS services and VPN services, help users to unblock geo-blocking technical measures so that they can continue committing copyright infringements.[93] While geo-blocking is not illegal per se,[94] the use of such services might pose serious threats to host ISPs' welfare. Therefore, it seems that a transparency obligation would erode the efficiency of an algorithm since users would be aware of its peculiarities and flaws and thus be able to circumvent them.[95]

The third reason supporting maintaining the secrecy of algorithms touches upon the lack of usefulness of disclosure of an algorithm to users. Take the example of a 65 year-old individual. Although she uses social networks and auction platforms, she is considered the average unskilled internet user. Whether the algorithm is revealed to her or not, it will not clarify her concerns why her content has been removed or why she bought a counterfeit product. Unless someone is experienced in understanding and interpreting complicated algorithms, it seems that the average user will not benefit from the revelation of the algorithm. This is because it is not possible to interpret an algorithm in simple words or at least in a way that is understood to the average user.[96] For instance, the Windows Vista algorithm includes 50 million lines with numerical and mathematical symbols.[97] Subsequently, the full disclosure of this algorithm code to most users would not help them understand the main reasons that justify the removal of their content.

Undoubtedly, the criticism against the full disclosure of an algorithm has its own merits. However, although full disclosure of their algorithms would be detrimental for host ISPs' business welfare, it could be argued that some level of transparency is acceptable. The primary aim of this type of transparency would be to accommodate the needs of users without neglecting host ISPs' interests.

[92] K Huszti-Orban, 'Countering Terrorism and Violent Extremism Online: what role for social media platforms?' in Belli and Zingales (n 45) 204; J Urban, J Karaganis and B Schofield, 'Notice and Takedown in everyday practice' (2017) *Berkeley Law Policy Paper* 4.

[93] Ernesto, 'PayPal starts banning VPN and SmartDNS services' (*Torrentfreak*, 5 February 2016) torrentfreak.com/paypal-starts-banning-vpn-and-smartdns-services-160205/.

[94] M Trimble, 'Geoblocking and Evasion of Geoblocking – Technical Standards and the Law' in R Lobato and J Meese, *Geoblocking and Global Video Culture* (2016) 55 where Trimble argues that geoblocking is used as a tool of regulation and enforcement of intellectual property rights.

[95] N Diakopoulos citing Goodhart, pointed out 'when a measure becomes a target, it ceases to be a good measure' in Diakopoulos (n 84) 12.

[96] Noto La Diega (n 38) 23.

[97] Introna (n 69) 7.

This book posits that a transparency obligation in the algorithmic decision-making process should be understood either as a right of an individual to request explanation of the content removal,[98] or as 'qualified transparency'[99] which means that the full disclosure of an algorithm can only be made to a governmental authority.

With regard to the first option, to set out a right to explanation for online intellectual property infringements seems a novelty. For this reason, in order to gain a better understanding of this right, an analogy can be drawn from the General Data Protection Regulation.[100] Looking closely at Articles 13, 14 and 15 of the GDPR, it is possible to observe that data controllers must reveal their rationale behind their decision-making processes. More specifically, as per Articles 13 and 14 of the GDPR, data controllers must disclose the existence of and the logic behind the algorithmic decision-making process while Article 15 notes that the data controller must provide to the data subject information about '... the significance and the envisaged consequences of such processing for the data subject'.[101]

Although it has been argued that the abovementioned Articles do not include any right to explanation,[102] the prevailing view seems in favour of a right to explanation. This is because scholars who support the right to explanation adopt a broader interpretation of these Articles. For instance, Maglieri and Comande argue that the new GDPR offers a right to explanation which is based on a wide interpretation of Articles 13, 14 and 15 along with Recital 71.[103] To my understanding, in order to have a right to explanation, there must be an ex-post information to data subjects about their personal data. This means that a data subject can request after the process of personal data more information about the process. By contrast, the provision of ex-ante information does not constitute a right to explanation. In this regard, while Maglieri and Comande found that Articles 13, 14 and 15 offered ex-ante information to data subjects, they argue that if these articles are examined through the lens of Recital 71, they can be interpreted as provisions of ex-post information and thus a right to explanation emerges. Recital 71 endorses a right to explanation and notes that '.... such processing should be subject to suitable safeguards, which should include specific information to the data subject and the right to obtain human intervention, to express his or her point of view, to obtain an explanation of the decision reached after such assessment ...'.

Yet, as pointed out at judicial level, from a European law perspective a recital is non-binding and its value is 'normative supplementary; and not interpretative'.[104]

[98] J Kroll argues that the ability of internet users to understand the reasons behind the removal of content safeguards procedural regularity. This means that 'each participant will know that the same procedure was applied to her and that the procedure was not designed in a way that disadvantages her specifically' in J Kroll et al, 'Accountable algorithms' (2017) 165 *University of Pennsylvania Law Review* 22.

[99] Pasquale (n 3) 9; F Pasquale, 'Beyond Innovation and Competition: The Need for Qualified Transparency in Internet' (2014) 104 *Northwestern University Law Review* 105.

[100] Hereinafter GDPR.

[101] Article 15(h) GDPR.

[102] L Edwards and M Veale, 'Slave to the algorithm? Why a right to an explanation is probably not the remedy you are looking for' (2016) 16 *Duke Law and Technology Review* 18.

[103] G Malgieri and G Comande, 'Why a right to legibility of automated decision-making exists in the General Data Protection Regulation' (2017) 7 *International Data Privacy Law* 254–55.

[104] ibid.

This understanding has been clarified in the *Nilsson* case.[105] In this case, in paragraph 54 the CJEU outlined that 'on this point, it must be stated that the preamble to a Community act has no binding legal force and cannot be relied on as a ground for derogating from the actual provisions of the act in question'.[106] At the same time, the Court concluded that the interpretation of a Recital shall not be in conflict with the existing provisions in the Directive.[107]

It is this clarification that is made by the Court that urged Maglieri and Comande to posit that since the interpretation of Recital 71 does not contradict the existing legal provisions, it could provide an 'explanatory value' to the existing legal provisions of the GDPR and thus a wide interpretation of Articles 13, 14, 15 and 22 of GDPR is warranted.

Such a stance has been maintained by Noto La Diega, who argues that a right to explanation is endorsed in Articles 13, 14, 15 and 22 of the GDPR after taking into consideration Recital 71.[108] This is because, as he argues, a 'purposive approach and a correct valorisation of the role of the recitals'[109] shall be taken into consideration. This means that the right to explanation in the recital shall signal the main purpose of the GDPR which is to safeguard data subjects' personal data in the course of the processing. Along similar lines, the Council of Europe outlined that '... the data subject should be entitled to know about the personal data concerning him or her and the logic which served as a basis for the profiling ...'.[110] Article 29 Working Party in its report on Guidelines on Automated individual decision-making and Profiling and its report on Guidelines on consent outlines the need to provide information to the data subject about the process of personal data.[111]

On the basis of the above, it could be argued that a right to explanation could be endorsed with regard to online intellectual property infringements. However, in this case, instead of processing personal data, host ISPs filter the content that internet users upload within the networks through automated process. For instance, with regard to the case of algorithms that social networks or video-exchange music platforms use and as discussed earlier, whereas it is prohibitory to reveal the full algorithm to users, the negative effects could be mitigated if users were aware of the parameters under which algorithms operate. In particular, excluding the commercial keywords and any fundamental technical

[105] This example has been given by Malgieri and Comande in order to reinforce the view that the preamble to a Community act is normative supplementary; see C-162/97 *Nilsson* (1998) ECR I- 7477.

[106] C-162/97 *Nilsson* (1998) ECR I-7477, para 54.

[107] Malgieri and Comande (n 103) 255.

[108] Noto La Diega (n 38) 23.

[109] ibid.

[110] Council of Europe, 'The protection of individuals with regard to automatic processing of personal data in the context of profiling' Recommendation CM/Rec (2010)13 and explanatory memorandum 50–51.

[111] Article 29 Working Party, 'Guidelines on Automated individual decision-making and Profiling for the purposes of Regulation 2016/679' (2018) 25 notes that 'nevertheless good practice to provide the above information. In any event the controller must provide sufficient information to the data subject to make the processing fair and meet all the other information requirements of Articles 13 and 14'; Article 29 Working Party, 'Guidelines on consent under Regulation 2016/679' (2018) 13 where it is stated that 'Providing information to data subjects prior to obtaining their consent is essential in order to enable them to make informed decisions, understand what they are agreeing to, and for example exercise their right to withdraw their consent. If the controller does not provide accessible information, user control becomes illusory and consent will be an invalid basis for processing.'

details of algorithms, users must be in a position to question host ISPs for more information about the ways filtering algorithms operate.[112] For instance, after their content has been removed, users must be in a position to interrogate online platforms about their decision-making process. In this way, it would not only the users who would be eligible to challenge the host ISPs' decisions, but also host ISPs' actions would be in accordance with the right to fair remedy and right to fair trial as enshrined in the European Convention of Human Rights and European Charter of Fundamental Rights.[113] This understanding was also reinforced by the Council of Europe's Recommendations in 2008 and 2015. More specifically, the Recommendations on promoting the respect of freedom of expression in 2008 noted that, in case host ISPs deploy filtering-based technologies, internet users should be offered the option to question the removal of their content as well as other remedies in order to protect their fundamental rights.[114] In a similar fashion, the Recommendations on media and information society in 2015 note that host ISPs must 'ensure that internet users have access to effective remedies when their rights and freedoms have been restricted or when they believe that their rights have been violated'.[115]

However, it could be argued that among the users whose content has been unreasonably removed, there are also infringer-users who uploaded or shared unauthorised content online. Thus, it may be considered why these infringer-users should be made aware of the parameters fed within an algorithm. Drawing parallels with democratic values, clear and codified procedures are in conformity with the principles of due diligence and the rule of law. Every individual shall be aware of the legal rules and the potential penalties which exist in case an individual breaks the law. Likewise, in the case of taking down material, every user that interacts with this kind of online platform should be made aware of the practices it follows. Yet, it is up to the internet user to decide whether she will upload or share illegal material online.

Apart from individuals who have the right to explanation, another interpretation of a transparency obligation with regard to algorithms is 'qualified transparency', as introduced by Pasquale.[116] 'Qualified transparency' is understood as the partial disclosure of an algorithm in order to balance the interests of the parties involved, namely host ISPs, internet users and rights holders. In this case, after taking into consideration trade secrecy laws and the reasons that encourage host ISPs to refrain from disclosing their algorithms, Pasquale explains that the revelation of an algorithm should be made only towards a governmental body that would be in charge of examining the accuracy of algorithms.[117]

[112] Romero-Moreno (n 34) 196.

[113] Noto La Diega (n 38) 23.

[114] Committee of Ministers, 'Recommendation to member states on measures to promote the respect for freedom of expression and information with regard to Internet filters' CM/ Rec (2008) search.coe.int/cm/Pages/result_details.aspx?ObjectID=09000016805d3bc4.

[115] Committee of Ministers, 'Recommendations in the field of media and information society Media and Internet Division' (2015) rm.coe.int/CoERMPublicCommonSearchServices/DisplayDCTMContent?documentId=0900001680645b44.

[116] F Pasquale, 'Beyond Innovation and Competition' (n 99) 126.

[117] ibid.

Interestingly, although Pasquale introduced the concept of qualified transparency with regard to search engines' search results, it could be argued that qualified transparency can also be extended to other kinds of host ISPs such as social networks and video-exchange platforms. In this case, the algorithm could be disclosed to an authority to which host ISPs would be accountable. This authority would assess the algorithm and identify any flaws embedded therein.[118] In this way, marginal errors in cases of material removals would be eliminated and users and consumers' rights would be safeguarded to a great extent. Otherwise, as Frosio points out 'unsupervised AI pervasiveness has the capacity to lower dramatically human rights standards online'.[119] This means that the lack of supervision of algorithmic enforcement might encroach upon fundamental rights of users such as the right to freedom of expression and information and thus lead to censorship. Further elaboration on the nature of this authority is discussed in chapter nine where the principles and main functions of the proposed host ISP supervisory authority are set out.

However, apart from the right to explanation that internet users should have towards the removal of their material and the possibility of a partial disclosure of the algorithms that host ISPs use in order to remove material from their networks to a proposed host ISP supervisory authority, it could be argued that another type of a transparency obligation could be adopted at operational level of host ISPs, namely the terms of service of host ISPs.

B. Operational Transparency

The terms of service of host ISPs usually make users aware of the practices that they adopt towards their subscribers. These terms of services give online users the opportunity to submit a counter-notification for the removal of the content that users have uploaded. For instance, YouTube gives the opportunity to its users to submit a counter-notification when their content has been removed.[120]

However, this does not mean that every host ISP gives this opportunity to its subscribers or, if it is offered, it might cover different kinds of material. For example, a survey conducted by a non-profit online censorship organisation found that Instagram and Facebook offer a counter-notification option only in cases where the profile of the user has been removed.[121] On the other hand, Twitter offers the possibility for counter-notification to any form of removal,[122] while Google, following the right to be forgotten case,[123] implemented a particular content removal request at the bottom

[118] T Harford, 'Algorithms judge us so know their rules' *Financial Times* (22 November 2019) www.ft.com/content/e155f91a-0b86-11ea-b2d6-9bf4d1957a67.

[119] Frosio (n 68) 33.

[120] support.google.com/youtube/answer/2807684?hl=en-GB.

[121] Online censorship, 'Unfriending censorship: insights from four months of crowdsourced data on social media censorship' (2016) 17, www.onlinecensorship.org/en/news-and-analysis/44.

[122] ibid.

[123] Case 131/12 *Google Spain SL, Google Inc. v Agencia Española de Protección de Datos and Mario Costeja González* [2014] ECR I-000; see also O Lynskey, 'Control over personal data in a digital age: Google Spain v AEPD and Mario Costeja Gonzalez' (2015) 78 *Modern Law Review* 522–34.

of its search listings results.[124] Ebay gives the opportunity for counter-notification of listings that include counterfeit goods but those counter-notices shall only be sent to the rights holders[125] whilst Amazon seems to offer this opportunity to the sellers whose listings have been removed in the US.[126]

By introducing a right to counter-notify the erroneous removal of content, internet users would be offered the appropriate legal remedy to claim their legal rights. The right to have the appropriate remedy is explicitly included in Article 47 of the EU Charter of Fundamental Rights.

However, the right of internet users for a counter-notification might lack essence if it is not accompanied by a notification sent to internet users when their content has been removed. The importance of notifying the affected parties of a dispute is not a novelty since it has already been endorsed at judicial level. For instance, with regard to blocking injunctions, in the *Cartier II* case,[127] it has been outlined that when a blocking injunction is ordered, the blocking website shall not just note that this specific site is blocked. Rather, it shall give information to the parties that requested the blocking injunction and provide further information on affected internet users who wish to challenge the order.[128] In a similar fashion, in the *FAPL v BT* case, which was about a live blocking order,[129] it was deemed that a notification shall be sent to host ISPs each week when their IP address is blocked as well as to subscribers of the providers in case they wish to challenge the blocking order.

This understanding implies that a transparency obligation at operational level of host ISPs shall not restrict appeal mechanisms in cases of counter-notifications. Rather it shall also cover users' notifications upon the take down of their content by host ISPs. This view stems from Article 6(1) of the European Convention of Human Rights and Article 47 of the EU Charter of Fundamental Rights. Both Articles address the right to a fair trial and a right to the appropriate remedy or more informally the equality of arms. This means that each party in a dispute shall be granted the same rights and not be placed in a disadvantageous position against the other party. In the case of host ISPs, this means that users shall be informed that their material has been removed and thus can seek a recourse of their rights. In doing so, users will be aware that their material has been removed and could thus challenge the decision.[130] Therefore, an effective review system, as Kaleda refers to it, will come to the forefront and safeguard internet users' rights.[131] Otherwise, procedural users' rights will be jeopardised and, since the material would remain hidden, users' rights to impart information and prevent other users from accessing it would be impeded.

[124] Google, EU Privacy Removal, Personal Information Removal Request Form.

[125] eBay, pages.ebay.com/seller-center/listing-and-marketing/verified-rights-owner-program.html#m22_tb_a1__4.

[126] sellercentral.amazon.com/gp/help/external/G202017130?language=en_US.

[127] *Cartier v BskyB* (2014) EWHC 3354 (Ch).

[128] ibid 264.

[129] *FAPL v BT* (2017) EWHC 27.

[130] Citron (n 67) 1253–54 where Citron notes that 'Inadequate notice will discourage some people from seeking hearing.'

[131] S Kaleda, 'The role of the principle of effective judicial protection in relation to website blocking injunctions' (2017) 8 *Journal of Intellectual Property, Information Technology and E-Commerce Law* 7.

This understanding excludes the belief that a transparency obligation with regard to the terms of services of host ISPs amounts to a detailed exposition of terms and conditions of the operation of host ISPs. This would be impossible and without any practical sense. For example, it has been reported that most users do not read the terms and conditions when they subscribe to an online service. For example, a study conducted by Ben-Shahar and Schneider found that the length of terms and conditions discourage internet users from reading them while the linguistic complexity of terms and conditions is not understandable by internet users at all.[132] Therefore, it seems that including all the decision-making processes and full details about the terms under which host ISPs operate might not be beneficial to users.

From a policy perspective, the adoption of appeal mechanisms and users' notifications have been supported by a wide number of sectors. For instance, the European Commission has introduced several recommendations with regard to transparency in online platforms in its recently issued Recommendation on battling illegal online content. In particular, the European policy makers outlined that there is a need to adopt an appeal mechanism and notify users as a matter of transparent procedures host ISPs must adopt.[133] Similarly, the Recommendation of the Council of Europe on the promotion of respect for freedom of expression and information with regard to internet filters has pointed out that in cases where filtering-based technologies are deployed, 'effective and readily accessible means of recourse and remedy' shall be provided to internet users.[134] Likewise, another Recommendation of the Council of Europe in the field of media and information society notes the need to 'ensure that internet users have access to effective remedies when their rights and freedoms have been restricted or when they believe that their rights have been violated'.[135] In addition, at UK level, the British and Irish Law Education and Technology Association is in favour of adopting transparent procedures with regard to counter-notification procedures for internet users whose material has been erroneously taken down.[136] Finally, the Platform to Business Relations Regulation sets forth in Article 4 that sellers whose accounts have been removed or suspended would need to be given a notice 30 days in advance and provided with a statement of reasons.[137]

[132] O Ben-Shahar and CE Schneider, 'The Failure of Mandated Disclosure' (2011) 159 *University of Pennsylvania Law Review* 647 where the authors found that '… when mandates are too detailed, both disclosers and disclosees have trouble. Forms become so long and elaborate that disclosers have problems assembling and organizing the information, and disclosees do not read them and cannot understand, assimilate, and analyze the avalanche of information'; see also F Marotta-Wurgler, 'Will Increased Disclosure Help? Evaluating the Recommendations of the ALI's 'Principles of the Law of Software Contracts' (2014) 78 *University of Chicago Law Review* 172.

[133] *FAPL v BT* (2017) EWHC 480 Ch. (27).

[134] Committee of Ministers (n 114).

[135] Committee of Ministers (n 115).

[136] British and Irish Legal Education and Technology Association, 'Written evidence submitted for the House of Lords, Select Committee on Communications, "The internet: To Regulate or Not to Regulate? Summary of Response' (2018) 1.

[137] Regulation (EU) 2019/1150 of the European Parliament and of the Council of 20 June 2019 on promoting fairness and transparency for business users of online intermediation services (Text with EEA relevance) PE/56/2019/REV/1, OJ L 186.

Such a stance has been maintained by Frank La Rue, the UN Rapporteur on the promotion and protection of the right to freedom of opinion and expression in his report of April 2018. La Rue criticised the lack of transparent procedures in relation to the removal of content online. More specifically, he stressed that transparency and notifications to users are directly correlated.[138] This is because, as he explains, operational transparency 'alleviates the pressure on notifications in individual cases, while weaker overall transparency increases the likelihood that users will be unable to understand individual removals in the absence of notifications tailored to specific cases'.[139] Otherwise, users would be unaware of the removal of their content in the first place and they would not be able to challenge it. Along similar lines, in light of the practices that Facebook uses in order to remove terroristic content from its platform, the UN Rapporteur addressed a letter to Facebook's CEO stressing the need to apply the Guiding Principles on Business and Human Rights that encourage the approach of 'respect, protect, remedy'.[140] In this sense, Facebook shall notify its users after their content has been removed and offer them the appropriate procedural safeguards to contest the removal.[141]

Lastly, this view has been echoed by prominent voices in academic scholarship who outline the need for sending notifications to users/traders after their content is removed. In particular, De Gregorio recommends a human rights approach towards the removal of content online.[142] Such an approach, he argues, should include notification to users, along with the opportunity for them to appeal the decision. This approach should be introduced on a mandatory basis. In similar fashion, Riordan[143] and Kaleda,[144] in the context of a blocking injunction, explain that it has been observed that many users are not aware that specific websites are blocked. For this reason, they argue that a notice to individual users or at least a general notice would enhance their awareness of the reasons that trigger the blocking of the site as well as the review process.

In addition, operational transparency presupposes that terms are not only clear with regard to policies on terminating accounts or appealing accounts' blocking but also visible to the internet users/consumers. For instance, the Memorandum of Understanding on the sale of counterfeit goods on the internet outlines a number of terms that should be made clear at the website when consumers are purchasing a specific product.[145] Amidst the points to address, there must be information about the seller,

[138] European Commission, 'Recommendation of 1.3.2018 on measures to effectively tackle illegal content online Brussels' COM (2018) 1177 final.

[139] Report of the Special Rapporteur on the promotion and protection of the right to freedom of opinion and expression (6 April 2018) 13.

[140] Guiding Principles on Business and Human Rights on Implementing the United Nations, 'Protect, Respect and Remedy Framework' www.ohchr.org/documents/publications/GuidingprinciplesBusinesshr_eN.pdf.

[141] Mandate of the Special Rapporteur on the promotion and protection of human rights and fundamental freedoms while countering terrorism (2018) 7.

[142] G De Gregorio, 'Expressions on Platforms: Freedom of Expression and ISP liability in the European Digital Single Market' (2018) *CoRe* 214.

[143] J Riordan, *The Liability of Internet Intermediaries* (Oxford, Oxford University Press, 2016) 457–58.

[144] Kaleda (n 131) 7.

[145] European Commission, 'Report on the functioning of the Memorandum of Understanding on the sale of counterfeit goods on the internet' (2020) 12.

the reviews and ratings of the sellers must be visible to the consumer, any complaints or refund policy must be clearly stated on the website. Further, with regard to the termination of sellers' accounts due to counterfeit goods, rights holders urge the need to refer to the website information regarding the number of notifications before the suspension or termination of a seller's account and the evidence that is needed to be provided if the removal is due to a fake report by the right holder. In similar fashion, the European Committee in the House of Lords urges for visible policies with regard to the listings of goods. In particular, the report states that 'The rating and review systems used by online platforms are instrumental in creating the trust necessary for consumers to engage in online transactions. To ensure transparency, however, we believe that all online platforms should have publicly accessible policies for handling negative reviews, and clearly distinguish between user reviews and paid-for promotions …'[146] Finally, the Platforms to Business Relations Regulation[147] sets forth in Article 3 paragraph 5 that the identity of the seller needs to be visible while the Proposal for a Digital Services Act Regulation follows the same rationale and notes that 'Providers of intermediary services shall include information on any restrictions that they impose in relation to the use of their service in respect of information provided by the recipients of the service, in their terms and conditions. That information shall include information on any policies, procedures, measures and tools used for the purpose of content moderation, including algorithmic decision-making and human review. It shall be set out in clear and unambiguous language and shall be publicly available in an easily accessible format.'[148] In this way, traders' awareness of policies and consumers' confidence will be promoted, thus attributing to the overall trust to e-commerce.

On the basis of the above, a transparency obligation at operational level of host ISPs would address an effective review mechanism. Such mechanism shall include users' notification as well as the appropriate appeal mechanisms to contest the decision of host ISPs with regard to the removal of their content. In this way, internet users' rights would be safeguarded, and potential abuses would be mitigated.

C. Transparency Reports

Finally, another context where transparency should be applicable can be found in transparency reports. Transparency reports are already issued on a voluntary basis from a handful of host ISPs while European policy makers have also stressed the mandatory need for issuing transparency reports.

Google was the first to introduce transparency reports in September 2010.[149] Following Google's reports, a handful of host ISPs followed suit in response to the requests they

[146] European Committee, 'Chapter 7: Consumer protection and online platforms' publications.parliament.uk/pa/ld201516/ldselect/ldeucom/129/12910.htm#_idTextAnchor.

[147] Regulation (EU) 2019/1150 of the European Parliament and of the Council of 20 June 2019 on promoting fairness and transparency for business users of online intermediation services (2019) OJ L 186.

[148] Proposal for a Regulation of the European Parliament and of the Council on a Single Market For Digital Services (Digital Services Act) and amending Directive 2000/31/EC COM/2020/825 final.

[149] Global Information Society Watch, 'The internet and corruption: Transparency and accountability online' (2012) 26.

receive in order to remove content from their platforms.[150] Likewise, at policy level, a number of European documents have also reinforced the need for issuing transparency reports. For instance, the Communication on tackling illegal content online notes that host ISPs 'should publish transparency reports with sufficiently detailed information on the number and type of notices received and actions taken, as well as the time taken for processing, and the source of the notification'.[151] What is more, at legislative level, Germany is the first European Member State that has issued a special Law for Social Media with regard to the removal of unlawful content from their networks.[152] According to this Network Enforcement Law, host ISPs have an obligation to issue transparency reports every six months, entailing the number of removal requests and the final removals of illegal content. Refusing to comply with the transparency obligation might trigger fines of between 5–10 million euros for host ISPs.

The main idea behind the issue of such transparency reports, as MicKinnon reveals, 'involves censorship and surveillance carried out not by government agents or Internet police but by the private sector'.[153] This means that with transparency reports, companies want to communicate to the public the criteria that trigger the removal of online content and defend themselves against potential criticism. Such criticism relies on thorny issues of censoring content online and overseeing internet users' activities. While the matter of surveillance is out of the scope of this research, censoring content is one of the central issues. For instance, a number of civil society organisations, such as Open Rights Group, argue that host ISPs tend to overzealously block material in order to exonerate themselves from liability under the safe harbour provisions of the ECD.[154]

To tackle this criticism, host ISPs include in their transparency reports more information about the removal of the content. For instance, they specify the reasons that generate the removal of the material and, in particular, whether it was for issues related to copyright, hate speech, nudism or violation of community standards. In addition, they include information about who made this request, for instance, whether it is a private or governmental request. In this way, internet users' trust towards the services host ISPs offer is reinforced.[155]

However, the issue of transparency reports might not only promote users' trust towards the online services. Indeed, transparency reports would enable a proposed host ISP supervisory authority, which is discussed in chapter nine, to oversee the right functioning of host ISPs' operation. As already seen in chapter two, host ISPs' role nowadays is not restricted to the role of an intermediary. Rather, host ISPs enforce intellectual property rights and shape our information environment. The majority of

[150] A Holland et al, 'NOC online intermediaries case studies series: intermediary liability in the United States' (18 February 2015) *Berkman Center for Internet and Society* 60; Urban, Karaganis and Schofield (n 92) 9.

[151] European Commission, 'Communication on tackling illegal content online towards an enhanced responsibility of online intermediaries' (2017) COM 555 final 16.

[152] Bundesministerium der Justiz and fuer Verbraucherschutz, Netzwerkungsdurchgesetz, see www.bmjv.de/SharedDocs/FAQ/EN/NetzDG/NetzDG.html.

[153] R McKinnon, *Consent of the Networked: The Worldwide struggle for Internet Freedom* (New York, Basic Books, 2012) 210.

[154] Open Rights Group, Web Blocking, see www.openrightsgroup.org/issues/web-blocking.

[155] Holland et al (n 150) 63.

consumers rely on their e-commerce services in order to purchase goods. Given that the activities of host ISPs directly affect rights holders and internet users, the issue of transparency reports would enable their compliance with the existing legal provisions and the rule of law.

Yet, it could be argued that a mandatory issuing of transparency reports would not receive a warm welcome from the majority of host ISPs. Indeed, host ISPs claim that the mandatory publication of transparency reports will place an additional burden on host ISPs since such reports may increase their transaction costs.[156] This means that host ISPs might need to engage a higher number of human labour resources in order to formulate such reports as well as additional employees to manage the system. In this way, host ISPs with higher revenues would be able to issue such reports, whereas new entrants on the market might face difficulties in issuing such reports annually.

In light of this discrepancy, this book argues for the issue of transparency reports for companies with a certain annual turnover. To attribute responsibilities to host ISPs according to their size is not a novelty at European level.[157] Supporting this argument, Article 17 of the DSMD addresses OCSSPs that host large amounts of content.[158] Although it lacks clarity, this Article implies that filtering mechanisms should be deployed from those host ISPs which enable the dissemination of a large amount of content such as the GAFA group.[159] Along similar lines, the text from the EU Parliament excludes from the adoption of a filtering mechanism those host ISPs that have less than €10M annual turnover and employ fewer than 50 employees.[160]

However, other critical voices against the issue of transparency reports argue that they might meet with criticism from civil society organisations and associations for the enforcement of rights online. This is because the reports would reveal the internal mechanisms host ISPs adopt in order to take down material from the platforms. It is these internal mechanisms that might generate criticism towards host ISPs' practices. Such criticism could address the thresholds of unlawfulness that should be embedded into a work or different view as to how ISPs should handle notices for copyright infringements. This understanding may lead to an influx of notices from rights holders to host ISPs. Given that rights holders would now know the thresholds of illegality that trigger the removal of the content, they could send notifications for removal to host ISPs. Yet, this understanding might have a dual effect. On the one hand, if host ISPs removed the allegedly infringing material upon receiving notification, rights holders would be satisfied. On the other hand, if host ISPs did not respond or ignored the notices from rights holders, there would be a high risk of lawsuits against them.[161] This is mainly because rights holders would be aware of the instances where host ISPs did not comply with the procedures.

[156] Urban, Karaganis and Schofield (n 92) 50.

[157] C Angelopoulos, 'EU Copyright Reform: Outside the Safe Harbours, Intermediary Liability Capsizes into Incoherence' (*Kluwer Copyright blog*, 6 October 2016) copyrightblog.kluweriplaw.com/2016/10/06/eu-copyright-reform-outside-safe-harbours-intermediary-liability-capsizes-incoherence/.

[158] Council Directive 2019/790/EC of the European Parliament and of the Council of 17 April 2019 on copyright and related rights in the Digital Single Market and amending Directives 96/9/EC and 2001/29/EC (Text with EEA relevance) PE/51/2019/REV/1, OJ L 130, 17.5.2019 (hereinafter DSMD).

[159] Angelopoulos (n 157); GAFA: Google, Amazon, Facebook, Apple.

[160] J Reda, 'Article 13 is back on – and it got worse, not better' (*Julia Reda's website*, 5 February 2019) juliareda.eu/2019/02/article-13-worse/.

[161] Urban, Karaganis and Schofield (n 92) 50.

Yet, this pitfall could be eliminated by applying a different level of transparency to this kind of report. This means that a detailed explanation of the internal procedures would amount to citing copyright removals depending on countries who requested them and what were the thresholds of unlawfulness. This type of concern has emerged in light of all the transparency reports issued by host ISPs nowadays on a voluntary basis. On closer examination, it can be observed that the great majority of reports do not indicate the country from which the request has been sent.[162] For example, Twitter refrains from specifying the country of origin of the request,[163] as do Facebook,[164] and YouTube.[165] This information is valuable since it enables rights holders to assess whether host ISPs' removals abide by the copyright rules. Given copyright standards vary from country to country, sometimes the requirements for a work to constitute a parody in the UK differ from the requirements for that work to be considered as a parody in the Greek legal system.[166] This means that a right holder could more easily assess whether the removal of the specific content in this jurisdiction complied with the national legislation.

With regard to trade mark infringements, transparency reports should include specific information about the removal of counterfeit goods, any counter-notices and the justifications for removal. This would offer a benefit for brand owners who would be able to assess whether host ISPs safeguard their platforms from fake goods and services. For instance, as per the report on the Memorandum of Understanding on the sale of counterfeit goods on the internet, rights holders ask for transparency reports that consist of '… URLs of the removed listings, information on the reasons for removing the listings, details of sellers on whom restrictions have been imposed'.[167] This implies that brand owners would be in a position to examine whether the host ISPs fulfil their duty of care and therefore remove the allegedly infringing listings from their networks.

Overall, it could be extrapolated that different contexts require different levels of transparency. This is because, as discussed earlier, one single type of transparency would not accommodate the different interests at stake, namely the interests of host ISPs, rights holders and internet users. For instance, if full transparency was applicable to algorithms, host ISPs' business welfare would be endangered while at the same time it would not be beneficial to average unskilled users. In contrast, it is only highly skilled users, potential hackers or competitors of a host ISP that could benefit from the disclosure of the full algorithm. Therefore, this book argues for two measures to be introduced. Firstly, the introduction of a right to explanation would mean that users can request more information about the removal of their content, and secondly, an authority should be established to audit the algorithms that host ISPs use. Another context where a

[162] Global Information Society Watch, 'The Internet and corruption: Transparency and accountability online' (2012) 26.

[163] transparency.twitter.com/en/copyright-notices.html.

[164] transparency.facebook.com/.

[165] transparencyreport.google.com/copyright/overview?hl=en.

[166] www.copyrightuser.org/understand/exceptions/parody-pastiche/.

[167] European Commission, 'Report on the functioning of the Memorandum of Understanding on the sale of counterfeit goods on the internet' (2020) 12.

transparency obligation should be applicable is the terms of service of host ISPs. In this case, this book argues that host ISPs should be compelled to notify users after their content has been removed and offer the appropriate counter-notification procedures so that users can appeal host ISPs' decisions. In this way, fundamental rights such as the right to effective remedy and to a fair trial would be respected. Finally, a transparency obligation would amount to the issue of transparency reports. Such transparency reports would not include internal technical procedures of host ISPs, thus preventing users from being able to circumvent them. Rather, they would include a list of removals related to copyright or trade mark classified per country and the specific reasons that lead to the removal of the content. Subsequently, users would be aware of the requests that had originated from each country and the reasons that triggered the removal or non-removal of their content.

V. Conclusion

This chapter has engaged in a critical discussion to endorse a statutory transparency obligation for host ISPs. This is because, as discussed in section III of this chapter, from a normative perspective, a transparency obligation would promote the rule of law. For instance, it would give users information about the content management policies that host ISPs follow. Therefore, users would be able to observe whether the host ISP abides by the rules and either justify or challenge the decision. The non-disclosure of information about the conditions that lead to the removal of content would undermine the rule of law and the principle of due process. This is because internet users would be deprived of the right to effective remedy and to a fair trial as enshrined in the EU Charter of Fundamental Rights and the European Convention on Human Rights respectively.

Further, the imposition of a transparency obligation would warrant the legitimacy of host ISPs' activities and thus enhance confidence for e-commerce services to online consumers. This is because transparency users would be aware of the thresholds that generated the removal of their material. Without disclosing the thresholds that generated the removal of the content, users would have doubts about the conditions that led to their material being removed and this would call into question the legitimate basis of this removal.

Apart from enhancing important democratic values, a transparency obligation would have a positive impact on transactions between host ISPs and consumers. This is because it would curb the existing information asymmetries. This understanding finds applicability mainly in the trade mark context where transactions between consumers and online auction platforms take place. In particular, with a transparency obligation, consumers in the online world would have more information about the goods that are displayed online and, therefore, their trust in the online services would be enhanced.

However, the introduction of a transparency obligation would not only safeguard users' rights but also induce host ISPs to adopt better practices. Under the fear of being disgraced or publicly criticised about their methods, host ISPs would be induced to undertake a prior assessment of their practices before they put them into practice and observe their outcomes. In this way, it is possible to argue that transparency would mitigate any errors or malfunctions and thus improve the principles of good governance.

It should be noted that, given that 'different contexts require different levels of transparency',[168] such a transparency obligation should be shaped accordingly. For instance, if the algorithms that host ISPs use were fully disclosed, the competitors of host ISPs along with potential hackers might either copy or more easily circumvent them. As a corollary, if the competitors of a host ISP copy its algorithm, then the host ISP might lose its competitive edge. Further, if potential hackers manage to more easily circumvent the algorithm, its business model and thus its credibility would be in serious doubt.

Therefore, this book argues for the introduction of a right to explanation so that users can request more information about the decision-making process of host ISPs. At the same time, the algorithms would only be disclosed in front of the previously proposed host ISP supervisory authority that would control its proper operation.

Another context to which a transparency obligation should apply is the terms of services of host ISPs. For instance, by notifying the users when their content has been removed as well as providing them with counter-notification mechanisms would enhance users' fundamental rights such as the right to fair trial and the right to appropriate remedy. Such terms shall not only be clear but also visible to online consumers. This means that host ISPs shall indicate in a clear and visible manner for the sake of online consumers the seller's details, the reviews and ratings for the products, refunds or complaints policies. For sellers, host ISPs need to be clear and provide information on the conditions for blocking or suspending sellers' accounts along with guidance on appealing the termination of the account.

Finally, a transparency obligation should include the issue of transparency reports. Such transparency reports would refrain from including internal technical procedures that host ISPs use in order to remove material from their networks. Rather, these transparency reports would include a list of removals for copyright and trade mark violations per country and the reasons that warrant such a removal. In this way, users would be aware of which requests come from a specific country, the reasons that justified their removal and thus their trust in the host ISP would be enhanced. In addition, with regard to fake goods and services, the transparency reports shall include specific information about the removal of counterfeit listings and the specific URLS so that sellers are aware of the reasons for taking down the products while brand owners would be able to assess whether host ISPs comply with their duty of care. These transparency reports would also enable the proposed host ISP supervisory authority to check the operation of host ISPs and assess the compliance of their practice with the existing rule.

In this light, the following chapter engages with the proposed host ISP supervisory authority and, in particular, it discusses the normative considerations for the proposed host ISP supervisory authority as well as the principles and functions of the proposed host ISP supervisory authority and schemes for funding.

[168] Caplan, Donovan, Hanson and Matthews (n 63).

9

Establishing a Supervisory Authority: A Proposal

I. Introduction

As elaborated in chapters seven and eight, within the proposed responsibility framework based on co-regulation, host ISPs shall be assigned with a set of responsibilities. Such proposed responsibilities shall focus on curbing the growth of online infringements, while at the same time they shall respect the fundamental rights of internet users. For instance, it was suggested in chapter seven that host ISPs should have a duty of care towards the unlawful content or counterfeit goods that are disseminated within their networks, while at the same time and as discussed in chapter eight, they should have an obligation of transparency towards their users with regard to the removal of the content they host and the goods they circulate within their networks.

As discussed in chapter seven, the proposed responsibility framework shall be based on a co-regulation scheme. Drawing on the internet regulatory theories discussed in chapter one, a co-regulatory regime implies a state interference to regulate internet users' actions via host ISPs. It is this state interference that could be illustrated in the establishment of a host ISP supervisory authority to which host ISPs shall be accountable.[1]

The idea of a supervisory authority has already been exemplified at policy and scholarship level. For instance, it can be traced in Article 17(9) of the DSMD that envisages the creation of a mechanism whose main purpose is to deal with users' complaints: 'Member States shall also ensure that out-of-court redress mechanisms are available for

[1] RJ Barcel and K Koelman, 'Intermediary liability in the E-Commerce Directive: so far so good, but it's not enough' (2000) 16 *Computer Law and Security Report* 237; M Bunting, 'Keeping Consumers Safe Online Legislating for platform accountability for online content' (2018) *Communications Chambers* 33; K Garstka, 'Looking above and beyond the blunt expectation: specified request as the recommended approach to intermediary liability in cyberspace' (2016) 7 *European Journal of Law and Technology* 15; M Tessier, J Herzog and L Madzou, 'Regulation at the Age of Online Platform-Based Economy: Accountability, User Empowerment and Responsiveness' in L Belli and N Zingales (eds), *Platform Regulations: How Platforms are Regulated and How They Regulate Us – Official Outcome of the UN IGF Dynamic Coalition on Platform Responsibility*, United Nations Internet Governance Forum Geneva (2017) 182–83; S Jacques and K Garstka, 'Automated anti-piracy systems: A call for further evidence-based policies' (*Kluwer Copyright blog*, 4 April 2019) kluweriplaw.com/2019/04/04/automated-anti-piracy-systems-a-call-for-further-evidence-based-policies; E Laidlaw, 'Private Power, Public Interest: An Examination of Search Engine Accountability' (2009) 17 *International Journal of Law and Information Technology* 141.

the settlement of disputes.'[2] The creation of such a body has also been discussed in the course of the whole legislative process of drafting this Directive. The Council's compromised text noted in Article 13(7) that 'Member States shall endeavor to put in place independent bodies to assess complaints related to the application of the measures',[3] while in similar terms the EU Parliament's compromised text Article 13(2b) noted that 'Member States shall ensure that users have access to an independent body for the resolution of disputes ....'[4]

Likewise, the proposed DSA Regulation envisages in Article 38 the creation of Digital Services Coordinators, which would be competent authorities within the jurisdiction of each EU Member State.[5] Such authorities would be responsible for the application and enforcement of the provisions in the Regulation. Finally, the Audiovisual Media Services Directive envisages the development of regulatory bodies in each EU Member State. In particular, Article 28(b)(5) states, 'Member States shall establish the necessary mechanisms to assess the appropriateness of the measures referred to in paragraph 3 taken by video-sharing platform providers. Member States shall entrust the assessment of those measures to the national regulatory authorities or bodies.'[6]

Apart from the DSMD which requires the establishment of an independent body to handle emerging disputes online, initiatives or suggestions for creating independent bodies that deal with disputes, either between host ISPs and online users or between host ISPs and right holders, have been witnessed at national level in Member States,[7] or have been recommended through empirical studies by academic scholarship, respectively.[8]

[2] Council Directive (EC) 2019/790/EC of the European Parliament and of the Council of 17 April 2019 on copyright and related rights in the Digital Single Market and amending Directives 96/9/EC and 2001/29/EC (Text with EEA relevance) PE/51/2019/REV/1, OJ L 130 (hereinafter DSMD).

[3] Council, Proposal for a Directive of the European Parliament and of the Council on copyright in the Digital Single Market – Agreed negotiating mandate, Interinstitutional File: 2016/0280 (COD).

[4] EU Parliament, P8_TA-Prov (2018) 0337, Copyright in the Digital Single Market, Amendments adopted by the European Parliament on 12 September 2018 on the proposal for a directive of the European Parliament and of the Council on copyright in the Digital Single Market (COM (2016) 0593- C8-0383/2016- 2016/0280 (COD)).

[5] Proposal for a Regulation of the European Parliament and of the Council on a Single Market For Digital Services (Digital Services Act) and amending Directive 2000/31/EC COM/2020/825 final 2.

[6] Directive 2010/13/EU of the European Parliament and of the Council of 10 March 2010 on the coordination of certain provisions laid down by law, regulation or administrative action in Member States concerning the provision of audiovisual media services (Audiovisual Media Services Directive) (Text with EEA relevance) OJ L 95, 15.4.2010.

[7] In France, Autorité de régulation de la communication audiovisuelle et numérique (ARCOM) https://www.arcom.fr/; In the UK, HM Government, 'Online Harms (White Paper)' (April 2019) 57; In Germany, Bundesministerium der Justiz and fuer Verbraucherschutz, Netzwerkungsdurchgesetz, see www.bmjv.de/SharedDocs/FAQ/EN/NetzDG/NetzDG.html; EU Parliament, 'Legislative resolution of 17 April 2019 on the proposal for a regulation of the European Parliament and of the Council on preventing the dissemination of terrorist content online' (COM(2018)0640 – C8-0405/2018 – 2018/0331(COD)); Council Directive (EU) 2018/1808 on the coordination of certain provisions laid down by law, regulation or administrative action in Member States concerning the provision of audiovisual media services (Audiovisual Media Services Directive) in view of changing market realities (2018) OJ L 303.

[8] Tessier, Herzog and Madzou (n 1) 182, United Nations Internet Governance Forum Geneva (2018) 182; 'UK Gov Aim to Make ISP Piracy Website Blocks Cheaper and Easier' (*ISP review*, 15 June 2018) www.ispreview.co.uk/index.php/2018/06/uk-gov-to-make-isp-piracy-website-blocks-cheaper-and-easier.html; L Edwards suggests the appointment of 'An Ombudsman able to get remedies for users' in L Edwards, 'With Great Power Comes Great Responsibility? The Rise of Platform Liability' in L Edwards (ed), *Law, Policy and*

Against this background, this chapter explores the underlying needs for the establishment of a supervisory authority for host ISPs with regard to copyright and trade mark infringements that accrue within their networks. In particular, it discusses the normative considerations of introducing such an authority, the scope of the proposed authority, as well as the principles and functions under which it would operate.

II. Normative Considerations for the Proposed Host ISP Supervisory Authority

Although a co-regulatory approach is not common in the field of Intellectual Property Law, there is a plethora of reasons that would justify the establishment of a host ISP supervisory authority. Such an authority would be established in each Member State and would operate under the umbrella of an EU authority, such as the Directorate-General for Communications Networks, Content, and Technology.[9]

Firstly, the creation of a host ISP authority for copyright and trade mark infringements might enhance legal certainty among right holders, host ISPs, and internet users. This is because, as discussed in chapter three, the current legal legislative framework under the ECD seems outdated. This is mainly due to the lack of harmonisation of secondary liability rules at European level, along with the different interpretations of Article 14(1) of the ECD. What is more, as my findings indicate, the current legal framework under the DSMD is controversial since it entails an array of problematic aspects that aggravate the existing legal uncertainty which has already been triggered by the ECD. As a corollary of this framework, right holders are unsure about the protection of their rights, and host ISPs are not sure of the specific conditions under which they may evade liability. For this reason, to hold host ISPs to account to a host ISP supervisory authority for fulfilling specific obligations would provide a more robust legal framework for right holders and host ISPs, respectively. Indeed, Hugenholtz has pointed out that in cases where fundamental rights come to the forefront, only clear and codified legal provisions may safeguard rights holders' interests, but they will also promote internet users' rights to freedom of expression and personal data.[10] Yet, this does not mean that users or right holders should not seek redress from the courts. The establishment of a

the Internet (Oxford, Hart Publishing, 2019) 289; K Garstka, 'Guiding the Blind Bloodhounds: How to Mitigate the Risks art. 17 of Directive 2019/790 poses to the Freedom of Expression' in P Torremans (ed), *Intellectual Property and Human Rights* (Alphen aan den Rijn, Kluwer Law International, 2020); M Vermeulen, 'Online content: to regulate or not to regulate – is that the question?' (2019) *Association for progressive communications* 10–11; S Kulk, *Internet Intermediaries and Copyright Law: EU and US perspective* (Alphen aan den Rijn, Kluwer Law International, 2019) 305; F Wilman, *The Responsibility of Online Intermediaries for Illegal User Content in the EU and US* (Cheltenham, Edward Elgar, 2020) 322, 326.

[9] DG Communications Networks, Content and Technology, see ec.europa.eu/info/departments/communications-networks-content-and-technology_en#responsibilities, The same approach is followed in data protection field with the European Data Protection Board, see further in N Lomba and T Evas, 'Digital Services Act: European Added value assessment' (2020) *European Parliamentary Research Service* 223; see also in the financial sector with the European Systemic Risk Council in J Larosiere, 'Report on High-level on financial supervision in the EU' (2009) 44.

[10] PB Hugenholtz, 'Codes of Conduct and Copyright enforcement in cyberspace' in I Stamatoudi (ed), *Copyright Enforcement and the Internet* (Alphen aan den Rijn, Kluwer Law International, 2010) 320.

host ISP supervisory authority needs to be applied without prejudice to the fundamental right of internet users and right holders to resort to the courts' legal arena when their rights have been violated.[11]

The establishment of a host ISP supervisory authority might not only enhance legal certainty to rights holders, but also to host ISPs. As mentioned above, due to the outdated legal framework under the ECD, along with the controversial regime under the DSMD (each elaborated on in chapters three and four, respectively), the existence of such an authority would promote legal certainty to host ISPs. This understanding might safeguard their right to conduct business as per Article 16 of the EU Charter of Fundamental Rights since host ISPs would be sure of how to adjust their business models in order to comply with the rules. Further, another corollary to the creation of a host ISP supervisory authority is the adoption of clearer rules about the procedures they follow. Finally, to avoid being highly sanctioned for non-compliance with the rules, host ISPs might be forced to deploy even more sophisticated technology to mitigate online infringements. Therefore, a host ISP supervisory authority might not only safeguard content owners' and brand owners' rights, but also encourage host ISPs to adopt more efficient practices in order to prevent sanctions.

Secondly, another reason that indicates the need to create a host ISP supervisory authority revolves around the facilitation of internet users' and right holders' access to justice.[12] Access to justice is understood as the access of citizens to judicial redress mechanisms in order to protect their rights. This is because, as explained in chapters three and four, the current legislative framework under the ECD and the DSMD seems to fail to meet the expectations of the parties involved. As Laidlaw points out, there is a risk that the lack of effective judicial redress could lead to internet users turning to host ISPs for complaints.[13] Indeed, this understanding was exemplified in Article 17(9) of the DSMD which dictates,

> Member States shall also ensure that out-of-court redress mechanisms are available for the settlement of disputes. Such mechanisms shall enable disputes to be settled impartially and shall not deprive the user of the legal protection afforded by national law, without prejudice to the rights of users to have recourse to efficient judicial remedies.

In similar fashion, the proposed DSA Regulation envisages the creation of independent bodies that would be entitled to the compliance of rules in the digital world.[14] In particular, Article 38 states that

> Member States shall designate one of the competent authorities as their Digital Services Coordinator. The Digital Services Coordinator shall be responsible for all matters relating

[11] As set out in Articles 47–50 of the EU Charter of Fundamental Rights, fra.europa.eu/en/charterpedia/title/vi-justice.

[12] E Laidlaw, 'Are We Asking Too Much from Defamation Law? Reputation Systems, ADR, Industry Regulation and Other Extra-Judicial Possibilities for Protecting Reputation in the Internet Age: Proposal for Reform' (2017) 6, see www.lco-cdo.org/wp-content/uploads/2017/07/DIA-Commissioned-Paper-Laidlaw.pdf; P Chapdelaine, 'Copyright User Rights and Remedies: An access justice perspective' (2018) *Laws* 7–10; I Barral-Vinals, 'Enforcing e-consumer protection beyond alternative dispute resolution (ADR): ODR' in J Devenney and M Kenny (eds), *European Consumer Protection: Theory and Practice* (Oxford, Oxford University Press, 2012) 88.

[13] Laidlaw (n 12) 75.

[14] Proposal for a Regulation of the European Parliament and the Council on a Single Market For Digital Services (Digital Services Act) and amending Directive 2000/31/EC COM/2020/825 final (hereinafter Proposed DSA Regulation).

> to application and enforcement of this Regulation in that Member State, unless the Member State concerned has assigned certain specific tasks or sectors to other competent authorities.

Yet, as explained in chapter four, the establishment of dispute resolution mechanisms by host ISPs might prompt reflections on their credibility, thus they would not guarantee redress for users whose rights have been infringed. A number of instances that criticise the inadequacy of dispute resolution mechanisms operated by host ISPs can be found in empirical studies and academic scholarship contributions. For instance, a study conducted by Jacques and others on the impact of YouTube on cultural diversity[15] found that 'the current online creative ecosystem already relies on private agreements reached between right holders and host ISPs at the expense of the wider public'.[16] In support of this finding, they cite the example of the PRS-YouTube deal. PRS for Music is an association that protects songwriters, singers, and musicians. The deal between PRS and YouTube states that in case of derogatory use, PRS will send a notification to YouTube and cooperate with the host ISP in order to take down the specific work.[17] Therefore, it may be possible to observe that the dispute resolution mechanisms operated by host ISPs might favour their business interests and exclude users' right of access to justice.

Yet, given there is 'no right without a remedy',[18] internet users must be offered an efficient redress mechanism. This role would be played by a host ISP supervisory authority which would serve as a place where users' complaints would be addressed. Otherwise, internet users' access to justice might be restricted.

Thirdly, the creation of a host ISP supervisory authority might enhance legitimacy and accountability. This is because the power and legitimacy of a supervisory authority stems from authorised government bodies. This means that the authority is accountable to government actors for its actions or omissions. In this sense, citizens' rights, such as the freedom of expression or the right to privacy, would be safeguarded. Indeed, in the context of a discussion of the advantages of co-regulatory approaches, Marsden has pointed out that co-regulatory approaches address issues which promote accountability, enhance legitimacy, and respect human rights in the online world.[19]

What is more, the creation of a host ISP supervisory authority might ensure the proper functioning of the duty of care and the transparency obligations that host ISPs must undertake.[20] This is because, within the responsibility framework suggested in this

[15] S Jacques et al 'An Empirical Study of the Use of Automated Anti-Piracy Systems and their Consequences for Cultural Diversity' (2018) 15 *Scripted* 277.

[16] ibid 308.

[17] Music Business Worldwide, 'PRS deal with YouTube: what does it mean for songwriters?' (6 September 2009) www.musicbusinessworldwide.com/prs-deal-with-youtube-what-does-it-mean-for-songwriters; Electronic Frontier Foundation considers this as a 'fair use massacre' is in S Mcsherry, 'The Fair Use Massacre Continues: Now Warner's Going After the Babies' (*EFF*, 12 March 2009) www.eff.org/deeplinks/2009/03/fair-use-massacre-continues-now-warner-s-going-aft.

[18] Footnote (61) in E Katsh and O Rabinovich- Einy, 'It is a settled and invariable principle in the laws of England, that every right when with-held must have a remedy, and every injury it's [*sic*] proper redress.' See E Katsh and O Rabinovich-Einy, *In Digital Justice: Technology and the Internet of Disputes* (Oxford, Oxford University Press, 2017) 15.

[19] C Marsden, *Internet Co-regulation* (Cambridge, Cambridge University Press, 2011) 128.

[20] Ch 9, Section V 1.

book, host ISPs would terminate and prevent further exposure upon notification of the appearance of online infringements within their platforms.[21] However, as seen earlier in chapter eight, a handful of host ISPs prefer to resort to algorithmic enforcement due to the massive scale of content transmitted via their networks. How such algorithms operate remains a 'black box'. For this reason, a number of scholars have suggested that an independent authority could audit the algorithms and identify any flaws which could lead to false removals of content from online platforms.[22] As a corollary of this approach, any restriction to users' free speech rights might be eliminated. At the same time, a host ISP supervisory authority would make sure that host ISPs exercise controls with regard to the goods displayed within their platforms, and thus prevent counterfeit goods from reaching end-consumers. In this way, consumers' rights would be safeguarded.

Moreover, another reason that justifies the creation of a host ISP supervisory authority revolves around the promotion of the rule of law. This is because adjudication duties must only be imposed on entities that are authorised by government institutions and act under the principles of independence, proportionality, and accountability. This governmental institution could be the host ISP supervisory authority that would reach decisions on issues relating to online copyright and trade mark infringements. Otherwise, any decision issued by a non-government body might undermine the rule of law. However, it could be argued that the duty of care proposed for host ISPs would amount to adjudicative duties. This is because it is up to the host ISPs to penalise the alleged infringers, either by removing content or even blocking users' access to specific websites.[23] Yet, a duty of care is not an adjudication instrument. Conversely, duty of care is an instrument that aims to terminate, or at least curb, intellectual property violations within host ISPs' networks. It must be seen as a fundamental tool against piracy online. In any case, it seems ironic to impose adjudicate duties on host ISPs when it is mainly their services that accentuate the rates of copyright and trade mark violations online.[24]

Further justification for the establishment of a host ISP supervisory authority is the protection it affords to the diversity of content. Indeed, it has already been seen that the removal of content by host ISPs can endanger the diversity of content.[25] Considering the use of parody as a study case, it has been found that technological tools used for content identification might remove videos that entail parodies of songs because it may be difficult to identify them as fair dealing. In addition, an empirical study conducted by Erickson and Kretschmer raises concern about the skills and knowledge of human moderators employed by host ISPs to distinguish between fair dealing content

[21] This understanding has been also exemplified in the report of Committee on Economic and Monetary Affairs on the overview and structure of financial supervision and regulation in the U.S Report of the Committee on Economic and Monetary Affairs on the overview and structure of financial supervision and regulation in the U.S (2015), www.europarl.europa.eu/RegData/etudes/STUD/2015/492470/IPOL_STU%282015%29492470_EN.pdf; in particular, the report points out that the disclosure of practices and mechanisms which the companies adopt will eliminate any risks for non-compliance or any other illegality.

[22] F Pasquale, *Black Box Society: The secret algorithms that control money and information* (Harvard University Press, 2015) 3; F Romero-Moreno, '"Notice and stay down" and social media: amending Article 13 of the Proposed Directive on Copyright' (2018) 33 *International Review of Law, Computers and Technology* 1.

[23] M Perel and N Elkin-Koren, 'Accountability in algorithmic copyright enforcement' (2016) 19 *Stanford Technology Law Review* 513.

[24] Edwards (n 8) 288.

[25] The diversity of the content includes parodies, political speeches, educational videos, historical documentaries; Jacques et al (n 15) 308.

and infringing content.[26] The online world facilitates the circulation of content so that end-users from every corner of the world may have access to it. Given that the aim of copyright is to encourage creativity and the dissemination of works,[27] a supervisory host ISP authority would guarantee the availability of works online to a greater extent than previously possible.

Further, the proposed host ISP supervisory authority would enhance the enforcement and protection of trade marks online by taking into consideration their peculiarities. This is because the proposed ISP supervisory authority and its qualified staff would be aware of what constitutes trade mark infringement and the acts that are not exclusive to the trade mark owner. As opposed to copyright, trade mark infringements do not take place by merely uploading a similar or identical trade mark online. Rather, trade mark infringements occur in cases where the trade mark is used in the course of trade, or there is a likelihood of confusion, or the trade mark would take unfair advantage of the reputation of the registered trade mark.[28] Further, the proposed ISP supervisory authority would consider the scope of trade mark protection, which differs from the scope of copyright protection.[29] More specifically, trade mark defences are cases where the trade mark is descriptive, or if the trade mark is used in order to indicate the intended purpose of a product or service, or if it is used in comparative advertising. In this way, unclear cases could be eliminated. For example, brand owners may argue that the placement of lists of goods under an undetermined category where goods are deemed to infringe trade mark protection, and for which there is no evidence, can trigger uncertainty with regard to the enforcement of their rights by host ISPs.[30] Therefore, the proposed supervisory authority might ensure whether host ISPs correctly identify trade mark infringements and brand owners would safeguard the different functions of their trade marks, while at the same time online consumers would not be deprived of information about the availability of goods that are offered online.[31]

Another reason that warrants the creation of a host ISP supervisory authority is the prospect of a higher level of protection for consumers' rights. This is because online consumers seem to be unprotected in cases where they are deceived by retailers selling counterfeit goods online. More specifically, due to the information asymmetry that exists in online commercial transactions, it seems almost impossible for online consumers to bring legal proceedings against individual traders.[32] Moreover, due to the limitation of liability clause, online consumers are not contractually entitled to turn to

[26] K Erickson and M Kretschmer, 'Empirical approaches to intermediary liability' (2019) 6 *Create Working Paper* 17.

[27] S Karapapa and L McDonagh, *Intellectual Property Law* (Oxford, Oxford University Press, 2019) 13–14; T Cotter, 'Some observations on the Law and Economics of Intermediaries' (2005) 1 *Michigan State Law Review* 9.

[28] S Senftleben, 'An uneasy case for notice and takedown: context-specific trademark rights' (2012) *VU Centre for Law and Governance* 15.

[29] L Bently, B Sherman, D Gangjee and P Johnson, *Intellectual Property Law* (Oxford, Oxford University Press, 2018) 1129.

[30] EU Commission, 'Commission staff working document: Report on the functioning of the Memorandum of Understanding on the sale of counterfeit goods on the internet' SWD(2020) 166 final 18–19.

[31] Senftleben (n 28) 15.

[32] Although the European Commission's Communication on New Deal for Consumers has announced new measures for protecting online consumers, its suggestions are non-binding.

host ISPs for compensation of any losses as a result of purchasing counterfeit goods from online marketplaces. A telling example can be found in eBay's terms and conditions where Section 6 on the Limitation of Liability states,

> We are not liable for any loss of money, goodwill or reputation, or any special, punitive, indirect or consequential damages arising, directly or indirectly, out of your use of or your inability to use our eBay Now Services or the items you purchased through our eBay Now Service. Some jurisdictions do not allow the disclaimer of warranties or exclusion of damages, so the above disclaimers and exclusions may not apply to you.[33]

However, whilst the creation of a host ISP supervisory authority would offer several advantages to all parties at stake, it might suffer from drawbacks. In particular, it has been argued that holding host ISPs accountable to a supervisory authority might increase their transaction costs. In particular, it is likely that host ISPs will be required to keep documentation in order to prove compliance with the supervisory authorities. For instance, within the data protection context, the report of the Information Commissioner's Office notes that the new accountability rules will give rise to compliance costs. In particular, it notes that the GDPR 'places too much emphasis on compliance paperwork, rather than results'.[34] This is because, as per Article 28 of the General Data Protection Regulation (GDPR),[35] business corporations are required to keep the necessary documentation in order to prove their compliance with the existing provisions. However, to keep documents, on the one hand, does not mean that the organisation employs the appropriate technical measures to comply with the rules while, on the other hand, such documentation might add an extra burden on the host ISPs.[36]

Although this argument has its own merit, it has to be borne in mind that such a negative effect could be prevented with the adoption of the 'one stop shop' principle, similar to the data protection framework. In particular, as per the GDPR's Articles 55–56, the concept of a one stop shop has been introduced.[37] The 'one stop shop' principle enables data processors to account for their actions to the data protection authority located in the same jurisdiction as the main establishment, regardless of its activities in other Member States. This tempers their compliance costs to a certain extent. In this light, within the context of intellectual property law, only the leading supervisory authority would request the host ISP to demonstrate compliance with the requirements set in existing law. In any case, it is important to outline that keeping documentation in order to prove to the host ISP supervisory authority that a host ISP undertook the appropriate set of responsibilities with which it was assigned seems a necessary evil in order to comply with those measures.

Further, the creation of a host ISP supervisory authority that deals exclusively with secondary intellectual property infringements would prove more efficient in terms of

[33] eBay terms of service are available at pages.ebay.com/ebaynow/terms.html.

[34] ICO, Documentation, ico.org.uk/for-organisations/guide-to-data-protection/guide-to-the-general-data-protection-regulation-gdpr/accountability-and-governance/documentation/.

[35] Council Regulation (EC) 2016/679 of the European Parliament and of the Council of 27 April 2016 on the protection of natural persons with regard to the processing of personal data and on the free movement of such data, and repealing Directive 95/46/EC (2016) O.J. L 119.

[36] ICO, Documentation (n 34).

[37] Article 29 Data Protection Working Party, 'Guidelines for identifying a controller or processor's lead supervisory authority' adopted on 13 December 2016.

tackling copyright and trade mark infringements. The value of this consideration can be understood if one imagines an authority that deals with all types of intellectual property infringements. This means that the authority would address primary as well as secondary intellectual property infringements. However, to add to the scope of a host ISP supervisory authority, primary infringements might prove either inefficient or devoid of legal basis. For instance, it is difficult to identify alleged infringers since they mostly hide behind fake IP addresses or use Virtual Private Networks,[38] thus making the disclosure of their identities almost impossible.[39] On the other hand, a number of legislative pieces that targeted primary infringer users have failed due to negative criticism. For instance, in 2009, under the mandate of Nicolas Sarkozy, the French government initiated the Hadopi Law,[40] according to which users' identity would be disclosed to right holders if they did not comply with three notices.[41] This law received severe criticism from civil society organisations that denounced the blatant violation of the right to privacy and outlined the lack of a legal basis for the disclosure of personal details of internets users without a court order.

What is more, with regard to the scope of the proposed host ISPs' supervisory authority, it might be called into question that this authority only addresses copyright and trade mark infringements that accrue in the digital ecosystem. For instance, it could be questioned as to why this host ISP supervisory authority would not deal with other online infringements, such as defamation, terroristic content, or fake news. As discussed in the introduction, the scope of this research focuses on copyright and trade mark violations. This is due to the fact that these two types of intellectual property infringements are the most common in the digital ecosystem and their violations have preoccupied, at most, a handful of courts at European and national levels.[42] Although there is an option to add to the scope of a host ISP supervisory authority, other types of online infringements cannot be precluded and a further examination of this is required. However, given that defamatory comments, or fake news, or hate speech issues fall outside the scope of this research, this further examination could be the subject of a future research project.

Finally, whilst the establishment of a supervisory authority for internet intermediaries has its own merits, one might argue that a supervisory authority would postpone an effective solution to the enforcement of rights online. This is because an ISP supervisory authority would be a bureaucratic authority that could suffer from the complexities and disadvantages of state regulation. Consider, for instance, the White Paper of the World Economic Forum states that '… relying only on government legislation and incentives

[38] Edwards (n 8) 282.

[39] Cited fn 50 in GB Dinwoodie, 'A comparative analysis of the secondary liability of online service providers' in GB Dinwoodie (ed), *Secondary Liability of Internet Service Providers* (Berlin, Springer, 2016).

[40] S Datoo, 'France drops controversial "Hadopi law" after spending millions: The "three strikes" anti-piracy measure, introduced under Nicolas Sarkozy, would have cut off users' access to the internet' *The Guardian* (9 July 2013) www.theguardian.com/technology/2013/jul/09/france-hadopi-law-anti-piracy.

[41] P De Filippi and D Bourcier, 'Three-Strikes' Response to Copyright Infringement: The Case of Hadopi' in F Musiani, D Cogburn, L DeNardis and NS Levinson (eds), *The Turn to Infrastructure in Internet Governance* (London, Palgrave-Macmillan 2016); J Phillips, 'Three Strikes … … and then?' (2009) 4 *Journal of Intellectual Property Law and Practice* 521; A Strowel, 'The Graduated reponse in France: Is it The good reply to online copyright infringements?' in Stamatoudi (n 10) 147; V Benabou, 'The Chase: The French Insight into the "Three strikes" System' in Stamatoudi (n 10) 163.

[42] *L'Oreal v eBay Int'l AG* (2009) EWHC 1094 AT; *eBay Inc v LVMH* Case 11-10505 (Cour de Cassation of France, 3 May 2012); OLG Düsseldorf, *Rapidshare I*, 27 April 2010, I-20 U 166/09.

to ensure the right outcomes is ill advised. These are likely to be out of date or redundant by the time they are implemented'.[43]

The vast array of EU Directives and Regulations that have succeeded each other over the last years with the aim of capturing the advanced technological developments in sector-specific issues offer an example. The Audiovisual Directive, the Copyright in the Digital Single Market Directive, the General Data Protection Regulation and the Directive against Terrorism are but a few examples of legislative pieces that regulate the thorny issues that arise with the rapid progress of technology, while the Proposal for a Digital Services Act and a Proposal for a Digital Markets Act have been introduced in order to cover the latest developments in technology.

Yet, this discrepancy might be mitigated if the duties of the supervisory authority would be clearly carved out. This means that the supervisory authority would operate under specific principles. Such principles might concern the independence of the authority, the consistent and proportionate decisions it would issue and the accountability it should have towards a hierarchically superior administrative body.[44] In this way, any complexity or peculiarities of the state regulatory framework would be avoided.

Bearing in mind the above, one might conclude that the creation of a host ISP supervisory authority would, to a greater extent, safeguard the different interests of the parties involved. In contrast to the current outdated framework under Article 14(1) of the ECD and the problematic aspects of Article 17 of the DSMD, the creation of a host ISP supervisory authority might offer a more robust legal framework for host ISPs, right holders, and internet users by enhancing legal certainty and due process principles.

Having demonstrated the need for the introduction of a host ISP supervisory authority for copyright and trade mark infringements, as well as its scope, the next question concerns the principles and functions of such an authority. In order to determine this, the operation of representative authorities established in two jurisdictions are explored, namely those in Greece[45] and those in Italy.[46] For this reason, their examination can inform this research. However, as is demonstrated in the following section, while these authorities are not ideal they offer a good start on which a host ISP supervisory authority could build.

III. Examples of Supervisory Authorities for Copyright and Trade Mark Infringements: Not Ideal but a Good Start

A. Administrative Agency in Greece

Within the context of Intellectual Property Law, a Committee on Internet Violations of Intellectual Property has been established. Pursuant to Article 66E of the Greek Intellectual Property Law 4481/2017, this Committee operates under the auspices

[43] 'Values and the Fourth Industrial Revolution: Connecting the Dots Between Value, Values, Profit and Purpose' (World Economic Forum).

[44] See further in section IV of this chapter.

[45] An analysis of the Greek agency follows.

[46] An analysis of the Italian agency follows.

of the Hellenic Copyright Organisation and its main duties are to adjudicate private disputes between host ISPs and rights holders for the circulation of unlawful material within their networks. In this way, instead of initiating civil proceeding in courts and requesting blocking injunctions or damages, right holders can file an application to the Committee asking for the removal of content posted online without their permission.[47]

The scope of Article 66E(1) of the Greek Intellectual Property Law covers those ISPs which provide internet access or hosting services, operators of websites, and users who upload unauthorised material online. However, it does not cover those activities of internet users who download, stream, or file-share unauthorised material.[48]

In order to seek redress in front of the Committee, the copyright holder must have already notified the host ISP with regard to the infringing content that exists within its platform and show that the host ISP either has not processed the notification or has dismissed it. In this case, the copyright holder can resort to the Committee by filing an application against the specific host ISP. The Committee issues its decision within 10 days. If the application is not rejected, then the host ISP is obliged to remove the infringing content. In the case of ISPs which offer internet access, the Committee orders them to terminate internet access for users of websites which carry unlawful material, such as those where users can upload or download illegal films. In the case of non-compliance with the Committee's decision, a fine of between €500 and €1000 might be imposed.[49]

In this way, the Greek Committee's procedure appears to offer advantages to right holders. Firstly, it provides them with fast redress of the rights which have been violated online. For instance, right holders receive a positive or negative answer to their application with regard to the infringements of their rights within 10 days of application. Secondly, this procedure offers an efficient way for right holders to seek legal protection in cases where their rights have been infringed. As demonstrated in chapter three, due to the outdated legal framework of the ECD and its befuddled national implementation, right holders have been unsure about the protection of their rights. However, a clear framework representing this procedure could offer legal certainty to right holders. Thirdly, a representative example of how right holders might appeal this procedure is reflected in the 56 decisions the Committee has issued since its establishment in 2017. These decisions concern blocking websites from carrying unlawful material, which reinforces the view put forward in this book that right holders would seek redress for violations of their rights through this new procedure.

However, this Committee also comes with disadvantages. Indeed, several concerns about its scope and its legal basis have been expressed. Firstly, activities such as downloading or peer to peer file-sharing are not included in the scope of this Committee. As explained in chapter three, there have been many cases which have preoccupied

[47] General information on the Greek Committee on intellectual property violations is available at www.opi.gr/en/committee/general-information.

[48] T Chiou, 'Greece: new notice and take down administrative mechanism for online copyright cases now in force' (*IPKat*, 5 March 2018) ipkitten.blogspot.com/2018/03/greece-new-notice-and-take-down.html.

[49] C Tsigou, 'Notice and Takedown Procedure under Greek Intellectual Property Law 4481/2017' (2018) 9 *Journal of Intellectual Property, Information Technology and E-Commerce Law* 206; Infographique about the complaints procedure for copyright infringements online, available at opi.gr/images/various/infographic_en.jpg.

national courts with regard to file-sharing, The Pirate Bay saga is an illustrative example which has involved the courts at both national and European levels.[50]

Secondly, some scholars have commented on the legitimacy of this Committee. This is because, as Chiou[51] and Tsigou[52] state, the creation of this agency does not fulfil the criteria of Greek Administrative Law. In particular, the Committee is not accountable to a higher administrative authority. Such lack of a hierarchical authority may undermine the legitimacy of the decisions issued by this administrative agency. Certainly, courts could annul the decisions of the Committee since the Committee's structure does not fulfil the requirements of a public administrative body. This understanding seems crucial for the establishment of the recommended supervisory authority. An independent supervisory authority must be accountable to a public administrative institution, such as the Ministry of Culture, which would oversee its decisions and its activities. Otherwise, the decisions issued by the authority would lack legitimacy and would be very easily challenged by the courts.[53]

Nevertheless, it should be borne in mind that this Committee is still in its infancy and there is room for improvement in the near future. In any case, the operation of the Committee has shown positive steps so far.

B. Administrative Agency in Italy

Another example of a national administrative authority that deals with copyright violations is found in the Italian jurisdiction. This authority was introduced via a Regulation[54] issued by the Italian Authority for Communication Industries.[55] Article 2 of the Regulation covers activities of those users who upload unauthorised material on the online platforms. Excluded from the scope of the Regulation are individual users as well as peer to peer networks that enable users to exchange illegal files of films or music.[56]

Unlike the Hellenic Committee on intellectual property violations, whose legal nature is not yet clear,[57] the Italian Authority for Communication Industries is integrated into the public administrative structure since it is accountable to the Italian Parliament. The Parliament appoints a member of the Authority whose main purpose is to issue decisions relating to the removal of unlawful content within the online platforms. In addition, it handles requests depending on their degree of urgency. More specifically, the Authority examines a request for removal within either 35 or 12 working days. The latter is described as the '*fastissimo*' process which takes place under certain

[50] Case C-610/15 *Stichting Brein v Ziggo BV and XS4ALL Internet BV* (2017) ECLI:EU:C:2017:456.

[51] Chiou (n 48).

[52] Tsigou (n 49) 204.

[53] ibid 205.

[54] Regolamento in materia di tutela del diritto d'autore sulle reti di comunicazione elettronica e procedure elettronica e procedure attuative ai sensi del decreto legislative 9 April 2003, N. 70, see www.agcom.it/documents/10179/0/Documento/b0410f3a-0586-449a-aa99-09ac8824c945; in English see wipolex.wipo.int/es/text/367415.

[55] Autorità per le Garanzie nelle Comunicazioni (Hereinafter AGCOM); its legal basis lies on Article 182 of Italian Copyright Law.

[56] Similar to the Greek Committee for intellectual property violations online.

[57] Tsigou (n 49) 204–05.

circumstances, such as massive copyright infringements. Further, according to the Regulation, non-compliance fines can be imposed on the internet access providers within three days of issuance of the order. Such fines may vary from €10,000 to €258,000 and may be appealed in front of the Italian Administrative Court within 60 days.[58]

Similar to the Hellenic Committee on intellectual property violations, the main purpose of the Italian authority's procedure is to offer to right holders a 'fast' and 'user friendly' recourse for those whose rights have been infringed.[59] In this area, this authority seems to be successful since there have already been a number of decisions made with regard to the termination of websites carrying unlawful material. For example, in the case of www.cineblog-01.net, rights holders filed two complaints to AGCOM alleging copyright infringements of 11 movies that were made available on a website without their permission. After examining the request, the Italian Authority treated the unlawful availability of 11 films as massive infringements and ordered the '*fastissimo*' process, thus blocking the entire website.[60] Finally, it is worthwhile to note is that AGCOM's procedures and services do not replace the courts. Rather, the authority offers an alternative remedy to rights holders whose rights have been violated online.[61]

However, despite the advantages this authority might offer to right holders, it has been argued that more clarification of the terms introduced in the Regulation is required. For instance, Article 1 of the Regulation introduces the new concept of 'the webpage manager', which is 'the information society service provider, other than those referred to in Articles 14, 15 and 16 of the Decree, who, within a website, manages a space where are present digital works or parts thereof or hyperlinks (link or torrent) to the same, also uploaded by third parties'.[62] This concept is a new term that is not included in the provisions of the ECD; indeed the absence of any clarification, or understanding of how its concept departs from the existing terminology of ECD and DSMD, might create confusion for right holders. What is more, further clarification is required with regard to the threshold that generates the fast or the slow procedure for examining a complaint with regard to the termination of the operation of a website with infringing material.[63]

Overall, as noted at the outset of this section, both administrative agencies aim to offer a fast and efficient recourse to right holders. While a few flaws have been identified, this does not mean that they cannot be seen as a good start upon which the recommended host ISP supervisory authority should be built.

In this regard, the following section articulates the principles the proposed host ISP supervisory authority should entail. Such principles, however, are not a novelty.

[58] Andy, 'Italian ISPs Say New Copyright Amendment Infringes Human Rights' (*Torrentfreak*, 27 July 2017) torrentfreak.com/italian-isps-say-new-copyright-amendment-infringes-human-rights-170728/; M Tavassi, 'Copyright and the Internet' in M Frazosi et al (eds), *The Digital Single Market Copyright; Internet and Copyright Law in the European Perspective* (Rome, Aracne Editrice, 2016) 188.

[59] Tavassi (fn 58).

[60] A Belan, 'BREAKING NEWS: AGCOM issues the first fastissimo administrative blocking injunction' (*IPKat*, 24 April 2014) ipkitten.blogspot.com/2014/04/breaking-news-agcom-issues-first.html.

[61] Tavassi (n 58) 188.

[62] Regolamento in materia di tutela del diritto d'autore sulle reti di comunicazione elettronica e procedure elettronica e procedure attuative ai sensi del decreto legislative 9 April 2003, N. 70, see www.agcom.it/documents/10179/0/Documento/b0410f3a-0586-449a-aa99-09ac8824c945.

[63] It has been argued that in the case of www.cineblog-01.net, the blocking of the whole website could prompt serious concerns over censorship as well as the proportionality of the measure in force; Andy (n 58).

Existing supervisory authorities at European level in other legal contexts, such as in Data Protection, Competition Law, or Finance Law, operate under the same principles. For this reason, it would be beneficial for this study to draw parallels with those authorities from other fields of law. Yet, it could be argued that a clear distinction should be made here in terms of the scope of a host ISP supervisory authority and the existing Data Protection or National Competition authorities. This is because it could be viewed that Data Protection authorities, or competition law authorities, do not have a similar scope of activities to the proposed host ISP supervisory authority. Indeed, a company may bring a case against the competition authority for anti-competitive behaviour, and another may face the scrutiny of the Information Commissioner's Office for engaging in profiling and data breaches. In contrast, a host ISP supervisory authority would deal with copyright and trade mark infringements committed by the users of host ISPs, not the host ISPs themselves. The purpose of the following section is simply to outline the principles under which the proposed host ISP supervisory authority should operate, it does not aim to analyse the spectrum of its activities.

IV. Principles of the Proposed Host ISP Supervisory Authority

The following section suggests a number of principles that could address the operation of the host ISP supervisory authority and the decisions it issues.

A. Independence

The concept of independence would be an important principle for a host ISP supervisory authority. This is because, as explored in chapter four, the existing mechanisms for dispute resolution that host ISPs adopt might be under pressure from the major copyright industry representatives. In this sense, they might favour their own interests and subordinate those of users, consumers, and smaller right holders.

This ascription of an independent status to an authority has already been widely applied by a handful of authorities at European level. Consider, for instance, the recommendations of the EU Commission to national Member States when they were establishing competition law and data protection law authorities. For instance, in 2014 in the context of the European Semester, the EU Commission made a recommendation to Spain to establish a competition law authority that is 'effective, autonomous and independent'.[64] In similar fashion, within the Data Protection framework, Article 52 of the GDPR dictates that each national supervisory authority shall perform its duties and make decisions independently.[65]

[64] G Monti, 'Independence, interdependence and legitimacy: the EU Commission, National Competition Authorities, and the European Competition Network' (2014) *Working Papers* 3.

[65] Article 52(1)(2) GDPR states that 'Each supervisory authority shall act with complete independence in performing its tasks and exercising its powers in accordance with this Regulation.

Scholars have identified two kinds of independence, formal and actual.[66] On the one hand, formal independence concerns the legal provisions that guarantee the independent function of the supervisory authority.[67] This means that in order to safeguard the independence of an authority, statutory legal provisions must prescribe its independent status.[68] This is illustrated in the case of cartels in the context of competition law. Cartel is a practice among companies which is illegal, thus it is prohibited by European competition law.[69] Lack of legal provisions that safeguard the independence of the authority which oversees and imposes sanctions would lead to fragmented situations, such as countries where cartels are highly sanctioned and countries where cartel practice is tolerated.[70] Having been documented in statutory provisions, the independent status of competition law authorities has enabled the authorities to act and issue decisions taking into consideration the existing legal framework.

On the other hand, actual independence amounts to the way the supervisory authority accomplishes its duties and mainly stems from the interaction between the authority and the external stakeholders or governmental bodies.[71] As the OECD report on the Governance of regulators points out, actual independence is achieved through 'an appropriate working relationship with government and other stakeholders'.[72] This is because the way under which the decisions are issued is also contingent upon the members who issue such decisions. These issues include, among others, the degree of independence those members have from political actors or relevant stakeholders when a decision is made.

Further, personal independence of the staff employed under the authority also falls within the scope of actual independence. In *Commission v Hungary*,[73] the Hungarian Commissioner was dismissed before the completion of his six-year mandate due to actions undertaken by the Hungarian government aimed at replacing all members of their Data Protection Authority.[74] In response, the EU Commission initiated legal proceedings against the Hungarian government on the basis of Article 16 of the Treaty on the Functioning of the European Union and Article 8 of the EU Charter of fundamental Rights, the purpose of each being to safeguard the independence of data protection supervisors. After careful consideration of the facts, the Court ruled

The member or members of each supervisory authority shall, in the performance of their tasks and exercise of their powers in accordance with this Regulation, remain free from external influence, whether direct or indirect, and shall neither seek nor take instructions from anybody.'

[66] S Alves, J Capiau and A Sinclair, 'Principles for the Independence of Competition Authorities' (2015) 11 *Competition Law Journal* 15–16.

[67] ibid.

[68] C Hanretty and C Koop, 'Shall the law set them free? The formal and actual independence of regulatory agencies' (2012) 7 *Regulation and Governance* 3.

[69] European Commission, Competition, Cartels, see ec.europa.eu/competition/cartels/overview/index_en.html.

[70] AM Mateus, 'Why should National Competition Authorities be Independent and how should they be Accountable?' (2007) 3 *European Competition Journal* 21.

[71] Alves, Capiau and Sinclair (n 66) 16.

[72] OECD, 'The Governance of Regulators' (2014) *OECD Best Practice Principles for Regulatory Policy*.

[73] C-288/12 *Commission v Hungary* ECLI:EU:C:2014:237.

[74] EU Commission, 'Court of Justice upholds independence of data protection authorities in case against Hungary' (8 April 2014), available at http://europa.eu/rapid/press-release_MEMO-14-267_el.htm, last accessed 9 September 2021.

that the replacement of the Data Protection Commissioner prior to completion of his service encroached upon existing EU law provisions because independence includes the 'obligation for the Member State concerned to allow that authority to serve its full term of office'.[75]

In light of the above case, it is possible to argue that to ascribe an independent status to the proposed host ISP supervisory for copyright and trade mark infringements could have merits for the parties whose interests are involved. Such merits could amount to the completion of policy objectives of copyright and trade mark law. Given that the outdated framework under the ECD and the problematic regime under the DSMD, as discussed in chapters three and four respectively, give rise to legal uncertainty to right holders and users, an independent host ISP supervisory authority might offer better protection of their interests. For instance, with regard to copyright law, the independence of the authority may create legal certainty to content owners. This, in turn, would give incentives to rights holders to further create works. Likewise, in the context of trade marks, brand owners would feel that their rights were protected, and that enforcement was not being left to host ISPs which are mainly private corporations with business interests. In this way, some cases could be avoided, such as one in 1970 when Louis Vuitton decided to withdraw its products from the market due to the high volume of counterfeit bags being sold.[76]

This understanding of the completion of policy objectives has been outlined in other sectors where supervisory authorities exist. For instance, with regard to competition law policies, an OECD survey has evidenced that one third of its respondents outlined 'greater independence' as enhancing the objectives of competition law.[77] With the establishment of an authority outside the public sector, or quasi-incorporated into the public sector, external influence towards the member of the authority may be limited. In this light, core competition aims, such as an increase in the competitive process and higher economic efficiency, will likely be achieved.[78] A similar understanding could be equally applied within the context of copyright and trade mark violations online. Independence of the host ISP supervisory authority could complete the goals of copyright law, such as the dissemination of creative works, while for trade mark rights it would boost innovation within the business market since a high degree of protection would be offered to brands.

B. Accountability

Another principle the proposed host ISP supervisory authority would possess is accountability.[79] As discussed in section III(A) of this chapter, the lack of accountability

[75] C-288/12 *Commission v Hungary* ECLI:EU:C:2014:237, para 50.

[76] A Radon, 'Counterfeit Luxury Goods Online: An Investigation of Consumer Perceptions' (2012) 4 *International Journal of Marketing Studies* 74.

[77] OECD Global Forum on Competition, 'The objectives of competition law and policy' (2003) www.oecd.org/daf/competition/2486329.pdf.

[78] ibid.

[79] The concept of accountability emerges from the latin word *accomptare* that means *to account* and *computare* which means calculate, see R Weber, 'The legitimacy and accountability of the Internet's

of the Greek administrative agency for copyright infringements online has given rise to criticism that might undermine the legitimacy of its decisions.

From a general point of view, accountability is to be understood as 'the obligation of a person to another person according to which the former must give account of, explain and justify her actions or decisions in an appropriate way'.[80] Endorsing this definition into the current narrative, the entity, who in this case is the host ISP supervisory authority, must be accountable to a hierarchical higher institutional body. This means that a supervisory authority would have vertical accountability.

Vertical accountability may include either the sharing of information to the superior institution with regard to previous actions, or sharing of information in the course of their supervisory duties.[81] In both cases, this means that the decisions and the actions undertaken by the authority would be under the scrutiny of the superior institution whose aim is to supervise the authority which deals with copyright and trade mark infringements online.

The application of the principle of accountability to the supervisory authority would have merits for the different parties at stake. In particular, accountability might enhance the legitimacy of their decisions and actions. This means that those decisions issued by the proposed host ISP supervisory authority would be legally binding, thus they could be challenged only in the courts. Otherwise, the legal validity of the decisions issued by the ISP supervisory authority would be questionable. This was the case in Greece with the Committee on Intellectual Property violations, as discussed in section III(A) of this chapter. Given that the Hellenic Committee does not account for its actions to either a higher administrative body or to the Ministry of Culture,[82] its decisions do not have the same legal effect on individuals. Conversely, ascribing accountability to a host ISP supervisory authority means that individuals cannot ignore its decisions, while its annulment can only be ordered after the issue of a court ruling. As a corollary, this understanding might promote the credibility and the efficiency of the host ISP supervisory body.[83]

Other examples of accountable supervisory bodies can be found in different legal contexts. A very recent example of this is understood through the *Schrems* ruling,[84] which draws on the data protection framework in light of the Snowden revelations. In this case, Michael Schrems, a doctoral researcher on privacy and a Facebook user, lodged a complaint with the Irish National Data Protection Authority requesting the termination of the transfer of his data from Facebook Ireland to Facebook Inc. in the US.

governing institutions' in I Brown (ed), *Research Handbook on Governance of the Internet* (Cheltenham, Elgar Publishing, 2013) 100; it has been widely used in Ancient Greece where Athenians were holding the public servants accountable for their actions, see DD von Dornum, 'The Straight and the Crooked: Legal Accountability in Ancient Greece' (1997) 97 *Columbia Law Review* 1483.

[80] Weber (n 79) 100.

[81] OECD, 'Working party on regulatory management and reform designing independent and accountable regulatory authorities for high quality regulation, Proceedings of an Expert Meeting in London, United Kingdom' (2005) 54.

[82] Tsigou (n 49) 204.

[83] Weber (n 79) 100.

[84] Judgment of the Court (Grand Chamber) of 6 October 2015, *Maximillian Schrems v Data Protection Commissioner* [2015] ECLI:EU:C:2015:650.

At European level, the EU Commission, under the Safe Harbor agreement, considers the transfer of data from Europe to US as safe and valid.[85] In this light, the Authority declined his request, reasoning that the Safe Harbor agreement was valid, and that he was bound by it.[86] Following this outcome, Schrems decided to challenge the decision of the Irish Data Protection Authority and brought legal proceedings against the Authority in front of the Irish High Court.

At European level, a pertinent example of an accountability mechanism is the EDPB.[87] EDPB is the European Data Protection Board[88] which replaced the Article 29 Working Party and undertook its activities. It is an independent European body whose purpose is to ensure the consistent application of data protection provisions across Europe. Such a body is answerable for its actions and decisions to European agencies.[89] In practice, this means that the EU Commission can control, on the basis of Article 17(1) of the Treaty on European Union,[90] the legitimacy of its decisions and Member States and the relevant stakeholders can challenge its decisions in front of the courts, pursuant to Article 263(1)[91] of the Treaty on the Functioning of the European Union.[92]

Therefore, to hold the proposed ISP supervisory authority accountable to a hierarchical superior government body could promote the legitimacy of its decisions, and thus offer an extra layer of protection for all the parties involved in the dispute.

C. Proportionality

Another principle that a host ISP supervisory authority would have is proportionality with regard to the decisions that this authority issues. In other words, a host ISP supervisory authority would examine any case under the lens of proportionality. This may

[85] S Monteleone and L Puccio, 'From safe harbour to privacy shield: advances and shortcomings of the new EU-US data transfer rules' (2017) 4, see www.europarl.europa.eu/RegData/etudes/IDAN/2017/595892/EPRS_IDA(2017)595892_EN.pdf.

[86] M Škrinjar Vidović, 'Schrems v Data Protection Commissioner (Case C-362/14): Empowering National Data Protection Authorities' (2015) *Croatian Yearbook of European Law and Policy* 262.

[87] At national level, the national data protection authority in every Member State is accountable to a higher institution. In Greece, for instance, it is the Greek Parliament, see in Hellenic Parliament archive, available at www.hellenicparliament.gr/UserFiles/c0d5184d-7550-4265-8e0b-078e1bc7375a/7873691.pdf.

[88] For more information on EDPB, see edpb.europa.eu/.

[89] O Lynskey, 'The Europeanisation of data protection law' (2016) 19 *Cambridge Yearbook of European Legal Studies* 252.

[90] Article 17(1) of the TEU: 'The Commission shall promote the general interest of the Union and take appropriate initiatives to that end. It shall ensure the application of the Treaties, and of measures adopted by the institutions pursuant to them. It shall oversee the application of Union law under the control of the Court of Justice of the European Union. It shall execute the budget and manage programmes. It shall exercise coordinating, executive and management functions, as laid down in the Treaties. With the exception of the common foreign and security policy, and other cases provided for in the Treaties, it shall ensure the Union's external representation. It shall initiate the Union's annual and multiannual programming with a view to achieving interinstitutional agreements.'

[91] Article 263(1) of the TFEU: 'The Court of Justice of the European Union shall review the legality of legislative acts, of acts of the Council, of the Commission and of the European Central Bank, other than recommendations and opinions, and of acts of the European Parliament and of the European Council intended to produce legal effects vis-à-vis third parties. It shall also review the legality of acts of bodies, offices or agencies of the Union intended to produce legal effects vis-à-vis third parties.'

[92] ibid.

concern either the adoption of proportionate measures in order to oversee the actions of host ISPs, or proportionate sanctions when host ISPs do not comply with the orders of the authority.

From a general point of view, the principle of proportionality traces its roots back to the Prussian courts of the nineteenth century and after World War II was diffused globally as a constituent of constitutional review in a handful of national jurisdictions.[93] At European level, the principle of proportionality is perceived as the 'cornerstone of EU law'.[94] This is because it is considered a substantial legal principle upon which the European legal system rests. As Stone, Sweet, and Matthews point out, '[a]fter the consolidation of the ECJ's "constitutional" doctrines of supremacy and direct effect, the emergence of proportionality balancing as a master technique of judicial governance is the most important institutional innovation in the history of European legal integration'.[95] This means that the principle of proportionality constitutes a fundamental principle of the EU Law, thus it could be equally placed next to the fundamental principles of EU Law that recognise the supremacy and the direct effect of EU legislation to the national legislation of EU Member States.

The principle of proportionality was officially included for the first time in Article 52 of the EU Charter of Fundamental rights, which dictates:

> any limitation on the exercise of the rights and freedoms recognised by this Charter must be provided for by law and respect the essence of those rights and freedoms. Subject to the principle of proportionality, limitations may be made only if they are necessary and genuinely meet objectives of general interest recognised by the Union or the need to protect the rights and freedoms of others.

This implies that proportionality is the most appropriate mechanism to warrant the limitation of fundamental rights, and thus could serve as a legitimate basis to weigh up the different interests at stake.

Given the seminal importance of proportionality to maintaining a balance between the different interests at stake, it seems that a handful of supervisory authorities at European level operate under the principle of proportionality.[96] By using this principle, the proposed ISP supervisory authority for copyright and trade mark infringements would ensure that a balance is reached between 'the means used and the intended aim'.[97]

Relevant examples of supervisory authorities that adopt the principle of proportionality can be found in the data protection framework. For instance, in order to impose fines on companies where data breaches have taken place, the Information Commissioner's Office in the UK takes into consideration the gravity of a data breach. This occurred in the case of Uber whose systems were hacked, resulting in a severe breach of passengers' and drivers' data. Crucially, instead of notifying the competent regulatory authorities of the data breach, Uber chose to pay the hackers a considerable amount of

[93] W Sauter, 'Proportionality in EU Law: A Balancing Act?' (2013) *TILEC Discussion Paper* 1.

[94] J Schwarze, *European Administrative law* (London, Sweet and Maxwell, 2006) 677.

[95] A Stone Sweet and J Matthews, 'Proportionality Balancing and Global Constitutionalism" (2009) 47 *Columbia Journal of Transnational Law* 73.

[96] EDPS, 'Report on assessing the necessity of measures that limit the fundamental right to the protection of personal data: A toolkit' (2017) 12.

[97] K Lenearts and P Van Nuffel, *European Union Law* (Sweet and Maxwell, 2011) 141.

money on the understanding that the stolen data would be destroyed.[98] After reports of this incident were leaked to the media, the ICO examined the case and imposed a very high fine on Uber. This is because, as the investigator of the ICO explained, this breach resulted in the theft of the personal data of 47 million passengers and drivers, thus it not only demonstrated Uber's incomplete security measures, but it also highlighted the disrespect of Uber towards its clients and employees whose rights and freedoms were severely violated without them being notified.[99]

The principle of proportionality is also applicable in the competition law sector. For example, the Spanish Competition Authority imposes fines after taking into consideration the principle of proportionality.[100] However, the Spanish Court noted that between November 2010 and February 2012, a handful of decisions issued by the Spanish Competition Authority have been considered disproportionate and have been annulled as a result.[101] Such disproportionate decisions were about the imposition of high fines irrespective of the gravity of harm.

In light of the above, the principle of proportionality could be used by the proposed host ISP supervisory authority when the authority examines disputes between copyright holders and brand owners with host ISPs. In this way, through the lens of proportionality, the host ISP supervisory authority would take into consideration the business model of host ISPs, as well as the impact of the decisions on the fundamental rights of third parties, such as the internet users.

D. Consistency

Another principle that the proposed host ISP supervisory authority would have is consistency. Consistency is understood as the compatibility of decisions taken by two separate national supervisory authorities in similar case scenarios.

The ascription of the principle of consistency would have benefits for a host ISP supervisory authority. Such benefits could include the promotion of legal certainty. In light of this understanding, it is possible to observe that a number of national supervisory authorities in different legal contexts attempt to follow a consistent approach with regard to the decisions they issue. For example, according to the report of the Article 29 Working Party of the Data Protection framework,[102] Data Protection Authorities must cooperate with other Data Protection Authorities with the aim of applying the

[98] BBC News, 'Uber pays $148m over data breach cover-up' (27 September 2018) www.bbc.co.uk/news/technology-45666280.

[99] Information Commissioner's Office, 'ICO fines Uber £385,000 over data protection failings' (27 November 2018) is available at ico.org.uk/about-the-ico/news-and-events/news-and-blogs/2018/11/ico-fines-uber-385-000-over-data-protection-failings/; ICO investigator noted 'This was not only a serious failure of data security on Uber's part, but a complete disregard for the customers and drivers whose personal information was stolen. At the time, no steps were taken to inform anyone affected by the breach, or to offer help and support. That left them vulnerable.'

[100] Spanish Supreme Court, Judgment of 24 May 2004, case nº 7600/2000.

[101] Van Bael and Bellis, 'VBB on Competition Law' (April 2019) www.vbb.com/media/Newsletters/VBB_on_Competition_Law_Volume_2019_No._4.pdf.

[102] THE ARTICLE 29 WORKING PARTY CEASED TO EXIST AS OF 25 MAY 2018, ec.europa.eu/newsroom/article29/item-detail.cfm?item_id=629492.

enforcement of data protection laws in a consistent manner.[103] As per Article 57(1)(g) of the GDPR, each supervisory authority shall 'cooperate with, including sharing information and provide mutual assistance to, other supervisory authorities with a view to ensure the consistency of application and enforcement of this Regulation'. In line with this, consistency in cases of ascription of administrative fines should also be maintained. This means that when a supervisory authority decides to impose fines or sanctions on a host ISP, a consideration of similar scenarios where other national authorities have ascribed penalties must be undertaken. In this regard, pursuant to Article 83(2) of the GDPR, a Data Protection Authority must assess a number of points before reaching a decision about fines. Such points may vary from the degree of responsibility of the data controller to the degree of cooperation with the supervisory authority. However, this understanding presupposes a pre-coordination and information exchange between the relevant authorities.

In a similar fashion, the principle of consistency is applicable to competition law authorities. This means that the authorities must ensure that their decisions are not in conflict with EU statutory rules, as well as court rulings handed down by the CJEU and the European Court of Human Rights.[104] For instance, the European Competition Network requires the close cooperation of the national competition authorities with an exchange of information in order to ensure the full enforcement of competition law rules.[105] Such information is only appropriate when it is used to complement EU legal rules and in cases where the outcome is the same.[106] Additional measures, such as investigations and fact-finding measures, are also available.[107]

The same understanding of the principle of consistency has been adopted by financial supervisory authorities at European level. Unlike the data protection authorities which are established in all 27 EU Member States, the financial supervisory authorities are not established at this level. Rather, they are based in only one Member State which oversees the activities of national financial institutions across all 27 EU Member States. However, their decisions must be consistent. For example, the Joint Committee of the three European Supervisory Authorities initiated a set of Guidelines whose purpose is to preserve consistency between the decisions of the financial authorities.[108] In particular, the Guidelines focus on the promotion of information exchange between the authorities, the conduct of impact assessments relating to the progress of the financial authorities, and supervision of the decision-making rules the authorities follow.[109] In this way, any threat of diverging enforcement practices for copyright and trade mark rights would be eliminated.[110]

[103] Article 29 Working Party, 'Guidelines on the application and setting of administrative fines for the purposes of the Regulation 2016/679' (adopted on 3 October 2017) ec.europa.eu/newsroom/article29/item-detail.cfm?item_id=611237.

[104] European Commission, 'EU Competition Law: Rules applicable to antitrust enforcement' 2013, ec.europa.eu/competition/antitrust/legislation/handbook_vol_1_en.pdf.

[105] European Commission, 'Notice on cooperation within the Network of Competition Authorities' (2004/C 101/03), para 2.2.3.

[106] European Commission, 'EU Competition Law: Rules applicable to antitrust enforcement' (n 104).

[107] ibid.

[108] European Securities and Markets Authority, 'Final report on Joint guidelines on cooperation and information exchange for the purpose of Directive (EU) 2015/849 between competent authorities supervising credit and financial institutions: The AML/CFT Colleges Guidelines ESMA' (2019) 5.

[109] ibid.

[110] Lomba and Evas (n 9) 224.

To summarise, drawing parallels with data protection, competition and finance law authorities enables illustration of the principles a host ISP supervisory authority should have. Such principles concern the independence of the authority, the consistent and proportionate decisions it would issue, and finally, the accountability it should have towards a hierarchically superior administrative body. Following this, the narrative moves to the functions the proposed host ISP supervisory authority should exercise. As discussed in the following section, such functions would include: enforcement duties; the adoption of a mediator role for disputes via its mechanism designed exclusively for complaints sent by either users, right holders, or host ISPs; and educative duties.

V. Functions of the Proposed Host ISP Supervisory Authority

The following section critically discusses the ascription of different functions to the authority and illustrates how those functions can be performed in the copyright and the trade mark context, accordingly.

A. Enforcement Duties for Copyright and Trade Mark Law

By ascribing enforcement power to the administrative authorities, the state validates the legitimacy of their operation.[111] Such enforcement duties may extend to ensure the right application of rules to either adjudicate disputes or to impose administrative fines.[112]

Amidst its enforcement duties, the host ISP supervisory authority would ensure that host ISPs comply with their responsibilities. Such proposed responsibilities, as discussed in chapters seven and eight, concern the duty of care host ISPs have to prevent the dissemination of counterfeit goods or unauthorised works within their platforms, as well as their obligation for transparency. However, to prevent the circulation of unlawful content within their platforms, host ISPs could resort to filtering technology. Apart from the merits filtering systems can offer, it has been found that marginal errors can occur with content identification technology.[113] In this sense, the host ISP supervisory authority would audit the algorithms before their use, or in the course of the operation, to ensure the correct functioning of the filtering technology.[114] Therefore, any restriction of users' free speech would be avoided to a great extent.

The same approach could be adopted for trade mark law. The proposed ISP authority shall examine whether the host ISPs are ensuring that counterfeit goods are not available within their networks, and that keyword advertising services do not trigger trade mark

[111] L Belli and C Sappa, 'The Intermediary Conundrum: Cyber-regulator, cyber-police or both?' (2017) 8 *Intellectual Property Information and Technology and Electronic Commerce* 185.

[112] ibid.

[113] House of Lords, Select Committee on Communications, 'The Internet: To regulate or not to regulate: Summary or response' 3; E Engstrom and N Feamster, 'The limits of filtering: a look at the functionality and shortcomings of content detection tools'(2017) 17, www.engine.is/the-limits-of-filtering.

[114] Pasquale (n 22) 3; Romero-Moreno (n 22) 183.

infringements. Given that appropriate measures are already taken on a voluntary basis by some host ISPs, the proposed ISP would be entitled to monitor their effectiveness. For instance, eBay has introduced the Verified Rights Owner Program which identifies counterfeit goods online.[115] In particular, the authority would examine whether the measures take into consideration the peculiarities of trade mark law, such as the use of the product in cases of comparative advertising, its use for criticism or parody, or the use of a trade mark to describe the characteristics of a product.[116] Otherwise, consumers will be deprived of valuable information about available products and services in the digital world.

With regard to the correct functioning of the transparency obligation, the host ISP supervisory authority might ensure that host ISPs publish transparency reports with regard to their content management, as well as provide users with the opportunity to submit counter-notifications in case their material has been removed. As discussed in chapters three and four, there have been instances where host ISPs have concluded agreements with industry representatives and, in doing so, neglected users' counter notifications.[117] In other instances host ISPs have resorted to over-enforcement of intellectual property rights in order to evade liability under Article 14(1) of the ECD.[118] Against this background, it is possible to argue that it could be reasonable to hold host ISPs accountable to a supervisory authority in order to demonstrate that they issue transparency reports and provide the opportunity to their internet users to appeal the removal of their content.

Further, within the trade mark context, the host ISP supervisory authority might ensure that host ISPs have increased transparency with regard to the methods used to place keyword advertising services, and to rank results for brands and any fake or misleading reviews about products. In particular, host ISPs would need to provide the grounds upon which they rank each result and their relationship with suppliers and trading partners. This understanding has also been supported by the European Union Committee on Online Platforms and the Digital Single Market. In particular, with reference to the Unfair Consumer Directive, it has been stated, 'We recommend that the Commission amend the Unfair Consumer Practices Directive so that online platforms that rank information and provide search and specialised results are required to clearly explain on their website the basis upon which they rank search results …'.[119] In this way, increased transparency would prevent potential consumer confusion, or eliminate threats to the goodwill of well-known trade marks.

This understanding has already been exemplified in a handful of court rulings. In these cases, the courts have noted that individuals who are being monitored should be offered a legal remedy to safeguard their rights. Thus, in *Tele2 Sverige AB v Post-och telestyrelsenk*, where the CJEU examined the impact of surveillance of communications

[115] pages.ebay.com/seller-center/listing-and-marketing/verified-rights-owner-program.html.

[116] Senftleben (n 28) 2.

[117] M Husovec, 'How Europe Wants to Redefine Global Online Copyright Enforcement' in T Synodinou (ed), *Pluralism or Universalism in International Copyright Law* (Alphen aan den Rijn, Kluwer Law International, 2019) 516–17.

[118] See further in ch 3.

[119] European Union Committee, 'Online Platforms and the Digital Single Market', see publications.parliament.uk/pa/ld201516/ldselect/ldeucom/129/12902.htm.

on the privacy of individuals, it has been stated that national Member States shall ensure, via independent authorities such as the Data Protection Authorities, that individuals could exercise their right to effective legal remedy in cases where their personal data was processed for unlawful reasons.[120]

Further, being entitled to ensure the correct functioning of their responsibilities towards the material that is disseminated within their platforms, this research recommends that the proposed host ISP supervisory authority should impose fines on host ISPs in cases of non-compliance. This means that in cases where a host ISP does not deploy the appropriate measures to prevent the dissemination of infringing material, as well as failing to publish transparency reports, or not offering counter-notifications options, the host ISP would be subject to the imposition of fines. This power to impose fines, as Laidlaw comments, would strengthen the status of the host ISP supervisory authority.[121] In support of this claim, it has been found that the role of the Information Commissioner's Office has been empowered since it took on the duty to impose penalties on companies for breach of their duties.[122]

In the trade mark context, the same approach would also be applicable. More specifically, the host ISPs would be fined by the proposed host ISP supervisory authority in cases of non-compliance. Such cases might be due to the failure to issue transparency reports, or the lack of a clear identification of third-party sellers, or unclear conditions with regard to the search listings. Indeed, the need for verification of the identity of the seller has been accentuated in the report by the European Committee on Online Platforms and Digital Single Markets. More specifically, the report states, with reference to the Unfair Consumer Practices Directive,

> … online platforms that rank information and provide search and specialised results are required to clearly explain on their website the basis upon which they rank search results. We also recommend that the Commission amend the Directive to require online platforms to provide a clear explanation of their business models and relationships with suppliers, which should also be prominently displayed on their websites.[123]

In addition, the report on the functioning of the Memorandum of Understanding on the sale of counterfeit goods on the internet demonstrates that some host ISPs already have in place Brand Protection Programs and other identification mechanisms in order to verify the sellers. Meanwhile, other host ISPs introduced additional layers of security for those sellers whose accounts link to a business, or which have a high level of sales.[124] In this light, host ISPs would be accountable to the proposed host ISP supervisory authority and would need to provide evidence of such for their operation. Lack of compliance would trigger penalties or fines on the host ISPs.

[120] Case C-203/15 *Tele2 Sverige AB v Post- ochre telestyrelsen and Secretary of State for the Home Department v Tom Watson and Others* (2016) ECLI:EU:C:2016:970.

[121] Laidlaw (n 12) 51.

[122] Laidlaw (n 12) 51; E Laidlaw, 'Internet Gatekeepers, Human Rights and Corporate Social Responsibilities' (PhD thesis 2012) 237.

[123] European Committee, 'Chapter 7: Consumer Protection and online platforms', publications.parliament.uk/pa/ld201516/ldselect/ldeucom/129/12910.htm.

[124] European Commission, 'Commission staff working document: Report on the functioning of the Memorandum of Understanding on the sale of counterfeit goods on the internet' SWD(2020) 166 final 18–19.

Finally, another enforcement duty recommended for the proposed host ISP supervisory authority is the adjudication of disputes. This means that right holders would resort to the host ISP supervisory authority in order to protect their rights against host ISPs which host their material without their permission. On the one hand, the attribution of adjudicative duties could be warranted. This is because, as explored in chapters three and four, respectively, the outdated approach under the ECD and the problematic approach under the DSMD might give rise to legal uncertainty among right holders whose rights have been violated, but where no redress has been achieved in the courts' legal arena.

On the other hand, the proposed host ISP supervisory authority could rely on existing authorities that deal with host ISP secondary infringements in Greece and Italy. Regardless of the flaws identified, such authorities could be seen as having the merit of being easy to implement and administer. This advantage seems to attract right holders who resort to those authorities when they seek redress for the violation of their rights. Consider, for instance, the Greek Committee on intellectual property violations. Following its establishment in 2017, the Committee has issued 56 decisions so far.[125] They mainly focus on the removal of copyright infringing works and ensure the compliance of the host ISPs with the decisions. To name a few, the first two, 1/2018[126] and 2/2018,[127] confirmed the compliance of host providers and website operators with the request to take down infringing content from their online platforms. The third decision, 3/2018, for the first time ordered the blocking of 38 websites whose purpose was to provide links that enabled internet users to view unauthorised films.[128] These websites offered classified links with the titles of the films that redirected internet users to third party websites and permitted them to watch the films. Taking into consideration the massive scale of copyright infringements that have lasted for a long period of time and the popularity of those websites to internet users, the Committee ordered the blocking of the entirety of the websites for three years. In case of non-compliance, fines of €850 per day for every day of non-compliance have been imposed. The fourth decision, 4/2019, confirmed the compliance of the host providers and website operators with the request of right holders to remove the unlawful material,[129] while the fifth decision, 5/2019, ordered the termination of access to websites that provided hyperlinks to unauthorised music files.[130]

These 56 decisions undoubtedly provide a promising example of a supervisory authority that adjudicates disputes between right holders and host ISPs.

In particular, with regard to copyright disputes, the right holders would be able to resort to the proposed ISP supervisory authority and provide evidence that copyright infringements are taking place within the network of the host ISPs. Having already asked the host ISPs to remove the allegedly copyright infringing work but receiving no response, the copyright holder would be entitled to seek legal redress from the proposed

[125] OPI, www.opi.gr/en/committee/decisions-committee.
[126] OPI, www.opi.gr/images/epitropi/apofaseis/edppi_1_2018.pdf.
[127] OPI, www.opi.gr/images/epitropi/apofaseis/edppi_2_2018.pdf.
[128] OPI, www.opi.gr/images/epitropi/apofaseis/edppi_3_2018.pdf.
[129] OPI, opi.gr/images/epitropi/apofaseis/edppi_4_2019.pdf.
[130] OPI, opi.gr/images/epitropi/apofaseis/edppi_5_2019.pdf.

host ISP supervisory authority. The proposed authority, following a careful examination of the claim and taking into consideration the scope of copyright law and the compliance of the host ISPs with the rules, would be expected to deliver the decision within a specific timeframe. Such a decision could vary from the imposition of fines on the host ISPs, to an order to block or remove the allegedly infringing work. The decision could be appealed in front of the courts in case the copyright holder or the host ISPs may require further litigation.

A similar approach might be followed in the case of trade mark infringements. If the brand owner perceives that the specific host ISP does not respond or act appropriately on notification of counterfeit goods or lists of counterfeit goods on a site, a request can be made to the proposed ISP supervisory authority for an investigation to be made. This might take into consideration the trade mark peculiarities and the competing interests involved; in this way the proposed ISP supervisory authority would consider the economic and social interests of trade marks, namely the freedom of competition and the promotion of innovation. Should the host ISP be found liable, the suggested authority would be entitled to order the removal of the infringing content or the blocking of the website, and also to impose fines for non-compliance with the order. Finally, the proposed ISP supervisory authority might be entitled to impose fines in cases of a breach of duty of care. For instance, fines might be imposed in cases where the host ISPs do not request details of the identity of the sellers, or fail to prevent the circulation of counterfeit goods.

To ascribe enforcement duties on supervisory authorities is not a novelty, however. As demonstrated below, a number of supervisory authorities are already entrusted with enforcement duties at European level, for example the Data Protection Authorities. These duties may vary from investigative powers to the imposition of sanctions in cases of non-compliance. For instance, the Spanish DPA imposed fines on Facebook for processing the personal data of its users without complying with the Spanish Data Protection Act.[131] The fine imposed reached up to €1.2 million for data protection violations. In Greece, the Greek DPA has dealt with a number of cases of illegal transmission of patients' data to insurance companies.[132] More specifically, there was a case where an insurance company accessed the medical records of a patient without his consent and denied him compensation. For this action, the insurance company was fined €20,000.

By the same token, the Competition Law Authorities' main goal is to enforce competition law. This means that they either carry out investigations for cartel violations or adjudicate disputes and impose fines. For instance, according to the report on an academic view of their roles and tools, the National Competition Authorities, in the majority of the countries, can go to the business premises of the company and take control, while in Poland a court warrant is required to enable the national competition authority to investigate.[133] Furthermore, upon finding that a company does not comply

[131] C O' Donoghue and K Albrecht, 'Spanish DPA fines Facebook €1.2 million for data protection infringements' (*Reed Smith*, 26 September 2017) www.technologylawdispatch.com/2017/09/privacy-data-protection/spanish-dpa-fines-facebook-e1-2-million-for-data-protection-infringements/.

[132] ARTICLE 29 – DATA PROTECTION WORKING PARTY, 'Recent examples of enforcement actions carried out by data protection authorities' (January 2005) ec.europa.eu/justice/article-29/documentation/opinion-recommendation/files/2004/wp101a_en.pdf.

[133] Economic and Monetary Affairs Committee, 'Report on an academic view on the Role and Powers of National Competition Authorities' (2016) 23.

with competition law rules, the authority may impose fines that vary according to the gravity of the violation. Consider, for example, in Germany the Federal Cartel Office can impose fines in cases of a breach of national or European competition rules which could amount to up to 10 per cent of their yearly profits.[134] The gravity and the duration of the breach are also considered in the imposition of fines. Finally, in France, the French Competition Authority can impose a fine of 10 per cent of their yearly profits and, if the company continues to breach the European competition rules, a daily fine of 5 per cent may also be imposed.[135]

However, the proposed host ISP supervisory authority would not be limited to enforcing intellectual property rights online. Indeed, it is recommended that this authority provide a mechanism for complaints from internet users or online consumers whose rights have been violated by content management policies, or consumers who have been deceived on online auction platforms.

B. Complaint Mechanisms for Internet Users and Consumers

Following the recommendation for enforcement duties of the proposed host ISP supervisory authority, it is suggested that a complaints mechanism be created for users or consumers whose rights are endangered. Their rights could be restricted either because host ISPs have wrongfully removed legitimate content users have uploaded to the platforms, or because counterfeit goods have reached end-consumers. This suggestion is based primarily on Article 17 of the DSMD which, as mentioned at the outset of this chapter, dictates in Article 17(9) that,

> Member States shall provide that online content-sharing service providers put in place an effective and expeditious complaint and redress mechanism that is available to users of their services in the event of disputes over the disabling of access to, or the removal of, works or other subject matter uploaded by them.[136]

In similar vein, the proposed DSA Regulation envisages the creation of out-of-court dispute bodies. Article 18 states,

> Recipients of the service addressed by the decisions referred to in Article 17(1), shall be entitled to select any out-of-court dispute that has been certified in accordance with paragraph 2 in order to resolve disputes relating to those decisions, including complaints that could not be resolved by means of the internal complaint-handling system referred to in that Article. Online platforms shall engage, in good faith, with the body selected with a view to resolving the dispute and shall be bound by the decision taken by the body.[137]

This complaints mechanism would ensure, to a greater extent, the protection of internet users and online consumers, as well as enhance their trust, itself considered a cornerstone

[134] ibid.
[135] ibid.
[136] Council Directive (EC) 2019/790/EC of the European Parliament and of the Council of 17 April 2019 on copyright and related rights in the Digital Single Market and amending Directives 96/9/EC and 2001/29/EC (Text with EEA relevance PE/51/2019/REV/1, OJ L 130 (hereinafter DSMD).
[137] Proposal for a Regulation of the European Parliament and of the Council on a Single Market for Digital Services (2020) COM/2020/825 final.

for e-commerce services.[138] Indeed, Barral-Vinals outlines that 'e-commerce will only grow if consumers have confidence in it'.[139] This implies the consumers' trust of online sales is contingent upon the host ISPs and, in particular, the appropriate safeguards they can offer those consumers who make purchases online.

At legislative level, the Regulation for promoting fairness and transparency for business users of online intermediation services[140] offers this possibility to users, it states in Article 11,

> Providers of online intermediation services shall provide for an internal system for handling the complaints of business users. That internal complaint-handling system shall be easily accessible and free of charge for business users and shall ensure handling within a reasonable time frame. It shall be based on the principles of transparency and equal treatment applied to equivalent situations, and treating complaints in a manner which is proportionate to their importance and complexity ….[141]

However, as commented on in chapter four, it has been observed that host ISPs conclude agreements with right holders.[142] Such agreements include terms that are often one-sided and neglect internet users' fundamental rights. A pertinent example can be found in the YouTube platform that dismisses any counter-notification for content that belongs to right holders with whom YouTube has entered into contractual agreements.[143]

What is more, the terms and conditions of host ISPs means they are subject to limited liability. Therefore, they are not liable should they remove any users' material. Consider the example of YouTube. In its terms and conditions there is an explicit section which limits the site's liability towards its users.[144] More specifically, it is noted that YouTube is not responsible towards its users for 'any loss or damage that was not, at the time that this Agreement was formed between you and YouTube, a reasonably foreseeable consequence of YouTube or its Affiliates breaching this Agreement'.[145] In a similar fashion, Facebook's terms note, 'Provided that we have acted with reasonable skill and care, we do not accept responsibility for: losses not caused by our breach of these Terms or otherwise by our acts …'.[146] Likewise, Instagram's terms and conditions state that 'Instagram shall not, under any circumstances, be liable to you for any indirect, incidental, consequential, special or exemplary damages arising out of or in connection with use of the Instagram Platform'.[147] Finally, Amazon's terms and conditions explicitly state,

[138] H Hallikainen and T Laukkanen, 'National culture and consumer trust in e-commerce' (2018) 38 *International Journal of Information Management* 97–106; P Dittrich, 'Online Platforms and how to regulate them: an EU overview' (2018) *Jacques Delors Institute* 28.

[139] Barral-Vinals (n 12) 93.

[140] The Council Regulation (EU) 2019/1150 of the European Parliament and of the Council of 20 June 2019 on promoting fairness and transparency for business users of online intermediation services (2019) OJ L 186.

[141] Article 11(1) of the Council Regulation (EU) 2019/1150 of the European Parliament and of the Council of 20 June 2019 on promoting fairness and transparency for business users of online intermediation services (2019) OJ L 186.

[142] Jacques et al (n 15) 308; A Ramahlo, 'Copyright law-making in the EU: what lies under the 'internal market' mask?' (2014) 9 *Journal of Intellectual Property Law & Practice* 224 where she notes that '… EU Copyright legislation that is partly industry-orientated, while other players seem to have fallen behind'.

[143] Perel and Elkin-Koren (n 23) 473.

[144] YouTube, Terms of service at www.youtube.com/static?gl=GB&template=terms.

[145] ibid.

[146] Facebook, legal terms are available at en-gb.facebook.com/legal/terms.

[147] Instagram, legal terms are available at www.instagram.com/about/legal/terms/api/.

'We and our affiliates and licensors will not be liable to you for any direct, indirect, incidental, special, consequential or exemplary damages including damages for loss of profits, revenues, customers, opportunities, goodwill, use of data.'[148] This implies that host ISPs do not have any legal responsibility for any direct or indirect losses of their online customers when they use their online services for either disseminating content or buying goods online. It is this limitation of liability of host ISPs that diminishes the possibilities of internet users to seek redress and ask for damages against host ISPs in case their content has erroneously been removed, or they have been deceived by purchasing counterfeit goods online.

Further, any attempts that have been initiated by users against host ISPs alleging erroneous removal of their content have failed. To my knowledge, such a case has not emerged at the European level, so far. It is only in front of the US courts where such cases have been brought and dismissed due to the binding contractual terms between the parties at stake. This was the case of *Lewis v YouTube* where Lewis brought legal proceedings against YouTube alleging a breach of contract since YouTube terminated his YouTube channel account alleging Lewis violated its terms of service.[149] Yet, the Superior Court of California dismissed the case, concluding that a claim for damages is not valid. To the court's reasoning, the non-commercial nature of the plaintiff's YouTube channel, along with YouTube's terms of service, precludes the request for damages. Accordingly, it may be assumed that a similar understanding could be equally applied at European level.

Finally, a further reason which reinforces the need for a complaints mechanism is the need for a higher degree of protection for online consumers. This is because, as Riefa has observed,[150] whilst in the bricks and mortar environment buyers could bring legal proceedings against owners of marketplaces, there is no adequate legal protection for online consumers who decide to purchase goods online. This is because online marketplaces are not considered auction places. For instance, Clause 2 of eBay's User agreement states, 'eBay is not a traditional auctioneer'.[151] Likewise, Amazon, pursuant to Clause 13, notes, 'Amazon is not an auctioneer, neither is it an intermediary between the buyer and the seller.'[152] Instead, Amazon's business is based on providing a platform for sellers to display their goods and consumers to purchase and complete transactions online. In a similar fashion, Etsy seller's agreement presents its activities as 'a marketplace where you can sell your handmade goods, vintage items, and craft supplies directly to buyers around the world'.[153] Any reference to online marketplaces or a description of its services as auction places are not included.

Such a stance has been maintained in policy documents issued at the European as well as national level. Within the European context, the EU Commission's impact assessment on promoting fairness and transparency on host ISPs refrains from treating

[148] Amazon, legal terms available at aws.amazon.com/agreement/.

[149] *Lewis v YouTube LLC*, 197 Cal. Rptr. 3d 219 (2015).

[150] C Riefa, 'To be or not to be an auctioneer? Some thoughts on legal nature of online "ebay" auctions and the protection of consumers' (2008) 31 *Journal of Consumer Policy* 167.

[151] eBay user agreement, www.ebay.com/help/policies/member-behaviour-policies/user-agreement?id=4259; cited in Riefa (n 150) 167.

[152] Amazon, seller participation agreement, sellercentral-europe.amazon.com/forums/t/who-is-contract-between/8636; cited in Riefa (n 150) 167.

[153] Etsy seller agreement, available at www.etsy.com/legal/sellers/.

online marketplaces as auction places. Rather it considers online marketplaces as places in which a commercial transaction between a customer and a business user takes place, or as online platforms bringing together users with the aim of 'facilitating' commercial transactions.[154] In addition, at national level, UK authorities explicitly inform online consumers that online marketplaces are not considered auction places. In particular, the Office of Fair Trading warns consumers that current host ISPs that facilitate the purchase of goods online do not fulfil the requirements of traditional auctions.[155] This means that such host ISPs do not have the same strict legal obligations of auctioneers, thus it is difficult for online consumers to hold them liable in cases of misconduct. Along similar lines, the Department of Trade and Industry clarifies that online auctions or internet auctions are simply terms to refer to websites were buyers place goods and consumers choose to buy them.[156] In any case, the consumers must not consider them auction places when they purchase goods from their platforms.

However, as discussed at the outset of this chapter, it is not only the DSMD that envisages the establishment of a mechanism for the disputes between host ISPs and internet users and consumers. Indeed, a growing body of academic scholarship encourages the creation of such a mechanism. For instance, a recommendation for such a mechanism has been expressed by Laidlaw, but not without scepticism. Within the context of search engines, she highlights the need to establish an independent complaints mechanism as a safeguard against the manipulation of search result rankings.[157] For instance, she argues that Ofcom in the UK illustrates a representative example since it entails a complaints mechanism.[158] Ofcom acts as a regulator for the broadcasting sector, it focuses on the protection of consumers' privacy rights and ensures the correct functioning of broadcasting standards. In particular, the complaints mechanism enables consumers to submit a complaint in cases when broadcasters do not comply with the rules. Upon submission of a complaint, within 15 working days Ofcom primarily assesses the complaint and decides whether it should be evaluated further. If so, after informing the broadcaster, Ofcom opens an investigation which should be concluded within 50 working days.[159]

Along similar lines, Fiala and Husovec conducted an experiment based on empirical studies whose purpose was to suggest an alternative dispute resolution model for users whose content has been removed by host ISPs. Focusing only on content removals, the two researchers recommended the development of an independent external body for

[154] European Commission Staff Working Paper, 'Impact assessment on Proposal for a Regulation of the European Parliament and of the Council on promoting fairness and transparency for business users of online intermediation services, Online Services, Including E-Commerce, in the Single Market' (2018) 238 final.

[155] Riefa (n 150) 175.

[156] ibid.

[157] Laidlaw (n 1) 143–44.

[158] ibid, in particular Laidlaw notes that 'The complexity and concerns regarding an OFCOM structure are far more than indicated herein. Such complexities are exacerbated if one attempts to apply it to the internet, because of the political ramifications of attempting public regulation of a transnational communications network. However, at this stage a fundamental question is whether a complaints mechanism is better run by the industry, with government involvement, or by international collaboration and so on. OFCOM is merely one example of a quasi-governmental approach. It is advantageous in binding the industry to the Code, and the threat of licence removal is significant to deter certain behaviour. Whether it is effective, or used for that matter, is uncertain as OFCOM is still in its infancy.'

[159] Ofcom, 'General procedures for investigating breaches of broadcast licences' (2017) www.ofcom.org.uk/__data/assets/pdf_file/0019/31942/general-procedures.pdf.

handling complaints about removals of material within the host ISPs.[160] According to the study, the creator of a video can pay a fee to submit a counter-notice to the independent body, termed an alternative dispute resolution mechanism (ADR). This means that the costs of the submission are undertaken by the internet users. However, if the body decides that the removal was unfair, the host ISP must pay back the creator's fee, as well as extra costs to the ADR.[161] In this light, the creators have incentives to submit counter notices since their complaints will be meticulously evaluated. In addition, the fees they pay for the counter-notice are returned to them.[162] With regard to host ISPs, the ADR mechanism gives them incentives to review more carefully the allegedly infringing material,[163] and take into consideration the fair dealing principle, before removing the content.

Such a stance has been maintained by Tessier and others who, in their report for the host ISPs' coalition, recommended the establishment of an independent agency, which they named the Agency for Trust in the Digital Platform Economy.[164] More specifically, this body would be entrusted with a mediator role that would deal with users' and consumers' complaints against host ISPs, while at the same time it would promote a dialogue between host ISPs and users/consumers. In addition, the staff of this independent agency would have the appropriate expertise to evaluate the comments and attempt to give a solution.

In the light of the above, an optimal complaints mechanism offered by the proposed host ISP supervisory authority could operate as follows: under the condition that the user has submitted a counter-notification requesting the reinstatement of the content that has been removed and the host ISP has either ignored its claim or rejected it, the user/consumer can resort free of charge to the complaints' mechanism of the proposed host ISP supervisory authority. With regard to trade mark disputes, an online consumer, or a brand owner, would resort to the complaints' mechanism and lodge a complaint against the host ISPs in cases of the purchase of counterfeit goods, or of offers of search listings with counterfeit goods or services, or of a lack of measures taken to detect fake products within their networks.

It is suggested that this complaints mechanism follow the EU Commission's Regulation on promoting fairness and transparency for business, offering online intermediation services,[165] and the EU Commission's Regulation[166] on ADR mechanisms.[167] The level of success of those ADR schemes has been outlined by the EU Commission's report in 2017, it reveals that users' complaints to the alternative dispute mechanism

[160] L Fiala and M Husovec, 'Using experimental evidence to design optimal notice and takedown process' (2018) *TILEC Discussion Paper* 7.

[161] ibid.

[162] ibid.

[163] ibid.

[164] Tessier, Herzog and Madzou (n 1) 182.

[165] Article 11 of Regulation (EU) No 2019/1150 of the European Parliament and of the Council of 20 June 2007 on promoting fairness and transparency for business users of online intermediation services, OJ L 156, 11.7.2019, p 57.

[166] Article 5 of Council Regulation (EU) No 524/2013 of the European parliament and of the Council on online dispute resolution for consumers (2013) OJ L 165.

[167] See also out-of-court settlement of consumer disputes, eur-lex.europa.eu/legal-content/EN/TXT/HTML/?uri=LEGISSUM:l32031&from=EN; see also Consumer access to justice (Green Paper), eur-lex.europa.eu/legal-content/EN/TXT/HTML/?uri=LEGISSUM:l32023&from=EN.

reached 3,000 per month in 2017, online consumers from Germany and the UK being the pioneers.[168] In similar fashion, another report, conducted by the EU Commission in 2019, on assessing the ADR mechanism confirms the findings of the 2017 report and outlines that such a mechanism 'has become an integral part of the EU's toolbox for the public and private enforcement of consumer law'.[169] Indeed, in 2018, over 4,500 users submitted complaints about online purchases per month.

Extrajudicial systems for disputes include a number of principles, such as: the independence of the body that deals with the disputes; transparent, effective, fast, non-costly, and fair procedures; and decisions compatible with the consumer protection framework. In this way, internet users whose material has been removed and whose counter-claim has been ignored or rejected could be given the option to submit their complaints against host ISPs to this mechanism. Alongside this, online consumers could also be entitled to resort to this mechanism for complaints against host ISPs which circulate infringing material.[170]

Therefore, it is possible to argue that with this complaints mechanism it would be more likely that users' fundamental rights would be safeguarded, thus avoiding the extent of their violation. In addition, it is likely that this mechanism would offer a higher degree of consumer protection, thus reaching the goals of consumer protection laws. Such goals address the need for consumer laws to adapt to the digital age,[171] as set out in the Communication of consumer law, as well as enable consumers to 'enjoy a high common level of protection across the Union',[172] as per Recital 7 of the Preamble of the Consumer Directive of 2011/83/EU.

However, apart from the enforcement duties and resolution of disputes between internet users/consumers and host ISPs that the proposed host ISP supervisory authority should have, another role of the proposed host ISP supervisory authority should be an educative one.

C. Promoting Awareness Among Users and Consumers

Informing users about the negative implications of piracy is also an important policy initiative that the proposed host ISP supervisory authority could offer.

[168] European Commission, 'Report on the functioning of the European Online Dispute Resolution platform established under Regulation (EU) No 524/2013 on online dispute resolution for consumer disputes' COM (2017) 744 final.

[169] European Commission, 'Report on the application of Directive 2013/11/EU of the European Parliament and of the Council on alternative dispute resolution for consumer disputes and Regulation (EU) No 524/2013 of the European Parliament and of the Council on online dispute resolution for consumer disputes' COM (2019) 425 final 17.

[170] J Devenney, 'The legacy of the Cameron-Clegg coalition programme of reform of the law on the supply of goods, digital content and services to consumers' (2018) 6 *Journal of Business Law* 488 where Devenney argues that in relation to clear consumer rights 'much will depend on, for example, dissemination of information on rights to consumers, consumer education and redress mechanisms and assistance.

[171] European Commission, 'A European Consumer Agenda – Boosting confidence and growth' COM(2012) 225 final.

[172] Council Directive (EC) 2011/83/EU of the European Parliament and of the Council of 25 October 2011 on consumer rights, amending Council Directive 93/13/EEC and Directive 1999/44/EC of the European Parliament and of the Council and repealing Council Directive 85/577/EEC and Directive 97/7/EC of the European Parliament and of the Council.

With regard to copyright infringements, the promotion of awareness among users would have merits with regard to the limitation of piracy and enhancement of creativity. This is because users would be informed about the negative impact on authors and creators, such as the economic loss that the transmission of their work without their permission might cause, as well as the imposed fines in cases where users upload, download, or exchange unauthorised material.[173] In this sense, users would be encouraged to refrain from illicit activities, and thus turn to lawful alternatives.

This understanding has been outlined in a number of studies conducted by private stakeholders. For instance, the Irdeto Global Consumer Piracy survey reports that 45 per cent of the individuals who participated in their survey stated that they would refrain from exchanging unauthorised works online after being made aware of the high revenue losses to creators.[174]

Such awareness campaigns have already shown positive results in other sectors.[175] A representative example can be found in the campaigns against teenage smoking.[176] These initiatives have had a positive result since it has been found that they have persuaded around 522,000 smokers to cease smoking in the long term.

At policy level, with regard to copyright infringements, educational campaigns that inform individuals about the negative impact of copyright violations are endorsed. The UK Government's funded programme[177] is a representative example of users' awareness of the implications of illegal downloading.[178] This initiative is called 'Get it right from a genuine site',[179] and is part of the Creative Content UK campaign. Its aim is to make users aware of the time and efforts creators invest in their works and it appears it has already led to positive outcomes. Indicatively, the pioneers of this initiative report stated 'We are very pleased with the progress of the campaign to date and as awareness continues to build, we expect to see strong results for the creative sectors in the coming year.'[180] In addition, the World Intellectual Property Organisation organises awareness events at schools in order to educate children about intellectual property rights.[181] Finally, in June 2021, the European Intellectual Property Office organised a Pan-European awareness campaign for the risks and damages posed by Intellectual Property Infringements in all EU Member

[173] Electronic Frontier Foundation, 'How SOPA Affects Students, Educators, and Libraries' (14 December 2011) www.eff.org/deeplinks/2011/12/how-sopa-affects-students-and-educators.

[174] Irdeto, 'Nearly half of consumers around the globe are willing to stop or watch less pirated video content' (8 March 2017) irdeto.com/news/nearly-half-of-consumers-around-the-globe-are-willing-to-stop-or-watch-less-pirated-video-content/.

[175] JM Crotty, 'Education Is Best Weapon Against Web Piracy, not SOPA' (*Forbes*, 31 January 2012) www.forbes.com/sites/jamesmarshallcrotty/2012/01/31/better-than-sopa-public-education-best-weapon-against-web-piracy/#76f84b504228.

[176] Public education campaigns reduce tobacco, www.tobaccofreekids.org/assets/factsheets/0051.pdf.

[177] While the UK is no longer an EU member state, it is a very useful initiative; Ernesto, 'UK Anti-Piracy 'Education' Campaign Launched, Quietly' (*Torrentfreak*, 1 December 2015) torrentfreak.com/uk-anti-piracy-education-campaign-launched-quietly-151201/; 'Get it right from a genuine site', www.getitrightfromagenuinesite.org/.

[178] www.wipo.int/wipo_magazine/en/2016/02/article_0007.html.

[179] www.getitrightfromagenuinesite.org/.

[180] Ernesto (n 177); 'Get it right from a genuine site' (n 177).

[181] World Intellectual Property Organisation, 'Building Respect for IP: Awareness Raising' www.wipo.int/enforcement/en/awareness-raising/.

States in light of the exponential growth of online purchases during the COVID-19 pandemic.[182]

Moreover, the importance of promoting awareness of the circulation of unlawful material is exemplified by initiatives introduced by copyright representatives, as well as host ISPs. For instance, reports from the International Federation of the Phonographic Industry (IFPI) demonstrate a handful of initiatives in different countries designed to inform users of the negative consequences of exchanging or downloading unauthorised music files. A spectrum of different countries is engaged in anti-piracy education campaigns, thus informing users about piracy and alternative legitimate ways to acquire music files, such as licensing.[183]

However, it is not only policy makers or copyright representatives who use user education as a weapon towards the decrease of piracy rates in the digital ecosystem. Indeed, host ISPs have adopted policies on a voluntary basis in order to enhance awareness for those uploading or sharing unauthorised material. For instance, YouTube's Copyright School[184] is a tool that educates users on what is lawful to upload on their platform. While the Copyright School tutorial video is entertaining, it stresses the negative implications of piracy for users, focusing on the imposition of monetary damages to individual users and the termination of alleged infringer users' YouTube's accounts.

Further, with regard to trade mark infringements, a similar initiative has been included in the EU Commission's Communication on New Deal for Consumers.[185] This Communication addresses the challenges that consumers face in the Digital Single Market. Amidst the initiatives undertaken by the European policymakers is the maintenance of consumer classroom tutorials which focus on informing consumers about their rights and how to protect them in the context of online purchases made in online marketplaces.

At the same time, host ISPs that display goods within their networks are taking initiatives to organise campaigns in order to make consumers aware of counterfeit goods and how to understand them.[186] For instance, Alibaba founded the Alibaba Anti-Counterfeiting Alliance along with other host ISPs from 16 countries; the Alliance promotes awareness of fake goods and their detrimental effect on different sectors of society.[187] Further, eBay collaborated with Industry Trust and organised a campaign

[182] European Intellectual Property Office, 'Risks and damages posed by IPR infringement in Europe' (2021) euipo.europa.eu/ohimportal/en/web/observatory/risks-and-damages-posed-by-irp-infringement-in-europe.

[183] IFPI Global Music Industry report 2021, www.ifpi.org/wp-content/uploads/2020/03/GMR2021_STATE_OF_THE_INDUSTRY.pdf; IFPI Digital Music Report 2013: 'Engine of a digital world', www.musikindustrie.de/fileadmin/bvmi/upload/06_Publikationen/DMR/ifpi_digital-music-report-2013.pdf; IFPI Digital Music Report 2019: 'State of the industry', www.ifpi.org/wp-content/uploads/2020/07/Global_Music_Report-the_Industry_in_2019-en.pdf, www.ifpi.org/ifpi-global-music-report-2018/.

[184] YouTube Copyright School is available at www.youtube.com/copyright_school.

[185] European Commission, 'Consumer Classroom' is available at www.consumerclassroom.eu/; European Commission, 'A New Deal for Consumers' COM (2018) 183 final 14, eur-lex.europa.eu/legal-content/EN/TXT/PDF/?uri=CELEX:52018DC0183&from=EN.

[186] European Commission, 'Commission staff working document: Report on the functioning of the Memorandum of Understanding on the sale of counterfeit goods on the internet' SWD(2020) 166 final 30.

[187] World Trade Mark Review, 'Alibaba Anti-Counterfeiting Alliance seized $536.2 million in fake goods last year: WTR exclusive' (28 March 2019) www.worldtrademarkreview.com/anti-counterfeiting/alibaba-anti-counterfeiting-alliance-seized-5362-million-fake-goods-last.

to educate consumers, enabling them to distinguish between legitimate and illegitimate DVDs.[188]

In light of the above, this book argues that the proposed host ISP supervisory authority should initiate education campaigns on the negative consequences of piracy on right holders and users/consumers. Such initiatives could be fostered by national governments and could entail educational material that would emphasise the importance of boosting creativity in the Digital Single Market, along with the need for alternative and legitimate ways to enjoy creative content online, such as the conclusion of licensing agreements. The same understanding could be equally applied to online consumers with regard to the protection of their rights against the circulation of counterfeit goods in the digital world.

In short, it is suggested that the proposed host ISP supervisory authority should play an educative role. In parallel with its enforcement duties and users' complaints resolution, it should promote educational campaigns and awareness among users about the negative impact of piracy on right holders' rights, and on creativity in general. Alongside this, education of consumers on the existing remedial mechanisms could offer them a higher degree of protection of their rights.

Yet, in order to offer a complete picture of the suggested ISP supervisory authority that would deal with copyright and trade mark infringement, it is imperative to explore available funding schemes that would support its activities. The following section discusses options for funding sources that are either contingent upon EU funding or represent an industry-based financial contribution.

VI. Funding Scheme for the Proposed Host ISP Supervisory Authority

The proposed ISP supervisory authority would require a structured funding scheme in order to operate. Potential fundings schemes and resources are available and representative examples can be drawn from existing national supervisory authorities in the fields of Data Protection and Audiovisual, as well as European agencies.

More specifically, a possible option could be to fund the operation of the proposed ISP supervisory authority through the imposition of fees from the industry. A telling example can be found in Ofcom. For instance, Ofcom's budget comes from the fees that are charged to the industry sectors which the authority regulates. This has been illustrated in the recent annual report which demonstrates that the annual budget for 2020–21 was £135 million and stems from a spectrum of posts, networks and services, broadcasters, the Telecoms security bill, online harms, and video sharing platform sectors.[189] The suggested ISP supervisory authority would attract fees from the brand

[188] Ebay, 'eBay Helps Users Say "No" to Knock-Off Nigels' (28 October 2014) www.ebayinc.com/stories/press-room/uk/ebay-helps-users-say-no-to-knock-off-nigels/; in addition, see further PE Chaudhr, *Handbook of Research on Counterfeiting and Illicit Trade* (Cheltenham, Edward Elgar, 2017) 214.

[189] Ofcom, 'The Office of Communications Annual Report and Accounts', www.ofcom.org.uk/__data/assets/pdf_file/0025/221686/annual-report-2020-21.pdf.

owners, copyright holders, and ISPs. Such fees need to vary between national authorities due to their different sizes and workloads. For instance, smaller EU jurisdictions would require a smaller budget than EU jurisdictions with a higher number of intellectual property infringements online.

Further, the proposed supervisory authority could also draw financial resources from the EU annual budget. For instance, ENISA, the EU Cyber security Agency's annual budget for 2019 was €17 million. Its funding mainly stems from EU financial resources, it includes a contribution from the Greek government since the Agency is situated in Greece, and financial support from countries that participate in the activities of the Agency.[190] Similarly, the European Data Protection Board's annual budget for 2019 was €16,638,572,[191] in the same year the European Union Aviation Safety Agency's budget was €161 million, with 23 per cent derived from EU funding and 64 per cent from the industry sector.[192] Finally, in 2020 the European Ombundsman received support in order to finance its activities from the EU budget of €10,825,382.[193]

Yet, one might argue that the development of an ISP supervisory authority in each national jurisdiction might require a large financial budget. Indeed, it has been estimated that Data Protection Authorities in national Member States have a very high budget. For instance, in 2019 the Belgian Data Protection agency had a budget of €6,345,000, the Croatian agency had €890,610, the Greek Data Protection agency had €2,849,000 while the UK Information Commissioner's Office had €36,047,932.[194]

However, an ISP supervisory authority could operate under the umbrella of an existing governmental body. Consider, for instance, the case of Greece. Within the context of Intellectual Property Law, a Committee on Internet Violations of Intellectual Property has been established. Pursuant to Article 66E of the Greek Intellectual Property Law 4481/2017, this Committee operates under the auspices of the Hellenic Copyright Organisation, its main duties are to adjudicate private disputes between online intermediaries and right holders for the circulation of unlawful material within their networks.[195] This means that the Committee operates under the Copyright Organisation's funding. That funding comes from the fees paid by the members of the Organisation, financial contributions from the EU Institutions, International Organisations such as the World Intellectual Property Organisation, and donations.[196]

Another example may be found in the Italian Authority for Communication Industries, which is integrated into the public administrative structure since it is accountable to the Italian Parliament. The funding for the authority mainly comes from an annual contribution from the State, and from fees paid by the members of the Authority, namely

[190] ENISA, accounting and finance, www.enisa.europa.eu/about-enisa/accounting-finance.

[191] European Data Protection Board, 'Memorandum of Understanding between the European Data Protection Board and the European Data Protection Supervisor' edpb.europa.eu/sites/default/files/files/file1/memorandum_of_understanding_signed_en.pdf.

[192] EASA is available at www.easa.europa.eu/the-agency/the-agency.

[193] Ombudsman is available at www.ombudsman.europa.eu/en/annual/en/141317.

[194] Report on EU Data Protection Authorities, Part 4: Resources Deloitte Privacy Services – Privacy Response, www2.deloitte.com/content/dam/Deloitte/nl/Documents/risk/deloitte-nl-risk-reports-resources.pdf.

[195] General information on the Greek Committee on intellectual property violations, www.opi.gr/en/committee/general-information.

[196] Tsigou (n 49) 204; Chiou (n 48).

online intermediaries. The annual budget and the amount of fees are decided on a yearly basis, as per Articles 65 and 66 of the Law on Disposizioni per la formazione del bilancio annuale e pluriennale dello Stato – legge finanziaria 2006.[197]

Overall, it seems that there is an array of funding schemes available at European level. Either the authority could draw financial resources from the EU budget, national governments' contributions, or members' fees, or it can operate under an existing authority, such as the example of the Greek Committee.

VII. Conclusion

This chapter has discussed the establishment of a host ISP supervisory authority for copyright and trade mark infringements and has built on the findings of the previous chapters in order to justify this need. In particular, as elaborated in chapter three, it has been found that the current legal framework under Article 14(1) of the ECD appears to be outdated, thus it undermines right holders' interests and poses serious threats for the restriction of the fundamental rights of internet users and host ISPs. In addition, as presented in chapter four, the legal framework that regulates the OCSSPs' liability, ie, the DSMD, seems to be problematic since while it favours copyright holders' interests, it interferes with the rights of OCSSPs and internet users.

In order to establish a robust legal framework that strikes a fair balance between the interests of the parties involved, this chapter recommended the creation of a co-regulatory regime that entails a set of responsibilities for host ISPs. The aim of this would be to terminate or curb online infringements within their networks through which they should be accountable to a host ISP supervisory authority.

In this regard, this chapter explored the normative considerations of a host ISP supervisory authority. In contrast to the current legal framework under Article 14(1) of the ECD and Article 17 of the DSMD, it was argued that a host ISP supervisory authority would enhance legal certainty to users, rights holders, and host ISPs. It would promote access to justice for users and right holders, while it would also enhance the rule of law by providing remedial mechanisms to internet users and online consumers.

Having discussed the normative considerations for creating such a host ISP supervisory authority, this chapter moved on to the question of the principles and functions this authority should have. In order to identify the principles, parallels with existing supervisory authorities at European level were drawn, such as Data Protection and Competition Law Authorities. With regard to the functions of a host ISP supervisory authority, it was suggested that proportionality, consistency, accountability, and independence would make this host ISP supervisory authority's role and decisions legitimate.

Further, this chapter suggested the functions that the proposed host ISP supervisory authority should have. The first function concerned the enforcement of intellectual property rights. In particular, it was argued that the host ISP supervisory authority would verify the completion of the set of responsibilities of host ISPs relating to the

[197] AGCOM's official website, www.agcom.it/contributo-dovuto-all-autorita.

dissemination of infringing content within their platforms. Non-compliance with the set of responsibilities would amount to the imposition of fines. In addition, right holders could resort to this authority in order to enforce their rights. The second function of this host ISP supervisory authority should be to examine complaints submitted by internet users whose material has been erroneously removed by host ISPs, or online consumers who have been deceived by purchasing counterfeit goods from online marketplaces. The third function of the proposed host ISP supervisory authority should represent an educative role. This means that the authority would be assigned the duty to promote awareness among internet users about the legal implications of online piracy for right holders. These include economic losses, legal consequences to those users who upload, download, and exchange material without permission, and information on existing remedies for those internet users whose content has been erroneously taken down. Moreover, information for online consumers should also be included with advice on how to protect themselves from fake goods online and existing mechanisms for safeguarding their rights.

Finally, the narrative finished with a discussion on potential financial schemes that could support the creation of a supervisory authority. More specifically, the financial contribution of the industry sector, members' fees or the governmental economic support could be offered as schemes for funding the operation and the functions of the proposed authority.

Conclusion

This book has now come to an end. Its aim, to critically examine the current legislative framework about the liability of host ISPs for copyright and trade mark infringements that take place within their networks and then to flesh out a more balanced legislative framework, taking into consideration the interests of host ISPs, rights holders, and internet users/consumers, has been achieved.

The reader will recall that Part I offered an overview of the theoretical and political background that revolves around the activities of host ISPs. In particular, chapter one presented the internet regulatory theories of self-regulation, state regulation, and co-regulation, and their advantages and drawbacks. This enabled the reader to gain an understanding of the different theories, their boundaries, and their scope of application within the online environment. It also provided a thorough analysis of the moral and utilitarian theories involved in order to justify the ascription of liability rules to host ISPs. Following this, chapter two engaged with policy and practical considerations upon which liability rules to host ISPs are warranted.

Part II evaluated the current legislative framework on host ISPs' liability with a focus on copyright and trade mark infringements that accrue within their networks. More specifically, in light of the exponential growth of e-commerce and rapid technological developments, host ISPs have evolved from being purely communication tools to becoming the main source of information and goods for internet users/consumers. At the same time, this transformation enabled rights holders to reach a broader audience for their goods and works, and therefore to increase their revenues.[1] However, a number of EU documents and court cases demonstrate that the activities of host ISPs attract a high rate of copyright and trade mark violations.[2]

In order to protect their works and brands, rights holders seek redress against host ISPs. Yet, the current legislative tools, namely the ECD and the DSMD, seem inefficient. In particular, the current legal framework, as discussed in chapters three, four, and five, fail to protect the rights of intellectual property holders. Rather, as the findings indicate, both legislative tools might severely interfere with internet users' fundamental rights to access information as well as pose serious risks to host ISPs' rights to conduct business, pursuant to Article 16 of the EU Charter of Fundamental Rights.

More specifically, in chapter three, it was argued that the legal framework with regard to host ISPs' liability for trade mark infringements under the ECD, is outdated.

[1] See also A Bridy and D Keller, 'U.S. Copyright Office Section 512 Study: Comments in Response to Notice of Inquiry' (31 March 2016) 14–15.

[2] EU Commission, 'Public Consultation on the evaluation and modernisation of the legal framework for the enforcement of intellectual property rights: Summary of responses' (14 September 2016) 8.

In this respect, it was noted that Article 14(1) of the ECD introduces a secondary liability regime for host ISPs with regard to trade mark infringements, it requires the element of knowledge in order to attribute liability to host ISPs. As many commentators have argued, the introduction of a secondary liability regime in 2000 was welcome. This is because the requirement of knowledge could be used by host ISPs as a defence in cases of legal proceedings against them. However, while this understanding has its own merits from a theoretical point of view, in practice it is far from reality.

As the findings indicate, this is mainly due to three factors. Firstly, Article 14 of the ECD failed to provide a definition for host ISPs' liability. By contrast, it offers defences to host ISPs in order to escape liability. In other words, this implies that the legal provisions specify only the requirements that shelter host ISPs from liability and state what host ISPs should not do in order to escape liability.

Secondly, the national implementation of the ECD also failed. It was noted that the selected jurisdictions this research looked at follow verbatim the ECD, and thus they follow its rationale by offering defences to host ISPs rather than offering the circumstances under which host ISPs could be held liable. What is more, it was noted that the selected jurisdictions fail to give concrete guidance with regard to the interpretation of the defences that host ISPs would use in order for them not to be liable for the infringements that accrue within their networks. For example, with regard to the requirement of knowledge, the UK Laws state that only a competent notice that allocates the precise location of the infringing content could obtain knowledge of the illicit activity, while the French legal system endorses the concept of the diligent economic operator.

Thirdly, by not defining host ISPs' liability along with the heterogenous interpretations of the requirements of knowledge and expeditious removal of the allegedly infringing content, domestic courts were forced to resort to their national tortious secondary liability doctrines in order to attribute liability to host ISPs for intellectual property violations committed by their users. Interestingly, even though it was noted that national tortious secondary liability doctrines could offer a definition for host ISPs' liability, a number of problematic issues were identified.

In particular, it was noted in chapter three that domestic courts faced discrepancies in order to apply tortious secondary liability doctrines to host ISPs' activities. Indeed, secondary tortious liability rules in some jurisdictions treat host ISPs as primary infringers. For instance, the joint-tortfeasance doctrine, which has an application in the UK and German legal systems, considers the host ISP as a primary infringer of the tortious act.[3] This doctrine, therefore, might raise concerns with regard to the appropriateness of applying joint-tortfeasance doctrines to the host ISPs' activities. In addition, tortious secondary liability doctrines impose a duty of care which can only be assessed on a case by case basis. Yet, the imposition of a duty of care on host ISPs has been subject to intense debate since Article 15(1) of the ECD explicitly prohibits the imposition of monitoring obligations on host ISPs.

Finally, another problematic issue is that tortious secondary liability rules differ from jurisdiction to jurisdiction, thus creating a patchwork of miscellaneous tort law doctrines and accentuating the existing legal uncertainty. As the findings indicate,

[3] Chapter 3 section III(C) i, ii, iii.

based on the analysis of the selected jurisdictions, the French tort law system extends the direct breach of tort law provisions to additional actors and imposes a duty of care on host ISPs which forces them to deploy preventive measures and mechanisms in order to eliminate future infringements online.[4] In similar fashion, the German legal system, based on case law, shapes the notion of disturber liability and imposes a reasonable duty of care on host ISPs.[5] With regard to the UK, although the courts apply the doctrine of joint-tortfeasance within the context of host ISPs' activities, to attribute a duty of care to host ISPs for the infringements online seems not to be applicable.[6] In Greek Law, it seems difficult to fit the doctrine of causal link within the host ISPs' context[7] while in Spanish legal system the duty of care appears to be a plausible but unexplored solution for host ISPs.[8]

As a corollary, in chapter three, it was concluded that the current legal framework under Article 14 of the ECD undermines the rights of intellectual property holders, while at the same time it subordinates the rights of host ISPs and internet users.

In light of this finding, in chapter four, the narrative continued to the second legislative tool that regulates OCSSPs' liability for copyright infringements, the DSMD. The DSMD[9] is relatively new since it was voted in on 26 March 2019 by the EU Parliament. Consequently, any assumption with regard to its implications rests on a theoretical basis. Yet, as the findings in chapter four indicate, Article 17 of the DSMD, which regulates the liability of OCSSPs for copyright infringements, is controversial because it entails an array of problematic features.

Firstly, it was noted in chapter four section III(B) that a problematic feature of Article 17 of the DSMD is the introduction of primary liability rules. In particular, Article 17(1) states that an OCSSP performs an act of communication to the public or an act of making available copyrighted content to the public. The imposition of primary liability rules goes against the rationale of secondary liability theories that have been the cornerstone of e-commerce since 2000. Such theories have safeguarded the operation of business for many host ISPs and the internet as a space for exchanging information between users. This is because the defence of knowledge, which is a requisite for triggering secondary liability rules, enabled them to escape from liability in cases where intellectual property owners were bringing lawsuits against them alleging violation of their rights. Indeed, as discussed in chapter three and as per Article 14 of the ECD, host ISPs can escape liability if they expeditiously remove the infringing content of which they have been made aware. In contrast, primary liability rules, which are now endorsed in Article 17 of the DSMD, do not require the element of knowledge. In other words, under Article 17 of the DSMD, OCSSPs would be held liable for any copyright infringement that occur within their networks.

In order to escape liability, OCSSPs have two options. Pursuant to Article 17(4) of the DSMD, OCSSPs must either make their best efforts to seek to conclude licensing

[4] Chapter 3 section III(C) iii.
[5] Chapter 3 section III(C) ii.
[6] Chapter 3 section III(C) i.
[7] Chapter 3 section III(C) v.
[8] Chapter 3 section III(C) iv.
[9] Chapter 4 section I.

agreements or to terminate the dissemination, as well as prevent the reappearance of copyright infringements. However, it was noted that both requirements present challenges. On the one hand, the conclusion of licensing agreements seems impossible. Indeed, even though the full licensing of the circulated content can only be achieved via umbrella licences, such extended collective licences that are issued by collective societies cover only the works of their members.[10] On the other hand, it was noted that a notice and stay down mechanism has been introduced without identifying what it entails and without defining its limits.[11] Indeed, it is questionable whether the notice and stay down system requires the implementation of technological filtering tools. What is more, the limits of this notice and stay down mechanism might be subject to different interpretations. Indeed, it is questionable whether this system points to the emergence of copyright infringements of the same nature, or by the same user, or of the same nature by different users, or of the same nature by the same user.[12]

Secondly, another problematic aspect addresses Article 17(8) of the DSMD which explicitly prohibits general monitoring obligations. It was noted in chapter four section III(E) that this paragraph lacks practical significance since Article 17(4) of the DSMD requires OCSSPs to prevent the reemergence of unlawful content online. The prevention of the reappearance of unlawful content can be achieved via either filtering tools or human review.

Finally, the problematic framework of Article 17 of the DSMD culminates with the creation of a redress mechanism by OCSSPs as well as the creation of an out of court body that would address any potential disputes between OCSSPs and internet users. This is because, as the findings indicate in chapter four section III(F), if those out of court mechanisms are established without a specific set of principles, they would be jeopardised. Such principles are those of accountability, consistency, proportionality, and due process, and the right of access to justice for internet users as enshrined in the EU Charter of Fundamental Rights and the European Convention of Human Rights.

However, as discussed in chapter four section V, it is not only Article 17 of the DSMD that appears to be problematic. Indeed, the intersection of Article 17 of the DSMD with Article 14 of the ECD is also problematic. Firstly, it was argued that a divide in the existing trend of case law might incur since there might be cases where host ISPs that do not fall within the definition of OCSSPs provide services that fall under the scope of Article 17 of the DSMD.

Secondly, Article 17 of the DSMD is considered *lex specialis* to Article 14 of the ECD. However, a dual liability regime would occur. Secondary liability rules would apply in the case of trade mark infringements within the networks of host ISPs, and primary liability rules would be applicable for OCSSPs in the case of copyright violations within their networks. This dual liability regime is contradictory since the rationale of both liability regimes are diametrically opposed. As presented in chapter three section III, the rationale of secondary liability rules is to enable host ISPs to avoid liability under

[10] JP Quintais, 'The New Copyright in the Digital Single Market Directive: A Critical Look' (2019) 1 *European Intellectual Property Review* 19.

[11] Chapter 4.

[12] This is the so called Kerntheorie and has been discussed in ch 3 section III(B) ii; see also in Case C-494/15 *Tommy Hilfiger Licensing* (2016) ECLI:EU:C: 2016:528, para 34.

the defence of a lack of knowledge of the illicit activity. It is this rationale that permitted e-commerce to thrive and enabled the European Digital Single Market to compete with its US counterparts. In contrast to secondary liability rules, primary liability rules do not offer the defence of a lack of knowledge. Indeed, under the regime of primary liability, once the infringement takes place, OCSSPs would be subject to liability.

What is more, this dual liability regime would split the burden of proof for the parties at stake. Under Article 14 of the ECD, right holders must provide evidence that they identified the infringing content and sent a valid notice to host ISPs detailing the precise allocation of the allegedly infringing content. In contrast, under Article 17 of the DSMD, which includes a notice and stay down regime, OCSSPs must demonstrate that they deployed all the preventive mechanisms to terminate the dissemination of unauthorised content within their networks as well as prevent its reappearance in the future.

As elaborated in chapter five section IV, this understanding might lead to the creation of a monopoly in the field of OCSSPs. For instance, popular OCSSPs would be empowered in the Digital Single Market since they have already developed their own technological tools, and thus they own the technological know-how required to terminate online infringements. What is more, given that the burden of proof rests on the OCSSPs to prove that they undertook all necessary measures to stop the infringements, many new OCSSPs will be hesitant to enter the Digital Single Market since they would prefer to invest in business models with a lower burden of proof in the context of liability. Therefore, the main aim of the European policymakers, namely to facilitate e-commerce players and boost innovation within the Digital Single Market, would be in peril.

Based on this analysis, what the implications of an outdated and problematic framework under the ECD and the DSMD would be for the parties whose interests are involved is questionable. Therefore, it was necessary to examine the implications of both legislative tools to intellectual property holders, internet users, and host ISPs. This has been discussed in chapter five Part II.

Firstly, it was noted that legal uncertainty might pose a serious interference to the business model of host ISPs. This is the case of dual use technologies which can 'be used to violate third parties' rights as well as promote social beneficial uses'.[13] Indeed, in order to be exonerated from liability, host ISPs might be forced to undertake expensive precautionary measures, thus their right to conduct business as per Article 16 of the EU Charter of Fundamental Rights would be disrupted. In this vein, new host ISPs that wish to enter the Digital Single Market would be hesitant. Therefore, one of the core elements of the Digital Single Market, which is the creation of new business models, would be jeopardised at supranational and national levels.[14]

Secondly, legal uncertainty might encroach upon internet users' fundamental right of freedom of expression, as per Article 11 of the EU Charter of Fundamental rights.

[13] G Frosio, 'Why keep a dog and bark yourself? From intermediary liability to responsibility' (2017) *Centre for International Intellectual Property Studies* 8.

[14] JS Marcus, G Petropoulos and T Yeung, 'Contribution to Growth: The European Digital Single Market Delivering economic benefits for citizens and businesses' (2019) *IMCO Committee* 11, www.europarl.europa.eu/RegData/etudes/STUD/2019/631044/IPOL_STU(2019)631044_EN.pdf; EU Commission, 'A Digital Single Market Strategy for Europe' COM (2015) 192 final 3.

Being subject to liability rules, host ISPs might act as 'overzealous police officers'.[15] Subsequently, this could lead to an over-enforcement of rights online or the blocking of websites without adequate investigation of the allegedly illicit activities that might occur. Therefore, this outcome might limit the amount of information available online, and thus restrict users' rights to information.

Thirdly, legal uncertainty might interfere with intellectual property holders' rights. The lack of a definition for host ISPs' liability, along with a patchwork of diverse tortious secondary liability doctrines under the ECD liability regime, might result in an uncertain enforcement of intellectual property rights. As a corollary, intellectual property holders might not be able to successfully seek redress for the violation of their rights and thus compensate their losses in cases of intellectual property infringements. What is more, under Article 17 of the DSMD, intellectual property holders might encounter difficulties when seeking redress for their damages. As discussed in chapter 5 section II, it is questionable how intellectual property holders might seek redress for the infringements of their rights within the platforms that fall outside the scope of Article 17 of the DSMD but who provide services that fall within the meaning of giving 'the public access to copyright-protected works or other protected subject matter uploaded by its users'.

Based on this analysis, in chapter six, the narrative continued to the third legislative tool that aims to regulate host ISPs for trade mark and copyright infringements, which is the Proposal for a Digital Services Act Regulation. The Proposal for a Regulation was introduced on 15 December 2020 and is not legally binding at this stage. It has received a warm welcome from human rights associations and rights holders because it appears to take into consideration the interests of online consumers and endorses the principle of transparency and the duty of care. However, more granularity in certain provisions is required while at the same time it is unclear how the final draft of the Regulation might look due to the long EU legislative process.

In light of the above, Part II of this book offered a critical examination of the current legislative tools that regulate the activities of host ISPs with regard to copyright and trade mark infringements online, and outlined the inefficiencies and the implications for the interests of the parties involved. These findings offered the normative justifications for a new regulatory framework for host ISPs that have been explicitly explored in Part III.

In particular, Part III presents an alternative legal framework based on a set of responsibilities for host ISPs that would be accountable to a host ISP supervisory authority. From a normative perspective, in chapter seven section II it was argued that host ISPs nowadays do not merely host content stored by their users, rather their new role has extended so they have become information gatekeepers, creators of public policies, enforcers and adjudicators of intellectual property rights. Yet, these new roles cannot be compromised by host ISPs' private interests. Host ISPs are private corporations with business partners and interests, a simple fact which could lead them to adopt a lower standard for protecting internet users' rights.[16] In this light, the establishment

[15] D Rowland, U Kohl and A Charlesworth, *Information Technology Law*, 5th edn (London, Routledge, 2017) 87.

[16] O Lysnkey, 'Regulation by Platforms: The Impact on Fundamental Rights' in L Belli and N Zingales (eds), *Platform Regulations: How Platforms are Regulated and How They Regulate Us* (2017) 92.

of a responsibility framework for ISPs might offer a greater degree of protection for the rights of internet users/online consumers.

Having discussed the normative considerations for imposing a responsibility framework for host ISPs through which they would be accountable to a proposed host ISP supervisory authority, a set of responsibilities for host ISPs were presented. More specifically, in chapter seven it was argued that a duty of care should be imposed on host ISPs with regard to the dissemination of infringing content within their networks. Such a duty of care amounts to the responsibility of host ISPs to terminate the dissemination of infringing content and also prevent its reappearance.

However, the imposition of a duty of care does not come without criticism. Firstly, it has been argued that the duty of care contravenes Article 14 of the ECD which states that the nature of host ISPs is passive. Yet, this argument is not solid. This is because, as the findings indicate, a growing trend in case law treats host ISPs as active entities. For instance, as noted in chapter seven, a number of judgments at European and national level confirm this tendency.

Moreover, it was argued that a duty of care is outside the rationale of the ECD because its Article 15 prohibits the adoption of general monitoring obligations. I have argued that a duty of care does not amount to general monitoring obligations. Rather, as stated in Recital 48, 'This Directive does not affect the possibility for Member States of requiring service providers, who host information provided by recipients of their service, to apply duties of care, which can reasonably be expected from them and which are specified by national law, in order to detect and prevent certain types of illegal activities.' Otherwise, there would be no reason to state in the preamble of the ECD that a duty of care could be imposed overall.

Further, it has been argued that a duty of care would amount to the implementation of filtering-based technology or human review of the content that is disseminated online. However, it shall be up to the host ISPs to decide which option better fits their business model.

This means that if filtering-based technology would be preferred, host ISPs would not be able to argue that they lack knowledge of the illicit activities online. This is a very likely scenario which could make host ISPs subject to liability rules. I have argued that the adoption of proactive measures would not result in the liability of host ISPs. In order to eliminate this outcome, in chapter seven section VI(A), I referred to the US legal system and examined the principle of the Good Samaritan clause. It has been suggested that a similar principle could be embedded in the proposed responsibility framework for host ISPs in order to avoid any serious interference with the right of host ISPs to conduct business, as set forth in Article 16 of the EU Charter of Fundamental Rights.

However, although the imposition of the Good Samaritan clause could safeguard host ISPs' fundamental right to business, the imposition of a duty of care might pose risks to internet users' rights. For instance, although filtering technology is highly sophisticated and a small margin of error may be incurred with regard to the removal of infringing content, a risk to censorship of the content that users have uploaded is apparent.

Accordingly, to eliminate the negative impact of a wide scope for transparency, in chapter eight it was noted that a transparency obligation should be implemented in host ISPs' activities with regard to the removal of infringing content or counterfeit goods.

However, even though many commentators argue that transparency might increase the transaction costs of host ISPs, I have argued that a transparency obligation would have merits not only for users' fundamental rights but also for host ISPs' interests.

With regard to users' fundamental rights, a transparency obligation would enhance the rule of law and due process. Indeed, as explained in chapter eight section III, users will be provided with information relating to the removal of their content, thus they would be able to ascertain whether host ISPs have complied with the rules. Also, in the context of transparency, users would be able to challenge the decision of removal if they do not agree. Moreover, the transparency obligation might enhance the trust of internet users since they would be aware of the thresholds that triggered the removal of their content and whether this decision was based on legitimate reasoning. Finally, consumers' trust in online sales in general would be increased since the provision of information would make consumers aware of how the online market places supervise the circulation of goods online and their methods to combat the spread of pirated goods.

Nevertheless, the introduction of a transparency obligation would not only safeguard users' rights but also induce host ISPs to adopt better methods. Given that their practices would be disclosed to their internet users/online consumers, host ISPs would be incentivised to conduct a prior examination of their practices, before they put them into practice, and evaluate their results. Hence, transparency would eliminate any errors or malfunctions in the practices that host ISPs adopt, thereby improving the principles of good governance.

Chapter eight argued that however necessary a transparency obligation might be, it is crucial to identify the limits within which such an obligation would be exercised. Otherwise, the potential advantages a transparency obligation might have would lead to adverse results for host ISPs. It was suggested that a transparency obligation would be required in different contexts. In this respect, it was recommended that a partial transparency obligation should be imposed with the introduction of a right to explanation so that users can request more information about the removal of their content, while at the same time host ISPs' algorithms would not be disclosed and their business model would be safeguarded. Moreover, it was recommended that a transparency obligation should be applicable to the terms of service of host ISPs. This means that users would be notified when their content has been removed and would be able to challenge the removal via the counter-notification procedures of host ISPs. As a result, the right to a fair trial and the right to appropriate remedy of internet users/online consumers would be safeguarded. Finally, a transparency obligation should include the issue of transparency reports. Those reports would inform the users about the removals related to unauthorised content or fake goods per country as well as the specific reasons that trigger their removal.

Finally, chapter nine presented the last recommendation to complete a responsibility framework for host ISPs based on co-regulation, namely the establishment of a host ISP supervisory authority. This recommendation has already been instigated at European and national levels. For instance, an authority envisaged in Article 17(9) of the DSMD states, 'Member States shall also ensure that out-of-court redress mechanisms are available for the settlement of disputes.' Although Article 17(9) of the DSMD does not entail any precise guidance as to the principles and functions of this authority, it offers a hint of such an authority. What is more, as the findings indicate in chapter nine, a number of national Member States have already created such authorities to deal with disputes between host ISPs and right holders. Representative examples can be found in Greece and Italy. Although certain flaws in the operation of such authorities were identified, this does not mean that they are not a good start.

In this regard, the creation of an ISP supervisory authority was recommended in chapter nine. Building upon the previous chapters, the proposed host ISP supervisory authority would function through a number of principles. Such principles concern the independence of the authority, the consistent and proportionate decisions it would issue, and the accountability it should have towards a hierarchically superior administrative body. Further, the proposed supervisory authority would enforce intellectual property rights online, offer a complaints mechanism for users, and promote awareness to users and consumers for online piracy. With regard to the enforcement of intellectual property rights, the current legal framework, under Article 14 of the ECD and Article 17 of the DSMD, does not offer adequate protection for the rights of content owners and brand owners. In this light, the proposed ISP supervisory authority would provide right holders a better redress mechanism in order to safeguard their rights.

Further, the proposed ISP supervisory authority would offer a complaints mechanism for internet users and online consumers and would be accessible to those whose counter-notifications have been dismissed or ignored by host ISPs. In this sense, a complaints mechanism for users would enhance the right of users to access justice since they would be able to submit a complaint against the host ISP to the proposed ISP supervisory authority. Following this, the complaint of the user would be thoroughly examined and a fine would be imposed on the host ISP if the removal lacks legitimate basis.

Moreover, the proposed ISP supervisory authority might also play an educative role. As explored in chapter nine section V(C), in parallel with its enforcement duties and users' complaints resolution, educational campaigns and promotion of awareness among users about the detrimental effect of piracy on right holders' rights, as well as about the access to remedy mechanisms, would have merits.

Therefore, on the basis of the recommendations provided, a responsibility framework based on a co-regulatory approach might offer a more balanced framework for the rights of all the parties at stake, namely intellectual property holders, internet users, and host ISPs. This balanced framework would be in accordance with the existing EU case law that advocates in favour of an equilibrium between the different interests at stake. In addition, this framework would be in accordance with the rationale of the secondary liability regime, of which the requirement of knowledge is a substantial part, and would enable host ISPs to use it as a defence in order to escape liability.

In light of the above, the recommendations detailed in this book aim to enhance the academic discourse on host ISPs' liability, offer an alternative path for legal practitioners to resolve copyright and trade mark disputes online, and to assist and influence the policy-making process at European level in order to craft a more robust legal framework that considers the interests of all parties involved.

APPENDIX

I. European Commission's Proposal for a Copyright in the Digital Single Market Directive on 14 September 2016

Article 13

Use of protected content by information society service providers storing and giving access to large amounts of works and other subject-matter uploaded by their users

1. Information society service providers that store and provide to the public access to large amounts of works or other subject-matter uploaded by their users shall, in cooperation with rightholders, take measures to ensure the functioning of agreements concluded with rightholders for the use of their works or other subject-matter or to prevent the availability on their services of works or other subject-matter identified by rightholders through the cooperation with the service providers. Those measures, such as the use of effective content recognition technologies, shall be appropriate and proportionate. The service providers shall provide rightholders with adequate information on the functioning and the deployment of the measures, as well as, adequate reporting on the recognition and use of the works and other subject-matter.
2. Member States shall ensure that the service providers referred to in paragraph 1 put in place complaints and redress mechanisms that are available to users in case of disputes over the application of the measures referred to in paragraph 1.
3. Member States shall facilitate, where appropriate, the cooperation between the information society service providers and rightholders through stakeholder dialogues to define best practices, such as appropriate and proportionate content recognition technologies, taking into account, among others, the nature of the services, the availability of the technologies and their effectiveness in light of technological developments.

II. Council Text 25 May 2018

Article 13

Use of protected content by online content sharing service providers

1. Member States shall provide that an online content sharing service provider performs an act of communication to the public or an act of making available

to the public when it gives the public access to copyright protected works or other protected subject matter uploaded by its users. An online content sharing service provider shall obtain an authorisation from the rightholders referred to in Article 3(1) and (2) of Directive 2001/29/EC in order to communicate or make available to the public works or other subject matter. Where no such authorisation has been obtained, the service provider shall prevent the availability on its service of those works and other subject matter, including through the application of measures referred to in paragraph 4. This subparagraph shall apply without prejudice to exceptions and limitations provided for in Union law. Member States shall provide that when an authorisation has been obtained, including via a licensing agreement, by an online content sharing service provider, this authorisation shall also cover acts of uploading by the users of the service falling within Article 3 of Directive 2001/29/EC when they are not acting on a commercial basis.

2. Deleted.
3. When an online content sharing service provider performs an act of communication to the public or an act of making available to the public, it shall not be eligible for the exemption of liability provided for in Article 14 of Directive 2000/31/EC for unauthorised acts of communication to the public and making available to the public, without prejudice to the possible application of Article 14 of Directive 2000/31/EC to those services for purposes other than copyright relevant acts.
4. In the absence of the authorisation referred to in the second subparagraph of paragraph 1, Member States shall provide that an online content sharing service provider shall not be liable for acts of communication to the public or making available to the public within the meaning of this Article when: (a) it demonstrates that it has made best efforts to prevent the availability of specific works or other subject matter by implementing effective and proportionate measures, in accordance with paragraph 5, to prevent the availability on its services of the specific works or other subject matter identified by rightholders and for which the rightholders have provided the service with relevant and necessary information for the application of these measures; and (b) upon notification by rightholders of works or other subject matter, it has acted expeditiously to remove or disable access to these works or other subject matter and it demonstrates that it has made its best efforts to prevent their future availability through the measures referred to in point (a).
5. The measures referred to in point (a) of paragraph 4 shall be effective and proportionate, taking into account, among other factors: (a) the nature and size of the services, in particular whether they are provided by a microenterprise or a small-sized enterprise within the meaning of Title I of the Annex to Commission Recommendation 2003/361/EC, and their audience; (b) the amount and the type of works or other subject matter uploaded by the users of the services; (c) the availability and costs of the measures as well as their effectiveness in light of technological developments in line with the industry best practice referred to in paragraph 8.
6. Member States shall ensure that online content sharing service providers and rightholders cooperate with each other in a diligent manner to ensure the effective

functioning of the measures referred to in point (a) of paragraph 4 over time. Online content sharing service providers shall provide rightholders, at their request, with adequate information on the deployment and functioning of these measures to allow the assessment of their effectiveness, in particular information on the type of measures used and, where licensing agreements are concluded between service providers and rightholders, information on the use of content covered by the agreements.

7. Member States shall ensure that the measures referred to in paragraph 4 are implemented by the online content sharing service provider without prejudice to the possibility for their users to benefit from exceptions or limitations to copyright. For that purpose, the service provider shall put in place a complaint and redress mechanism that is available to users of the service in case of disputes over the application of the measures to their content. Complaints submitted under this mechanism shall be processed by the online content sharing service provider in cooperation with relevant rightholders within a reasonable period of time. Rightholders shall duly justify the reasons for their requests to remove or block access to their specific works or other subject matter. Member States shall endeavour to put in place independent bodies to assess complaints related to the application of the measures.
8. The Commission and the Member States shall encourage stakeholder dialogues to define best practices for the measures referred to in point (a) of paragraph 4. Member States shall also endeavour to establish mechanisms to facilitate the assessment of the effectiveness and proportionality of these measures and provide the Commission regularly with information on those mechanisms. The Commission shall, in consultation with online content sharing service providers, rightholders and other relevant stakeholders and taking into account the results of the stakeholder dialogues and the national mechanisms, issue guidance on the application of the measures referred to in point (a) of paragraph 4.

III. EU Parliament Text 12 September 2018

Article 13

Use of protected content by online content sharing service providers storing and giving access to large amounts of works and other subject-matter uploaded by their users

1. Without prejudice to Article 3(1) and (2) of Directive 2001/29/EC, online content sharing service providers perform an act of communication to the public. They shall therefore conclude fair and appropriate licensing agreements with right holders.
2. Licensing agreements which are concluded by online content sharing service providers with right holders for the acts of communication referred to in paragraph 1, shall cover the liability for works uploaded by the users of such online content sharing services in line with the terms and conditions set out in

the licensing agreement, provided that such users do not act for commercial purposes. 2a. Member States shall provide that where right holders do not wish to conclude licensing agreements, online content sharing service providers and right holders shall cooperate in good faith in order to ensure that unauthorised protected works or other subject matter are not available on their services. Cooperation between online content service providers and right holders shall not lead to preventing the availability of non-infringing works or other protected subject matter, including those covered by an exception or limitation to copyright. 2b. Members States shall ensure that online content sharing service providers referred to in paragraph 1 put in place effective and expeditious complaints and redress mechanisms that are available to users in case the cooperation referred to in paragraph 2a leads to unjustified removals of their content. Any complaint filed under such mechanisms shall be processed without undue delay and be subject to human review. Right holders shall reasonably justify their decisions to avoid arbitrary dismissal of complaints. Moreover, in accordance with Directive 95/46/EC, Directive 2002/58/EC and the General Data Protection Regulation, the cooperation shall not lead to any identification of individual users nor the processing of their personal data. Member States shall also ensure that users have access to an independent body for the resolution of disputes as well as to a court or another relevant judicial authority to assert the use of an exception or limitation to copyright rules.

3. As of [date of entry into force of this directive], the Commission and the Member States shall organise dialogues between stakeholders to harmonise and to define best practices and issue guidance to ensure the functioning of licensing agreements and on cooperation between online content sharing service providers and right holders for the use of their works or other subject matter within the meaning of this Directive. When defining best practices, special account shall be taken of fundamental rights, the use of exceptions and limitations as well as ensuring that the burden on SMEs remains appropriate and that automated blocking of content is avoided.

Article 13a. Member States shall provide that disputes between successors in title and information society services regarding the application of Article 13(1) may be subject to an alternative dispute resolution system. Member States shall establish or designate an impartial body with the necessary expertise, with the aim of helping the parties to settle their disputes under this system. The Member States shall inform the Commission of the establishment of this body no later than (date mentioned in Article 21(1)).

Article 13b. Use of protected content by information society services providing automated image referencing Member States shall ensure that information society service providers that automatically reproduce or refer to significant amounts of copyright-protected visual works and make them available to the public for the purpose of indexing and referencing conclude fair and balanced licensing agreements with any requesting rightholders in order to ensure their fair remuneration. Such remuneration may be managed by the collective management organisation of the rightholders concerned.

IV. Compromised Text after the Trilogues' Negotiations 20 February 2019

Article 17

Use of protected content by online content sharing service providers

1. Member States shall provide that an online content-sharing service provider performs an act of communication to the public or an act of making available to the public for the purposes of this Directive when it gives the public access to copyright-protected works or other protected subject matter uploaded by its users. An online content-sharing service provider shall therefore obtain an authorisation from the rightholders referred to in Article 3(1) and (2) of Directive 2001/29/EC, for instance by concluding a licensing agreement, in order to communicate to the public or make available to the public works or other subject matter.
2. Member States shall provide that when an authorisation has been obtained, including via a licensing agreement, by an online content sharing service provider, this authorisation shall also cover acts carried out by users of the services falling within Article 3 of Directive 2001/29/EC when they are not acting on a commercial basis or their activity does not generate significant revenues.
3. When an online content-sharing service provider performs an act of communication to the public or an act of making available to the public under the conditions laid down in this Directive, the limitation of liability established in Article 14(1) of Directive 2000/31/EC shall not apply to the situations covered by this Article. The first subparagraph of this paragraph shall not affect the possible application of Article 14(1) of Directive 2000/31/EC to those service providers for purposes falling outside the scope of this Directive.
4. If no authorisation is granted, online content-sharing service providers shall be liable for unauthorised acts of communication to the public, including making available to the public, of copyright-protected works and other subject matter, unless the service providers demonstrate that they have: (a) made best efforts to obtain an authorisation, and (b) made, in accordance with high industry standards of professional diligence, best efforts to ensure the unavailability of specific works and other subject matter for which the rightholders have provided the service providers with the relevant and necessary information; and in any event (c) acted expeditiously, upon receiving a sufficiently substantiated notice from the rightholders, to disable access to, or to remove from, their websites the notified works or other subject matter, and made best efforts to prevent their future uploads in accordance with point (b).
5. In determining whether the service provider has complied with its obligations under paragraph 4, and in light of the principle of proportionality, the following elements, among others, shall be taken into account: (a) the type, the audience and the size of the service and the type of works or other subject matter uploaded by the users of the service; and (b) the availability of suitable and effective means and their cost for service providers.

6. Member States shall provide that, in respect of new online content-sharing service providers the services of which have been available to the public in the Union for less than three years and which have an annual turnover below EUR 10 million, calculated in accordance with Commission Recommendation 2003/361/EC20, the conditions under the liability regime set out in paragraph 4 are limited to compliance with point (a) of paragraph 4 and to acting expeditiously, upon receiving a sufficiently substantiated notice, to disable access to the notified works or other subject matter or to remove those works or other subject matter from their websites. Where the average number of monthly unique visitors of such service providers exceeds 5 million, calculated on the basis of the previous calendar year, they shall also demonstrate that they have made best efforts to prevent further uploads of the notified works and other subject matter for which the rightholders have provided relevant and necessary information.
7. The cooperation between online content-sharing service providers and rightholders shall not result in the prevention of the availability of works or other subject matter uploaded by users, which do not infringe copyright and related rights, including where such works or other subject matter are covered by an exception or limitation. Member States shall ensure that users in each Member State are able to rely on any of the following existing exceptions or limitations when uploading and making available content generated by users on online content-sharing services: (a) quotation, criticism, review; (b) use for the purpose of caricature, parody or pastiche.
8. The application of this Article shall not lead to any general monitoring obligation. Member States shall provide that online content-sharing service providers provide rightholders, at their request, with adequate information on the functioning of their practices with regard to the cooperation referred to in paragraph 4 and, where licensing agreements are concluded between service providers and rightholders, information on the use of content covered by the agreements.
9. Member States shall provide that online content-sharing service providers put in place an effective and expeditious complaint and redress mechanism that is available to users of their services in the event of disputes over the disabling of access to, or the removal of, works or other subject matter uploaded by them.

   Where rightholders request to have access to their specific works or other subject matter disabled or those works or other subject matter removed, they shall duly justify the reasons for their requests. Complaints submitted under the mechanism provided for in the first subparagraph shall be processed without undue delay, and decisions to disable access to or remove uploaded content shall be subject to human review. Member States shall also ensure that out-of-court redress mechanisms are available for the settlement of disputes. Such mechanisms shall enable disputes to be settled impartially and shall not deprive the user of the legal protection afforded by national law, without prejudice to the rights of users to have recourse to efficient judicial remedies. In particular, Member States shall ensure that users have access to a court or another relevant judicial authority to assert the use of an exception or limitation to copyright and related rights.

   This Directive shall in no way affect legitimate uses, such as uses under exceptions or limitations provided for in Union law, and shall not lead to any identification of individual users nor to the processing of personal data, except in accordance with Directive 2002/58/EC and Regulation (EU) 2016/679.

Online content-sharing service providers shall inform their users in their terms and conditions that they can use works and other subject matter under exceptions or limitations to copyright and related rights provided for in Union law.

10. As of … [date of entry into force of this Directive] the Commission, in cooperation with the Member States, shall organise stakeholder dialogues to discuss best practices for cooperation between online content-sharing service providers and rightholders. The Commission shall, in consultation with online content-sharing service providers, rightholders, users' organisations and other relevant stakeholders, and taking into account the results of the stakeholder dialogues, issue guidance on the application of this Article, in particular regarding the cooperation referred to in paragraph 4. When discussing best practices, special account shall be taken, among other things, of the need to balance fundamental rights and of the use of exceptions and limitations. For the purpose of the stakeholder dialogues, users' organisations shall have access to adequate information from online content-sharing service providers on the functioning of their practices with regard to paragraph 4.

V. Final Text of the Copyright in the Digital Single Market Directive as voted by the EU Parliament on 26 March 2019

Article 17

Use of protected content by online content-sharing service providers

1. Member States shall provide that an online content-sharing service provider performs an act of communication to the public or an act of making available to the public for the purposes of this Directive when it gives the public access to copyright-protected works or other protected subject matter uploaded by its users. An online content-sharing service provider shall therefore obtain an authorisation from the rightholders referred to in Article 3(1) and (2) of Directive 2001/29/EC, for instance by concluding a licensing agreement, in order to communicate to the public or make available to the public works or other subject matter.
2. Member States shall provide that, where an online content-sharing service provider obtains an authorisation, for instance by concluding a licensing agreement, that authorisation shall also cover acts carried out by users of the services falling within the scope of Article 3 of Directive 2001/29/EC when they are not acting on a commercial basis or where their activity does not generate significant revenues.
3. When an online content-sharing service provider performs an act of communication to the public or an act of making available to the public under the conditions laid down in this Directive, the limitation of liability established in Article 14(1) of Directive 2000/31/EC shall not apply to the situations covered by this Article.

   The first subparagraph of this paragraph shall not affect the possible application of Article 14(1) of Directive 2000/31/EC to those service providers for purposes falling outside the scope of this Directive.

4. If no authorisation is granted, online content-sharing service providers shall be liable for unauthorised acts of communication to the public, including making available to the public, of copyright-protected works and other subject matter, unless the service providers demonstrate that they have: (a) made best efforts to obtain an authorisation, and (b) made, in accordance with high industry standards of professional diligence, best efforts to ensure the unavailability of specific works and other subject matter for which the rightholders have provided the service providers with the relevant and necessary information; and in any event (c) acted expeditiously, upon receiving a sufficiently substantiated notice from the rightholders, to disable access to, or to remove from, their websites the notified works or other subject matter, and made best efforts to prevent their future uploads in accordance with point (b).
5. In determining whether the service provider has complied with its obligations under paragraph 4, and in light of the principle of proportionality, the following elements, among others, shall be taken into account: (a) the type, the audience and the size of the service and the type of works or other subject matter uploaded by the users of the service; and (b) the availability of suitable and effective means and their cost for service providers.
6. Member States shall provide that, in respect of new online content-sharing service providers the services of which have been available to the public in the Union for less than three years and which have an annual turnover below EUR 10 million, calculated in accordance with Commission Recommendation 2003/361/EC20, the conditions under the liability regime set out in paragraph 4 are limited to compliance with point (a) of paragraph 4 and to acting expeditiously, upon receiving a sufficiently substantiated notice, to disable access to the notified works or other subject matter or to remove those works or other subject matter from their websites. Where the average number of monthly unique visitors of such service providers exceeds 5 million, calculated on the basis of the previous calendar year, they shall also demonstrate that they have made best efforts to prevent further uploads of the notified works and other subject matter for which the rightholders have provided relevant and necessary information.
7. The cooperation between online content-sharing service providers and rightholders shall not result in the prevention of the availability of works or other subject matter uploaded by users, which do not infringe copyright and related rights, including where such works or other subject matter are covered by an exception or limitation. Member States shall ensure that users in each Member State are able to rely on any of the following existing exceptions or limitations when uploading and making available content generated by users on online content-sharing services: (a) quotation, criticism, review; (b) use for the purpose of caricature, parody or pastiche.
8. The application of this Article shall not lead to any general monitoring obligation. Member States shall provide that online content-sharing service providers provide rightholders, at their request, with adequate information on the functioning of their practices with regard to the cooperation referred to in paragraph 4 and, where licensing agreements are concluded between service providers and rightholders, information on the use of content covered by the agreements.

9. Member States shall provide that online content-sharing service providers put in place an effective and expeditious complaint and redress mechanism that is available to users of their services in the event of disputes over the disabling of access to, or the removal of, works or other subject matter uploaded by them.

   Where rightholders request to have access to their specific works or other subject matter disabled or those works or other subject matter removed, they shall duly justify the reasons for their requests. Complaints submitted under the mechanism provided for in the first subparagraph shall be processed without undue delay, and decisions to disable access to or remove uploaded content shall be subject to human review. Member States shall also ensure that out-of-court redress mechanisms are available for the settlement of disputes. Such mechanisms shall enable disputes to be settled impartially and shall not deprive the user of the legal protection afforded by national law, without prejudice to the rights of users to have recourse to efficient judicial remedies. In particular, Member States shall ensure that users have access to a court or another relevant judicial authority to assert the use of an exception or limitation to copyright and related rights.

   This Directive shall in no way affect legitimate uses, such as uses under exceptions or limitations provided for in Union law and shall not lead to any identification of individual users nor to the processing of personal data, except in accordance with Directive 2002/58/EC and Regulation (EU) 2016/679. Online content-sharing service providers shall inform their users in their terms and conditions that they can use works and other subject matter under exceptions or limitations to copyright and related rights provided for in Union law.
10. As of 6 June 2019 the Commission, in cooperation with the Member States, shall organise stakeholder dialogues to discuss best practices for cooperation between online content-sharing service providers and rightholders. The Commission shall, in consultation with online content-sharing service providers, rightholders, users' organisations and other relevant stakeholders, and taking into account the results of the stakeholder dialogues, issue guidance on the application of this Article, in particular regarding the cooperation referred to in paragraph 4. When discussing best practices, special account shall be taken, among other things, of the need to balance fundamental rights and of the use of exceptions and limitations. For the purpose of the stakeholder dialogues, users' organisations shall have access to adequate information from online content-sharing service providers on the functioning of their practices with regard to paragraph 4.

VI. Proposal for a Digital Services Act Regulation (Relevant Provisions)

Article 5 – Hosting

1. Where an information society service is provided that consists of the storage of information provided by a recipient of the service the service provider shall not

be liable for the information stored at the request of a recipient of the service on condition that the provider.

(a) does not have actual knowledge of illegal activity or illegal content and, as regards claims for damages, is not aware of facts or circumstances from which the illegal activity or illegal content is apparent; or
(b) upon obtaining such knowledge or awareness, acts expeditiously to remove or to disable access to the illegal content

2. Paragraph 1 shall not apply where the recipient of the service is acting under the authority or the control of the provider.
3. Paragraph 1 shall not apply with respect to liability under consumer protection law of online platforms allowing consumers to conclude distance contracts with traders, where such an online platform presents the specific item of information or otherwise enables the specific transaction at issue in a way that would lead an average and reasonably well-informed consumer to believe that the information, or the product or service that is the object of the transaction, is provided either by the online platform itself or by a recipient of the service who is acting under its authority or control.
4. This Article shall not affect the possibility for a court or administrative authority, in accordance with Member States' legal systems, of requiring the service provider to terminate or prevent an infringement.

Article 6 – Voluntary Own-Initiative Investigations and Legal Compliance

Providers of intermediary services shall not be deemed ineligible for the exemptions from liability referred to in Articles 3, 4 and 5 solely because they carry out voluntary own-initiative investigations or other activities aimed at detecting, identifying and removing, or disabling of access to, illegal content, or take the necessary measures to comply with the requirements of Union law, including those set out in this Regulation.

Article 7 – No General Monitoring or Active Fact-Finding Obligations

No general obligation to monitor the information which providers of intermediary services transmit or store, nor actively to seek facts or circumstances indicating illegal activity shall be imposed on those providers.

Article 8 – Orders to Act Against Illegal Content

1. Providers of intermediary services shall, upon the receipt of an order to act against a specific item of illegal content, issued by the relevant national judicial or administrative authorities, on the basis of the applicable Union or national

law, in conformity with Union law, inform the authority issuing the order of the effect given to the orders, without undue delay, specifying the action taken and the moment when the action was taken.

2. Member States shall ensure that the orders referred to in paragraph 1 meet the following conditions:
   (a) the orders contains the following elements:
      - a statement of reasons explaining why the information is illegal content, by reference to the specific provision of Union or national law infringed;
      - one or more exact uniform resource locators and, where necessary, additional information enabling the identification of the illegal content concerned;
      - information about redress available to the provider of the service and to the recipient of the service who provided the content;
   (b) the territorial scope of the order, on the basis of the applicable rules of Union and national law, including the Charter, and, where relevant, general principles of international law, does not exceed what is strictly necessary to achieve its objective;
   (c) the order is drafted in the language declared by the provider and is sent to the point of contact, appointed by the provider, in accordance with Article 10.
3. The Digital Services Coordinator from the Member State of the judicial or administrative authority issuing the order shall, without undue delay, transmit a copy of the orders referred to in paragraph 1 to all other Digital Services Coordinators through the system established in accordance with Article 67.
4. The conditions and requirements laid down in this article shall be without prejudice to requirements under national criminal procedural law in conformity with Union law.

Article 9 – Orders to Provide Information

1. Providers of intermediary services shall, upon receipt of an order to provide a specific item of information about one or more specific individual recipients of the service, issued by the relevant national judicial or administrative authorities on the basis of the applicable Union or national law, in conformity with Union law, inform without undue delay the authority of issuing the order of its receipt and the effect given to the order.
2. Member States shall ensure that orders referred to in paragraph 1 meet the following conditions:
   (a) the order contains the following elements:
      - a statement of reasons explaining the objective for which the information is required and why the requirement to provide the information is necessary and proportionate to determine compliance by the recipients of the intermediary services with applicable Union or national rules, unless such a statement cannot be provided for reasons related to the prevention, investigation, detection and prosecution of criminal offences;

  - information about redress available to the provider and to the recipients of the service concerned;

(b) the order only requires the provider to provide information already collected for the purposes of providing the service and which lies within its control;

(c) the order is drafted in the language declared by the provider and is sent to the point of contact appointed by that provider, in accordance with Article 10;

3. The Digital Services Coordinator from the Member State of the national judicial or administrative authority issuing the order shall, without undue delay, transmit a copy of the order referred to in paragraph 1 to all Digital Services Coordinators through the system established in accordance with Article 67.
4. The conditions and requirements laid down in this article shall be without prejudice to requirements under national criminal procedural law in conformity with Union law.

BIBLIOGRAPHY

I. Primary Sources

EU Legislation

Al White Paper, 'Artificial Intelligence at the service of the citizen' ai-white-paper.readthedocs.io/en/latest/.

Article 29 Working Party, 'Guidelines on the application and setting of administrative fines for the purposes of the Regulation 2016/679' adopted on 3 October 2017.

Article 29 Working Party, 'Guidelines on Automated individual decision-making and Profiling for the purposes of Regulation 2016/679' (2018) 25.

Article 29 Working Party, 'Guidelines on consent under Regulation 2016/679' (2018) 5.

Article 29 Working Party, 'Opinion 4/2007 on the concept of personal data' (WP 136) 20 June 2007.

Article 29 Data Protection Working Party, 'Guidelines for identifying a controller or processor's lead supervisory authority' adopted on 13 December 2016.

Article 29 Data Protection Working Party, 'Recent examples of enforcement actions carried out by data protection authorities' adopted on January 2005.

Article 29 Data Protection Working Party, 'WP 37: Privacy on the Internet – An integrated EU Approach to On-line Data Protection' adopted on 21 November 2000.

ARTICLE 19, 'Germany: Responding to 'hate speech: Country report' (2018) www.article19.org/wp-content/uploads/2018/07/Germany-Responding-to-%E2%80%98hate-speech%E2%80%99-v3-WEB.pdf.

ARTICLE 19, 'Germany: The Act to Improve Enforcement of the Law in Social Networks' (2017) www.article19.org/wp-content/uploads/2017/09/170901-Legal-Analysis-German-NetzDG-Act.pdf.

Citizens' summary EU action plan on 'enforcing intellectual property rights' (2015) ec.europa.eu/docsroom/documents/10058.

Council Directive (EC) 2000/31 on certain legal aspects of information society services, in particular electronic commerce, in the Internal Market [2000] O.J. L 178.

Council Directive (EC) 2001/29 on the harmonisation of certain aspects of copyright and related rights in the information society (2001) O.J. L 167.

Council Directive (EC) 2004/48/EC on the enforcement of intellectual property rights (2004) O.J. L 157.

Council Directive (EC) 2003/33/EC on the approximation of the laws, regulations and administrative provisions of the Member States relating to the advertising and sponsorship of tobacco products (2003) O.J. L 152.

Council Directive (EC) 2019/790/EC of the European Parliament and of the Council of 17 April 2019 on copyright and related rights in the Digital Single Market and amending Directives 96/9/EC and 2001/29/EC (2019) OJ L 130.

Council Directive (EU) 2018/1808 on the coordination of certain provisions laid down by law, regulation or administrative action in Member States concerning the provision of audiovisual media services (Audiovisual Media Services Directive) in view of changing market realities (2018) OJ L 303.

Council Directive (EU) 2014/104/EU of the European Parliament and of the Council of 26 November 2014 on Certain Rules Governing Actions for Damages under National Law for Infringements of the Competition Law Provisions of the Member States and of the European Union Text with EEA Relevance.

Council Directive (EU) 2013/11/EU of the European parliament and of the Council on Alternative Dispute Resolution for consumers (2013) OJ L 165.

Council Regulation (EU) 2016/679 of the European Parliament and of the Council of 27 April 2016 on the protection of natural persons with regard to the processing of personal data and on the free movement of such data, and repealing Directive 95/46/EC (2016) O.J. L 119.

Council Regulation (EU) No 524/2013 of the European parliament and of the Council on online dispute resolution for consumers (2013) OJ L 165.

Council Regulation (EU) 2019/1150 of the European Parliament and of the Council of 20 June 2019 on promoting fairness and transparency for business users of online intermediation services (Text with EEA relevance) PE/56/2019/REV/1, OJ L 186.

Committee on Economic and Monetary Affairs, 'On the overview and structure of financial supervision and regulation in the US Report of the Committee on Economic and Monetary Affairs on the overview and structure of financial supervision and regulation in the U.S' (2015) www.europarl.europa.eu/RegData/etudes/STUD/2015/492470/IPOL_STU%282015%29492470_EN.pdf.

Committee of Ministers, 'Recommendation to member states on measures to promote the respect for freedom of expression and information with regard to Internet filters' CM/ Rec (2008).

Committee of Ministers, 'Recommendation to member states on measures to promote the public service value of the Internet' CM/ Rec (2007).

Committee of Ministers, 'Recommendation to member States on the roles and responsibilities of internet intermediaries' CM/Rec (2018).

Committee of Ministers, 'Guide to good practice in respect of domestic remedies (adopted by the Committee of Ministers on 18 September 2013)' www.echr.coe.int/Documents/Pub_coe_domestics_remedies_ENG.pdf.

Communications Decency Act, 47 U.S.C. §230.

Council text, Proposal for a Directive of the European Parliament and of the Council on copyright in the Digital Single Market – Agreed negotiating mandate, Interinstitutional File: 2016/0280 (COD).

Department for Digital, Culture, Media and Sport, 'Centre for data ethics and innovation consultation' (June 2018) assets.publishing.service.gov.uk/government/uploads/system/uploads/attachment_data/file/715760/CDEI_consultation__1_.pdf.

Digital Millennium Copyright Act, H.R. 2281, 105th Cong. (1998).

Data Protection Act 1998.

Danish Government, 'Strategy for Denmark's Digital Growth' (2018) eng.em.dk/media/10555/digital-growth-strategy-report_uk_web-1.pdf.

E-Commerce Regulations 2002.

EDPS, 'Report on Assessing the necessity of measures that limit the fundamental right to the protection of personal data: A toolkit' (2017) 12.

Estonian Government, 'Prime minister: to implement artificial intelligence, countries need a unified approach and ability to adapt' (16 October 2018) www.valitsus.ee/en/news/prime-minister-implement-artificial-intelligence-countries-need-unified-approach-and-ability.

Economic and Monetary Affairs Committee, 'Report on an academic view on the Role and Powers of National Competition Authorities' (2016) 23.

EU Agency for Fundamental rights, 'Report on freedom to conduct a business: exploring the dimensions of a fundamental right' (2015).

European Union, Charter of Fundamental Rights of the European Union, 26 October 2012, 2012/C 326/02.

EU Commission, 'Public Consultation on the evaluation and modernization of the legal framework for the enforcement of intellectual property rights: Summary of responses' (2016).

EU Commission, 'Public Consultation on the role of online intermediaries: Summary of responses' (2016).

EU Commission, 'Public Consultation on the future of electronic commerce in the Internal Market and the implementation of the Directive on electronic commerce: Summary of response' (2010).

EU Commission, 'Towards a renewed consensus on the enforcement of Intellectual Property Rights: An EU Action Plan Strasbourg' COM (2014) 392 final.

EU Commission, 'Online Platforms and the Digital Single Market Opportunities and Challenges for Europe' COM (2016) 288 final.

EU Commission, 'A New Deal for Consumers' COM (2018) 183 final.

EU Commission, 'Study for the assessment of the implementation of the code of practice on disinformation: final report' (2020) 67.

EU Commission, 'Overview of the functioning of the Memorandum of Understanding on the sale of counterfeit good via the internet' COM (2017) 430 final.

EU Commission, 'A Digital Single Market Strategy for Europe' COM (2015) 192 final.
EU Commission, 'Recommendation on measures to effectively tackle illegal content online' COM (2018) 1177 final.
EU Commission, 'Digital Single Market Creating a Digital Single Market European Commission actions since 2015' (2018).
EU Commission, 'Study on the role of intermediaries – Summary of the public consultation' (2016).
EU Commission, 'A balanced IP enforcement system responding to today's societal challenges' (2017) 430 final.
EU Commission, 'Online Platforms and the Digital Single Market Opportunities and Challenges for Europe' COM (2016) 288 final.
EU Commission, 'Behavioural Study on the transparency of online platforms- Executive summary' (2018).
EU Commission, 'Tackling illegal content online: Towards an enhanced responsibility of online platforms' COM (2017) 555 final.
EU Commission, 'Towards a modern, more European copyright framework' COM (2015) 626 final.
EU Commission, 'Online platforms and the Digital Single Market opportunities and challenges for Europe' COM (2016) 0288 final.
EU Commission, 'Memorandum of Understanding on the online sale of counterfeit goods' (2016) 1.
EU Commission, 'Report on the functioning of the European Online Dispute Resolution platform established under Regulation (EU) No 524/2013 on online dispute resolution for consumer disputes' COM (2017) 744 final.
EU Commission Staff Working Paper, 'Piracy Watch List' SWD (2018) 492 final.
EU Commission Staff Working Paper, 'Online Services, Including E-Commerce, in the Single Market' SEC (2011) 1641 final.
EU Commission Staff Working Document, 'A Digital Single Market Strategy for Europe- Analysis and Evidence' COM (2015) 192 final.
EU Commission Staff Working Paper, 'Impact assessment on Proposal for a Regulation of the European Parliament and of the Council on promoting fairness and transparency for business users of online intermediation services, Online Services, Including E-Commerce, in the Single Market' COM (2018) 238 final.
EU Commission Staff Working Paper, 'Overview of the functioning of the Memorandum of Understanding on the sale of counterfeit goods via the internet' SWD(2017) 430 final 6.
EU Commission's Directorate-General for Communications Networks, Content and Technology, 'Algo: aware; Raising awareness on algorithms' (2018).
EU Commission, 'Overview of the legal framework of notice and action procedures in Member States SMART 2016/0039' (2018).
EU Commission, 'Notice on cooperation within the Network of Competition Authorities' (2004/C 101/03).
EU Commission, 'EU study on the New rules for a new age? Legal analysis of a Single Market for the Information Society 6. Liability of online intermediaries' (2009) 24.
EU Commission, 'Shaping Europe's Digital Future' (February 2020) 2.
EU Commission, 'Open Public Consultation on the Digital Services Act Package: Summary Report on the open public Consultation on the Digital Services Act Package' (2020) 5.
European Commission, Proposal for a Regulation of the European Parliament and the Council on a Single Market For Digital Services (Digital Services Act) and amending Directive 2000/31/EC COM/2020/825 final.
EU Commission staff working document, 'Executive summary of the impact assessment report' SWD (2020) 1–3.
EU Commission, 'Consumer market study on online market segmentation through personalised pricing/offers in the European Union' (2020) 131.
EU Commission, 'Consumer Conditions Scoreboard' (2019) 14.
EU Commission, 'Communication on the Guidance on Article 17 of Directive 2019/790 on Copyright in the Digital Single Market' (2021) COM/2021/288 final 2.
EU Parliament, 'Legislative resolution of 17 April 2019 on the proposal for a regulation of the European Parliament and of the Council on preventing the dissemination of terrorist content online' (COM(2018)0640 – C8-0405/2018 – 2018/0331(COD)).
EU Parliament, 'Copyright in the Digital Single Market, Amendments adopted by the European Parliament on 12 September 2018 on the proposal for a directive of the European Parliament and of the Council on copyright in the Digital Single Market' (COM (2016) 0593- C8-0383/2016- 2016/0280 (COD)).
EU Parliament, 'The rise of e-commerce and the cashless society' (2021).

EU Parliament resolution of 20 October 2020 with recommendations to the Commission on a Digital Services Act: adapting commercial and civil law rules for commercial entities operating online.

European Parliament, 'Briefing Legislation on Digital Services Act' (2021) 1.

European Intellectual Property Office, 'Online copyright infringement in the European Union: music, films and TV (2017–2018), trends and drivers' (November 2019).

European Data Protection Supervisor, 'Opinion 1/2021 on the Proposal for Digital Services Act' (2021).

European Patent Office and OECD, 'Report on trends in trade in counterfeit and pirated goods' (2019).

European Patent Office and the European Union Intellectual Property Office, 'A joint project on IPR-intensive industries and economic performance in the European Union' (2019).

European Securities and Markets Authority, 'Final report on Joint guidelines on cooperation and information exchange for the purpose of Directive (EU) 2015/849 between competent authorities supervising credit and financial institutions: The AML/CFT Colleges Guidelines ESMA' (2019) 5.

General Secretariat of the Council on 'Draft Directive of the European Parliament and of the Council on copyright and related rights in the Digital Single Market and amending Directives 96/9/EC and 2001/29/EC, Joint statements' (15 April 2019).

Government of the Netherlands, 'Dutch Digitization Strategy' (2018) www.government.nl/documents/reports/2018/06/01/dutch-digitalisation-strategy.

Greek Intellectual Property Law 4481/2017.

High Commissioner for Human Rights, 'Letter to the President of the European Commission on the Proposal on a Digital Services Act Regulation' (September 2020).

HM Government, 'UK Government Response to EU public consultation on Digital Platforms: Including the regulatory environment for platforms, online intermediaries, data and cloud computing and the collaborative economy' (2016).

HM Government, 'Online Harms White Paper: Full Government Response to the consultation' (2020) 53–54.

Human Rights Council of the United Nations, 'Resolution on the Promotion, Protection and Enjoyment of Human Rights on the Internet' (2012) documents-dds-ny.un.org/doc/UNDOC/GEN/G14/082/83/PDF/G1408283.pdf?OpenElement.

Information Commissioner's Office, 'The principles' ico.org.uk/for-organisations/guide-to-data-protection/guide-to-the-general-data-protection-regulation-gdpr/principles/storage-limitation/.

Intellectual Property Office, 'IP Crime and Enforcement Report 2018–2019' (2019) 54.

Loi no 2004-575 du 21 juin 2004 pour la confiance dans l'economie numerique, Art. 6-I-5.

Mandate of the Special Rapporteur on the promotion and protection of human rights and fundamental freedoms while countering terrorism (24 July 2018).

Mandate of the Special Rapporteur on the promotion and protection of the right to freedom of opinion and expression (13 June 2018).

Ministry of National Development, 'NTD/N&A procedures regulated in law (Hungary)' ec.europa.eu/transparency/regexpert/index.cfm?do=groupDetail.groupDetailDoc&id=32318&no=6.

Opinion of the European Economic and Social Committee, Proposal for a Regulation of the European Parliament and of the Council on a Single Market For Digital Services (Digital Services Act) and amending Directive 2000/31/EC [COM(2020) 825 final – 2020/0361 (COD)] 3.4.

Opinion of the Civil Liberties Committee, 'P9_TA(2020)0274 – Digital Services Act and fundamental rights issues posed European Parliament resolution of 20 October 2020 on the Digital Services Act and fundamental rights issues posed' (2020/2022(INI)) 19.

OECD, 'The economic and social role of internet intermediaries' (2010).

OECD, 'The Economic Impact of Counterfeiting and Piracy' (2008).

OECD, 'Guidelines on the Protection of Privacy and Transborder Flows of Personal Data' (2013).

Propriete Industrielle et economie numerique, 'Part 1: A law for a digital French Republic – online platforms' www.dreyfus.fr/en/new-technologies/part-1-a-law-for-a-digital-french-republic-online-platforms/.

Regolamento in materia di tutela del diritto d'autore sulle reti di comunicazione elettronica e procedure elettronica e procedure attuative ai sensi del decreto legislative 9 April3 2003, N. 7 www.librari.beniculturali.it/export/sites/dgbid/it/documenti/Eventi/2014/35.REGOLAMENTO_AGCOM.pdf.

Report of the Special Rapporteur, 'On the promotion and expression of the right to freedom of expression' (The United Nations General Assembly, 16 May 2011) www2.ohchr.org/english/bodies/hrcouncil/docs/17session/A.HRC.17.27_en.pdf.

Regulatory Scrutiny Board Opinion, 'Proposal for a Regulation of the European Parliament and of the Council on a Single Market For Digital Services (Digital Services Act) and amending Directive 2000/31/EC' 6.11.2020SEC(2020) 432.

Spanish legislative approach to notice and action procedures /ec.europa.eu/transparency/regexpert/index.cfm?do=groupDetail.groupDetailDoc&id=32315&no=3.

United Nations Office on Drugs and Crime, 'The Globalization of Crime: A Transnational Organized Crime Threat Assessment' (2010) www.unodc.org/documents/data-and-analysis/tocta/TOCTA_Report_2010_low_res.pdf.

White Paper, 'Chinese courts and internet judiciary' (2019) 66 wlf.court.gov.cn/upload/file/2019/12/03/11/40/20191203114024_87277.pdf.

World Economic Forum, 'Report on the Global Governance of Online Consumer Protection and E-commerce Building Trust' (2019).

World Economic Forum, 'White Paper on The Global Governance of Online Consumer Protection and E-commerce Building Trust' (2019) www3.weforum.org/docs/WEF_consumer_protection.pdf.

Secondary Sources

Books and Book Chapters

Angelopoulos C, *European intermediary liability in copyright: a tort-based analysis* (Alphen aan den Rijn, Kluwer Law International, 2016).

Balkin RP and Davis JLR, *Law of Torts*, 2nd edn (London, Butterworths, 2002).

Barral-Vinals I, 'Enforcing e-consumer protection beyond alternative dispute resolution (ADR): ODR' in James Devenney and Mel Kenny (eds), *European consumer protection: theory and practice* (Oxford, Oxford University Press, 2012).

Benabou V, 'The Chase: The French Insight into the "Three strikes" System' in Irini Stamatoudi (ed), *Copyright Enforcement and the Internet* (Alphen aan den Rijn, Kluwer Law International, 2010).

Belli L and Zingales N, 'Law of the Land or Law of the Platform? Beware of the Privatisation of Regulation and Police' in Luca Belli and Nicolo Zingales (eds), *Platform Regulations: How Platforms are Regulated and How They Regulate Us* (2017).

Berendschot H, 'Summary and analysis of Case C-494/15' in Huib Berendschot and Karel Janssens (eds.), *Landmark IP decisions of the European Court of Justice 2014–2018* (ELS Belgium 2019) 139–44.

Birks P, 'Civil Wrongs: A New World' in FMB Reynolds and Peter Birks (eds), *Butterworths Lectures 1990–1991* (1991).

Bowen H R, *Social Responsibilities of the Businessman* (Iowa, University of Iowa Press, 2013).

Broeders D and Taylor L, 'Does Great Power Come with Great Responsibility? The Need to Talk about Corporate Political Responsibility' in Mariarosaria Taddeo and Luciano Floridi (eds), *The responsibilities of online service providers* (Berlin, Springer, 2017).

Brownsword R, *Rights, Regulation and the technological revolution* (Oxford, Oxford University Press, 2008).

Buijze A, *The Principle of transparency in EU Law* (Utrecht, Unpublished PhD Thesis, 2013).

Calhoun CJ, *Dictionary of the social sciences* (New York, Oxford University Press, 2000).

Caroll B, 'A History of Corporate Social Responsibility: Concepts and Practices' in Andrew Crane, Dirk Matten, Abagail McWilliams, Jeremy Moon and Donald S Siegel (eds), *The Oxford Handbook of Corporate Social Responsibility* (Oxford, Oxford University Press, 2009).

Dinwoodie GB, 'A comparative analysis of the secondary liability of online service providers' in Graeme B Dinwoodie (ed), *Secondary Liability of Internet Service Providers* (Berlin, Springer, 2016).

De Filippi P and Bourcier D, 'Three-Strikes' Response to Copyright Infringement: The Case of Hadopi' in Francesca Musiani, Derrik L Cogburn, Laure DeNardis and Nanette Levinson (eds), *The Turn to Infrastructure in Internet Governance* (London, Palgrave-Macmillan, 2016).

Downie RS, 'Collective responsibility; in Stacey Hoffman (ed., *Collective responsibility: Five decades of debate in theoretical and applied ethics* (Studies in Social, Political and Legal Philosophy, 1992).

Edwards L, 'With Great Power Comes Great Responsibility? The Rise of Platform Liability' in Lilian Edwards (ed), *Law, Policy and the Internet* (Oxford, Hart Publishing, 2019).

Fischman Afori O, 'Universal measures in the service of global challenges: proportionality, blocking orders, and online intermediaries as hybrid bodies' in Tatiani Synodinou, *Pluralism or Universalism in international copyright law* (Alphen aan den Rijn, Kluwer Law International, 2019) 657.

Frabboni M, 'File-sharing and the role of intermediaries in the marketplace' in Irini Stamatoudi (ed.), *Copyright enforcement and the Internet* (Alphen aan den Rijn, Kluwer Law International, 2010).

Frosio G and Husovec M, 'Accountability and Responsibility of Online Intermediaries' in Giancarlo Frosio (ed), *The Oxford Handbook of Online Intermediary Liability* (Oxford, Oxford University Press, 2020).

Frosio G, 'Algorithmic enforcement online' in Paul Torremans (ed), *Intellectual Property and Human Rights, 4 edn* (Alphen aan den Rijn, Kluwer Law International, 2020).

Garstka K, 'Guiding the Blind Bloodhounds: How to Mitigate the Risks art. 17 of Directive 2019/790 Poses to the Freedom of Expression' in Paul Torremans (ed), *Intellectual Property and Human Rights* (Alphen aan den Rijn, Kluwer Law and Business, 2020).

Geiger C, 'Fundamental Rights as Common Principles of European (and International) Intellectual Property Law' in Matthias Leistner (ed), *Common principles of European Intellectual Property Law* (Heidelberg, Mohr Siebeck, 2012).

Giampiero G, *National Governments and Control of the Internet: A Digital Challenge* (London, Routledge, 2005).

Gibblin R, *Code Wars: 10 Years of P2P software litigation* (Cheltenham, Edward Elgar, 2011).

Goldstein G and Hugenholtz B, *International Copyright: Principles, Law and Practice* (Oxford, Oxford University Press, 2010).

Goldsmith J and Wu T, *Who Controls the Internet?: Illusions of a Borderless World* (Oxford, Oxford University Press, 2006) 175.

Guadamuz A, 'Internet Regulation' in Lilian Edwards (ed), *Law, policy and the internet* (Oxford, Hart Publishing, 2019).

Guadamuz A, 'Developments in Intermediary Liability' in Andrej Savin and Jan Trzaskowski (eds) *Research Handbook on EU Internet Law* (Cheltenham, Edward Elgar, 2014).

Guadamuz A, *Networks Complexity and Internet Regulation: Scale Free Law* (Cheltenham, Edward Elgar, 2011).

Hart LA and Honore' T, *Causation in the Law*, 2nd edn (Oxford, Oxford University Press, 1985).

Holland HB, 'Section 230 of the CDA: Internet Exceptionalism as a Statutory Construct' in Berin Szoka and Adam Marcus (eds) *The next digital decade: Essays on the future of the Internet* (TechFreedom, 2011).

Hugenholtz PB, 'Codes of Conduct and Copyright enforcement in cyberspace' in Irini Stamatoudi (ed), *Copyright enforcement and the Internet* (Alphen aan den Rijn, Kluwer Law International, 2010).

Husovec M, *Injunctions Against Intermediaries in the European Union: Accountable but not liable* (Cambridge, Cambridge University Press, 2017).

Husovec M, 'How Europe Wants to Redefine Global Online Copyright Enforcement' in Tatiani Synodinou (ed), *Pluralism or Universalism in International Copyright Law* (Alphen aan den Rijn, Kluwer Law International, 2019).

Jougleux P, 'The role of internet intermediaries in copyright law online enforcement' in Tatiani Synodinou, Philippe Jougleux, Christianna Markou and Thalia Prastitiou (eds), *EU Internet Law: Regulation and Enforcement* (Berlin, Springer, 2017) 273.

Karapapa S and McDonagh L, *Intellectual Property Law* (Oxford, Oxford University Press, 2019).

Katsh E and Rabinovich-Einy O, *In Digital Justice: Technology and the Internet of Disputes* (Oxford, Oxford University Press, 2017).

Keller D and Leerssen P, 'Facts and Where to Find Them: Empirical Research on Internet Platforms and Content Moderation' in Nathaniel Persily and Joshua Tucker (eds), *Social Media and Democracy: The State of the Field and Prospects for Reform* (Cambridge, Cambridge University Press, 2020) 14–17.

Kulk S, *Internet Intermediaries and Copyright Law: EU and US perspective* (Alphen aan den Rijn, Kluwer Law International, 2019).

Kuczerawy A, *Intermediary Liability and Freedom of Expression in the EU: from Concepts to Safeguards* (Wellington, Intersentia, 2018).

Kuczerway A, 'General Monitoring obligations: a new cornerstone of Internet Regulation in the EU?' in KU Leuven Centre for IT and IP Law (ed), *Rethinking IT and IP Law* (Wellington, Intersentia, 2019).

Laddie H, Prescott P, Vitoria M and Speck A, *The Modern Law of Copyright and Designs*, 3rd edn (London, Butterworths 2000).
Laidlaw E, 'Notice-and-Notice-Plus: A Canadian Perspective beyond the Liability and Immunity Divide' in Giancarlo Frosio (ed), *The Oxford Handbook of Intermediary Liability Online* (Oxford University Press 2020, Forthcoming).
Laidlaw E, 'Internet Gatekeepers, Human Rights and Corporate Social Responsibilities' (LSE, PhD Thesis, 2012).
Leistner M, 'Common Principles of Secondary Liability?' in Ansgar Ohly (ed), *Common Principles of European Intellectual Property Law* (Heidelberg, Mohr Siebeck, 2012).
Leistner M, 'Intermediary liability in a global world' in Tatiani Synodinou (ed), *Pluralism and Universalism in international copyright law* (Alphen aan den Rijn, Kluwer Law International, 2019).
Lenearts K and Van Nuffel P, *European Union Law* (Sweet and Maxwell, 2011).
Lessig L, *Code and other Laws of cyberspace* (New York, Basic Books, 1999).
Lessig L, *Code: version 2.0* (New York, Basic Books, 2006).
Lichtman D, 'Copyright as Information Policy: Google Book Search from a Law and Economics Perspective' in Josh Lerner and Scott Stern (eds), *Innovation Policy and The Economy* (National Bureau of Economic Research, 2008).
List C and Pettit P, *Group agency: The possibility, design, and status of corporate agents* (Oxford, Oxford University Press, 2011).
Litmam J, *Digital Copyright: Revising Copyright Law for the Information Age* (New York, Prometheus Books 2001).
Lodder A, 'Directive 2000/31/EC on certain legal aspects of information society services, in particular electronic commerce, in the internal market' in Arno Lodder and Andrew Murray (eds), *EU Regulation of E-Commerce: A commentary* (Cheltenham, Edward Elgar, 2017).
Luetge C, 'Responsibilities of OSPs from a Business Ethics Point of View' in Mariarosaria Taddeo and Luciano Floridi, *Responsibilities of internet service providers* (Berlin, Springer, 2016).
Lynskey O, 'Regulation by Platforms: The Impact on Fundamental Rights' in Luca Belli and Nicolo Zingales (eds), *Platform Regulations: How Platforms are Regulated and How They Regulate Us* (2017).
Marsden C, *Internet co-regulation* (Cambridge, Cambridge University Press, 2011).
Marsden C, 'Co- and Self-regulation in European Media and Internet Sectors: The Results of Oxford University's Study www.selfregulation.info' in OECD, *Self-Regulation, Co-Regulation and State Regulation* (2003) 80.
Marsoof A, *Internet intermediaries and trade mark rights* (London, Routledge, 2019).
Matthews P and Malek H M, *Disclosure*, 5th edn (Sweet and Maxwell, 2012).
Maturana H and Varela F, *Autopoiesis and Cognition* (Berlin, Springer, 1928) 32;
McIvor C, *Third Party Liability in Tort* (Oxford, Hart Publishing, 2006).
McKinnon R, *Consent of the Networked: The Worldwide struggle for Internet Freedom* (New York, Basic Books, 2012).
Murray A, *Information Technology Law: The law and society* (Oxford, Oxford University Press, 2009).
Murray A, *The Regulation of Cyberspace: Control in the Online Environment* (London, Routledge-Cavendish, 2006).
Nissenbaum H, 'Accountability in a Computerized Society' in Batya Friedman (ed), *Human Values and the Design of Computer Technology* (Cambridge, Cambridge University Press, 1997).
Pasquale F, *The Black Box Society – The Secret Algorithms that Control Money and Information* (Cambridge MA, Harvard University Press, 2015).
Pasquale F, *New Laws of Robotics* (Cambridge MA, Harvard University Press, 2020)
Price M and Verhulst S, 'The Concept of Self-Regulation and the Internet' (2000) in J Waltermann and M Machill (eds), *Protecting our children on the internet: Towards a new culture of responsibility* (Gütersloh, Bertelsmann Foundation Publishers) 75.
Revolidis I, 'Internet intermediaries and copyright enforcement in the EU: In search of a balanced approach' in Marcelo Corrales, Mark Fenwick and Nikolaus Forgó (eds), *New Technology, Big Data and the Law* (Berlin, Springer, 2017).
Riefa C, *Consumer Protection and Online Auction Platforms: Towards a Safer Legal Framework (Markets and the Law)* (London, Routledge, 2015).

Riordan J, 'Website Blocking Injunctions under United Kingdom and European Law' in Graeme Dinwoodie (ed), *Secondary liability of internet service providers* (Berlin, Springer, 2017).
Riordan J, *The liability of internet intermediaries* (Oxford, Oxford University Press, 2016).
Rosati E, *Copyright in the Digital Single Market: Article-by-Article Commentary to the Provisions of Directive 2019/790* (Oxford, Oxford University Press, 2021).
Rosen F, 'Reading Hume Backwards: Utility as the Foundation of Morals' in Frederick Rosen (ed), *Classical Utilitarianism from Hume to Mill* (London, Routledge, 2003).
Rowland D, Kohl U and Charlesworth A, *Information Technology Law*, 4th edn (London, Routledge, 2011).
Ruben E, 'The internet, consumer protection and practical knowledge' in Jane Winn, *Consumer Protection in the Age of the 'Information Economy'* (London, Routledge, 2006) 37.
Sadeghi M, 'The Knowledge Standard for ISP Copyright and Trademark Secondary Liability: A Comparative Study on the Analysis of US and EU Laws' (Brunel, Unpublished PhD Thesis, 2013).
Schack H,'Täter und Störer: Zur Erweiterung und Begrenzung der Verantwortlichkeit durch Verkehrspflichten im Wettbewerbs- und Immaterialgüterrecht' in *Festschrift für Dieter Reuter zum 70. Geburtstag am 16. Oktober 2010* (Berlin, De Gruyter, 2010).
Shapiro L, *The control revolution: How the internet is putting individuals in charge and changing the world we know* (New York: Public Affairs 2000).
Schruers M, 'Copyright, Intermediaries and Architecture' in Francesca Musiani, Derrik L. Cogburn, Laure DeNardis, Nanette Levinson (eds), *The Turn to Infrastructure in Internet Governance* (London, Palgrave-Macmillan 2016).
Schwarze J, *European Administrative law* (London, Sweet and Maxwell, 2006).
Sørensen MJ, 'Draft Model Rules on Online Intermediary Platforms' in Bram Devolder (ed), *The Platform Economy: Unravelling the Legal Status of Online Intermediaries* (Wellington, Intersentia, 2019) 182.
Stalla-Bourdillon S, 'Internet intermediaries as responsible actors? Why it is time to rethink the e-Commerce Directive as well' in Mariarosaria Taddeo and Luciano Floridi (eds), *The Responsibilities of Online Service Providers* (Berlin, Springer, 2017).
Storskrubb E, 'Access to Justice in European Comparative Law' in Francesco Francioni (ed), *Access to Justice as a Human Right* (Oxford, Oxford University Press, 2007).
Strowel A, 'The Graduated response in France: Is it the good reply to online copyright infringements?' in Irini Stamatoudi (ed), *Copyright Enforcement and the Internet* (Alphen aan den Rijn, Kluwer Law International, 2010).
Taddeo M and Floridi L, 'The Moral Responsibilities of Online Service Providers' in Mariarosaria Taddeo and Luciano Floridi (eds), *The Responsibilities of Online Service Providers* (Berlin, Springer, 2017).
Tessier M, Herzog J and Madzou L, 'Regulation at the Age of Online Platform-Based Economy: Accountability, User Empowerment and Responsiveness' in Luca Belli and Nicolo Zingales (eds), *Platform regulations – How to regulate them and how they regulate us* (2017).
Trimble M, 'Geoblocking and Evasion of Geoblocking – Technical Standards and the Law' in Ramon Lobato and James Meese, *Geoblocking and Global Video Culture* (Institute of Network Cultures, 2016).
Tusikov N, *Chokepoints: Global private regulation on the Internet* (University of California Press, 2017).
Van Dam C, *European Tort Law* (Oxford, Oxford University Press, 2007).
Wang J, *Regulating Hosting ISPs' responsibilities for copyright infringement: The freedom to operate in the US, EU and China* (Berlin, Springer, 2018).
Watkins D and Burton M, *Research Methods in Law* (London, Routledge, 2017).
Weber R, 'The legitimacy and accountability of the Internet's governing institutions' in Ian Brown (ed), *Research Handbook on Governance of the Internet* (Cheltenham, Edward Elgar, 2013).
Williams G, *Joints Torts and Contributory Negligence* (Stevens & Sons Ltd 1951).
Wilman F, *The responsibility of online intermediaries for illegal user content in the EU and* US (Cheltenham, Edward Elgar, 2020).
Yoo C, *The dynamic Internet: How technology, users and businesses are transforming the network* (American Enterprise Institute, 2014).

Articles in Journals and Conferences and Reports

Addink GH and ten Berge BJM, 'Study on Innovation of Legal Means for Eliminating Corruption in the Public Service in the Netherlands' (2007) *Netherlands Comparative Law Association* 12.

Angelopoulos C, 'On Online Platforms and the Commission's New Proposal for a Directive on Copyright in the Digital Single Market' (2017) 1.

Angelopoulos C, Brody A, Hins W, Hugenholtz B, Leerssen P, Margoni T, McGonagle T, van Daalen O, van Hoboken J, 'Study of fundamental rights limitations for online enforcement through self-regulation' (2015) *IVRi* 3.

Angelopoulos C and Smet S, 'Notice and Fair Balance: How to reach a compromise between fundamental rights in European Intermediary Liability' (2016) 8 *Journal Media of Law* 266.

Angelopoulos C, 'Digital Services Act and Digital Markets Act: Commission presents legislative proposals' (2020) *EU Law live* 30–31.

Angelopoulos C, 'Filtering the Internet for copyrighted content in Europe' (2009) *IRIS* 3.

Angelopoulos C, 'Beyond the safe harbors: harmonizing substantive intermediary liability for copyright infringement in Europe' (2013) 3 *Intellectual Property Quarterly* 254.

Angelopoulos C and Quintais JP, 'Fixing copyright reform: a better solution to online infringement' (2019) 10 *Journal of Intellectual Property, Information Technology and E-Commerce Law* 153.

Ahlert C, Marsden C and Yung C, 'How 'Liberty' Disappeared from Cyberspace: The Mystery Shopper Tests Internet Content Self-Regulation' (2014) www.academia.edu/686683/How_Liberty_Disappeared_from_Cyberspace_The_Mystery_Shopper_Tests_Internet_Content_Self_Regulation.

Alves S, Capiau J and Sinclair A, 'Principles for the Independence of Competition Authorities' (2015) 11 *Competition Law Journal* 15–16.

Amadei X, 'Standards of liability for Internet for Internet Service Providers: A comparative study of France and the United States with a specific focus on copyright, defamation and illicit content' (2002) 35 *Cornell International Law Journal* 204.

Arnold M, Darmon E, Dejean S and Penard T, 'Graduated Response Policy and the Behavior of Digital Pirates: Evidence from the French Three-Strike (Hadopi) Law' (2014) *Working Papers 14-07* 3.

Appel H, 'The Ideological Determinants of Liberal Economic Reform: The Case of Privatization' (2000) 52 *World Politics* 520, 528–29.

Baird S, 'The Government at the standards Bazaar' (2007) 18 *Stanford Law and Policy Review* 66, 84.

Boni-Saenz A, 'Public-Private Partnerships and Insurance Regulation' (2008) 121 *Harvard Law Review* 1367.

Balkin J, 'Old-School/New-School Speech Regulation' (2014) 127 *Harvard Law Review* 2309.

Balkin J, 'The Future of Free Expression in a Digital Age' (2009) 36 *Pepperdine Law Review* 437.

Baratta R, 'Complexity of EU Law in the domestic implementing process' (2014) 2 *The Theory and Practice of Legislation* 296.

Barazza S, 'Secondary liability for IP infringement: converging patterns and approaches in comparative case law' (2012) 7 *Journal of Intellectual Property Law and Practice* 882.

Barcelo R J and Koelman K, 'Intermediary liability in the E-Commerce Directive: so far so good, but it's not enough' (2000) 16 *Computer Law and Security Report* 235.

Bartholomew M and Tehranina J, 'The secret life of legal doctrine: the divergent evolution of secondary liability in trademark and copyright law' (2006) 21 *Berkeley Technology Law Journal* 1419.

Barzilai-Nahon K, 'Toward a theory of network gatekeeping: a framework for exploring information control' (2008) 59 *Journal of the American Society for Information Science and Technology* 1493.

Barlow JP, 'A Declaration of the Independence of Cyberspace' (8 February 1996) www.eff.org/cyberspace-independence.

Belli L and Sappa C, 'The Intermediary Conundrum: Cyber-regulator, cyber-police or both?' (2017) 8 *Intellectual Property Information and Technology and Electronic Commerce* 185.

Benhamou Y, 'Compensation of Damages for Infringements of Intellectual Property Rights in France, Under Directive 2004/48/EC and its Transposition Law – New Notions?' (2009) 40 *International Review of Intellectual Property and Competition Law* 126.

Ben-Shahar O and Schneider C E, 'The Failure of Mandated Disclosure' (2011) 159 *University of Pennsylvania Law Review* 647.

Bertolini A, 'Liability of online platforms' (2020) *European Parliamentary Research Service* 78.

Black J, 'Decentring Regulation: Understanding the Role of Regulation and Self-Regulation in a "Post-Regulatory" World' (2001) 54 *Current Legal Problems* 106.

Blevins J, 'Uncertainty as Enforcement Mechanism: The New Expansion of Secondary Copyright Liability to Internet Platforms' (2013) 34 *Cardozo Law Review* 1829.

Bonadio E, 'File-Sharing, Copyright and Freedom of Speech' (2010) 33 *European Intellectual Property Review* 620.

Bonnici JP Mifsud and de vey Mestdagh CNJ, 'Right Vision, Wrong Expectations: The European Union and Self-regulation of Harmful Internet Content' (2005) 14 *Information and Communications Technology Law* 189.

Boroughf B, 'The Next Great YouTube: Improving Content ID to foster creativity, cooperation and fair compensation' (2014) 25 *Albany Law Journal of Science and Technology* 8.

Bohte S M, Langdon W B and La Poutre H, 'On Current Technology for Information Filtering and User Profiling in Agent-Based Systems, Part I: A Perspective' (2000) 9.

Braithwaite J, 'The Regulatory State?' in RE Goodin (ed), *The Oxford Handbook of Political Science* (Oxford, Oxford University Press, 2011) 219–20.

Bridy A, 'Graduated Response and the Turn to Private Ordering in Online Copyright Enforcement' (2010) 89 *Oregon Law Review* 101.

Bridy A and Keller D, 'U.S. Copyright Office Section 512 Study: Comments in Response to Notice of Inquiry' (2016) 14–15.

Brill J, 'Transparency, Trust, and Consumer Protection in a Complex World' Keynote Address Before Coalition for Networked Information Fall 2015 Membership Meeting (15 December 2015).

Bredow H, 'Final Report Study on Co-Regulation Measures in the Media Sector' (2006) 11.

Bunting M, 'Keeping Consumers Safe Online Legislating for platform accountability for online content' (2018) *Communications Chambers* 20–27, 33.

British and Irish Legal Education and Technology Association, 'Written evidence for the House of Lords, The Internet: To Regulate or Not to Regulate? Summary of Response' (2018) 1.

Bucher T, 'The algorithmic imaginary: exploring the ordinary effects of Facebook algorithms' (2017) 20 *Information, Communication and Strategy* 40.

Burk DL, 'How state regulation of the internet violates the commerce clause' (1998) 17 *Cato Journal* 151.

Caplan R, Donovan J, Hanson L and Matthews J, 'Algorithmic Accountability: A primer' (2018) 7.

Castells M, 'Materials for an Exploratory Theory of the Network Society' (2000) *The British Journal of Sociology* 5.

Carrier M A, 'Copyright and Innovation: The Untold Story' (2012) 891 *Wisconsin Law Review* 923–49

Carsten U, 'Standards for Duty of Care? Debating Intermediary Liability from a Sectoral Perspective' (2017) 8 *Journal of Intellectual Property, Information Technology and E-Commerce Law* 116.

Carty H, 'Joint tortfeasance and assistance liability' (1999) 19 *Legal studies* 10.

Castillo A, 'The Digital Services Act Package: Reflections on the EU Commission's policy options' (2021) *ETUI Policy Brief* 4.

Center for Democracy and Technology, 'Chile's notice and takedown system for copyright protection: an alternative approach' (August 2012).

Cerf V G, 'First, do no harm' (2011) 24 *Philosophy & Technology* 463.

Chadelaine P, 'Copyright User Rights and Remedies: An access justice perspective' (2018) *Laws* 7–10.

Cheung C, Chiu P and Lee M, 'Online social networks: Why do students use facebook?' (2011) 27 *Computers in Human Behaviour* 1337.

Chen S, 'Corporate Responsibilities in Internet-Enabled Social Networks' (2009) *90 Journal of Business Ethics* 523.

Citron D, 'Technological Due Process' (2008) 85 *Washington University Law Review* 1253–54.

Citron Keats D and Wittes B, 'The Internet Will Not Break: Denying Bad Samaritans Section 230 Immunity' (2017) *University of Maryland Legal Studies Research Paper No. 2017-22* 17.

Citron Keats D and Pasquale F, 'The Scored Society: Due Process for Automated Predictions' (2014) 89 *Washington Law Review* 19.

Coase R, 'The Problem of Social Cost' (1960) 3 *Journal of Law and Economics* 1, 19.

Cohen J, 'The Regulatory State in the Information Age' (2016) 17 *Theoretical Inquiries in Law* 6.

Daly M, 'Life after Grokster: analysis of US and European approaches to file-sharing' (2007) 29 *European Intellectual Property Review* 2.

Davies P, 'Accessory liability for assisting torts' (2011) 70 *The Cambridge Law Journal* 353.

Davies P, 'Accessory liability: protecting intellectual property rights' (2011) 4 *Intellectual Property Quarterly* 390.

De Gregorio G, 'Expressions on Platforms: Freedom of Expression and ISP liability in the European Digital Single Market' (2018) 2 *CoRe* 214.

Devenney J, 'The legacy of the Cameron-Clegg coalition programme of reform of the law on the supply of goods, digital content and services to consumers' (2018) 6 *Journal of Business Law* 488.

Easterbrook FH, 'Cyberspace and the Law of the Horse' (1996) *University of Chicago Legal Forum* 210–11.

Edwards L and Waelde C, 'Online Intermediaries and Liability for Copyright Infringement' (2005) *WIPO* 2.

Edwards L, 'Privacy, security and data protection in smart cities: a critical EU law perspective' (2016) 2 *European Data Protection Law Review* 48.

Edwards L, 'Should ISPs be compelled to become Copyright Cops?' (2009) 19 *Magazine of the Society for Computers and Law* 29.

Edomsowan S, 'The history of social media and its impact on business' (2011) 16 *The Journal of Applied Management and Entrepreneurship* 4.

Diakopoulos N, 'Algorithmic accountability reporting: on the investigation of black boxes' (2013) *Town Center for Digital Journalism* 14.

Dittrich P J, 'Online platforms and how to regulate them: an overview' (2018) *Jacques Delors Institute Policy Paper No. 227* 5.

Dusollier S, 'The 2019 Directive on Copyright in the Digital Single Market: Some Progress, a few bad choices and an overall failed ambition' (2020) 57 *Common Market Law Review* 979.

Eberle E, 'The Methodology of Comparative Law' (2011) 16 *Roger Williams University Law Review* 52.

Economides N, 'The Economics of networks' (1996) 14 *International Journal of Industrial Organization* 673.

Economides N, 'The Economics of Trademarks' (1988) 78 *Trademark Reporter* 523.

Edwards L and Veale M, 'Slave to the algorithm? Why a right to an explanation is probably not the remedy you are looking for' (2016) 16 *Duke Law and Technology Review* 18.

Elkin-Koren N, Nahmias, Y and Perel M, 'Is It Time to Abolish Safe Harbor? When Rhetoric Clouds Policy Goals' (2020) 31 *Stanford Law & Policy Review* 1.

Epstein RA, 'Can Technological Innovation Survive Government Regulation?' (2013) 36 *Harvard Journal of Law and Public Policy* 87

Erickson K and Kretschmer M, 'Empirical approaches to intermediary liability' (2019) 6 *Create Working Paper* 2, 4, 7.

Farano M, 'Internet Intermediaries' Liability for Copyright and Trademark Infringement: Reconciling the EU and US Approaches' (2012) *TTLF Working Paper* 47.

Ferrel O C and Ferrel L, 'The Responsibility and Accountability of CEOs: The Last Interview with Ken Lay' (2010) *Journal of Business Ethics* 11.

Fiala L and Husovec M, 'Using experimental evidence to design optimal notice and takedown process' (2018) *TILEC Discussion Paper* 7.

Finck M, 'Digital Regulation: Designing a Supranational Legal Framework for the Platform Economy' (2017) *LSE Law, Society and Economy Working Papers* 15.

Fisher W, 'CopyrightX: Lecture 11.1, Supplements to Copyright: Secondary Liability' (18 February, 2014) cyber.harvard.edu/people/tfisher/cx/CopyrightX_Lecture11_Illustrations.pdf.

Ferri F, 'The dark side(s) of the EU Directive on copyright and related rights in the Digital Single Market' (2020) 7 *China EU Law Journal* 1.

French High Council for Literary and Artistic Property, 'Mission to Link Directives 2000/31 and 2001/29 – Report and Proposals' (2016) 7 *Journal of Intellectual Property, Information Technology and E-Commerce Law* 70.

Friedman L W and Friedman H, 'The New Media Technologies: Overview and Research Framework' (2008) *SSRN Electronic Journal* 1.

Friedmann D, 'Sinking the Safe Harbour with the legal certainty of strict liability in sight' (2014) 9 *Journal of Intellectual Property Law and Practice* 148–55.

Freeman D, 'Collaborative governance in the administrative state' (1997) *UCLA Law Review* 12.

Frosio G, 'Why Keep a Dog and Bark Yourself? From Intermediary Liability to Responsibility' (2017) 26 *International Journal of Law and Information Technology* 7–12.

Frosio G, 'Reforming intermediary liability in the platform economy: a European Digital Single Market Strategy' (2017) 112 *Northwestern University Law Review* 43.

Frosio G and Mendis S, 'Monitoring and filtering: European reform or Global trend?' (2019) *Center for International Intellectual Property Studies Research Paper* 21.

Frosio G, 'Reforming the C-DSM Reform: a user-based copyright theory for commonplace creativity' (2019) papers.ssrn.com/sol3/papers.cfm?abstract_id=3482523.

Fourberg N et al, 'Online advertising: the impact of targeted advertising on advertisers, market access and consumer choice' (2020) *IMCO Committee* 39–40.

Gardner J, 'The Many Faces of the Reasonable Person' (2015) 113 *Law Quarterly Review* 563.
Garstka K, 'Looking above and beyond the blunt expectation: specified request as the recommended approach to intermediary liability in cyberspace' (2016) 7 *European Journal of Law and Technology* 1.
Geiger C and Frosio G, 'Taking fundamental rights seriously in the Digital Services Act's platform liability regime' (2021) *European Law Journal* 35.
Geiger C and Jütte JB, 'The EU Commission's Guidance on Article 17 of the Copyright in the Digital Single Market Directive – A Guide to Virtue in Content Moderation by Digital Platforms?' (2021) *European Intellectual Property Review* 625.
Giannopoulou A, 'Copyright enforcement measures: the role of the ISPs and the respect of the principle of proportionality' (2012) 3 *European Journal for Law and Technology* 1.
Giblin R, 'Evaluating Graduated Response' (2014) 37 *Columbia Journal of Law and the Arts* 147.
Gill L, Redeker D and Gasser U, 'Towards Digital Constitutionalism? Mapping attempts to craft an Internet Bill of Rights' (2015) 80 *The International Communication Gazette* 302.
Ginsburg J C, 'Separating the Sony Sheep from the Grokster Goats: Reckoning the Future Business Plans of Copyright-Dependent Technology Entrepreneurs' (2008) 50 *Arizona Law Review* 591.
Global Information Society Watch, 'The Internet and corruption: Transparency and accountability online' (2012) 26.
Goldberg J and Zipursky B, 'Tort Law and Responsibility' (2013) *Fordham Law Legal Studies Research Paper* 7.
Goldman E, 'Search Engine Bias and the Demise of Search Engine Utopianism' (2006) 8 *Yale Journal Law and Technology* 189.
Goold P, 'Unbundling the tort of copyright infringement' (2016) 102 *Virginia Law Review* 1842.
Grisse K, 'After the storm – examining the final version of Article 17 of the new Directive (EU) 2019/790' (2019) 14 *Journal of Intellectual Property Law & Practice* 887.
Guerra-Pujol, FE and Martínez-García, Orlando I, 'Does the Prisoner's Dilemma Refute the Coase Theorem?' (2013) 47 *John Marshall Law Review* 2.
Hallikainen H and Laukkanen T, 'National culture and consumer trust in e-commerce' (2018) 38 *International Journal of Information Management* 97.
Hamdan A, 'Gatekeeper liability' (2005) 77 *Southern California Law Review* 98.
Hanretty C and Koop C, 'Shall the law set them free? The formal and actual independence of regulatory agencies' (2012) 7 *Regulation and Governance* 3.
Harvard Law Association, 'Developments in the Law: The Law of Cyberspace' (1999) *Harvard Law Review* 1680.
Hays T, 'The evolution and decentralisation of secondary liability for infringements of copyright-protected works: Part 1' (2006) 12 *European Intellectual Property Review* 617.
Heaven D, 'Not like us: Artificial Minds we can't understand' (2013) *New Scientist* 32–35.
Helman L and Parchomovsky G, 'The best available technology standard' (2011) 111 *Columbia Law Review* 1230.
Hilty R and Moscon V, 'Modernisation of the EU Copyright Rules Position Statement of the Max Planck Institute for Innovation and Competition' (2018) *Max Planck for Innovation and Competition Research Paper* 99.
Hoeren T and Yankova S, 'The Liability of Internet Intermediaries – The German Perspective' (2012) 43 *International Review of Intellectual Property and Competition Law* 501.
Horten M, 'Content responsibility: The looming cloud of uncertainty for internet intermediaries' (2016) *Center for Democracy and Technology* 12–13.
Hurwitz J, 'Trust and Online Interaction' (2013) 161 *University of Pennsylvania Law Review* 1593.
Husovec M and Leenes R, 'Study on the role of online intermediaries Summary of the public consultation: a study prepared for the European Commission DG Communications Networks, Content & Technology' (2016) 1.
Husovec M, 'Accountable, Not Liable: Injunctions Against Intermediaries' (2016) *TILEC Discussion Paper* 36.
Husovec M, 'Injunctions against Innocent Third Parties: The case of Website Blocking' (2016) 4 *Journal of Intellectual Property, Information Technology and E-Commerce Law* 116.
Husovec M, 'The promises of algorithmic copyright enforcement' (2018) 42 *Columbia Journal of Law and Arts* 59.
Husovec M and Quintais JP, 'How to License Article 17? Exploring the Implementation Options for the New EU Rules on Content-Sharing Platforms' (1 October 2019) papers.ssrn.com/sol3/papers.cfm?abstract_id=3463011&download=yes.

Huszti-Orban K, 'Countering Terrorism and Violent Extremism Online: what role for social media platforms?' in L Belli and N Zingales (eds), *Platform Regulations: How Platforms are regulated and how they regulate us* (2017) 204.

Ives A, 'Neoliberalism and the concept of governance: Renewing with an older liberal tradition to legitimate the power of capital' (2015) Mémoire(s), identité(s), marginalité(s) dans le monde occidental contemporain. Cahiers du MIMMOC.

Introna L, 'Algorithms, Governance and Governmentality: on governing academic writing' (2016) 41 *Science, Technology and Human Values* 17.

Introna L and Nissenbaum H, 'Shaping the web: Why the Politics of search engines matters' (2000) 13 *The Information Society* 169.

Ibrahim D, 'Venture impact: the economic importance of venture capital-backed companies to the US Economy' (2012) 65 *Vanderbilt Law Review* 1.

Jacques S, Garstka K, Hviid M and Street J, 'Automated anti-piracy systems as copyright enforcement mechanism: a need to consider cultural diversity' (2018) 40 *European Intellectual Property Review* 218.

Jondet N, 'The silver lining in Dailymotion's copyright cloud' (2008) *Juriscom. Net* 2.

Jones J, 'Internet pirates walk the plank with article 10 kept at bay: Neij and Sunde Kolmisoppi v Sweden' (2013) 35 *European Intellectual Property Review* 5.

Johnson DR and Post D, 'Law and Borders: The Rise of Law in Cyberspace' (1996) 48 *Stanford Law Review* 1367.

Kaleda S, 'The role of the principle of effective judicial protection in relation to website blocking injunctions' (2017) 8 *Journal of Intellectual Property, Information Technology and E-Commerce Law* 7.

Karapapa S, 'The requirement for a "new public" in EU copyright law' (2017) 42 *European Law Review* 63.

Karapapa S and Borghi M, 'Search engine liability for autocomplete suggestions: personality, privacy and the power of the algorithm' (2015) 23 *International Journal of Law and Information Technology* 261–89.

Kaspersen H, 'Liability of Providers of the Electronic Highway' (2006) 12 *Computer Law and Security Report* 290.

Katyal N K, 'Criminal Law in Cyberspace' (2001) 149 *University of Pennsylvania Law Review* 1097.

Kiat Boon Seng D, 'The State of the Discordant Union: An Empirical Analysis of DMCA Takedown Notices' (2014) 18 *Virginia Journal of Law and Technology Association* 369.

Kleinschmidt B, 'An International Comparison of ISP's Liabilities for Unlawful Third-Party Content' (2010) 18 *International Journal of Law and Information Technology* 332.

Kleinsteuber HJ, 'State – Regulation – Media: OSCE Conference Amsterdam-Guaranteeing Media Freedom on the Internet' (2004) 3.

Köhler C and Burmeister K, 'Copyright liability on the Internet today in Europe (Germany, France, Italy and the E.U.)' (1999) 21 *European Intellectual Property Review* 485.

Kochanowski J, 'The 'reasonable man' standards in continental law' (2007) 1 *The Journal of Legislative studies* 1.

Koch CH, 'Policymaking by the Administrative Judiciary' (2003) SSRN Electronic Journal 693 www.ssrn.com/abstract=460520.

Koop C and Lodge M, 'What is regulation? An interdisciplinary concept analysis' (2015) *Regulation and Governance* 7.

Kraakman R H, 'Gatekeepers: The Anatomy of a Third-Party Enforcement Strategy' (1986) 2 *Journal of Law, Economics and Organization* 61.

Krokida Z, 'Towards a wider scope for the duty of care of host internet service providers: The case of Eva Glawischnig-Piesczek v Facebook' (2021) 43 *European Intellectual Property Review* 313–21.

Krokida Z, 'Use of Filters by Online Intermediaries and the Rights of Users: Developments in the European Union, Mexico, India and China' in IFLA, *Copyright Reader for Librarians* (Berlin, De Gruyter 2022).

Kroll J et al, 'Accountable algorithms' (2017) 165 *University of Pennsylvania Law Review* 640.

Kulesza J, 'Due diligence in international internet law' (2014) *Journal of Internet Law* 28.

Kulk S and Borgesius FZ, 'Filtering for Copyright Enforcement in Europe after the Sabam Cases' (2012) 11 *European Intellectual Property Law Review* 791.

Laidlaw E, A framework for identifying Internet information gatekeepers' (2010) 24 *International Review of Law, Computers and Technology* 264.

Laidlaw E, 'Private Power, Public Interest: An Examination of Search Engine Accountability' (2009) 17 *International Journal of Law and Information Technology* 113.

Laidlaw E, 'Are We Asking Too Much from Defamation Law? Reputation Systems, ADR, Industry Regulation and Other Extra-Judicial Possibilities for Protecting Reputation in the Internet Age: Proposal for Reform' (2017) www.lco-cdo.org/wp-content/uploads/2017/07/DIA-Commissioned-Paper-Laidlaw.pdf.

LaFontaine A, 'Adventures in software licensing: SCO v. IBM and the future of the open source model' (2006) 4 *Journal on Telecommunications and High Technology Law* 449.

Landes W M and Lichtman D, 'Indirect Liability for Copyright Infringement: An Economic Perspective (2003) 16 *Harvard Journal of Law and Technology* 409.

Landes W and Lichtman D, 'Indirect Liability for Copyright Infringement: Napster and Beyond' (2003) 16 *The Journal of Economic Perspectives* 20.

(St.) Alphonsus Liguori, *Theologia Moralis*. 4 volumes ed by L Gaude (Rome: Ex Typographia 1912) 357 archive.org/details/theologiamoralis01inligu.

Lee E, 'Recognizing Rights in Real Time: The Role of Google in the EU Right to Be Forgotten' (2016) 49 *U.C. Davis Law Review* 1066

Leistner M, 'Structural aspects of secondary provider liability in Europe' (2014) 9 *Journal of Intellectual Property Law and Practice* 75.

Leistner M, 'Störerhaftung und mittelbare Schutzrechtsverletzung' (2010) *GRUR-Beilage zu Heft* 1.

Leistner M, 'Copyright law on the internet in need of reform: hyperlinks, online platforms and aggregators' (2017) 12 *Journal of Intellectual Property Law & Practice* 136.

Leistner N, 'The Commission's vision for Europe's Digital Future: Proposals for the Data Governance Act, the Digital Markets Act and the Digital Services Act – Acritical primer' (2021) 10.

Levinson D, 'Collective sanctions' (2003) 56 *Stanford Law Review* 365.

Lichtman D and Posner E, 'Holding Internet Service Providers Accountable' (2006) 14 *Supreme Court Economic Review* 221.

Lodder A and Van der Meulen N, 'Evaluation of the Role of Access Providers: Discussion of Dutch Pirate Bay Case Law and Introducing Principles on Directness, Effectiveness, Costs, Relevance, and Time' (2013) 4 *Journal of Intellectual Property, Information Technology and E-Commerce Law* 130.

Lovejoy N, 'Standards for determining when ISPs have fallen out of Section 512(A)' (2013) 27 *Harvard Journal of Law and Technology* 257.

Lomba N and Evas T, 'Annex II: Digital Services Act: Adapting commercial and civil law rules for commercial entities operating online: legal assessment' (2021) 73.

Lynskey O, 'Control over personal data in a digital age: Google Spain v AEPD and Mario Costeja Gonzalez' (2015) 78 *Modern Law Review* 522.

Lynskey O, 'Regulating "Platform Power' (2017) *LSE Law, Society and Economy Working Paper* 3.

Lynskey O, 'The Europeanisation of data protection law' (2016) 19 *Cambridge Yearbook of European Legal Studies* 252.

Mansell R, 'Platforms of power' (2015) 43 *Intermedia* 20–24.

Mayer-Schonberger V, 'Demystifying Lessig' (2008) 4 *Wisconsin Law Review* 713.

Mac Sithigh D, 'The road to responsibilities: new attitudes towards internet intermediaries' (2019) 29 *Information and Communications Technology Law* 18.

Malgieri G and Comande G, 'Why a right to legibility of automated decision-making exists in the General Data Protection Regulation' (2017) 7 *International Data Privacy Law* 254.

Mann R and Belzley S, 'The promise of internet intermediary liability' (2005) 47 *William and Mary Law Review* 26.

Manner M, Siniketo T and Polland U, 'The Pirate Bay ruling' (2009) 20 *Entertainment Law Review* 198.

Marsoof A, 'Notice and take down: a copyright perspective' (2015) 5 *Queen Mary Journal of Intellectual Property Law* 24.

Martens B, 'JRC Technical Support reports: An economic policy perspective on online platforms' (2016) *Institute for prospective technological studies digital economy working paper* 34.

Marchill M, Neuberger C and Schindler F, 'Transparency on the Net: Functions and Deficiencies of Internet Search Engines' (2003) 5 *The Journal of policy, regulation and strategy* 52.

Margoni T and Perry M, 'Online intermediary liability and privatized enforcement: the Content ID case' (2016) *The Tenth International Conference on Digital Society and eGovernments* 36.

Mateus M, 'Why should National Competition Authorities be Independent and how should they be Accountable?' (2007) 3 *European Competition Journal* 21.

Marsden C, 'Co-Regulation in European Media and Internet Sectors' (2005) 33 *Intermedia* 28.

Marsden C, 'Internet Co-Regulation and Constitutionalism: Towards a More Nuanced View' (2011) ssrn.com/abstract=1973328 or dx.doi.org/10.2139/ssrn.1973328.

McGinnis JL and Heinisch O, 'Eyes across the Atlantic: coordination and management of global private antitrust litigation' (14 April 2017).

Moravcsik A, 'Taking Preferences Seriously: A Liberal Theory of International Politics' (1997) 51 *International Organisation* 518.

McDougal MS, 'Law as a Process of Decision: A Policy-Oriented Approach to Legal Study' (1956) 1 *Natural Law Forum* 67.

McIntyre K, 'The Evolution of Social Media from 1969 to 2013: A Change in Competition and a Trend Toward Complementary, Niche Sites The Journal of Social Media in Society' (2014).

Mimler M, 'First things first: German Federal High Court provides guidance on ISP liability in online copyright infringement cases' (2016) 11 *Journal of Intellectual Property Law and Practice* 485.

Montagnani ML and Trapova A, 'Safe harbours in deep waters: a new emerging liability regime for Internet Intermediaries in the Digital Single Market' (2018) 26 *International Journal of Law and Information Technology* 294.

Monti G, 'Independence, interdependence and legitimacy: the EU Commission, National Competition Authorities, and the European Competition Network' (2014) *Working Paper* 3.

Moohr GS, 'The crime of copyright infringement: an inquiry based on morality, harm and criminal theory' (2009) 83 *Boston University Law Review* 731.

Mulgan R, 'Accountability issues in the New Model of Governance' (2008) *Discussion Paper* 8.

Narveson J, 'Collective responsibility' (2002) 6 *Journal of Ethics* 179–98.

Lecture by Sjoera Nas, Bits of Freedom 'The Multatuli Project ISP Notice & take down' (2004) www-old.bof.nl/docs/researchpaperSANE.pdf.

Nissenbaum H, 'Computing and Accountability' (1994) 37 *Communications of the ACM* 76.

Negreiro M, 'The rise of e-commerce and the cashless society' (2020) *European Parliamentary Research Service* 6.

Nordemann JB, 'Report for Liability of Online Service Providers for Copyrighted Content- Regulatory Action needed?' (2017) *IMCO Committee* www.europarl.europa.eu/RegData/etudes/IDAN/2017/614207/IPOL_IDA(2017)614207_EN.pdf.

Nordemann JB, 'Annex III: Digital Services Act: Improving the functioning of the single market' (2020) 299.

Nordemann JB, 'Internet Copyright Infringement: Remedies against Internet Intermediaries- The European Perspective on Host and Access Providers' (2012) *59 Journal of the Copyright Society of the USA* 773.

Nordemann JB, 'Liability for Copyright Infringements on the Internet: Host Providers (Content Providers) – The German Approach' (2011) 2 *Journal of Intellectual Property, Information Technology and Electronic Commerce Law* 37.

Noto La Diega G, 'Against the Dehumanisation of Decision-Making: Algorithmic Decisions at the Crossroads of Intellectual Property, Data Protection and Freedom of Information' (2018) 9 *Journal of Intellectual Property, Information Technology and E-Commerce Law* 23.

OECD, 'The Economic Impact of Counterfeiting and Piracy' (2008) www.oecd.org/sti/ind/theeconomicimpactofcounterfeitingandpiracy.htm.

OECD, 'The economic and social role of internet intermediaries' (2010) 9 www.oecd.org/internet/ieconomy/44949023.pdf.

OECD, 'An Introduction to Online Platforms and Their Role in the Digital Transformation' (2019) 28, 29.

Ohly A, 'The broad concept of "communication to the public" in recent CJEU judgments and the liability of intermediaries: primary, secondary or unitary liability?' (2018) 13 *Journal of Intellectual Property Law and Practice* 670.

Okoye A, 'Theorising Corporate Social Responsibility as an Essentially Contested Concept: Is a Definition Necessary?' (2009) 89 *Journal of Business Ethics* 613.

Online censorship, 'Report on unfriending censorship: insights from four months of crowdsourced data on social media censorship' (2016) 17.

Oswald L, 'International issues in secondary liability for intellectual property rights infringement' (2008) 45 *American Business Law Journal* 247.

Oxford Economics, 'The economic impact of the UK film industry' (June 2010) www.bfi.org.uk/sites/bfi.org.uk/files/downloads/economic-impact-of-the-uk-film-industry-2010-06.pdf.

Oxera, 'Report on behalf of Google on the economic impact of safe harbours on Internet intermediary start-ups' (2015) 10 www.oxera.com/wp-content/uploads/2018/07/The-economic-impact-of-safe-harbours-on-Internet-intermediary-start-ups.pdf.pdf.

Papadaki E, 'Hyperlinking, making available and copyright infringement: lessons from European national courts' (2017) 8 *European Journal of Law and Technology* 2–14.

Parti K and Marin L, 'Ensuring Freedoms and Protecting Rights in the Governance of the Internet: A comparative analysis on blocking measures and internet providers' removal of illegal internet content' (2013) 9 *Journal of Contemporary European Research* 149.

Pasquale F, 'Beyond Innovation and Competition: The Need for Qualified Transparency in Internet Intermediaries' (2014) 104 *Northwestern University Law Review* 173.

Pasquale F, 'Restoring transparency to automated authority' (2011) *Seton Hall Research Paper* 254.

Palzer c, 'Self-Monitoring v. Self-Regulation v. Co-Regulation' (2003) *IRIS Special: Co-Regulation of the Media in Europe* 31.

Peguera M, 'The DMCA Safe Harbors and their European Counterparts: a comparative analysis of some common problems' (2008) 32 *Columbia Journal of Law and the Arts* 482.

Peguera M, 'Internet Service Providers' Liability in Spain: Recent Case Law and Future Perspectives' (2010) 10 *Journal of Intellectual Property, Information Technology and E-Commerce Law* 159.

Perel M and Elkin-Koren N, 'Black Box Tinkering: Beyond Disclosure in Algorithmic Enforcement' (2017) 69 *Florida Law Review* 181.

Perel M and Elkin-Koren N, 'Accountability in Algorithmic Copyright Enforcement' (2016) 19 *Stanford Technology Law Review* 483.

Penney J, 'Privacy and Legal Automation: The DMCA as a Case Study' (2019) 22 *Stanford Technology Law Review* 456.

Phililips J, 'Three Strikes … and then?' (2009) 4 *Journal of Intellectual Property Law and Practice* 521.

Pilutik S, 'eBay's Secondary Trademark Liability Problem and its VeRO Program' (2007) www.cs.cmu.edu/~dst/Secrets/E-Meter/eBay-VERO-pilutik.html.

Posner RA, 'Guido Calabresi's 'The Costs of Accidents': A Reassessment' (2005) *University of Chicago Law School* 12.

Poort J and Quintais JP, 'Global online piracy study' (2018) *University of Amsterdam* 50, 51.

Quintais JP, 'Untangling the hyperlinking web: In search of the online right of communication to the public' (2018) 21 *The Journal of World Intellectual Property* 408.

Quintais JP, 'The New Copyright in the Digital Single Market Directive: A Critical Look' (2019) 1 *European Intellectual Property Review* 19.

Quintais JP and Schwemer SF, 'The Interplay between the Digital Services Act and Sector Regulation: How special is copyright?' (2022) *European Journal of Risk Regulation* 1–31.

Radon, 'Counterfeit Luxury Goods Online: An Investigation of Consumer Perceptions' (2012) 4 *International Journal of Marketing Studies* 74.

Ramahlo A, 'Copyright law-making in the EU: what lies under the "internal market" mask?' (2014) 9 *Journal of Intellectual Property Law and Practice* 224.

Reidenberg J, 'Governing Networks and Rule-Making in Cyberspace' (1996) 45 *Emory Law Journal* 911.

Reidenberg J, 'Lex Informatica: The formulation of Information Policy Rules through Technology' (1997) 76 *Texas Law Review* 577.

Du Rausas MP et al, 'Report of McKinsey Global Institute, Internet matters, the net's sweeping impact on growth, jobs, and prosperity' (2011) www.mckinsey.com/~/media/McKinsey/Industries/Technology%20Media%20and%20Telecommunications/High%20Tech/Our%20Insights/Internet%20matters/MGI_internet_matters_exec_summary.ashx.

Rendas T, 'How Playboy Photos Compromised EU Copyright Law: The GS Media Judgment' (2017) 20 *Journal of Internet Law* 11.

Reda J, Selinger J and Servatius M, 'Article 17 of the Directive on Copyright in the Digital Single Market: A Fundamental Rights Assessment' (2020) www.ssrn.com/abstract=3732223.

Reuters Institute for the Study of Journalism, 'Reuters Institute Digital News Report 2016' (2016) reutersinstitute.politics.ox.ac.uk/sites/default/files/research/files/Digital%2520News%2520Report%25202016.pdf.

Reuters Institute for the Study of Journalism, 'Reuters Institute Digital News Report 2019' (2019) reutersinstitute.politics.ox.ac.uk/sites/default/files/2019-06/DNR_2019_FINAL_0.pdf.

Romero-Moreno F, 'Notice and stay down and social media: amending Article 13 of the Proposed Directive on Copyright' (2019) 33 *International Review of Law, Computers and Technology* 187.

Rosati E, 'The CJEU Pirate Bay judgment and its impact on the liability of online platforms' (2017) 12 *European Intellectual Property Review* 748.

Rosati E, 'GS Media and Its Implications for the Construction of the Right of Communication to the Public within EU Copyright Architecture' (2017) 54 *Common Market Law Review* 1242.

Rosati E, 'Why a Reform of Hosting Providers' Safe Harbour is Unnecessary Under EU Copyright Law' (2016) 38 *European Intellectual Property Law Review* 668.

Rubenstein W, 'The concept of equality of in civil procedure' (2002) 23 *Cardozo Law Review* 1.

Sander B, 'Freedom of Expression in the Age of Online Platforms: The Promise and Pitfalls of a Human Rights-Based Approach to Content Moderation' (2020) 43 *Fordham International Law Journal* 939.

The Santa Clara Principles on Transparency and Accountability in Content Moderation, newamericadotorg.s3.amazonaws.com/documents/Santa_Clara_Principles.pdf.

Savin A, 'The EU Digital Services Act: Towards a more responsible Internet' (2021) *Copenhagen Business School Law Research Paper Series* No. 21

Sartor G, 'Providers Liability: From the e-commerce directive to the future: In depth analysis' (2017) *IMCO Committee* www.europarl.europa.eu/RegData/etudes/IDAN/2017/614179/IPOL_IDA(2017)614179_EN.pdf.

Sartor G and Loreggia A, 'The impact of algorithms for online content filtering or moderation: Upload filters (2020) *Report for the JURI Committee* 50.

Sauter W, 'Proportionality in EU Law: A Balancing Act?' (2013) 2013 *TILEC Discussion Paper* 1.

Sawyer MS, 'Filters, Fair Use & Feedback: User-Generated Content Principles and the DMCA' (2009) 24 *Berkeley Technology Law Journal* 380.

Savin A, 'The EU Digital Services Act: Towards a more responsible Internet' (2021) *Copenhagen Business School Law Research Paper Series No. 21-04.*

Schellekens M, 'Liability of Internet Intermediaries: a slippery slope?' (2011) 8 *SCRIPTed* 154.

Senftleben M, 'Content censorship and Council carelessness – Why the Parliament must safeguard the open, participative Web 2.0' (2018) 4 *AMI* 141.

Senftleben M et al, 'The Recommendation on Measures to Safeguard Fundamental Rights and the Open Internet in the Framework of the EU Copyright Reform' (2016) 1–24.

Senftleben M, 'Content censorship and Council carelessness – Why the Parliament must safeguard the open, participative web 2.01' (2018) 4 *AMI – tijdschrift voor auteurs-, media- en informatierecht* 139.

Senftleben M, 'An uneasy case for notice and takedown: context-specific trade mark rights' (2012) *VU Centre for Law and Governance* 3.

Seng D, 'Comparative analysis of the national approaches to the liability of internet intermediaries- Part I' (2010) *WIPO* 46.

Seltzer W, 'Free speech unmoored in copyright's safe harbour: chilling effects of the DMCA on the first Amendment' (2010) 24 *Harvard Journal of Law and Technology* 172.

Sims C and Figueira E, 'YouTube, google find safe harbour in New York Court' (2010) *Communications Lawyer* 3.

Škrinjar Vidović M, 'Schrems v Data Protection Commissioner (Case C-362/14): Empowering National Data Protection Authorities' (2015) *Croatian Yearbook of European Law and Policy* 262.

Spinello RA, 'Secondary Liability in the Post Napster Era: Ethical Observations on MGM v. Grokster' (2005) 3 *Journal of Information, Communication and Ethics in Society* 12.

Spinello RA, 'Intellectual Property: Legal and Moral Challenges of Online File Sharing' in Kenneth Einar Himma and Herman Tavani (eds), *Handbook of Information and Computer* Ethics (2008) 553.

Spindler G and Leistner M, 'Secondary Copyright Infringement – New Perspectives from Germany and Europe' (2006) 37 *International Review of Intellectual Property and Competition Law* 788.

Stalla-Bourdillon S, 'Online Monitoring, Filtering, Blocking ... What is the Difference? Where to Draw the Line?' (2013) *Southampton Research Paper* 19.

Stalla-Bourdillon S et al, 'Open Letter to the European Commission – On the Importance of Preserving the Consistency and Integrity of the EU Acquis Relating to Content Monitoring within the Information Society' (2016) 1–5.

Stigler G, 'The theory of economic regulation' (1971) 2 *The Bell Journal of Economics and Management Science* 4.

Stanford report on 'Similarities in Managing Supply Chain Sustainability and Intellectual Property' (2014) 4 www.gsb.stanford.edu/sites/gsb/files/publication-pdf/white-paper-vcii-sustainability-ip-supply-chains.pdf.

Strathern M, 'Improving ratings': audit in the British University system' (1997) 5 *European Review* 308.

Synodinou T, 'Intermediaries' liability for online copyright infringement in the EU: evolutions and confusions' (2015) 31 *Computer Law and Security Review* 57–67.

Sylvain O, 'Internet Governance and Democratic Legitimacy' (2010) 62 *Federal Communications Law Journal* 207–08.

Spoerri T, 'On Upload-filters and other competitive advantages for big tech companies under Article 17 of the Directive on Copyright in the Digital Single Market' (2019) 10 *Journal of Intellectual Property, Information Technology and E-Commerce Law* 173.

Stone Sweet A and Matthews J, 'Proportionality Balancing and Global Constitutionalism' (2009) 47 *Columbia Journal of Transnational Law* 73.

Swiss Institute of Comparative Law, 'Comparative study on filtering, blocking and take-down on illegal content on the Internet, Report commissioned by the Council of Europe' (2015) 5.

Tavassi M, 'Copyright and the Internet' in M Frazosi et al (eds), *The Digital Single Market Copyright: Internet and Copyright Law in the European Perspective* (Rome, Aracne Editrice, 2016) 188.

Taddeo M and Floridi L, 'The Debate on the Moral Responsibilities of Online Service Providers' (2016) 22 *Science and Engineering Ethics* 1575.

Thompson M, 'Beyond Gatekeeping: The Normative Responsibility of Internet Intermediaries' (2016) 18 *Vanderbilt Journal of Entertainment and Technology Law* 783.

Tsigou C, 'Notice-and-Takedown Procedure under Greek Intellectual Property Law 4481/2017' (2018) 9 *Journal of Intellectual Property, Information Technology and E-Commerce Law* 201.

Tuch A, 'The limits of Gatekeeper liability' (2017) 73 *Washington and Lee Law Review Online* 619.

Utting P, 'Rethinking business regulation: from self-regulation to social control' (2005) *Technology, Business and Society Programme-United Nations Research Institute for Social Development* 5–6.

Van Couvering E, 'Is relevance relevant? Market, Science and War: Discourses of search engine quality' (2007) 12 *Journal of Computer-Mediated Communication* 866.

Van Hoboken J, 'Hosting intermediary services and illegal content online: an analysis of the scope of article 14 ECD in light of the developments in the online service landscape' (2018) 27 op.europa.eu/en/publication-detail/-/publication/7779caca-2537-11e9-8d04-01aa75ed71a1/language-en.

Van Eecke P, 'Online service providers and liability: A plea for a balanced approach' (2011) 48 *Common Market Law Review* 1483.

Van der Sloot B, 'Welcome to the Jungle: The Liability of Internet Intermediaries for Privacy Violations in Europe' (2015) 6 *Journal of Intellectual Property, Information Technology and E-Commerce Law* 212.

Van Ecke P and Ooms B, 'ISP Liability and the E-Commerce Directive: A growing trend toward greater responsibility for ISPs' (2007) 11 *Journal of Internet Law* 5.

Vedder A, 'Accountability of and service providers – strict liability entering ethics?' (2001) 3 *Ethics and Information Technology* 71.

Verbiest T, Spindler G, Riccio G and Van der Perre A, 'Study on the Liability of Internet Intermediaries: general trends in the EU' (2007) EU Commission study (MARKT/2006/09/E) papers.ssrn.com/sol3/papers.cfm?abstract_id=2575069.

Villeneuve N, 'The Filtering Matrix: Integrated Mechanisms of Information Control and the demarcation of borders in cyberspace' (2006) 11 *First Monday* journals.uic.edu/ojs/index.php/fm/article/view/1307/1227.

Volkmann C, 'Trademark Use and Liability of Referencing Service In Keyword Advertising – Google AdWords and Trademark Law' (2011) 3 *European Journal of Risk Regulation* 450.

Von Dornum D, 'The Straight and the Crooked: Legal Accountability in Ancient Greece' (1997) 97 *Columbia Law Review* 1483.

Von Blanckenburg K, 'Google search abuses dominant position to illegally favour Google Shopping: an economic review of the EU decision' (2018) 20 *Digital Policy, Regulation and Governance* 211.

Wachter S, Mittelstadt B and Floridi L, 'Why a right to explanation of automated decision-making does not exist in the General Data Protection Regulation' (2017) 7 *International Data Privacy Law* 76.

Wallberg K, 'Notice and takedown of counterfeit goods in the Digital Single Market: a balancing of fundamental rights' (2017) 12 *Journal of Intellectual Property Law and Practice* 922.

Wexler R, 'Life, Liberty, and Trade Secrets: Intellectual Property in the Criminal Justice System' (2018) 70 *Stanford Law Review* 1383.

Weiser P, 'The Future of Internet Regulation' (2009) 43 *UC Davis* 585.

Wilman F, 'The EU's system of knowledge-based liability for hosting service providers in respect of illegal user content – between the e-Commerce Directive and the Digital Services Act' (2021) 12 *Journal of Intellectual Property, Information Technology and E-Commerce Law* 340.

Wright C, 'Actual versus legal control: Reading vicarious liability for copyright infringement into the Digital Millennium Copyright Act of 1998' (2000) 75 *Washington Law Review* 1005.

Wu FT, 'Collateral Censorship and the Limits of Intermediary Immunity' (2011) 87 *Notre Dame Law Review* 295–96.

Wyckoff A and Colecchia A, 'The Economic and Social Impact of Electronic Commerce' (1992) *OECD* 12.

Yakowitz Bambauer J and Zarsky T, 'The Algorithm Game' (2018) 94 *Notre Dame Law Review* 1.

Yu H, Xie L and Sanner S, 'The Lifecyle of a Youtube Video: Phases, Content and Popularity' (2015) *Proceedings of the Ninth International AAAI Conference on Web and Social Media* 533.

Zerilli J, Knott A, Maclaurin J and Gavaghan C, 'Transparency in Algorithmic and Human Decision-Making: Is there a double standard?' (2018) 9 *Philosophy and Technology* 5.

Zittrain J, 'A History of Online Gatekeeping' (2006) 19 *Harvard Journal of Law and Technology* 253.

Websites and Blogs

Anderson N, 'Verizon to forward RIAA warning letters (but that's all) Verizon looks set to forward RIAA copyright infringement notices to its …' (*Ars Technica*, 13 November 2009) arstechnica.com/tech-policy/2009/11/verizon-to-forward-riaa-warning-letters-but-thats-all/.

Anderson N, 'Swedish court rules TPB admins too broke to pay damages' (*Ars Technica*, August 2009) arstechnica.com/tech-policy/2009/08/swedish-court-rules-tpb-admins-too-broke-to-pay-damages/.

Anderson M R, 'Twenty years on from Deep Blue vs Kasparov: how a chess match started the big data revolution' (*The Conversation*, 11 May 2017) theconversation.com/twenty-years-on-from-deep-blue-vs-kasparov-how-a-chess-match-started-the-big-data-revolution-76882.

Andy, 'YouTube's deal with universal blocks DMCA counter notices' (*Torrentfreak*, 5 April 2013) torrentfreak.com/youtube-deal-with-universal-blocks-dmca-counter-notices-130405/.

Andy, 'Italian ISPs Say New Copyright Amendment Infringes Human Rights' (*Torrentfreak*, 27 July 2017) torrentfreak.com/italian-isps-say-new-copyright-amendment-infringes-human-rights-170728/.

Angelopoulos C, 'CJEU Decision on Ziggo: The Pirate Bay Communicates Works to the Public' (*Kluwer Copyright blog*, 30 June 2017) copyrightblog.kluweriplaw.com/2017/06/30/cjeu-decision-ziggo-pirate-bay-communicates-works-public/.

Angelopoulos C, 'AG Szpunar in Stichting Brein v Ziggo: An Indirect Harmonisation of Indirect Liability' (*Kluwer Copyright blog*, 23 March 2017) copyrightblog.kluweriplaw.com/2017/03/23/ag-szpunar-stichting-brein-v-ziggo-indirect-harmonisation-indirect-liability/.

Angelopoulos C, 'EU Copyright Reform: Outside the Safe Harbours, Intermediary Liability capsizes into incoherence' (*Kluwer Copyright blog*, 6 October 2016) copyrightblog.kluweriplaw.com/2016/10/06/eu-copyright-reform-outside-safe-harbours-intermediary-liability-capsizes-incoherence/.

Angelopoulos C, 'C-494/15 – Tommy Hilfiger: No Difference between Online and Real World Marketplaces for IP Enforcement' (*Kluwer Copyright blog*, 10 August 2016) copyrightblog.kluweriplaw.com/2016/08/10/c-49415-tommy-hilfiger-no-difference-online-real-world-marketplaces-ip-enforcement/.

ARTICLE 19, 'EU: The draft Digital Services Act and the Digital Markets Act must protect freedom of expression' www.article19.org/resources/digital-rights/.

Belan A, 'BREAKING NEWS: AGCOM issues the first fastissimo administrative blocking injunction' (*IPKat*, 24 April 2014) ipkitten.blogspot.com/2014/04/breaking-news-agcom-issues-first.html.

Bernal N, 'EU Parliament approves sweeping digital copyright reforms' *The Telegraph* (12 September 2018) www.telegraph.co.uk/technology/2018/09/12/eu-parliament-approves-sweeping-copyright-reforms-reshape-internet/.

Berners-Lee T, 'Commentary on Web architecture on Axioms of Web Architecture. Links and Law: Myths' www.w3.org/DesignIssues/LinkLaw.

Bickert M, 'At Facebook we get things wrong – but we take our safety role seriously' *The Guardian* (22 May 2017) www.theguardian.com/commentisfree/2017/may/22/facebook-get-things-wrong-but-safety-role-seriously.

Boffey D, 'Google fined record €2.4bn by EU over search engine results' *The Guardian* (27 June 2017) www.theguardian.com/business/2017/jun/27/google-braces-for-record-breaking-1bn-fine-from-eu.

Boscher H, 'YouTube takes copyright law into their own hands with new policy on music infringement' (*IPKat*, 2 September 2019) ipkitten.blogspot.com/2019/09/youtube-takes-copyright-law-into-their.html.

Canada: Innovation, Science and Economic Development Canada, 'Notice and Notice Regime' www.ic.gc.ca/eic/site/oca-bc.nsf/eng/ca02920.html.

Chee FY, 'Privacy app maker files EU antitrust complaint against Google' (*Reuters*, 2 June 2015) www.reuters.com/article/us-eu-google-antitrust/privacy-app-maker-files-eu-antitrust-complaint-against-google-idUSKBN0OI1Z220150602.

EU Commission, 'Press release on State of the Union 2016: Commission proposes modern EU copyright rules for European culture to flourish and circulate' (Strasbourg 14 September 2016) europa.eu/rapid/press-release_IP-16-3010_en.htm.

EU Commission, 'Press release on antitrust: Commission fines Google €2.42 billion for abusing dominance as search engine by giving illegal advantage to own comparison-shopping service' (27 June 2017) europa.eu/rapid/press-release_MEX-17-1805_en.htm.

EU Commission, 'Press release on copyright reform clears final hurdle: Commission welcomes approval of modernised rules fit for digital age' (15 April 2019) europa.eu/rapid/press-release_IP-19-2151_en.htm.

EU Commission, 'Press release on Antitrust: Commission fines Google €2.42 billion for abusing dominance as search engine by giving illegal advantage to own comparison-shopping service' europa.eu/rapid/press-release_IP-17-1784_en.htm.

EU Commission, 'Joint statement by Vice-President Ansip and Commissioner Gabriel on the European Parliament's vote to start negotiations on modern copyright rules' (12 September 2018) europa.eu/rapid/press-release_STATEMENT-18-5761_en.htm.

EU Commission, 'Press release on Court of Justice upholds independence of data protection authorities in case against Hungary' (8 April 2014) europa.eu/rapid/press-release_MEMO-14-267_el.htm.

Chiou T, 'Greece: new notice and take down administrative mechanism for online copyright cases now in force' (*IPKat*, 5 March 2018) ipkitten.blogspot.com/2018/03/greece-new-notice-and-take-down.html.

Crotty JM, 'Education Is Best Weapon Against Web Piracy, not SOPA' (*Forbes*, 31 January 2012) www.forbes.com/sites/jamesmarshallcrotty/2012/01/31/better-than-sopa-public-education-best-weapon-against-web-piracy/#76f84504228.

Dansby A, 'Napster Files for Bankruptcy: Action part of Bertelsmann-initiated financial restructuring' (*Rolling stone*, 4 June 2002) www.rollingstone.com/music/music-news/napster-files-for-bankruptcy-246468/.

Datoo S, 'France drops controversial 'Hadopi law' after spending millions: The "three strikes" anti-piracy measure, introduced under Nicolas Sarkozy, would have cut off users' access to the internet' *The Guardian* (9 July 2013) www.theguardian.com/technology/2013/jul/09/france-hadopi-law-anti-piracy.

DSA Observatory, dsa-observatory.eu/.

European Digital Rights (EDRi), 'Leaked document: Does the EU Commission really plan to tackle illegal content online?' (21 September 2017) edri.org/leaked-document-does-the-eu-commission-actually-aim-to-tackle-illegal-content-online/.

European Digital Rights (EDRi), 'Spanish case law about hyperlinks' (23 April 2003) edri.org/edrigramnumber7spanish-case-hyperlinks/.

European Digital Rights (EDRi), 'The Slide from "Self-Regulation" to "Corporate Censorship"' www.edri.org/files/EDRI_selfreg_final_20110124.pdf.

Electronic Frontier Foundation, 'Section 230 of the Communications Decency Act 47 U.S.C. § 230: a Provision of the Communication Decency Act' www.eff.org/issues/cda230.

Electronic Frontier Foundation, 'How SOPA Affects Students, Educators, and Libraries' (14 December 2011) www.eff.org/deeplinks/2011/12/how-sopa-affects-students-and-educators.

Electronic Frontier Foundation, 'Lawrence Lessig Strikes Back Against Bogus Copyright Takedown: EFF Sues Liberation Music for Forcing Harvard Professor's Video Off YouTube' (22 August 2013) www.eff.org/press/releases/lawrence-lessig-strikes-back-against-bogus-copyright-takedown.

Ernesto, 'YouTube's copyright protection is a total mess. Can it be fixed?' (*Torrentfreak*, 22 December 2018) torrentfreak.com/youtubes-copyright-protection-system-is-a-total-mess-can-it-be-fixed-181222/.

Ernesto, 'UK Anti-Piracy "Education" Campaign Launched, Quietly' (*Torrentfreak*, 1 December 2015) torrentfreak.com/uk-anti-piracy-education-campaign-launched-quietly-151201/.

Ernesto, 'YouTube's Deal with Universal Blocks DMCA Counter Notices" (*Torrentfreak*, 5 April 2013) torrentfreak.com/youtube-deal-with-universal-blocks-dmca-counter-notices-130405/.

European Copyright Society, 'Opinion on the Reference to the CJEU in Case C-466/12 Svensson' (15 February 2013) europeancopyrightsociety.org/opinion-on-the-reference-to-the-cjeu-in-case-c-46612-svensson/.

Edwards J, 'This child being abused in a cobalt mine is why Apple is trying to fix the mining business' (*Business Insider UK*, 14 May 2017) uk.businessinsider.com/apple-cobalt-mine-child-labor-2017-5?r=UK&IR=T.

Elgot J, 'VW scandal: emissions cheats could face criminal charges' *The Guardian* (February 2018) www.theguardian.com/business/2018/feb/02/vw-scandal-emissions-cheats-could-face-criminal-charges.

Engstrom E and Feamster N, 'The limits of filtering: a look at the functionality and shortcomings of content detection tools' (2017) 17 www.engine.is/the-limits-of-filtering.

Ernesto, 'PayPal starts banning VPN and SmartDNS services' (*Torrentfreak*, 5 February 2016) torrentfreak.com/paypal-starts-banning-vpn-and-smartdns-services-160205/.

Erikson K, 'The EU copyright directive creates new legal uncertainties' (*LSE Blog*, 6 April 2019) blogs.lse.ac.uk/businessreview/2019/04/06/the-eu-copyright-directive-creates-new-legal-uncertainties/.

EFF, 'Preserve What Works, Fix What is Broken: EFF's Policy Principles for the Digital Services Act' (2020) www.eff.org/issues/eu-policy-principles.

Fairless T, 'EU Digital Chief Urges Regulation to Nurture European Internet Platforms: Speech illustrates policy makers' concerns over threat posed by U.S. tech companies to European industry' (*Wall Street Journal*, 14 April 2016) www.wsj.com/articles/eu-digital-chief-urges-regulation-to-nurture-european-internet-platforms-1429009201.

Hartmans A, '15 fascinating facts you probably didn't know about Amazon' (*Business Insider*, 23 August 2018) www.businessinsider.com/jeff-bezos-amazon-history-facts-2017-4?r=US&IR=T#in-the-early-days-of-amazon-a-bell-would-ring-in-the-office-every-time-someone-made-a-purchase-and-everyone-would-gather-around-to-see-if-they-knew-the-customer-2.

Hempel J, 'UN Right to connectivity, Zuckerberg to the UN: the Internet belongs to everyone' (*Wired*, 28 September 2015) www.wired.com/2015/09/zuckerberg-to-un-internet-belongs-to-everyone/.

Hempel J, 'Zuckerberg to the UN: The Internet Belongs to Everyone' (*Wired*, 28 September 2015) www.wired.com/2015/09/zuckerberg-to-un-internet-belongs-to-everyone/.

Hills M, 'Survey: YouTube Is America's Most Popular Social Media Platform' (*Forbes*, 23 March 2018) www.forbes.com/sites/meganhills1/2018/03/23/social-media-demographics/#59f74a57783a.

Horten M, 'Liability and responsibility: new challenges for Internet intermediaries' (*LSE Media Policy Project Blog*, 20 October 2016) blogs.lse.ac.uk/medialse/2016/10/20/liability-and-responsibility-new-challenges-for-internet-intermediaries/.

Husovec M, 'Compromising (on) the Digital Single Market? A Quick Look at the Estonian Presidency Proposal(s) on Art 13' (*Kluwer Copyright blog*, 8 September 2017) copyrightblog.kluweriplaw.com/2017/09/08/compromising-digital-single-market-quick-look-estonian-presidency-proposals-art-13/.

Husovec M, 'Why There Is No Due Process Online?: New Controversies in Intermediary Liability Law' (*Balkan.com*, 7 June 2019) balkin.blogspot.com/2019/06/why-there-is-no-due-process-online.html.

Hydra Greek mythology (Encyclopedia Britannica) www.britannica.com/topic/Hydra-Greek-mythology.

International Federation of the Phonographic Industry (IFPI), 'Digital Music Report 2013: Engine of a digital world' www.musikindustrie.de/fileadmin/bvmi/upload/06_Publikationen/DMR/ifpi_digital-music-report-2013.pdf.

International Federation of the Phonographic Industry (IFPI), 'Digital Music Report 2019: State of the industry' www.ifpi.org/downloads/GMR2019.pdf.

International Federation of the Phonographic Industry (IFPI), 'Global Music Report 2018' www.ifpi.org/downloads/GMR2018.pdf.

Information Commissioner's Office, 'ICO fines Uber £385,000 over data protection failings' (27 November 2018) ico.org.uk/about-the-ico/news-and-events/news-and-blogs/2018/11/ico-fines-uber-385-000-over-data-protection-failings/.

Infographique about the complaints procedure for copyright infringements online opi.gr/images/various/infographic_en.jpg.

Ingham T, 'YouTube's content ID fails to spot 20%-40% of music recordings' (*Music Business worldwide*, 13 July 2016) www.musicbusinessworldwide.com/youtubes-content-id-fails-spot-20-40/.

Investor relations, 'Facebook Reports Fourth Quarter and Full Year 2018 Results' investor.fb.com/investor-news/press-release-details/2019/Facebook-Reports-Fourth-Quarter-and-Full-Year-2018-Results/default.aspx.

Internet Governance Forum, 'Dynamic Coalition on Platform Responsibility (DCPR)' www.intgovforum.org/multilingual/content/dynamic-coalition-on-platform-responsibility-dcpr.

Irdeto, 'Nearly half of consumers around the globe are willing to stop or watch less pirated video content' (8 March 2017) irdeto.com/news/nearly-half-of-consumers-around-the-globe-are-willing-to-stop-or-watch-less-pirated-video-content/.

Jacques S and Garstka K, 'Automated anti-piracy systems: A call for further evidence-based policies' (*Kluwer Copyright blog*, 4 April 2019) copyrightblog.kluweriplaw.com/2019/04/04/automated-anti-piracy-systems-a-call-for-further-evidence-based-policies/.

Jasserand C, 'France: The Court of Cassation puts an end to the Notice and Stay Down Rule' (*Kluwer Copyright blog*, 14 August 2012) copyrightblog.kluweriplaw.com/2012/08/14/france-the-court-of-cassation-puts-an-end-to-the-notice-and-stay-down-rule/.

Keller D, 'DMCA classic, DMCA turbo: major new empirical research on notice and takedown operations' (*The Center for Internet and Society*, 20 April 2016) cyberlaw.stanford.edu/blog/2016/04/dmca-classic-dmca-turbo-major-new-empirical-research-notice-and-takedown-operations.

Keller D, 'Filtering Facebook: introducing dolphins in the net, a new Stanford CIS White Paper – or- why internet uses and EU policymakers should worry about the Advocate General's opinion in Glawischnig-Piesczek' (*The Center for Internet and Society*, 5 September 2019) cyberlaw.stanford.edu/blog/2019/09/filtering-facebook-introducing-dolphins-net-new-stanford-cis-white-paper-or-why.

Kiss J, 'Mark Zuckerberg defends Facebook's motives in free internet project in India' *The Guardian* (28 December 2015) www.theguardian.com/technology/2015/dec/28/mark-zuckerberg-facebook-india-internet-free-basics.

Kuczerawy A, 'The EU Commission on voluntary monitoring: Good Samaritan 2.0 or Good Samaritan 0.5?' (*KULeuven blog*, 24 April 2018) www.law.kuleuven.be/citip/blog/the-eu-commission-on-voluntary-monitoring-good-samaritan-2-0-or-good-samaritan-0-5/.

A Kuczerawy, 'The Good Samaritan that wasn't: voluntary monitoring under the (draft) Digital Services Act' (*Verfassungsblog*, 12 January 2021) verfassungsblog.de/good-samaritan-dsa/.

Letter of CEO Birkenstock Americas, 'Amazon, our valued Birkenstock Retail Partners' www.washingtonpost.com/news/business/wp-content/uploads/sites/8/2017/07/Amazon-retailer-letter-7.20.17.pdf?tid=a_inl&noredirect=on.

Levi A, 'Amazon's plan to fight counterfeiters will cost legit sellers a ton' (*cnbc*, 29 August 2016) www.cnbc.com/2016/08/29/amazons-plan-to-fight-counterfeiters-will-cost-legit-sellers-a-ton.html.

Lianos I and Botwright K, 'Five ways to increase trust in e-commerce' (*World Economic Forum*, 22 March 2019) www.weforum.org/agenda/2019/03/five-ways-to-restore-trust-in-e-commerce/.

Matsa K E and Shearer E, 'News Use Across Social Media Platforms 2018' (*Pew Research Centre*, 10 September 2018) www.journalism.org/2018/09/10/news-use-across-social-media-platforms-2018/.

Moscon V, 'The Council Negotiating Position on Article 13: Warning, Creators are also Part of the Game!!!' (*Kluwer Copyright Blog*, 4 July 2018) copyrightblog.kluweriplaw.com/2018/07/04/council-negotiating-position-article-13-warning-creators-also-part-game/.

Music Business Worldwide, 'PRS deal with YouTube: what does it mean for songwriters?' (6 September 2009) www.musicbusinessworldwide.com/prs-deal-with-youtube-what-does-it-mean-for-songwriters.

Niklas J, 'The regulatory future of algorithms' (*LSE Media Policy Project Blog*, 15 August 2017) blogs.lse.ac.uk/mediapolicyproject/2017/08/15/the-regulatory-future-of-algorithms/.

Nordemann JB, 'The German Bundesgerichtshof applies the latest CJEU case law on liability for linking to search engines' (*Kluwer Copyright blog*, 6 March 2018) copyrightblog.kluweriplaw.com/2018/03/06/german-bundesgerichtshof-applies-latest-cjeu-case-law-liability-linking-search-engines/.

Nordemann JB, 'Are preventive duties on hosting service providers in line with EU law? Some comments from a legal perspective on Art. 13 Draft DSM Directive and "upload filters"' (*Kluwer Copyright blog*, 28 June 2018) copyrightblog.kluweriplaw.com/2018/06/28/preventive-duties-hosting-service-providers-line-eu-law-comments-legal-perspective-art-13-draft-dsm-directive-upload-filters/?print=pdf.

Nordemann JB, 'YouTube is a hosting provider, but one with extensive duties of care, say two German Courts' (*Kluwer Copyright Blog*, 6 November 2015) copyrightblog.kluweriplaw.com/2015/11/06/youtube-is-a-hosting-provider-but-one-with-extensive-duties-of-care-say-two-german-courts/.

O' Donoghue C and Albrecht K, Spanish DPA fines Facebook €1.2 million for data protection infringements' (*Reed Smith*, 26 September 2017) www.technologylawdispatch.com/2017/09/privacy-data-protection/spanish-dpa-fines-facebook-e1-2-million-for-data-protection-infringements/.

Ofcom, 'General procedures for investigating breaches of broadcast licences' (2017) www.ofcom.org.uk/__data/assets/pdf_file/0019/31942/general-procedures.pdf.

Oltermann P, 'Tough new German law puts tech firms and free speech in spotlight' *The Guardian* (5 January 2018) www.theguardian.com/world/2018/jan/05/tough-new-german-law-puts-tech-firms-and-free-speech-in-spotlight.

O' Reilly T, 'What is Web 2.0' (30 September 2005) www.oreilly.com/pub/a/web2/archive/what-is-web-20.html.

Ortiz-Urculo, 'Madrid court of appeals upholds YouTube's liability safe harbor in Telecinco case' (*Hogan Lovells website*, 14 February 2014) www.hlmediacomms.com/2014/02/14/safe-harbor-victory-telecincos-appeal-v-youtube-dismissed/.

Out-Law.com, 'Spain legislates for out-of-court copyright enforcement' (29 November 2018) www.out-law.com/en/articles/2018/november/spain-out-of-court-copyright-enforcement/.

Pasquale F, 'Secret Algorithms Threaten the Rule of Law' (*MIT Technology Review*, 1 June 2017) www.technologyreview.com/s/608011/secret-algorithms-threaten-the-rule-of-law/.

Press release BGH, 'Keine Urheberrechtsverletzung bei der Bildersuche durch Suchmaschinen' juris.bundesgerichtshof.de/cgi-bin/rechtsprechung/document.py?Gericht=bgh&Art=en&Datum=Aktuell&Sort=12288&nr=79566&linked=pm&Blank=1.

Price R, 'Google has been hit with a record-breaking €2.4 billion fine by the EU over its antitrust case' (*UK Business Insider*, June 2017) uk.businessinsider.com/eu-fines-google-record-breaking-antitrust-shopping-case-2017-6.

Public education campaigns reduce tobacco www.tobaccofreekids.org/assets/factsheets/0051.pdf.

Quintais JP, 'The New Copyright Directive: A tour d' horizon- Part II (of press publishers, upload filters and the real value gap)' (*Kluwer Copyright Blog*, 17 June 2019) copyrightblog.kluweriplaw.com/2019/06/07/the-new-copyright-directive-a-tour-dhorizon-part-i/.

Reda J, 'The text of Article 13 and the EU Copyright Directive has just been finalised' (*Julia Reda's website*, 13 February 2019) juliareda.eu/2019/02/eu-copyright-final-text/.

Reda J, 'Censorship machines are coming: It's time for the free software community to discover its political clout' (*Julia Reda's website*, 6 April 2018) juliareda.eu/2018/04/free-software-censorship-machines/.

Reda J, 'When filters fail: These cases show we can't trust algorithms to clean up the internet' (*Julia Reda's website*, 28 September 2017) juliareda.eu/2017/09/when-filters-fail/.

Reda J, 'Article 13 is back on – and it got worse, not better' (*Julia Reda's website*, 5 February 2019) juliareda.eu/2019/02/article-13-worse/.

Rosati E, 'More on the Swedish application of GS Media' (*IPKat*, 15 December 2016) ipkitten.blogspot.co.uk/2016/12/more-on-swedish-application-of-gs-media.html.

Rosati E, 'Italian court finds Google and YouTube liable for failing to remove unlicensed content (but confirms eligibility for safe harbour protection)' (*IPKat*, 20 April 2017) ipkitten.blogspot.co.uk/2017/04/italian-court-finds-google-and-youtube.html.

Rosati E, 'Athens Court of Appeal applies CJEU GS Media linking decision and interprets 'profit-making intention' restrictively' (*IPKat*, 20 November 2017) ipkitten.blogspot.co.uk/2017/11/athens-court-of-appeal-applies-cjeu-gs.html.

Samuels, 'Amazon May Have a Counterfeit Problem: The company is facing multiple lawsuits from brands who say it does not do enough to prevent fakes from being listed on its website' (*The Atlantic*, 20 April 2018) www.theatlantic.com/technology/archive/2018/04/amazon-may-have-a-counterfeit-problem/558482/.

Sandvig C, 'Seeing the Sort: The Aesthetic and Industrial Defense of "The Algorithm"' (*Journal of the New Media Caucus* median.newmediacaucus.org/art-infrastructures-information/seeing-the-sort-the-aesthetic-and-industrial-defense-of-the-algorithm/.

Shipp J, 'A more transparent and accountable Internet? Here's how' (*LSE Media Policy Project Blog*, 24 May 2018) blogs.lse.ac.uk/mediapolicyproject/2018/05/24/a-more-transparent-and-accountable-internet-heres-how/.

Smith S, 'Birkenstock accuses Amazon of failure to tackle fake replicas' (*The Telegraph*, 22 December 2017) www.telegraph.co.uk/business/2017/12/22/birkenstock-accuses-amazon-failure-tackle-fake-replicas/.

Stalla-Bourdillon S, 'On Delfi v Estonia … Is it time to adopt a good-Samaritan style exemption? – Sophie Stalla-Bourdillon' (*Inforrm's Blog*, 24 June 2015) inforrm.org/2015/06/24/on-delfi-v-estonia-is-it-time-to-adopt-a-good-samaritan-style-exemption-sophie-stalla-bourdillon/.

Starzak A, 'When the Internet (Officially) Became the Public Square' (*Cloudfare*, 21 June 2017) blog.cloudflare.com/internet-became-public-square/.

Statista, 'Most popular social networks worldwide as of April 2019, ranked by number of active users (in millions)' www.statista.com/statistics/272014/global-social-networks-ranked-by-number-of-users/.

Tassi P, 'The Injustice Of The YouTube Content ID Crackdown Reveals Google's Dark Side' (*Forbes*, 19 December 2013) www.forbes.com/sites/insertcoin/2013/12/19/the-injustice-of-the-youtube-content-id-crackdown-reveals-googles-dark-side/#5336a67866c8.

UNCTAD, 'How COVID-19 triggered the digital and e-commerce turning point' (2021) unctad.org/news/how-covid-19-triggered-digital-and-e-commerce-turning-point.

United Nations, 'Covid-19 and e-commerce: a global review' (2021) unctad.org/system/files/official-document/dtlstict2020d13_en_0.pdf.

Venkant S, 'When an algorithm isn't' (*Medium*, 2 October 2015) medium.com/@geomblog/when-an-algorithm-isn-t-2b9fe01b9bb5.

INDEX

Lightning Sour=e UK Ltd.
Milton Keynes JK
UKHW021950 40622
404432UK00003B/141

9 781509 948529